iLife™ Bible

Dennis Cohen
Bob LeVitus

Wiley Publishing, Inc.

iLife™ Bible

Published by
Wiley Publishing, Inc.
909 Third Avenue
New York, NY 10022
www.wiley.com

Library of Congress Control Number: 2003105651

ISBN: 0-7645-4172-2

Manufactured in the United States of America

10 9 8 7 6 5 4 3 2 1

1O/RT/QW/QT/IN

Published by Wiley Publishing, Inc., Indianapolis, Indiana
Published simultaneously in Canada

About the Authors

Dennis R. Cohen has written or contributed to many books, including *iTunes, iPhoto, iMovie, & iDVD Bible, Macworld Mac OS X Bible, Macworld Microsoft Office 2001 Bible, Macworld AppleWorks 6 Bible, AppleWorks 6 For Dummies*, and *Mac Secrets*, 6th Edition, as well as being the technical editor for over 70 titles in just the past few years. A software developer for over 20 years and a Mac developer since 1984, he brings a history not only with the Mac, but also with other platforms (including Unix). Dennis lives in Sunnyvale, California, with his Boston Terrier, Spenser.

Bob "Dr. Mac" LeVitus is the author of over 40 books, including *Dr. Mac: The OS X Files, or, "How to Become a Mac OS X Power User,"* and *Mac OS X For Dummies* for Wiley, and *The Little iTunes Book* and *The Little iDVD Book* for Peachpit Press. He's been a newspaper columnist for the *Houston Chronicle* for five years penning the popular "Dr. Mac" column every Friday for their award-winning Business section, and has been published in most magazines with the word "Mac" in their title. He's known for his expertise, trademark humorous style, and ability to translate "techie" jargon into usable and fun advice for regular folks.

Authors' Dedication

Thanks to all my friends and family, especially Spenser (who gets me out from in front of the computer for regular walks). —drc

Thanks to my family, once again, for putting up with me. —BL

Authors' Acknowledgments

Dennis would like to thank Bob LeVitus for agreeing to work on this project with him; Apple Computer for providing software that is not only useful, but fun to use; Wiley Acquisitions Editor Tom Heine for believing in this book, Maureen Spears for coordinating all the logistics, Lisa Spangenberg for her careful and insightful technical review, and Beth Taylor for catching our typos and style goofs. He'd also like to thank his brother, Michael, and sister-in-law, Lisa, for their assistance in researching and help in Chapters 15 and 20, respectively. Finally, he'd like to thank various folks at Apple, in particular Peter Lowe (iLife Product Manager), Greg Scallon (iLife Assistant Product Manager), Ken Bereskin (Mac OS X Product Manager) and Sal Soghoian (AppleScript Product Manager and iDVD guru) for their help, intentional or not, in providing some very cool tips and ideas. He would also like to join Bob in thanking Carole McClendon, their agent, for her help in making this project a reality.

All Bob has to say is: "Ditto."

Credits

Acquisitions Editor
Tom Heine

Project Editor
Maureen Spears

Technical Editor
Lisa Spangenberg

Copy Editor
Beth Taylor

Editorial Manager
Rev Mengle

Vice President and Executive Group Publisher
Richard Swadley

Vice President and Executive Publisher
Bob Ipsen

Vice President and Publisher
Barry Pruett

Project Coordinator
Ryan Steffan

Graphics and Production Specialists
Amanda Carter
Lauren Goddard
Michael Kruzil
Lynsey Osborn

Quality Control Technician
John Greenough
Charles Spencer

Proofreading and Indexing
Sossity R. Smith, TECHBOOKS
Production Services

Cover Illustration
Authony Bunyon

Introduction

Popular folklore suggests that Macs are so easy to use that manuals and books aren't necessary. Apple has bought into that philosophy by not providing a user manual for any of the applications in this book. In fact, Apple doesn't provide a user manual for Mac OS X or AppleWorks, either. We disagree with this philosophy; and most of the user base seems to agree with us as the demand for books and other documentation grows.

Apple's online help is pretty good as online help systems go, but it leaves a lot out, is slow, and requires that you know what questions to ask in the first place.

Who Should Read This Book

Anyone who uses or wants to use Apple's wonderful "digital hub applications" (now called "iLife") — iTunes, iPhoto, iMovie, and iDVD — will benefit from this book.

We do make a few assumptions, though. The primary ones are that you're using Mac OS X (all four applications work only in Mac OS X) and that you already know Mac and OS X fundamentals — point and click, dragging items, opening windows, choosing commands from menus, selecting items in a window or list, editing text, and what a Home directory is. If you don't have this knowledge, we'd recommend either *Mac OS X For Dummies* (by one of the authors of this book) or *Macworld Mac OS X Bible* (co-authored by the other author of this book).

Apple frequently updates the subject applications, so we had to draw the line somewhere as to what versions of the iLife application programs to cover — iTunes 3.0.1, iPhoto 2, iMovie 3.0.2, and iDVD 3 are current as we went to print and the ones on which this book is based. These applications require Mac OS X (10.1.5 or later, with 10.2.2 or later recommended).

Note

Although the main body of text covers iTunes 3.0.1, we wanted to bring you the most current information possible. To that end, we added iTunes 4 coverage while the book was in production. The iTunes 3 material is still applicable in iTunes 4, but Appendix B covers what's new in iTunes 4 and the changes to various commands and dialogs.

Normally, a Bible title is a little dry, but normally the subject matter is, too — word processors, spreadsheets, databases, operating systems, and so forth. We're blessed with software that, while productive, is primarily fun to use. Because of this, we're going to present the material in a lighter style than is usual, with a little repartee, some personal anecdotes, and occasional (okay, maybe more than occasional) opinions.

iTunes, iPhoto, and iMovie come with all currently shipping Macs and with boxed copies of Mac OS X. iDVD comes with all current Macs that include a SuperDrive. You might (but probably won't) find it on some other Macs, but it won't run unless a SuperDrive is present. If you have older versions of these applications, you can download iTunes, iPhoto, and iMovie from Apple's Web site. iDVD 3 is only available (on DVD-ROM) in the boxed iLife product ($49).You have the software; now you can read this book and learn how to use the software Apple provided.

What's Inside

The *iLife Bible* covers each of the title applications in detail. Not only does it tell you what the applications do and how to use them, but it also points out the limitations and suggests software or hardware to augment the applications or function as alternatives. The book is divided into six parts:

✦ **Part I:** Provides a very basic overview of the four applications and lays some groundwork for what is to follow.

✦ **Parts II through V:** Cover iTunes, iPhoto, iMovie, and iDVD, respectively. Each part consists of five chapters, as follows:

- Introduction
- Getting Started
- Getting Advanced
- Tips, Tricks, and Techniques
- Hardware and Software Enhancements

✦ **Part VI:** Covers ways to share your work between the different applications and what software to consider if one of the applications no longer satisfies your needs.

Conventions Used in This Book

We use the following conventions in this book in an effort to assist you through the material:

Version references

Apple regularly updates Mac OS X and the applications described in this book, each update bringing with it a new version number. When we don't list a version number, you can assume that we are talking about the book's subject versions: iTunes 3.0.1 (iTunes 4 coverage is in Appendix B), iPhoto 2, iMovie 3.0.2, and iDVD 3. If we list a version without a decimal point (such as iMovie 3 rather than iMovie 3.0), we're talking about all versions whose version numbers start with that digit.

Mac OS X (10.2, aka "Jaguar") was current while we were writing this book. Our screen shots and discussions were taken with Mac OS X (10.2.3). If Apple releases an update to the operating system between the time we wrote this material and the time you read it, some minor visual differences might exist.

Sidebars

Certain discussions are expanded with sidebars. These are shaded boxes containing background information, advanced technical details and references, and other helpful ancillary information.

Icon paragraphs

We augment the basic discussion of our topics with special information, set apart from the regular text and marked with one of the following distinctive icons:

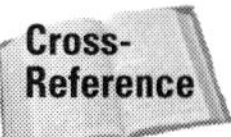

These icons point you to other places in the book where you can find more information on a given topic.

A note icon is an "aside," calling attention to an interesting or unexpected aspect of the current topic. This often includes our personal opinions and experiences where we feel them germane to the discussion.

A tip icon indicates an advisory discussion. When you see one of these, you can expect to learn a shortcut or other useful information concerning the current topic.

A caution icon warns you of possible pitfalls and will include workarounds (even if that workaround is "don't do that.")

We hope you enjoy using this book at least as much as we enjoyed writing it. If you have feedback or suggestions for future editions, please let us know about them.

Contents

P A R T

I

Getting Started with Digital Media

✦ ✦ ✦ ✦

In This Part

✦ ✦ ✦ ✦

The Big Picture: What's the Digital Hub All About?

In This Chapter

Bringing the studio into your home

Sharing your work with others

On October 5, 1999, Apple rolled out the iMac DV, the first iMac ready for digital filmmaking that did not require any additional hardware or software. Every iMac DV came with iMovie, Apple's revolutionary new digital video editing software. For the first time ever, you could edit high-quality digital video at home for well under $2,000. Fourteen months later, Steve Jobs premiered iTunes and iDVD, and ballyhooed Apple's new digital hub strategy: To make the Mac "the Hub of your digital lifestyle." Amid great speculation and phenomenal hype, Apple announced the iPod on October 23, 2001. It was a huge hit, selling far more units than Apple had forecasted. Then, on January 7, 2002, Jobs introduced iPhoto, "the missing link," according to Apple, in digital photography and the missing spoke on Apple's digital hub.

On January 7, 2003, Jobs announced the new iLife bundle—including updates to iPhoto 2, iMovie 3, and iDVD 3—that, in addition to many nice enhancements to the individual products, introduced a great new level of integration. Your iTunes library is accessible within the other three applications. Your iPhoto library is available in iMovie and iDVD, and your iMovies are available within iDVD.

On April 28, 2003, Apple introduced iTunes 4 and debuted the Apple Music Store. You can find iTunes 4 coverage in Appendix B.

As you've probably noticed, none of the digital hub products has a printed User's Manual or any documentation beyond a ReadMe file or short Getting Started pamphlet. You're expected to rely upon the often terse, and occasionally helpful Help files. That's where this book comes in. In this single volume, you get what amounts to a manual for each of the four applications — iPhoto, iTunes, iMovie, and iDVD — packed with easy-to-follow, step-by-step instructions for just about anything you'll ever need to do, topped off with plenty of tips, tricks, and techniques. (And some puns, jokes, and old song references at no additional charge.) Think of the book you hold in your hand as our version of the four missing (MIA) iManuals.

Bringing the Studio into Your Home

Apple's iPhoto Web page used to start with the caption, "Shoot like Ansel. Organize like Martha." While the first sentence may be a bit of an exaggeration, iPhoto certainly provides tools making such a result less improbable. Similar claims, with different names, could be made about the other hub applications. That's the whole point of Apple's digital hub: You now have the tools in hand to be all that you can be as a multimedia producer. All you have to provide is the vision and talent.

For years, we've all been reading and hearing about "the computer revolution" and the "digital revolution." Being in the industry, your savvy authors knew that "revolution" was generally an overstatement. Since the iMovie debut, "revolution" stopped being an exaggeration, and each new hub application and upgrade adds momentum to this ongoing revolution from Apple.

In just the past three years, we've watched iMovie take filmmaking out of the hands of professionals and dedicated hobbyists and put it squarely in the grasp of the average consumer. iDVD now lets that typical consumer create DVDs — a process, which not too long ago was the exclusive province of studios with hundreds of thousands of dollars worth of equipment. iTunes can enable anybody to become a DJ or album maker. iPhoto and a digital camera (an increasingly affordable tool) provide an escape from film and photo developers.

You're now the master of your own digital destiny. Here's just a sample of what you can do:

✦ **iPhoto:** Lets you use your photographs as more than just prints to frame, paste in albums, or store in a drawer. If you want prints, you've got them, but you also have slide shows, bound and printed albums, screen savers, Web pages, desktop backgrounds, and on and on.

  And you get all of this without any fancy professional equipment, smelly chemicals, or darkroom. (Save the closet for your clothes.)

✦ **iTunes:** Lets you create your own recording mixes and burn your own CDs without splicing tapes.

✦ **iMovie:** Eliminates all the nastiness of splicing scenes together as well as the fancy and expensive equipment required to add special effects and transitions. And, through the wonders of FireWire and QuickTime, you can easily save the finished product to videotape or to disk.

✦ **iDVD:** You can take your iMovies and burn your own DVDs, complete with static and live-motion menus just like the ones on commercial DVDs.

Only a few short years ago, the software and hardware required to perform these tasks cost astronomical amounts. Now, you find the software included in your OS X Dock when you first start up your $1500 eMac or $1900 flat panel iMac (or a number of other Mac configurations), as shown in Figure 1-1. Additionally, these hub applications have rendered a lot of the hardware unnecessary. Of course, you still need to own digital still and video cameras to make full use of iPhoto and iMovie, but even without cameras, the programs can be useful, as you'll see in Parts III ("iPhoto") and IV ("iMovie") of this book.

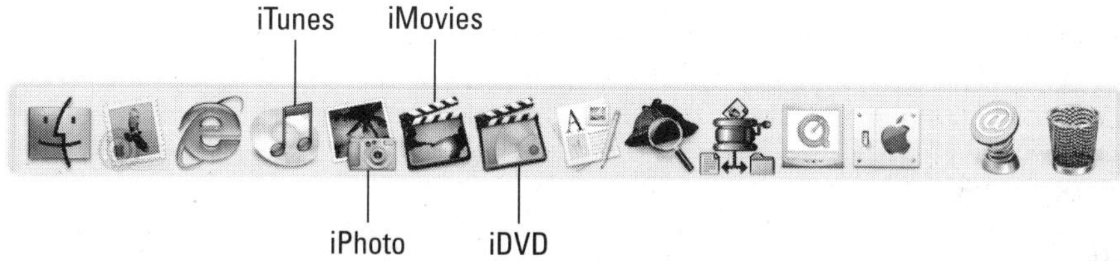

Figure 1-1: The standard OS X Dock, with iPhoto, iTunes, iMovie, and iDVD all ready to use.

With some additional software, most notably Roxio's Toast 5 Titanium, you can also create VideoCDs from your iMovies and your iPhoto Slide Shows or create photo collections on CD directly from iPhoto.

Note

VideoCDs, also referred to as VCDs, are a popular distribution format for video almost everywhere in the world except the United States, with quality equivalent to that found on prerecorded videotapes. Because most, but not all, DVD players also play VCDs, the format is starting to gain momentum in the US, as well. And why not? Eighty minutes of VHS-quality video on a 19-cent CD-R disc that you can view on your set-top DVD player, almost any Mac, or even a PC is a very good thing.

You may cringe when you encounter phrases using words like *empower,* but it's hard to think of a better word to use when describing what the digital hub applications do. They empower you, turning your Mac into a combination Hollywood studio and Fotomat.

Sharing Your Work with Others

Although there are exceptions, most people enjoy sharing music, movies, and their photographic memories. Of course you enjoy being reminded of your trip to London, your tour of the Smithsonian, or the way Junior looked as a baby, but more than that, you like to show the photos and home movies to your friends and family. Similarly, no matter how much we enjoy just sitting back and listening to music, most of the time we enjoy it even more at a party or with friends.

Because of this normal human desire to share our pleasures and memories, Apple has included lots of sharing capabilities in both the Mac OS and in the hub applications.

On the Web

The Web is a little over ten years old now and, for the past few years, ISPs (Internet Service Providers) have touted personal Web page space as one of their selling points. Unfortunately, except for some truly awful automated tools (usually Windows-only), creating and publishing your own Web pages required a Web page editor or knowledge of HTML, or HyperText Markup Language. Transferring these files to your ISP-provided space requires using an FTP, or File Transfer Protocol.

Apple decided to make this whole process easier for their customers, and created iTools, a collection of Internet-related tools for Mac users (OS 9 and later). The two iTools of particular interest to us here are the iDisk, a mountable 20MB disk volume, and HomePage, Apple's Mac-only Web page builder that uses your iDisk as your personal Web space. At the July, 2002 Macworld Convention, Apple morphed iTools into a for-pay service named .Mac and increased the mountable iDisk's size from 20MB to 100MB.

The first hub application to exploit Apple's HomePage iTool was iMovie, which isn't surprising as it's also the oldest of the four hub programs. In fact, Apple has promoted the Web presence of home iMovies with the iMovie Gallery. At `http://homepage.mac.com/imovie/`, Apple not only provides a few iMovies on its own .Mac page to amuse and entertain, but also demonstrates how easy it is to provide a Web browser interface to your finished movie.

Using your own products both for everyday operations and to show what they can do is often referred to as, "eating our own dog food." If you want to see a can of Bob's, it's on his Apple HomePage:

`http://homepage.mac.com/boblevitus/iMovieTheater1.html`

If you have a dial-up modem connection, it may not stream but you can control-click and download it since it's only about 5MB.

With iPhoto, Apple automates the page-creation process even more by having iPhoto interact directly with both iDisk and HomePage; iDisk loads the photos into the iDisk's Pictures folder for you and HomePage links directly into HomePage's PhotoAlbum page themes without using your Web browser. An example of a Web page created in this manner (photos of Dennis's canine companion) is shown in Figure 1-2.

So far, we haven't seen a Music page linking iTunes with iDisk and HomePage, but there is a Music folder on your iDisk. Who knows what the future holds in this area? Apple's probably wise not to provide tools for sharing music at this time. The RIAA (Recording Industry Association of America) doesn't have much tolerance for companies that facilitate sharing music. Remember what happened to Napster?

Note

We don't *know* that the RIAA has anything to do with Apple's omission of MP3 distribution in its HomePage and e-mail tools. That's just a guess on our part, owing partly to our skeptical natures and partly to the fact that we read the newspapers and follow the battles between the recording industry and consumers with great interest and mixed emotions.

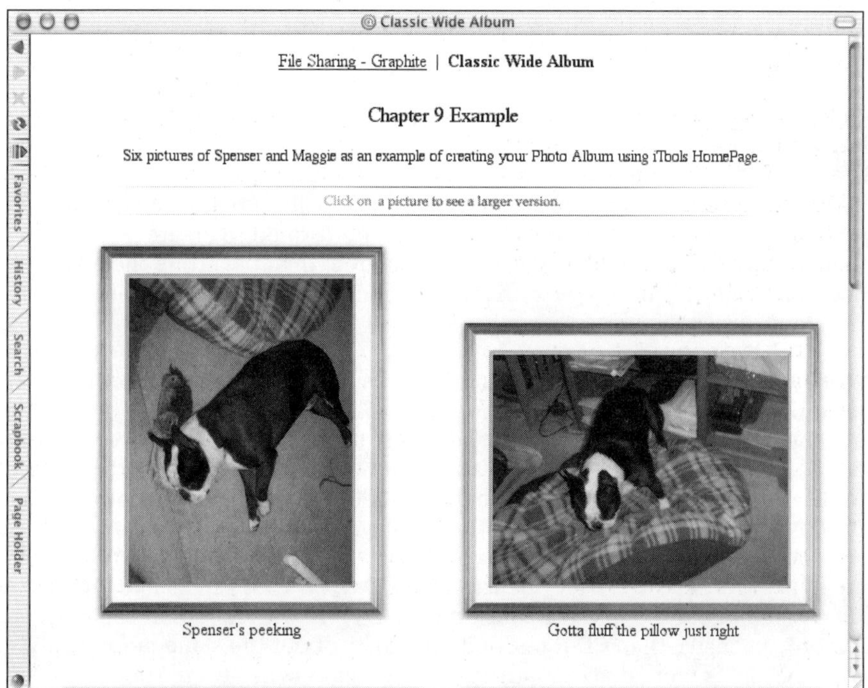

Figure 1-2: iPhoto's HomePage connection makes creating and posting a Web page easy.

Suffice it to say, if you're willing to design your own Web pages, it isn't difficult to make a few MP3s available, as you'll see in Chapter 6.

Caution

Be very careful about what songs you post on the Web. Make sure that you have the right to post them. The DMCA (Digital Millennium Copyright Act) was used to go after Napster and others for just this sort of thing. "Sharing" copyrighted music is a no-no without specific, written permission from the copyright holder.

Via e-mail

Once again, Apple concentrates on iPhoto and iMovie when dealing with e-mail. Of course, sending a DVD by e-mail doesn't make much sense, even with a very fast connection. Transferring an MP3, though, does make sense, but Apple hasn't automated that process — again, probably something to do with the RIAA.

One of iMovie's default formats for exporting is designed specifically for e-mail attachment. This is the Save As in most Mac programs. Just fire up your e-mail program, create a new message, address it, drag the movie file(s) into it, and click Send.

Just as with Web pages, iPhoto automates sending photos via e-mail. iPhoto does everything for you except address the message and click Send.

On CD/DVD

Don't get us wrong, sharing via Web pages and e-mail is great when the files are few and small. But, even with all the compression performed to create MP3s, QuickTime movies, and JPEG photo files, you sacrifice a lot of quality getting them small enough to transfer quickly over an Internet connection, especially for folks dialing in via modem.

In today's world of large multimedia files and massive hard disks, portable media like floppy disks are all but useless (which might be why they aren't built into Macs any more); and Zip disks are often inadequate and are very expensive. Apple was one of the pioneers in delivering software on CD and including CD drives as a standard feature in some models as far back as 1990. CDs and DVDs become even more attractive when you can create music CDs playable in your CD players, and can play DVDs on the DVD player hooked to your TV set. With 650MB to 700MB capacities and a very low per-MB cost, optical media (CD-R, CD-RW) seems like the next evolutionary step in backup and transport media. DVD-R, with its 4.7GB capacity, is a little more expensive than CD-R per unit, but costs about the same per megabyte. As DVD-R becomes more common, the price is going down — even Apple's DVD-R 5-packs are now selling for $15. Three dollars for 4.7GB (between six and seven CDs) makes it comparable to 50-cent CD–Rs.

The Care and Labeling of Optical Media

We're going to focus on CD-R media here, but what we write also applies to CD-RW and DVD-R discs.

Before Apple introduced the Macintosh with its Sony 3.5" floppy disk, floppies really were, well, floppy. The thin Mylar disk was enclosed in an insubstantial, flexible case and writing on that case with anything other than a soft felt-tip pen was likely to damage the disk inside. Adhesive labels came with floppies. You wrote on the label, indicating what the disk held, then affixed the label to the case. This was fine, so long as you didn't have to change what was on the label by adding to the disk's contents or replacing them. If so, you were back to square one.

With CDs, you have much the same problem. Writing on the (nondata) surface can, if you don't use a soft writing implement, apply sufficient pressure to deform the substrate layer behind it, where the laser burns your data.

On the other hand, applying a label can unbalance the disc, resulting in problems when the drive has the disc spinning and tries to read from it. This is less of a problem with full-coverage labels, properly applied using the tool that comes with your labels and/or labeling software, but it's still a consideration.

Just writing on a CD or DVD that you want to give as a gift looks tacky, so what are you to do?

For backups and the like, we just scribble something with a soft pen designed for this purpose, such as the TDK CD Mark (`www.tdk.com`). On some discs, though, presentation is important and we create our labels using various software. Dennis has templates for both Photoshop and Illustrator that match his label stock, Bob collects Avery products and has templates in Word and Photoshop, and a script that exports a playlist from iTunes and lays it out in a jewel box insert template in AppleWorks. Then, very carefully, making sure that the label is applied evenly, we use an applicator. (The one that comes with CD Stomper [`www.cdstomper.com`] is our favorite.)

One tip, though: The instructions that come with the label applicators suggest using fingertip pressure in the center ring to press the CD onto the label. We've found something better, eliminating the risk that our fingers will slip and damage the recorded surface. If you purchase your CDs in bulk on spindles, there are usually clear plastic CD-sized protective "discs" at the top and bottom of the stack. These protective discs can serve the same purpose when you're applying a label. Just put the non-label side down on the plastic, flip the pair of discs over and press the discs down onto the label. Because you only touch the protective disc, you can actually spread your fingers more, ensuring a more even application.

Oh, and don't try to peel labels off the discs. You're guaranteed to flex the media and that will separate the disc's layers, resulting in an unusable disc.

Apple also recognized the importance of integrating disc-burning capabilities into the Finder (data CDs and DVDs), iTunes (Audio CDs and MP3 CDs), and iDVD (DVDs), and at about the same time (early 2001) started including burners for CDs and/or DVDs in most Mac models. The integrated disc burning is simple, straightforward, and for most people, adequate to meet their disc burning needs. We're going to mention Roxio's Toast 5 Titanium frequently in this book. In our opinion, it is an invaluable tool for anyone who burns more than an occasional CD. Roxio (`www.roxio.com`) includes an iMovie and QuickTime plug-in for creating VideoCDs. El Gato Software (`www.elgato.com`) created a free iPhoto plug-in so that you can burn photo collections directly to CD using Toast.

Summary

In this chapter, you've seen the evolution of Apple's digital hub. You've also seen how the digital hub applications integrate with Apple's Internet strategy and take advantage of Mac OS's built-in disc-burning software, which makes sharing your digital creations much easier.

✦ ✦ ✦

Tools and Terms

✦ ✦ ✦ ✦

In This Chapter

Meeting the iApplications

Learning a little jargon

✦ ✦ ✦ ✦

Because Apple continues to expand the scope of their digital hub concept and frequently updates the applications and services comprising the hub, anything we write will, eventually, become outdated. Dealing with an evolving technology base (like the digital hub) just means that "eventually" isn't a very long time.

Our snapshot in time is iTunes 3, iPhoto 2, iMovie 3, and iDVD 3. It's possible, even likely, that one or more of these applications will be out in a newer version by the time you read this, but that's the nature of software.

Fortunately, when new versions of these applications appear, the things you learned about the previous version still apply — you just have some new tools to use. Thus, even with a newer version, the information in this book is still useful — it may just be a little less complete with respect to the new version and some things may have moved or look a little different.

Having said that, here's an introduction to the four applications and some of the jargon (including acronyms) that we'll be using throughout the book.

Meeting the iApplications

Although this isn't the order in which we'll cover them in the book, Apple introduced iMovie first, followed by iTunes and iDVD, and then iPhoto. The order we're following is the order of most users to fewest users, which has nothing to do with the applications' relative complexity and everything to do with the dollar or equipment cost of entry. Interestingly, it is also a hierarchic ordering where the earlier discussed programs are accessible from within those discussed later. Here, though, we'll introduce them in the order Apple presented them. We will occasionally refer to the collection of these four applications as the *iApps*.

Rolling out iMovie

With the release of the iMac DV models in autumn 1999, Apple shook up the digital video world by bundling iMovie, the industry's first easy-to-use and affordable digital video editing program. Taking advantage of the iMac DV's high-speed FireWire connectors, common on most digital camcorders (though usually referred to as i.LINK or IEEE-1394), iMovie made the iMac the least expensive platform for editing high-quality video.

Figure 2-1 shows you the iMovie 3 screen you see when you first launch iMovie. In Chapter 13, we cover what all the parts are for.

iMovie comes with a very nice tutorial to give you practice using the application. We believe in hands-on use, so if you want some ready-made footage to use when you're reading this book, the tutorial is a good place to look.

Figure 2-1: iMovie welcomes you with just a hint of its capability.

Hitting the high notes with iTunes

In January 2001's Macworld Expo keynote, Apple introduced both iTunes and iDVD. In that keynote, Steve Jobs commented that Apple was late to the game in including CD burners with their hardware, but they were making up for it in a big way. And, to make the CD burners even more useful, he showed iTunes burning audio CDs directly from user-created playlists.

As the second half of this one-two punch, Jobs also demonstrated burning a CD directly from the Finder, eliminating the requirement for third-party applications for basic CD burning.

Eighteen months later, iTunes had two major revisions and now stands at version 3. Figure 2-2 shows what you see the first time you run iTunes after you answer a number of configuration questions.

Figure 2-2: iTunes is ready to shake, rattle, and roll.

Be your own producer with iDVD

At the same time Jobs announced CD-R availability in Macs, he announced an industry breakthrough with the first consumer-priced DVD burner, the Apple SuperDrive, which is based on the Pioneer A103 mechanism. Using a simple drag-and-drop metaphor, iDVD enables anyone with a suitably configured Mac to create DVDs with navigation menus virtually indistinguishable from those on commercial DVDs that play in most set-top DVD players.

Now in version 3, iDVD has added some bells and whistles, such as motion menus (animated menus and buttons), without sacrificing any of its simplicity of use. Figure 2-3 shows the initial iDVD screen, which starts you off ready to work with the iDVD tutorial.

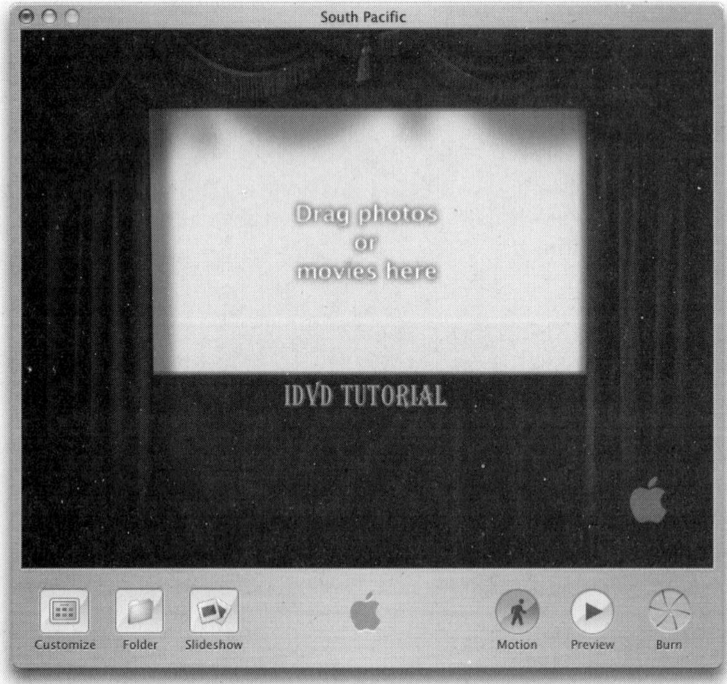

Figure 2-3: iDVD starts out ready to create a menu-driven DVD.

Smile for iPhoto

January 2002's Macworld Expo saw Apple introduce iPhoto, hailing it as the "missing link" in digital photography. Sporting a simple, yet elegant, user interface, iPhoto leverages OS X's Image Capture technology to recognize a wide variety of USB-connected digital cameras without any user configuration, as well as Picture CDs and various Smart Media readers. With iPhoto's organizational tools, a typical user can manage photo collections containing hundreds or even thousands of images. Basic built-in editing tools let you crop, rotate, adjust hue and saturation, remove red-eye, remove scratches and imperfections, and auto-enhance the contrast and brightness. And, if those tools prove insufficient, you can specify an external editing program to use when a photo is double-clicked. Finally, iPhoto includes a number of ways to share your photos, including printing, commercial print processing, coffee table books, slideshows, screensavers, Web pages, and many others.

The initial iPhoto window is shown in Figure 2-4, although it seems a bit barren with no pictures yet imported. The current iPhoto version is 2.

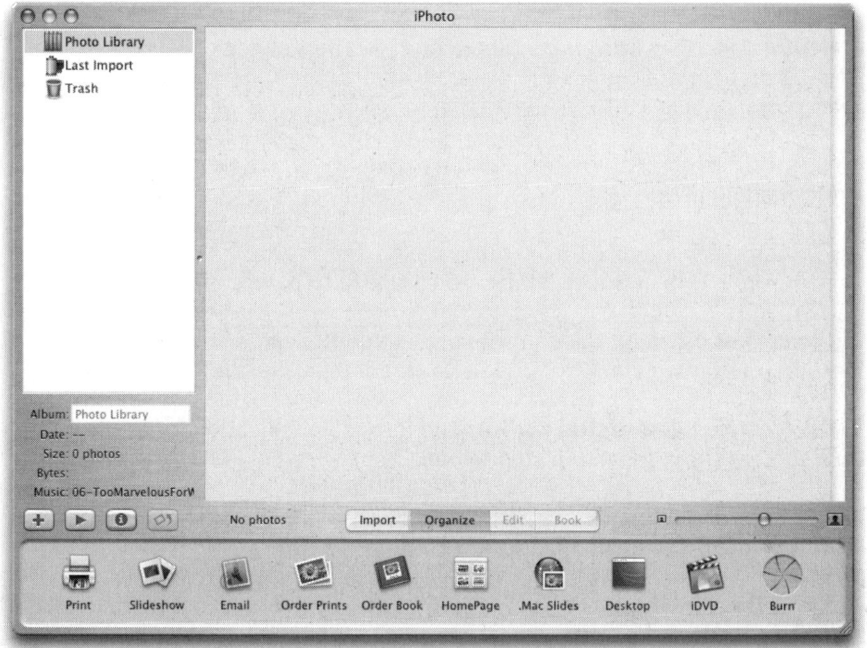

Figure 2-4: iPhoto starts you out with an empty photo library, just waiting to be filled.

Learning a Little Jargon

Every vocation and avocation has its own lingo. Photography, cinematography, and music are great examples of this, and the addition of computers to the mix has spawned additional verbage.

There's no way we can give you an exhaustive list (an unabridged dictionary, as it were), but we can get you started with those words, phrases, and acronyms you're most likely to encounter — in fact, you'll run across a number of them while reading this book.

AIFF (Audio Interchange File Format): The Apple-standard specification for audio such as that used on CDs.

aspect ratio: The horizontal to vertical ratio. For example, 320 x 240 and 640 x 480 are both 4:3 aspect ratios.

authoring: The act of assembling the various elements of a video production and creating a consumer-ready end product including navigational aids. One example is creating the menus and background music that present the video and slideshows on a DVD and then encoding and burning the result.

bit depth: Describes how many bits define the color space of each pixel in an image. A bit depth of 8 gives 256 possible colors, 16-bit depth allows for 65,536 possible colors.

burner: A CD or DVD drive that has the capability of writing CDs and DVDs in addition to reading them.

cap: Digital video captured from other media. For example, when you transfer video footage from a VHS or Super-8 tape, you are said to have capped it.

CBR (constant bit rate): Used in reference to digital video streams that transfer data with the same number of bits-per-second, regardless of the content.

CD-DA (compact disc-digital audio): The format specification for audio compact discs such as those played in standalone CD players.

CD-R (CD-recordable): An inexpensive write-once, read-many disc format that has become popular for use in CD burners.

CD-RW (CD-rewritable): Similar to CD-R, but you can erase and write over the CD content.

chapter: a scene-break in a movie or clip to which your viewing program can jump automatically.

decoding: The conversion process that reads compressed audio or video and reconstructs the sounds and images you hear and see.

dpi (sometimes ppi): Dots, or pixels, per inch, dpi (ppi) describes the density of an image. You primarily use it as a measurement for how well, or poorly, an image will print.

DVD: Can either be digital versatile disc or digital video disc, depending on the context and whom you ask.

DVD-R (DVD-recordable): A user-writable disc medium that you can play in most modern DVD players.

encoding: Changing the format of the data to comply with a transmission standard. The term is used most often when referring to the process of creating the MPEG files from DV stream source material for video or the MP3 file from AIFF or WAV files for audio.

FireWire: Apple's name for the IEEE-1394 data transmission standard, a high-bandwidth technology. Also known, primarily on Sony products, as i.LINK, it is the standard high speed data transfer technology used on current Macs and almost all digital camcorders.

fps (frames per second): Tells how many digital images per second are being decoded for display.

JPEG: Joint Photographic Experts Group, also the image-compression algorithms that organization developed and which are in common use by digital cameras and for use on Web sites.

kbps, mbps: Kilobits/megabits per second.

kBps, MBps: Kilobytes/Megabytes per second.

lossy: Describes data compression techniques that involve removing detail as part of the compression process. When you employ lossy compression, the decompressed image will differ from the original. *Lossless* compression, on the other hand, completely reconstructs the original from the compressed data. JPEG and the various MPEG formats are lossy, GIF and PNG are lossless.

MP3 (MPEG-1, Audio Layer 3): Audio compression technology specified by MPEG and in common use for digital audio to produce near-CD quality encodings in substantially less disk space.

MPEG: Motion Picture Experts Group, an industry organization that has developed the algorithms and formats used for DVD, VideoCD, SuperVideoCD, and streaming video.

NTSC (National Television System Committee): Group that specifies the U.S. television standard and for whom the standard is named.

PAL (phase alternating line): The European TV standard.

resolution: The number of pixels in an image's horizontal and vertical dimension.

rip: Extracting audio from CD, tape, or record.

SCSI (small computer systems interface): A medium-to-high bandwidth data transfer technology that, until recently, was the standard on Macintoshes. Although still available as an extra-cost option, FireWire has supplanted SCSI as the Mac standard.

SuperDrive: Apple's name for the DVD-R/CD-RW drive available on many Mac models. It was originally based upon the Pioneer A103 mechanism, but now uses the Pioneer A104, which allows 2x writing.

SVCD (Super VideoCD): A format based on MPEG-2 and developed by Philips for use in China on enhanced VCD players. It has achieved significant popularity due to its near-DVD quality while still allowing the use of inexpensive CD media.

USB (universal serial bus): A standard for the transmission of serial data between electronic devices. It is the current standard for low-bandwidth transfers on the Mac, such as between the keyboard and the computer.

VBR (variable bit rate): Used in reference to digital video streams that vary the amount of data transferred per second depending upon the content.

VCD (VideoCD): A format based on MPEG-1 for digital video that plays on both computers and standalone VideoCD players. The format is playable on most commercial DVD players as well, with quality approximately equal to VHS tape.

WAV: The Windows standard format for phase-encoded audio such as that used on CDs.

Summary

In this chapter you've learned the history and purpose of our four title applications and how Apple has positioned the iApps. You've also picked up some of the jargon common to these applications and their venues. Every vocation and avocation has terminology (jargon) specific to it, and computers, audio, and video sometimes carry that to an extreme—knowing these terms in context will help you follow not only our discussion, but what you read on the Web and in magazines as well.

✦ ✦ ✦

iTunes

PART

II

✦ ✦ ✦ ✦

In This Part

✦ ✦ ✦ ✦

Introducing iTunes

In This Chapter

Discovering iTunes

What you need to use iTunes

Getting started with iTunes

Exploring the iTunes window

Using iTunes Help

Setting iTunes preferences

Since time immemorial (or at least a decade ago), Mac users have listened to music in a variety of formats on their Macs, with programs such as QuickTime Player, HyperCard, AppleCDAudio Player, SoundJam, and a plethora of other players by non-Apple third-party developers. These all-Mac solutions were popular in their day, but none came close to the universal and ubiquitous popularity MP3 has today.

Today, regardless of what kind of computer you have, what operating system it runs, or even what portable device you choose for your listening enjoyment, chances are it understands MP3 files.

MP3 is a file format that uses compression to create smaller audio files that sound almost as good as the original. Most computers, regardless of make, model, or operating system, can read and write MP3 files either by using included software such as iTunes, or third-party software such as Toast. Many portable music playing devises also use the MP3 file format. These devices come in all sizes and shapes — from software players for the Mac or PC to teeny-tiny wearable players that weigh less than an ounce, including the ear-buds!

Note

The very coolest (in our opinion) is Apple's revolutionary 5GB, 10GB, and 20GB, 1000 – 4000 song, FireWire-fast, iTunes-savvy iPod.

Photo courtesy of Apple Computer

Many portable CD players and DVD players sold today play MP3-formatted disks as well as regular Audio CDs. MP3 discs, which you can burn with iTunes (as you'll see shortly), let you pack up to ten times more music on each CD you burn (versus the Audio CD format).

Bob once burned his whole Beatles boxed set—around 250 songs—onto one 700MB CD and listened to it on his pre-iPod music player, a RioVolt.

Now consider the phenomenal popularity of peer-to-peer file sharing services such as Napster and Gnutella, and you'll realize that the MP3 file format has become the proverbial 900-pound gorilla. And, as such, we've seen a profusion of cool Mac programs to play, organize, manage, burn, and transfer MP3 files.

iTunes can do all that and more. When Steve Jobs showed iTunes to the Mac faithful during his January 9, 2001 Macworld Expo keynote, jaws were dropping all over the room.

Of course, there were those few jaded individuals who gleefully noted that iTunes was actually the spawn of best-selling MP3 player SoundJam (written by Jeffrey Robbin and published by Casady & Greene), and that Apple must have made Casady & Greene and Robbin an offer they couldn't refuse to get it.

In this chapter, we discuss what iTunes can do for you and explore the iTunes interface. In the next few chapters, we show you how to perform specific tasks using iTunes.

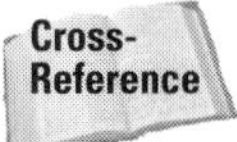

For the latest on iTunes 4, see Appendix B.

Discovering iTunes and What It Does

Ask a half-dozen Mac users what iTunes is, and you're likely to get at least a dozen different descriptions. You've been told that iTunes is a Mac's CD player, and it is. You've also been told that it is the way to burn audio CDs, and it is that, too. In addition, you've been told (also accurately) that it is the conduit to our MP3 players, such as the iPod or Rio; our radio connection to Internet radio station broadcasts; and the database managing our Mac's collection of MP3s, AIFFs, and WAVs.

We use the words *song* and *track* interchangeably and generically throughout the book. And we do it even though we know that not every track on a CD is a song. For example, the CD might be a book on disc. We also know that not every item in your library will be a song even though that is what iTunes calls them.

iTunes is all these things and more. You can use it to play the MP3 files on your hard disks and the Red Book CD-audio files on your CDs. You can use it to display soothing, stimulating, or otherwise satisfying visual effects. And you can use it to send information to AppleWorks, which can automatically generate jewel-box covers and CD labels, complete with artist names, song titles, and track lengths.

Most would agree, however, that iTunes' ability to rip songs — encode Red Book audio files from a music CD and magically turn them into great sounding yet much smaller MP3 files on your hard drive — is its most valuable capability.

WARNING: Some So-Called "CDs" May Damage Your Macintosh!

You should be careful of so-called audio CDs that are "copy-protected." Check new CDs you purchase. According to Apple KnowledgeBase article #106882, the industry is starting to produce CDs that not only won't play in your computer's optical drive, but may actually cause damage to your computer.

These renegade discs shouldn't even be called CDs—they don't conform to the Red Book, the standards document that describes a properly created audio CD. And, in fact, the aforementioned article says as much:

The (copy protected) audio discs are technically and legally not Compact Discs (CD format), and the CD logo has been removed from the disc. In the logo's former place is the printed message:

"Will not play on PC/Mac"

This appears both on the cover and on the disc. Inserting this disc in a computer may cause the system to stop responding. It might not be possible to eject the disc on computers without a manual eject hole.

Unfortunately, not all Mac users notice the fine print in time to prevent damage to their Macs. Some Macs reportedly require hardware repairs not covered by Apple's warranty, which only covers "real" CDs, and states:

If a disc with copyright protection technology remains inside the drive after following the procedures above, or if the computer does not start up normally, it is recommended that you contact an Apple Authorized Service Provider (AASP) or Apple Technical Support. Audio discs that incorporate copyright protection technologies do not adhere to published Compact Disc standards. Apple designs its optical disc drives to support media that conform to such standards.

The first such disk that came to our attention was Sony's *A New Day Has Come* by Celine Dion. Released in Europe, this disk reportedly causes some Macs to crash. Apple rightfully places the blame squarely on the record label. If a copy-protected disk (note that we avoided calling it a "CD") messes up your Mac, blame it on labels like Sony, not on Apple.

The bottom line is to be very careful about what you stick into your Mac's mouth. Shiny discs that look like, but are not really, CDs may be hazardous to your Mac's health.

Now, although the music industry tries to equate this ripping with the idea that you're ripping them off, it's not true unless you start giving away or, worse, selling copies of copyrighted material. If you're just enjoying copies of songs you've purchased on another device, such as your computer, iPod, cassette player, or car stereo, you're probably okay under the U.S. Court of Appeal's (Ninth Circuit)

BetaMax decision. You're even okay if you're playing the copy you made on your regular CD player to prevent risking damage to the original.

However, posting these files on your Web site is an infringement unless you have the copyright holder's express written consent. (Good luck getting that, by the way, in most cases.)

As the MP3 craze has gathered momentum, manufacturers of CD and DVD players have found a niche to fill. Creating players that play not only standard audio CDs, but also properly formatted data CDs containing MP3 files seemed like a natural evolution. Although they are not yet in the majority, the number of CD and DVD players that boast MP3 CD support is rapidly growing. In Chapter 5, we discuss how to create an MP3 CD. We also describe the differences in formatting between an audio CD (called a CD-DA, for Compact Disc-Digital Audio) and a data CD (sometimes called an MP3-CD). iTunes has a Preferences setting to create an MP3 CD instead of a CD-DA. And iTunes converts AIFF, WAV, and MP3 files to Red Book audio files automatically when it creates an audio CD (CD-DA).

Caution

Don't convert between formats more than once, especially between MP3 and either AIFF or WAV. MP3 is a *lossy* compression format. Therefore, when you apply the compression, some (hopefully) unnecessary data is thrown away (lost) to reduce the file's size. The bad news is that if that lost data is lost forever. So, if you later convert that MP3 file to either AIFF or WAV, it won't sound as good as the original. Further, if you were to re-encode the resulting AIFF or WAV file back into an MP3, even more data is discarded, and the sound quality deteriorates further. As you can imagine, looping through this cycle a few times seriously degrades the quality of the recording.

What You Need to Use iTunes

iTunes requires a Mac with at least one USB port running Mac OS X. Technically, that is all iTunes requires. But unless you have some of the things in this section, you won't be able to do much with it. For starters, you're also going to need some free disk space — probably a lot of it — if you're going to rip tracks to disk and build a library of songs.

Note

Bob's music collection uses more than 6GB of disk space and contains over 1500 songs. All of the songs fit easily on his 10GB iPod, with room to spare for such items as a cleanly-installed bootable System Folder (Mac OS 9.2.2), DiskWarrior, Disk First Aid, Norton Disk Doctor, and some folders he backed up from his PowerBook the other day in a hotel room somewhere.

Dennis's music collection, not including the stuff he has yet to put on the computer, uses more than 8 gigabytes of disk space and doesn't come close to fitting on his 5GB iPod. But that's okay, because he mostly sits at home writing and finds listening to a CD in his computer or listening to audio files with iTunes more convenient than listening to music straight from his iPod.

CD burner

A CD-R, CD-RW, or SuperDrive isn't required to use iTunes, but you won't be able to create (burn) your own CDs without one.

Fortunately, most current Mac models come with such a drive as a standard component or offer it as an optional configuration. If your Mac doesn't have such a drive, you can always hook one up through USB or FireWire. We'd say SCSI, too, except that SCSI support, particularly in OS X, is limited.

Note

Be sure to verify that any external CD burner you acquire is compatible with iTunes and your Mac's built-in burner software. The iTunes Web page at `www.apple.com/iTunes` maintains a list of compatible drives.

We also encourage you to seriously consider FireWire drives over USB. USB is much slower and, due to other activity on the USB bus, rarely burns successfully at speeds beyond 2x. Failed burns result in what we long-time burners call *coasters,* which are worthless CDs useful as a drink coaster and nothing more.

Media

No, you don't need a newspaper, magazine, TV station, or radio station to enjoy iTunes. In this instance, when we say *media* we mean blank discs. Blank discs are necessary if you're planning to burn CD-DAs or MP3 discs, but because that's half the fun, you'll want to try it if your hardware supports it.

Note

We strongly recommend that you stick to CD-R media rather than CD-RW because CD-R discs are much more compatible with audio CD players. Also, most drives burn CD-R discs two or three times faster than CD-RWs. Finally, although you can erase and reuse CD-RW discs, they cost more than even high-quality blank CD-R discs. Many users don't use CD-RW discs at all because they find them not worth the additional cost, burn-time, and bother. Finally, Apple includes a cautionary note concerning CD-RW media in Knowledge Base article 58585: "Apple CD-RW Drive: Cannot Write to High Speed CD-RW Discs."

Some audio CD players might not even recognize CD-R media. This is mostly true for older models.

Please note that some Audio CD and DVD players can be sensitive to the color or brand of the CD-R. We have encountered players that have only liked silver, only liked blue, only liked gold, or liked just two of the three. There's no rule to follow here—trial and error is your best method.

For all these reasons, it is best to buy small quantities of media at first until you find a brand/color of CD-R that works well on the player(s) you're going to use. As to the brand, CD-burning folklore says that Verbatim, Fuji, TDK, and other so-called name brands are usually your best bet. Bob has had good luck lately with spindles of 50 top-of-the-line discs from Memorex (Black; 700MB; 16X) and iMation (Silver; 700MB; 16X).

You can be sure that the cheapest no-name CD-R discs, often sold under the store's own brand name, are usually no bargain unless you have a thing for coasters.

Be very careful if you stumble across CD-Rs that advertise greater than 80 min/700MB capacity. Some burners won't recognize them, and we have heard stories about damage to burners when they were used. We haven't experienced this, but we haven't ever used such questionable media.

Speakers or headphones

Although your Mac does have built-in speakers, you can probably use external speakers or headphones. If you work in an office or not everyone in your household appreciates your excellent musical taste, you certainly need a set of headphones. And, unless you have more of a tin ear than Dennis does, you'll really enjoy the extra sound quality from a set of good external speakers.

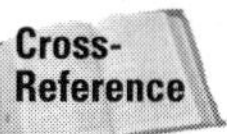

Turn to Chapter 7 for more information on specific speakers and headphones.

An iPod or other MP3 player

Although having an MP3 player (particularly the iPod) is not a necessity, after you start using this device, you'll be hooked. Being able to download your favorite play lists to a pocket-sized portable device that you can take with you to the park, the pool, or on a trip is habit-forming. We'll also discuss these in Chapters 6 and 7.

Internet access

If you never intend to make use of iTunes' Internet radio capabilities, don't want to download MP3s from newsgroups and Web sites, and don't want iTunes to automatically look up the track names and lengths when you insert an audio CD, then Internet access isn't necessary.

Otherwise, it is, and having it makes iTunes that much more fun (and useful).

In the interest of full disclosure, both authors believe Internet access is as necessary as water, shelter, and even food. We also believe that the faster the Internet connection, the better.

Getting Started with iTunes

You might find it convenient to be in front of your Mac with iTunes running for this section. We include pictures as we go along, but keep in mind that they are in black-and-white whereas your Mac screen is in living color.

You are more likely to remember if you explore as you read. Experimentation is a great way to learn, and you rarely hurt anything experimenting with software as forgiving and friendly as iTunes.

Start by launching iTunes, which is located in the Applications directory. Note that *directory* is OS X/UNIX-speak for that thing we longtime Mac OS 9 users called a *folder*. When you find it, double-click the iTunes icon to launch it.

Or, because Apple assumes that you'll be using iTunes often, it comes preinstalled in the Dock, as shown in Figure 3-1.

Figure 3-1: Apple is so thoughtful that they've put iTunes in your Dock for easy access.

When you launch iTunes for the first time, the first screen you see is brought to you courtesy of the Apple legal eagles. Fortunately, no trees were killed to bring you the iTunes Software License Agreement screen (Figure 3-2).

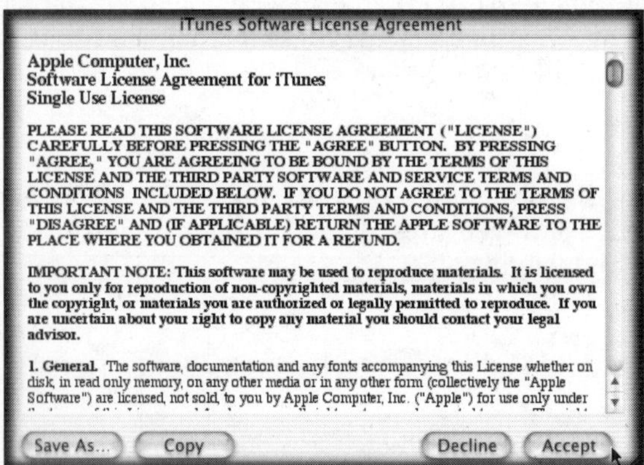

Figure 3-2: Count on the lawyers to get into the act nice and early.

You have four options, from left to right:

- ✦ **Save As:** Click the Save As button to save a copy of the license agreement to disk.
- ✦ **Copy:** Click the Copy button to copy the license agreement to the Clipboard This comes in handy when you want to paste the agreement into another application, such as TextEdit.
- ✦ **Decline:** Click the Decline button to exit the license agreement and the iTunes installer. If you want to read the agreement, you'll have to scroll down quite a few times. Or, do what everyone does:
- ✦ **Accept:** Click the Accept button to proceed.

The iTunes Setup Assistant's Welcome screen (Figure 3-3) should now appear. Read it and then click Next.

The polite iTunes assistant helps you get iTunes configured quickly. It asks if you want your Web browser to play audio MP3 streams from the Internet and whether you want iTunes to automatically connect to the Internet. If you select the appropriate option, iTunes will connect to the Internet when you choose a streaming radio broadcast or when you want to obtain a track list upon inserting an audio CD. As you can see in Figure 3-4, iTunes defaults to enabling both options.

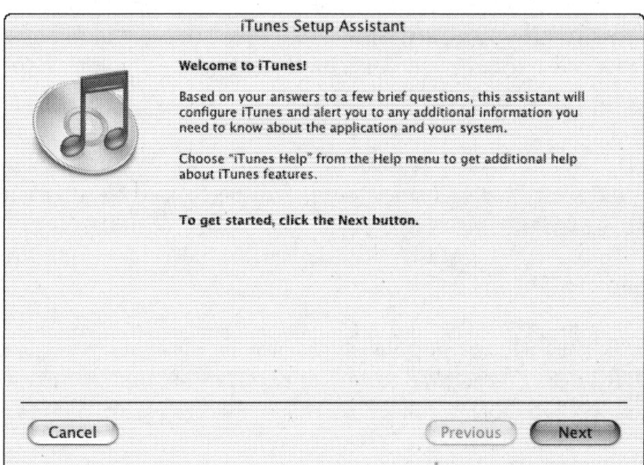

Figure 3-3: Welcome to the iTunes Setup Assistant.

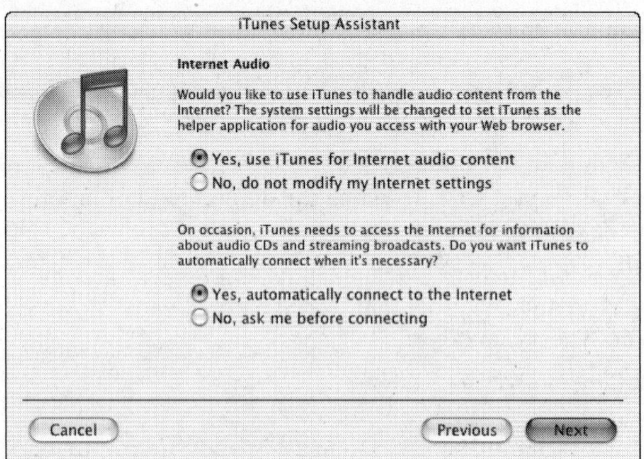

Figure 3-4: Set your iTunes Internet access preferences here.

Set these radio buttons as you desire. If you have a broadband Internet connection (cable or DSL), we suggest you answer Yes to both. If you have dial-up (telephone/modem) access to the Internet, you may want to change the settings to No and No.

When you're done, click Next.

iTunes generously offers to search your hard disk (really just the areas accessible to you as a user under Mac OS X), locate any MP3 files, and add copies to your music library for easy access, as shown in Figure 3-5.

If you change the setting to "No, I'll add them myself later," you'll be on your own when it comes to populating your iTunes Library and will be forced to drag the MP3 files into the iTunes window or to choose File ⇨ Add to Library. Which you choose depends primarily upon whether you want to duplicate the disk space and whether you want everything or just certain items in your iTunes Library.

Note that if you answer "Yes," iTunes populates your music library with every single MP3 file on your hard disk. If you have games or applications that include MP3 files, you may end up with a library full of so-called "songs" with names like "DwarfHeadExplosion" and "MortalWoundScreamLong."

After making your choice, click Done.

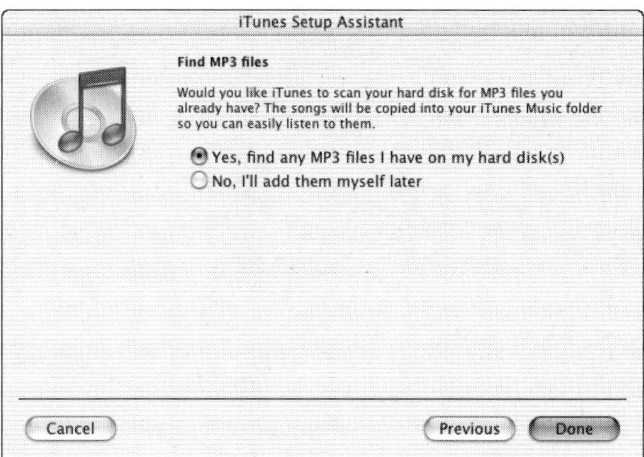

Figure 3-5: iTunes asks if you want it to find all your MP3 files.

Assuming that you answered affirmatively in the previous step, iTunes searches all available files looking for MP3s and copies them to the iTunes Library (Figure 3-6).

When the search is complete, you see a populated iTunes Library window similar to the one in Figure 3-7, the difference being that it shows your music collection rather than Dennis's.

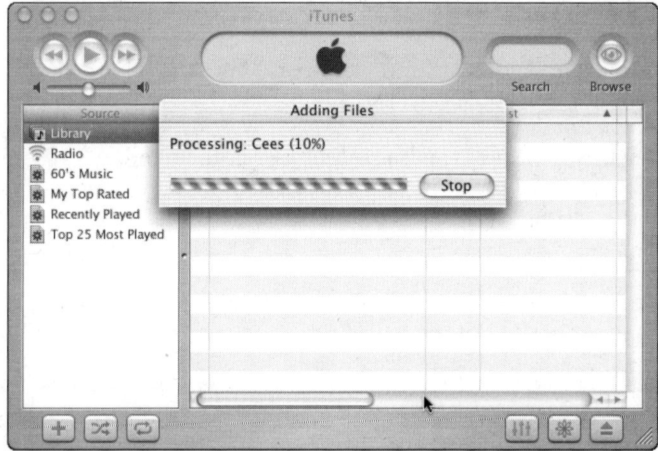

Figure 3-6: iTunes searches your hard disk for MP3 files.

Figure 3-7: The iTunes window with all the MP3 files iTunes could find.

As mentioned previously, iTunes finds *all* files that contain MP3 tracks (or any other format it recognizes, such as AIFF or WAV), even games, applications, and MPEG video files, as shown in Figure 3-7. We discuss MPEG video in the iMovie and iDVD sections of this book.

Exploring the iTunes Window

The iTunes window, shown in Figure 3-8, sports the brushed-metal look made (in)famous by QuickTime when Apple released QuickTime 4. Using this window type has some advantages over that used in most OS X windows. You can drag the window by clicking in any part of the frame, not just in the window's title bar. If that's not enough, the brushed-metal look is evocative of high-end audio and video equipment's finish, letting folks know right away that this is a multimedia application.

As you can see, the iTunes window has many parts. In fact, if you have an iPod plugged in, an iPod button appears to the left of the equalizer button on the bottom of the window.

For more about the iPod button, see Chapter 5, where we also discuss the iPod and MP3 players.

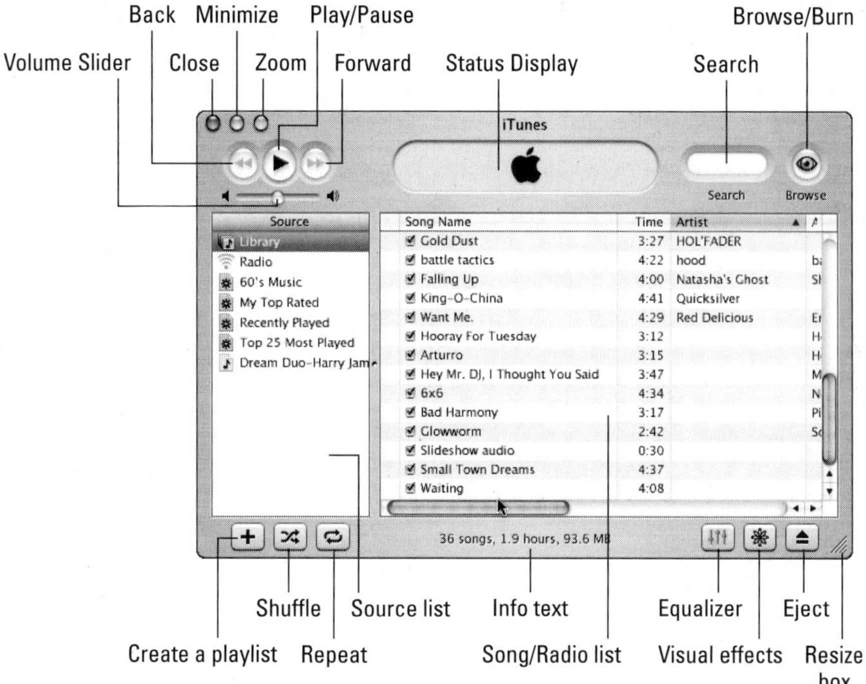

Figure 3-8: Welcome to iTunes. Here's a brand spanking new iTunes Library.

Here are the features of the iTunes window:

- ✦ **Close, Minimize, and Zoom:** You find these buttons in the upper-left corner of virtually every window in OS X. As usual, Close (red) is self-explanatory; Minimize (amber) reduces the window to an icon in your Dock; and Zoom (green) switches you back and forth between the window shown in Figure 3-8 and a much reduced window, as shown in Figure 3-9.

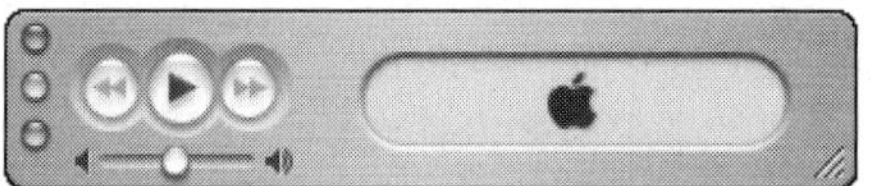

Figure 3-9: Clicking the zoom box shrinks the iTunes window down to this basic status display.

✦ **Status Display:** This little area tells you a lot when a song is playing, as shown in Figure 3-10a. There are three rows in the Status Display that enable you to do the following:

- **Top Row:** You can view the song name, artist name, and album name, which appear in rotation. Or, you can force this row to switch at your whim just by clicking on it.
- **Second Row:** You can view how much of the song has played, how much is remaining to play, and the full length of the song.
- **Bottom Row:** Contains a graphic bar indicating the current position of the virtual playhead within the song. You can drag the little diamond (which is called, not coincidentally, the *playhead*) or just click on the bar where you want the playhead to be.

The Status Display also has another mini-icon that looks like an arrowhead inside a circle. Clicking this icon toggles the display between the information described above and the animated graphic equalizer, shown in Figure 3-10b, which is an audio display.

When you're connected to a streaming radio broadcast, the Status Display shows the station you're playing and how long you've been connected, as shown in Figure 3-10c.

When you're ripping a CD, the Status Display also shows the name of the track (if known) and the speed at which the song is being ripped. This speed represents the number of minutes being imported per minute of real time. For example, if the display says 6.6x, as shown in Figure 3-10d, then 6.6 minutes of content is being imported each minute.

✦ **Source List:** The Source List specifies all the various sources iTunes accesses to play songs (or whatever) for you. At the top of the list is your iTunes Library, the master database of all the songs iTunes tracks for you. This is followed by any external sources, such as inserted audio CDs, iPods, and supported MP3 players that are currently connected to your computer. Next is your portal to Internet radio, called the *Radio Tuner.* Finally, you'll have a list of *playlists*. Playlists are subsets of your library that you've created. *Smart playlists* are dynamic playlists whose contents change according to criteria you specify. Smart playlists appear at the top of the playlists and bear the distinctive icon shown next to them. For example, see the icon next to My Top Rated, in Figure 3-8. We'll discuss all of these source types in Chapter 4 and Chapter 6.

Tip

Double-clicking an item in the Source List opens that item in its own window.

✦ **Song/Detail List:** After you select an item in the Source List (the Library is the default), its contents will be enumerated in this large list area. There is one exception to this, covered under the Search option later in this section. When you select the Radio Tuner, you'll see categories of stations with disclosure triangles to their left, as shown in Figure 3-11. Clicking one of the disclosure triangles presents an indented list of stations within that category. You must have an active Internet connection for this to work. In all other cases, you see a list of the songs available in that Library, device, or playlist.

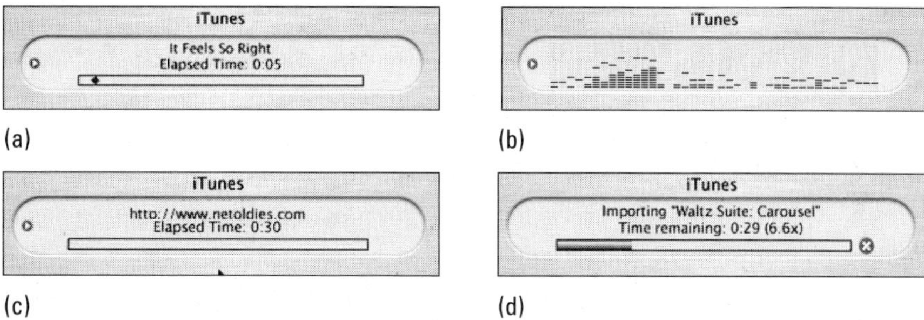

Figure 3-10a–d: The Status Display when a song is playing (a); with the equalizer shown (b); when listening to Internet radio (c); and when ripping songs from a CD (d).

Figure 3-11: Internet radio stations are grouped just like folders in a Finder list view.

Following guidelines almost as old as the Mac itself (dating back to the introduction of the List Manager in 1985) you can select multiple items in a list by holding down the Command button (⌘) as you click the items you want. Or, you can select a contiguous range by clicking the first item you want and then holding down the Shift button when you select the last item.

You also have control over which columns display for a particular source item by choosing Edit ⇨ View Options (or ⌘-J), which opens the View Options dialog (Figure 3-12).

Figure 3-12: In the View Options dialog you can specify which columns are displayed for a source item.

✦ **Back:** This is your rewind button. Hold it down to move back through the song being played or click it to move back to the beginning of the current song. When no song is playing, but you have a song selected in the song list, this button moves you to the previous song in the list. If you have no song selected in the song list, the button becomes disabled.

✦ **Forward:** This is the opposite of the Back button. It provides a Fast Forward feature when you hold it down, or it moves to the next song when you click it.

For both Back and Forward, if you've enabled Shuffle (described later in this chapter), the previous or next item will be based upon the shuffle order and not the one displayed.

✦ **Play/Pause:** When nothing is playing, this button is the right-pointing triangle shown in Figure 3-13a. When a song is playing this button becomes the two vertical line Pause button shown in Figure 3-13b.

(a)

(b)

Figure 3-13a–b: To start a song playing, click the Play button (a), which then changes to the Pause button (b). You can click the Pause button to pause play.

✦ **Volume slider:** You can adjust iTunes' volume to anything from Mute (far left) to maximum (far right) by sliding the little knob.

These volume settings are relative to the current system volume setting, so if you have your system volume (Sound Preferences panel) set low, a maximum setting will still be quite low.

✦ **Browse/Burn:** This button takes on many appearances and functions, depending upon what is displayed in the center of the window. When you select the Library, this button is a colorful eyeball named Browse. Selecting a playlist changes it to the camera shutter Burn button. With Radio Tuner selected, it changes to Refresh, and so forth. We'll cover its many faces in Chapters 5 and 6 where we discuss iTunes capabilities in greater detail. One major point is that when you click Browse for the Library, an additional pane with three columns displays above the detail list. You will see this in Chapter 5 when we cover browsing the Library.

✦ **Search:** Typing in this field allows you to search for a string of characters in the detail list. iTunes displays only those entries containing the string. This is called *filtering* the list.

✦ **Add playlist:** Click this button to create a new, untitled playlist in the source list. When you create the list, iTunes turns an *untitled playlist* into an editable text field so that you can begin typing immediately to (re)name it. Chapter 5 contains an extensive discussion of playlists.

✦ **Shuffle:** Click this button to have iTunes play the songs in the current list in (pseudo) random order.

✦ **Repeat:** You get two different repeat functions for the price of one with this little button. Clicking it once loops the current list, repeating it over and over until you intervene. A second click of the button changes the repeat from focusing on the list to just repeating the current song. When just the current song is being looped, the button changes appearance slightly, as shown in Figure 3-14a–c. If you can't tell the difference between the buttons shown in Figure 3-14a and Figure 3-14b, it's because they're in black-and-white. On your computer screen, you'll see the looped arrows change from gray to blue when Repeat List is on.

(a)

(b)

(c)

Figure 3-14a–c: The three faces of Repeat: (a) Repeat off; (b) Repeat list; (c) Repeat song.

✦ **Eject CD:** This is a quick way to eject an inserted CD-DA or CD-ROM. Don't press this while burning a CD unless you want to ruin your CD.

✦ **Equalizer:** Clicking this button displays the dialog shown in Figure 3-15. Using this dialog and all its various controls and menu selections allows you to adjust specific sound frequencies, working much like the treble and bass controls on stereo equipment. We discuss the Equalizer in Chapter 6.

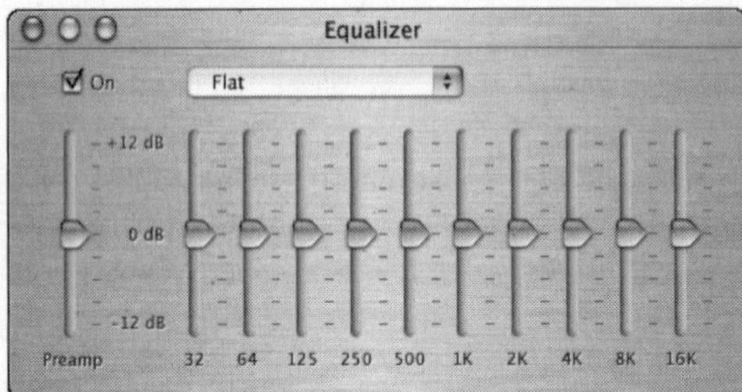

Figure 3-15: The Equalizer dialog lets you fine-tune the sound.

✦ **Visual Effects:** We don't think this button has a practical application, but it sure is fun to play with. When you click it, iTunes replaces the source and detail lists with a colorful animated display, as shown in Figure 3-16. Okay, so you can't see the color or the animation in this black-and-white still shot— that's one of the reasons we recommended that you read this material in front of your Mac!

When you have Visual Effects turned on, the Browse/Burn button turns into an Options button (see Figure 3-16). We'll cover iTunes Visual Effects in Chapter 5.

✦ **Resize box:** You can resize both the shrunken and full-sized iTunes windows by clicking and dragging the resize box at the lower-right corner of the window. The shrunken window resizes only horizontally with a minimum size showing just the control buttons and hiding the status box, and a maximum size just large enough to show the buttons and the status field. Resizing the regular iTunes window resizes the status box, resizes the search field, and hides/reveals columns in the detail list, leaving everything else intact.

✦ **Info text:** iTunes displays text here that tells you how many items are in the detail list and, if the selected item in the Source List is either the library or a playlist, how long it takes to play them all, as well as how much disk space they consume.

As you can see, iTunes packs a lot of buttons and other items into its window and there's going to be a lot to learn if you want to learn it all.

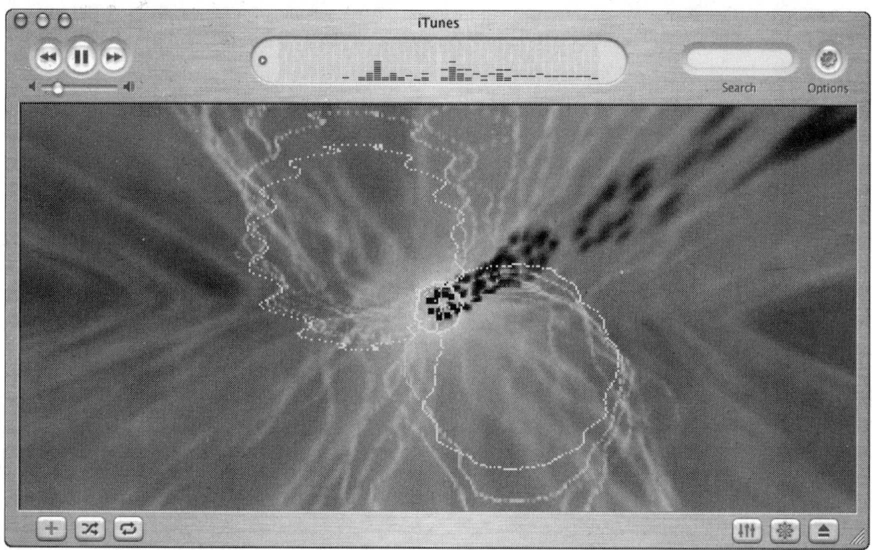

Figure 3-16: Visual Effects can relax or entertain.

Getting Help

Apple actually does a pretty decent job with its iTunes Help files. That's a good thing, because iTunes doesn't come with a manual—hence the reason for this book. Unfortunately, as with most help systems, you must have some clue about what you want to ask before you can get the help you need. If you don't know whether a feature is available then you can't ask about it and, thus, probably won't ever discover that feature or how to use it.

Because this is the first of the four applications, we'll just say it here. Apple doesn't include manuals for any of its iLife applications (or other consumer software, such as AppleWorks). This creates a larger market for books such as this, simply because these products pack so much power and capability that just can't be adequately expressed and demonstrated with the Help systems available.

Obtaining Help with iTunes is the same as other OS X applications—choose *application-name* Help from the Help menu. In this case it is iTunes Help (⌘-?). After a short wait, Help Viewer starts up and displays the window shown in Figure 3-17 or something very similar, if you have a different version of iTunes or Help Viewer (which is a possibility, considering how often Apple revises the software).

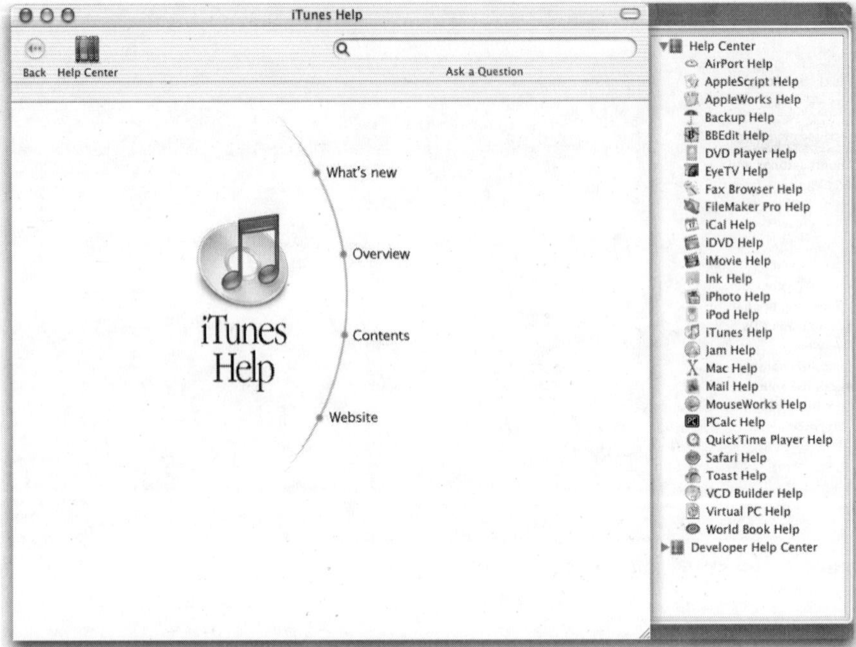

Figure 3-17: The initial iTunes Help window.

The text field above the Ask a Question label is your friend. Type a word or phrase and press Return to get some help. The Help Viewer searches the entire iTunes Help database for anything that might answer your question or provide information about the words you entered. In Figure 3-18, you can also see the result of a query about MP3s. The barcodes to the right of a listed topic are relevancy rankings. The longer the bar, the more relevant Help Viewer believes the topic to be. In other words, that's an approximation of how appropriate the topic might be. When you see a really long bar, you can bet that the topic is completely germane to the discussion, unless you weren't very specific in the words you entered. When you see a short bar, the topic probably won't be too helpful, but there is some wording in it that is related to your query.

Note The Help Viewer displayed here is the one that comes with Jaguar (Mac OS X 10.2 and later). A different version might have a different appearance.

When you click a topic in the scrolling list, a brief excerpt from that topic displays in the bottom pane, as shown in Figure 3-18.

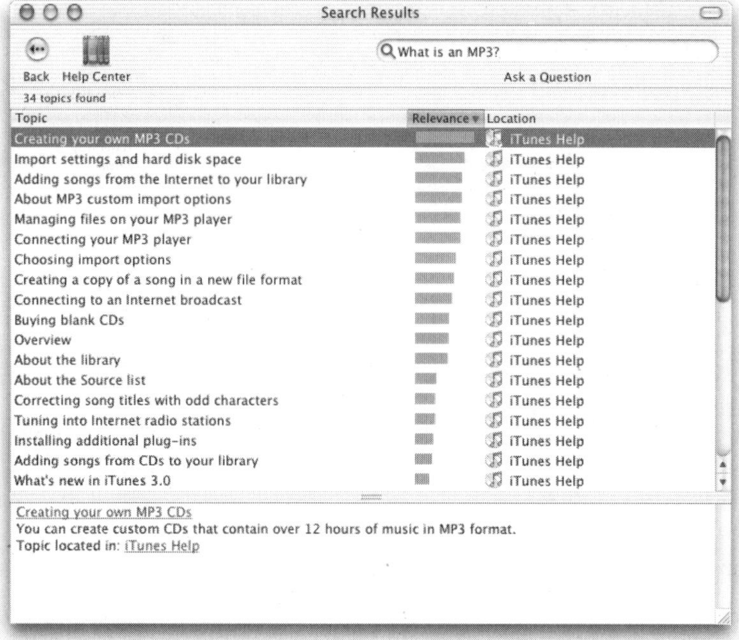

Figure 3-18: iTunes Help answering a query about MP3s.

Setting iTunes Preferences

iTunes allows you to customize a number of settings through the iTunes Preferences dialog. To access Preferences, choose iTunes ➪ Preferences (or ⌘-Y). You'll be presented with a dialog with five buttons in its toolbar: General, Effects, Importing, Burning, and Advanced.

General

As shown in Figure 3-19, the General display has three sections. The top section has two pop-up menus and a checkbox that control how things look in the main iTunes window. If you have trouble making out the text in either the Source List or the Song List, you can choose to make them larger. Apple doesn't let you set the actual size, just Small (which is about 10 pt) and Large (which is about 14 pt). The Show genre when browsing checkbox determines whether the Genre column joins the Artist and Album columns when you browse. (See Chapter 5 for a full discussion of browsing the Library.)

Figure 3-19: General Preferences control basic iTunes appearance and behavior. The On CD Insert pop-up menu is to the right of the label.

Clicking the On CD Insert pop-up menu presents you with four choices as shown in Figure 3-20.

Figure 3-20: The On CD Insert pop-up menu.

✦ **Show Songs:** The default option, tells iTunes to check with its database and, if necessary, to check the Internet database for the CD's track list.

✦ **Begin Playing:** Tells iTunes to automatically start playing with the first track.

✦ **Import Songs:** Tells iTunes to start ripping the tracks from the CD into MP3 files stored in your Library.

✦ **Import Songs and Eject:** A variation on Import Songs where iTunes ejects the CD when the import is done.

The bottom section of the General Preferences tab should be familiar to you, because it is very similar to the iTunes Setup Assistant discussed earlier in this chapter in the "Getting Started with iTunes" section.

Remember that if you enable Connect to Internet when needed, iTunes attempts to dial your modem whenever you insert an audio CD or do anything else that might need Internet access. If you're using just one phone line for both your modem and your (real) life, you might want to leave this unchecked and manually make the connections either beforehand or when iTunes complains about not being able to communicate with the cyber world.

Effects

The Effects display, shown in Figure 3-21, lets you specify whether and how much each of two sound effects is used. You can also tell iTunes to do the math and equalize sound playback volume for all songs, regardless of how you manually adjust the volume slider.

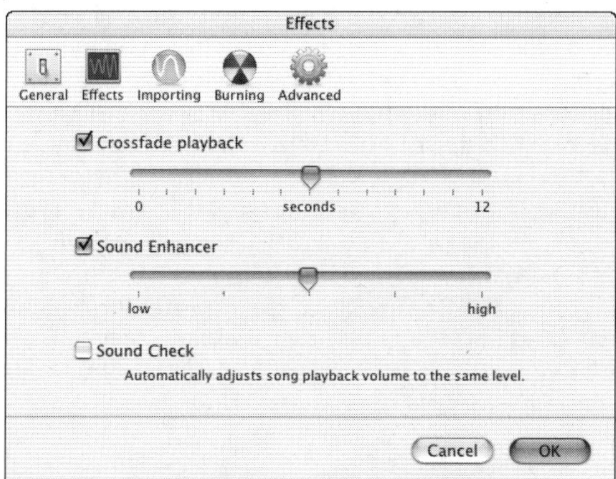

Figure 3-21: The Effects display lets you specify whether and how the Sound Enhancer is employed, as well as whether and how much cross fade is used between songs.

Cross fade playback controls whether iTunes has silent gaps between songs or whether finishing songs fade out while new songs fade in. You can specify how many seconds (from 0 to 12) of fade are employed.

Note

Bob thinks this may be iTunes' most annoying "feature." Songs, for the most part, should start and end the way the performer recorded them. "Cross fade is the music industry equivalent of colorization. In both cases the end product is not what the artist intended. It also attenuates the beginning and ending of songs, possibly losing notes and words. We both suggest that you set this feature to 0 if you want to hear the music as it was recorded."

The Sound Enhancer lets you control the *depth* and *liveliness* (Apple's terms) of your music. Barring really good speakers, you're probably not going to notice much difference, but you can see a difference in the Equalizer status display. A high Sound Enhancer setting raises the level near the display's center.

The Sound Check checkbox provides an override to the volume slider. If you have this box checked, all songs play at the same volume. iTunes goes through your entire library to determine the various volume levels, and evens them out.

Importing

The Importing display (Figure 3-22) enables you to specify whether tracks imported from CDs should be encoded as MP3, AIFF, or WAV. When you choose either AIFF or WAV, the Configuration pop-up menu offers two choices: Automatic and Custom. Specifying Custom displays the dialog shown in Figure 3-23, where you can specify whether your rip will be mono or stereo, 8-bit or 16-bit, and what the Sample Rate will be (from 8kHz to 48kHz). Unless you really have a specific need and know what you're doing, it is advisable to leave this set to Automatic.

Most of the time, you'll probably be importing your songs as MP3s where iTunes offers three choices for CBR (constant bit rate) importing (Figure 3-24a) and a Custom choice, which displays the MP3 Encoder dialog (Figure 3-24b). If you turn on the Use Variable Bit Rate Encoding (VBR) checkbox, the bit rate pop-up menus specify the minimum rates to be used and the Quality pop-up menu becomes enabled. In the Quality pop-up menu, you can choose from seven quality levels, which iTunes attempts to maintain by varying the compression bit rate. If the music is relatively complex, like an orchestral offering, using VBR can help reduce the file size.

Tip

If you're importing voice recordings, such as speeches or narratives, you should consider lower bit rates. Unless your ears are even worse than Dennis's, you should probably keep music at 128 Kbps or greater, disk space permitting, because higher bit rates mean larger files and, usually, better fidelity. Bob, who claims he used to hear like an audiophile, rips his MP3s at 160 Kbps and can tell the difference.

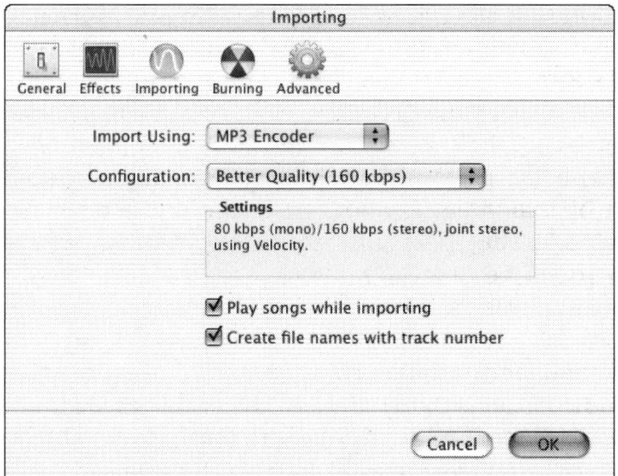

Figure 3-22: The Importing tab is where you can specify how songs are ripped from disc and in what format they're to be stored.

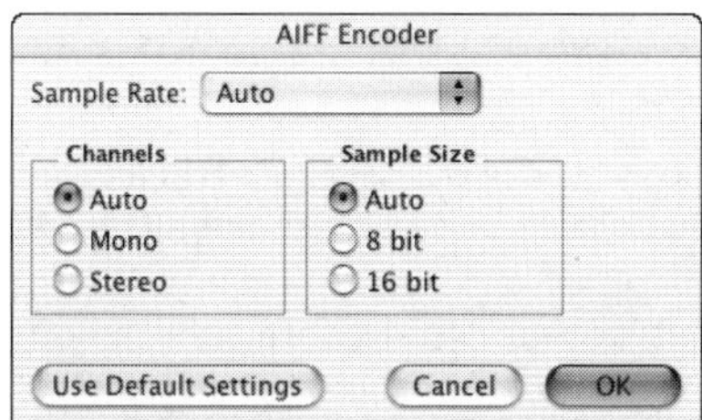

Figure 3-23: A true audiophile can control AIFF and WAV imports using the Custom dialog.

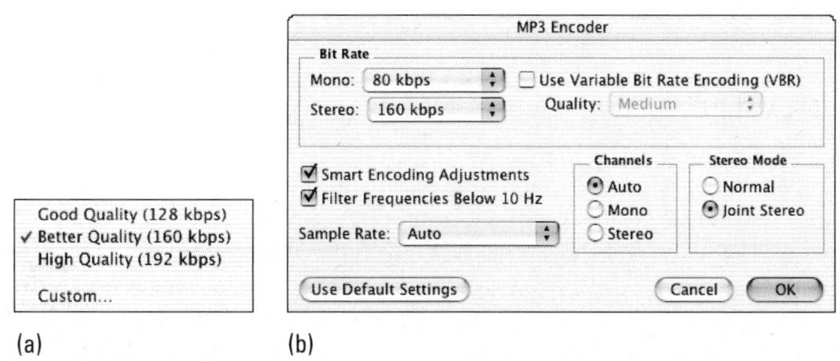

Figure 3-24: The MP3 Encoder's Configuration pop-up menu (a) and the Custom choice's MP3 Encoder dialog (b).

The Smart Encoding Adjustments checkbox tells iTunes to compare your encoding settings to the source music and, when beneficial to the quality, modify your settings. The Filter Frequencies Below 10Hz checkbox tells iTunes to eliminate these (essentially) inaudible frequencies from your encoding, which results in smaller files.

The Channels settings let you specify whether iTunes should create one (Mono) or two channels (Stereo) of sound. Mono files are about half the size of stereo files. Auto tells iTunes to use the same setting as the incoming data: Mono input is saved as mono and stereo input as stereo.

In the Stereo Mode settings, selecting Normal Stereo means your MP3 files will contain one track for the left stereo channel and one track for the right stereo channel. Frequently, this means that information is duplicated on the two channels. The Joint Stereo option allocates one channel to the duplicated information and the other channel to be unique information. At lower bit rates (128 Kbps and below), this often improves the quality of your encoding.

Choosing Auto for the Sample Rate tells iTunes to use the same rate as the music being imported. This gives you the highest possible quality for the space consumed, but you won't be in control of how much space is consumed.

The Play Songs While Importing checkbox is self-explanatory.

CD Burning

The CD Burning display, shown in Figure 3-25, tells you what CD burner is going to be used. You can specify the speed at which the disk should be burned and whether to burn an Audio CD or MP3 CD. When you choose Audio CD, you can also specify how large a gap to place between song tracks.

Although the pop-up menu allows you to specify up to 24x as a burn speed, iTunes ignores settings greater than the maximum speed your burner supports and resets to the maximum for your burner.

Advanced

Figure 3-26 shows the Advanced display. One of iTunes' best-kept secrets is the Change button, which allows you to change the location of your iTunes music folder. The iTunes Music folder's default location is in your Home directory's Music folder. Click the Change button to specify a different folder or to create a new folder in another location in the standard Choose a Folder dialog. You do this if, for example, you want to keep your iTunes music in the Shared folder so that other users of your Mac can access it. You also do this if, on another hard disk, you want to offload it to a portable FireWire disk, which you can move from computer to computer. Here are the features on the Advanced display:

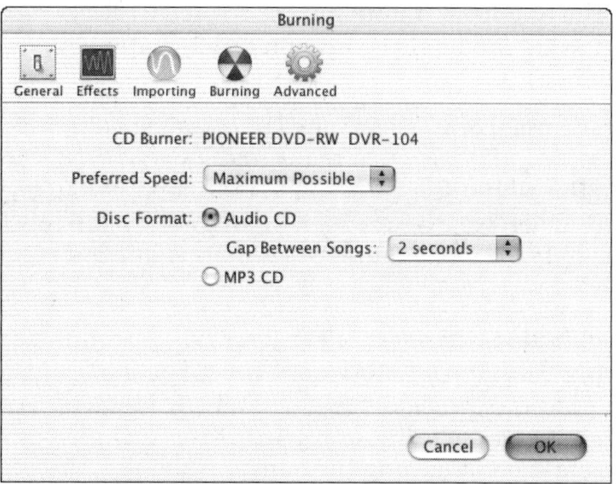

Figure 3-25: The CD Burning preferences tab is where you specify the type of CD you want to burn and how fast you'll burn it.

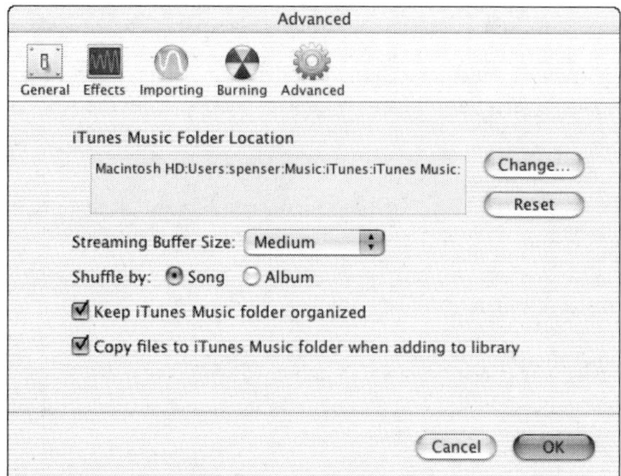

Figure 3-26: In the Advanced tab you can set your Music Folder Location, how much memory to provide the Radio's streaming buffer, how Shuffle operates, and two organizational preferences.

✦ **Streaming Buffer Size:** Choose among a Small, Medium, and Large buffer when listening to Internet radio stations in the Streaming Buffer Size pop-up menu. By allocating a larger buffer size, you are less susceptible to breaks in the sound resulting from short Internet connection interruptions.

- **Shuffle by:** You can use the Shuffle by radio buttons to specify that iTunes shuffle the songs when playing or shuffle the album order (but maintain the song order within the albums).
- **Keep iTunes Music folder organized:** Tells iTunes to organize your library into folders for each artist, with folders for albums under each artist's name and then for discs within the album (for those multi-disc sets). When you change song information (which we discuss both in Chapters 4 and 5), iTunes (if necessary) moves the song from one folder to another when you check this box.
- **Copy file to iTunes Music folder when adding to library:** This option can be a boon or a curse, depending upon your individual style. The major upside is that the Library is always intact, even if you accidentally delete a folder containing a song from elsewhere on your disk or if one of your disks is not connected. The major complaint is that making the copy consumes more disk space, which isn't too bad if you're religious about deleting the original MP3s after you've added them to iTunes.

Summary

This chapter gave you a very brief overview of iTunes and its multifaceted interface. Now turn to Chapter 4 to learn how to really start using iTunes!

✦ ✦ ✦

Getting Started with iTunes

✦ ✦ ✦ ✦

In This Chapter

Checking out the Library

Creating and managing playlists

Importing songs

Making your own CDs

Listening to Internet radio

Introducing Smart Playlists

✦ ✦ ✦ ✦

In Chapter 3, we gave you a thorough overview of iTunes and showed just how many capabilities are crammed into the deceptively simple iTunes interface. Now, we're going to get right down to the real nitty-gritty and examine the iTunes features you're likely to use most.

For iTune 4 coverage, see Appendix B.

Checking Out the Library

The very first item in the iTunes Source List is Library, with its own distinctive icon. You can neither remove the Library from the Source List, nor can you create another one. Sure, you can create a playlist (see "Creating and Managing Playlists" later in this chapter) and name it Library, but it won't have the same capabilities as the real thing. For example, the button in the upper-right of the window will be Burn rather than Browse—the wonderful browser capability we discuss shortly will be missing.

Okay, so what is the Library? The Library is the database of all the songs on all the volumes connected to your Mac that iTunes knows about. iTunes keeps track of all the songs you show it, regardless of where you have them stored on disk or disc—as long as the disk is online and accessible. But iTunes reserves a favorite place, in your Music folder (which iTunes Help calls the Music Library), for the songs it manages. In Chapter 3, we discussed the (Advanced) Preferences settings that tell iTunes where to look for this folder. We like it in our Music folder, but that's just us being a bit compulsive. Wherever you choose to keep it, be aware that when you let iTunes manage songs for you, this is where they'll be, neatly organized by artist and album.

As we've just mentioned, the Library is a database. Entries in a database are called records (one for each song, in this case). Records are divided into fields and, in the case of iTunes, these fields are named "Song," "Track," "Artist," "Album," "Rating," and so forth. We use these terms when talking about the Library.

Adding songs to your Library

There are four ways to add songs to your Library:

- ✦ **Choose File ➪ Add to Library:** This displays a standard Choose Object dialog, named Add to Library as shown in Figure 4-1. You can select either a file or a folder and click the Choose button. iTunes adds any song (MP3, WAV, or AIFF) files to your Library.

Figure 4-1: Select a file or folder in the Choose Object dialog to add songs to your Library.

If the file isn't a song file and the folder doesn't contain any song files, then nothing will get added to your Library, although iTunes won't tell you that. You just won't see any change to your Library.

Based upon your Advanced Preferences settings (refer to Chapter 3), iTunes either adds the file references or copies the songs into your iTunes Music folder. Figure 4-2 shows the copying process in operation — note the slightly dimmed items that have not yet been copied as well as the progress information in the Status Display area.

Figure 4-2: iTunes copies the songs into your Music Library by default.

In previous versions (before iTunes 3), iTunes didn't copy the files to your Library, leaving you to do so manually and it displayed a warning alert that the files wouldn't really be in your Library for iTunes to manage, just references to them elsewhere on your disk. We both avail ourselves of, and applaud, the new default. We strongly recommend that you leave the Copy files to the iTunes Music folder when adding to library box checked. It's just too easy to end up with unresolved references if you don't.

Now, your Library will be populated with some songs, as shown in Figure 4-3. By the way, this figure and the others in this section reflect Dennis's taste in music, not Bob's (which tends more to Heavy Metal and Hard Rock).

✦ **Drag a song file:** You can drag a song file or folder full of (folders of) song files to either the Library item in the Source List or to the detail list area when Library is selected in the Source List. Figure 4-4 shows a folder being dragged onto the Source List's Library icon.

iTunes automatically creates Playlists for folders (or disks) dragged directly into the Source List. This is a handy feature. If you don't want the Playlists created, drag the folders onto the Library icon.

✦ **Choose Advanced ⇨ Convert Selection to MP3:** This converts any file from which QuickTime can extract the audio to an MP3 file. This is a very powerful feature and makes full use of QuickTime's broad support for multiple formats.

Not only can you convert (as expected) sound files like AIFF and WAV to MP3, but you can also extract the sound tracks from QuickTime-readable movie files, as shown in Figure 4-5. Just add the file to your iTunes Music Library and choose Convert Selection to MP3 from the Advanced menu. iTunes starts the extraction and then the conversion process, places a small Converting Songs entry in the Source List if a playlist is being converted, and tells you how things are progressing in the Status Display while the extraction and conversion takes place. When the conversion is done, the converted file(s) will play.

Figure 4-3: Your Library now has some songs on the shelf.

Figure 4-4: You can also drag files and folders from the Finder into the Library.

Figure 4-5: iTunes converts anything with a sound track it can read into an MP3 file for you.

This is a handy way to extract and convert the sound track from movies you create with iMovie, which we discuss in Part IV of this book.

✦ **Import songs:** You can convert songs from a CD. We cover ripping (importing) from a CD later in this chapter in the "Importing Songs" section.

Removing songs from the Library

In true Macintosh fashion, deleting one or more files from your Library is simplicity itself. You just select them in the Library's detail list and press the Backspace (Delete) key on your keyboard or the Clear key on the numeric keypad or, if you like to work with the mouse, choose Edit ➪ Clear. In each of these cases, iTunes produces one of its cautionary "Are you sure?" alerts (Figure 4-6a), but you can check a box in the alert telling iTunes not to bother you with it again. If any file you're deleting is in your Music Library folder, iTunes asks, with yet another alert, whether you also want it removed from the disk (Figure 4-6b). iTunes doesn't provide this service unless the songs are in your iTunes Music folder.

If you want the file removed from the folder, click Yes. If you want the song deleted from the Library, but the file left on the disk, click No. One would expect Cancel to tell iTunes to ignore the request and leave the song in the Library and the file on disk. However, you already confirmed in the previous alert that you wanted the file removed from the list, so clicking Cancel is the same as clicking No.

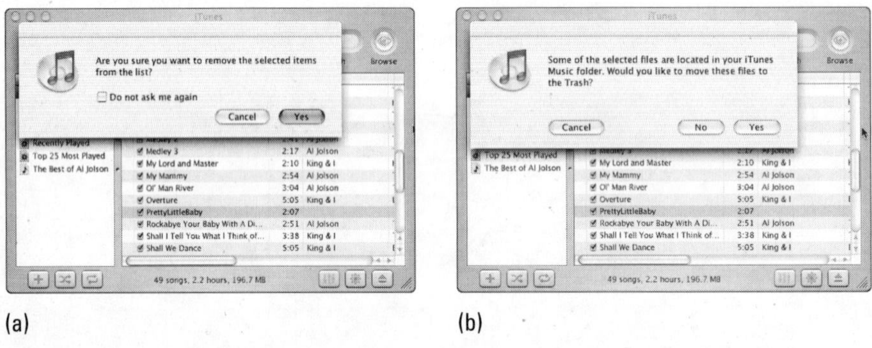

(a) (b)

Figure 4-6: iTunes asks whether you really want to delete files (a); iTunes offers to trash files you remove if they're in your Music Library (b).

Dealing with the Detail List

The iTunes detail list has a lot in common with a Finder list view. Click a field title, such as Artist or Rating, and iTunes sorts the list based upon that field's contents. Click the triangle on the right end of that title and reverse the sort order from low-to-high to high-to-low, or vice versa. An up-pointing triangle indicates an ascending (A–Z, 0–9) sort and a down-pointing triangle indicates a descending sort. Reorder the fields (other than the Song field) dragging a field title into a new position.

So, how does all this data get into the fields? As you see in the Import songs bullet, when iTunes can get the information from the Internet database, it fills the fields automatically. Sometimes, though, the information isn't there or is inaccurate or you may not have an Internet connection available while you're ripping a CD.

You can enter data into these fields in two ways. You can always type directly into the detail list, but you'll probably find it easier to click the song in the detail list and choose File ➪ Get Info (or type ⌘-I) and click the Tags tab to display the dialog shown in Figure #1. We cover the Song Information dialog and ID3 tags in Chapter 5.

This technique is especially handy when you select multiple songs and choose File ➪ Get Info. iTunes now (after presenting another nagging "Do you really wanna..." alert) presents the Multiple Song Information dialog with all the common fields filled in, as shown in Figure #2. You should be very careful before clicking OK in this dialog because every selected song will have the check marked fields replaced with the values displayed in this dialog. Therefore, be sure that you have checkmarks next to only those fields that you want changed. iTunes automatically checks the box on any field in which you type and, if you remove the change but don't uncheck the checkmark, you could inadvertently wipe out the contents of that field in every song you selected.

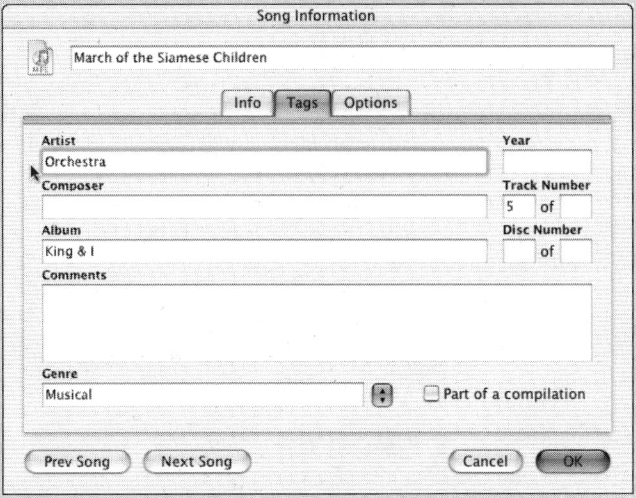

Figure #1: Change the song's detail information in the Tags tab.

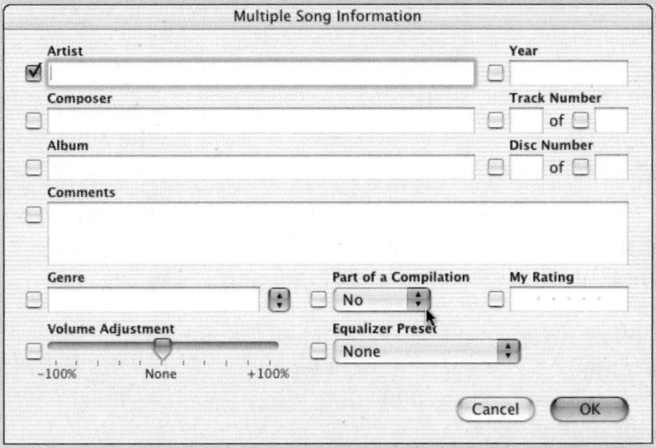

Figure #2: Make bulk changes to multiple songs using the Multiple Song Information dialog.

By the way, the little checkbox to the left of the song title (we're back in the detail list now) tells iTunes whether to play or skip the song when it plays songs sequentially. You can also use it to designate which songs to download to your iPod. (There's an iPod preference for this; if you have an iPod you can choose to ignore checkmarks or not.)

Other than the leftmost column, which does nothing in the Library (it shows the sequence order in a playlist), and the song column, which always appears in both the Library and your playlists, you can control which columns display in the Detail List and playlists, by choosing Edit ➪ View Options (⌘-J).

Searching the Library

We told you that the Library is a database. No database interface is complete without a search capability. After all, databases are often large collections of information and it is easy to overlook an entry you're trying to find if you scan manually.

iTunes provides a very basic search facility with the Search text box. Type a string into that Search box, and your detail list shrinks down to just those records that contain the string in one of the text fields, as shown in Figure 4-7.

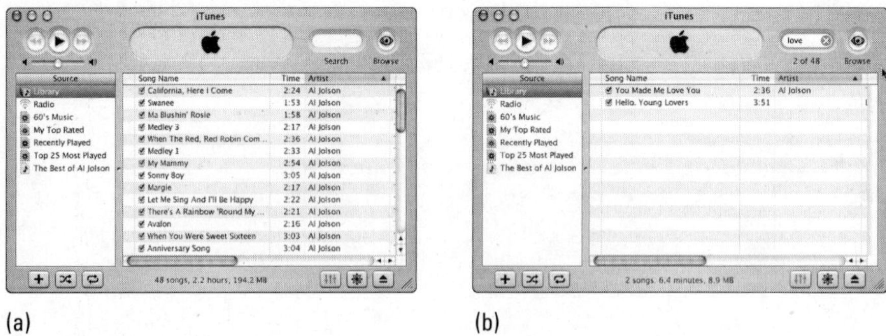

(a) (b)

Figure 4-7: Before you search (a); After you search (b).

In addition to displaying only those songs that match your search string, iTunes tells you how many songs were found out of however many were displayed in the window originally. It does this by displaying the information directly below the Search field at the top of the iTunes window (16 of 420 in Figure 4-7b).

iTunes only searches the text fields displayed in the detail list. If the string appears in a hidden field – one turned off in View Options, it won't be displayed. Similarly, if you enter digits, iTunes still won't search the Time, Size, Date, or similar fields because they are numeric and not text.

The advantages of Search are that it is blindingly fast and incredibly easy to use. The disadvantage is that it isn't very discriminating. You can't, for example, tell it to search only one or more specific fields.

Browsing the Library

It is now time to discuss the "button of many faces" in the iTunes window's upper-right corner. When the Library is selected in the Source List, this button is an eyeball called "Browse." Clicking the Browse button changes the detail list appearance, as shown in Figure 4-8, adding the number of columns you specify at the top. These columns list all the genres, all the artists, and all the albums included in your database.

The number of columns that display in the iTunes window when you click the Browse button depends on whether you have Genre display turned on or off in your Preference settings. For more on Preference settings, see Chapter 3.

Figure 4-8: Browse lets you filter your detail list display on three criteria.

Figure 4-8 also gives an example of the possible inconsistencies and misspellings that occur in Internet-downloaded Song Information. The album, "The King and I" is spelled three different ways, and the artist, Al Jolson, is spelled two different ways. This is why you should check the information obtained from the Internet and, when necessary, edit it.

Select an item from any of the three columns, and the other two columns rearrange themselves to include only items shown after the filter is applied. Click an entry in one of the two remaining columns and the third will get even smaller, as shown in Figure 4-9. Simultaneously, the detail list is filtered, displaying only those songs that match the criteria specified. Figure 4-9 shows the result of filtering a database to display only songs on Soundtracks (Genre) where F. Sinatra is the Artist. Another difference you note is that, where a search looks for an occurrence of the search string within any field, Browse only finds exact matches. Thus, in the example shown in Figure 4-9, those songs where the artist field contains "G. Kelly, F. Sinatra" are not displayed.

Figure 4-9: Multiple Browse criteria further narrow the search.

Be consistent in entering the data if you want to take advantage of browsing. For example, using both "Platters" and "The Platters" as the artist on different songs by that group results in two different Artist entries. A filter on one won't catch songs with the other entry in the Artist field.

Browsing and searching are not mutually exclusive activities. Trimming a list down by browsing and then doing a search lets you search subsets of your Library.

Creating and Managing Playlists

Playlists are groupings of songs in your Library constructed according to your whims. They may be an album, all the songs by a specific group, or just some random collection of songs that you think complement each other. It doesn't matter or have to make sense to anyone but you. They do have one very important function, though, because iTunes uses playlists as its interface to burning CDs, as you see later in this chapter in the "Making Your Own CDs" section.

Playlists work almost exactly like the Library, which is not surprising because playlists are subsets of the Library. You select, sort, search, and edit items in the Library and playlists the exact same way. The biggest difference is that you can't use the three-column browse mode in a playlist — that feature is only available in the Library.

Creating and deleting playlists

iTunes provides several methods for creating playlists. You can click the Create a playlist button at the bottom-left of the iTunes window, or you can choose File ⇨ New Playlist (⌘-N) to create a new, empty playlist. Alternatively, and the method we employ most often, you can select a group of songs by Shift- or ⌘-clicking them in the Library and choosing File ⇨ New Playlist From Selection (Shift-⌘-N). This last method creates an already populated playlist that shows up untitled in the Source List, ready for you to type in a real name for it (Figure 4-10). Finally, when you have a folder full of songs you want to add, you can drag the folder from the Finder into the blank area at the bottom of the Source List. iTunes adds all the songs to the Library as well as creating a playlist named the same as the dragged folder.

Tip

To rename a playlist, click once to select it in the Source List, pause briefly and then click again (not a double-click) to make the name editable. Doing this is just like renaming a file in the Finder.

Note

Unlike the rest of the pictures in this chapter, Figure 4-10 was created by Bob, not Dennis. Could you tell from the song list?

Deleting a playlist is simplicity itself. Select it in the Source List and choose Edit ⇨ Clear or press Backspace (Delete) or Clear. iTunes asks you, unless you turn the alert off by clicking the Do not ask me again checkbox, whether you really want to delete the playlist.

Note

In general, iTunes provides these cautionary alerts for any activities that are not undoable. So, if you see one of these "do you really wanna?" alerts, you can be pretty sure that Undo won't be available if you change your mind.

You can even open a playlist in its own window by double-clicking the playlist in the Source List. There is no menu equivalent for this operation.

Tip

This feature is useful when you're copying a song or songs from one playlist to another. Open both in their own windows, arrange them on screen just the way you like, and drag songs from one list to the other to your heart's content.

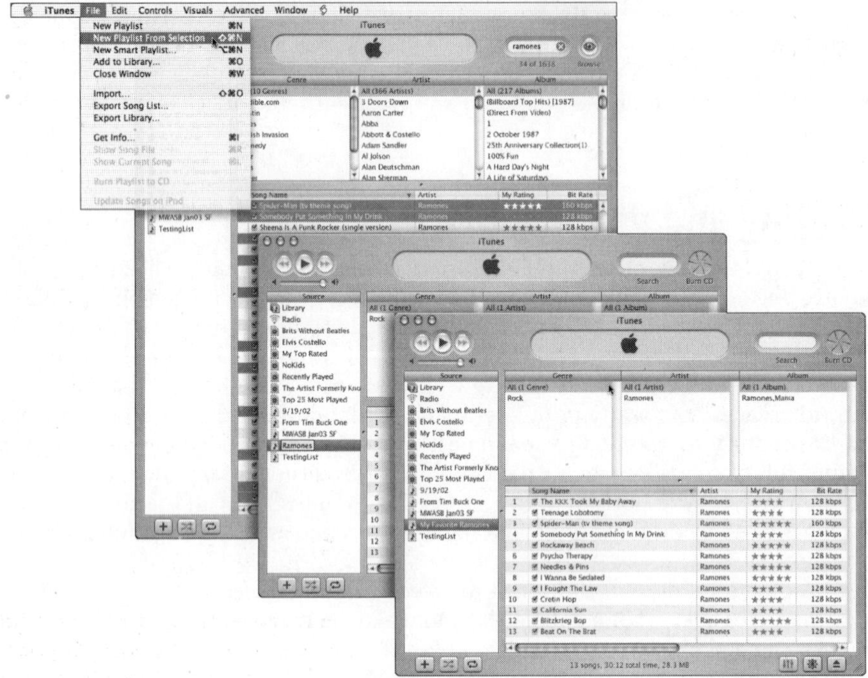

Figure 4-10: It's easy as 1-2-3.... Select the songs and then choose New Playlist From Selection (rear); a new untitled playlist with those songs is created for you (middle); rename the playlist (front) and you're done.

Modifying playlists

You can add songs in your Library (or another playlist) to a playlist by dragging the song to the target playlist's entry in the Source List. You can also drag songs from the Finder onto the playlist's Source List entry or, if the playlist is selected, to its detail list area. Figure 4-11 illustrates the process of dragging a couple of files from the Finder onto a playlist entry.

Figure 4-11: Dragging songs from the Finder to a playlist.

Dragging from the Finder is a "kill two birds with one stone" approach. You not only add the song(s) to the Library (remember, the playlist can only display songs that are in the Library), but you get them in the playlist in one fell swoop.

If you have a playlist opened in its own window, you can drag Library entries or songs from other playlists directly to the playlist window's detail list.

Removing playlist entries is Mac-easy. Select the entry or entries and choose Edit ⇨ Clear or press Backspace (Delete) or Clear on your keyboard. The entry is gone, again with the warning because you can't use Undo. Fortunately, removing a playlist entry does nothing to the underlying Library entry. The song is still in your Library.

You may have noticed that a playlist has a number in the leftmost column, a column that is empty in the Library. If you select this column as the sort column, iTunes lets you drag songs into a different order, as shown in Figure 4-12. iTunes automatically renumbers the play order.

When Shuffle is turned on, you don't control the sequence of play, so iTunes doesn't let you reorder the playlist. You can turn Shuffle off by either clicking the Shuffle button (turning it back to black crossed arrows) or by choosing Controls ⇨ Shuffle.

(a)

(b)

Figure 4-12: You can drag songs into a different play order in a playlist: (a); after you let go (b).

Importing Songs

Commonly called ripping, importing tracks from an audio CD and converting them to smaller MP3 files is one of iTunes great strengths. In Chapter 3, you learned that you can import MP3, AIFF, or WAV format into iTunes (see Chapter 2 for definitions of these formats). The default behavior is to import as MP3 files, because they are the smallest (typically about 10 percent the size of an AIFF or WAV), and they are the format recognized by the iPod, portable players like the Rio, and the growing number of CD and DVD players that also recognize MP3 CDs.

Because iTunes can play the tracks directly from your audio CD, why should you import them? Good question. Here are just a few of the answers:

✦ **Convenience:** If they're on an accessible hard disk, iTunes need only look them up in your Library and play them with a double-click. You don't have to go to the shelf, find the CD, take it out of the case, insert it in your CD drive (thus rendering it unavailable for other uses), and start it playing.

✦ **Customization:** You can easily build playlists that play only the songs you want, in the order you want. Although many CD players are programmable, using them is always considerably more complicated than using a playlist to create that program, and the program isn't as easily modified.

✦ **Searchability:** As we saw, finding the song(s) you want in iTunes is really fast and easy. If you know a manual system for doing this with CDs that is anywhere near as fast, we'd love to hear about it.

✦ **Burnability:** You can create your own CDs — either audio CDs or MP3 CDs — with the songs you want in the order you want them. We don't know about you, but with rare exceptions we usually are only interested in a small number of songs from the CDs we purchase.

✦ **Flexibility:** You can download the songs into your iPod or other MP3 player for convenient, portable use.

Again, the best reason to import songs as MP3s rather than using AIFF or WAV is the size difference. On the other hand, if your goal in ripping songs from a group of CDs is solely to construct a tailored composite of your favorite tracks on those CDs and burn that composite to a new CD, you should probably import them as AIFF and avoid any of the data loss that comes with MP3 compression (however minor).

Preparing to rip

Unless you're a masochist, if you have an Internet connection available, have it up and running when you insert a CD for ripping. If you don't, you'll get no help with names or titles, as you can see at the top of Figure 4-13. But if your connection is up and active, you almost always get a filled-in display, as you see at the bottom of Figure 4-13.

We say that you can "almost always" get the CD information online because sometimes you run across a CD that isn't in the Internet database. If you're ambitious and want to help out others who might have the same CD, you can enter the information manually and choose Advanced ➪ Submit CD Track Names, as we discuss in Chapter 5.

Deciding whether to have iTunes connect to the Internet automatically whenever you insert a CD depends on your connection type and, possibly, your patience level. Frankly, if you have an "always-on" connection, such as a cable-modem, DSL, or T1 line, we can't think of any good reason to disable the automatic connection. However, if you use a dial-up connection, you may want automatic connection disabled because your Mac will attempt to dial in every time you insert a CD and you're not connected. This can try your patience as you wait for the connection to establish.

With such a dial-up connection and automatic checking disabled, you can still get the information. When you're ready, with the CD already inserted and showing in your Source List, initiate your Internet connection and choose Advanced ➪ Get CD Track Names. iTunes fills in the information just as if you had automatic checking enabled.

It's time to rip

Assuming that you have all the track information displayed, click the Import button (refer to Figure 4-13) at the top-right of the iTunes window—yes, it's another face for the "button of many names." iTunes proceeds to import the CD's tracks and store them in your Music Library.

You don't have to import every song on the CD. Those little checkmarks to the left of the song names tell iTunes which tracks to rip. Uncheck any songs you don't want to rip. If you have either Import Songs or Import Songs and Eject chosen in your iTunes General Preferences for On CD Insert (see Chapter 3 for more on Preferences), iTunes will rip the first track before you can uncheck its box.

While iTunes is importing the songs, the Status display reports which song is being ripped, how much time it estimates the remainder of that song will require, and how fast the import is progressing, as shown in Figure 4-14. Songs display a green-circled checkmark when they're completed; the song currently ripping has an orange-circled, animated squiggle (that's supposed to look like a sine-wave, for those of you who know about such things). Though not in color, you can see both marks—the green checkmark for tracks one and two; the orange squiggle for track three—in Figure 4-14. Unless you unchecked the default preference on the Preferences' Importing tab, iTunes plays the songs while importing. The import will finish well before the CD is done playing unless your Mac is really, really slow.

(a)

(b)

Figure 4-13: iTunes can't get the information when you aren't connected to the Internet (a); iTunes gets the CD information when you are connected (b).

Figure 4-14: iTunes shows you which songs have been ripped, which one is being ripped, and the status of the song being ripped.

When iTunes finishes ripping everything you want imported from the CD, it notifies you with a chime sound. You can locate all of your songs in your Music Library (Figure 4-15), neatly organized by Artist and then by Album for that artist, or as compilations (such as our "The Wizard of Oz" soundtrack).

Figure 4-15: iTunes keeps your Music Library organized when it imports a CD.

iTunes organization is fine, as far as it goes. Additional soundtrack CDs are stored alongside "The Wizard of Oz" (to use the pictured example). Assume, however, that you're importing Ella Fitzgerald albums — if the Internet database has an album marked as just "Ella" for the artist, they'll be stored separately, as will the albums she made with Louis Armstrong.

If you're concerned about the size versus quality trade-off when importing as MP3 files, see Chapter 5 for more about the correct bit rate to select when you import.

Making Your Own CDs

Now that you know how to create a playlist, how to add songs to your Library, and how to import songs from CDs, you pretty much know all you need to know to burn your own CDs.

In addition to what you know, there are just a few things you need to burn a CD: the desired songs in your Library organized into a playlist, a supported CD-R or CD-RW drive, and a blank CD-R.

✦ **Songs:** Because CD-Rs are "burn once" media, you only get one chance to write to them. Whatever you burn will be all you get on that CD. Thus, you should have everything you want, up to the 74 or 80 minutes (depending upon your media) capacity of your blank CD-R. If you only burn 26 minutes, that's all you're ever going to have on that CD.

✦ **CD Burner:** Most Macs these days come with built-in CD burners — some of them also burn DVDs. If you have such a Mac, this requirement is solved. If not, make sure that whatever CD-R(W) drive you attach is compatible with iTunes and your version of MacOS. You can find a compatibility list at `www.apple.com/itunes/notes.html`.

✦ **Blank CDs:** Originally, Apple recommended only using 74-minute (650MB) CD-R media; however, they've relented and are now selling Verbatim 80-minute (700MB) media as their preferred media. We'll repeat the advice we gave in Chapter 3: Check out whether a particular brand and style works in your CD player before buying in bulk.

✦ **Soft-tipped Pen:** Never use anything sharp to write on your CDs. We tend to use Fine or Extra-Fine Sharpies, which aren't sharp, or pens like the TDK CD Mark, made specifically for writing on CD-Rs, to keep track of what we put where.

Burning the CD

iTunes places a gap (default is 2 seconds) between tracks on CDs it burns. You can alter this (as mentioned in Chapter 3) in your CD Burning Preferences. Remember these gaps when you're figuring out how many songs will fit on the CD you're going to burn. Thirty songs adds a full minute to the time. iTunes helps you out by showing the playtime of your playlist at the bottom of its window.

Okay, it's time to burn a CD. Here's how:

1. **Create your playlist.** See the section "Creating and Managing Playlists" earlier in the chapter for more on how to do.
2. **Put the songs you want on your CD in the playlist, in the order you want them.** See Figure 4-16 for an example.
3. **Click the Burn CD button.** The Burn CD button looks like a closed camera shutter. The Burn CD button changes to look like a radiation warning symbol (Figure 4-17) and you're prompted to insert a blank CD.
4. **Insert your CD and click the button again.** After checking the media, iTunes displays the status and tells you to click Burn CD to start.
5. **Click Burn CD.** Only do this when you're sure that you're ready. The iTunes Status display keeps you informed as to what's happening as it prepares the data.

Make certain that your Mac doesn't go to sleep. As per Apple's Knowledge Base document 60841, you'll end up with ruined CDs and your Mac may stop responding, requiring a restart. So, set Sleep to Never in your System Preferences' Energy Saver panel before burning CDs.

But There's More than 700MB on That CD!

If you rip to AIFF files, avoiding any audio degradation, you will find considerably more data in 80 minutes of audio than the 700MB listed as the CD's capacity. We're going to explain how that happens.

Primarily, the two capacities—80 minutes and 700MB—have (almost) nothing to do with each other. Every sector of a CD is 2,352 bytes in size. The 80 minutes describes how much audio data can fit on the CD if it is formatted according to CD-DA specification. One thing about the CD-DA specification is that it mandates a packet size of 2,324 bytes. The 700MB lists how much data can fit when the CD is formatted as a data disk, and a data disk's packet size is 2,048 bytes (so is DVD data, by the way). What this means is that audio CDs get 276 more bytes of data into each sector of the disk, about 23 percent more data. Therefore, a CD-DA can contain over 850MB of data to the data disk's 700MB.

Figure 4-16: Fill your playlist and order the songs the way you want them to occur.

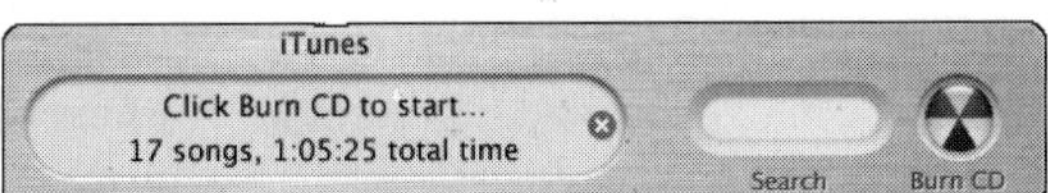

Figure 4-17: Click Burn CD again when you're ready to start the burn.

The first thing iTunes does is prepare the CD tracks. A major part of this preparation is converting the MP3 files back to CD-DA format. iTunes computes whether it needs to convert the files before starting to burn or whether your Mac is fast enough for it to do the conversion while burning. How long this takes depends on how fast your Mac is, how much data has to be prepared, how much memory is available to iTunes, how fast your hard disk is (temporary files are created), and how many other things your Mac is doing at the same time. After iTunes is done preparing the data, the Status display tells you that it is now writing tracks, at what speed, and which track is currently being burned, as shown in Figure 4-18. In another typical Apple touch, the Burn CD button animates, pulsing slowly while the disk is burned.

Again, the burn time depends on multiple factors, especially how much data has to be burned and how fast your burner is. How long the burning takes is roughly the length of the CD divided by the burn speed of your burner, plus a little extra for closing out the CD burn. For example, Dennis's 8x drive takes about 9 minutes plus just short of a minute of preparation and closing to burn the 71-minute CD used in the example illustrated in Figure 4-18. On completion, iTunes notifies you by playing a chime.

A nice feature of the CDs you burn is that, if you Insert them back into your Mac's CD drive, iTunes finds the track list in its internal database without going out to the Internet (where it probably won't find the disk listed).

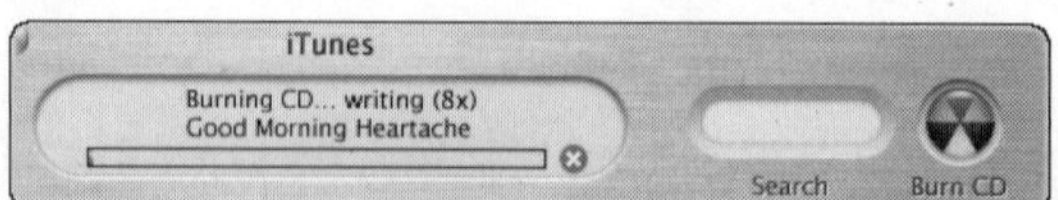

Figure 4-18: iTunes tells you when it starts actually burning tracks to the CD.

If something goes wrong

Being true paranoids, we verify our newly burned discs immediately. You can stick it back in your Mac's CD drive, although even if your Mac recognizes it that doesn't mean other CD players will. We generally use audio CD players for that purpose. Bob, being a true audiophile, has some top-flight equipment, whereas Dennis slips it into a small CD boombox to try it out.

Here are some of the things that can go wrong with a burned CD:

- **The burn fails partway through.** This can be caused by various problems, but the most common are
  - **You were burning data at a higher speed than the Mac could deliver.** This is particularly common with USB burners, but can also occur when your Mac is doing so much that iTunes doesn't get enough time to deliver the data. If you're using USB, burn at 2x or even 1x instead of 4x (you can set the speed on the CD Burning tab of iTunes Preferences). If you're connected via FireWire or using an internal burner, you can try slowing the burn or you can quit some of the other activity on your Mac. (Heavy network activity with a lot of disk access sometimes causes this problem for Dennis.)
  - **You were using media with defects.** Remember what we've said about using quality CD-R blanks.
- **The burn completes, but the CD has odd noise (pops, hisses, and clicks) when played back.** The first thing to do when you encounter this problem is to check the MP3s from which you burned. If the MP3s have the same problem, you probably want to rip the song again (maybe to AIFF this time) but check the source CD first — the problem may have been on the original.

✦ **The burn completes and the CD plays fine in your Mac but fails in some audio CD players.** First, not all audio CD players can handle CD-R media, particularly older models. Check it in a player known to support CD-Rs. Second, some audio players are sensitive to the brand/color of CD-Rs. If you've burned other CDs that were recognized in this player, try to use the same brand and color media.

Listening to Internet Radio

The iTunes Radio tuner lets you listen in to a growing number of Internet radio stations transmitting music and conversation. (Yes, even the Internet has talk radio.) So long as the stations *netcast* (transmit over the Internet) in streaming MP3 format, iTunes can connect and play their netcasts. Unfortunately, some Internet radio stations lock themselves into proprietary formats, such as WMA (Windows Media Audio) or RealAudio (requires RealPlayer).

What's available on Internet radio

iTunes comes with access information for hundreds of Internet radio stations organized in 22 (at the time we wrote this) categories, as shown in Figure 4-19.

Figure 4-19: Twenty-two categories of radio come prepackaged with iTunes.

In addition to the hundreds of stations Apple packs into these categories for you, you can add more from the thousands of other stations available. We show you how to do that later in the "Adding your own stations" section.

Listening to the built-ins

Few things are easier than listening to one of the built-in stations. Just follow these steps:

1. **Make sure that you have an active Internet connection.**
2. **Select Radio Tuner in iTunes' Source List.**
3. **Find a category that interests you in the detail list and click its disclosure triangle.**
4. **In the list of stations that gets revealed (Figure 4-20), double-click a station that interests you (or select it and either click the Play button or press Return).**

Figure 4-20: Find a station that interests you in whatever category you chose.

Very shortly (it's just about immediate with Dennis's cable modem connection), the station will start playing. While you're listening, iTunes tells you about the current station in the Status display, as shown in Figure 4-21.

Figure 4-21: Internet radio does live radio one better – it tells you what's playing while you listen.

As you can also see in Figure 4-20, some stations, such as Puregold ROCK'N'ROLL, offer multiple bit rates from which to choose. The higher the bit rate, the higher the quality; however, the higher the bit rate, the faster the connection needed to support it. You should choose a bit rate no faster than your Internet connection. For example, with a 56K dial-in connection, choose 56kbps or less.

Tip Use the Refresh button periodically to update iTunes database of available stations.

Adding your own stations

We previously told you that you can add your own stations and that's true. Unfortunately, this process isn't as easy as some things you can do with iTunes. First, you have to know the URL of the netcast. Unfortunately, that is almost never anything but a string of four numbers separated by periods (an IP address), so they aren't the easiest things to remember for most people.

Fortunately, there is a wonderful Web site called Live365.com that maintains a database of thousands of Internet radio stations, which are organized (like iTunes) by genre. Just launch your Web browser and go to `www.live365.com`. You can search its genres using keywords (like Redneck in the Comedy genre, for example, if you're looking for Jeff Foxworthy-style comedy). Live365 presents a list of matches. Click on one of them and, when the pop-up window tells you that you need an MP3 player, tell it you have one. (They even give iTunes top-billing in their list of compatible players.) The next thing you know, iTunes will be back in front with a new entry in your Library's detail list, as shown in Figure 4-22.

If you select the entry and choose File ⇨ Get Info (⌘-I), you will see the Song Information dialog shown in Figure 4-23. Check out the "Where" field — aren't you glad you didn't have to type in that URL?

Figure 4-22: iTunes adds new stations to your Library's detail list.

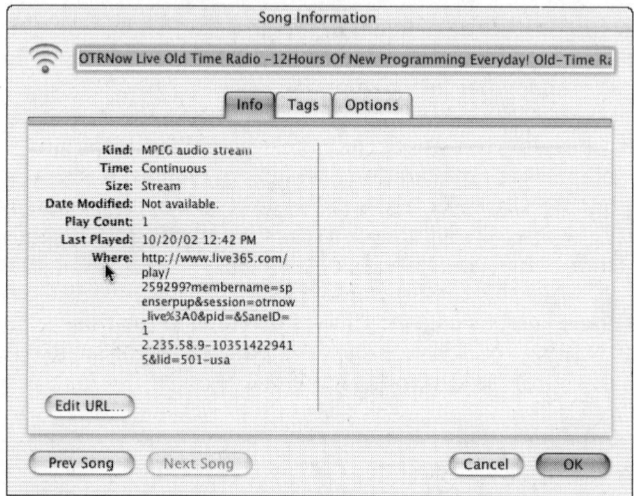

Figure 4-23: The Info dialog shows that the URL isn't easy to remember.

If this doesn't satisfy your craving for Internet radio, you can also do searches using various search engines such as Google (`www.google.com`) or Bob's favorite Big Mamma (`www.mamma.com`). Good keywords are Internet, radio, and MP3. Additionally, you can check Internet newsgroups such as `alt.radio.internet` to find station announcements and references.

The biggest problem we have with adding your own stations is that they go in your Library and don't appear in the Radio Tuner. Therefore, if you want to change stations, you might have to change lists as well. On the other hand, you can easily make a playlist with all your favorite Internet radio stations.

Introducing Smart Playlists

We could have buried this topic under "Creating and Managing Playlists"(earlier in this chapter), but we feel it is a really cool feature and deserves its own heading. Introduced with iTunes 3, Smart Playlists are dynamic — you set criteria and iTunes fills the list for you. Even better, iTunes updates the list automatically, keeping the list in compliance with your specifications as you continue to use iTunes.

iTunes 3 comes with four predefined Smart Playlists, just to give you a headstart:

✦ **60's Music:** Songs (and other MP3s) whose tags indicate that they were recorded between 1960 and 1969, inclusive.

✦ **My Top Rated:** Songs that you've rated as better than 3-star.

✦ **Recently Played:** Songs you've played in the past two weeks.

✦ **Top 25 Most Played:** The 25 songs you've played the most often.

You rate a song by clicking a star from 1 to 5 to indicate your opinion. After you've rated a song, you can re-rate it by clicking a different star. Unless you delve into AppleScript (see Chapter 7) you can't unrate a song.

If all you could do is make use of the provided Smart Playlists, this feature wouldn't be very interesting, but iTunes lets you create your own Smart Playlists and modify them as well as the ones it provides, when and as you like.

Creating a new Smart Playlist

You start the creation process by choosing File ➪ New Smart Playlist (Option-⌘-N), at which point iTunes displays the Smart Playlist dialog (Figure 4-24).

Figure 4-24: The Smart Playlist dialog.

You can also create a new Smart Playlist by holding down the Option key and clicking the New Playlist button at the lower-left of the iTunes window. When you do this, the New Playlist button changes to display a cog.

We're only going to deal with the Simple tab at this point, and discuss the Advanced tab, along with other advanced iTunes topics, in Chapter 5.

Although they're not outlined or otherwise separated, each of the three rows is a group of related controls, as follows:

- ✦ **Checkbox, pop-up menu (defaults to Artist), and the large text field:** This is where you specify the criteria by which you want to make selections. The pop-up menu limits you to Artist, Composer, or Genre and you can enter any text by which you want to filter the specified field. As a nice touch, if you start to type in the text field, iTunes checks the box for you, so you don't have to take your hands off the keyboard.
- ✦ **Checkbox, Limit to text item, units pop-up, and selected by criterion:** These let you control the size of the playlist. Using the text field and the units pop-up, you control either the number of songs, the duration of the playlist, or the amount of disk space the playlist consumes. The selected by pop-up tells iTunes to select the playlist's constituents at random. Alternatively, iTunes can sort by a criterion and then take as many songs as it requires to meet your limit from the start of that list. You can choose artist, last played, most played, or song name as your criterion.
- ✦ **Live updating:** When checked, iTunes will continually adjust the playlist as you continue to use iTunes. For example, if you limited your Smart Playlist to your 15 most played Beatles tunes and then you started playing a newly-added Beatles song over and over, that song automatically appears in the Smart Playlist when its play count surpassed whatever song was previously fifteenth on your list.

As an example, creating the simple playlist shown in Figure 4-25a generates the Smart Playlist shown in Figure 4-25b. Notice that the Smart Playlist takes its name from the criterion specified in the Contains text field, if it is non-blank. Otherwise it gets a numbered name of the form *untitled playlist n*, where “n” is whatever number is next in iTunes’ automated numbering sequence.

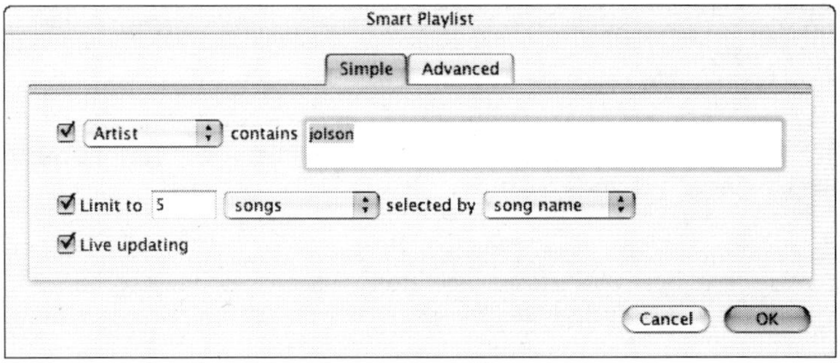

(a)

(b)

Figure 4-25: The criteria specified in (a) result in the Smart Playlist shown in (b).

Editing a Smart Playlist

To edit or view an existing Smart Playlist's criteria, select the Smart Playlist in the Source List and choose File ➪ Get Info (⌘-I).

Summary

In this chapter you learned about building, organizing, and searching your Library; creating playlists; burning CDs; listening to Internet Radio; and how to create and modify simple Smart Playlists. In Chapter 5, you'll learn even more about these and other (more advanced) iTunes features.

✦ ✦ ✦

Getting Advanced with iTunes

In This Chapter

Exploring the Song Information Dialog

Working with MP3 players

Adjusting sound with the Equalizer

Exploring the Visualizer

Burning MP3 CDs

Choosing the right bit rate

Advanced importing and converting

Advanced Smart Playlists

Accessing Audible.com

Now that we've covered the basics of using iTunes to manage our collections of MP3s, burn audio CDs, listen to CDs, rip songs from CDs, and listen to Internet Radio, we're going to explore other things you can do.

Exploring the Song Information Dialog

As we mentioned in Chapter 4, the Song Information dialog lets you enter and modify information displayed in your Library: title, artist, year, album track number, genre, and comments. It also displays information about the song that can't be modified (at least not by changing something in this dialog): time, size, date, location on your hard disk, kind, bit rate, sample rate, channels, ID3 tag, and encoder.

This dialog, accessed by selecting a song and choosing File ➪ Get Info (⌘-I), is subdivided into three parts (each in its own tab), each of which you explore in detail. But before you even get to those tabs, look at the top of the dialog at the icon with a text field to its right. The icon echoes the file's Finder icon and the text field lets you change the title of the song displayed in the Library and playlists, but it does not rename the actual song file on your hard disk.

Note

If you're like Bob and Dennis, you'll use this text field often, if only to correct spelling and punctuation errors you didn't make. The database iTunes uses to automatically fetch song titles via the Internet is notorious for mistakes; they drive us nuts.

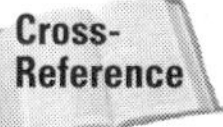

For iTune 4 coverage, see Appendix B.

What Are ID3 Tags?

When MP3 was a very young standard there was no way to include such textual information about songs as title, artist, album, year, genre, and other user-specific information. After all, MP3s were originally "computer only" files. At that time, no players existed for them other than computer programs, and many operating systems (such as MacOS pre-X) didn't allow for much information to be encoded into the name. Someone (reputedly Eric Kemp) came up with a 128-byte text block to be added at the end of the music data and named it ID3, supposedly because it was ID information for MP3s.

As with any software implementation that acquires a following, enhancements were made. The first was an "upgrade" to ID3 Version 1.1, for which a Windows developer created an extension to Windows Explorer that allowed the user to edit the ID3 information and to add the track number as a field in the ID3 block.

Various folks, in particular Martin Nilsson, decided that this 128-block, located at the end of the stream/file was inadequate to the descriptive task set for ID3. Thus was born ID3 Version 2 (popularly known as ID3v2). At the time we're writing this (March, 2003), the current version is ID3v2.4.0 and the tags can now specify a lot more than just the fields listed previously. The tags are now divided into frames and can store a wealth of data in addition to the textual information for which the tags were initially intended. For more detail, check out `www.id3.org/easy.html`.

You can only have one text frame of a given type within a tag, and there are now a slew of text frame types in addition to the initial ones. In fact, iTunes doesn't display much more than what was possible with ID3v1.1.

If you want to know virtually everything there is to know about ID3, check out the Web site, `www.id3.org`, the home of the ID3 standards group.

And now, back to our regularly scheduled programming . . . .

Viewing the Info tab

The first tab, Info (Figure 5-1), has no user-modifiable fields. It just tells you about the song selected.

iTunes separates the information into two categories: General Information and Detail Information. You may want to think of General Information as the "What, Where, and When" data and the Detail Information as the "How" data. The "Why and Who" is left to you — after all, you're the one who acquired it and put it in your Library.

The first three General Information items (Kind, Time, and Size) tell you what the file is. In the example shown in Figure 5-1, you see that we have a 2 minute 16 second MPEG audio file that consumes 2.7MB of disk space. Next, you get to see when the file was created, how often it has been played, when it was last played, and finally we get to see where it is stored.

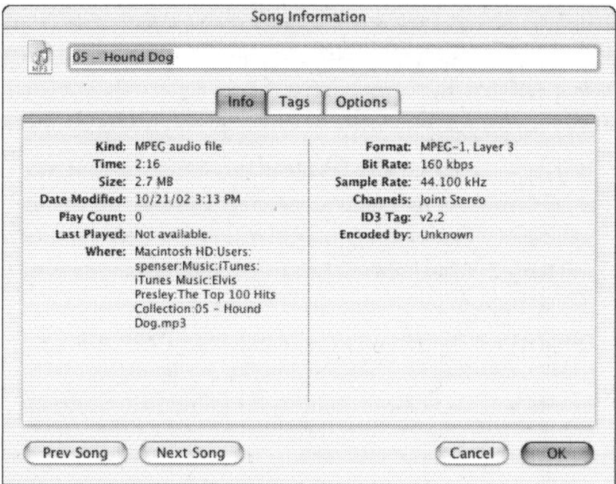

Figure 5-1: The Info tab tells you a lot about the selected song.

Under Detail Information, you see how the file is formatted and how it will play back. In the same example, the MP3 was created at 160kbps (kilobits per second) with 44,100 samples taken per second, two-channel joint stereo, version 2.2 ID3 tags, and with no information stored as to who/what did the encoding.

Using the Tags tab

The Tags tab (Figure 5-2) should be somewhat familiar from Chapter 4. This tab is where you can change most of the text fields associated with the song. Information that you place in the text fields is not checked for accuracy. For example, you could enter that it was track 31 of 14 and recorded in the year 2131, and iTunes wouldn't object in the least. Think of these tags as your own personal, embedded notes about the file.

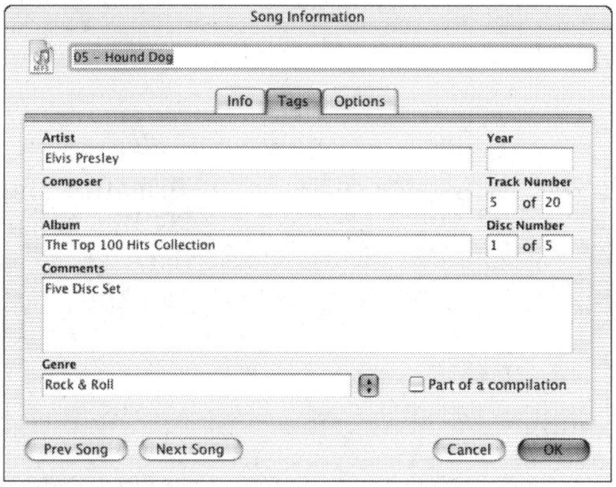

Figure 5-2: The Tags tab is where you can record and edit information about the song.

As you can see in Figure 5-3, the Genre pop-up comes preset with a number (26) of provided genres, to which you can add. Bob likes to add British Invasion and Dennis likes to add Rock & Roll and Broadway to the list (as shown in Figure 5-3). You can add a genre by selecting the text in the Genre field and typing in a new value, which is the same as clicking the pop-up menu button and choosing Custom, which highlights the text for editing. Similarly, if the genre information downloaded from the Internet is not in iTunes list, it gets added.

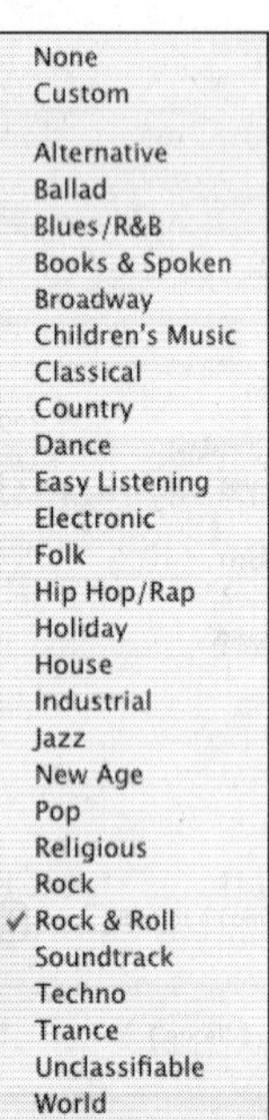

Figure 5-3: The Genre pop-up menu helps you classify the song type.

Other tags, such as time, size, and date added, are calculated and not user-editable and appear on the Info tab.

It's a good thing that the fields on this tab are user-editable, because, as we mentioned before, you find that many song, album, and artist entries are misspelled in the Internet database. Additionally, not all the fields are populated with data (such as genre or number of tracks on an album), and you'll often want to supply that data.

Adjusting on the Options tab

The Options tab is one of the more powerful tools in iTunes (Figure 5-4). By modifying the default settings you can significantly alter the way a song sounds when you play it in iTunes (or on an iPod). You can increase or decrease the volume, set the beginning or end point, and specify an Equalizer preset (see the "Adjusting Sound with the Equalizer" section later in this chapter) for the selected song (Figure 5-5).

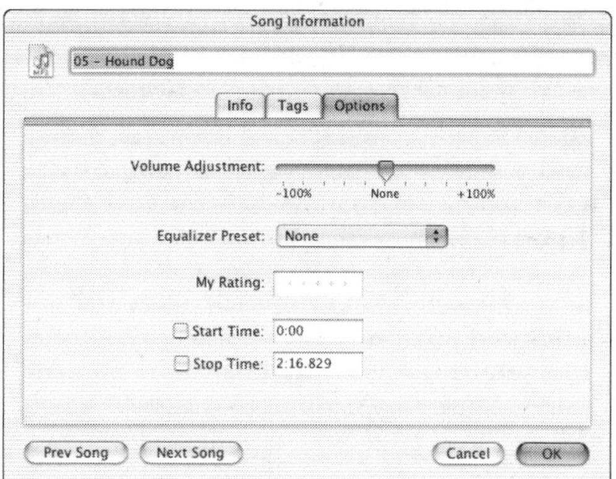

Figure 5-4: The Options tab lets you specify how a song plays.

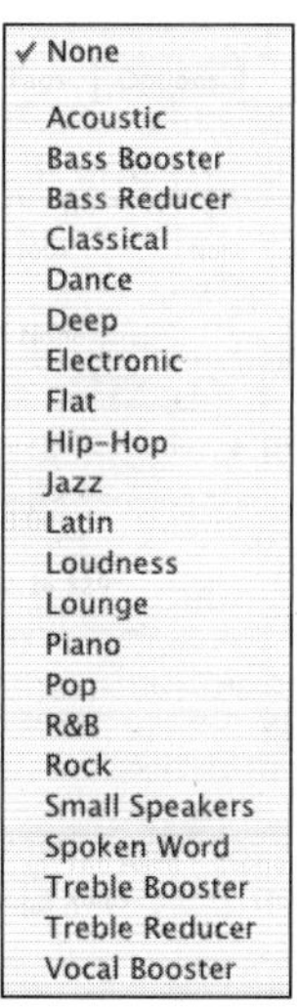

Figure 5-5: The Equalizer preset pop-up menu lists all the Equalizer adjustments of which iTunes is aware.

Working with MP3 Players

MP3 CD players aren't the only inexpensive and compact way to take your music on the road with you. You can choose from a broad range of small, dedicated MP3 player devices. Some of the most popular are from SonicBlue and Creative Technologies.

Until Apple released the iPod, a compatibility list of MP3 players was prominently displayed on the iTunes Web pages. The page is still there at `www.apple.com/itunes/notes.html`, but you probably won't find a link to it from the main iTunes pages and it hasn't been updated in a while. Be forewarned that even though some of these devices are linked to the Apple Online Store, the only one Apple sells is the iPod.

For the purposes of this discussion, we're going to divide MP3 players into two categories: the iPod and everything else. We do this partly because the iPod is cooler than any of the other MP3 players we've seen or used and partly because iTunes treats it differently from other MP3 players.

Interfacing the iPod to iTunes

Although we have lots of gadgets hooked to our Macs either permanently or intermittently (scanners, digital cameras, digital camcorders, external hard disks, printers, Zip drives, and so forth), the single coolest item is the little iPod that Apple introduced in late 2001. You can see a photo of one in Figure 5-6. Fitting easily in a shirt pocket, it contains a 5GB, 10GB, or 20GB FireWire hard disk and, without recharging, the battery has stood up to over ten hours of steady use for us. It comes with earbuds, a FireWire cable, and a recharger that plugs into a standard electrical outlet and, get this, uses the FireWire cable and connection to do the recharging. The 10GB and 20GB models also come with a carrying case and a remote control. In addition to being an MP3 player, your iPod can also serve as a portable hard disk, allowing you to copy files between it and your Mac's hard drives.

You cannot see or access the iPod's Library from the Finder. Similarly, the iPod's MP3-playing feature does not recognize songs that are placed on the iPod's hard disk any way other than via iTunes. At least, Apple intended this feature to work that way. Enterprising hackers (in the best sense of the word) have gotten around these limitations with utilities like Podestal, PodMaster 1000, XPod, and iPod2iTunes—all of which (and others) can be obtained through Version Tracker (`www.versiontracker.com`).

Figure 5-6: The iPod: compact, light, and just plain cool in looks and functionality.

IWhen you connect your iPod to your Mac with iTunes running, the iPod appears in your Source list as shown in Figure 5-7a. Select the iPod in the Source, and iTunes sprouts an iPod button just to the left of the Equalizer button along the window's bottom and shows you how much of the iPod is filled and how much free space remains below the detail list (Figure 5-7b).

(a)

(b)

iPod status iPod button

Figure 5-7: The iPod shows up in your Source list (a); Select the iPod and iTunes displays a new button and status area (b).

iPod preferences

That little button opens the iPod Preferences dialog (Figure 5-8). Your choices include allowing iTunes to copy all your songs and playlists to the iPod, copying only the playlists you specify, or copying manually, as shown in Figure 5-8.

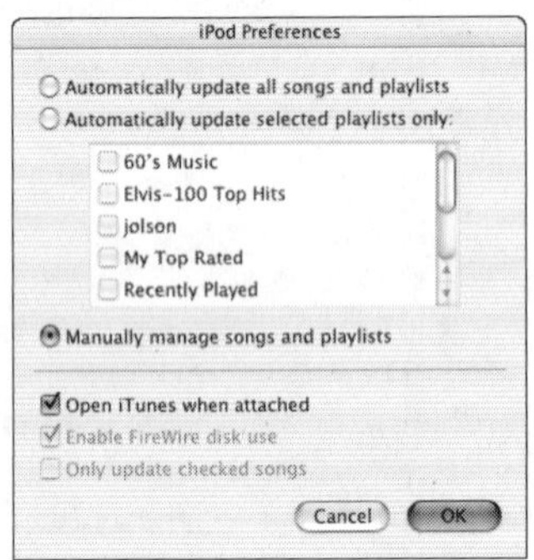

Figure 5-8: The iPod Preferences dialog is where you tell iTunes just how much control it should exert over the iPod's contents.

When you choose to manually manage the iPod, the Enable FireWire disk use checkbox is automatically selected and the item disabled—in other words, you can't turn off FireWire disk use if you manually manage your iPod. Similarly, the Only update checked songs option is off and disabled because you're going to be in complete control. If, however, you select either of the Automatic options, you can update only those songs with a checkmark next to their names in your various playlists.

Note

Your iPod is also a Contact Manager, if you wish. You can obtain AppleScripts to export your contact database to your iPod from a wide variety of e-mail clients and contact managers, including the OS X Address Book, Microsoft Entourage, FileMaker Pro, and Now Contact. Applications, written in AppleScript Studio, for the first two (Address Book and Entourage) are available as free downloads at `www.apple.com/iPod/contacts.html`. For other scripts, you should check at `www.versiontracker.com` (a good place to check for just about any Macintosh software) or ask the developer of the contact database program. The contacts interface expects *Virtual business Card Files* (.vcf), a standard (if not completely universal) format for text transmission of contact information.

Enterprising folks have also _adapted" the contacts interface, allowing you to store notes and various other types of data, rather than just the .vcf files that were originally intended. Check for iPod at Version Tracker to see what is current—new items appear almost daily.

Apple has also made it a clock and calendar application, interfacing with the iCal application in Mac OS X 10.2 (more commonly known as "Jaguar_), so you can take your iCal calendars with you.

Between the Contacts, Calendar, and Clock, the iPod is looking more and more like a PIM (Personal Information Manager) every day.

Automatic updating

Your iPod will synchronize with only one iTunes Library. Choosing Automatically update all songs and playlists tells iTunes to check whether the iPod "belongs" to it. If not, you get the alert shown in Figure 5-9. Assuming you answer affirmatively, iTunes erases the current iPod Library and copies your iTunes Library and all your playlists to the iPod.

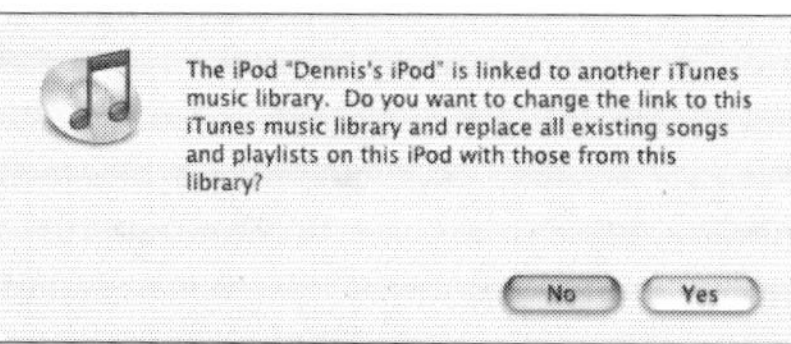

Figure 5-9: You get the option of starting with a clean slate when you connect your iPod to a different Mac.

You also get the same alert if you choose Automatically update selected playlists only. The difference is that now, only the playlists you checked in the iPod Preferences dialog will be copied, replacing the previous iPod Library contents.

In either Automatic case, songs deleted from the iTunes Library are also removed from the iPod on the next synchronization. The same holds true for playlists. If you don't want these songs removed, choose Manually manage songs and playlists, as described in the next section.

If you want your iPod to be a reflection of your iTunes Library, without any conscious involvement on your part, choose one of the Automatic settings. All you have to do is plug in the iPod and let iTunes do all the work for you. Well, at least up until the point where the iPod is full, at which point iTunes informs you that no more space is available and stops copying files to the iPod.

Manually updating

The selection, Manually manage songs and playlists, appeals to those people (like your authors) who have libraries larger than the iPod can hold or who might want to keep songs and playlists on the iPod that they've already removed from their iTunes Library. For example, on a recent trip Dennis wanted an audiobook on his iPod in addition to his tunes, but saw no reason to keep the book around on his PowerBook's hard disk, chewing up hard disk space that he needed for work. If he had chosen to update automatically, the audiobook would have disappeared when he hooked up the iPod.

Additionally, using manual updating allows you to create a new iPod playlist and drag files from your hard disk, MP3 CD, Zip, or other storage device, which are not in your iTunes Library, directly to the iPod playlist item in the Source list, as shown in Figure 5-10.

Figure 5-10: You can add tunes and playlists to your iPod that aren't in your iTunes Library when you use manual updating.

After you release the mouse, iTunes starts adding the selected items to your iPod, as indicated by the Status display shown in Figure 5-11.

Figure 5-11: iTunes lets you know what it is adding to your iPod.

Using MP3 players other than the iPod

Before Apple announced and shipped the iPod, it touted compatibility with a wide range of portable MP3 players, to the point of selling devices like the Rio (Figure 5-12) through the Apple Store and advertising them on the iTunes Web pages.

These devices connect to your Mac via USB, so the transfer of songs to such a device is significantly slower than to an iPod with its FireWire connection. More importantly, you can't play from these MP3 players in iTunes; you can only copy files to the device or erase the player's contents. They also have substantially smaller capacities (generally between 32 and128MB), much shorter battery life, and a much higher cost of storage per song. The primary advantages are that they tend to cost less than an iPod (between $100 and $300 for the Rio and similar devices compared to $300 for a 5GB, $400 for a 10GB, and $500 for a 20GB iPod), and you can use them with computers other than a Mac, or with other Macintoshes.

Figure 5-12: The Rio 600 from SonicBlue, one of the many iTunes-compatible MP3 players.

Note

We both have Diamond Rio MP3 players, made before SonicBlue took over the product from Diamond. Since we got our iPods, about the only time the Rios get any use is when we're writing about them. They're okay, but they're really slow, have limited battery life, and are severely restricted compared to the iPod.

As you can see in Figure 5-13, iTunes sports two new buttons to the left of the Equalizer button when a Rio (or other MP3 player) is selected in addition to the status line below the detail list. The Preferences button (cog wheel) invokes the player's Preferences dialog and the Erase button (lightning bolt) erases the player's memory. For the Rio 600, the only things you can do in Preferences is rename the device and apply firmware upgrades. Other players might (probably will) offer other options.

Tip

If you want to delete individual tracks rather than all the songs in the player's memory, select them and press Backspace (Delete) or Clear (or choose Clear from either the Edit menu or the contextual menu).

To add songs to your MP3 player's memory, either drag them from the Library or another playlist within iTunes or, if it's an MP3 file, drag it from the Finder. iTunes displays transfer progress in the Status Display, as shown in Figure 5-14. Many of these devices also play WMA files (Windows Media Audio) and dragging from the Finder is the only way to add them to the player's memory, because iTunes can't play them.

Note

Microsoft's Windows Media format files (both audio and video) are proprietary formats. Few tools (other than those from Microsoft) exist to create or edit Windows Media files, and those tools are almost never available for MacOS.

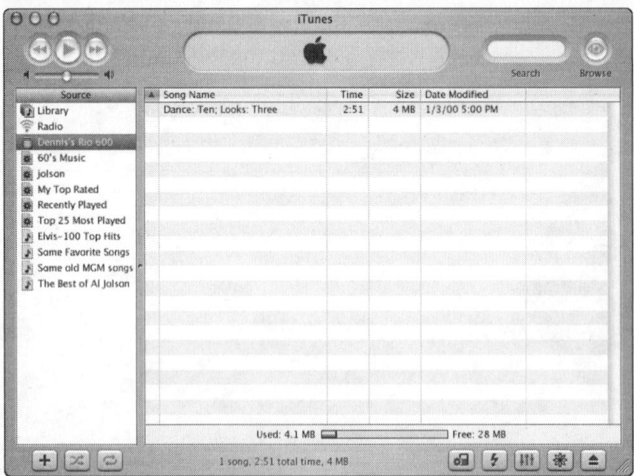

Figure 5-13: Connecting the Rio adds it to the Source list and sprouts two new buttons at the bottom of the iTunes window, to the left of the Equalizer button.

We don't go into more specifics here because you absolutely must read the manual that comes with your particular MP3 player. Every one of them is a little (some are a lot) different. For example, the Rio 600s we have do not support multiple playlists, but your player might. So, check the user manual or the company's Web site.

It is possible that there is a plug-in for your MP3 player, even if it isn't one of the ones iTunes already knows about. Check the Web site for the company, which made your player to see whether they have such a plug-in for your version of MacOS. If so, download it and install it in Library:iTunes:iTunes Plug-ins (creating the subdirectories of Library if necessary). If you're going to be the only one using this plug-in, you can instead place it in your Home directory's Library:iTunes:iTunes Plug-ins folder (again, creating the directory path if necessary). Also, be aware that the underlying software is Unix and the names are case-sensitive, so capitalize as we did.

Figure 5-14: iTunes displays the transfer status. USB transfers can take a long time.

Adjusting Sound with the Equalizer

In Version 1, iTunes had no equalizer, and audiophiles who wanted to tweak their sound based upon the type of music being played were screaming bloody murder.

Adding an equalizer was among the most-requested features for iTunes 2. Luckily, Apple responded with a quality tool.

Clicking the Equalizer button at the bottom of iTunes' window displays the Equalizer window shown in Figure 5-15. Flat is the default setting and all sliders are at their midpoints.

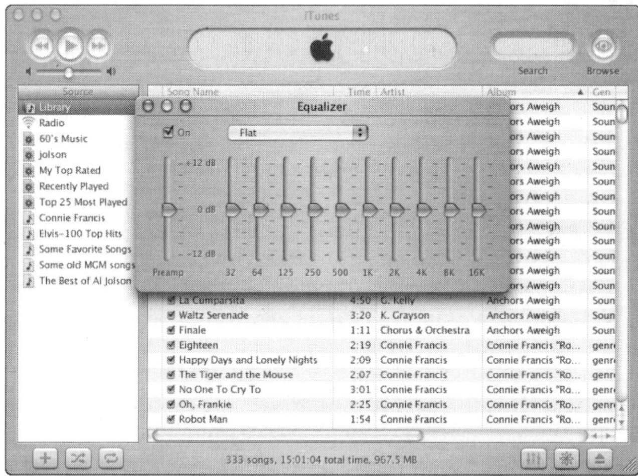

Figure 5-15: The Equalizer lets you change the sound level at a number of different frequencies.

What is an equalizer?

Okay, we hear you screaming, "But what does it all mean?"

This is going to get a bit technical, but we'll try to make it as clear as possible. The human ear can hear across a range of frequencies, but not across the entire sound spectrum. For example, you've probably all seen those whistles that produce a sound so high that dogs can hear it but we can't. Typically, the frequency range for human hearing is from about 32Hz (a deep bass) to about 16kHz (a high treble). This is not a linear scale. What we consider *mid-tones* (normal frequencies) tend to lie in the 250–500Hz range. Each of these frequencies has a volume, expressed in decibels (abbreviated dB) and these are also nonlinear. (They're logarithmic.) The sliders (called *faders*) on the different frequency bars in Figure 5-15 allow you to adjust the volume of sounds only in that frequency range without affecting any others. Dropping below the midpoint mutes the sound while raising the fader above the midpoint enhances the volume in that range.

The *preamp* is a secondary adjustment and applies equally to all the frequency ranges. You might want to employ preamp if the original recording was particularly quiet or particularly loud.

Roll your own or use presets

As you saw earlier, in Figure 5-5, iTunes comes with a wide range of presets (predetermined equalizer settings provided by Apple). The names are descriptive and cover a broad range of likely settings to enhance your audio experience.

Note

If you've never used an audio equalizer, here's how to get up to speed quickly. Choose a song you're familiar with and select each of the built-in presets for a few seconds. Watch the *faders* (the technical term for those blue dohickies you slide up and down) and notice how they affect the way the music sounds. The leftmost fader controls the lowest (bass) frequency; the rightmost fader controls the highest (treble) frequency; the faders in the middle control the rest. Move a fader up to make that frequency louder; move it down to make that frequency softer. That's how it works. Play around with it for a few minutes and you'll have it mastered.

After you have everything just so, you want to save these equalizer settings. Click on the pop-up menu and choose Make Preset (it's at the top of the menu). In the dialog that appears, give your preset a name and click OK. From now until you delete it, that preset is available to you in the Equalizer window and on the Song Information dialog's Options tab.

Tip

Tweak the faders until it sounds the best to you. Now save the preset and forget about the equalizer. Bob says his older ears don't hear high or low sounds as well as they once did. So, as you can see in Figure 5-16, he's boosted the lowest and highest frequencies more than the others. He uses this preset for all the songs he listens to and swears that it sounds much richer, fuller, and better this way. Your mileage, of course, may vary.

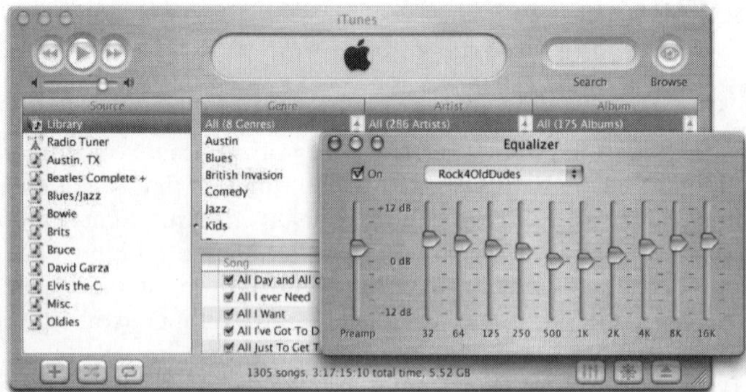

Figure 5-16: Bob's Rock4OldDudes setting.

Choose Edit List from the pop-up menu to use the dialog, as shown in Figure 5-17 to delete or rename a preset. Just select the preset in the list and click the appropriate button. If you click Delete, iTunes will ask if you really want to do so. Clicking Rename just brings up a naming dialog where you can enter a different name.

Figure 5-17: You can remove or rename presets on the list.

Exploring the Visualizer

Visual Effects is probably the iTunes feature Bob enjoys most. Clicking the Visual Effects button (between Equalizer and Eject) at the bottom-right of iTunes' window lets you play with this electronic lava lamp and light show. If you're more menu- or keyboard-oriented, you can choose Visuals ➪ Turn Visual On (⌘-T). iTunes comes with some Visual Effects built-in, but you can add more as we describe in a bit.

The Visualizer is the software component in iTunes that plays the Visual Effects. The built-in Visual Effects are what we're referring to as the lava lamp and light show.

Adjusting Visual Effects

Just to be agreeable, iTunes lets you choose any size for your Visual Effects, providing that you choose one of Small, Medium, Large, or Full Screen. The first three sizes are shown in Figure 5-18, and we're going to let you guess (we're sure you can do it) what Full Screen looks like.

Just choose your size from iTunes' Visuals menu.

Visual Effects even has some built-in help. With the Visualizer at play, press the Help key (?) on the keyboard, and you'll see some information appear, as shown in Figure 5-19. The listed keystrokes are modifiers for the visual effect being shown.

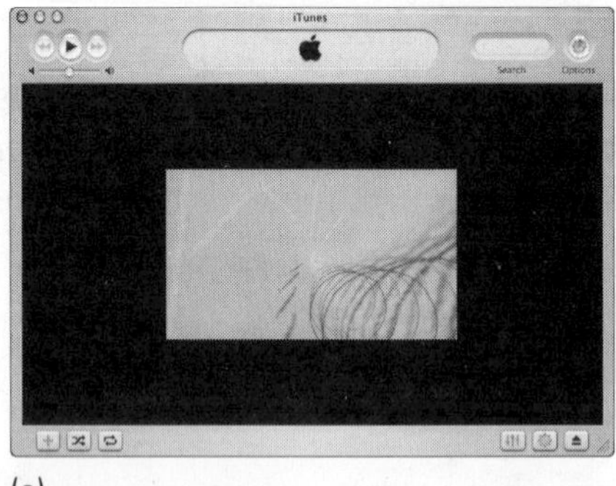

(a)

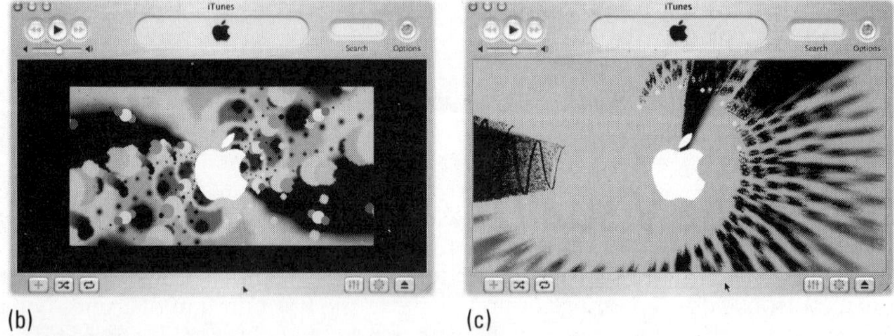

(b) (c)

Figure 5-18: Small (a), Medium (b), and Large (c) Visual Effects displays.

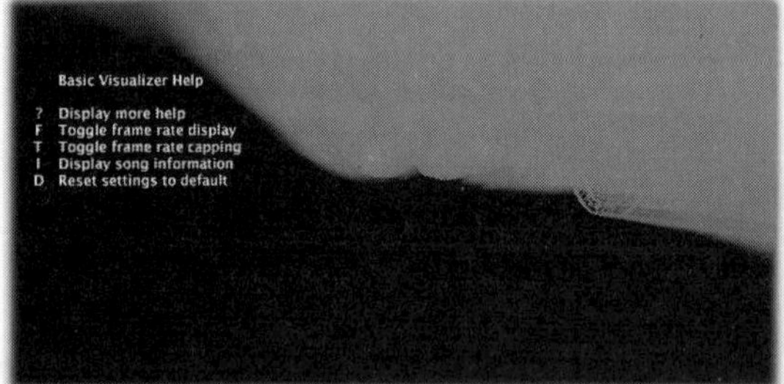

Figure 5-19: Press the Help key on the keyboard to display a list of which keys modify the Visual Effect's behavior.

Clicking the Options button, which is what the multipurpose button becomes when Visual Effects are active (Figure 5-18), displays the Visual Options dialog (Figure 5-20) for the built-in Visual Effects. Different Visual Effects (see the following section, "Installing additional Visual Effects") have their own Options dialogs. In this dialog, you set bounds on the speed at which the Visualizer plays and determine whether the frame rate and song information (assuming a song is playing) is always displayed.

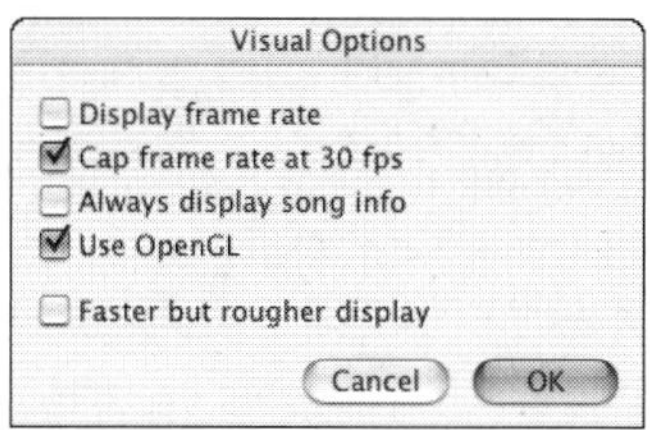

Figure 5-20: The Visual Options dialog lets you control Visual Effects' speed and information display.

Here are the choices in the Visual Effects dialog for the built-in Visual Effects:

✦ **Display frame rate:** When you check this box, the frame rate being employed displays in the visual.

✦ **Cap frame rate at 30fps:** This box is checked by default and limits the number of visual frames calculated and displayed per second to 30 (about the same as a TV picture in the U.S.).

✦ **Always display song info:** Checking this box tells the visual to display the song title, artist, and album information in the corner of the display.

✦ **Use OpenGL:** This tells iTunes to use OpenGL (a library of two-dimensional graphics functions) to generate its displays. Using OpenGL accelerates graphics performance.

✦ **Faster but rougher display:** Checking this box tells the Visualizer to display the effect as fast as it can, and not worry about keeping the flow smooth.

Installing additional Visual Effects

Like the Equalizer, the ability to add Visual Effects was very high on the list of most-requested features for iTunes 2, and Apple responded again. Additional Visual Effect plug-ins are available on the Internet through such sites as Version Tracker. (At the time we wrote this there were 15 listed and all were freeware.) Make sure that the plug-ins you download are appropriate for your version of MacOS. (Some are for OS 9, some for OS X.)

Here's how to make the Visual Effect available to all users of your Mac:

1. **Make sure that there is a folder named iTunes Plug-ins inside a folder named iTunes inside the Library folder at the top level of your startup disk.**

2. **If the folders aren't present, create them (you need to be running from an Administrator account to do this).**

3. **Drag the plug-in or plug-ins to this iTunes Plug-ins folder.**

Now, wasn't that easy? If, on the other hand, you want the plug-ins to be available only to your account, drag them to the Library:iTunes:iTunes Plug-ins folder in your Home directory (creating the folder[s] if necessary). You need to quit from iTunes if it is running and relaunch to have the new Visual Effect show up at the bottom of the Visuals menu. Choose the Visual Effect you want from the Visuals menu and you're good to go. Figure 5-21 shows the DHG-FlowerPowerX plug-in in action. Because it has no Options dialog, the Options button is disabled.

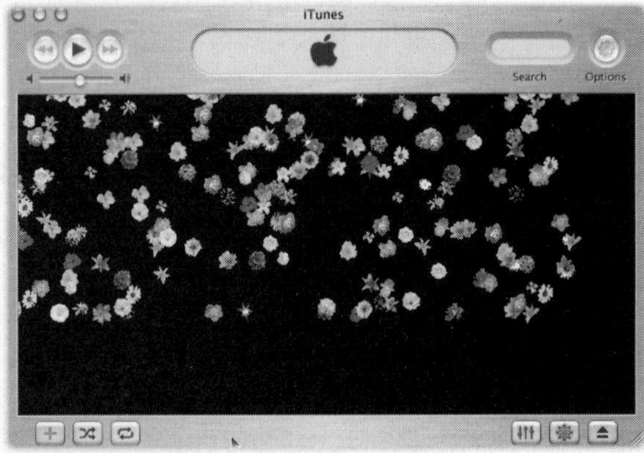

Figure 5-21: Flowers, flowers, everywhere: the DHG-FlowerPowerX Plug in.

If you're into programming, check out `developer.apple.com/sdk` for the software development kit allowing you to create your own visual effects plug-ins.

Burning MP3 CDs

As we've said over and over, MP3s take up a lot less space than the equivalents on an Audio CD. Further, more and more CD players and DVD players are appearing that can play properly formatted discs containing MP3s. Not surprisingly, these are called MP3 CDs.

Calling them MP3 CDs is a bit of a misnomer. They're really just PC-standard ISO9660 CDs, but your burning software generally makes sure that the names of all the MP3 files end in the .mp3 extension.

iTunes makes burning MP3 CDs a breeze. All you have to do is choose iTunes ⇨ Preferences (⌘-Y) and, on the CD Burning tab, click the MP3 CD radio button instead of the Audio CD radio button and then click OK. Chapter 3 covers iTunes Preferences.

Now, you just burn the CD as described for Audio CD burning in Chapter 4. Doesn't iTunes make this simple?

Choosing the Right Bit Rate

There is very little about bit rate selection that is cut-and-dried. What can generally be stated is that the higher the bit rate, the larger the file and the more faithfully the original will be reproduced.

After you get past that point, things get a little murkier. Usually, any bit rate below 128kbps should be reserved for such things as recordings of the spoken word (books on disc, comedy monologues, lectures, and so on) Although 128kbps is pretty much the default used for most MP3 music, the folks who are serious about their MP3s trade some disk space and insist on 192kbps at a minimum and some opt for 320kbps. All of this is, of course, for stereo. Mono material is captured at half the bit rate of stereo for equivalent reproductive fidelity.

The only way you can tell which bit rate to use for a particular album or genre is to run some tests on the music you're going to rip. First, rip a representative track at one bit rate and then do it at least one more time at a different bit rate. Play them both on the device and through the speakers you intend to use and, if you can hear the difference, choose the bit rate that sounds better to you. If you can't hear a difference, you might as well use the smaller one.

Typically, we encode anything where there is significant audio range (such as an orchestra recording) at no less than 192kbps and usually at 320kbps. In fact, Dennis keeps his default set at 192kbps as a reasonable balance between fidelity and size.

Advanced Importing and Converting

Because iTunes can recognize and play MP3, AIFF, and WAV files, it isn't surprising that iTunes can also convert between the formats. This is one of the few places where iTunes doesn't make an operation straightforward. You would think that converting a song from one format to another would be a simple matter of selecting the song and choosing a conversion format. Unfortunately, in an effort to make the conversion as general-purpose as possible, you need to take several steps:

1. **Choose iTunes ➪ Preferences (⌘-Y) .**
2. **On the Importing tab, select your desired format (from the Import Using pop-up menu) and configuration. Click OK when done.**
3. **Select the song(s) in your Library.**
4. **You'll see that the Advanced ➪ Convert to <format> menu item now specifies your destination format rather than, necessarily, MP3.**

   For example, if you set AIFF as the Import Using selection in your Importing Preferences, you would see the Advanced menu shown in Figure 5-22.

Figure 5-22: The Advanced menu reflects your destination format in the Convert to item.

When we described this process as "general-purpose" we really meant it. You can convert a 320kbps MP3 to 192kbps using this same method. We think that Apple could have simplified this process while retaining its flexibility by making the menu selection bring up a dialog similar to the Importing Preferences tab. For now, you'll have to make the trip back to Importing Preferences when you're done with the conversion to reset your Importing Preferences.

Be aware that you cannot improve the quality of an MP3 by converting it to a higher bit rate. Any data that was lost in the original encoding is still lost. All re-encoding to a higher bit rate does is make the file larger. Similarly, re-encoding as AIFF does not improve the quality, but it does allow you to use the song in programs that require AIFF files.

Advanced Smart Playlists

We promised in Chapter 4 to cover the Smart Playlist Advanced tab, and that's where we are now. At a cursory glance (Figure 5-23a and 5-23b), the Simple and Advanced tabs look very similar, but that small visual difference conceals significant functionality differences.

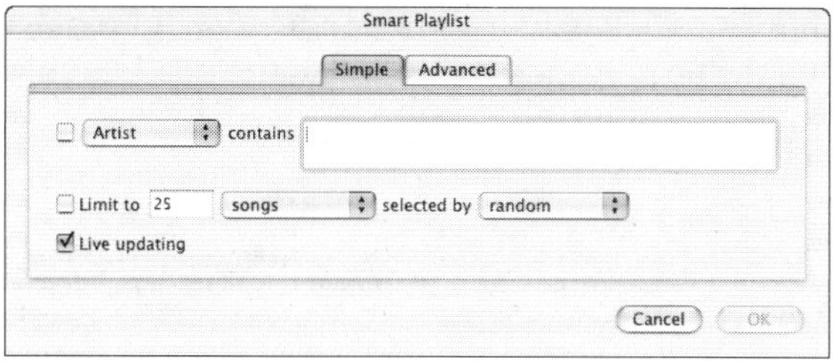

(a)

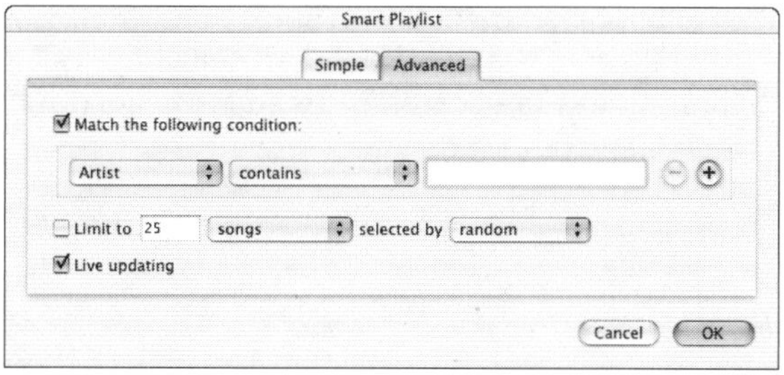

(b)

Figure 5-23: The Smart Playlist's Simple tab (a) doesn't look that different from the Advanced tab (b).

All of those differences reside in the condition-matching area — first row of the Simple tab and the "Match the following condition" checkbox and area in the Advanced tab. The most significant of these differences are

✦ You're no longer limited to Artist, Composer, and Genre for your conditions. You can now use any field that might be shown in the Detail List except for Disc # and Equalizer — that's 18 fields at your disposal instead of 3.

✦ You can create multiple criteria, used simultaneously. For example, you could search for all Elvis Presley songs recorded in 1961–1963 that you've played at least four times and rated four stars or better.

Note When you specify multiple criteria, you can tell iTunes to match all conditions or any condition.

✦ You're no longer limited to "contains" as the match condition, but also have exact matches (is) and a variety of comparison matches: "is not" is greater than, is less than, and is in the range for numeric and time fields; "does not contain" is not, starts with, and ends with for text fields.

The plus and minus buttons shown here allow you to add and remove conditions as you develop your Smart Playlist. Click a + button and a new condition line is added immediately after the line whose + button you clicked. Click a – button and that button's line disappears.

iTunes' four presupplied Smart Playlists all use the Advanced tab, but are a single condition. They use the Advanced tab because they're based on criteria other than Artist, Composer, and Genre.

Figure 5-24 shows one of Dennis's Smart Playlists. Growing up an Elvis Presley fan, he has dozens of Elvis CDs and he's imported them into iTunes. Some songs, though, he likes far more than others, so he has this playlist to select all his 5-star, Rock & Roll, Elvis songs and then randomly choose up to 78 minutes worth (in case he wants to burn a CD of the selected songs).

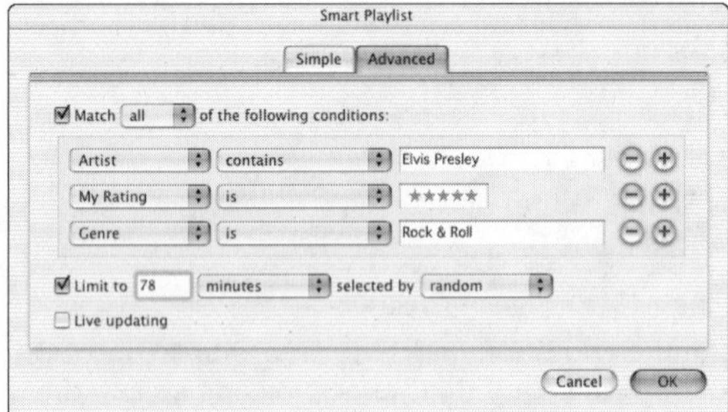

Figure 5-24: Create a playlist of 5-star, Rock & Roll, Elvis songs that fit on a CD.

To view or edit a Smart Playlist, select it in the Source List and choose File ➪ Get Info (⌘-I).

Accessing Audible.com

Books on disk, books on tape, and all the variations arising from these technologies have grown by leaps and bounds in the past few years. Audible.com is a Web-based service providing these audiobooks, audiomagazines, and even radio programs as downloadable items you can listen to in iTunes, transfer to your iPod, or even burn to CD. Something like a book-of-the-month club, you can choose one audiobook and one periodical per month for $14.95 or two audiobooks per month (no periodicals) for $19.95 per month. If you're into books on disk or tape, these prices are generally lower than purchasing the books through traditional channels.

When you purchase a book from audible.com, you don't have to worry about losing it—you can store it in your personal space at audible.com and redownload it if and when necessary.

The files you download aren't MP3 files, though. They're audible.com files and have the filename extension .aa. All you have to do in iTunes is open General Preferences (iTunes ➪ Preferences and click General in the toolbar), click the Set button next to "Use iTunes for Internet Music Playback" and click OK in the dialog that appears, and in the Preferences dialog. From then on, you can download audiobooks from audible.com and work with them in iTunes almost as though they were MP3 files (the big difference is that you can't convert between aa and other formats).

Neither of us is a fan of audiobooks, but we know many people who are. The ones whose opinions we value all think that audible.com is great and a big improvement over purchasing the books on CD or tape. If you're into audiobooks, check out `www.audible.com`. We think that you'll be pleased.

If you ever want to remove audible.com access, choose Advanced ➪ Remove Audible Account.

Summary

In this chapter, you learned how to work with the song information dialog, in particular how to enter and edit song information. You learned about using MP3 players with iTunes, with an emphasis on the iPod. Additionally, you saw how to adjust sound levels with the Equalizer and provide yourself with some visual entertainment using iTunes Visual Effects. You also learned how to burn your own CDs in iTunes, convert between file formats (WAV, AIFF, and MP3), and select bit rates for encoding. Finally, you learned how to use the Smart Playlist's Advanced tab and obtain audiobooks from audible.com.

✦ ✦ ✦

iTunes Tips, Tricks, and Techniques

In This Chapter

At its core, iTunes is a database. The player, the Smart Playlists, the Visualizer, and the disc-burning interface are all just ways of presenting the (audio) data stored in the database. The ID3 tags are text data and the songs are audio data.

If you treat iTunes as a database and approach it as a database, you'll be more productive and iTunes will be more responsive.

In this chapter, we point out a few ways that you can work with your iTunes 3 data that might not be immediately obvious.

For information on iTunes 4, see Appendix B.

Smarten Up Smart Playlists

Smart Playlists got a big play (pun intended) when Steve Jobs showed them off at Macworld Expo, New York in July 2002. By adding a few fields to the database record, such as times played, user rating, and last played date/time, Apple enables us to apply some numerically-based selection and sorting criteria to the data in our iTunes database. That's really all Smart Playlists are: sorted selections of songs based upon the text and numeric fields in the database.

Looking at a Smart Playlist's Advanced tab (Figure 6-1) makes this very clear. You can make selections based on one or more fields, either as an AND condition (select "all" in the Match pop-up menu) or an OR condition (select "any") and then limit the selection based upon a sorting criteria such as "most played."

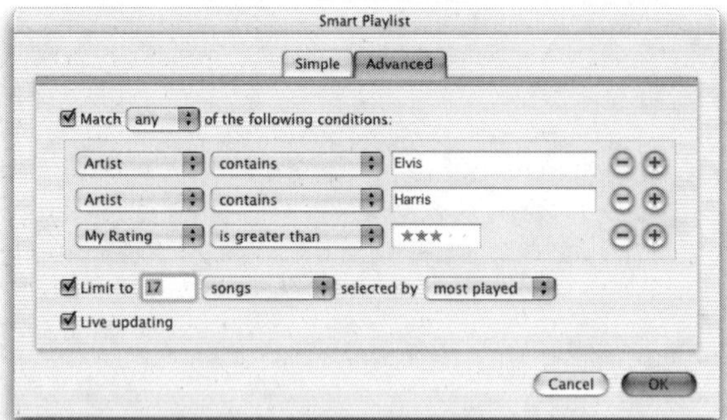

Figure 6-1: Smart Playlists are dynamic database searches.

Because you can't mix AND and OR conditions, we expect (okay, hope) that the Smart Playlist feature continues to evolve, allowing even more complex and useful criteria specifications. We know that we would like to be able to create a playlist of our 20 most frequently played Beatles and Elvis songs that have a 4- or 5-star rating. We'll show you a little later in this chapter how to use AppleScript to create a normal playlist that meets the criteria we specified, though.

The Internet lookup is a mixed blessing. While it gives you a lot of really good information, you sometimes find misspellings, abbreviations, or different artist naming conventions. For example, songs by the King might be up there as Elvis Presley or just Elvis. If you want to build a Smart Playlist of your 25 favorite Elvis Presley numbers, you'll surely want to include the ones with just Elvis as the artist. However, if you make "Elvis" the "contains" criteria for Artist, you're also going to have songs by Elvis Costello. The Advanced tab lets you work around this by allowing you to specify multiple criteria (any), for example, choosing "is" Elvis or "contains" Presley as your criteria.

You can also use "contains" Elvis and "does not contain" Costello for this example. The NOT options are worth exploring to exclude specific items. For example, if you wanted all the songs that had Frank Sinatra in a duet or trio performance, you can choose "contains" Frank Sinatra and "is not" Frank Sinatra.

Remember, to get maximum use out of Smart Playlists, use the Advanced tab to construct useful filters. The Simple tab is a very small subset of it, and not nearly as useful.

Relocating Your iTunes Library

MP3s are compressed, but that doesn't necessarily make them small. Just because they only take up about 1MB/minute instead of 10MB/minute, a 72-minute CD will still be over 70MB in size. To paraphrase Everett Dirksen: A megabyte here and a megabyte there, before you know it, you're talking about some real disk space.

Even in these days of multigigabyte hard disks, dedicating 10 or 20 gigabytes to MP3s is a bit extravagant. If you think those numbers are out-of-line, just remember that Apple is selling iPods in those capacities and some people are still asking for bigger disks. After all, even your small iMovie projects chew up gigabytes of space and your steadily growing digital photo collection will rapidly consume additional gigabytes. Then, of course, there are your "real" documents — word processing, spreadsheets, and all the rest. Before you know it, your internal hard drive is going to be getting cramped for space. Thirty gigabytes (or whatever your internal disk size is) just doesn't go very far in a digital media world.

In Chapter 7 and Chapter 17, we recommend that you get an external hard drive for your songs and movies. In the case of iTunes, there are benefits beyond freeing internal hard drive space — you can carry your iTunes Library to other computers (say at the office) with a minimum of fuss.

The key here is to use the iTunes Preferences' Advanced pane to change the iTunes Music Folder Location. Do this by choosing iTunes ➪ Preferences or ⌘-Y and then click the Advanced icon in the toolbar. Click the Change button shown in Figure 6-2 and select a location on your external hard disk.

Note Both Dennis and Bob use lightweight external 30GB FireWire drives (a FireLite and a FireWireDirect, respectively) and recommend them. They're reliable and compact in addition to being light.

Tip If all the Macs you're using have drives that read DVDs and your main Mac has a SuperDrive, you might consider creating an archive library containing your favorite 4+ GB of songs, and burning it on a DVD-R disc. This is close to the capacity of the original iPod and only costs you about $3 (or roughly $0.75/GB) for the storage. Then, moving your library from computer to computer becomes very inexpensive.

Figure 6-2: Click the Change button to relocate your iTunes Library to another drive (or folder).

Backing Up Your Music

Dr. Mac's (that's Bob) most frequently (m)uttered advice is "Back up your data. There are only two types of users: those who have lost data and those who are going to lose data." And Dennis concurs in that admonition. We both back up our data, though Bob is more thorough in this respect than Dennis. Even so, we've both lost data, but we've lost a *lot* less than we would have without our backups.

Do your MP3s qualify as data worth backing up? We would respond with a resounding and unequivocal "maybe." The larger your collection, the more likely the answer is a "yes." You can re-rip a small collection with a minimum of effort and all you'll have to do is recreate your playlists. Of course, if you have a .Mac account, you can use the Backup utility almost effortlessly to back up your collection to CD-R or DVD-R — even a small collection quickly overflows a 100MB iDisk Backup folder.

If you have an iPod and your collection all fits on the iPod, you could (rightly) consider that a backup, assuming that you have one of the myriad utility programs we mention in Chapter 7, which are capable of copying your songs back off the iPod and onto your hard disk. Dennis currently uses Christian Vick's iPod2iTunes, available through Version Tracker (`www.versiontracker.com/macosx`), because it also handles recreating the playlists. (Other similarly useful programs will almost certainly come out after this book is published.)

Tip

Backing up a large iTunes Library can run into lots of CDs or DVDs. Be sure to label them and have a catalog – both on your computer and on paper – of where you can find everything. While you might not be the packrats we are, when archiving music, video, book projects, and so forth to CDs, it is likely that you will get to the point where you start grumbling, "Where in the <expletive-deleted> is the disc with 'Yellow Submarine' on it?" (or whatever). We recommend iView Media as an excellent cataloging tool – it comes with Toast Titanium – or the even more powerful iView Media Pro. Dennis uses Unikeeps CD cases (`www.univenture.com`), which he buys in lots of 20 and each of which holds 10 CDs and their catalog sheets. They look great; Bob ordered his own 5-pack of them after reading the previous line.

Assuming that you want to back up to CD/DVD, you have essentially two choices. You can manually drag the files and folders to the CD and then burn. This is a cumbersome and error-prone method because you have to remember what needs to be backed up and make sure that you have the latest copy of everything. This method is best suited to archiving material you're going to delete from your hard disk. Alternatively, you can use a backup program, which does the bookwork for you — tracking what has already been backed up and what still needs to be, thus minimizing your effort and the amount of backup disk space consumed. Until recently, our unequivocal recommendation would have been Retrospect (`www.dantz.com`). If you're going to back up to anything other than CD/DVD, it is still our recommendation. If you have a .Mac account, you have a decent CD/DVD backup tool called Backup (a very suggestive but not very innovative name) included with your membership.

Adding Visual Effects

As noted elsewhere (Chapters 3, 4, and 5), Bob loves the iTunes Visualizer. Dennis considered it just a cute and, occasionally, relaxing display until he started trying out some of the downloadable visual plug-ins so that he could write about them in this book. While still not the fan that Bob is, he is using the Visualizer occasionally, even when not showing it to a Mac-deprived friend. You'll find lots of possibilities to explore at Version Tracker, just search the Mac OS X section for "iTunes Visual" and you'll get page after page of potential additions to your software collection and, best of all, most of them are freeware.

Some of the visual effects plug-ins come with installers, making installation a trivial matter. Luckily for all of us, Apple made it almost as easy to add plug-ins even if they don't have an installer.

In your Home folder's Library folder, you should find a folder named iTunes. Inside that folder should be two additional folders, iTunes Plug-ins and Scripts. We're interested in the iTunes Plug-ins folder. Deposit a downloaded plug-in in this directory and relaunch iTunes. You'll now have additional entries in iTunes' Visuals menu, as shown in Figure 6-3.

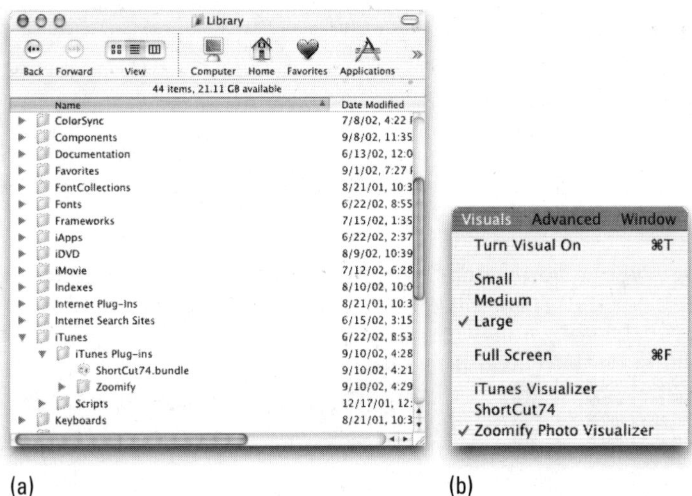

Figure 6-3: Place your visual plug-ins in your Home/Library/iTunes/iTunes Plug-ins folder (a); they'll be available next time you launch iTunes (b).

AppleScript and iTunes

We both find it a little hard to believe that AppleScript hasn't generated a cottage industry abounding with freeware and shareware to dwarf the HyperCard revolution of the late 1980s. The only reason we can come up with is that the visual metaphor provided by the cards in a HyperCard stack made the difference. As a language, there is virtually no difference in complexity between AppleScript and HyperTalk and the fact that AppleScript can drive program operation of numerous commercial products (such as Entourage, BBEdit, StuffIt, and Photoshop) instead of self-contained stacks makes AppleScript enormously powerful.

We're not going to attempt to teach you AppleScript. That's not what this book is about and, frankly, to do the job properly would require at least a few hundred pages. Apple makes extensive AppleScript documentation and tutorials available via their Web site at `www.apple.com/applescript`.

Apple made iTunes scriptable starting with iTunes 2.0.3, and iTunes 3.0's scriptability is enhanced beyond that initial offering. Enhancing iTunes functionality, Apple has made a number of iTunes-related AppleScripts available at `www.apple.com/applescript/itunes`. You can find even more at such sites as AppleScript Central (`www.applescriptcentral.com`) or MacScripter (`www.macscripter.net`). Many (we're tempted to say "most") such scripts are available in source form, giving you the opportunity to learn how to script various functions and to modify scripts that do almost what you want so that they do precisely what you want.

When we talked about plug-ins in the previous section, we mentioned the Scripts folder within your Home Library's iTunes folder. Placing your iTunes AppleScripts in this folder gives you quick and convenient access to them. This is because the AppleScripts appear under the script icon, between Window and Help, in your menu bar when you run iTunes.

An application hosting a Scripts menu so that you may invoke AppleScripts from within the application as if they were built-in commands is called *being attachable*.

Using AppleScript won't let you match Smart Playlists' dynamic capabilities, but you can do some things that Smart Playlists won't do, in particular mix AND and OR conditions when constructing a playlist. For example, you can build a playlist that includes all your unrated songs featuring Elvis Presley or Janis Martin. The script for that is shown here:

```
property required_version : "2.0.3"
property artist1 : "Elvis Presley"
property artist2 : "Janis Martin"
property targetrating : "0"
```

```
tell application "iTunes"
    activate
    try
        -- VERSION CHECK
        set this_version to the version as string
        if this_version is not greater than or equal to the required_version
then
            beep
            display dialog "This script requires iTunes version: " &
required_version & ù
                return & return & ù
                "Current version of iTunes: " & this_version buttons {"Update",
"Cancel"} default button 2 with icon 2
            if the button returned of the result is "Update" then
                my access_website("http://www.apple.com/itunes/download/")
                return "incorrect version"
            end if
        end if

        display dialog "Creating a playlist for "" & artist1 & " & " & artist2 &
" that have not been rated"." buttons {"•"} default button 1 giving up after 1
        set this_playlist to make new playlist
        set the name of this_playlist to artist1 & "-" & artist2

        display dialog "Adding tracks to the playlist." & return & return & ù
            "One moment..." buttons {"•"} default button 1 giving up after 1
        tell source "Library"
            tell playlist "Library"
                duplicate (every track whose (rating is targetrating) and
(artist is artist1 or artist is artist2)) to this_playlist
            end tell
        end tell

        display dialog "Process completed." buttons {"•"} default button 1
giving up after 2
    on error error_message number error_number
        if the error_number is not -128 then
            beep
            display dialog error_message buttons {"Cancel"} default button 1
        end if
    end try
end tell

on access_website(this_URL)
    ignoring application responses
        tell application "Internet Explorer"
            GetURL this_URL
        end tell
    end ignoring
end access_website
```

Notice that we used constants (properties) at the top of the script to handle the rating and artists' names. By the way, for ratings, each star is worth 20 points, so if you're looking for songs with ratings greater than 3 stars, you should check for ratings greater than 60.

We'd like to thank Apple for their example scripts, from which we shamelessly cadged the version check code and the `access_web site` routine.

Using parentheses for grouping your conditions, you can quickly create complicated conditionals that are not remotely possible via Smart Playlists. AppleScript opens a wealth of possibilities when it comes to managing your iTunes database (for example, deleting all tracks that have a 1-star rating), building playlists (as discussed previously), and communicating between iTunes and other scriptable programs (such as the Apple-provided script that creates CD jewel box covers in AppleWorks corresponding to your selected iTunes playlist). Check out `www.apple.com/applescript/itunes` for the Build CD Tray Insert and other scripts.

Summary

Treating iTunes as the (programmable) database that it is and its contents as the valuable data that it comprises can pay dividends. You've seen that following a backup strategy saves you from a great deal of unnecessary effort in the event of a disk crash or other related problem and that relocating your iTunes Library can pay dividends both in your enjoyment of iTunes and, to a lesser extent, in your use of OS X on your Mac. You've seen that using AppleScript with iTunes, or just employing the scripts Apple and others make available enhances iTunes functionality. You've also seen how to add visual effects plug-ins to iTunes. Additionally, you've learned that the Smart Playlist Advanced tab is the secret to getting truly useful Smart Playlists.

✦ ✦ ✦

CHAPTER 7

Enhancing Your iTunes Experience

✦ ✦ ✦ ✦

In This Chapter

Picking hardware accessories

Choosing software add-ons

✦ ✦ ✦ ✦

We haven't done a scientific survey or anything like that, but we'd guess from talking to people and watching the traffic in user group forums on Usenet and on the Web that more people use iTunes than any of the other iApps (the term for all the iLife applications). This isn't surprising when you realize that you can enjoy iTunes with less investment than any of the other programs in this book. Every OS X-capable Mac comes with a CD drive. You don't need a CD burner (though it helps), you don't need a peripheral device like a digital camera, digital camcorder, or set-top DVD player (much less the SuperDrive) to make the program useful. Stick in a CD or download some music from the Internet (paying the obligatory attention to not violating copyright) and you're good to go.

However, this doesn't mean that you can't add hardware and software to make your iTunes experience richer, just that you can get pretty decent use out of iTunes with your basic Mac.

Now we're going to start tempting you with some of the things you can add to create an even better iTunes world for yourself.

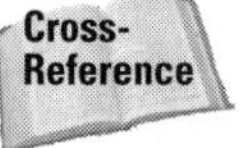

For information on iTunes 4, see Appendix B.

Hardware Accessories

One thing that will become clear throughout this book is that each of the four iApps programs is useful in and of itself. Beginning with iTunes, see how you can enjoy using your iLife programs even more by adding hardware and software accessories.

These accessories have a price range from free (for some software) to "Do I have enough credit before I max out this card?" When making the decision whether to shell out large chunks of money for something, try to decide whether the pleasure you'll derive henceforth is worth the short-term, stabbing pain in the wallet.

The Apple iPod

You have to know that this wonderful combination MP3 Player, PIM, and portable FireWire hard drive is right at the top of the iTunes user's hardware wish list. Coming in 5MB, 10MB, and 20MB sizes (as of March 2003) and priced at $300, $400, and $500 respectively, you're looking at a versatile tool that provides good value relative to its price. Check out the "Working with MP3 Players" section in Chapter 5 for a picture and some more detail.

One iPod accessory worth mentioning is an auto adapter that allows you to listen to your iPod while driving, because using headphones (or plugs) while driving is illegal in many jurisdictions. Dennis likes the iRock 300W (`www.myirock.com`). You just plug it into your iPod, choose one of four available FM frequencies, tune your car stereo to that station, and enjoy. For $25, it's a great buy, especially if you don't have a cassette player in your car that will utilize the Dr. Bott adapter Bob likes (see the next couple of paragraphs).

Bob bought an iRock also, but wasn't happy with it. With iRock, you must use one of four FM radio stations — 88.1, 88.3, 88.5, and 88.7. Unfortunately, in Austin, Texas, where Bob lives, there are FM stations on all four frequencies and they interfere with the iRock no matter which station you choose.

Bob recommends the cassette audio adapter he bought from Dr. Bott (`www.drbott.com`) for about the same price as the iRock. It does the same thing as the iRock (albeit, with a little cord instead of wirelessly) but doesn't suffer from FM bleed-through. The downside of this device is that it requires your car stereo have a cassette player (Dennis's doesn't).

Announced while we were writing this edition was the Griffin Technology iTrip (`http://griffintechnology.com/products/itrip`), which not only works with whichever FM frequency you select but also is designed to look like a part of your iPod. Because this device appears to answer Bob's complaint, it might be worth considering.

Speakers and headphones

iTunes is an auditory experience. Unless you can hear what's playing, it really isn't very compelling. The better sound you have, the greater the enjoyment (assuming it's music to which *you* want to listen). All Macs have built-in speakers, but there is a reason that they also have jacks to connect external speakers and/or headphones.

Bob's attitude on speakers is that Mac speakers are significantly better than those found on other PCs, but that isn't saying much because he thinks that even the Mac's are pretty bad. Dennis, who has a less discerning ear, thinks that the built-in speakers aren't acceptable for listening to music, but the external Apple Pro Speakers that came with his flat-panel iMac are more than adequate. We both agree, though, that good external speakers (or headphones) are a must if you want to really enjoy iTunes.

Some Macs include just a stereo audio-out jack, some include both a headphone jack and an audio-out jack, and at least one (the discontinued G4 Cube) had neither, and requires you to use USB speakers. We're not done yet: Some audio-out jacks use a standard connector, but some newer models, like the flat-panel iMacs, take a shorter plug — plugs that have a shield around their base for Apple Pro Speakers. Some (the Summer 2002 G4s) have both the stereo audio-out jack and the Apple Pro jack. Although adapters are available in some cases, you're best advised to make certain the speakers you choose have the appropriate connectors for your Mac model.

Note At least currently (February 2003), you can only use Apple Pro Speakers with the Apple Pro jack that comes with the flat-panel iMacs and the G4s.

If you're playing your tunes in an isolated environment, speakers are a great investment; however, if you're in a shared office environment (like a Dilbertian cubicle farm) or you're at home but not everyone there shares your discerning musical taste, you should consider getting a good set of headphones. One advantage to headphones is that, while they prevent (or protect) others from sharing your music, they also shield you from distracting noises such as other people talking while you're trying to relax.

What to look for in a speaker

Obviously, the first thing you should check out is that the speakers plug into your Mac, either via USB or one of your Mac's available jacks. In some cases, it won't be possible without an adapter (and sometimes, such as for the Apple Pro Speakers and an iBook, no such adapter exists).

Note Adapters add an extra connection and, possibly, one more thing that can go wrong. We've (more than once) experienced signal loss or breakup when a stereo jack is plugged into an adapter. If you absolutely must have a certain speaker, by all means get the adapter and make sure the connection is solid and secure. But if there is an option that doesn't involve an adapter, you should opt for it.

When it comes to USB-connected speakers, we're in complete agreement. The Harman-Kardon Sound Sticks are the class act in the field. The only controversy is whether their appearance or their sound quality is their greatest strength. With a list price of $199, they aren't the least expensive offering available, but they look and sound great and will work with any USB-equipped Mac — including every iTunes 3-compatible Mac except for the Beige G3.

Bob's favorite non-USB speakers are also his overall favorite — the Sonigistix Monsoon iM700s. These flat-panel speakers with a separate subwoofer can really be cranked up without any quality loss. Priced at $170, they're not exactly inexpensive, but their quality warrants the price. The iM700 can also be used via a USB connection if that is your desire.

Dennis prefers a Harman-Kardon (`www.harmankardon.com`) product as his non-USB choice, the JBL Sonnet Power Satellite Speakers ($100). This is the Harman-Kardon M310J model; it can be plugged into any Mac with a headphone jack, as well as into other audio devices like the iPod. Because anything "cranked up" gives Dennis a headache, he really doesn't know how they perform compared to the Monsoons at high levels. (Nothing cranked up sounds good to him.) Although he uses them with his G4 tower on occasion, he mostly has them hooked to the iPod, running off its power adapter while he's working. Another Harman-Kardon offering, the $150 Creature series is more visually appealing and is, in fact, prominently displayed and demonstrated in Apple's Retail Stores.

For flexibility, you might consider speakers that also have a headphone jack. We regret that Apple no longer makes such speakers, but Dennis's old AppleDesign Powered Speakers still do a great job with current Macs and he can plug headphones into the left speaker when he wants to without having to unplug the speakers from the computer.

Another option, for those of you who have quality home stereo systems and a Mac with an Apple Pro Speaker jack, is the Griffin Technology ProSpeaker Breakout Cable. Using this cable you can connect your home stereo speakers (even high-end ones like Boston Acoustics or B&W) directly to your Mac's Apple Pro jack without requiring an amplifier. Priced at $25, it's a serious value.

Headphones for a personal listening experience

Like the Harman-Kardon M310Js, headphones with a ministereo plug can serve double-duty. You can plug them into either your Mac or your iPod (or Sony Discman, an MP3 player, and so forth). Additionally, you don't have to worry about speaker placement relative to where you're sitting or standing because you're always perfectly centered between the speakers.

Dennis hasn't yet found a compelling reason to purchase new headphones and still uses the old lightweight Sonys he bought in the early '90s to use at work. If your taste runs more toward ear buds, like those that come with the iPod, they'll also work just fine plugged into your Mac's headphone jack.

If you like the ear buds, you can purchase a set of ear buds bundled with an iPod remote for $39 at Apple's online store or most any other Apple dealer.

Near the high end in terms of price, features, and quality is the BOSE QuietComfort Acoustic Noise Cancelling Headset. This is not a common, cheap set of headphones and, at $300, it's not inexpensive either, but it is lightweight, with cushioned ear cups that are adjustable both in size and angle for a proper and comfortable fit. A nice touch is the inclusion of two adapters, one for standard home stereo systems and one dual-plug to fit those airline headphone jacks so that you don't need to rent their cheap headphones to listen to music or hear the movie's sound. (And the quality will be much higher.)

If, however, you have an aversion to cords and like to listen from the other side of the room or in an adjacent room, cordless headphones just might be your thing. Dennis is partial to the Sony MDR-IF630RK model and considers it the most likely candidate to replace his old corded headphones when the time comes. With a 33-foot (10-meter) range, he's tempted because he would still have "right there" sound, even if he had to go into another room. With a street price of $115, they're not exactly inexpensive, but they probably won't break the bank, either.

Bob's favorite headphones so far are the Grado SR-60s he bought on the Web for about $70. They're regular over-the-head style cup headphones but they sound so much better than any earbuds he's tried that he often stuffs them in his briefcase and uses them when he travels.

MP3 players

In addition to the iPod, there are a number of iTunes-supported MP3 players on the market. Check out Chapter 5 for more information on using them with iTunes and finding Apple's compatibility list.

With their slower USB interfaces, limited capacity and feature set, and (generally) shorter battery life when compared to the iPod, the primary redeeming feature of these players is price. Also, they are solid-state devices that can withstand more punishment than a hard disk-based device like the iPod.

Some MP3 players, like the Rio, provide all their storage on internal memory, and upgrading the memory is both awkward and costly. Others, like the iRock 530, provide a compromise with a certain amount of internal storage (the iRock 530 has 128MB) and a SmartMedia card slot for additional memory. One advantage of the card system is that you can purchase multiple cards, load each of them up with a collection of tunes, and then swap them in and out as desired. Of course, by the time you purchase the iRock ($130) and a four 128MB cards for $50 each, you still only have 640MB on a slow USB connection and you've spent more than the 5GB iPod's cost.

Note Of course, the SmartMedia cards can serve more than one purpose. You can also use them in a number of digital cameras, as described in our iPhoto chapters (Chapters 8–12).

If you aren't ready to spring for an iPod but want a way to carry your tunes with you, an MP3 player like the iRock 530, Rio, or Nomad provides a reasonable compromise.

External storage

If you're looking for a way to take your tunes with you from home to the office or vice versa, portable FireWire drives should be on your list. Even though MP3 files are compressed, it doesn't take long to accumulate a huge library. Dennis doesn't even have a tenth of his CD collection in iTunes yet and it's already way too big to fit on his 5GB iPod, to say nothing of the space it consumes on his main hard disk. Bob is in the same predicament (though the exact numbers vary a bit).

You can designate an external hard disk as your iTunes Library location, which will free up space on your boot disk, eliminate some contention between iTunes and other applications for disk access, and provide you with more flexibility if you (like we do) have more than one Mac.

Bob is partial to VST products and uses an ultrathin 30GB VST FireWire drive. Dennis opted for the SmartDisk FireLite 30GB drive as his solution. At just a few ounces each, they're easily transported and don't require an external power supply. (They draw their power from the FireWire bus.)

SmartDisk recently bought VST, so both of our drives actually come from the same company. Bob adds, "With prices so low, I've bought a variety of inexpensive FireWire drives from Other World Computing and FireWire Direct lately, and they've all performed flawlessly."

There are plenty of options in all price ranges, more than we can even start to cover here. As quickly as technology develops, no doubt there are new options for you to explore that weren't announced when we wrote this.

CD burners

Most Macs these days come with a CD burner, but if yours didn't you should really consider acquiring one. CD burners are great for backing up your Mac (you do back up, don't you?) and also provide a handy method for archiving your tunes to free up hard drive space. Those functions are in addition to a burner's main iTunes-related use—creating your own audio and MP3 CDs.

See Chapter 4 for more on making your own CDs and Chapter 5 for more information on how to burn CDs.

When looking for an external CD burner, USB burners are usually a little less expensive than FireWire burners, but we can't seriously recommend them. USB is just too slow to reliably burn CDs at any reasonable speed. Though most USB burners list a maximum speed of 4x, we've never successfully burned at higher than 2x, and have had failures even at that speed.

One critical feature to look for, in addition to the burn speed, is Buffer Underrun Protection. Without this protection, your burn failure rate will go up, especially if you're trying to do other work while burning CDs. Most built-in Apple drives (since 2002) have this feature built-in, but even today, not all third-party drives offer it.

Software Add-Ons

There are so many software enhancements available for iTunes and MP3 that we'll limit ourselves to a few of the high points in some different categories.

Roxio Toast with Jam

Roxio's Toast 5 Titanium ($90) is going to be a recurring recommendation throughout the book, but for iTunes we're going to recommend a variation: Toast with Jam, which at the time of this writing was retailing for $190.

Toast goes far beyond Mac OS's built-in disc-burning technology, supporting VideoCD, Multitrack CD-ROM XA, and other formats. Add in the QuickTime component to convert movies to VideoCD format and the iMovie plug-in to do so directly (covered in detail in Chapter 17), and Toast becomes a very compelling addition to the digital hub enthusiast's arsenal. Toast also includes some useful-in-their-own-right utilities: Discus for creating and printing CD labels and covers; iView Media for managing libraries of sounds, images, movies, and other documents; and Panic's Audion to import music from analog sources such as cassettes or LPs, removing hisses, clicks, and pops along the way.

Jam is a professional-quality audio editing package. In addition to supporting additional formats beyond MP3, AIFF, and WAV, Jam's editing tools let you tweak the actual waveforms. You can soften peaks, add reverb to vocals, and create a variety of audio special effects, all in real time. Additionally, you can create Red Book standard audio CD masters suitable for mass duplication. Along the way, you can create cross fades between tracks, edit the gain on individual audio channels, and introduce index points to break a live recording session into individual tracks.

Check out Figure 7-1 to see Jam in action, editing the cross fade between two tracks.

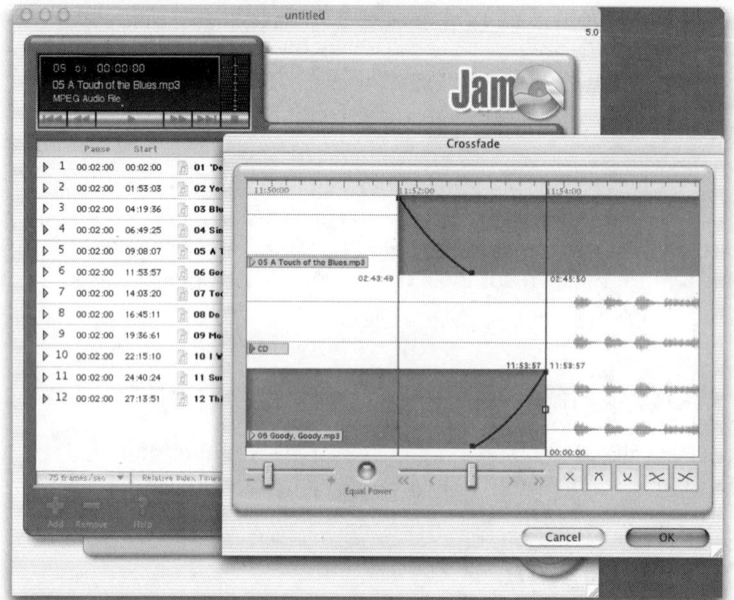

Figure 7-1: Use Jam to control cross fades between tracks.

AppleWorks and Apple's iTunes AppleScripts

If you're going to burn your own CDs, it's quite likely that you're going to want to have some way to find out what's on which disc. Apple has provided some AppleWorks jewel-case templates that are iTunes AppleScript targets. You can download the templates and relevant AppleScript from `www.apple.com/applescript/itunes`. A number of other useful iTunes-related scripts are also available on that page.

Frankly, we don't think that the artwork on Apple's supplied templates is very compelling, but one of the beauties of AppleWorks is that you can easily change the artwork or create your own templates based upon their model.

Figure 7-2 shows an example jewel case cover created using the Build CD Tray Insert AppleScript and the provided Party Mix template.

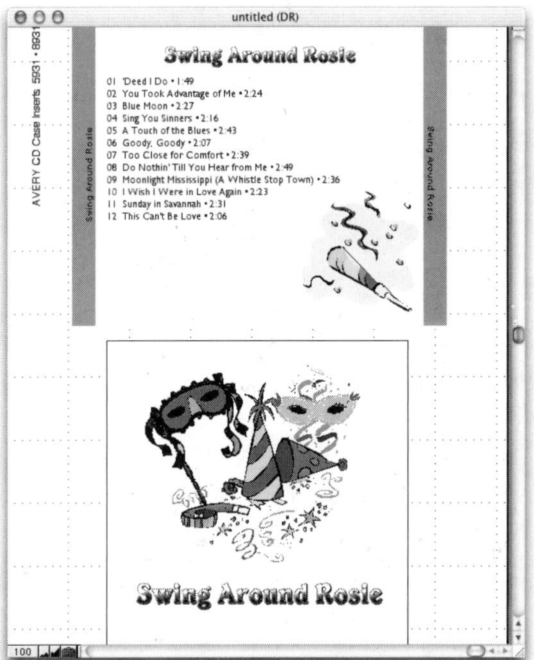

Figure 7-2: You can easily create CD tray inserts with AppleWorks and the iTunes AppleScripts.

MP3 Rage

Bob refers to MP3 Rage (shareware, $25, from Chaotic Software, `www.chaoticsoftware.com`) as a Swiss Army knife when it comes to working with MP3 files because it has everything in one compact bundle. Dennis thinks of it more as a Sears Tool Center — everything is there, but the selection is overwhelming. The MP3 Rage menu screen is shown in Figure 7-3 and you can decide how easily you can find the MP3-related tool you're looking for.

iTunes' search capabilities are pretty good, assuming that you display the fields in which you want to search and are willing to scroll around a bit (or a lot). MP3 Rage searches the ID3 tags in your iTunes database quickly and builds a list for you, as shown in Figure 7-4.

Figure 7-3: MP3 Rage's menu screen provides an almost overwhelming option set.

MP3 Rage is also helpful when you want a catalog of your MP3s. With iTunes, you can Export to text and end up with a lot of information you don't really want. MP3 Rage produces a tab-delimited report formatted with just the fields you specify, in the order you specify them, as shown in Figure 7-5. We admit that the specification syntax is a little geeky, but it isn't too difficult and you don't have to memorize anything with the cheat sheet displayed right below the text box.

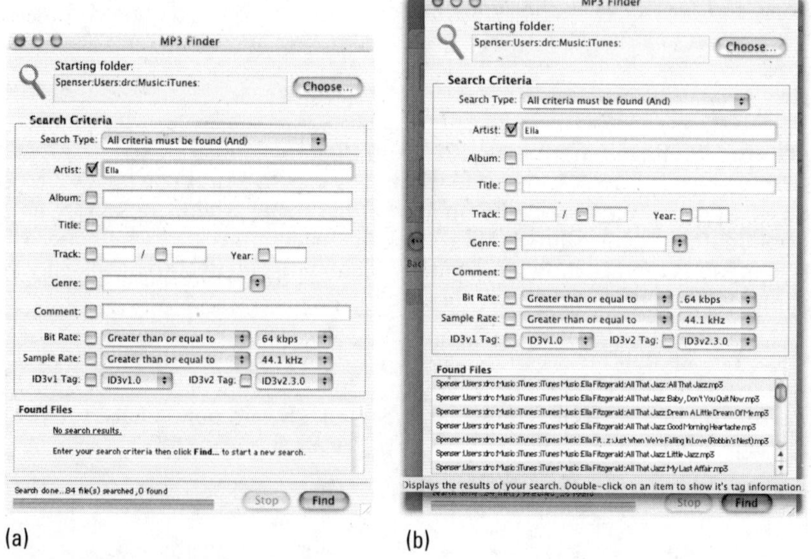

Figure 7-4: Setting your search criteria (a); MP3 Rage builds a list of all files with matching ID3 Tag information (b).

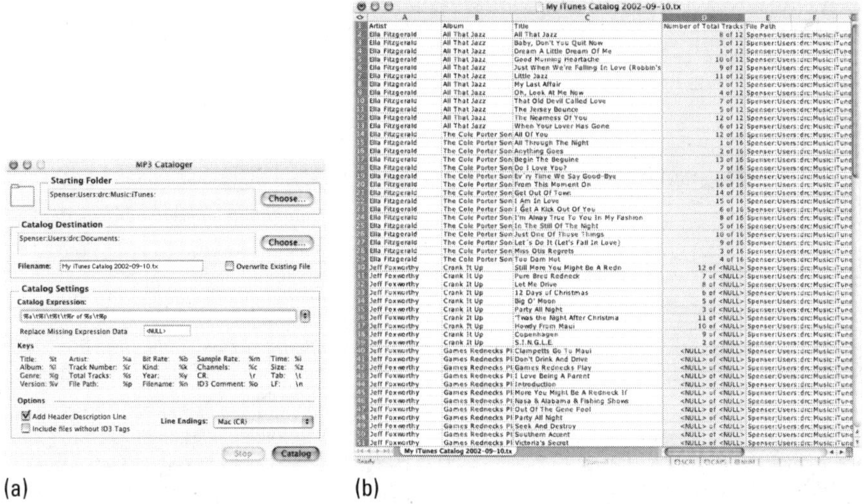

(a) (b)

Figure 7-5: You can specify the fields you want, in the order you want them (a); MP3 Rage will generate the catalog for you. This report was opened in Excel (b).

Amadeus II

A useful shareware tool ($25) from Hairer Soft (`www.hairersoft.com/Amadeus.html`), Amadeus II lets you generate, analyze, and edit MP3 files. You can use it to trim and combine MP3 files and actually process the audio waveforms. You can speed the music up or slow it down, either in toto or in chunks.

As Martin Hairer, the author of Amadeus II concedes in the program's Readme file, Amadeus II doesn't have the most intuitive of interfaces. What it does, it does well, at least on our Macs. In Figure 7-6, you can see Amadeus playing an MP3, displaying the combined waveform as well as the waveforms for both stereo channels.

Neither of us is audio geek enough to know what all of the functions do, but we each find a few of its functions very useful, particularly in cleaning up MP3s we bring in from older analog sources such as cassette or LP.

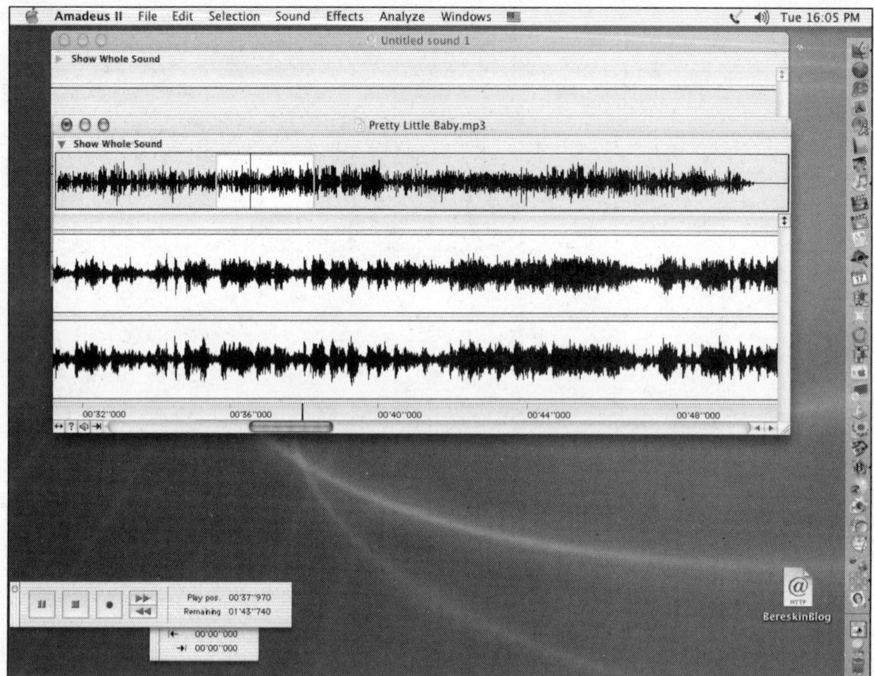

Figure 7-6: Amadeus II shows you both channels and the combined waveform.

Visualizer plug-ins

Bob is a huge fan of the iTunes Visual Effects functionality, while Dennis uses it primarily to entertain and amaze Windows-using friends. Wherever you fall on the continuum between these two positions, you should check out Version Tracker's collection of Visualizer plug-ins. The assortment grows steadily — far beyond the prosaic effects Apple includes with iTunes 3 — and you're almost sure to find something you'll like. Best of all, most of the visual effects plug-ins are *free*.

One of our favorites (and a big hit with guests) is the Zoomify plug-in, shown in Figure 7-7 transitioning from one photo to the next in a slide show.

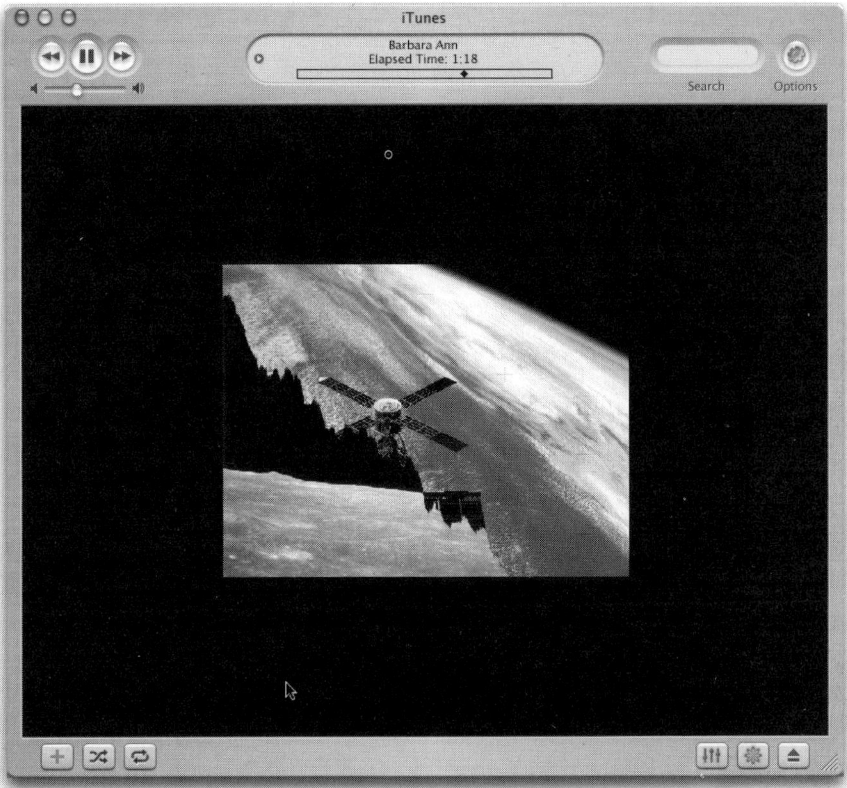

Figure 7-7: The freeware Zoomify plug-in plays a slideshow in the iTunes Visualizer.

Summary

Depending upon your interests and budget, the material in this chapter should start you on the road to even greater iTunes enjoyment. Whether hardware or software, there are plenty of items with which you can deck out both your Mac and iTunes. Some work directly with iTunes, while others work with the MP3 files that provide iTunes its fodder.

✦ ✦ ✦

P A R T

iPhoto

✦ ✦ ✦ ✦

In This Part

✦ ✦ ✦ ✦

Introducing iPhoto

✦ ✦ ✦ ✦

In This Chapter

Introducing digital photography and iPhoto

Exploring the iPhoto window

Setting iPhoto preferences

✦ ✦ ✦ ✦

The newest spoke in Apple's Digital Hub is iPhoto, introduced at Macworld San Francisco in January 2002 to a very appreciative audience and updated to iPhoto 2, with the introduction of iLife, at the January 2003 San Francisco Macworld. Paraphrasing Steve Jobs, iPhoto filled the gaping hole in the Macintosh digital hub strategy. Apple already had iTunes for digital music, iMovie for digital video editing, and iDVD for digital video production, but nothing for managing digital images.

This oversight is especially amusing and amazing to those of us who remember that Apple was among the first to seriously promote digital photography with their QuickTake 100 digital camera almost a decade ago. The first digital camera with a three-digit price tag at about $600 ($10,000-plus was the norm for even a 640 x 480 pixel digital camera in those days), the QuickTake once again demonstrated that Apple recognizes technology trends early. Since then, almost every major camera and printer manufacturer (and a whole slew of others) have been producing and selling digital cameras, offering more and more features and resolution for the same or lower prices. You can now purchase a pocket-sized equivalent of the QuickTake 100 for $29, and cameras costing $600 will have ten to fifteen times the resolution and a raft of special features (such as panoramas and minimovies).

Apple's Mac OS X Public Preview (Spring 2000) again highlighted digital photography, when the standard Steve Jobs demo featured Image Capture recognizing USB-connected digital cameras and mounting them on the desktop like any (other) volume, downloading pictures, and even automatically creating Web page photo albums. But thereafter, for 18 months, through two versions of iTunes, a major upgrade to iMovie 2, and the introduction of iDVD, digital photography on the Mac languished.

In contrast, Apple released the critically acclaimed iPhoto software, significantly upgraded it to iPhoto 1.1.1 in less than six months, and released iPhoto 2 about six months after that.

Introducing Digital Photography and iPhoto

If you're like most of the people we know, you have been exposed to albums, shoeboxes, envelopes, and drawers full of old photographs most of your life. Most of these photos are part of a totally disorganized mess, never looked at but never discarded. On the rare occasion that you think, "Aha, I have a photo of that event," you probably can't find it or, if you do, it is creased, smudged, or otherwise damaged.

Here comes digital photography, freeing you from the tyranny of purchasing film, the drudgery of hauling the exposed film rolls to wherever you choose to have your pictures developed, and the confusion of sorting through the results when you get the processed pictures back to see if any of them turned out the way you hoped. No film to deal with and no agonized wait to see how the pictures look—sounds like photographic nirvana, doesn't it?

In those respects, it is. When you take a picture with a digital camera, you can check it out immediately on the camera's LCD screen. If you don't like the result, just delete the picture from the camera's memory (or memory card) and take more pictures.

Resolution and Pixels

Because digital cameras don't use film, they require a different technology to acquire an image. Like most scanners, most digital cameras use a *CCD* (Charged Coupled Device). A CCD reacts to light, storing color information in the pixels (picture elements) that comprise it. Each of these pixels is one dot in your digital photo – the more dots you have, the more accurate the picture. A 640 x 480 image measures 640 dots in one (normally thought of as the horizontal) dimension and 480 dots in the other dimension. This is just over 39 percent of a typical 1024 x 768 monitor's display area. Because the image is smaller than the screen, scaling it to fill the screen will introduce blur and jagged edges. This explains the constant race for higher and higher resolution cameras. Similarly, if you want to print an 8 x10-inch photo on an inkjet printer that prints 360 dots per inch and not introduce any *interpolated* (estimated) pixels, you need 360 x 8 pixels in one dimension and 360 x 10 pixels in the other (2880 x 3600 resolution) – that's over 10 megapixels. Fortunately, those dots are so small and the interpolation is so good that you can get by with much less, about 2 to 3 megapixels, before your eye starts to notice a lack of fidelity.

Choosing a digital camera

You do pay a price for going digital, however. Pictures of just about any size printed from a photographic negative can look sharp, but digital photos don't print out well past a certain size, which is determined by the camera's *resolution*. For example, a camera that advertises 640 x 480 resolution is limited to about wallet size printouts, unless you like blocky artifacts in your picture. To print an 8 x 10 that looks like it came from film, you need at least 2 megapixels (about 1600 x 1200) and probably 3.3 megapixels (about 2048 x 1536).

Higher resolution cameras do have their upsides and downsides. The upsides:

- You can increase a printed image without pixelization (blocky artifacts).
- You can enlarge a portion of a picture and still print without pixelization.

The downsides:

- The higher the resolution, the fewer images you can store in memory at a time.
- The higher the resolution, the more the camera will cost.

Cap'n, we need more power

You'll quickly learn that digital cameras go through batteries like food through a goose. Most digital cameras take two to four AA batteries and will exhaust that set of alkaline AAs in twenty to thirty minutes of use. Lithium ion (sometimes called photo lithium or just lithium) batteries last longer (maybe 60 to 90 minutes of use), but cost a lot more than alkaline. The best way to go, at least at present, is with rechargeable NiMH (nickel metal hydride) batteries. NiMH batteries are even more expensive than lithium ion, but they don't get exhausted as quickly, lasting two to three hours in our informal testing, and you can recharge and reuse them. You can also find rechargeable lithium ion batteries, though they are far less common than NiMH.

Those cameras that don't take AAs generally have their own, proprietary batteries that require recharging while the camera is plugged into an electrical outlet. While the life of these batteries is good, you can't get too far from a power source and you have to wait for the camera to recharge before you can continue shooting pictures.

Possibly the best of the lot are cameras that have their own power packs, but will also run off AAs. These aren't common and tend to be high-end (read "expensive") purchases.

Tip

Although it negates one of the major advantages of digital cameras, instant feedback, turning off the LCD display greatly extends battery life. That little screen is a major power drain. So, you might want to turn it off while you're shooting and only turn it on to review groups of pictures during a lull.

Resolving resolution

If your only use (and don't get us wrong, it's a good use) of a digital camera is to take photos to use on Web pages and view on the computer, 640 x 480 resolution is all you'll ever need. For one thing, larger pictures take longer to download and for your Web browser to render. For another, anything much larger than 640 x 480 won't fit in a lot of users' browser windows without scrolling.

Note

It has long struck us as curious that even though the image aspect ratio of digital photographs is generally 4:3, that pictures are usually printed at 4 x 6 and 8 x 10, which aren't true 4:3 ratios. (True 4:3 ratios are 7.5 x 10 or 4.5 x 6.) We're also unsure if the film photography world knows how to measure. When we put the ruler to the allegedly 4 x 6 prints, we almost never get 4 x 6 (more like 4 x 5.875) on a full-bleed (edge to edge) print, and we know (from looking at the negative), that the picture's edges were cropped. The fact is you're going to be trimming and cropping if you want to print your digital photos at standard picture sizes. Fortunately, iPhoto makes that an easy task, as you'll see in Chapter 10.

Lies, Damn Lies, and Specifications

If you want to do the math, you can discover that camera manufacturers lie (okay, exaggerate) when they list a camera's resolution. For example, Dennis's Kodak DX-3500 is listed as 2.2 megapixels. The image is 1800 x 1200 (yes, we know that isn't a 4:3 ratio), which multiplies out to 2,160,000 pixels. With computers, "mega" generally means 1,048,576 (that's 1,024 times 1,024) and we're way short of the 2,306,867 that 2.2 megapixels should mean (1,024 x 1,204 x 2.2). Now, even using the generous definition of "mega" to mean "million," we still aren't at 2,200,000 pixels. The cameras advertised as 3.3 megapixel (2048 x 1576) are *exactly* 3 megapixels in computer terms, which makes the exaggeration a nice round 10 percent. Be aware of this, but don't worry about it too much – everybody lies, but at least they're all telling pretty much the same lies.

Yes, they lie about expected battery life, too. Of course, we're used to that because everybody in the electronics business lies about battery life. Ask any PowerBook owner. We've yet to encounter a single instance of *anyone* who got the stated battery life on their laptop computer in anything resembling normal use, or in their Walkman, or in their portable TV, or. . . Well, you get the picture. In fact, the only device we can think of that seems to get its advertised battery life is the iPod.

Our best advice is to take electronic product specifications with a grain of salt.

The next step up in resolution is the "megapixel" camera, generally with 1280 x 960 resolution. Because most computer screens are smaller than this, you'd have to scroll the picture or reduce it in size to view on-screen. The megapixel cameras (often listed as 1.1 megapixel) are good for printing pictures up to 4 x 6 inches.

The cameras in the 2-megapixel family (those designated as 2, 2.1, or 2.2 megapixels) are usually sufficient for images up to 8 x 10 inches. Three megapixel (usually marked as 3.3 megapixel) cameras generally suffice for pictures up to 11 x 14 and you can get good results at 12 x 16 inches with a 4-megapixel camera.

Trying to print a lower resolution picture than those listed results in a picture that appears pixilated or, to use a more common term, *jaggy*. For those of you who have been around a while, you might recall trying to print bitmap fonts on a laser printer, and the ugly jagged characters that would result. Those are the jaggies. Figure 8-1 shows an example of the jaggies in a photograph.

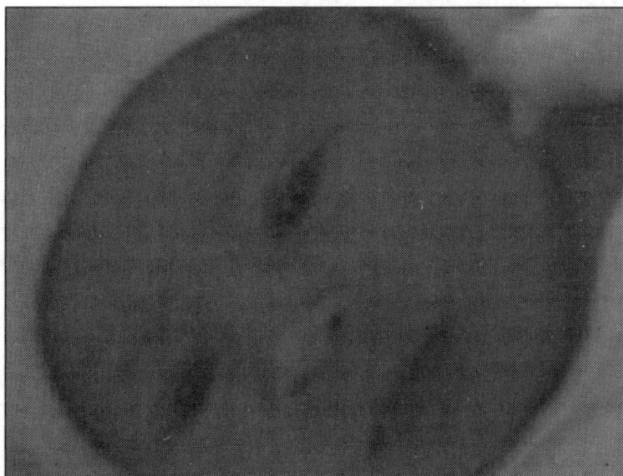

Figure 8-1: Attempting to print a low-resolution picture at too large a size introduces the jaggies.

The number of pixels is not, however, the only item affecting how good your printouts will look. You also need a good printer, appropriate paper, and a good clean shot from which to start. That last item is really not within our areas of expertise. Although we give you a few tips to produce a good clean shot in Chapter 11, we suggest taking a college-level course or purchasing a book dedicated to digital photography if you want to learn more about the photographic art.

Thanks for the memory

The bigger your picture (higher resolution), the more memory it is going to consume in your camera. Even with the JPEG compression used by most digital cameras, these pictures are going to fill your camera's built-in memory (usually 8MB or 16MB) pretty quickly. Using a 2-megapixel camera, you shouldn't expect to get more than about 7 to 15 pictures in 8MB of memory. That's why most digital cameras also accept memory cards, which come in a variety of flavors and sizes (both physical and capacity). The more common of these are

✦ **Smart Media:** Small (about 2 square inches), thin, reasonably priced, and commonly used cards that come in sizes ranging up to 128MB.

✦ **CompactFlash:** Another relatively inexpensive and widely used format, boasting capacities up to 1GB. They have varying write speeds, so if you're going to be taking pictures rapidly, you might want to make sure that yours are up to the task.

✦ **Memory Sticks:** Sony-only format that is used in Sony cameras, camcorders, and laptop computers. (Not that the latter should interest you — you have a Mac.) Memory sticks top out at 128MB and are not cheap.

✦ **Secure Digital:** Small (postage stamp-sized) card that comes in capacities up to 128MB. They aren't common, but are starting to appear in some handheld devices (Palms, for example). They're a little more expensive than Smart Media or CompactFlash in the same capacity, but a little less expensive than Memory Sticks.

If you have other devices that use memory cards (Dennis has an old MP3 player that uses Smart Media and a Sony digital camcorder that uses Memory Sticks), you might consider that an incentive to favor one format over another.

Manufacturer hype notwithstanding, there is almost never a quality difference between brands. We say "almost" just to cover our posteriors – we've never encountered a difference, nor do we personally know anyone who has, except with Memory Sticks. Although they're more expensive, Sony's seem more reliable, but then, Sony is just about the only manufacturer that uses them. Bob has been buying whichever brand of CompactFlash card is least expensive and hasn't had a problem with any of the four or five different brands he's purchased.

Fathoming feature lists

Digital cameras have other features in common with film cameras: bells and whistles. These bells don't ring and the whistles don't blow, but if you want to take the best pictures you can under a variety of conditions, you're going to have to know about them. Then the real problem arises — deciding how much you're willing to pay for the features. Adjustable f-stops, aperture control, shutter mode control, color balance, auto-focus assist, variable film speeds, swivel LCDs, and so forth give you more flexibility, but they come with a price that is measured in both dollars and, often, size.

Without these additional features, your digital camera, available for $19.95 and up, is roughly the digital equivalent of simple Instamatic film cameras. It'll work fine in normal conditions: outdoors on a sunny day or at relatively close range indoors, where the flash will be effective or you have a lot of natural light. But the camera will work poorly for action shots, night shots, pictures in mood lighting, or any of the other atypical conditions you're going to encounter when you really want to capture a memory.

Here are some of the more desirable options to look for in a digital camera:

✦ **Swivel or flip LCD:** Enables you to see what is in your shot when you're holding the camera somewhere other than right in front of you. For example, you could be holding the camera down low to take an eye-level shot of your child's first steps or up high to get an elevated perspective without climbing a ladder or standing on a chair.

✦ **Color balance:** You can adjust how the camera sees light. Our eyes automatically adjust to what's called the *color temperature* of light. Shots taken in the shade or indoors without a flash are "cool" and can display a bluish tint. Pictures taken under incandescent lighting are "warm" and display a yellow or reddish tint. Color balance is sometimes listed as white balance.

✦ **Aperture priority control:** You can specify how wide the shutter opens. This provides control over how much light gets in.

✦ **Shutter priority control:** You set how quickly (or slowly) the shutter cycles. You can use this to great effect in taking action shots (quick) or nighttime shots (slow).

✦ **Manual mode:** Control the aperture and shutter independently.

✦ **Variable film speeds:** Simulate the effects you achieve with different film speeds (ISO 100, 200, 400) in traditional cameras.

✦ **Optical zoom:** Gives you control over how close objects appear to be without sacrificing quality. Don't pay much attention to digital zoom numbers. Using digital zoom is just like taking the picture and cropping the edges — you end up with fewer pixels.

✦ **Attachment ready cameras:** You hook up real flashes (helps eliminate red-eye and other side effects of having the built-in flash right next to the lens) and different lenses and filters.

✦ **Burst mode operation:** You can take pictures one after another, just like you see the fashion photographers do in the movies and on TV. A camera with burst mode operation is going to be expensive because it requires a large memory buffer to hold these images. Storing the image on a memory card is not the world's fastest operation.

Finally, some digital cameras can record short movies and/or record audio.

Almost all digital cameras are threaded to attach a tripod, but you might want to check whether the threading is metal or plastic. Metal is better because it is less likely to go out of shape or strip the threads when used.

To get a rundown on these features and others, check out a Web site like `www.shortcourses.com`.

Focusing on iPhoto

Okay, you have your digital camera and you want to use your Mac to view, edit, organize, and print your pictures. Those are just some of the tasks iPhoto performs. iPhoto will download your pictures from your camera when you connect it to your Mac and store them in your photo library. iPhoto can even erase the pictures from your camera after they're downloaded, if you want.

You can find both pluses and minuses to automatically erasing pictures after they're downloaded. The biggest plus, obviously, is that it frees up room in your camera's memory (or on the memory card) for new pictures. Erasing the pictures from the camera also means that you won't be downloading the same pictures the next time you attach your camera. Weighing against these pluses is the fact that "stuff happens" and, if you accidentally erase a picture from your Library before doing a backup, it will be irrevocably lost. Paranoid, (uh, make that cautious), people eschew this option and make sure that everything got into the Library without a problem and that a backup has been made before manually erasing the camera's contents. Bob rarely follows this advice and hasn't lost a picture yet (though it's probably just a matter of time).

In addition to being a photo importer, iPhoto wears many other hats, as described in the sections that follow.

A photo organizer

When iPhoto downloads pictures from your camera, it adds them to your Photo Library. At first glance, this Library resembles nothing so much as a huge drawer full of apparently unrelated pictures. iPhoto keeps track of what is there by both roll number (groups of simultaneously imported photos) and by date. Additionally, iPhoto lets you create albums of related pictures, including sharing pictures between multiple albums (without having to pay for additional prints).

A basic photo editor

No one is going to seriously suggest that iPhoto is competition for Photoshop as a photo editor. iPhoto does, however, provide you with a handful of the basics for cleaning up your digital photos: trimming them to print on different paper sizes and at different aspect ratios, converting to black and white for that retro look, and adjusting the brightness and contrast.

A photo publisher

It matters not whether you're talking about publishing a book or a Web site containing your photos. iPhoto publishes both the traditional hardcover coffee table book and the Web photo gallery currently in vogue. Well, for the book it actually connects via the Internet to a printer/bindery, but what gets printed are your photos and text as you laid them out in one of the supplied iPhoto templates. When publishing your Web page, iPhoto can create a one-click page on your .Mac account or let you customize the layout and produce a page you can publish on either your .Mac homepage, or any other account.

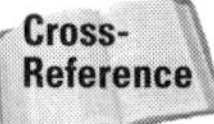

We cover .Mac Homepages in Chapter 10, and custom Web pages in Chapter 11.

A photo printer

Whether you want to print your photos on your own printer or order prints from Kodak, iPhoto fills the bill. In addition to individual prints in various sizes, you can print *contact sheets* (collections of miniatures on a single page).

A photo delivery service

Using the Mail program that comes with OS X, iPhoto creates messages with your chosen photos attached just waiting for you to address and send.

A photo jack-of-all-trades

iPhoto runs on a Mac and we all like to personalize our Macs. Apple realized this and made iPhoto capable of creating slideshows, desktop pictures, and screen savers using your photos.

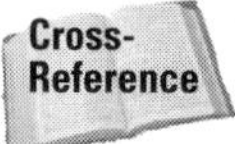

Turn to Chapter 10 to find out more in-depth information about iPhoto features. For more about creating custom Web pages, see Chapter 11.

Exploring the iPhoto Window

What you see when you first open iPhoto depends upon whether you launched it by connecting a digital camera through the USB connection (Import mode) or clicked the iPhoto icon in the Dock (Organize mode). iPhoto 2 has four modes, accessible via the buttons shown in Figure 8-2: Import, Organize, Edit, and Book.

Each mode displays its own set of tools in the iPhoto window's bottom panel. For those of you upgrading from iPhoto 1.1.1 to iPhoto 2, Share mode disappeared from the product and the Share tools now appear under Organize. The old Organize tools (keywords, for example) are still available via iPhoto's menus.

Figure 8-2: These buttons set iPhoto's mode, determining which controls show up in the toolbox at the bottom of the window.

Except for this mode-specific tool panel, the rest of the iPhoto window is the same regardless of the current mode (Figure 8-3).

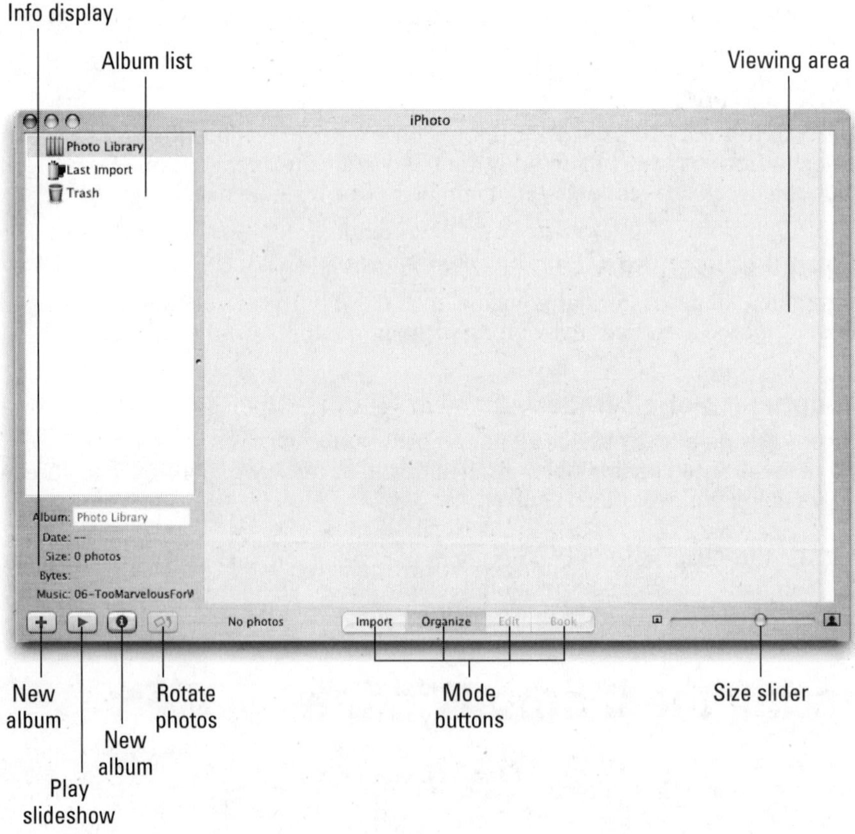

Figure 8-3: Most of the iPhoto window doesn't change if you change modes.

The parts and controls you see in Figure 8-3 are

- **Album list:** Reminiscent of the iTunes Source List (see Chapter 3). The first item is fixed and that's your Photo Library, the repository and database for all the photos iPhoto knows about. Working under the assumption that you're often going to want to work with your newest pictures, Last Import is a special album that contains whatever group of pictures you last imported into iPhoto. Any albums that you create appear beneath.
- **Viewing area:** Where you view your photos. Depending upon your mode, you'll see one (Edit) or more pictures or thumbnails.
- **Info display:** Can be hidden, normal-sized as shown in Figure 8-3, or expanded to include a Comments box. If no image or more than one image is selected, the name and date of the current album are displayed; otherwise, the current photo's name and date are shown. For a single image, the dimensions are shown next to Size; otherwise, the number of selected photos or photos in the album is displayed. Bytes shows the size on disk of the photo, photos, or album selected.
- **New album button:** Creates a new entry in the Album List when clicked, presenting the New Album dialog where you can name your new album.
- **Play slideshow button:** Starts playing a slide show of the currently selected photo(s) or Album, using the settings established in Preferences (see the "Setting iPhoto Preferences" section later in this chapter).
- **Show Info button:** Cycles the Info Display through its three states.
- **Rotate photos button:** Rotates the photos 90 degrees in the direction of the arrow, which you can set in Preferences (see the "Setting iPhoto Preferences" section later in this chapter). Pressing Option while clicking this button rotates the photo(s) 90 degrees in the opposite direction.
- **InfoDisplay:** iPhoto displays how many photos are in the current album and, if any are selected, just how many are selected.
- **Mode buttons:** Four buttons are used to switch between iPhoto's different operating modes.
- **Size slider:** Shrinks or expands the size of the thumbnails displayed in the Viewing Area. Moving it all the way to the left shrinks the thumbnails down to tiny images, nearly impossible to discern one from another when you're in Import or Organize mode (or when you've moved to Share from one of those modes) and to "fill the Viewing Area" size when in Edit or Book mode. Moving the slider right zooms in when in Edit or Book mode and expands the thumbnails until you get to one per row in Import or Organize mode. Once again, the Share mode display inherits the characteristics of the previous mode.

Import mode tools

When you connect a compatible digital camera, iPhoto switches to Import mode if you haven't bothered to do so. The iPhoto tool panel display resembles that shown in Figure 8-4. The camera type and contents will probably be different, but other than that, what you see is what you get.

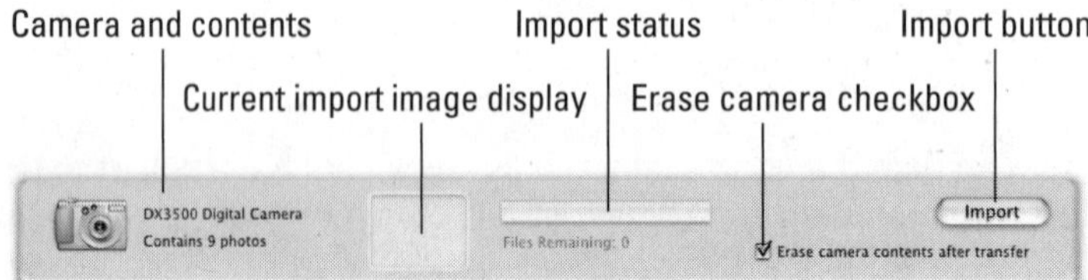

Figure 8-4: These are iPhoto's camera import controls and status display.

From left to right, you see

- ✦ The make of attached digital camera and how many images it currently holds
- ✦ A frame that displays the current image's thumbnail during import
- ✦ A status bar displaying the progress of the current import above a line telling how many images remain to be imported
- ✦ The Import button that initiates the import process when clicked
- ✦ A checkbox telling iPhoto whether to erase the camera's memory (or memory card) when the import is complete

Organize mode tools

Apple decided that Share mode was superfluous, and research indicated that users were constantly switching between Organize and Share mode to print, e-mail, specify desktop pictures, and so on. Now, in iPhoto 2, Share mode is gone, and its tools are available in the Organize toolbox, as shown in Figure 8-5. You also find a few new buttons: .Mac Slides, iDVD, and Burn (but Screen Saver is gone, now part of Desktop).

Figure 8-5: iPhoto's Organizational tools; they used to be Share mode tools.

Most of these buttons are self-explanatory, but we would be remiss not to enumerate them. From left to right, they are

- **Print:** Presents iPhoto's Print dialog so that you can print your photos on your Mac's printer.
- **Slideshow:** Asks you to verify your Slideshow settings and then plays your slide show.
- **Mail:** Creates a message in Apple's Mail application with your selected photos attached and, if you wish, resized for the convenience of your recipients (3-megapixel images are *really* big attachments, especially after they're encoded for e-mail transmission). See Chapter 9 for more on e-mailing your photos.
- **Order Prints button:** as an electronic Fotomat. Click it to order prints of your photos from Kodak.
- **Order Book button:** assembles your latest Book design and connects to Apple's Online Store to order one or more copies. Ordering books requires an Apple One-Click account, which is easy to create.
- **HomePage button:** to quickly create a Web page of your selected photos using your .Mac account (if you have one). Your design choices are limited, but it is a very quick way to get your page created and published.
- **.Mac Slides:** if you have a .Mac account and wish to publish a selection of photos as a slide show to which other people who are running Mac OS X 10.2 or later can subscribe. All they have to do is open their Screen Effects preference, select the .Mac screen effect, and supply your .Mac member name. iPhoto even prompts you to send an announcement e-mail when the upload to your iDisk completes.
- **Desktop button:** uses the selected photo (if you only have one selected) as your Desktop picture without you having to mess with System Preferences, until and unless you want to go back to a non-picture Desktop. If you select an album or multiple images, iPhoto communicates to your System Screen Effects Preferences that the selected images are to be used as your screen saver.
- **iDVD button:** specifies that the selected photos be used to create a slideshow in iDVD. Note that the iDVD button will **not** be present if you don't have iDVD installed.
- **Burn button:** has become available in iPhoto and you can use it to archive photos to CD or DVD. But, iPhoto doesn't just write the selected albums and/or photos, it writes them as an iPhoto Library that, when inserted, will appear in the iPhoto Album List (just like your iPod's music library appears in iTunes Source List).

For more on setting Slideshow preferences and the Mail tool's mail clients, see "Setting iPhoto Preferences" later in this chapter. For more on the Mail, Order Print, Order Book, HomePage, and Desktop buttons, see Chapter 9.

Edit mode tools

As we stated earlier, iPhoto's editing tools are no threat to Photoshop, but by adding the Enhance and Retouch tools to iPhoto 2, the gap is getting a lot smaller. iPhoto provides a minimal set of tools (shown in Figure 8-6) to perform the most common photo-editing tasks: cropping, adjusting brightness and contrast, red-eye elimination, and (sort of a bonus) converting your beautiful color photo to a classic black and white.

Figure 8-6: iPhoto's editing tools are a spartan but useful collection.

iPhoto's editing tool chest seems kind of empty, but does include the following useful tools:

✦ **Constrain pop-up menu:** Establishes the proportions of a selection. For example, if you're planning to print an 8 x 10 of your 2048 x 1536 image, some of the 2048 is going to have to go (1920 x 1536 works out to 10 x 8 at 192ppi).

✦ **Crop button:** Available when you select part of the photo. Click it and, poof, your picture has been trimmed to just the selection.

✦ **Brightness and Contrast controls:** Similar to the like-named controls on your TV set or computer monitor. Moving brightness to the right lightens your picture by moving the pixels closer to white, although light pixels move toward white at a faster rate than dark pixels. Similarly, turning brightness down makes the picture darker by darkening all the pixels, with the dark pixels moving toward black faster than the lighter pixels. Contrast moves dark toward black and light toward white, sharpening the demarcation between light and dark areas of your photo.

✦ **Red-eye reduction:** A technique to eliminate the flash's reflection off the blood vessels in your subject's cornea. Was that clinical enough?

✦ **Black & White:** Converts your color photo to an old-fashioned black-and-white photo (really, grayscale). You see the Black & White effect throughout this book — all of our screen shots were in color when we submitted them, but they were converted to black-and-white for printing.

✦ **Enhance:** New in iPhoto 2 and can be thought of as an intelligent brightness/contrast tool — it adjusts over- and under-exposed pictures so that the subject matter stands out.

✦ **Retouch:** Also new in iPhoto 2, bears a superficial resemblance to the Photoshop 7 Healing brush, except that you don't have to specify the background texture you seek. The tool uses the surrounding pixels to "fill in" the damaged section to remove scratches, blemishes, or (as Steve Jobs demonstrated when announcing iPhoto 2) freckles.

✦ **Previous** and **Next** buttons: Move from one picture to another, as do the left and right arrows on your keyboard.

Book mode tools

Book mode is where you design and lay out your coffee table books, which, for a relatively modest fee ($30 for a 10-page hardbound book, plus $3/page for additional pages), Apple's preferred bindery will print up and ship back to you. Figure 8-7 shows the Book mode toolbox.

Figure 8-7: Use iPhoto's Book tools to design, layout, and preview a picture book.

The Book mode tools are the following:

✦ **Theme pop-up list:** You select one of the limited number (six at the time we're writing this) of book designs as your starting point.

✦ **Show Guides checkbox:** Specifies whether light-blue guidelines are displayed while you're laying out your book. These guides delimit the editable areas on each page.

✦ **Titles, Comments, and Page Numbers checkboxes:** Tell iPhoto whether to include picture names and comments adjacent to each photo and whether page numbers should appear on each interior page of your book.

✦ **Page Design pop-up list:** Shows the layout choices for pages of your chosen Theme. For example, the Yearbook theme allows up to 32 pictures with captions and comments per page, but the Portfolio theme only allows up to four photos with captions and comments per page.

✦ **Lock Page checkbox:** Tells iPhoto not to reflow pictures onto or off of the chosen page if earlier pages have their design changed.

✦ **Preview button:** Opens a window where you can move from page to page, seeing how your book will look.

Setting iPhoto Preferences

All but the most single-purpose programs are incomplete without a Preferences dialog where you tailor an application's behavior to more closely match your way of working. To access the iPhoto Preferences dialog (Figure 8-8), choose iPhoto ⇨ Preferences (⌘-,).

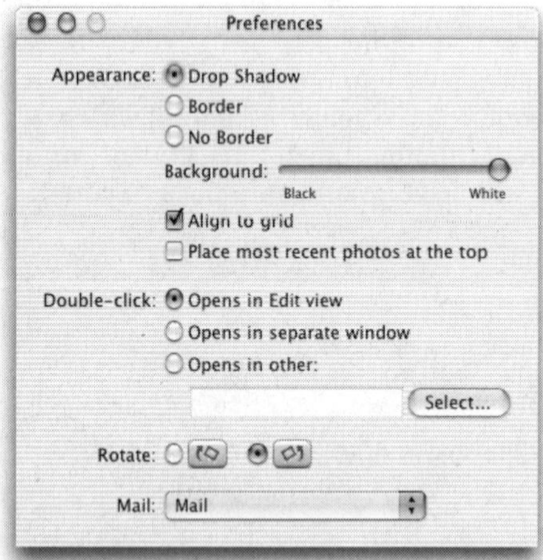

Figure 8-8: The iPhoto Preferences dialog crams a lot into one small window.

The iPhoto Preferences fall into four categories and, in an unusual move by Apple programmers, there are no dividing lines or tabbed panels separating the preference groups. You can set preferences as follows:

✦ **Appearance:** The controls in this group manage the presentation of photos in the Viewing Area.

- Drop Shadow displays your photos with a faint drop-shadow (the default) or with a frame. If you choose Border, a thin white border will surround your photo. Of course, if the Background slider is set to white (the default). This is the same as No Border, in which your photo's edges directly abut the background.
- Align to grid keeps your photo thumbnails in an orderly row and column display. Supposedly, turning this off lets you rearrange the photos into a pattern of your choosing, but everything stays aligned to the grid when we turn it off.

- Normally, iPhoto displays your photos with the oldest at the top left, working across rows and down the scrollable pane to the newest. Clicking Place most recent photos at top reverses this order.

✦ **Double-click:** offers three choices

- Opens in Edit view is the default and is the same as clicking the Edit mode button.
- Opens in separate window, as its name implies, opens the target image in its own window with some of the Edit mode controls in a toolbar, as shown in Figure 8-9. You can, as always, customize the toolbar and add in the Enhance and Retouch tools, which are, inexplicably, missing from the Edit window's default toolbar.

Figure 8-9: Editing a photo in its own window places Edit mode controls in the window's toolbar.

- If you click Opens in other, then you can click the Select button and choose a more powerful editing application. Some Macs come with GraphicConverter (a very powerful shareware image editing and creation tool) and PixelNhance (an application focused on manipulating existing images), either of which make an excellent choice if you find iPhoto's editing tools inadequate. Then, of course, there is the expensive crème de la crème of photo-editing tools: Adobe Photoshop (`www.adobe.com`) or its very capable, but less expensive, offspring: Adobe Photoshop Elements 2.

✦ **Rotate:** Offers two choices, Clockwise and Counter Clockwise (the default). These are depicted rather than spelled-out.

✦ **Mail pop-up:** You specify which of the four mail clients iPhoto supports (OS X Mail, Microsoft Entourage, America Online, or Eudora) and that you want to use for e-mail-related activities in iPhoto. If you choose a client other than OS X's Mail application, iPhoto will even change the icon used for the Mail button to indicate the client you chose.

Summary

In this chapter, you've learned a little about the history of digital photography, been introduced to the myriad features available and tradeoffs to consider when purchasing a digital camera, learned about the iPhoto window and its five modes, and perused the iPhoto Preferences window

✦ ✦ ✦

Getting Started with iPhoto

In This Chapter

Organizing your photos

Editing photos

Laying out books

Printing photos

Ordering photos

E-mailing your photos

Creating a slideshow

Using your photos on the desktop

Web publishing photos on your .Mac homepage

Sharing slideshows via a .Mac account

Burning CDs of your photos

iPhoto is an easy-to-use but still powerful photo collection organizer and manager. It can communicate with most current digital cameras. (See `www.apple.com/iphoto/compatibility/` for a long, though still incomplete, list of compatible cameras.)

Utilizing iPhoto's tools you can organize, search, print, edit, and use your digital photos in myriad ways. Not only can you produce the traditional 4 x 6, 5 x 7, and 8 x 10 prints, but you can print contact sheets and greeting cards, lay out coffee table books and have them professionally printed and bound, or send your digital images to Kodak to be professionally printed.

You can use your pictures in a screen saver, a slideshow (with background music), or place them on your desktop in place of the standard background. With just a few clicks, your photos can be on the Web to share with friends and family, published as a shared screensaver, or sent as e-mail attachments.

You can also drag copies directly from your iPhoto window into your report for school, your inventory database, or just about any other document you're creating with a drag-and-drop savvy application (such as AppleWorks or Microsoft Office). Think of iPhoto as your one-stop art collection, because the images don't have to be photographs — you can store and manage any graphic in a compatible format in iPhoto.

Importing Pictures

Your camera's memory is full, you have folders of photos you downloaded with Image Capture or the software that came with your digital camera before you got iPhoto, you have Kodak PhotoCDs or Picture CDs full of pictures from your film camera, or you have the ever-present drawer or shoebox full of snapshots. Maybe all, or at least more than one, of these are true.

iPhoto handles the first three alternatives neatly, with no fuss or mess. If you have a digital image, the odds are that iPhoto can handle it. iPhoto will not, however, work with digital images in obscure or proprietary formats. Dennis, for example, has an old Casio digital camera in his collection that saves its pictures in Casio's proprietary CAM format. In a case like this, you're going to need an external tool, such as GraphicConverter or the software that came with your uncooperative camera, to convert the image to a supported format.

The loose snapshots, though, are going to have to be digitized. If you have a scanner, you could scan them and save the images on your hard disk. Alternatively, you can take them to your Kodak outlet or some other development house and have them scanned to CD. After they're in digital form, you're ready to feed them to iPhoto.

Importing from a supported digital camera or equivalent

Using the USB connector, hook your camera up to your Mac, and iPhoto start up automatically in Import mode. You'll see information about your camera in the Import toolbox, including how many pictures it holds, as shown in Figure 9-1. Click the Import button, and iPhoto starts importing the photos, displaying a thumbnail of the photo it is currently reading and telling you how many photos still await import.

Tip If your Mac doesn't recognize that a camera is connected and you know your camera is supported, try turning the camera off and then back on while it is connected.

iPhoto even makes it easy for you to erase the photos from your camera's memory or memory card. Just select the "Erase camera contents after transfer" checkbox, if you wish. Selecting this checkbox means that you never import the same picture(s) twice because you forgot to erase them the first time you imported them. If you're a very cautious and organized sort, though, you may want to leave this checkbox cleared and manually delete the pictures after you've verified that everything was imported and that you have made backups of the photos of particular interest.

When iPhoto finishes importing your pictures, it is even obliging enough to switch to Organize mode, as shown in Figure 9-2, displaying your Photo Library. See "Organizing Your Photos" later in this chapter on how Organize mode works.

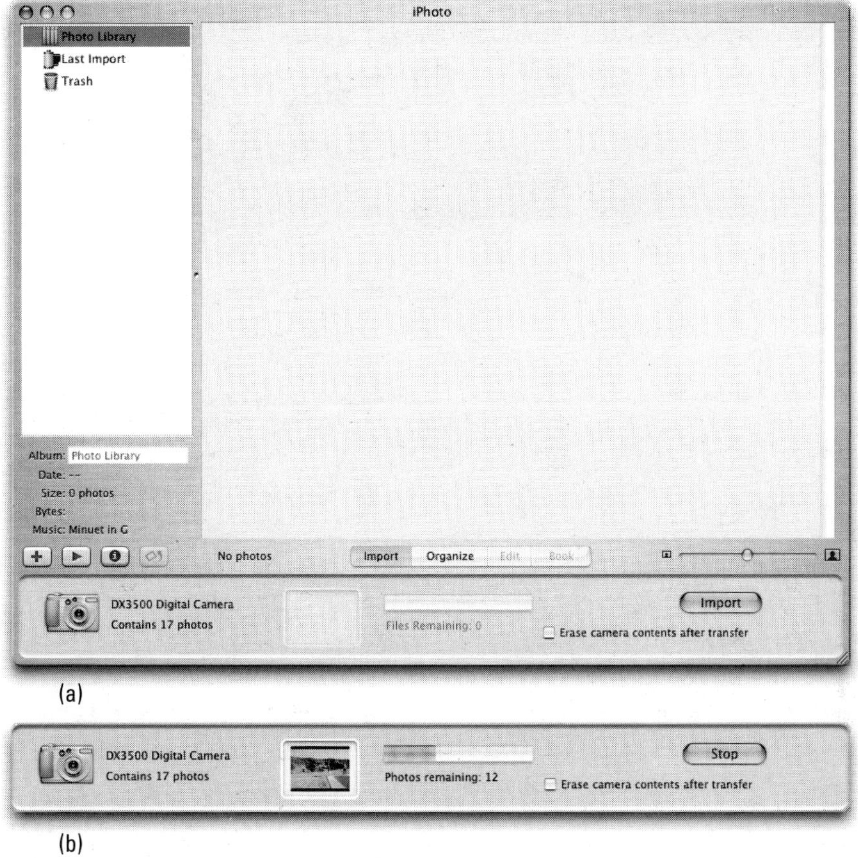

Figure 9-1: iPhoto's Import mode window, just waiting for you to click the Import button (a); iPhoto shows you what photo it's importing and how many remain (b).

If you are importing from a memory card in a memory card reader rather than a camera, you can switch to the Finder and locate the memory card as another disk at the Finder's Computer level. Double-click this icon and you can selectively delete or copy images from the card.

Depending upon your camera, it might behave like a memory card and mount as a disk. If so, be sure to eject the camera or card by choosing File ➪ Eject (⌘-E), dragging it to the Dock's Eject icon, or by Control-clicking the camera's icon and choosing Eject from the contextual menu before disconnecting the camera or turning it off.

Figure 9-2: iPhoto assumes that you want to organize your newly imported photos.

To iPhoto, a Kodak PhotoCD is just like a camera or memory card. Insert the CD with iPhoto running and click the Import mode's Import button. iPhoto does the rest.

If iPhoto doesn't detect a compatible camera, memory card reader, or a PhotoCD, the Import button is disabled (dimmed), and you'll need to choose File ⇨ Import or use drag-and-drop to get your images into iPhoto, as described in the next section.

Importing other digital images

You don't have to import your pictures directly from a camera. In fact, they don't have to be photographs at all. iPhoto can import images in a wide variety of formats: BMP, FlashPIX, GIF, JPG, MacPaint, PDF, PICT, PNG, PSD, SGI/Targa, or TIFF or anything else QuickTime reads.

Although iPhoto imports multipage PDF files, you can only see or work with the first page in iPhoto. You can still access the other pages using a separate program, like Adobe Acrobat or Photoshop, as described in Chapter 10. The same is true of multilayer TIFF files. All layers of multilayer Photoshop files are visible, though.

You can also use iPhoto as a Clip Art Gallery. Similarly, if you want iPhoto to be the graphics scrapbook where you store the charts and images that you might need someday, go for it. With the keyword and comment capabilities (see the "Organizing Your Photos" section later in this chapter) iPhoto can serve as a handy graphics document database and catalog.

You can add image files to iPhoto in two ways:

✦ **Choose File ⇨ Import.**

An Import Files dialog appears. Navigate to the file or directory you want imported and click the Import button. You can use the Shift and ⌘ keys to select multiple files within the same directory, as shown in Figure 9-3. iPhoto will switch, temporarily, to Import mode and display the Import's progress, just as if you were importing from a camera.

✦ **Drag the images or folder of images to iPhoto:** You can drag images from the Finder or another application that supports drag-and-drop, such as iView Media, GraphicConverter's Browser, or Photoshop's File Browser. Figure 9-4 shows an image being dragged from an GraphicConverter to iPhoto.

iView Media, covered in Chapter 12, overlaps iPhoto's organizational tools and, in many cases, surpasses them. Although a superb graphics database, iView Media doesn't recognize cameras. It also has no editing tools other than rotation, and lacks most of iPhoto's sharing capabilities.

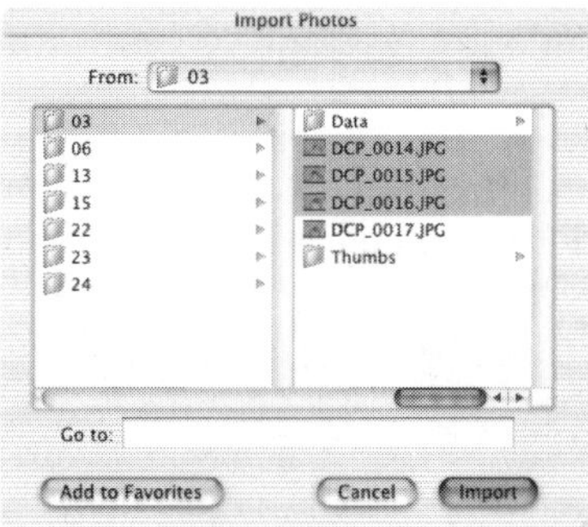

Figure 9-3: You can select multiple items in the Import Photos dialog.

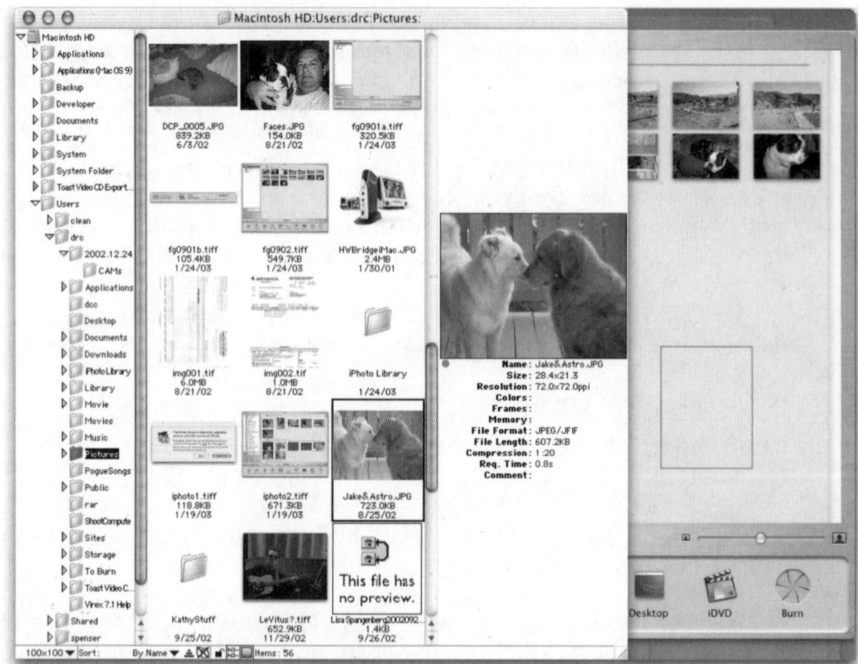

Figure 9-4: Drag pictures from other application documents to add them to iPhoto's Library.

Organizing Your Photos

Regardless of how you add your photos and images to iPhoto, they all end up in the Photo Library. To be more precise, copies of every photo and image go into the Photo Library. This distinction is important for two reasons:

1. More than double the hard disk space is consumed if the image was already on your disk. Not only does iPhoto make an exact copy of the file, it also creates a thumbnail image, and if you do any editing, it creates yet another copy beforehand and stores that as an "original" in case you decide to abandon your edits and revert to the original.

2. Unless you erased (or had iPhoto erase) your camera's memory or memory card, the original file remains where it was. This is also true for any images you drag into iPhoto's window. Therefore, you always retain a backup in case you delete the image from iPhoto. This backup feature is helpful if, for example, you need to import an image into iPhoto to include in a book or slideshow but have no further need of the image in your Library when that task is completed.

Understanding the iPhoto Library's Structure

iPhoto creates the iPhoto Library in your Home directory's Pictures folder. You can move the iPhoto Library folder to another location as long as you create an alias to it, placed in the Pictures folder, and named iPhoto Library.

If you open the Photo Library folder, you'll see other folders:

- **Albums:** Contains data files denoting which pictures appear in which of your albums and how they're organized.
- **Folders identified by year:** Contain folders for the month (by number), which contain folders for the day of month their images were added to iPhoto.

Also in each of the day of month folders are folders with the following names:

- **Data:** Contains data files for each image in your Library, chock-full of all the information about each image: size, modification date, dimensions, keywords, and so forth.
- **Thumbs:** Contains the thumbnails for each image.
- **Originals:** Contains the original copies of any photos you've cropped or otherwise edited. This folder only exists if you have edited at least one image in that group.

Although we appreciate that learning how iPhoto keeps track of things is interesting, we have one piece of strong advice: *Do Not Manipulate, Delete, Move, or Otherwise Edit These Files and Folders!* Doing so is a virtual guarantee that iPhoto won't be able to work with them and may even crash.

Your Photo Library will grow (and grow and grow). Before you know it, finding the photo you're looking for will become harder than finding the proverbial needle in a haystack. No one is going to stop you from scrolling randomly through your Photo Library looking for a particular photo or type of photo, but iPhoto provides a number of tools to help you group, annotate, and search for photos.

Tip

Hold down the Option key when scrolling to reduce the scroll speed and smooth out the presentation.

Organizing your iPhoto Library

Your Photo Library is presented in one of three ways, as shown in Figure 9-5: by Film Roll, by Title, or by Date. Before you start asking, "What's with this film roll business? I went digital so that I won't have to mess with film," we'll tell you. It's just a metaphor. Every group of pictures you import, whether from a camera, Kodak PhotoCD, or by choosing File ⇨ Import, or dragging and dropping is grouped by iPhoto into an entity that it calls a Film Roll, which is date- and time-stamped for future reference. You can switch between these presentations by choosing

View ➪ Arrange Photos ➪ by Film Roll, View ➪ Arrange Photos ➪ by Title, or View ➪ Arrange Photos ➪ by Date.

Note

Viewing by title might not look any different from viewing by date at first glance, unless you choose View ➪ Titles (Shift-⌘-T) to display photo titles under the pictures, as shown in Figure 9-5(c).

Note

In the View ➪ Arrange by submenu, you'll see a fourth choice, Manually, but it's disabled unless you're working in an album (see the "Creating your own albums" section later in this chapter).

The default ordering is "Honor your elders." In other words, if you're displaying Film Rolls, the first roll is at the top and the last roll added is at the bottom. Similarly, the oldest picture is at the top-left, continuing across the rows and down the scrollable pane until you get to the newest addition on the bottom-right. You can reverse this behavior by selecting "Most recent at top" in the iPhoto Preferences dialog (iPhoto ➪ Preferences or ⌘-,). With a by Title sort, the photos are arranged by name, from left-to-right and then top-to-bottom.

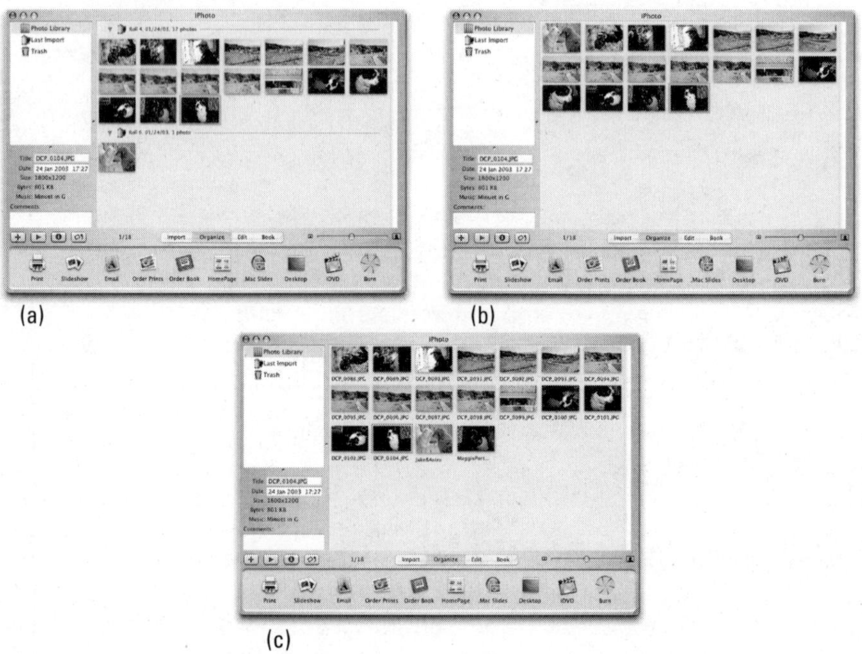

Figure 9-5: Your Photo Library can be displayed by roll (a), by date (b), or by title (c).

We both prefer the Film Roll display. As Figure 9-6 shows, you can collapse or expand an individual roll's display by clicking the disclosure triangle to the left of the roll's name. That's a very good thing.

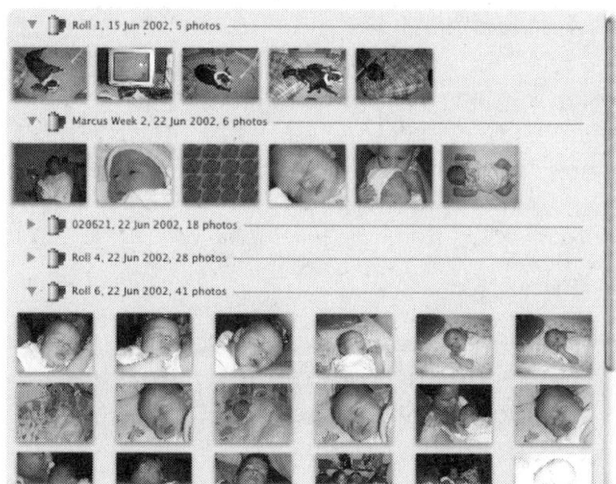

Figure 9-6: Use the disclosure triangle to hide a film roll's contents.

By hiding rolls, you also speed iPhoto's scrolling and display. When your Library has grown to significant size (even a couple hundred pictures is enough), you will really notice how much faster iPhoto responds if you collapse most of the rolls.

You can even arrange the Viewing pane's contents by Film Roll, without the disclosure triangles and lines. You can choose View ⇨ Arrange Photos ⇨ by Film Roll and then choose View ⇨ Film Rolls (Shift-⌘-F) to toggle the film roll display.

What's in a name?

The greatest annoyance in the iPhoto 1.0 release was that all photos, even those imported from your hard disk, had cryptic names, and you were stuck with those names. iPhoto 1.1.1 (1.1 was released and withdrawn in a matter of just a few hours) removed, or at least lessened, the annoyance. Since that time, when you import files, they retain their names. Of course, the name they come with from a camera probably won't be much better than the sequence naming iPhoto 1.0 used. (Names like DCP_0014 or MVC_011f aren't exactly descriptive.) To improve on the situation, Apple included editable titles via the Info pane. You can select a photo or roll and then you can change its name in the Info pane's Title text field.

You can even change the date of a photo or a roll. Although this is almost never necessary for photos you import from your camera, images you scan and import or obtain in other ways might not include valid date information. Similarly, a roll's date is the date and time you imported its images. If you have multiple memory cards, you might have imported the rolls out of order and this gives you a chance to fix the date/time to match when they were taken.

Note

Most digital cameras include what is called EXIF (EXchangeable Image Format) data (`www.pima.net/standards/it10/PIMA15740/exif.htm`). The EXIF record has a wealth of information, including date and time shot, all of which depends upon your camera's clock being properly set.

Tell me all about it

iPhoto provides two ways of attaching information to your photos. One, Keywords, is pretty rigid and primarily useful for categorizing your photos. The other, Comments, is freewheeling and lets you describe the image.

Categorizing by keyword

In iPhoto 1, Apple put a keyword grid and related controls in the Organization mode toolbox. Unfortunately, you were limited to a small number (16) of keywords, and Apple had "appropriated" some of those. Additionally, many (we're tempted to say "most") users found it a confusing interface. iPhoto 2 moves the keyword feature to a palette showing a user-controllable list of keywords, accessible by choosing Edit ➪ Keywords (⌘-K). The Keywords palette is shown in Figure 9-7. The Keywords button at the top of the palette is actually the title of a drop-down menu (indicated by the down-pointing triangle) where you can choose to add a new keyword to the list, rename a selected keyword, or delete selected keywords. This list-driven interface, besides being more flexible, seems to be a lot easier to use (and to explain).

Assigning keywords to photos is as easy as pie. Just select the photos in your iPhoto Library, select your keywords from the list in the Keywords palette (adding any new ones you might need along the way), and click the Assign button. Presto, all the selected photos now have all the specified keywords attached.

Note

As with just about any list in OS X, you select a range of items by clicking the first item and Shift-clicking the last item. Similarly, you specify multiple, not-necessarily-contiguous items by ⌘-clicking the items. You can even select a range and then remove specific items from that range by ⌘-clicking the ones you want omitted.

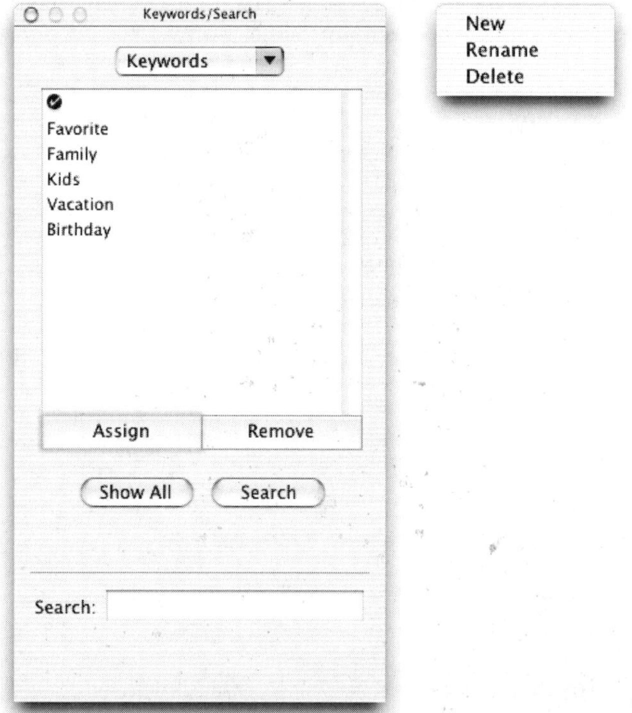

Figure 9-7: The iPhoto 2 Keywords palette lets you create as many keywords as you want by using the Keywords drop-down menu shown on the right.

Removing keywords from photos is just as easy. Follow these steps:

1. **Select all the photos from which you want to remove one or more keywords.**
2. **Choose Edit ⇨ Keywords (or press ⌘-K):** This displays the Keywords palette.
3. **In the list, select any keyword(s) you want to remove from these photos.**
4. **Click the Remove button.**

One benefit of this keyword removal method is that if the photo doesn't have one or more of the keywords associated, there's no problem — only selected keywords get removed.

You can see which keywords are associated with individual photos by choosing View ➪ Keywords (Shift-⌘-K), as shown in Figure 9-8. The keywords appear to the right of the photo.

For those of you who have used the Mac before OS X, you might remember labeling items in the Finder. Keywords are very similar to the text labels that accompanied the colors. If you rename a keyword, everything that had the old keyword gets the new keyword in its place. The significant difference between keywords and the old text labels is that an item can only have one label associated with it, but your photos can have as many keywords as you want to assign.

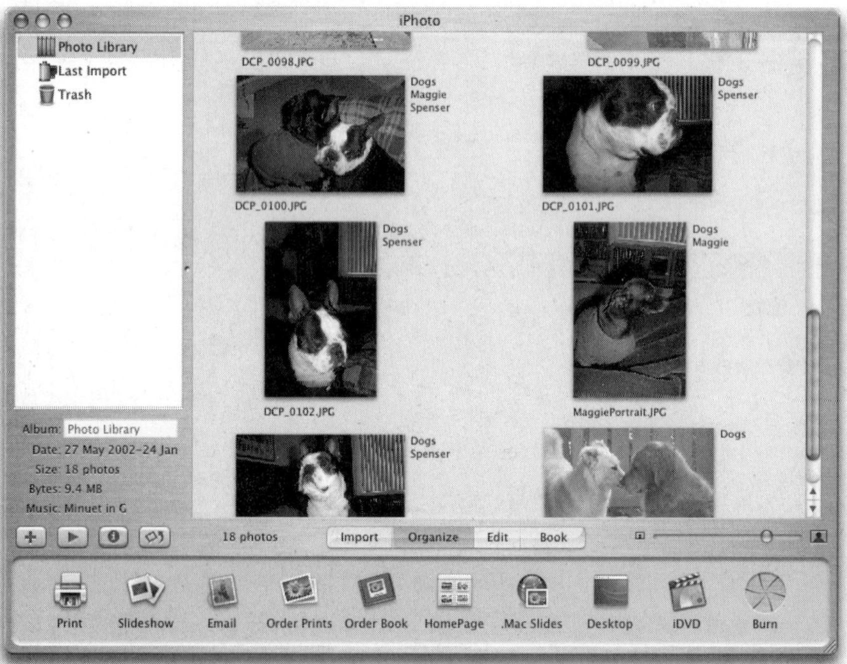

Figure 9-8: Keywords appear as a list to the right of your photo when you choose View ➪ Keywords (Shift-⌘-K).

Do you want to comment on this photo?

The old saying is that a picture is worth a thousand words. We don't know if that's true of all photos (it surely isn't of some of ours), but every photo has a story behind it. In fact, people have written notes on the backs of their photos for years, noting the names, locations, and people involved or telling how the photo came to be. iPhoto lets you tell your photo's story in the Info pane's Comments field, as shown in Figure 9-9. If the Comments field isn't visible, just click the circled-i (Info) button to make it so.

The Comments field doesn't scroll, but you can keep typing even after the cursor has disappeared from view. Alternatively, you can drag the handles (they look like small indentations) either above the Info pane or between the Album list and the Viewing pane to resize the panes, as shown in Figure 9-10.

Unlike keywords, you can enter comments for only one photo at a time. If you try to type in that inviting little Comment field after you select multiple items, iPhoto will beep at you. You can, of course, copy and paste the same comment into the Comments text box for as many photos as you like, although doing this is a bit more work than assigning keywords to multiple photos.

Figure 9-9: Write about your picture in the Comments field.

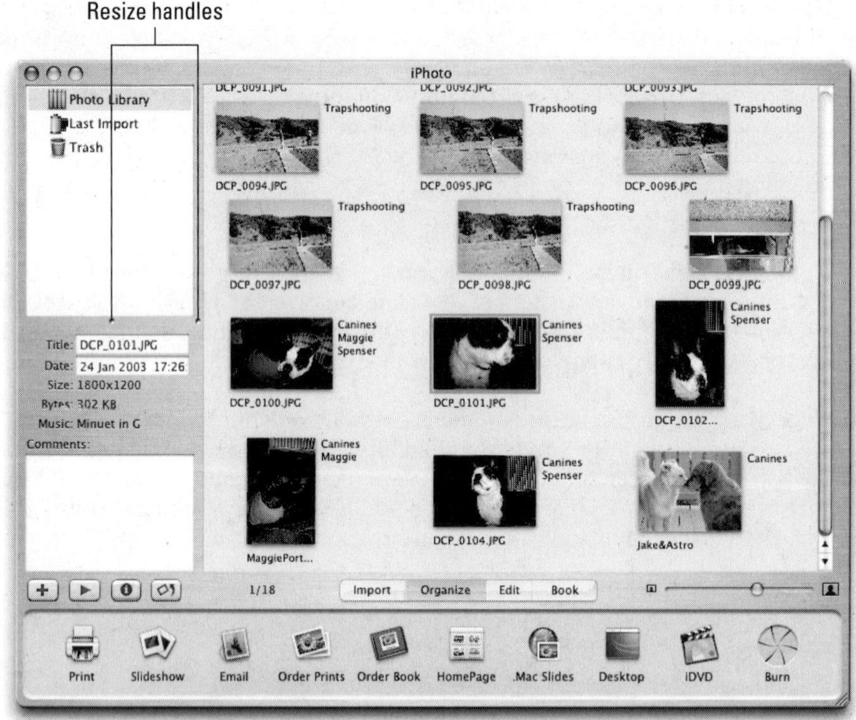

Figure 9-10: Drag the handles to resize the various iPhoto panes.

Creating your own albums

One easy way to organize your photos is to place them in albums. iPhoto recognizes this and provides virtual photo albums. You don't have to mess with tape, glue, plastic protective sheets, mounting corners, extra pages, a pair of scissors, or a paper cutter. If you want the same photo to appear in more than one album, you don't even have to bother creating extra prints. iPhoto does all the bookwork for you by keeping pointers (like aliases) to an album's photos. Albums form the basis for your slideshows, Web pages, screen savers, and books as we discuss later in this chapter.

iPhoto makes it easy to create albums. Here's four ways of doing it:

✦ **Select a group of photos, either from the Viewing pane or from the Finder, and drag it to a blank area of the Album list.** iPhoto creates a new album with the name Album-1 (or whatever number you're up to) containing the selected photos and selects it in the Album list. Double-click the name to make it editable if you want to rename the album.

If you drag a folder to the Album list, iPhoto is smart enough to give the album the same name as the folder.

✦ **Click [+] to create a new album in the Album list.** iPhoto displays the New Album dialog shown in Figure 9-11, asking you to give the album a name. (You're offered the very anonymous Album-n, where n is whatever number you're up to, as a default.) Name your album and you can now drag any photos you want to the album's name or icon in the Album list.

Figure 9-11: The New Album dialog offers a very forgettable default name. You can surely choose a better one.

✦ **Choose File ⇨ New Album (⌘-N).** You're now exactly where you would be if you clicked [+]. Proceed in the same way.

✦ **Control-click (or right-click, if your mouse is so blessed) in the white area of the Album List and choose New Album from the contextual menu.** Proceed as previously mentioned to name the album.

Adding photos to an album is as easy as dragging them to the album's name in the Album list, either from within iPhoto or from the Finder or another application. If the photos aren't dragged from the Photo Library or another album, iPhoto adds them to the Photo Library, creating a new Film Roll, while placing them in the album.

iPhoto doesn't know whether an image you're importing already exists in the Library. It assumes that anything you're importing is new, so you can easily end up with two or more copies of the same picture if you Import it more than once. That's why you should erase your camera's contents after you know the pictures are safely imported and why you should keep track of which files you've imported from your disk or a PhotoCD. Being conscientious in adding keywords and comments can also help you find photos if you're unsure whether a photo has already been imported, as you'll see in the "Searching your Photo Library" section, next.

Searching your Photo Library

Visually scanning hundreds or thousands of thumbnails to find specific photos is, at best, a tedious, time-consuming, and error-prone process. Adding keywords and comments to your photos (as described in the "Tell me all about it" section earlier in this chapter) and then searching for the keyword or a text string using iPhoto's built-in database search is much faster and more thorough. Of course, it does require that you have data there to find.

Dennis recalls that when he was a very young programmer, he learned a very valuable lesson. There are "good lazy programmers" and "bad lazy programmers." Bad lazy programmers do very little overall design work and cut corners while writing their code, just to say they're done quickly. Then, they have to spend a lot of time (usually, over and over again) fixing what isn't right, frequently creating new problems while fixing old ones. Being good lazy means that you are willing to do more work in the beginning to save you all that time and effort later. Working with a database — and iPhoto is definitely a database, among other things — offers you the same choice. Annotate your photos when adding them to the database and you'll easily find them when you want them; otherwise, you can laboriously pore through the thumbnails to find the photo(s) you seek. Creating a solid foundation makes future maintenance much easier.

Another way of looking at annotating/categorizing your photos is that you can pay iPhoto now, or you can pay it later. If you pay later, the interest charges mount up (rapidly), and the coin of the realm is your time.

iPhoto lets you search for matching keywords or for text in comments. Follow these steps to search for photos that match one or more keywords:

1. **Choose Edit ➪ Keywords (⌘-K).** This displays the Keywords palette.
2. **Click the Show All button.** This ensures that all your photos are available for searching.
3. **Click the keywords for which you want to search.** See Figure 9-12 for an example of this.

(a)

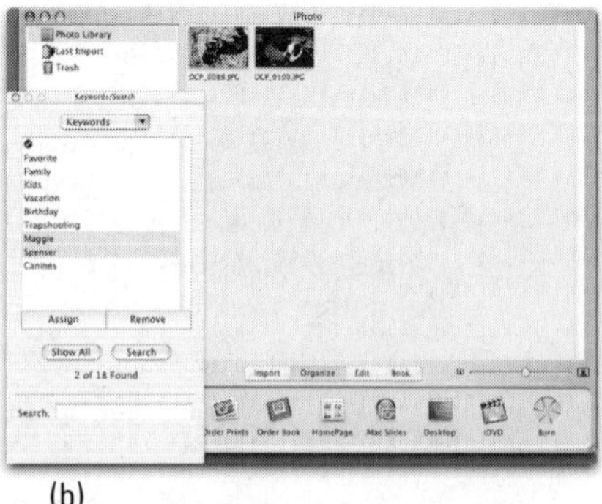

(b)

Figure 9-12: Before clicking a keyword, everything is available (a); Clicking a keyword reduces the displayed photos to just those that have the selected keyword assigned (b).

4. **Click the Search button at the bottom of the list box.** You can ⌘-click a selected keyword to remove it from the search set or click Show All to deselect all the selected search keywords.

These searches are sometimes called AND searches, which means that a photo has to match all the criteria to be included. Unfortunately, iPhoto doesn't provide an OR search (where matching any criterion would include the photo) — maybe if enough users request it, an OR search will show up in a future revision. We requested it at `www.apple.com/macosx/feedback` both with iPhoto 1.1.1 and iPhoto 2.

The Search textbox at the bottom of the Keywords window is not limited to keywords. This search finds matches in any photo's Comments field (Figure 9-13), and it also finds matches for keywords, photo titles, and filenames (Figure 9-14).

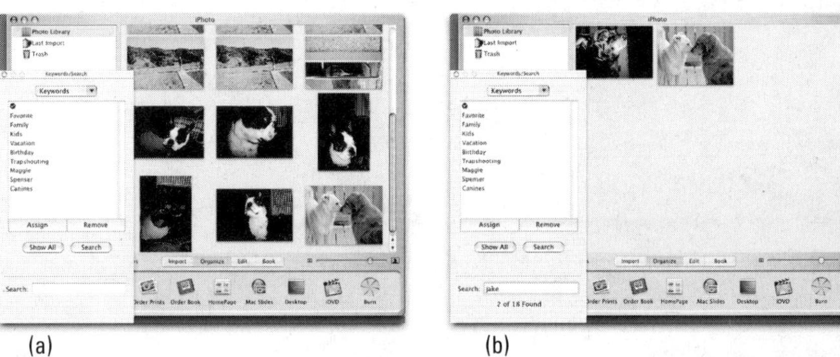

(a) (b)

Figure 9-13: Before entering a search string, the Viewing pane shows everything (a); Entering a search string finds all the photos with that string in the Comments (b).

In reality, iPhoto doesn't search for strings in a comment search, at least not in the traditional sense. The search more closely resembles a Sherlock Internet search, doing matches on each word individually. If you enter "baseball game" as the search string, iPhoto returns all photos that had both words anywhere in the searchable fields. For example, if a photo had "baseball" in the comments, and you had a "Games" keyword assigned to it, iPhoto displays the photo as a match.

Because a Comments search also matches on keywords, you might consider it the more flexible search. (We do.)

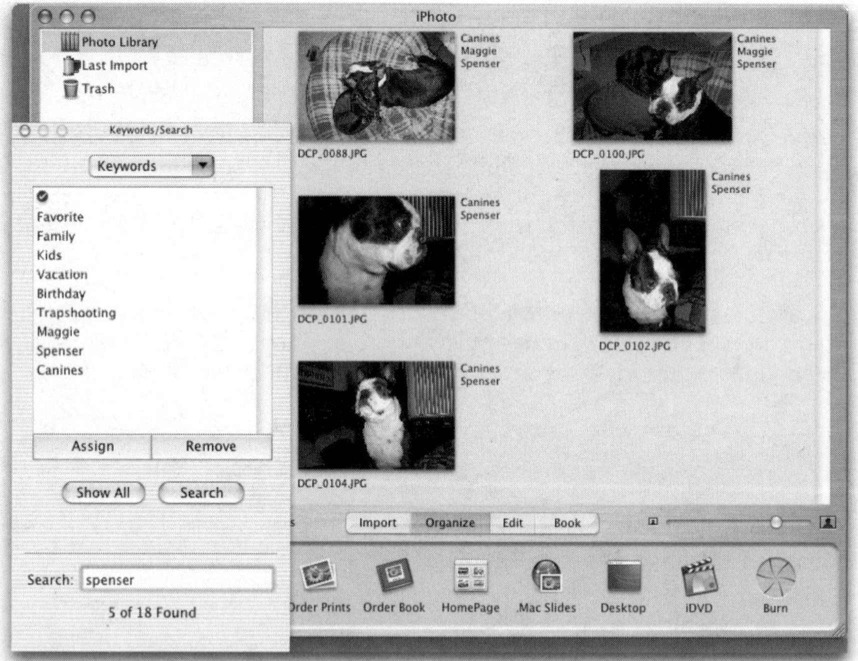

Figure 9-14: Searching Comments also finds matches in titles, filenames, and keywords.

Removing photos from albums and the Library

A day will come when you want to remove one or more photos from an album. In fact, if you take a lot of digital photos, you'll eventually want to remove photos from your Photo Library, just to speed up iPhoto.

Tip

We strongly recommend periodically archiving older photos to CD or some other medium, and then removing the photos from your Library. As an iPhoto Library fills up, performance degrades. Of all the wonderful things we can and do say about iPhoto, its speed and responsiveness don't make the list—and big Libraries only exacerbate the problem.

Removing photos from an album is a truly simple operation. Select the photo(s) you want to delete and choose File ➪ Remove from Album (⌘-Delete) or press the Delete key. Del also works, if your keyboard has a Del key. When you remove a photo from an album, iPhoto doesn't even ask whether you're sure. If you change your mind or delete a photo by mistake, choose Edit ➪ Undo Remove Photo From Album (⌘-Z).

iPhoto's Undo commands are very literal and occasionally long-winded. They spell out exactly what you'll be undoing.

iPhoto 2 added an internal Trash. When you remove a photo from the Library, the photo goes into iPhoto's Trash and, just like things that get thrown into the Trash from your Mac OS X desktop, it sits in the Trash until you choose to empty the Trash. When you empty the Trash (File ➪ Empty Trash or Control-clicking the Trash and choosing Empty Trash from the contextual menu), you see the alert shown in Figure 9-15, asking if you really want to permanently remove the photo. Other than the alert, though, the process is identical: Select the photos you want to remove and choose File ➪ Move to Trash (⌘-Delete) or press Delete (or Del) or ⌘-Delete.

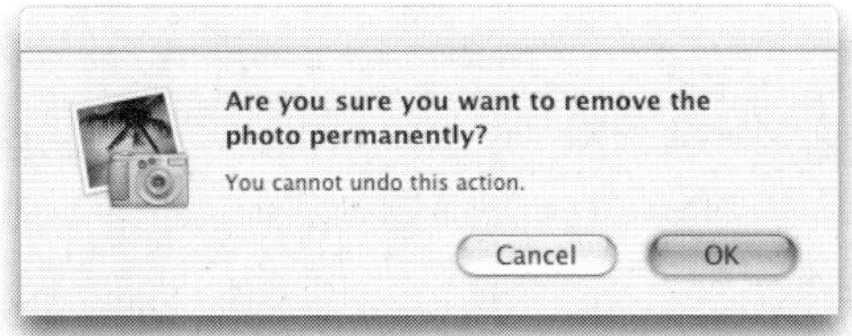

Figure 9-15: iPhoto asks for verification when emptying the Library's Trash.

Making Adjustments to a Photo

iPhoto's editing tools are no threat to Photoshop, GraphicConverter, or any other dedicated image-editing application. The iPhoto editing tools are, however, the tools you'll probably need the most often. And, with iPhoto 2's addition of the Retouch brush and the Enhance button, the gap in capability is significantly narrowed.

In general, whether you are editing in a separate window or editing in the iPhoto window's Edit mode, your tools are the same. Some differences exist, however. The primary one is that you no longer have the size slider on the iPhoto window to zoom in or out when you edit in a separate window. Instead you'll find two Zoom buttons on the Edit window toolbar's left end. The up-arrow zooms in, and the down-arrow zooms out.

Probably one of the best, unheralded features introduced with iPhoto 2 is the expansion of contextual menu support. You no longer have to go to iPhoto's Preferences and reset what double-clicking does to use a different editing style. The contextual menu that appears when you Control-click a photo has choices for Edit, Edit in separate window, and Edit in external editor. The last requires that you have at least specified the external editor in your preferences, even if that isn't your double-click default.

Customizing the Edit Window's Toolbar

Just like the toolbar in a Finder or Mail window, the toolbar in iPhoto's separate Editing window is customizable. With an Edit window open, choose Window ➪ Customize Toolbar to display the sheet shown in the following figure. You can also Control-click in the toolbar and choose Customize Toolbar from the contextual menu.

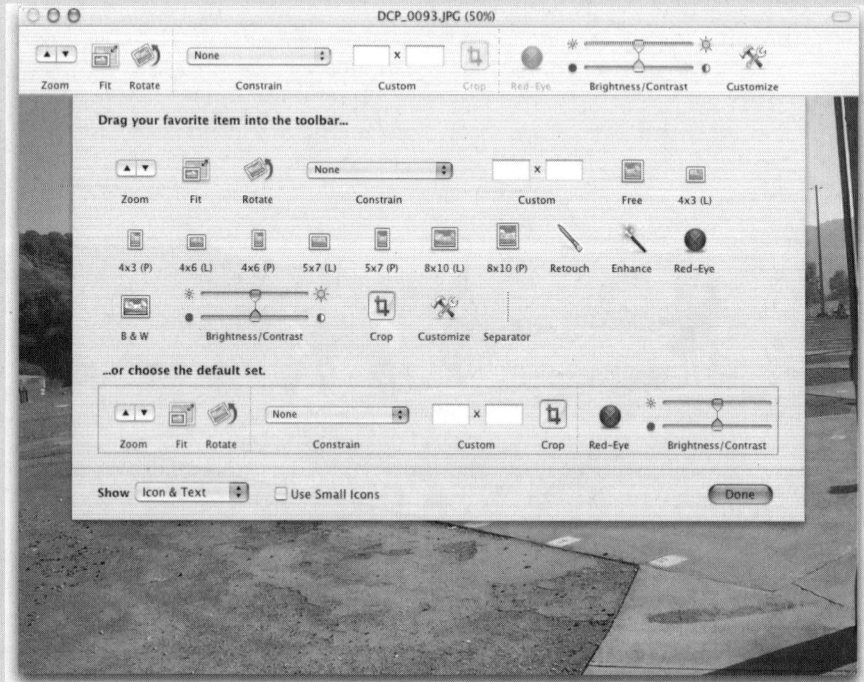

Customize the Edit toolbar using the objects on this sheet.

In addition to being able to remove, replace, or add buttons to the toolbar, you can choose whether the buttons display Icon & Text, Icon Only, or Text Only in the Show pop-up menu. iPhoto 2 also adds a checkbox allowing you to use small icons, if you find toolbar space in short supply (or it just appeals to your sense of aesthetics). ⌘-clicking the lozenge button at the top-right of the Edit window, in the window's title bar, cycles through the Show choices without you having to display the Customize sheet.

To us, the fact that neither the Enhance tool nor the Retouch brush appears in the default tool set is astonishing. Maybe we're unusual, but we find a lot more use for the Retouch and Enhance tools than we do for the Red-Eye tool or the Brightness/Contrast sliders.

Rotating an image

iPhoto assumes that all your photos are in landscape orientation. After all, there's no way for iPhoto to know you rotated your camera before shooting that picture of Uncle Joe and Aunt Betty. iPhoto doesn't even consider rotating a picture as an editing action and puts the Rotate button alongside the New Album, Play Slideshow, and Show Information buttons in the main window rather than in the Edit toolbox.

iPhoto's default rotation direction is counter-clockwise (the right edge becomes the top). You can change the rotation direction in iPhoto's Preferences or, if you only want to rotate an occasional picture clockwise, press the Option key while clicking the Rotate button when performing those rotations (or click Rotate three times).

Note The counter-clockwise default is a strange choice, considering that more people are right-handed than left. When a person rotates the camera for a shot, their tendency is to put the viewfinder (and shutter button) on the same side as their dominant eye: for right-handed people this is usually the right eye. If you're left-handed (or tend to put the viewfinder on the left side of the camera when taking a portrait shot), you'll probably like the default preference.

Cropping an image

Most digital cameras, like most computer monitors and TVs, have a 4:3 aspect ratio (well, at least they did until the advent of HDTV, Cinema Displays, Titanium PowerBooks, and the like). Some standard photo sizes are 4 x 6, 5 x 7, 8 x 10, and 11 x 14, and you'll notice that not one of those is a 4:3 ratio.

Note We've always considered it a little curious that photo sizes always list the smaller dimension first and monitor sizes (and aspect ratios) list the larger first.

You can fit a 4:3 image in a frame with a different aspect ratio three ways:

✦ **You can distort the picture by stretching or compressing in one dimension.** iPhoto doesn't provide any tools to affect distortion, so if you want a funhouse mirror effect, you're going to have to employ an image-editing application like Photoshop.

✦ **You can *letterbox* the picture, leaving a border along two edges.** Accomplishing this is simple, just tell iPhoto to print at the desired size, and it fits your picture into the frame. A 1280 x 960 photo printed to fit on 4 x 6 paper leaves a ⅓-inch border on the left and right.

✦ **You can crop part of the picture so the aspect ratio is the same.** iPhoto makes cropping easy with Edit mode's Constrain pop-up menu. Choose the image size with which you want to finish and perform your selection, as shown in Figure 9-16. iPhoto keeps the selection's proportions correct. After you slide the selection rectangle to surround the part of the picture you want kept, click the Crop button.

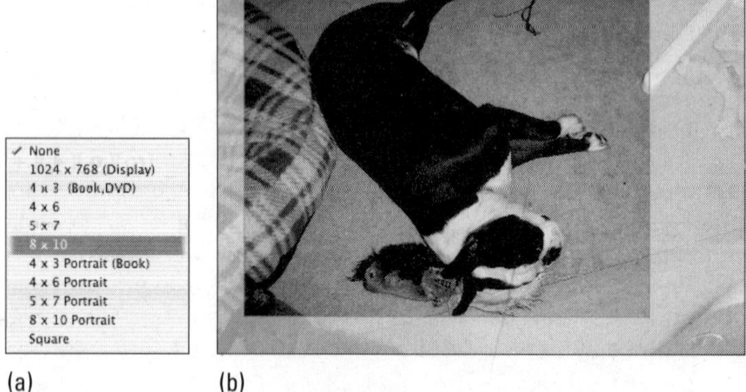

Figure 9-16: Choose 8 x 10 from the Constrain pop-up menu (a), and iPhoto's selection rectangle will maintain those proportions (b).

Cropping is also useful when you want to reduce a photo to show only your subject, eliminating distracting surroundings or backgrounds.

If you want to print the picture, be careful of cropping a picture too much unless you have a *really* high-resolution image to start with. Cropping a 2048 x 1536 image to 1500 x 1200 makes an 8 x 10 print of marginal quality; any lesser resolution and you have serious jaggies problems.

If your preferences are set so that double-clicking a photo opens it for editing in a separate window, or if you Control-click a photo and choose Edit in separate window from the contextual menu, you get one extra benefit. You can set a customized constraint, such as 3 x 5, by entering the values in the text boxes that show up between the Constrain pop-up menu and the Crop button.

Adjusting brightness and contrast

The brightness and contrast sliders behave just like the brightness and contrast controls on your TV set.

Increasing brightness moves all the pixels closer to white (light pixels move to white faster than dark pixels) and decreasing brightness moves all the pixels closer to black (dark pixels moving faster than light pixels). Figure 9-17 shows how a picture is altered when brightness is moved to the extreme settings.

Increasing contrast moves dark pixels toward black and light pixels toward white, resulting in greater discrimination between light and dark areas. Decreasing contrast moves dark and light pixels toward a midpoint (50 percent gray), dulling the picture. Using the same original image from Figure 9-17, Figure 9-18 demonstrates adjusting Contrast to its extreme settings.

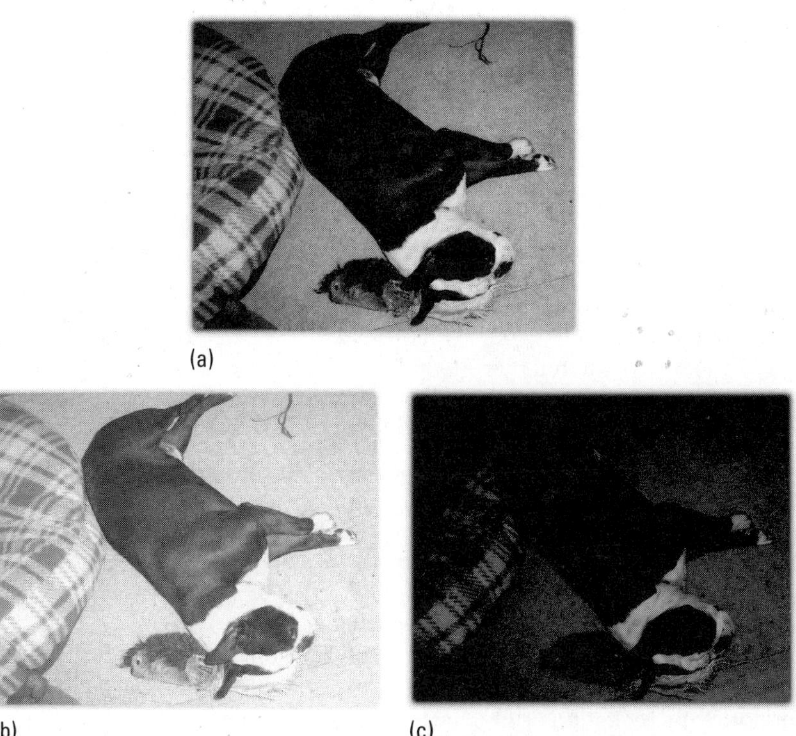

Figure 9-17: The original image (a); maximum brightness (b); minimum brightness (c).

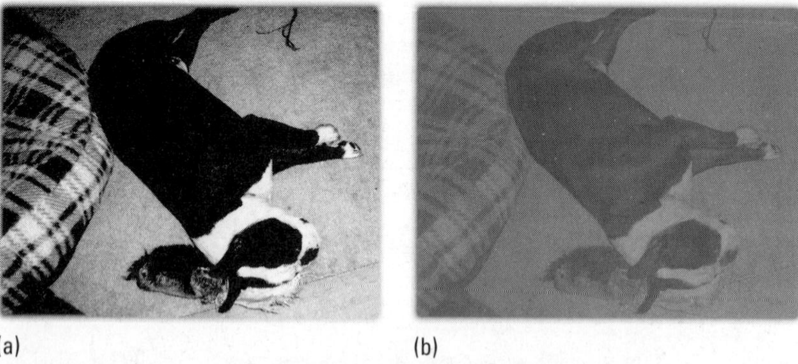

(a) (b)

Figure 9-18: Maximum contrast (a); Minimum contrast (b).

Removing red-eye from an image

How many times have you taken a photo, using your flash, and found the person dead-center in your picture looking as if red-hot coals had replaced their eyes? This phenomenon, called *red-eye*, is the result of your flash reflecting off the blood-red retinas at the back of your subject's eyes. The dimmer the room, the more open the subject's pupils and the more the light reflects.

Here's how to remove the red-eye effect:

1. **Zoom in so that you have a good view of the affected eye(s).**
2. **Select the eye and a significant amount of surrounding skin.** The red-eye tool works by distinguishing red from almost-red in a comparison with normal skin tones, so the more facial skin in your selection the better (so long as the person isn't sporting a bright sunburn).
3. **Click the Red-Eye tool.** The Red-Eye tool converts the red pixels to black; now your subjects don't look like victims of demonic possession.

Although this fix for red-eye is less than perfect (coal-black eyes are better than red, but not really realistic), you're better placed to avoid red-eye altogether if you use a flash that is separated from your camera by a few feet or if you use strong indoor or reflected light rather than a flash.

Enhancing a photo

Are some of your photos dull and lifeless? Do they frequently appear under- or over-exposed? iPhoto 2 introduces the Enhance button to put life back into your pictures. If your photo is too dark, you can use Enhance to lighten it; if it's too light, using Enhance darkens (and brighten) it. Figure 9-19 shows an example of Enhance working on an overly dark picture. We just hope that the difference is as visible in black & white as it is in color.

You can even invoke Enhance multiple times for a more profound effect. Be aware, though, that if you make a dark picture too light, the next click of the Enhance button will start to darken it (or vice versa, if you started with a too-light photo).

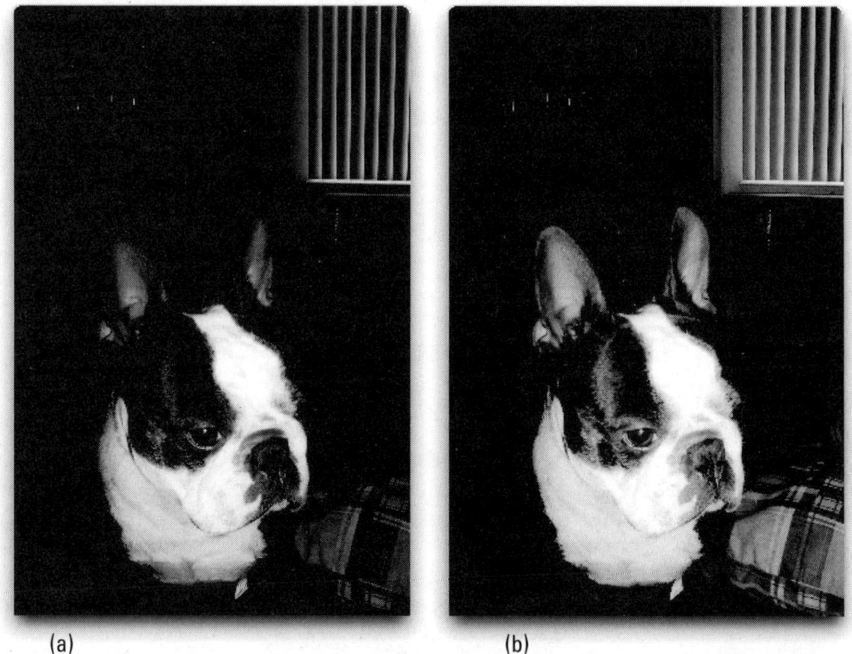

Figure 9-19: Enhance takes the dark picture (a) and brings out the highlights (b).

Makeup artistry with the Retouch brush

Removing unsightly blemishes from your photos has never been easier than with the iPhoto 2 Retouch brush. Not only can you repair minor scratches, but you can also remove freckles, birthmarks, acne scars, and so forth. Figure 9-20 shows an example of what a few simple strokes of the Retouch brush can accomplish.

When Steve Jobs demonstrated the Retouch brush at the iPhoto 2 announcement, he not only removed a scar from a child's face but showed that the Retouch brush could even eliminate the lad's freckles. If you look really closely, we also removed some reflected light patches on Dennis's nose and ear (assuming that it shows up after the conversion to black and white).

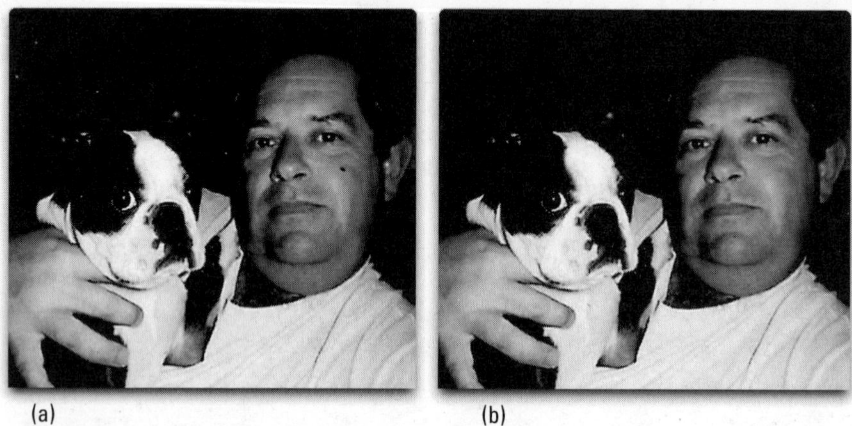

(a) (b)

Figure 9-20: A few strokes of the Retouch brush removes the smudge on Dennis's face seen in (a), leaving clear skin (b).

Converting to black-and-white

The screen shots and photos in this book were color when we submitted them. During the production process, they were converted to black-and-white for printing. (Color is a lot more expensive to print than black-and-white.) If you're going to be duplicating your photos in a newsletter or on a copy machine, you're better off using black-and-white images — then your copies will look like your originals.

iPhoto's Black & White button drains all the color out of your picture, reducing it to a grayscale image, commonly (and imprecisely) referred to as a black and white.

Note

If you're editing a picture in its own window (iPhoto ➪ Preferences, "Double-click: Opens in separate window"), the Black & White button will be called B&W, and it won't be present on the default toolbar. You'll need to click the Customize button and add B&W if you want to employ it.

Laying Out Books

What sets iPhoto apart from other photo organizers is that you can take one of your iPhoto albums and, with just a few clicks and a credit card, order a hard-bound book of your photos, professionally printed on acid-free glossy paper. We know this has to be a cool feature because when Steve Jobs announced it at Macworld in January 2002, he was clearly in awe (or an even better actor than many award-winners).

Although we're yet to be convinced that producing coffee table books of your photos is anything but a niche market today, the potential is clear. A well-designed, hardbound wedding album, baby album, or the like is a much more convenient and attractive gift or keepsake than the traditional "pasted-in photos" albums. They're even nicer than the vacation flipbook albums memorializing your first visit to the Australian outback. They're also a convenient way to create yearbooks, whether from a school class or to tell the story of a Little League team's season.

We'll cover the actual ordering process later in this chapter in the "Ordering photos: Coffee table books" section, but the cost of these books: $30 for the first 10 pages (or fraction thereof) and $3 for each subsequent page. Each page in a book is 9 x 11.5 inches, and a book's maximum size is 50 pages.

Now, we discuss the layout process.

Putting together your album

You first notice that iPhoto won't let you switch to Book mode unless you have an album selected (Figure 9-21). Everything you do in iPhoto's Book mode is tied to the album, and changes in the order of photos in the book are reflected back to the order of the photos in your album.

Before you enter Book mode, though, identify the photo you want on the book's cover and place it first (if it's not already there) in the album because iPhoto won't let you change the cover photo in Book mode (you'd have to return to Organize mode to do so).

iPhoto offers six *themes* (book design templates), only two of which places more than four photos on a page. This has an upside: You won't be reducing the size of your photos to the point where they're hard to see and lose their impact. On the downside: You'll burn up your ten pages quickly and go into the $3/page overflow. Even four photos on a page is a bit crowded, so you're probably going to end up with only about two dozen photos in a 10-page book (not including the photo on the cover), unless you have a lower-resolution camera. iPhoto puts low-resolution warnings on any photo that doesn't have enough pixels to print well, which pretty much means that if there's only one photo on the page, it should be at least a 2-megapixel photo (and 3 megapixels is a lot better). If you have a 1-megapixel digital camera, you're probably not going to be thrilled with the Picture Book theme if you ever employ the one-photo-per-page design option.

Figure 9-21: iPhoto's Book mode requires an album for its content.

iPhoto's themes all expect photos with a 4:3 aspect ratio. If you've cropped your figures to a different aspect ratio, you should revert them to their original condition or crop again back to a 4:3 ratio. If, like Dennis's Kodak DX3500, your camera creates photos with a different aspect ratio, you're going to need to crop them to 4:3 or have your book look bad. If you're a bit adept at using Apple's Interface Builder and editing XML, though, you can work around this (but we're not encouraging such activity, just acknowledging the possibility).

Although you can reorder most of the photos in Book mode, setting the photo sequence in Organize mode is a lot easier. Books are laid out horizontally (they're wider than they are tall), which is great for the typical landscape orientation photo when you're placing one, three, or four per page. However, you might consider grouping any portrait-orientation shots for two-per-page presentation. Figure 9-22 shows two portrait photos on a page at the top and two landscape photos on a page at the bottom (using the Picture Book theme).

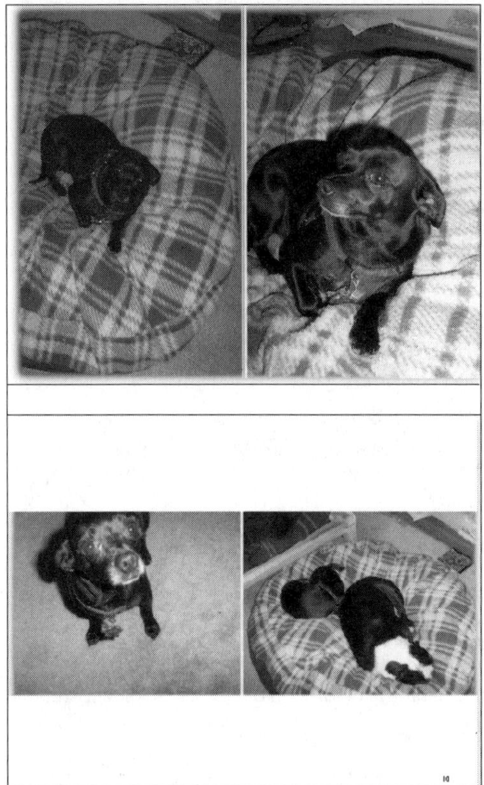

Figure 9-22: Two portrait pictures (top) fill a landscape page better than two landscape photos (bottom).

Choosing a theme

After you have your album populated and ordered the way you want it, you can build the book. Click the Book button, and the iPhoto window switches to the window shown in Figure 9-23 (except that your pictures will be used). By default, iPhoto uses the album name as the title on your book's cover page, but you can change the title if you want.

The Viewing pane is now divided into two parts — an editing pane and a horizontally scrolling list of numbered page thumbnails. Pay attention to those numbers, because they tell you how many pages your book is going to be, which tells you how big a dent the book will make in your credit card.

Figure 9-23: The Viewing pane splits into two parts when you enter Book mode.

Before you go any further, decide which of iPhoto's six themes you want to use. You can always change themes later but making that change costs you any text, captions, and other design work you've done.

Tip If you want to try out a different theme after you've done some work, duplicate the album and try the theme out on the duplicate. If you like the new theme, you can switch between albums and copy/paste the text rather than recreating it from scratch. If you decide that your first choice was better, you can go back to that.

Here are iPhoto's six themes:

✦ **Catalog:** Although well laid out for a product catalog, this is probably a bit expensive for just about any product line unless you're an exclusive jeweler or furrier. It's probably not an original idea, but Dennis chose this theme for an insurance inventory. Catalog offers one, four, or eight photos per page, with accompanying product name and large description boxes for each photo. In this case, we recommend landscape photos for the one-per-page and eight-per-page choices and portrait for the four-per-page design.

✦ **Classic:** A simple and aptly named design, Classic focuses on the photo, with page designs for one, two, three, or four photos per page with small name and description boxes beneath the photos. One advantage of this theme is that even the one-photo-per-page design accommodates a 1280 x 960 (1-megapixel) image without a low-resolution warning.

✦ **Picture Book:** An aptly named theme, the only text allowed in this book is on pages with Cover or Introduction (text-only) designs. With proper orientation choices, the picture pages are *full-bleed* (print from edge to edge), providing a striking presentation on each of the one-, two-, three-, and four-per-page designs.

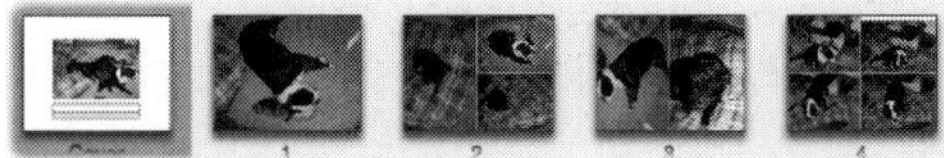

✦ **Portfolio:** Resembling a model's or artist's portfolio of work, this theme provides for full-bleed printing on the right side of each page, with the left side reserved for titles and commentary (or white space). Portfolio offers one-, two-, three-, and four-per-page designs.

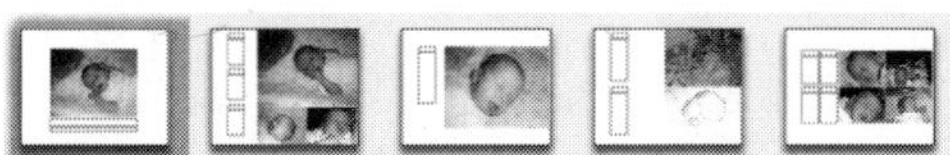

✦ **Story Book:** We don't know where this design got its name, other than the fact that every page has a large rectangular text box at the bottom or along the right edge where you can write a story about the one to three pictures on that page. If the text flowed from page to page, the name might be more appropriate. No photo is square to the page and when two or more photos are on a page, they overlap slightly.

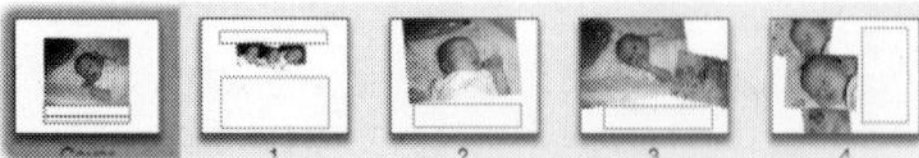

✦ **Year Book:** Allowing up to 32 photos per page, the Yearbook theme can cram many small pictures into a minimal number of pages. The text box for each photo is small, especially considering the font size used (11.8 points), so you have a very limited number of characters available before iPhoto puts a warning triangle on your caption. At 32 photos per page, you only get a Titles box. The Year Book theme is aptly named, serving well for a school or class yearbook.

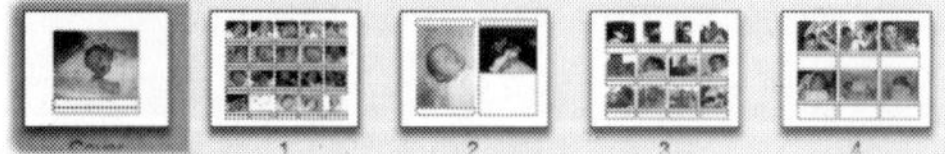

As you investigate the different themes' suitability for your book, you'll also notice that you still have a lot of design work ahead of you, arranging the photos so that they show to best advantage.

Designing your pages

After you select your photos and the theme, you can get down to the real work: laying out the design. Always keep in mind that iPhoto books are a sequence of photos, flowing from one to the next just as they appear in the Organize mode's Viewing pane.

When you move a photo in Organize mode, it induces a ripple effect on your book's pages. Suppose, for example, that your first page has three photos, your second page has one photo, and your third page has two photos (we're going to ignore subsequent pages, but you'll get the idea). If you were to go into Organize mode and move the photo that is on page 2 so that it immediately follows your cover photo and then switch back to Book mode, your page design sequence remains the same, but the photo on page 2 is now the one which was previously the third photo on page 1. On the other hand, if you drag page 2 to precede page 1, you get the same sequence of photos, but this does not affect which photos are grouped on a page.

Every page you create poses three questions:

✦ How many photos do you want on the page?

✦ What text, if any, do you want on the page?

✦ How do you want the text formatted?

The first photo of any album is your Cover photo. iPhoto won't let you move the Cover page, so if you want a different photo there, switch to Organize mode and move the photo you want to the top-left of the album's Viewing pane. The Cover photo appears, nicely centered, on your printed book's linen cover (see the "Ordering Photos: Coffee table books" section later in this chapter to learn about specifying your cover's color). iPhoto places the album name as your book's default title, as shown in Figure 9-24. You can edit the title, if you want. The second text field is for adding a subtitle.

Note We don't know why the subtitle field uses neither the album's, nor the cover photo's comment as a default as is the case with other page designs, if you have the Comments checkbox selected.

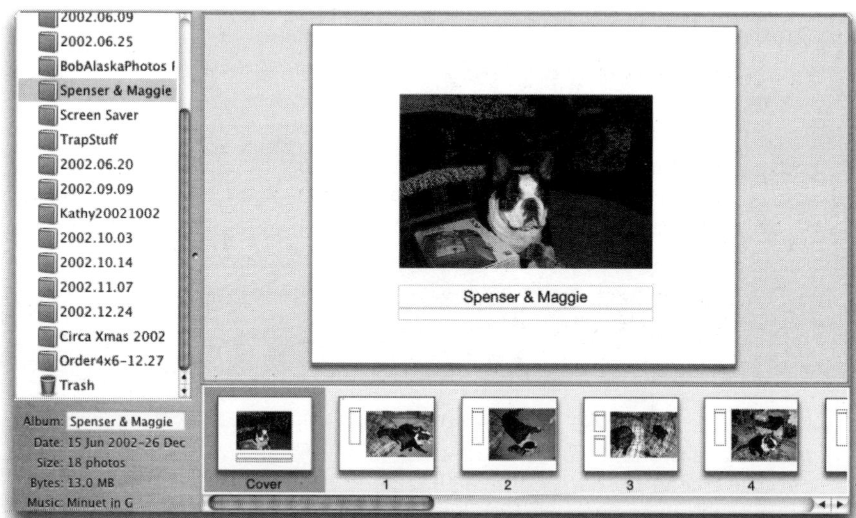

Figure 9-24: The book's cover uses the album name as the default title.

iPhoto's themes each have their own set of page designs, but these page designs fall into four general categories, as follows:

✦ **Cover:** The first page of your book must have the Cover design, but you can apply the cover design to internal pages as well. This is handy if you want to use the Cover design to introduce chapters.

✦ **Introduction:** With Story Book the sole exception, this is a text-only page with two text boxes. (Story Book also has two text boxes, but includes three photos.)

iPhoto starts you out with the album name in one box and your long name (the one the Mac knows you by) with the month and year the pictures were taken in the other box. Feel free (please!) to replace this text with something more appropriate.

✦ **One, Two, ... (number of photos per page):** iPhoto places the specified number of photos on the page, but they are arranged according to iPhoto's programmed sense of aesthetics. You can, with a little experimentation, determine how iPhoto arranges things. For example, refer to Figure 9-22, our earlier case of two portrait photos versus two landscape photos. Similarly, when displaying three photos per page, you often get superior results (depending upon the theme and the order in which the photos occur) with one portrait and two landscape prints as shown in Figure 9-25.

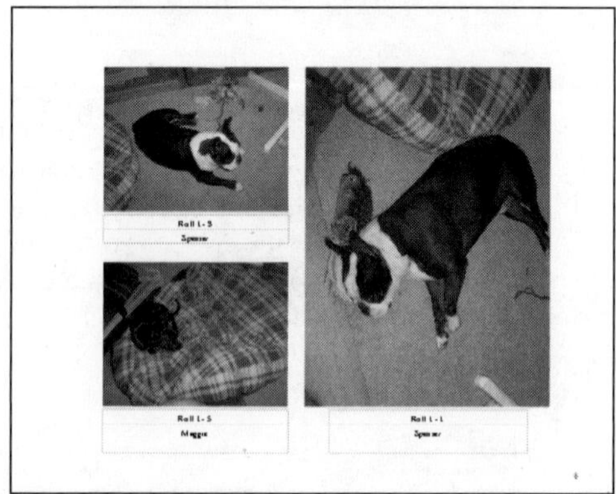

Figure 9-25: With three photos per page, one portrait and two landscapes are often an effective combination.

✦ **End:** This design exists only in the Story Book theme and has one photo, and that photo is partway off the page.

As you change the number of photos on a page, that change also affects which photos are on subsequent pages — another ripple effect. The ripple can be particularly annoying if you've already designed one of the later pages and had it just the way you wanted it, only to see your work go *poof*. The solution to this dilemma is the Lock Page checkbox. When you have a page exactly the way you want it, select the page and select the Lock Page checkbox. If you lock a page, the thumbnail sprouts a small lock icon in the lower-right corner, as shown in Figure 9-26.

Figure 9-26: Locked pages display a padlock icon in their thumbnail's lower-right corner.

There are a few "gotchas" associated with locking a page:

✦ **Cascading changes:** If, at some future time, you decide you want to make a change to the page design, you have to unlock it, possibly resulting in a wild cascade of changes as iPhoto realigns everything according to the theme's priorities. One way to avoid this cascade is to temporarily lock the preceding page before unlocking the one you want to modify.

✦ **Picture order:** Changes to picture order you make in Organize mode won't be reflected on the locked page. It is, essentially, a static item and all the other photos flow around it.

✦ **Changing themes:** Changing themes removes the lock as well as all your other design work. Choosing Edit ➪ Undo restores your designs, but the lock will still be gone.

The smallest book you create will have ten single-sided pages, even if some of them are blank. You're paying for a minimum of ten pages and, by George, Apple's going to make sure that you get those ten pages (but they will warn you first that some pages will be bereft of photos). The largest book available has 50 pages — and costs you $147! If you try to produce a book with more than 50 pages, you won't be allowed to have it printed. You should make these limits part of your design and layout process. Of course, if you're willing to pay for it, you really can get more than 50 pages printed, just split your book into volumes like the *Encyclopedia Britannica,* and pay accordingly.

Adding page numbers to your book

The three checkboxes beside the Theme pop-up menu control which elements, other than your photos, show up on your book's pages. The easiest element to deal with is Page Numbers, which are printed in the bottom-right corner of each page. Take them out or leave them in, depending how you feel about having numbered pages. Don't worry, though, if the page number location and a photo coincide — the photo wins, hiding the page number.

Adding titles and comments

Most numbered page designs allow accompanying each photo with two text boxes, whose appearance are predicated upon selecting the Titles and Comments checkboxes. In other words, if you want to place text in the boxes, you have to select Titles for the first field and Comments for the second — selecting just one displays just that one field. As shown in Figure 9-27, some designs can look really strange if you don't have the text, because iPhoto's themes don't use the space where the text would be to enlarge the photos' display. iPhoto puts the photo's title in the first field and any comments you've added to the photo in the second field, but you're welcome to edit, replace, or delete those entries as you want.

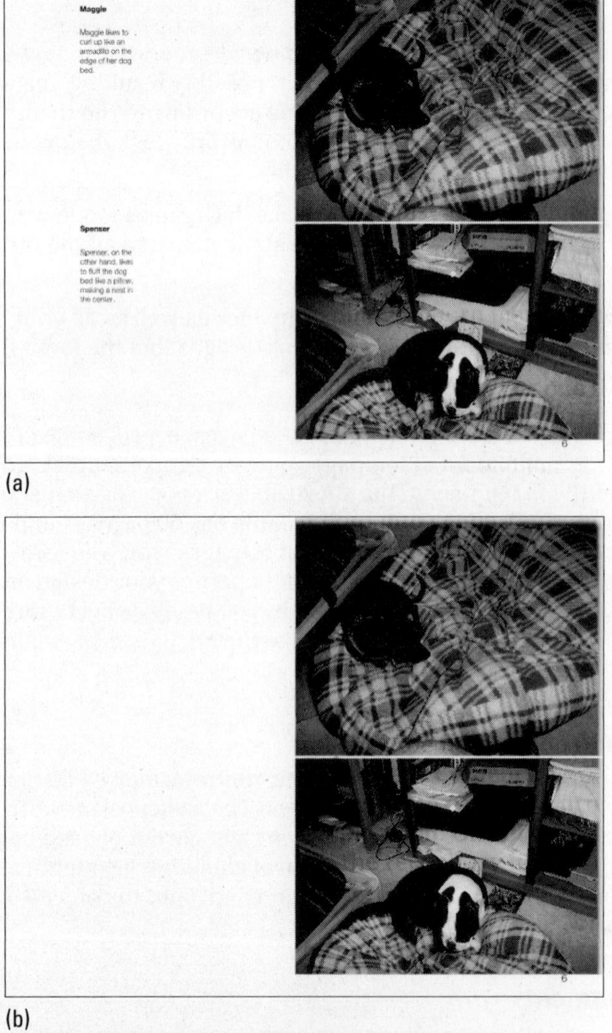

Figure 9-27: A Portfolio "Two" page with Titles and Comments on (a); The same page with Titles and Comments turned off (b).

Some themes and page designs have rather small boxes for Comments and, if your text overflows, iPhoto cuts it off and displays the ubiquitous exclamation point in a yellow triangle Caution icon to make sure that you're aware of that fact. Make sure that you edit that text before you have your book printed.

Spellchecking your book

iPhoto even includes an interface to the OS X spell checker, which is a good thing because iPhoto deviates from standard OS X application behavior by not including a Services submenu in the iPhoto application's menu. There are three ways to check your spelling in iPhoto and, with what you're going to pay to have the book produced, you really don't want any spelling errors making you look foolish.

✦ Choose Edit ➪ Spelling ➪ Spelling to check the spelling in whatever text block contains the cursor. The keyboard shortcut for this is ⌘-: (yes, normally you see this marked as Shift-⌘-;).

✦ Choose Edit ➪ Spelling ➪ Check Spelling (⌘-;) to check the current selection. If there is no selected text, the current text block is checked, just as if you had chosen Edit ➪ Spelling ➪ Spelling.

✦ Choose Edit ➪ Spelling ➪ Check Spelling As You Type to toggle. When this item is checked in the Spelling submenu, the spellchecker follows along as you type and, interactively, helps you correct your spelling as you work.

You can also choose any of the three spelling choices by control-clicking in a text box and choosing from the contextual menu's Spelling submenu.

Words that are not in the OS X dictionary or in your personal learned words list sprout a red dotted underline. Figure 9-28 shows the standard Spelling dialog where you can correct your errors, tell the spell checker to ignore a word in the future, or add the word to your learned words list.

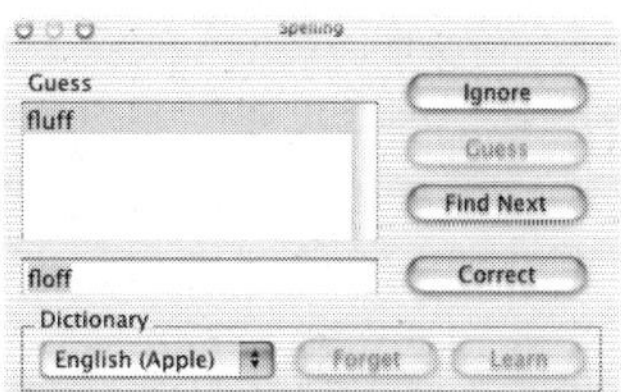

Figure 9-28: The OS X spell checker is on hand to help you catch typos in your book.

The learned words list is in your Home folder's Library/Spelling folder in a file named for the language you're using. For example, mine (and probably, yours) is in `~/Library/Spelling/English`.

iPhoto's Funny Font Handling

iPhoto's treatment of fonts is different from what we've all come to expect in a Mac application. You cannot change the font family or typeface or apply a bold or italic style to a single character or word — all changes of this type affect all the text in that field and, in the case of books, in all the fields of that type, as shown in the accompanying figure.

Change one word's font and you change the fonts for that whole field and all like fields.

Adding to this global font change property, iPhoto also teases you in the Font panel (Edit ➪ Font ➪ Show Fonts, or ⌘-T). It shows you the Sizes display, lets you edit the Sizes text box entry, and then rejects your change. Like the original Model T Ford's approach to color ("You can have any color you want, so long as it's black") iPhoto's approach to font sizes in books is, "You can print in any size you want, so long as it is the one we chose for this theme."

If, like Dennis, your spelling errors generally fall into the category of transposed letters that leave a real word ("filed" rather than "field" is one of his personal gotchas), iPhoto's contextual menu can come in handy. Control-click in a text block and choose Speech ➪ Start Speaking, as shown in Figure 9-29, to have the Mac read your text back to you. Dennis finds the available computer voices (System Preferences ➪ Speech ➪ Default Voice tab) annoying, but a lot of people find them cute, entertaining, or useful. At least you have the option.

We're very pleased to see that iPhoto 2 increases contextual menu usage. Many very useful capabilities are only accessible or are much more convenient via the contextual menus.

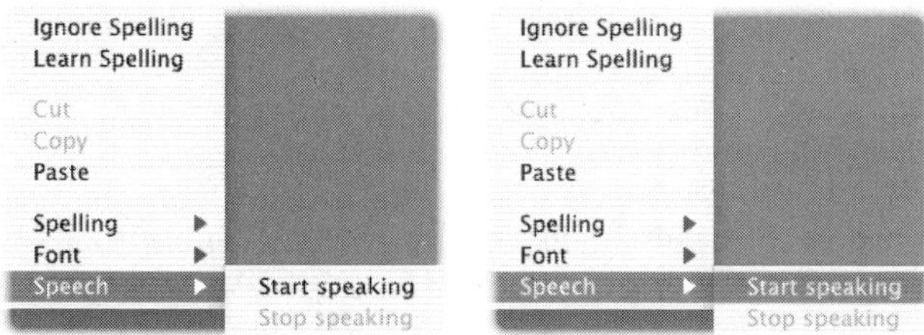

Figure 9-29: The contextual menu gives you the option of having the Mac read your text to you.

Previewing your book

When you are reasonably sure that you have the book you want, it's time to double-check. You can preview your book on-screen by clicking the Preview button at the right end of Book mode's toolbox. Alternatively, you can double-click one of the thumbnails. iPhoto presents a preview window, shown in Figure 9-30, with a current page text box at the top left, flanked by previous and next page arrow buttons. You can type a page number in the text box to go to a specific page if you don't like clicking the buttons repeatedly (page 0 is the cover). The Show Guides checkbox determines whether thin blue lines surround the text fields.

As you can see, the default window size makes the text well-nigh unreadable. Click the zoom (green gumdrop) button to make the window grow to maximum size so that you get a reasonable picture of the text as well.

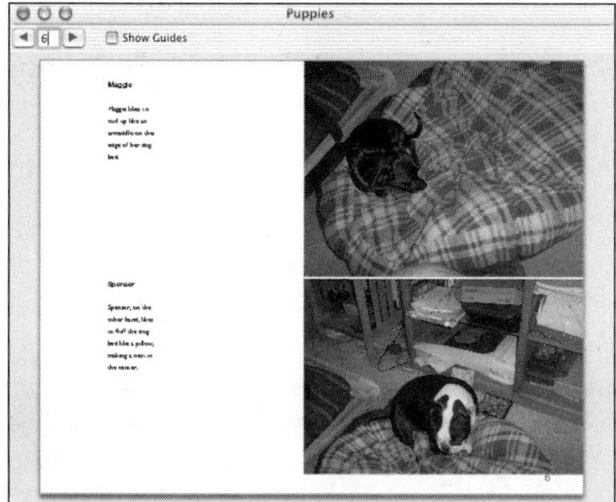

Figure 9-30: You can preview your book on-screen.

Although it won't have the fancy linen cover or the acid-free glossy paper (unless you decide to splurge), you can print your book on a color inkjet or, if you have one, a color laser printer to get a really good idea of how your book will look. Just choose File ➪ Print (⌘-P), select your printer if it isn't already chosen, and click Print. If you want a PDF file, just click the Save As PDF button at the bottom of your Print dialog. Alternatively, you can click the Print dialog's Preview button to generate a temporary PDF file, which will open in the Preview utility.

Preview displays the pages rotated 90 degrees clockwise with the top along the right edge. You can open the PDF in Adobe's Acrobat Reader and choose View ➪ Rotate Counterclockwise to see it as it is meant to be seen. Alternatively, assuming you're running MacOS X 10.2 or later, you can choose View ➪ Rotate Left command in Preview.

When you're really sure that you want to send the book off to be printed and bound, with your credit card charged, check out the "Ordering Photos: Coffee table books" section later in this chapter.

iPhoto "remembers" the last book created for each album, allowing you to go back later and print or order more without having to recreate your work.

Printing Photos

We can almost guarantee the time will arrive when you need a printed copy of one or more of your photos. Web pages and e-mail are nice, but Grandma wants an 8 x 10 of Junior's picture to put on the mantel, a wallet-size to carry around and show her friends, and a 4 x 6 to put in the family photo album, and you don't dare disappoint Grandma!

Of course, you could just use the easy iPhoto-Internet interface to order prints from Kodak (see the "Ordering Photos: Prints" section later in this chapter) and, if you don't have a color printer or just don't feel like a do-it-yourself type, that's certainly a reasonable way to go.

Preparing to print

With an appropriate color printer and photo quality paper, you can get a print just as good as the ones you order from Kodak. There are fine inkjet printers available for well under $100, but they typically only use a four-color cartridge. Although the output quality of these printers is usually quite good, if you want to challenge the professionals you'll need a printer with a six-color cartridge (such as an Epson Stylus Photo 780).

Many of these printers are quite inexpensive. Inkjet printer manufacturers have learned the lesson taught by Gillette and Schick in their razor business: You can just about give away the carrier, the profit is in the consumables. If you're paying retail, it can cost $60 or more just to replace both the black and color cartridges in an inkjet printer that only cost you $59 or $79 to begin with. And, just so you know, printing color photos on glossy photo paper will go through ink cartridges like a '65 Caddy goes through gasoline.

You need to do two things if you want quality inkjet photo printouts:

✦ **Use the right paper and tell your printer driver what kind of paper you're using and that you are going for quality rather than speed.** No matter how much you try, you're not going to get a decent photo on typical 20# bond typing paper. Paper like this just absorbs the ink and you get a dull, smeared look. Glossy paper made specifically for photo printing, such as Hewlett-Packard's PhotoSmart, Kodak's Inkjet Photo, or Epson's Glossy Photo, is the ticket. This paper is expensive, running as high as $1 per sheet, and with the amount of ink you'll use for an 8 x 10, your photos might cost a little over $2 each on average, but that is only half as much as an 8 x 10 from Kodak ($3.99 at this writing). If you can get a good buy on your paper and ink cartridges, you'll actually be well under half the cost. (Dennis buys his at Costco for about 60 percent of list.)

But, using the right paper doesn't do any good unless you let the printer driver know about it. In your Print dialog (File ➪ Print or click the Print button in Organize mode), there's a button labeled Advanced Settings. Click it to access OS X's standard Print dialog for your printer and, in the pop-up menu that says Copies & Pages, choose Advanced Settings. Use the controls (they might be pop-up menus or radio buttons, depending upon your printer model) to let the printer driver know what kind of paper you're using and that you want the highest quality setting.

✦ **Don't try to print a photo larger than its resolution supports.** Inkjet printers do their best work if they can work with photos that are between 220 pixels per inch and 300 pixels per inch. This is a separate consideration from how finely the printer can spray the ink. If the photo is 600 dpi and your printer can print 720 dpi, the picture won't look any better than if the photo was 300 dpi and you printed at 720 dpi unless you put it under a really good magnifying glass and had some fine detail to compare. In other words, bumping the photo's resolution above 300 dpi doesn't gain a *perceptible* advantage. Lower photo resolutions, though, can have a significant, visible, negative effect. Having written that, we admit that sometimes you get better results in practice than theory would indicate. For example, using the Epson Stylus Photo 780, we've gotten superb 8 x 10 prints from 180 dpi originals (1800 x 1440) and even some 1-megapixel (1280 x 960) photos. A lot depends upon the original photo's clarity and just how much detail the JPEG compression loses.

Many people will advise you to print draft copies on regular paper "to see how things look." We don't share that philosophy. The process uses a lot of expensive color ink and the results aren't indicative of what you'll produce with good paper and the proper settings — prints that look muddy and dull when printed on plain paper often turn out clean and crisp when printed at 720 (or 1440) dpi on glossy photo paper. What you see on your screen is a better indicator of how the final print will appear than a plain paper draft.

Printing from iPhoto

Select the photo or photos you want printed and choose File ➪ Print or, in Organize mode, click the Print button. iPhoto makes the actual printing process easier than most applications with a customized printing dialog, shown in Figure 9-31. iPhoto displays a preview of what your first page will look like on the left.

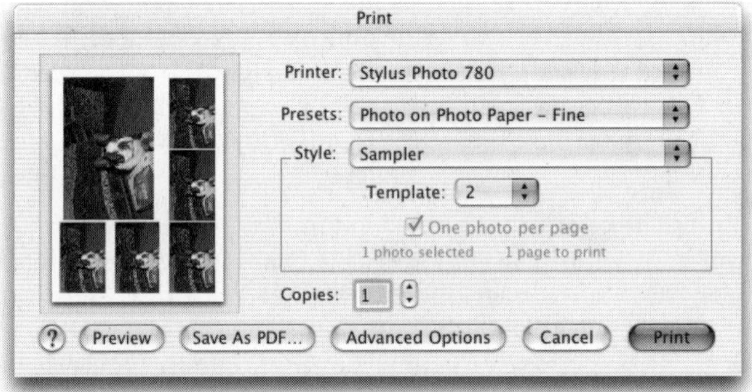

Figure 9-31: iPhoto presents a custom Print dialog.

Choose your printer from the Printer pop-up menu, if it isn't already displayed. Choose your paper and print quality combination from the Presets pop-up menu, if iPhoto offers choices for your printer. Finally, in the Style section, specify what you want to print and how you want things laid out. iPhoto offers six styles:

✦ **Contact Sheet:** Prints out a photo array. You can specify from one to eight photos per row. The more photos per row, obviously, the smaller the prints, as shown in Figure 9-32. Depending upon the printable area your printer supports, you can have up to 104 prints per page (13 rows of 8 photos) or 112 prints per page (14 rows of 8 photos). In fact, if your printer supports it and you choose to use 4 x 6 paper, you can get 15 rows of 8 really tiny pictures on a single sheet. If you select multiple photos, you get one copy of each laid out in the array. If you only select one photo, you get one full page containing multiple prints of that photo — a pretty decent shortcut to printing multiple wallet-size copies. When you select multiple photos, the Save Paper checkbox is enabled, allowing you to print closer to the edge of the paper.

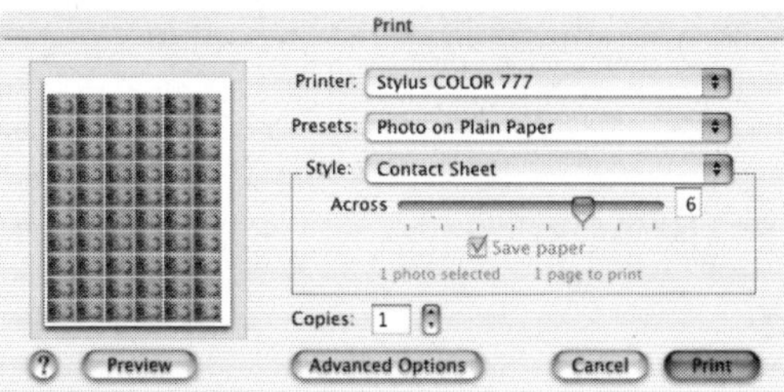

Figure 9-32: You can use the Contact Sheet to fill a page with the same photo.

✦ **Full Page:** Printing is pretty self-explanatory. Choosing Full Page rotates each selected picture and enlarges or reduces it to fill a page (subject to the margin, which you can set, up to 1 inch on each side). Figure 9-33 shows the Full Page selection.

Figure 9-33: Full Page printing fills the printable area, less any margins you set.

✦ **Greeting Card:** Rotate and resize your photo(s) to fill either a quarter (Double-fold) or half page (Single-fold), allowing you to fold your printout into a greeting card. Figure 9-34 shows the Greeting Card choice. This choice's name is a bit misleading, because you still have to add your message to the card, either in another program or by hand.

Figure 9-34: All set to add your message and fold into a greeting card.

✦ **N-Up:** This style is new to iPhoto 2. This style tells iPhoto to print N copies of the selected photo per page. You have a choice of 2, 4, 6, 9, or 16 pictures per page. If you select multiple photos, you'll almost certainly want to select the One photo per page checkbox. Doing this tells iPhoto to print N copies of each picture on its own page. In other words, if you select three photos and six per page, you'll get six copies of picture 1 on one page, six copies of picture 2 on the second page, and six copies of picture 3 on the third page. Figure 9-35 shows the N-Up choice.

Figure 9-35: N-Up printing gives you multiple copies of a picture on a page.

✦ **Sampler:** Offers two templates, one with a 6 x 8 and two 3 x 4 prints and the other with a 4 x 6 and 5 wallet-size (2 x 3) prints. Although not nearly so versatile as the Picture Package in Photoshop or Photoshop Elements, Sampler is much faster and easier to use. Figure 9-36 shows the Sampler choice.

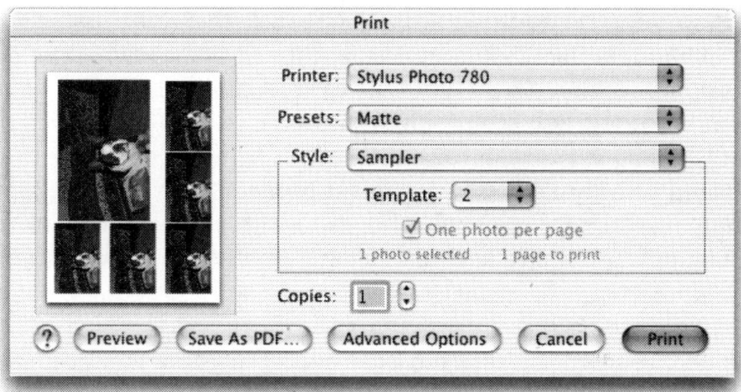

Figure 9-36: The Sampler is reminiscent of sheets of school photos. Certain photo sizes are considered standard.

✦ **Standard Prints:** This style as shown in Figure 9-37. When more than one photo is selected (and more than one at the size selected will fit on a page), the One photo per page checkbox is enabled, allowing you to restrict printing to one photo per page, centered on the page. The 2 x 3 (wallet-size) offering is new in iPhoto 2.

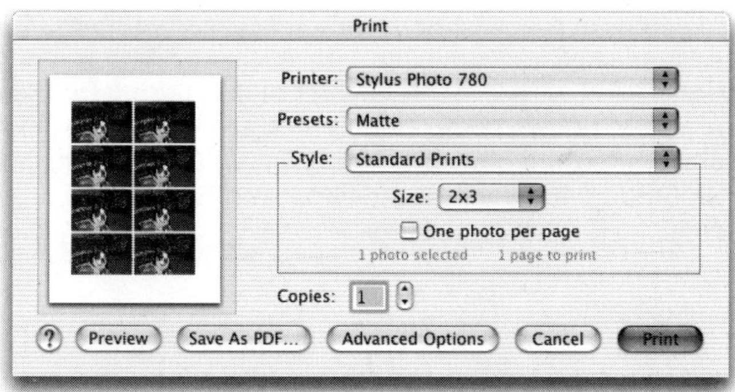

Figure 9-37: You can print standard photo sizes, all ready for trimming.

While making many things easier, iPhoto also makes a few printing operations more confusing by offering a Page Setup dialog and then ignoring some of the settings you make, such as print orientation. The one setting that iPhoto does honor from Page Setup is the paper size. We find it particularly annoying, though, that iPhoto says that it can't fit a 4 x 6 print on 4 x 6 Photo paper, as sold by Epson and Hewlett-Packard. Fortunately, there is a way around that: Choose Full Page rather than Standard Prints as your style after you've selected one of these paper sizes.

Tip

If the colors in your printouts look way off, click the Print dialog's Advanced Options button and, in the OS X Print dialog, choose Color Management from the unlabeled pop-up menu. Click the ColorSync radio button if it isn't already selected. One frequent type of problem is the presence of heavy "color casts" where a photo prints very green (or red, or blue...). This is often the result of one or more clogged print nozzles on your inkjet printer. Make sure that you test the printer before wasting a lot of ink and expensive paper. Most inkjet printers include a diagnostic program, such as Epson's Printer Utility, where you can run this test.

The Preview box on the Print dialog's left side can give you a rough idea of what your printout's first page will look like, but it won't tell you anything about subsequent pages, including whether there are low-resolution warnings on any of those photos. Fortunately, as with all good OS X programs, you can "print" to a PDF file by clicking the Print dialog's Preview button. iPhoto creates a temporary PDF file of your entire print job and opens it for you with the OS X Preview utility (where you can save the PDF file, if you want). If you just want a PDF file and don't care about going through Preview, just click the Save As PDF button in the Print dialog.

Ordering Photos

Whether you want copies of specific photos or a ready-made album, iPhoto makes it easy. Apple has established a relationship with Kodak that lets you order prints of your photos and, as we saw earlier in this chapter in the "Laying Out Books" section, you can assemble your own photo albums and, as we describe below, have them professionally printed and bound. The only limitation upon this feature is that, at least so far, this service is only available in North America.

Prints

If you don't have an appropriate printer, or you just don't want to hassle with buying and loading expensive special paper and then trimming the prints, you can order prints from Kodak with just an Internet connection, a few clicks of the mouse, and a credit card, as follows:

1. **Make sure that you have an active Internet connection.**
2. **Select the photos you want printed.** You can select an album and have its contents printed or select individual photos for printing.
3. **In Organize mode, click the Order Prints button.** Your Mac will (probably) ask whether it is okay to open an item in your Keychain. Your 1-Click settings are stored here, and they are necessary to the ordering process. If you haven't established a 1-Click account, you need to do so before you can order. iPhoto displays the Order Prints dialog, as shown in Figure 9-38.

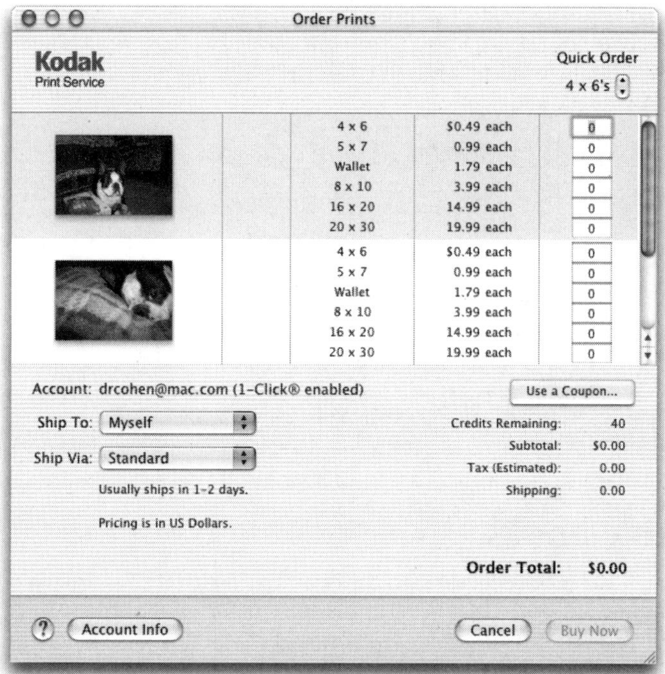

Figure 9-38: iPhoto presents the Kodak Print Service's Order Prints dialog.

4. **Specify that you want a set number of 4 x 6 prints of every selected photo using the two quantity boxes at the top-right of the dialog.** If you want varying quantities and sizes of the different prints, use the quantity boxes for the desired sizes of each photo.

   Notice that iPhoto displays low-resolution warnings next to any sizes that will not print well.

   After you have all your quantities filled in, check to see what the damages are and, if you still want to place the order, click the Buy Now button. iPhoto transfers the photos to Kodak over your Internet connection and Kodak processes the order and charges your credit card. Next, you see an alert similar to the one in Figure 9-39 telling you that your order has been received. You also receive an e-mail from Apple confirming and thanking you for the order.

Having Kodak print your photos is definitely convenient and not too much more expensive than printing the photos yourself, except on small orders where the shipping charges really inflate the per-print cost. Of course, if you're having them sent to Grandma, you don't have to find a photo mailer and put stamps on it, so the incremental cost is not too bad. Where Kodak really shines, if your camera can produce a high-enough resolution image, is printing really large photos — the 16 x 20s and the 20 x 30s that you frame and hang on the living room wall — but which you can't print out on most inkjet printers.

Figure 9-39: Your order's been placed; now you wait for the prints to show up.

Coffee table books

You've selected your album, gone into Book mode, created the book you want printed and bound, now what? iPhoto considers ordering a book to be an organizing experience, so click the Organize button and then click the Order Book button in Organize mode's tools panel, making sure that you have an active Internet connection beforehand. If you're not connected, iPhoto won't proceed.

iPhoto will spin the cursor for a while (how long depends upon the length of your book and the speed of your Mac) while it converts your book into something it can send over the Internet. When iPhoto is ready, you'll see a screen similar to the one in Figure 9-40.

There are two things about which iPhoto might warn you at this point. The first is about the presence of any low-resolution warnings still in your book. You can either go back and fix those problems or tell iPhoto to order the book anyway, but if you do so, be prepared for some blotchy prints. The second is if your book has fewer than ten pages. In this situation, you can either return to Book mode and modify the layout or Organize mode and add more photos to fill up the remaining pages, or just tell iPhoto to have them print the book with some blank pages.

If you haven't created an Apple ID and enabled 1-Click ordering, that lower-right button will be as shown in Figure 9-40. After you have 1-Click ordering enabled, the Tax and Shipping charges will fill in, and the buttons along the bottom will enable (with some changes) as shown in Figure 9-41.

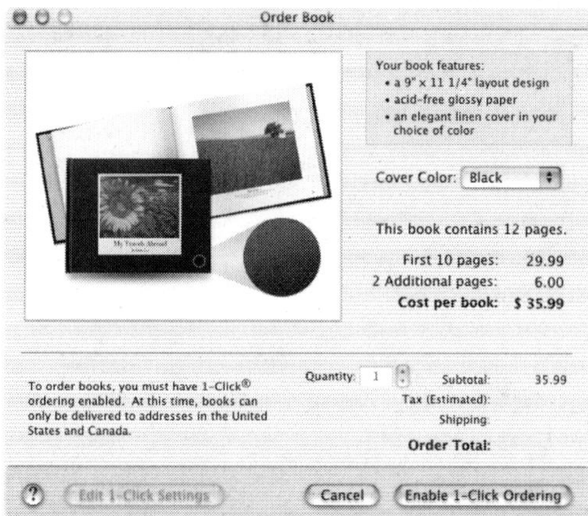

Figure 9-40: The Order Book dialog tells you the basic cost, but you have to enable 1-Click Ordering to place the order.

Figure 9-41: After you establish an account, all the gory pricing and shipping details are revealed.

Resolving Resolutions

Whether you're printing the photos yourself, ordering from Kodak, or having a book printed by Apple's designated bindery, you should follow some basic guidelines to avoid the yellow triangle warning.

According to Kodak's Ofoto Web site (`www.ofoto.com/PhotoTipsDigital.jsp`), use the following reference table:

Print Size	***Minimum Resolution***
Wallet-size (2" x 3")	320 x 240
4" x 6"	640 x 480
5" x 7"	1024 x 768
8" x 10"	1536 x 1024
16" x 20"	1600 x 1200
20" x 30"	1600 x 1200

Yes, we're surprised by the recommendations for 16 x 20s and 20 x 30s as well, although that makes Dennis's Kodak DX3500 (1800 x 1200 resolution) look like a better purchasing decision.

At any rate, those recommendations are *minimums*. Any resolution less than those in the list prompt you with a low-resolution warning flag when laying out a book or printing.

You should also be aware that edges of your photos will be cropped if the aspect ratios don't match. Ofoto calls this process Zoom & Trim. First they enlarge (Zoom) the photo so that it completely covers the print area, then they crop (Trim) any overflow.

Creating an Apple ID is easy. Your ID is just your e-mail address, with a password you create. The password must be at least eight characters long and at least one must be nonalphabetic. In case you forget your password at some future time, Apple gets two questions and answers from you to use for verification purposes so that you might create a new password for your account.

Answer a few more questions: credit card number and expiration date, billing address, one or more named shipping addresses and whether you prefer standard or expedited (faster, but more expensive) shipping.

Although the offer might not last forever, while we're writing this material Apple is offering a free ten-print (4 x 6s) order when you first activate your 1-Click account (you still pay the shipping charges, though). They also offer similar incentives for purchasers of .Mac accounts. We each got 100 free 4 x 6 prints for our .Mac signup.

Choose a color from the Cover Color pop-up menu. If you want more than one copy of the book, adjust the quantity in the text box or by clicking the up or down arrows next to it. Click the Buy Now With 1-Click button when you're ready to go.

Now, just sit back and wait for FedEx to deliver your book(s).

Dennis found the book both very nice and a little disappointing. The binding is excellent, the acid-free paper looks, feels, and even smells nice (or maybe that's the linen cover). The quality of the printout is pretty good, but nowhere near comparable to what you get when you order Kodak prints. Actually, side-by-side, the prints in the book don't look quite as good as those he gets from his Epson 780 Stylus Photo inkjet printer on glossy photo quality paper.

Apple doesn't do the printing/binding themselves; they outsource this work. They won't acknowledge which company actually does the work, but the most common guess is MyPublisher.com. You might want to check out the MyPublisher.com Web site, because they have a lot more themes than those in iPhoto (including do-it-yourself); however, you don't have the easy iPhoto interface to use while laying out your book.

E-mailing Your Photos

In some situations you're going to have to order prints or print them yourself and mail them (can you say, "Grandma?"), but other than those cases, you'll find e-mail the faster, more convenient way to distribute your photos. One e-mail message can send the photos to dozens of relatives, saving you not just the printing costs, but the photo mailers and the postage.

If you use the OS X Mail application, Eudora, AOL, or Entourage as your mail client, you're just a click or two away from sending your photos to friends and family. Plus, with the addition of a freeware utility named iPhoto Mailer Patcher (self-described as a hack and available at `homepage.mac.com/jacksim/software/`), you can do the same with Mailsmith, PowerMail, or QuickMail Pro.

iPhoto invokes AppleScripts to communicate with Mail. What the iPhoto Mailer Patcher does is rename the script in iPhoto's package and install a replacement script that invokes your mail client of choice. The patcher also replaces the picture used for the button in iPhoto's Organize tools panel.

Follow these steps to send photos to others via e-mail:

1. **Select the photo(s) you want to send.**
2. **Enter Organize mode (if you're not already there) by clicking the Organize button.**
3. **Click the Mail button in the Organize toolbox.** If you forgot to select any photos, iPhoto displays an alert telling you to do so and try again. Otherwise, iPhoto displays the dialog shown in Figure 9-42. Below the Size pop-up menu, iPhoto tells you how many photos you've selected to e-mail and how much disk space they use. Be aware that the size of the photo message is substantially larger because Mail has to encode the images for transmission over the Internet. The encoding typically adds 30 to 50 percent to the size of a binary file like a photo. If your recipients are using a dialup Internet connection (as opposed to broadband, like cable or DSL), they'll appreciate you keeping your messages as small as possible. iPhoto offers a little assistance here, as well, with the Size pop-up menu.

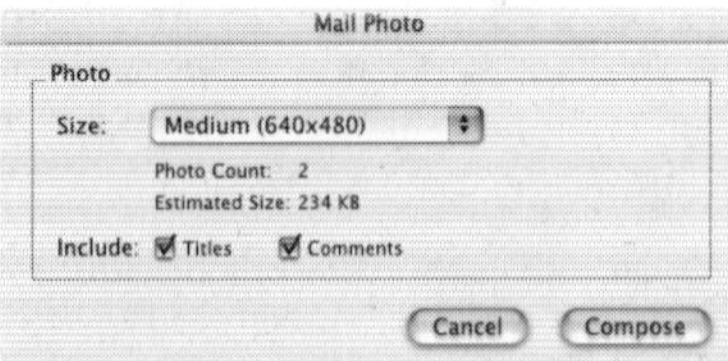

Figure 9-42: The Mail Photo dialog lets you set parameters for the mail message and resize the image(s) for quicker transmission.

4. **Choose an image size from the Size pop-up menu.** A typical 2-megapixel image is over one-half megabyte in size and approaches three-quarter megabytes when encoded. Attach four of these pictures and you're quickly looking at a mail message of 3MB that takes 10 to 15 minutes to upload on a dialup and 10 to 15 minutes to download using a dialup connection—all for photos too large to fit on a standard computer screen in the first place. Reduce them to 640 x 480 and you'll cut the size by over 75 percent, saving everyone involved some time, and your recipients can view your photos without resizing.
5. **Select the Titles and/or Comments checkbox if you want Mail to include the photos' Title and Comments information in the body of your e-mail message.** If you are only sending a single photo, selecting the Titles checkbox makes the photo's title the e-mail message's Subject.
6. **Click Compose.** iPhoto now goes to work, resizing the photos (if requested) and converting them to JPEG images (if they weren't already). It then sends a series of AppleEvent messages to launch Mail, if it isn't already running, and to tell Mail how to compose the message and what photo files to attach.
7. **Address your messages in Mail and click Send.**

Most e-mail boxes (such as the wonderful mac.com addresses available via .Mac) have size limitations — mac.com mailboxes are "full" when they contain 15MB. Think of the mailbox as your checking account and the 15MB as your overdraft protection. If an incoming message puts your mailbox over the limit, it and subsequent messages "bounce" like bad checks until you free up enough space. So, be considerate of others and keep the message sizes manageable.

Another unpublicized "gotcha" with mac.com addresses (and similar limitations when using other ISPs) is that although your mailbox can hold 15MB, no single message over 3MB in size is acceptable.

If you don't want iPhoto to convert the photo to JPEG (you might be sending a PDF, a TIFF, or a Photoshop PSD file that you want to have arrive intact), don't use Organize's Mail button. Launch your mail client and drag the photo(s) from iPhoto to the message window (Mail), Enclosure tab (Mailsmith), or whatever place your mail client uses to indicate attached files.

Publishing Your Pictures on Your .Mac HomePage

Creating a Web page of your photos and sending a simple message telling your friends and relatives where they can check out your latest offerings is actually far more versatile than sending a large group of recipients photos via e-mail. You don't have to restrict the number of photos so that everything fits in their mailboxes and you can post as many as you want, within the limits of what your Web server allows. The easiest way to post your photos on the Web is using a .Mac account.

If you don't have a .Mac account, by all means get one. They're only $100 a year, they provide 100MB of storage for your Web pages and assorted other items, and they provide a conduit for obtaining all sorts of OS X software. Just go to `www.mac.com` and follow the simple directions or pick up a copy of the *Macworld Mac OS X Bible* or *Mac OS X For Dummies* (Wiley Publishing, Inc.) and read all about it in there.

Assuming that you have an active Internet connection, iPhoto makes creating a .Mac HomePage almost effortless. If you aren't connected, establish a connection and follow along:

1. **Select the photos (or album) you want to publish.**
2. **If you're not already in Organize mode, click the Organize button.**

3. **Click the HomePage button in the Organize toolbox.** iPhoto connects to the .Mac Web pages and displays a Publish HomePage dialog similar to the one in Figure 9-43. We say "similar" because the frame styles and page layouts are subject to change and enhancement, and your photos, not Dennis's canine collection, will display.

4. **Select and edit any of the text on the page that you want, be it the page name, description block, or any/all of the photo names.** Though not documented, there appears to be a 40-character limitation on photo captions.

Apple puts a little ad at the bottom of your page telling your visitors that the page was "Created using .Mac." Although you can't remove that logo here, you can (after publishing the page) mount your iDisk and edit the HTML file iPhoto placed in your Sites folder to remove it, assuming that you have some familiarity with HTML. Turn to Chapter 10 for more information on this topic.

5. **Select a frame style for your thumbnails.**

Figure 9-43: The Publish HomePage dialog, ready for you to customize your page.

6. **Click Publish when you're ready.** iPhoto uploads the photos and thumbnails to your .Mac account. The photos and thumbnails will be in the Pictures folder, and the HTML file, named PhotoAlbum1.html, will be in your Sites folder. If you already have a PhotoAlbum1.html, this will be PhotoAlbum2.html, and so on. When the upload is completed, iPhoto asks whether you want to check your work, as shown in Figure 9-44.

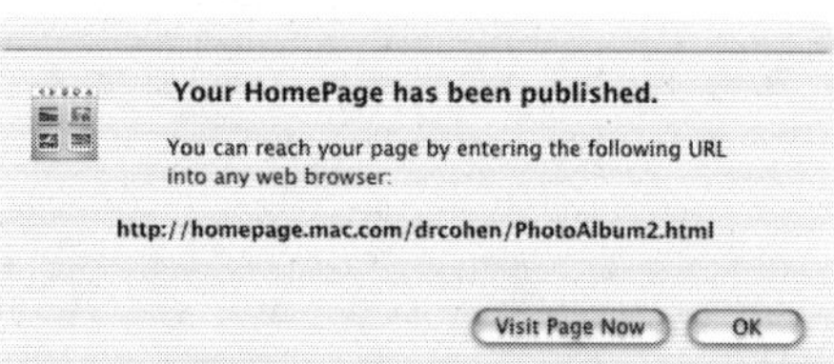

Figure 9-44: iPhoto tells you you're done and asks whether you want to visit your new page.

If you already have pages other than those managed by Apple's HomePage tools published in your .Mac account, do *not* publish the page in this manner unless you're willing to have your index.html file wiped out. iPhoto doesn't add the page to existing index.html files it doesn't manage, it replaces those index files with a new one that points to the PhotoAlbum collections.

Assuming that you clicked the Visit Page Now button, you'll see your handiwork, as Dennis did in Figure 9-45.

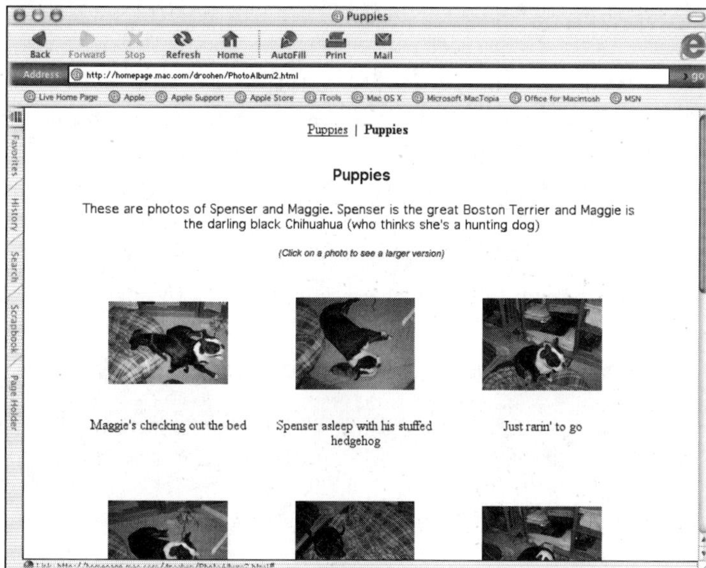

Figure 9-45: The finished Web page, displayed in Internet Explorer.

Clicking a thumbnail displays an enlarged copy of the photo, nicely placed in a Slideshow window (Figure 9-46). The Slideshow loops; if you're looking at the first picture on the page and click the left-pointing arrow button, you'll be taken to the last photo on the page, and vice versa.

Figure 9-46: Click on a thumbnail to see an enlarged version of the photo in a slideshow window.

If iPhoto's subset of the .Mac page designs don't satisfy your aesthetic sense, you can follow a more hands-on path to creating an .Mac photo HomePage, as follows:

1. **Open your iDisk in the Finder (Go ⇨ iDisk or Shift-⌘-I).**
2. **Create a new folder inside your iDisk's Pictures folder.**
3. **Drag the photos from iPhoto's Viewing pane to the folder you created in Step 2.**
4. **Start your Web browser and go to `www.mac.com` and log in.**

Some browsers don't interact well with the HomePage functions. If you're having problems, you might want to switch (temporarily) to Safari or Internet Explorer.

5. **Click the HomePage button on the .Mac Web page.**

6. **Click the Create a Page panel's Photo Album tab and select from the wide theme selection available (16 at the time we're writing this).**

   You can also find Photo Album styles on some of the other tabs, such as Personal and Education.

7. **When you click a theme, HomePage asks you to identify the folder containing your pictures.** You did perform Steps 2 and 3, didn't you? Select the folder in the list and click Choose. iTools now displays an "Edit your page" window.

8. **Click "Edit changes to Preview."**

9. **Click the Edit button and perform any editing you desire.** You can eliminate or replace the placeholder text. If you want, you can change the photo captions from the filename default.

10. **Click Preview when done to check your work.**

11. **Assuming that you like what you see in the Preview, click the Publish button, and HomePage creates your page and offers to send iCards announcing it to people you specify.** You can click on the link to check it out or go back into HomePage to create more Web pages by clicking the Return to HomePage button.

You can password-protect individual sites created by HomePage and group your HomePage sites into categories using the HomePage tools.

If this level of control is still insufficient, see Chapter 10 to create a custom Web page.

Creating a Slideshow

Photo slideshows have a long history, from the tedious vacation slides your grandparents projected onto a pull-down screen (or a wall) to the even more boring, but more high-tech, presentations you'll see if you ever attend a time-share sales pitch. But slideshows don't have to be boring. With iPhoto you can group your slides and set the show to music. Dennis's friends, Joseph and Tammy, had a baby boy just before Dennis started working on these chapters for the first edition. (You see a number of Marcus's pictures in the book.) Naturally, parents, grandparents, and friends took many pictures, and Dennis used iPhoto to create albums of the best photos for slideshows, each with its own "baby" background music (Nat King Cole's renditions of "Yes Sir, That's My Baby" and "Too Marvelous for Words," "Pretty Little Baby" by Connie Francis, and many others). Then he exported the slideshows to QuickTime (see Chapter 10 for more on sharing a slideshow) and using Toast Titanium burnt them to VideoCD. The young parents loved the gift.

Not only can iPhoto create slideshows, but it can play them right on your Mac, full-screen, in living color and stereophonic sound.

Playing a slideshow

If you're happy with your Slideshow Music preference, all you have to do is click the iPhoto window's Play the slideshow button to have your screen go completely black, the music start to play, and your selected photos or album to fade in and then start cross-fading from one to the next at two-second intervals (or whatever you changed your Slideshow: Play each slide for *n* seconds setting to be).

Note

iPhoto has a precedence it follows to determine which photos are shown in a slideshow. If you select no photos, all the photos in the Viewing pane (even if there is just one) are shown in sequence. If you select a single photo, the show starts with that photo and proceeds to the end of the Viewing pane before looping back to the beginning. If you select multiple photos, they are the only ones displayed in the slideshow.

The shorter the play time for each slide, the less visible the cross-fade transition will be.

Other than presenting photos that will actually interest your audience, appropriate background music does more to make a slideshow pleasurable than anything else. Clicking the Slideshow button in the Organize toolbox gives you direct access to your iTunes Library from the slideshow Settings dialog, shown in Figure 9-47. Your iTunes Library can be a great source and you can find more music on the Internet, both on the Web and in Internet newsgroups (Usenet).

Cross-Reference

Check out Chapters 3 through 5, in particular for tips on where to find music and how to get it on your Mac and into iTunes.

The pop-up menu (which says iTunes Library in Figure 9-47) gives you access to the two pieces of Sample Music with which iPhoto ships, Bach's *Minuet in G* and *Jesu, Joy of Man's Desiring*. More importantly, it lets you select, search for, and play anything in your iTunes Library and (via the pop-up) you can even narrow things down to your individual playlists.

Note

We really appreciate this new feature. No more hassling with adding music to a pop-up, one at a time, is a great boon.

Additionally, iPhoto 2 associates songs with albums, so you no longer have to either use one song for all your slideshows or laboriously change songs each time you switch to a different slideshow.

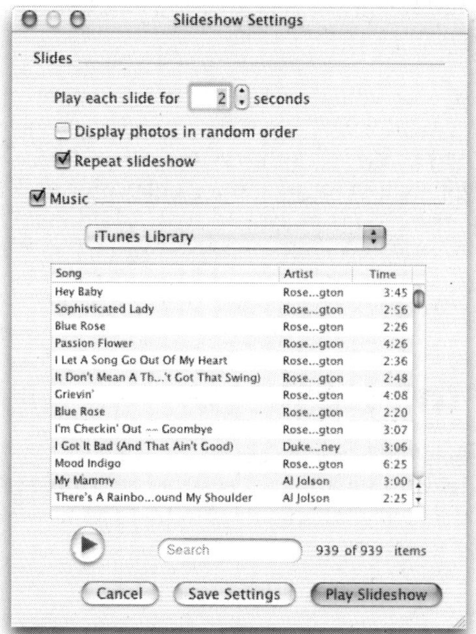

Figure 9-47: The Slideshow Settings dialog gives you access to all the Slideshow preferences and to your iTunes Library.

Controlling your slideshow

Although you don't have enough control to set different timings or transitions for your slides, iPhoto does give you some control over the presentation:

✦ Pressing the Space Bar pauses the slideshow until you press Space again.

  A small Pause or Play indicator appears briefly in the lower-right corner of your screen. Even though the slides don't advance while you're paused, the music plays on.

✦ Pressing the left-arrow (←) or right-arrow (→) keys disables the slideshow's automatic advance timing putting you in manual control. You now advance (→) or move backward (←) at your own pace. Once again, the music plays on.

  If you want to resume automatic advance timing, press Space.

✦ You can temporarily speed up or slow down slide advancement by pressing the up-arrow (↑) or down-arrow (↓) keys, respectively.

  One slide per second seems to be as fast as you can make iPhoto move. Maybe someday, with faster processors and hard disks, iPhoto will be able to advance fast enough to make a slideshow into a smooth animation.

✦ Clicking the mouse or pressing any key other than Space or the arrow keys terminates the slideshow.

If you want the best visual results from your slideshow, make all your photos the same size. Your screen resolution is a great choice, especially if you want the pictures to completely fill the screen and to avoid any letterboxing effect. By making them the same size and orientation, you avoid changing the display area in which the photos appear and this makes the transitions more effective. Additionally, if your photo's aspect ratio is different from your monitor's aspect ratio, you'll experience letterboxing.

Using Your Photos on the Desktop

Apple combined the Desktop and Screen Saver choices of iPhoto 1 into a single Desktop button in iPhoto 2. Integrating with the System Preferences Desktop panel and Screen Effects panel, iPhoto lets you designate pictures to be used as your Desktop picture or in your selected screensaver.

Desktop pictures

Since the beginning of the Mac, users have loved to plaster a picture on their screen to replace the patterned (or solid) background Apple provides as a default. A clever young programmer named Clay Maeckel achieved some measure of fame with his shareware DeskPict utility, making desktop pictures available to the Mac masses. With OS 8, Apple finally made desktop pictures a part of the new Appearance Manager and blessed them as a supported feature of the Mac OS. In Mac OS X, you have a Desktop System Preferences panel where you can set your Desktop picture and you can even specify background pictures for individual Finder windows.

The point of all this is that many people like to wallpaper their desktop with photographs of friends, family, pets, or cool scenery. iPhoto gives you two-click access to setting any photo in your Photo Library as your Desktop picture:

1. **Click to select the photo you want to use.**
2. **In Organize mode, click the Desktop icon in the toolbox.** (Okay, if you weren't already in Organize mode, it's three clicks.)

That's all there is to it. Your selected photo is now your Desktop picture, as shown in Figure 9-48. It's even a good reason to keep your Desktop tidy, hiding applications you aren't using and not leaving files and folders scattered around the Desktop.

You can change to any other photo just by following the above steps, but if you want to go back to a boring desktop pattern, you'll have to access the Desktop System Preferences panel and set it there, as shown in Figure 9-49.

Figure 9-48: This picture of Bob (sans his trademark shades) and family posing in front of an Eskimo totem while on vacation makes a great desktop picture.

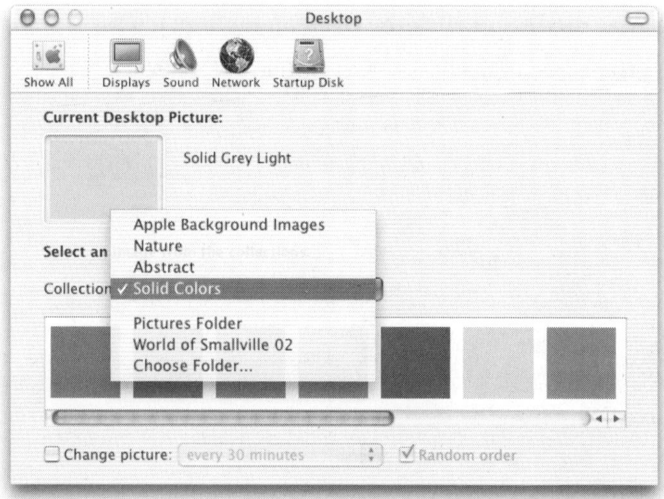

Figure 9-49: Choose a collection from the Collections pop-up menu and then select a dull replacement as your photographic backdrop.

Screen savers

In the old days of black-and-white computer displays (cathode-ray tubes or CRTs), leaving your screen on for long periods would result in a ghost of the static image being burned into the screen. Dennis remembers being able to see the menu bar on his Mac Plus (1986), even when the computer was turned off. In response to this situation, various clever individuals came up with screen savers for the Mac, the most famous of these being the After Dark "Flying Toasters" from Berkeley Systems.

With modern color CRTs and, even more so, with today's LCD screens, burn-in is not a problem. Regardless, screen savers are more popular than ever as they entertain, display messages, or just hide what's on the screen while you're away from the computer.

Recognizing that folks like screen savers, and probably to show off OpenGL technology, Apple includes a Screen Saver with OS X and places your interaction with it in System Preferences' Screen Effects panel.

In addition to the static displays, animated icons, and other variations on traditional screen savers, Apple includes some themed photo slideshows: beach scenes, stellar displays, and forest scenes. But these photo collections don't just transition from one still image to the next, they move slowly toward or away from you before cross-fading to the next image.

iPhoto makes it easy to use your own photos as a screen saver:

1. **Collect the photos you want to use into an album.**
2. **Switch to Organize mode and click the Desktop toolbox icon.**

   iPhoto displays the Screen Effects dialog shown in Figure 9-50.

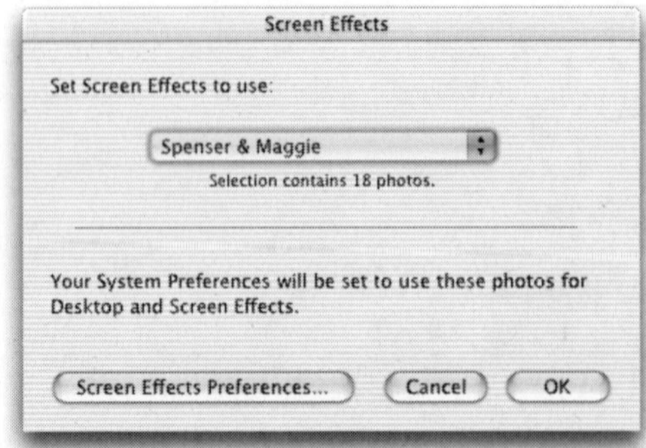

Figure 9-50: Choose your album in the Screen Effects dialog.

3. **If your preferred album isn't already selected in the pop-up menu, choose it.**
4. **Click the Screen Effects Preferences button to display the Screen Effects System Preferences panel, where you can check out your handiwork, as shown in Figure 9-51.**

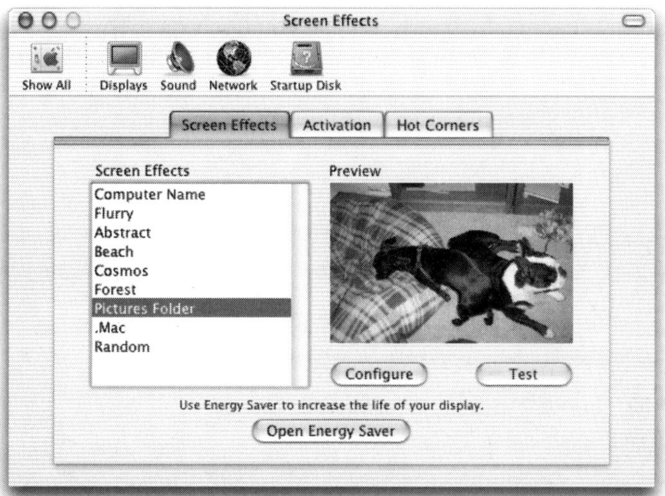

Figure 9-51: Preview your screen saver in System Preferences.

5. **If you like what you've created, Quit from System Preferences and click OK in iPhoto's Screen Effects dialog.** Now, when the OS X screen saver kicks in, you'll see your photos.

Two tips here, actually. First, use landscape photos for your screen saver because the software rotates portrait photos to landscape orientation before it displays them. Second, try to make sure the resolution of your photos is at least that of your monitor to avoid the jaggies and blurry pictures as the screen saver scales them to fill (or more than fill) the screen.

Sharing Your Slideshows via .Mac

If you don't have a .Mac account and don't intend to get one, this option will be of little interest to you. Similarly, if the folks with whom you want to share your slideshow don't run Jaguar (MacOS X 10.2, or later), this material won't be of much use. However, if you have a .Mac account, and your friends show the good judgment to use Macs running Jaguar, you can publish your slideshows to your .Mac account and your friends and family can connect to share your slideshow.

After you create the slideshow as described in “Creating a Slideshow,” earlier in this chapter, just proceed as follows:

1. **Open the album in Organize mode.**
2. **Click the .Mac Slides button in the Organize toolbox.** iPhoto connects to your .Mac account and displays the alert shown in Figure 9-52. The Learn More button is especially handy in case you don’t have this book around to remind you how it works (or if Apple changes something in the process down the road a bit).

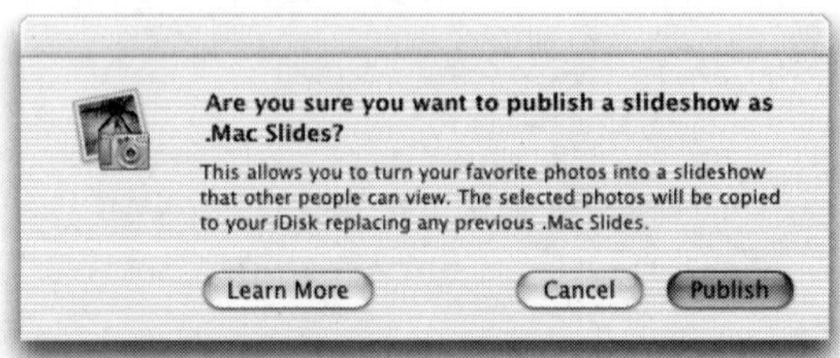

Figure 9-52: iPhoto 2 asks whether you are sure you want to proceed.

3. **Click the Publish button.** iPhoto starts to upload the photos to your iDisk, displaying the progress dialog shown in Figure 9-53.

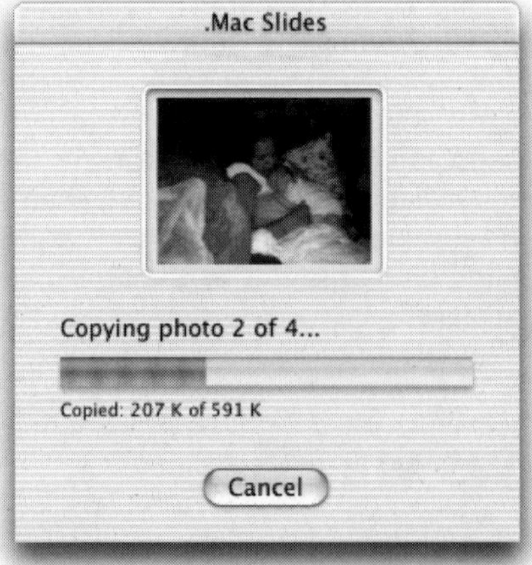

Figure 9-53: You can follow the progress as iPhoto uploads your photos to your iDisk.

4. **When the upload is complete, you'll see the alert shown in Figure 9-54.** The instructions in the dialog make further discussion of this point unnecessary.

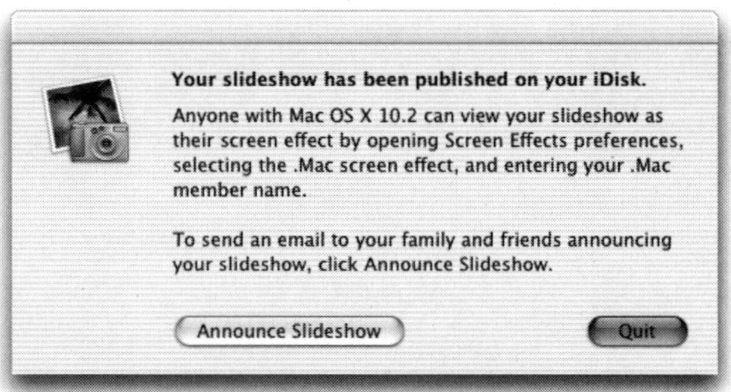

Figure 9-54: You can now send out announcements to your friends or just Quit and return to iPhoto.

Interestingly, iPhoto's developers went to the trouble of removing the Services submenu under the iPhoto menu – a standard by-product of Cocoa-developed applications (like iPhoto). Similarly, the Net Services entry, which appeared with iPhoto 1.1.1's installation, is now gone from the Services menu in general. Those Net Services are the tools iPhoto uses to order prints, order books, and interface with your iDisk (for HomePage and .Mac Slides, for example).

Burning Your Photos to CD or DVD

A glaring hole in iPhoto 1 was the inability to conveniently archive all or part of your Photo Library. As we've noted (more than once), large libraries slow things down a lot — both in terms of how fast your Mac operates and how quickly you can find what you want in an ever-growing photo collection.

iPhoto 2 plugs that hole and does so with panache. Using the Organize toolbox's Burn button, you can burn photos (or albums) to CD, just as you can burn MP3s to create audio CDs in iTunes. By itself, that doesn't mean too much. After all, you could have just used the built-in Disc Burner software or Toast Titanium to burn photos to CD (in fact, El Gato Software created an iPhoto plug-in to do just that with Toast Titanium). Apple added the fine touch, though, that when you burn a photo archive using iPhoto, that archive is also a Photo Library and will, when the disc is reinserted, appear in your album list as shown in Figure 9-55. Note that this is a subordinate library. You can copy items out of it, but not into it (after all, it's on read-only media). iPhoto even gives you a clue that the albums aren't part of your main library by coloring them green rather than blue in the album list.

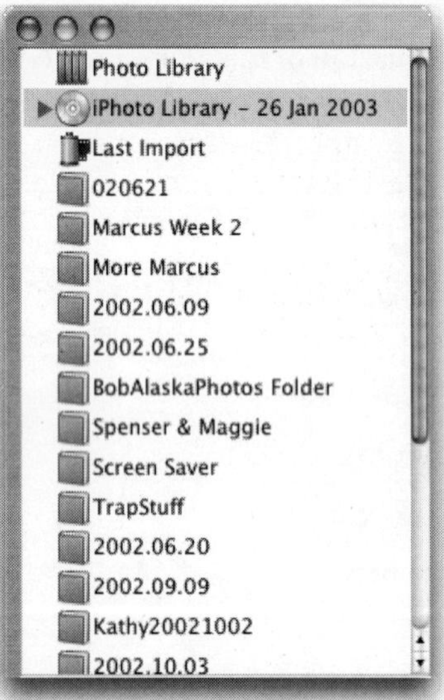

Figure 9-55: Archived photo collections appear in your album list when you reinsert the disc.

Another nice touch is that when you click Burn, iPhoto displays a small graph in the Info area under your Album list showing just how much of the CD (or DVD) will be used.

Archives that you create in this manner are going to have the same disc name, "iPhoto Disc." If you want to tell them apart, we strongly encourage you to label them in some fashion. Fortunately, iPhoto names the libraries in the archives as "iPhoto Library – dd mmm yyyy" where the *dd* is the day of month, *mmm* is the short month name, and *yyyy* is the four-digit year.

Figure 9-56: iPhoto shows you both textually and graphically how much of your disc is going to be used.

Summary

We covered a lot of ground in this chapter. You learned how iPhoto structures and manages your Photo Library. You also saw how to import pictures whether from camera, disk, or Kodak PhotoCD (sometimes called PictureCD) and perform minor editing. Additionally, you learned to create your own albums and use them to create books, slideshows, and screen savers. We covered printing your own photos as well as ordering prints from Kodak and linen-bound books from Apple. You also saw how to send your photos via e-mail and use a photo as your Desktop picture with a single click.

✦ ✦ ✦

Getting Advanced with iPhoto

As we saw in the last chapter, iPhoto provides a good return with minimal effort. But you can still do more with iPhoto, much of which you find by choosing File ⇨ Export (⌘-E) command.

Choosing File ⇨ Export lets you do the following:

- ✦ You can create photo album Web pages on a Web site other than your .Mac site, or if you don't care for the limited selection of .Mac HomePage photo album themes, don't worry — iPhoto makes it simple to export your pictures as Web pages you can tweak to your heart's content.
- ✦ You can make a slideshow for other folks. iPhoto teams up with QuickTime and, voila — you have a QuickTime movie slideshow you can put on the Web, burn to a CD, or e-mail to anyone, anywhere.
- ✦ You can make copies of photos in your Library, for any reason whatsoever, iPhoto exports to most popular graphic file formats.

Do you need more powerful tools than iPhoto offers to edit your photos? That's no problem either. As long as iPhoto knows what program you prefer, double-clicking any thumbnail opens the photo in your preferred program. iPhoto even lets you undo the editing session as well as keep an original copy if you choose to Revert at a later time.

Finally, iPhoto has an extensible plug-in architecture, so third-party developers can provide additional iPhoto functionality such as exporting to Roxio's Toast Titanium or a dedicated Web site creation tool like PhotoToWeb.

✦ ✦ ✦ ✦

In This Chapter

Exporting your photos

Sharing a slideshow

Creating custom Web pages

Using an external program for photo editing

Plugging in to iPhoto

Learning a little more about your photos

✦ ✦ ✦ ✦

Exporting Your Photos

Although iPhoto is the perfect tool for collecting, organizing, and otherwise managing your collection of digital images, it probably isn't the only program you will use with your pictures. After all, you can't easily create a newsletter, a business presentation, a montage, or a million other creations that have pictures in them using iPhoto.

And often when you share images with others, they want you to supply the files in a specific file format. For example, the pictures in this book have to be TIFF files; the files Bob submits to his editor at `www.osxfaq.com` for use online have to be .jpg files, and so on.

Tip

One way to avoid the issue of file formats is to drag the photo from iPhoto to another application's document window and hope it works. AppleWorks, Keynote, Microsoft Word, Microsoft PowerPoint, InDesign, and many other programs offer graphics tools that work on drag-and-dropped images. But we digress.

The File Export tab (shown in Figure 10-1) appears when you choose File ➪ Export (Shift-⌘-E).

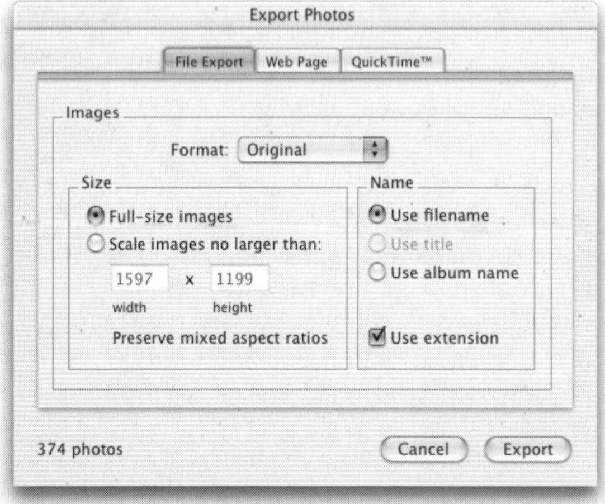

Figure 10-1: Export your photos for use in other programs via Export Photos' File Export tab.

The Format pop-up menu gives you four choices:

✦ **Original:** Tells iPhoto to export it in whatever format you imported: JPEG, PSD, PDF, TIFF, and so on.

✦ **JPG:** Tells iPhoto to convert any files in a different format to JPEG as they're exported.

✦ **TIFF:** Tells iPhoto to convert any non-TIFF files to TIFF as they're exported.

iPhoto saves TIFF files as a multipage TIFF, with the thumbnail saved as the second page. TIFF files tend to be much larger than the other formats because they are not compressed. Even though compression is available in the TIFF standard, many applications, particularly on the Windows platform, do not recognize compressed TIFFs.

✦ **PNG:** Stands for *Portable Network Graphics*, and is one of the three standard graphics formats recognized by standards-compliant Web browsers, at least those released in the past couple of years. PNG actually comes in two variants, PNG-8 and PNG-24. Because PNG-8, like GIF, only supports 256 colors, iPhoto uses PNG-24, which supports millions of colors. Although PNG doesn't compress as much as JPEG, it does compress losslessly, resulting in TIFF-quality images at much smaller file sizes.

The Size box gives you two choices. You can either export the file at its actual size (Full-size images) or you can scale it so that it fits within a rectangle of your definition.

Note

Although iPhoto labels the boxes with a (w) for width and (h) for height, these labels are not accurate. The (w) actually means "long edge" and the (h) means "short edge." For example, if you set the boxes to 640 and 480, respectively, and export a portrait photo that is 960 x 1280, the resulting photo, when opened in another application will be 480 pixels wide and 640 pixels tall.

If your photos and the rectangle you describe do not have the same aspect ratio, iPhoto scales the image so that it completely fits within the rectangle but does not fill it. This effect is called *letterboxing*—you see it on TV whenever a widescreen movie is shown. (The black stripes above and below the picture are the letterbox effect.) That's what the Preserve mixed aspect ratios message means.

The Name box gives you a choice between using the name that the photo started with, usually something cryptic from your camera, such as DVC-0013, the (hopefully less cryptic) title you assigned it in iPhoto, or the name of the album (followed by a dash and sequential numbers). You can even deselect the Use Extension checkbox, and the exported files won't have a file extension at the end of their name.

Caution

We advise against turning off the extension unless you're really sure you don't want to add filename extensions. Without the extension, your non-Mac-using friends will have a much more difficult time viewing the pictures and double-clicking the file will result in OS X telling you that no application is assigned to this file/filetype.

Sharing a Slideshow

When you choose File ➪ Export or click Organize mode's Export button, the Export Images dialog appears and its rightmost tab, shown in Figure 10-2, is QuickTime. Although the tab's name doesn't make it obvious, this tab's raison d'etre is exporting slideshows.

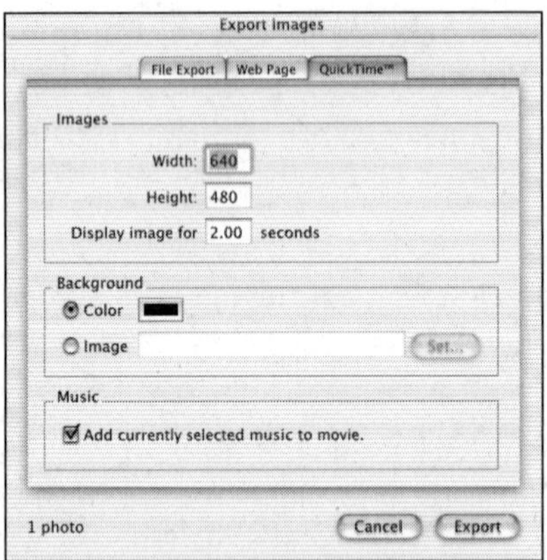

Figure 10-2: As far as iPhoto's Export is concerned, QuickTime and Slideshow are synonymous.

Exporting a slideshow means turning your slideshow into a movie. Apple, not surprisingly, chose their QuickTime technology—available for both Mac and Windows—as the means to this useful end.

Consider adding a title screen and possibly other narrative screens. Because iPhoto happily imports a number of different formats, you can use AppleWorks, Photoshop, GraphicConverter, or other programs to create and save text or other non-photographic images, then import the files into iPhoto.

Before you export a slideshow, make certain any title or narrative screens are in the proper position in the slideshow's album, and check one more time that everything looks just the way you want it to look.

See Chapter 9 for more on importing pictures or creating a slideshow.

Be sure to look at the Export Images dialog's lower-left corner (as shown in Figure 10-2) to see how many photos are going to be in your movie. You find a subtle difference between the way slideshows work inside iPhoto and the way iPhoto exports slideshows, and in this case, if you don't know, it could hurt you. If you select just one photo in an album and then play the slideshow within iPhoto, the selected photo is the starting point for the show and the show includes all the photos in the album. On the other hand, if you select just one photo in an album and export the slideshow, the slideshow includes just that one photo. So, if you want a slideshow to start with a specific photo and include all the photos in the album, reorder the photos to put the selected photo first and then export the entire album as your slideshow.

Click the QuickTime tab and then in the QuickTime's Images box, specify the dimensions for your movie. The default, 640 x 480, is generally considered a great compromise size between compatibility with older systems and maintaining image detail. Those dimensions also make the file small enough for comfortable play from CD (assuming that you don't put too many pictures in the slideshow), particularly on older hardware with 1x or 2x speed CD-ROM drives.

If you want to post the movie on the Web (see Chapter 15), even 640 x 480 may be too large.

Unlike exporting files, Width and Height mean what they say here. Not only will any photos with a different aspect ratio receive a letterbox effect on playback, but portrait orientation photos are reduced in size to fit within the height limit, as shown in Figure 10-3.

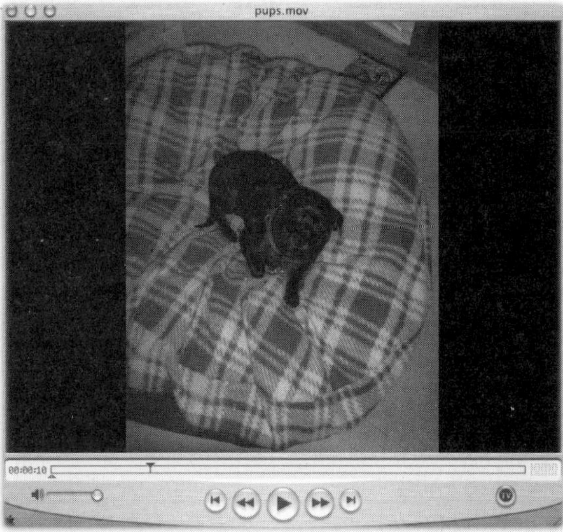

Figure 10-3: Portrait photos really shrink when displayed in a landscape slideshow.

Mixing landscape and portrait photos results in letterboxing, but if you are willing to have all your photos letterboxed with each photo at the same resolution, set the rectangle dimensions as square (such as 640 x 640). Be aware, however, that doing this increases the size of the QuickTime movie.

You can also set the duration of each photo's display in the Images box. By default, iPhoto uses the duration set in your Slideshow Settings (click Organize mode's Slideshow button). Unlike the on-screen slideshow, you can set durations in fractions of a second rather than just full seconds. Unfortunately, you are still limited to a maximum of 60 seconds per slide, but you can set the duration as low as 0.01 seconds. The only reasons we can see for setting a duration that low is if you have thousands of similar pictures and want to perform animation or embed subliminal messages, although there are easier ways to do this. Besides, values less than one second get treated as two seconds when you export your movie.

If, for example, you specify 1.5 seconds, you actually get a 3-second setting. We've reported this as a perceived anomaly to Apple via the iPhoto feedback page on their Web site, but haven't gotten a response.

The Background box controls what you see behind your photos. If all your photos are the same orientation and have the same aspect ratio as the Width and Height set mentioned previously, you're never going to be aware of the background. However, if any letterboxing occurs, the background (which defaults to Black) will fill the margins.

Click the color preview box next to the word Color to display the Colors dialog (Figure 10-4).

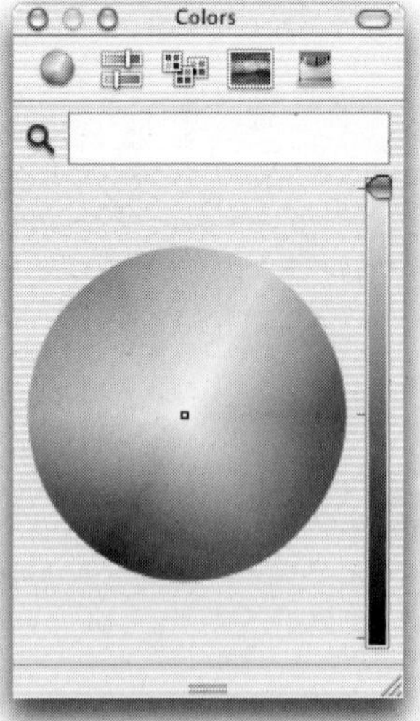

Figure 10-4: You can set your background color using the Colors dialog.

Initially, the Colors dialog displays the color wheel, where you adjust the colors available by raising or lowering the slider on the right and selecting your color by moving the square inside the circle. Besides the Color Wheel button, along the dialog's top are Color Sliders, Color Palettes, Image Palettes, and (in OS X 10.2 or later) Crayon buttons, each of which provides access to a different mode of color selection. Find the color picker that you feel comfortable with (Dennis prefers the color sliders and crayons) and set your background color.

Tip

The Colors dialog might not immediately be visible. If that is the case, move the Export dialog as the Colors dialog is probably hidden behind it.

If you would rather have a picture for your background, such as the swirling Aqua Blue that OS X uses for a default Desktop background, click the Image radio button (Figure 10-2) and navigate to the picture you want to use.

Tip

The OS X galleries of desktop pictures are in /Library/Desktop Pictures.

The Music box (Figure 10-2) has just one checkbox and it determines whether your slideshow has a sound track. If you select it, the song set in your iPhoto Slideshow Settings for this album will be used. You are now ready to export your movie. Click the Export button and iPhoto asks you to name the movie (it adds the .mov extension for you). By default, iPhoto offers to save the movie to your Movies folder, but you can choose any location. Depending on the number of pictures, their size, and the speed of your Mac, the Export process could take a while, so iPhoto displays a progress bar while rendering and saving your movie.

And that's all. Now double-click the movie to view it in QuickTime Player.

Creating Custom Web Pages

Don't get us wrong, we think that using iPhoto's or Apple's .Mac HomePage software, as described in Chapter 9, is a great way to post attractive and functional photo albums. But, you are limited to the designs that HomePage provides and the structure it imposes. Using HomePage tools to build and maintain a comprehensive Web site, of which your photo albums are just one part, is difficult — not impossible just difficult. Additionally, if you have Web space with your ISP, school, or business that you're trying to use, HomePage-built pages won't do you much good, because their functionality is totally dependent upon the services .Mac provides. Finally, MacOS X comes with the Apache Web-serving software included, letting you host Web pages directly from your Sites folder (in your Home directory) — not a bad solution for an intranet Web page or a home network.

Hosting a Web site on your Mac could violate your service agreement with your ISP. Check to see what is permissible before you start Web sharing with the outside world off your Mac.

iPhoto caters to the do-it-yourselfer with the (you guessed it) Export Images dialog's Web Page tab. As with most options, you gain some things and you lose some things. The main things you lose are the nice themes and some of the fancy designs. What you gain are flexibility of design and control over your page's presentation. The Export Images Web Page tab is shown in Figure 10-5.

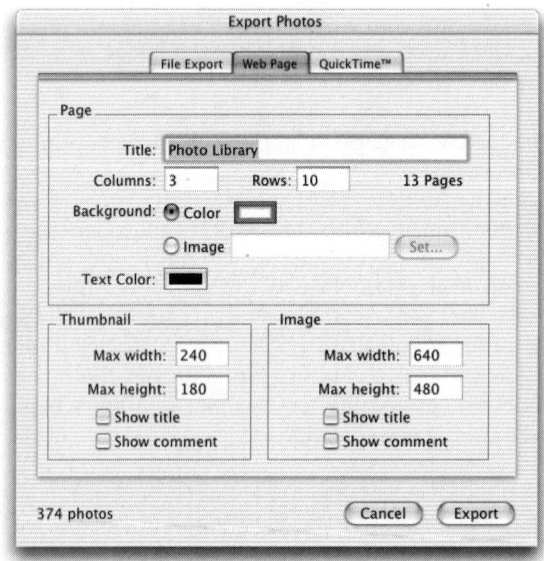

Figure 10-5: Control your photo album's presentation with the Web Page tab.

As you can see, the Web Page tab contains three sections, as follows:

✦ **Page box:** Manages the settings that describe your page as an entity.

  • **Title field:** Lets you specify the title that appears in the browser window's title bar and, centered in large bold letters, at the top of your page.

  • **Columns and Rows fields:** Here, you specify how many thumbnails you want to have in each row on your page and how many rows before iPhoto generates a second, linked page. iPhoto tells you, to the right of the text boxes, how many pages your configuration will create.

Limiting the number of images on a page, both to minimize scrolling by your page's visitors and to decrease the time needed for them to load a page into their browser, is a good idea. Even at only 12KB each, 30 to 40 thumbnails can take a while to download on a dial-up connection. iPhoto's default setting displays ten rows of three thumbnails, but we feel that is too many, especially if your visitors are likely to be dial-up users or are using older computers (or WebTV) where they scroll a lot and where the page takes a long time to load. Three rows of two thumbnails fit in most browser windows without any scrolling. More rows involve vertical scrolling, which seems to annoy visitors less than horizontal scrolling.

- **Background options:** This is where you specify a background color or image for your Web page. The default is a solid white background. You have two options.

  Color option: Clicking in the color preview box next to this option presents the Cocoa Colors dialog, where you can use one of the Cocoa color pickers to specify your background color, as described in the "Sharing a Slideshow" section earlier in this chapter.

  Image option: Clicking this radio button enables the Set button. Click it to present an Open dialog you can navigate to find the background picture you want to use. The image tiles, as shown in Figure 10-6, to fill the window as you scroll.

- **Text Color preview box:** New iPhoto 2, this button works like the Background Color preview box, but you use it to specify the color of your text (you might want light colors against a dark background).

✦ **Thumbnail box:** This is where you specify the maximum dimensions for the thumbnails your page will display.

Once again, the words "Width" and "Height" are misleading. iPhoto exchanges their meanings for portrait orientation photos.

Also new in iPhoto 2 are the Show title and Show comment checkboxes, which do exactly as the names imply. Titles and comments display centered below the thumbnails.

✦ **Image box:** Here, you specify the maximum dimensions on your photos. These photos are what your page's visitors see when they click on one of the thumbnails. Select the Show title checkbox if you want to display the photo's title left-justified beneath each photo. Select Show comment if you want anything you placed in the comments field to display beneath your pictures, also left-justified.

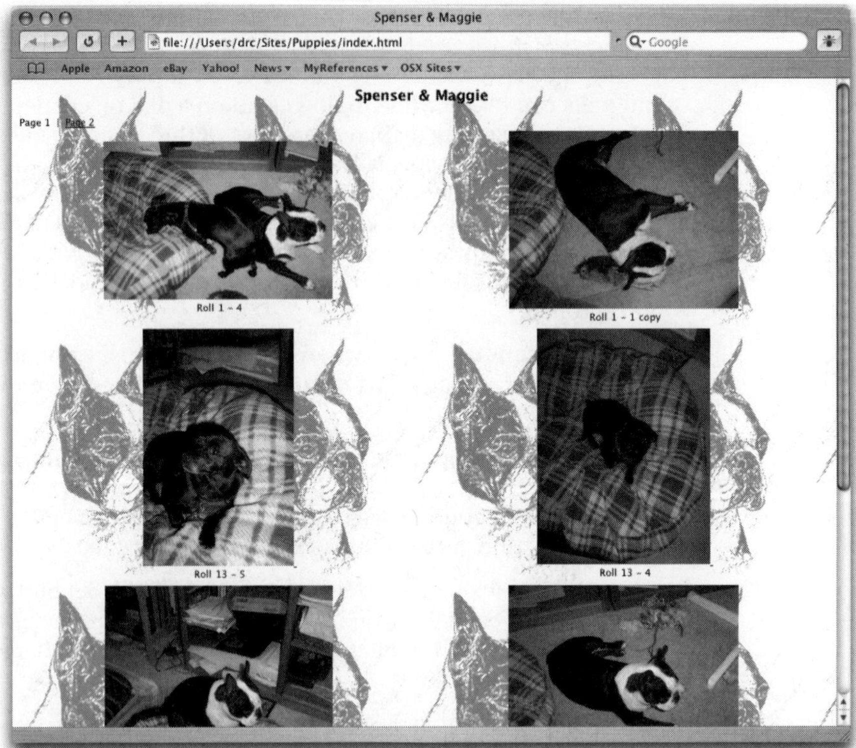

Figure 10-6: A small, faint GIF image can be nice background wallpaper for your photo album pages.

Unless you have selected a photo or group of photos, iPhoto assumes that you want to export the current album (or your entire Photo Library). Unlike Web pages created with the HomePage tools, exported Web pages do not limit the number of photos you can use. iPhoto generates another page each time the grid you specified in the Rows and Columns fields fills up.

When you have everything the way you want it, click the Export Photos dialog's Export button. iPhoto presents a sheet asking where you want to place the pages. By default, iPhoto suggests your Home folder's Sites folder. Unless you want to replace the contents of the Sites folder or whatever folder is currently displayed, we recommend that you click the New Folder button and name a new repository (which we'll refer to as *pagename* in the following discussion). Click OK, and iPhoto starts creating your Web pages.

After iPhoto is finished, you can check out what you and iPhoto created. In the Finder, navigate to the folder where you created your Web page and you should find the following items:

✦ A folder named *pagename*-Images, which contains each of your photos, scaled as you specified in the Image area and numbered starting from zero (0). If you specified a background image in the Page area, it will be numbered 99999 and will be converted to a JPEG.

✦ A file,*pagename*.html, which is the first page of your photo album.

✦ Files named Page1.html, Page2.html, and so on. These are the additional pages iPhoto generates each time your thumbnail array fills up. The file, Page1.html, corresponds to the Page 2 link on your Web pages. Page2.html corresponds to Page 3, and so forth. Just think of the *pagename*.html file as Page0.html, if that makes this a little easier to follow.

✦ A folder named *pagename*-Pages, which contains the HTML files a browser will load when your visitor clicks on a thumbnail. These files are named Image0.html, Image1.html, and so forth, corresponding to the photos in the Images folder.

✦ A folder named *pagename*-Thumbnails, which contains numbered JPEG files: 0.jpg, 1.jpg, 2.jpg, and so on, corresponding to the photos in the Images folder. The various Page.html files display these thumbnails.

Tip

You can now preview your work by opening the index.html file with your browser.

Now, all you have to do is upload them to your Web server (even the Sites folder on your iDisk), which probably involves using an FTP client like Interarchy or Fetch. Because each Web server is a bit different, get the particulars for your situation from your ISP. Alternatively, if you have a relatively fast, always-on Internet connection, such as a cable modem or DSL, you could use OS X's built-in Web Sharing, as follows:

1. **Make certain that you have the pages in your Sites folder hierarchy.**
2. **Open System Preferences and select the Sharing Preferences pane.**
3. **Turn on Web Sharing by clicking its Start button.**

   Write down the IP address that appears under Network Identity. This is the first part of the URL people need to enter in order to access your Web pages.
4. **Assuming that the IP address in Step 3 was 10.10.10.1, that the pages are in a folder named MyPages, and that your short login ID is drc (that's Dennis's), you can let folks know that your new pages are available at** `http://10.10.10.1/~drc/MyPages/`. Make sure that they don't forget that last `/`.

Caution

Again, we're going to suggest that you check your Terms of Service agreement with your ISP to determine whether hosting a Web site on your computer is in violation of that agreement. If traffic to your pages is very light, it's quite possible that your ISP may never actually become aware of your Web site; however, if you get a fair amount of activity (and loading in a lot of pictures can easily qualify), you might find yourself being warned by your ISP or even having your service cut off.

A (Very) Brief Overview of iPhoto's HTML

We're not going to teach you how to create pages from scratch or do anything fancy with Java or JavaScript. What we are going to do is show you the HTML of a typical iPhoto-generated Web page and what the various *tags* (HTML directives) and *attributes* (tag options) mean.

With a plain text editor such as BBEdit or TextEdit (if you turn off Rich Text) you can edit these files, changing the appearance, or adding functionality. Dennis uses BBEdit (`www.barebones.com`), which comes with excellent HTML reference material. If you're a more visual sort, you can load the page into a graphical page editor, such as Freeway (`www.softpress.com`) or WebDesign (`www.ragesw.com`) to make your changes. If you check Version Tracker for HTML editors, you'll find a large number available, many of them freeware or shareware. If you own Microsoft Word X, you can even do your page editing with it if you click the Save only display information radio button in Word's Save As Web Page dialog (also with AppleWorks, but its HTML support isn't nearly as complete).

The following HTML was generated by iPhoto:

```
<!DOCTYPE HTML PUBLIC "-//W3C//DTD HTML 4.01 Transitional//EN">
<html>
 <head>
  <meta http-equiv="Content-Type" content="text/html;
charset=utf-8">
  <title>
  Spenser &amp; Maggie
  </title>
 </head>
  <body background="Images/99999.jpg">
  <h2 align="center">
  Spenser &amp; Maggie
  </h2>
  <a href="SpenserMaggie.html">
  Page 1
  </a>
   | 
  Page 2
  <table cellspacing="2" width="100%" cellpadding="2">
   <tr>
    <td align="center" width="50%">
     <a href=" SpenserMaggie -Pages/Image8.html">
      <img src=" SpenserMaggie -Thumbnails/8.jpg" alt="Spenser"
width="240" height="160">
     </a>
     <br>Spenser
    </td>
```

```
      <td align="center" width="50%">
       <a href=" SpenserMaggie -Pages/Image9.html">
        <img src=" SpenserMaggie -Thumbnails/9.jpg" alt="Twosome"
 width="239" height="180">
       </a>
       <br>Twosome
      </td>
     </tr>
    </table>
   </body>
  </html>
```

HTML tags are enclosed in angle brackets (< and >) and the values assigned to attributes are enclosed in double quotes.

Most tags consist of a start tag and an end tag. The end tag is a slash (/) followed by the start tag's name. Some tags, those that don't apply to a block of data, such as insert a horizontal line (`<hr>`), insert a line break (`<br>`), or display this picture (`<img>`), don't take an end tag.

The first line is a comment, specifying what HTML revision is being used for the document, in this case 4.01. The next line, `<html>`, signifies the beginning of the HTML, describing the page a browser should render. The lines between `<head>` and `</head>` (start and end of header information), include the title for the page and any metainformation that might be of interest to browsers or search engines.

The actual page contents start with the `<body>` line and end with the `</body>` line. The body line tells the browser to find a background image named `99999.jpg` in the Images subdirectory of the directory holding the page's HTML file.

The page's heading, Spenser & Maggie, will center horizontally and display in the second largest heading style. Certain characters, such as the ampersand, have special meaning in HTML and must be described with a name, in this case `&`.

The next tag, called an *anchor* tag, tells the browser that Page 1 is a link and that, when clicked, the file `SpenserMaggie.html` should be loaded.

At this point, iPhoto generated an HTML table, each cell of which contains a thumbnail. The `cellspacing="2"` attribute tells the browser to keep a 2-pixel border around each cell and `cellpadding="2"` says to keep a 2-pixel margin between the cell's border and the cell's contents. The `width="100%"` attribute tells the browser to fill the window horizontally with the table.

The `<tr>` tag tells the browser that a new row is starting. The table datum (`<td>`) or cell tag tells the browser that the enclosed information should be placed in a table cell and that it should be centered, with the cell's width being 50 percent of the table's width. The anchor tag surrounding the image (`img`) tag tells the browser that the thumbnail specified in the `img` tag is a hyperlink and which page to load when the link is clicked.

iPhoto's HTML is straightforward, and the pages it generates aren't very fancy. If you're accustomed to editing HTML, you can add all sorts of bells and whistles to the pages iPhoto generates. Fortunately, iPhoto is extensible via plug-ins, as we discuss later in this chapter (see the "Plugging in to iPhoto" section), a very nice, free plug-in named BetterHTMLExport (`www.droolingcat.com`) that adds a Better Web Page tab to the Export Images dialog for those of you who want something a little nicer but don't want to soil your hands actually editing the HTML.

Using an External Program for Photo Editing

iPhoto's editing tools are good, but far from extensive. You can crop, adjust brightness and contrast, convert a color picture to black-and-white, retouch blemishes and scratches, enhance too-light or too-dark photos, and eliminate red-eye. After that, your editing toolbox is empty.

A wide variety of image-editing applications are available for you to use. For example, many desktop Macs come with licenses for Lemke Software's shareware GraphicConverter (`www.lemkesoft.com`) and Caffeine Software's free PixelNHance (`www.caffeinesoft.com`). Although Dennis considers GraphicConverter the best $35 he ever spent on software, the royal flush of photo-editing programs is Adobe's Photoshop (Version 7 is OS X-native), at almost 20 times the price of GraphicConverter. Photoshop Elements 2.0, at a list price of $99 is another excellent bargain, giving you all but the very high-end Photoshop features in an affordable package. Another very powerful and interesting image editor is TIFFany3, also from Caffeine Software.

Unfortunately, because they had nice products, Caffeine Software went out of business (March 2003) while we were writing this edition. If you have PixelNHance or TIFFany, you have a handy tool, but it is unlikely to ever be updated.

As you learned in Chapter 8, you can tell iPhoto to send images to another application when you double-click the thumbnail. You can also Control-click a photo and choose Edit in *application-name*, once you've designated an external editing application in your preferences. Using Photoshop or another external editor enables you to perform such tasks as eliminating shadows, adding distortions, correcting color, sharpening blurry edges (we told you to use a tripod), and adding objects to your image. In short, you can do (almost) all the cool things you see people do with computer-editing software on TV shows (such as *24*, *The Agency,* and so forth) and in the movies (although not as easily, nor nearly as quickly, as these fictional characters do it).

If you're asking, "Why can't I just drag the thumbnail to the application icon of any editor I want?" the answer is, "You can, but then iPhoto won't know about the changes, won't update the thumbnail and, if you hadn't edited it previously in iPhoto, you won't be able to Revert to Original."

One of the nicest things about designating an external program as your editor for double-clicked photos is that you still have Edit mode for when iPhoto's tools suffice. Additionally, if you press Option while double-clicking, iPhoto reverses the precedence and uses its own editing tools. And, again, the contextual menu is your friend — you can decide on a case-by-case basis just which method you want to use by Control-clicking and making a choice.

Plugging in to iPhoto

iPhoto, like iTunes, iMovie, and iDVD, provides a lot of functionality in a simple, straightforward interface. But Apple realizes that a significant minority of their users is going to want more, or slightly different, functionality than the basic program provides. Back in 1986, Apple introduced HyperCard. Realizing that people were going to want to do more with it than was possible out of the box, the XCMD interface was included so that users could extend HyperCard's power and flexibility. The plug-ins you see for today's Web browsers, which enable you to view PDF files and Flash animations or watch QuickTime movies on a Web page, perform the same function. Apple provides a similar plug-in architecture for iPhoto.

Think of iPhoto as the software equivalent of an iMac. Other than hooking up a printer (or, obviously, temporarily connecting their digital camera), most people rarely add anything to their iMac's hardware configuration. However, USB and FireWire ports are present so that you can plug in scanners, floppy disk drives, Zip drives, and a myriad of other devices. Any one of these would make the iMac larger and more expensive if they were part of the standard package. Most people never add anything to their basic iPhoto configuration, but if you want to do so, the capability is present via the plug-in architecture.

Discovering iPhoto plug-ins

iPhoto is still relatively new and, because it does so much so well, only a few plug-ins have appeared. Here are some that we like a lot:

✦ **BetterHTMLExport:** ($20 shareware from `www.droolingcat.com`) significantly outshines iPhoto's basic Web Page export, adding the following features:

  - Optional links on each thumbnail and image page so that you can easily integrate your photo album into a larger Web site
  - The option of exporting the original image rather than a scaled-down JPEG

- Navigation link placement placed under your control rather than fixed to the top-left of each thumbnail page
- The templates mechanism, which allows you to design an overall "look" for your pages (A few examples are included with the software.)

✦ **iPhoto Toast Export Plug-in** (`www.elgato.com`) adds something that we were amazed to see missing from the original iPhoto — the ability to burn CDs directly from the application, just as you can burn CDs from iTunes.

Admittedly, this plug-in requires Toast Titanium, but as we frequently mention, Roxio's Toast Titanium is one piece of software we both think that you should own if you're planning to burn many discs.

Although the plug-in is less necessary now, with archive burning built into iPhoto 2, this plug-in still has its place. For one thing, Toast lets you write *sessions* (separate volumes) on your CDs, so you can continue adding to the CD at a later time.

✦ **iPhoto to OmniGraffle Album Export** (`www.omnigroup.com`) lets you export photos directly from iPhoto into OmniGraffle albums. OmniGraffle is an excellent diagramming tool, great for laying out organization charts, family trees, and timelines.

Adding and removing plug-ins

iPhoto, like most Mac OS X applications, is really a folder masquerading as a single application file. If you Control-click the iPhoto icon (in the Finder), one of the contextual menu options is Show Package Contents. Choosing this opens the disguised folder in a new Finder window, and you can now burrow down to see all the folders and files that make up your application. One of the folders in iPhoto's Contents folder is named PlugIns and is the repository for both the plug-ins that came with iPhoto and any you add.

Obviously, adding plug-ins by digging into the application package is somewhat less than elegant and not what one expects from Apple. Rest assured, Apple has provided an easier way to add (and remove) plug-ins:

1. **With iPhoto not running, select the iPhoto icon in the Finder and choose File ⇨ Get Info (⌘-I).** Alternatively, you can Control-click the iPhoto icon and choose Get Info from the contextual menu.
2. **In the iPhoto Info window, choose the Plug-in panel as shown in Figure 10-7.** The currently installed plug-ins appear. The default installation of plug-ins is shown in Figure 10-8.

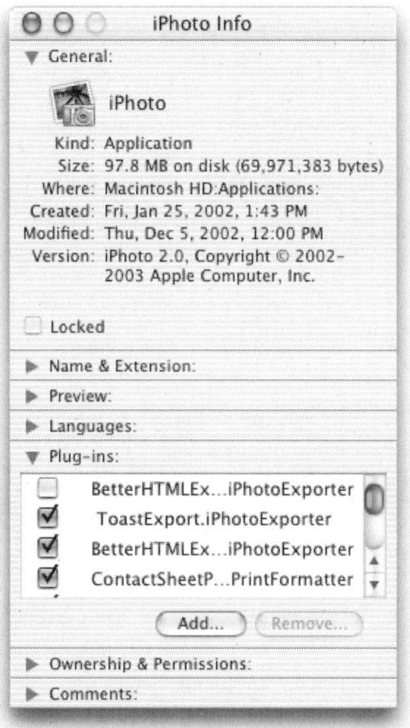

Figure 10-7: Select the Get Info dialog's Plug-ins panel.

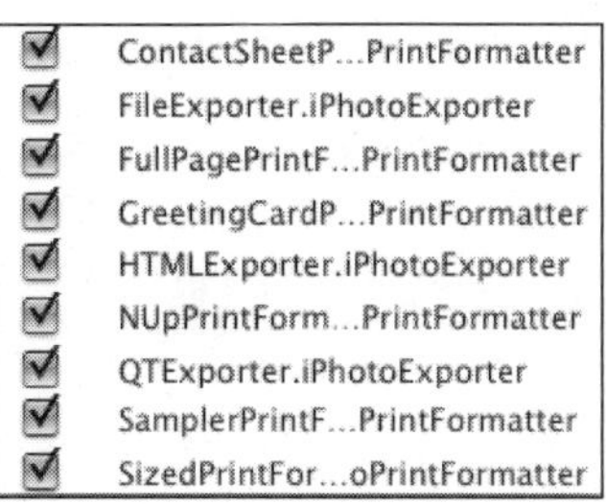

Figure 10-8: iPhoto's preinstalled plug-ins collection

3. **Click the Add button.** An Open-style dialog named Add appears.
4. **Navigate to the folder for the plug-in you want to install, as shown in Figure 10-9 and click Choose.** Your plug-in is now installed, as shown in Figure 10-10.

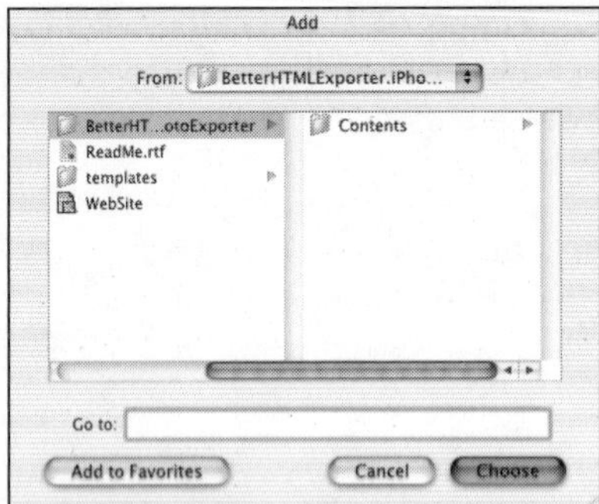

Figure 10-9: Find the plug-in you want installed.

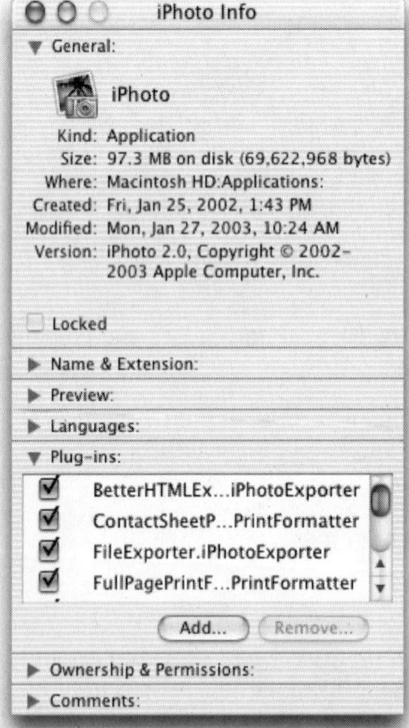

Figure 10-10: The newly installed plug-in has joined the club.

Note: Sometimes, the plug-in doesn't show up right away in the list and you have to close the plug-ins panel and reopen it. Hopefully, this bug will be fixed by the time you read this material. This bug has been around for quite a while, though, so you can't count on it.

The next time you choose File ➪ Export (Shift-⌘-E), you'll see your plug-in as yet another tab in the Export Photos dialog, as shown in Figure 10-11.

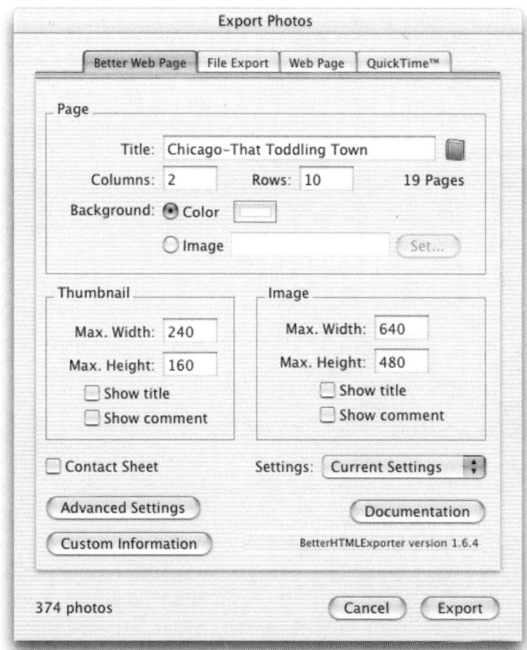

Figure 10-11: The new plug-in tab shows up in the Export Photos dialog.

We used BetterHTMLExport as our example. At first glance, you might not notice much difference between the Web Page tab that iPhoto provides and the Better Web Page tab. The Better Web Page tab sports an Advanced Settings button, a Current Settings pop-up list, a Contact Sheet checkbox, and a Custom Information button (also a Documentation button). About the only thing missing at the time we're writing this is the Text Color setting that was added in iPhoto 2. Clicking the Advanced Settings button exposes a lot of new functionality, as shown in Figure 10-12.

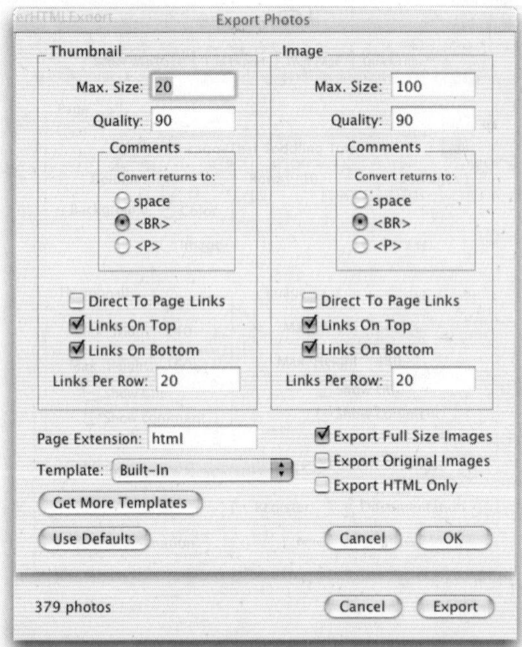

Figure 10-12: The Better Web Page's Advanced Settings sheet gives you a lot of options.

Removing a plug-in is just as easy. Select it in the list and click the Remove button. MacOS X warns you to make sure that you want to remove the plug-in, because if you remove something other than an added plug-in, you can disable basic application functionality. You can also disable a plug-in by clearing the checkbox next to its name. This eliminates its tab in iPhoto, but leaves it installed if you might want to use it at a later date.

Because we expect that more plug-ins will appear as iPhoto gains wider usage, the Export Photos dialog is going to get really crowded. Disabling a few plug-ins that you use only occasionally, without having to remove and later reinstall them, is a great way to simplify the row of tabs you'll see in the Export Photos dialog.

Getting More Photo Info

iPhoto's Info pane gives you a fair amount of basic information concerning your photographs. However, it doesn't delve into the deeper details available through EXIF information. Some cameras have more information than others, including your shutter speed, aperture settings, and focal length. Figure 10-13 gives you an example of what you can find on the Photo Info dialog's Exposure tab. To access the tab, choose File ➪ Show Photo Info, ⌘-I.

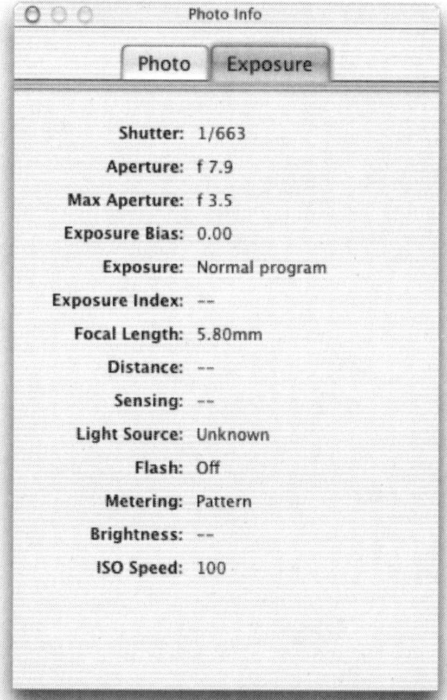

Figure 10-13: The exposure settings from Bob's Nikon E775, used to take the photo in the desktop picture in Figure 9-48.

The more you know about photography and the more information your camera provides, the more useful this information can be. However, all that is beyond the scope of this book (which is the iLife applications).

Summary

In this chapter, you saw how to export your files, slideshows, and Web pages. You also learned some advantages of using a dedicated graphics-editing program with iPhoto. Finally, you learned how to extend iPhoto's capabilities with plug-ins and reviewed a few of the currently available plug-ins.

✦ ✦ ✦

More iPhoto Tips, Tricks, and Techniques

♦ ♦ ♦ ♦

In This Chapter

Inside an iPhoto Library

Managing your iPhoto Library

Taking better pictures

AppleScripting iPhoto

♦ ♦ ♦ ♦

We used up most of our iPhoto keyboard shortcut tips in the last two chapters, but that's okay. The really good iPhoto tips involve planning, preparation, and organization. In fact, some of them don't even require iPhoto — they revolve around shooting the best shots you can, which, in turn, gives you something really good to work with in iPhoto.

In addition to these basic tips on taking snapshots, in this chapter we delve into how iPhoto stores and organizes your collection of digital images.

Inside an iPhoto Library

At heart, iPhoto is a database for pictures, with special tools for displaying, editing, printing, and sharing its contents. In fact, it is a relational database in which album files contain pointers into the *central store* (main database), thus eliminating redundant copies of those wonderful snapshots you want included in multiple albums. Further, the central store is divided into multiple files in nested folders, with the actual pictures stored four levels deep.

Figure 11-1 shows one of Dennis's iPhoto databases, in a Finder list view. You can see that the actual pictures are in a numbered folder, within another numbered folder, inside yet another numbered folder at the iPhoto Library folder's top level. This top-level numbered folder is the year. Within a year folder are numbered folders corresponding to months. Inside those are numbered folders for the days of the month, where you will find your pictures along with a few more folders.

iPhoto uses the creation date for pictures you add from the Finder and the camera-supplied date data to distribute camera-imported pictures into the various folders.

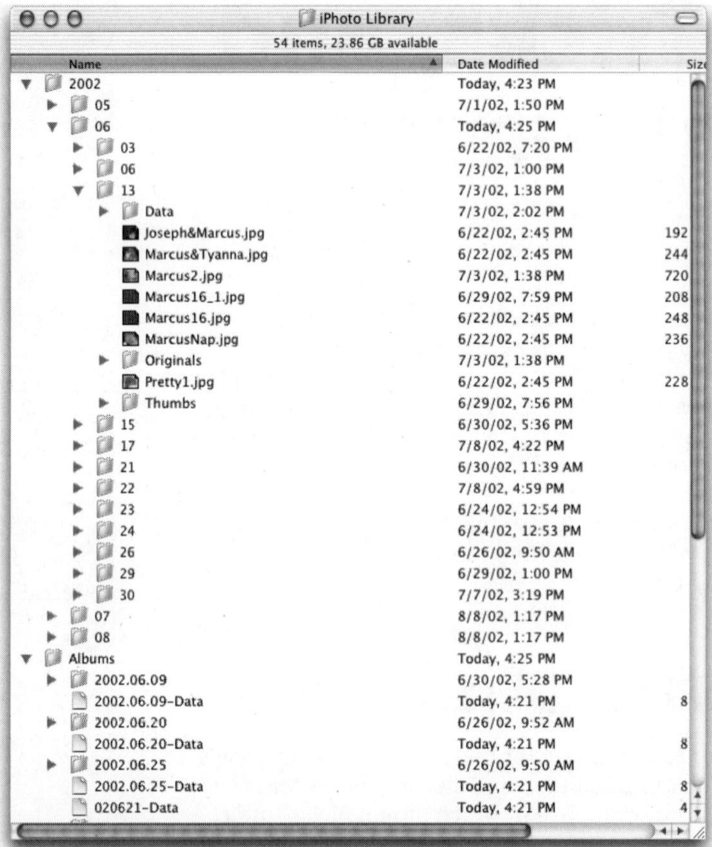

Figure 11-1: iPhoto organizes your photos by year, month, and day.

Do not, under any circumstances, move, rename, or otherwise mess with the files and organization in your iPhoto Library hierarchy. We're presenting this information for two reasons: So you can write AppleScripts that will copy pictures and albums into other applications; and so that you will have an understanding of what iPhoto is doing behind the scenes—knowledge is power. If you do abuse that power, don't hold us responsible—you have been warned!

Nestled in a day-of-month folder with your pictures are a few folders, as follows:

✦ **Thumbs:** Contains thumbnail images of your various pictures, but you won't recognize them from their names. All you'll see for names are a number (followed by a .jpg extension if you've set your Finder preferences to show filename extensions).

When iPhoto first appeared, you couldn't name your pictures. iPhoto assigned them sequential numbers and that was that. Internally, iPhoto still assigns the pictures numbers and that's how it deals with them, the names are just for your benefit.

✦ **Data:** iPhoto stores the information about what you've named the photos as well as other attributes, such as whether the photo has been rotated, edited, and so forth.

✦ **Originals:** May or may not be present. If you have edited any of the photos in this day's folder, you'll see an Originals folder, and it will contain the (surprise) original, pre-editing, image. This is how iPhoto lets you revert to the original if you don't like the editing you've done, by keeping a spare copy available. The downside is the extra disk space consumed keeping that copy around.

Located with your year folders at the top of your iPhoto Library hierarchy is the Albums folder. Nestled snugly within the Albums folder you find more folders, each bearing the name of one of your iPhoto albums and accompanied by a data file of the same name with `-data` appended. The folders contain aliases to each of the album's photos, and the data files tell iPhoto how they're arranged and other album-specific information, such as any book theme settings or slideshow settings.

Also at the iPhoto Library's top-level are three more files: Dir.data, Library.data, and Library.cache that iPhoto uses to manage your photo collection and load your Library.

Managing Your iPhoto Library

You've undoubtedly noticed by now that for all of iPhoto's wonderful features and ease-of-use, unfortunately, speedy performance is not among its attributes. As your iPhoto Library grows, iPhoto gets even slower. Lots of memory, a fast hard disk, and a speedy processor all help but only to a point. The main thing you can do to minimize your wait time is to cull photos from your Library when you're done with them. You can back them off to Zip or CD and eliminate them from the Library.

Chapter 12 lists some software (and hardware) you can use to help keep your Library's size under control. If you don't want to go that route, you should certainly take advantage of iPhoto's Burn capability to archive material. After burning material to an archive, you can remove it from your Library to free up the space—you can always insert the CD or DVD at a later time, and iPhoto will mount it as a subordinate library.

Unless you have a superb memory, your Library will rapidly grow to the point where you'll have trouble remembering just where that special photograph is located. As we note in Chapter 9, naming and adding comments to your photos when you import them can save you scads of time later on. Although Keywords are convenient, all they do is categorize your photos. By all means, apply keywords to your photos if you want, but remember that the real strength of iPhoto's searching comes from using the Search textbox at the bottom of the Keywords (Edit ➪ Keywords, ⌘-K) palette. Not only does it find keywords, it also finds matches on the title or any text in the Comments fields.

Taking Better Pictures

This topic could easily fill a book of its own, and it has, many times over. We even recommend a few good books for your consideration in Chapter 12.

We're not going to challenge those tomes, but we are going to cover a few basics that can get you off on the right foot (or the left, if you're a southpaw).

Photo composition

Unless you're just clicking the button, most photos you take have a subject. That subject is usually surrounded with extraneous items, called the background. How you position your subject relative to the background and how you take advantage of the background to focus attention on your subject is part of the art of composition.

Split things into thirds

Contrary to what you might think, the exact center of a picture is seldom the right place for your subject. Think of your picture as a tic-tac-toe board, divided into thirds both horizontally and vertically. When you have, for example, a portrait shot, try to position your subject's eye line on the line separating the upper and middle thirds. As you can see in Figures 11-2 and 11-3, positioning the subject's face in a landscape shot at the intersection points (Figure 11-2) is very effective in making their face the eye-catcher. Alternatively (Figure 11-3), positioning the subject in the exact center of the frame reduces the impact and allows background items to capture your viewers' attention.

Figure 11-2: Dividing lines and intersection points provide good positioning for your subjects.

Figure 11-3: Unless it's a close-up, your subject can disappear if centered in the frame.

Don't let the background overwhelm your subject

Having a lot of objects in your photograph is likely to cause your subject to fade into the background. Don't distract your viewer with nonessentials.

Some items to avoid (besides somebody holding up two fingers behind your subject's head) are poles, wires, signs and signposts, tree trunks, and fence lines. We all have a tendency toward tunnel vision when framing a shot in our viewfinder. Making an effort to check the edges and corners for these distractions is a good habit to acquire. These objects are more distracting the closer that they are to your subject. Figure 11-4 is a good example of bad positioning because the base of the fan on the left distracts the viewer's eye from the subject.

Figure 11-4: The base of that fan distracts the viewer's eye.

Ideally, your background should be composed of soft tones and indistinct shapes. If your background is subtle, your subject stands out.

How close can you get?

Until the edges of the picture start lopping off parts of your subject, you can probably get closer and take a better picture. Figure 11-5 shows a close-up on the left and a more distant shot on the right, showing clearly how much more compelling a close-up is.

Note

Getting up close has a beneficial side effect. Because you have less wasted background to crop out, you have a higher effective resolution and you'll get better prints when you print them, send them off to Kodak, or include them in your coffee-table book.

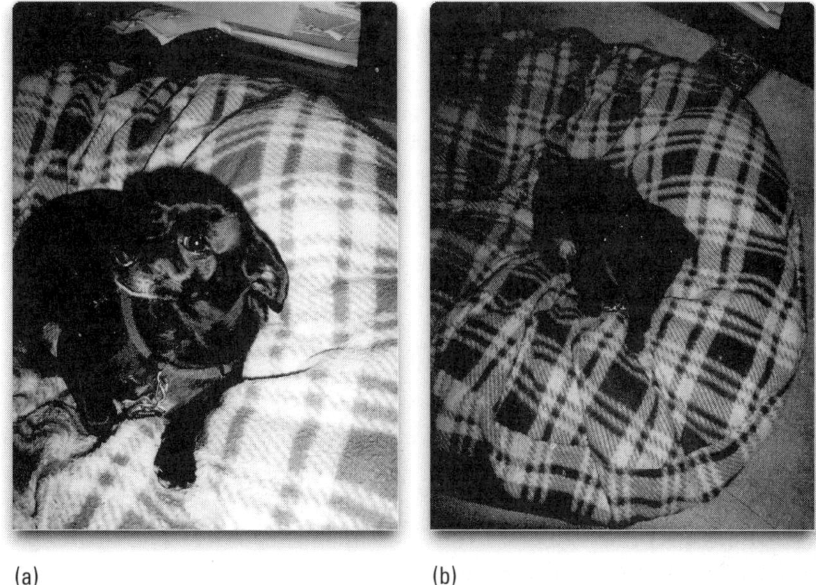

(a) (b)

Figure 11-5: A close-up of Maggie (a); a less effective shot taken from a few feet further away (b).

Look at things another way

The angle at which you take your photos can have tremendous impact. If you were to take a photo of Shaquille O'Neal from ground level, you'd be emphasizing his height in a way that just wouldn't come across if you stood on a chair to shoot him at eye-level.

Conversely, if you're trying to give a clear picture of a football play, you're well-advised to shoot it from an elevated position, say a press box. Those "blimp" shots you see during Bowl Game telecasts have impact for just this reason.

Take pictures of a stationary subject from as many perspectives as possible. We bet that the results surprise you and that your favorites will come from nontraditional angles.

Make use of your camera's capabilities

If you own something a little better than a simple point-and-shoot digital camera, you could well have the tools to take stop-action shots and create some other special effects that we'll describe in the next few paragraphs.

Freeze that shot

The secret to getting a good stop-action photo is being able to control your shutter speed and your lens aperture. The shutter has to open and close very quickly to freeze the action. However, if the shutter isn't open for very long, less light gets in and you're likely to end up with a dark picture. That's why you want the aperture larger than normal — to get the same amount of light in that you would with a slower shutter speed.

How you achieve this feat, assuming that your camera even supports it, varies from camera to camera. Some call it *shutter priority mode*, others call it *time value,* and you can find them on a switch or dial. With others, you have to hunt through the camera's menu system to find your feature.

In any case, turn on shutter priority mode and set your shutter speed to a very short time, like a millisecond (1/1000th of a second) and let the camera take care of adjusting the aperture.

Make your subject stand out

Backgrounds should be just that, something subtle that accentuates your subject. In most professional photos the backgrounds are indistinct and sometimes even hazy. You, too, can achieve this effect by controlling the focus and aperture. Use your optical zoom to make your subject stand out more and, if you have a manual aperture control, use a large opening (like f-2.8) while focusing on your subject. Additionally, the further you can separate your subject from the background, the better.

Avoid the flash

Natural lighting is best, but failing that, you should try to use lighting that is slightly away from the camera. Not only does the flash occasionally result in red-eye, but you also have no control over shadowing. By positioning lights at different angles, you can eliminate shadows created by facial features and uneven surfaces.

Bob often tapes a small piece of white cardboard to the left or right of the flash on his camera to achieve different types of flash lighting effects. This technique is low tech, but changing the amount and angle of flash can make a huge difference in a shot. Give it a try.

AppleScript and iPhoto 2

We stand amazed that Apple isn't touting iPhoto 2's scriptability more prominently (iPhoto 1 wasn't scriptable). Apple doesn't even point you at the wonderful page `www.apple.com/applescript/iphoto/`, where a number of useful scripts and some other examples are available.

Although Dennis finds many of these scripts useful, his favorite (while writing this book) is the Photo Summary script. Just select the photos you want summarized and invoke the script to get a table such as the one shown in Figure 11-6. The file is an HTML file, which you can save for use with a Web browser, such as Safari. But, the TextEdit application that comes with OS X also reads these files, and you can save the document as an RTFD file. This report is very handy to have available when you're submitting images to a colleague or editor.

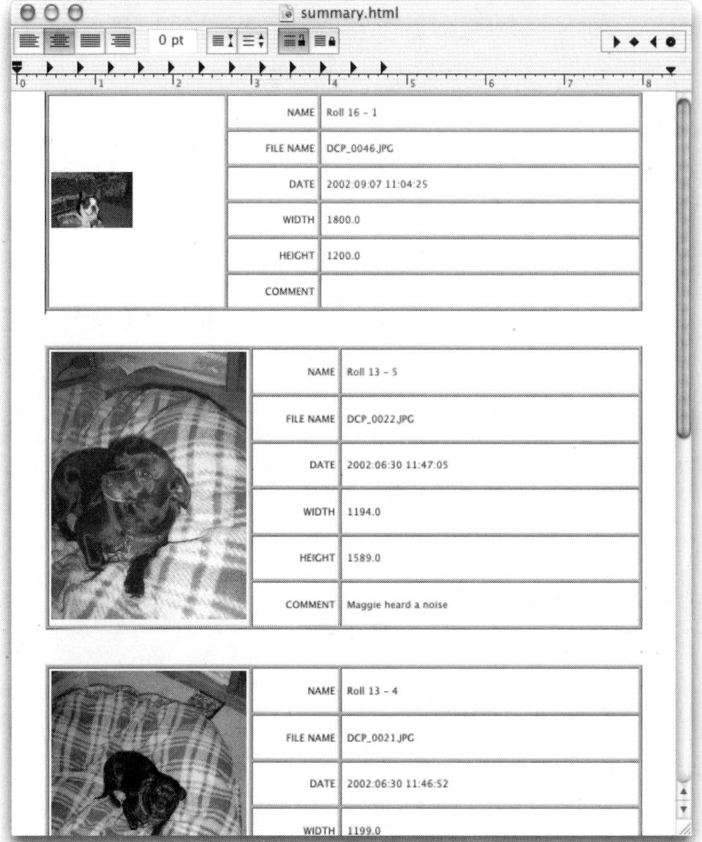

Figure 11-6: The Photo Summary opens up in TextEdit, where you can save it as an RTFD file to send along with the photos.

iPhoto doesn't sport its own Scripts menu, as iTunes and other attachable applications do. However, you can make use of the OS X Scripts menu by moving or copying the iPhoto Scripts folder that you downloaded to either /Library/Scripts or to ~/Library/Scripts. If you copy the folder to /Library/Scripts, the script becomes available to all accounts on your Mac, and the iPhoto Scripts menu item appears as shown in Figure 11-7(a). Placing the folder in your personal Library's Scripts folder restricts the contents to your account, and the iPhoto Scripts submenu appears at the bottom as in Figure 11-7(b). In either case, your scripts of choice will be ready at the drop of a menu.

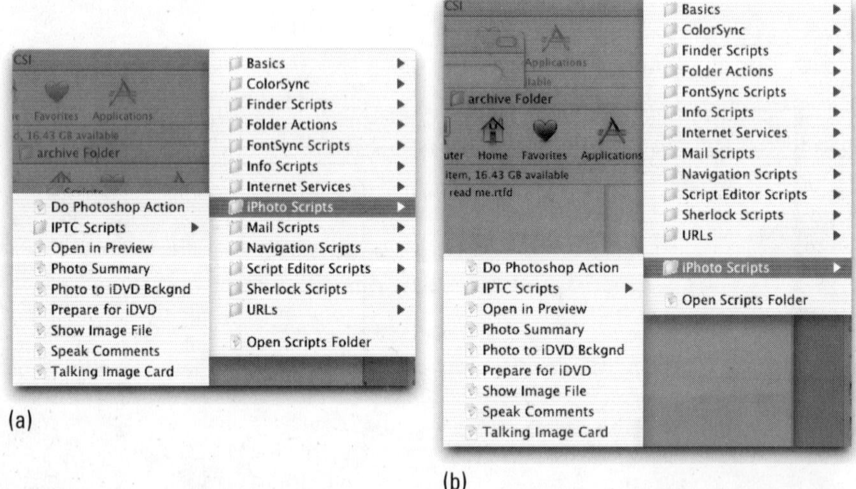

Figure 11-7: (a) shows an iPhoto Scripts submenu accessible by any user of the Mac while (b) shows one accessible only to the current account.

Check out the example scripts in Script Editor. These scripts provide a good starting point for writing your own scripts.

Summary

In this chapter, you learned how iPhoto stores your pictures, that large libraries can force iPhoto to a crawl, and that even just a few techniques can help you take better pictures. Finally, you learned that iPhoto 2 is scriptable and that Apple seeds the pot with some very handy example scripts.

✦ ✦ ✦

CHAPTER 12

Enhancing Your iPhoto Experience

✦ ✦ ✦ ✦

In This Chapter

Hardware purchases to consider

Software acquisitions to consider

✦ ✦ ✦ ✦

There's an old saying that goes, "a picture is worth a thousand words." We disagree. We'd say, "a good picture is worth much more than a thousand words; a lousy picture is worth much less."

Creating a good digital picture is the result of many things: good equipment, good software, good technique, and good subject matter are paramount among those. We can't help you with the last of these, nor can we help much with technique.

Note

If you're interested in learning more, try the *Digital Photography Handbook* by Mark Chambers (Wiley Publishing, Inc.), a handy guide to digital photography technique. It's somewhat biased toward Hewlett-Packard equipment, but still covers style, composition, and technique nicely. Another excellent resource is *50 Fast Digital Photo Techniques* by Gregory Georges (John Wiley & Sons, Inc.).

You're starting with good equipment and software—a Mac, Mac OS X, and iPhoto. But even a Mac running OS X and iPhoto can't make a silk purse out of a sow's ear. Fortunately, you can purchase accessories for your camera that may help you capture better pictures in the first place. And, you can also find hardware and software that can help iPhoto produce great results from your photos.

Hardware to Consider

Some of the items we're going to suggest might seem like "no-brainers"—items you'd expect to buy (like a digital camera or a color printer), but we're going to tell you what you should consider before you make that purchase. Other items might not be so obvious, at least until we mention them.

Digital camera

Although iPhoto works with most digital images, such as scanned photos (see the "Scanner" section later in this chapter) or photos imported from a Kodak PictureCD, a compatible digital camera and iPhoto make a dynamite combination. You can import your photos, erase the camera's memory (or stick in another memory card) and just keep shooting.

Most digital cameras have LCD screens that show you what your picture looks like right after you take it. That means no more waiting until they're developed to see whether you got the shot. If you don't like the Grand Canyon shot you just took, erase it and take another. If you chopped your husband's head off at the hairline, just do it over (unless that's what you *really* wanted to do).

Besides such obvious considerations as resolution, aspect ratios, battery life, and memory capacity, you need to consider some additional factors when choosing a digital camera, just as when you purchase a film camera.

Refer to Chapter 8 for more information on resolutions, aspect ratios, battery life, and memory capacity.

✦ **Camera size:** A camera's weight, size, and shape impact how willing you are to carry it around and have it available when those interesting shots appear. If it's too bulky or too heavy, you can't carry it around in your shirt or coat pocket. If it's too small, you'll have problems using it comfortably as you contort your fingers to click the shutter release without blocking the flash or lens.

✦ **Digital versus Optical zoom:** Don't be misled by digital zoom features. All digital zoom does is enlarge the pixels, resulting in a lower effective resolution. Optical zoom, on the other hand, is like a magnifying glass. You get your magnified image without losing resolution.

✦ **LCD screen:** Assuming that you're willing to put up with a little extra size, an LCD flip screen can be a great boon. By angling the screen, you can hold the camera down low or up high and still see what's framed in your shot. You can even position it to see yourself in the shot, for those self-portrait efforts.

✦ **Manual modes:** Manual controls get you out of the digital Instamatic equivalent's world and into that of professional Nikons and Leicas. The big three features here all deal with *aperture* (how wide the shutter opens when you take a shot) and *shutter speed* (how fast the shutter opens and closes):

   • Aperture priority mode lets you control aperture.

   • Shutter priority mode lets you control shutter speed.

   • Manual mode lets you adjust aperture and shutter speed independently.

✦ **Film Speed:** Some cameras offer you the digital equivalent of different film speeds. You can choose a faster film speed, often labeled ISO, such as 200 or 400, when you are working with more light. Doubling the ISO rating (say from 100 to 200) means that you can get the same exposure with one less F-stop on the lens.

✦ **Burst mode:** Burst mode lets you operate like the fashion photographers you see in movies and on TV, snapping picture after picture as if the camera were a machine gun. When you take multiple photos rapidly, you can choose the best of many similar shots as your final effort. The trick here is to get a camera with a large memory buffer, because memory cards are s-l-o-w. There is no way to write the data to a SmartMedia or CompactFlash card fast enough to keep up — the data has to be stored in the camera's fast RAM and downloaded to the memory card as time permits.

✦ **Sliding lens covers and Attachable lenses filters:** The last two features we'll mention, sliding lens covers and attachable lenses/filters, are pretty much mutually exclusive.

   Detachable lens covers are a royal pain. More than one professional, to say nothing of legions of hobbyists, have snapped pictures while forgetting to remove the lens cap. And, when you do remove the lens cap, it frequently gets lost or, if attached by a cord, flops around getting in the way. This makes the automatic, sliding lens cover integral to most point-and-shoot models quite attractive.

   Attachable lenses and filters, on the other hand, typically have to be threaded onto your camera. The finer the threads, the harder it is to attach things and the easier it is to mess up the threads. However, having the capability to use a telephoto or wide-angle lens or attach various lens filters lets you take a wider variety of pictures under varying conditions. See the "Lenses and filters" section later in this chapter.

All the major camera manufacturers (Sony, Nikon, Canon, Leica, Minolta, Olympus, and so on), as well as a plethora of companies that you might not ordinarily associate with cameras (Hewlett-Packard, Epson, Logitech, and Toshiba), are competing for your digital camera business. Every year, more and more powerful and feature-rich digital cameras become available at the same or lower prices as the previous year's models. Like buying a computer, figure out how much you need, add a little bit more for growth, close your eyes, and dive on in. If you're waiting for the absolute best deal, you'll never actually *buy* a camera because something better is always coming along and the price (at least on existing models) is always coming down.

Scanner

Until Apple shipped OS X, 10.2 (Jaguar), scanners were the forgotten stepchildren in the Mac's family of supported hardware. Now, with Image Capture recognizing many USB-connected scanners, you can easily connect compatible scanners and scan in your loose photos.

Epson, Hewlett-Packard, UMAX, Canon, and many other companies offer a wide variety of scanners, ranging in price from well under $100 to over $1000. You probably won't need anything more than 300 dpi resolution to scan your photos for use with iPhoto. After all, at 300 dpi, a 4 x 6 print is 1200 x 1800 resolution (2.2 megapixels, the way Kodak advertises their DX3500 and DX3600 models). Because even most inexpensive scanners give 600 dpi or better resolution, even a wallet-size photo (2 x 3) can be treated like a 2-or-more-megapixel image, and that means you'll get a good print even when you blow it up to 8 x 10.

The major feature to look for in a scanner is its *optical resolution*, which is the resolution at which it really scans. The *interpolated resolution* is the scanner's equivalent of a camera's digital zoom—the scanner approximates the pixels in between the ones it actually scans. With scanners under $100, like the Epson Perfection 1250U, providing 1200 x 2400 dpi optical resolution, your scanning needs can be satisfied at budget prices.

If you're interested, Epson 1250U has an interpolated resolution of 9600 dpi.

Be aware that the higher you set the scanning resolution, the more disk space your image consumes. A 4 x 6 photo scanned at 1200 dpi can require dozens of megabytes, depending upon the bit-depth (i.e., the number of colors).

Another feature to look for when purchasing a scanner is a *slide adapter*, a small case for holding photographic slides. If you have a collection of slides from your film camera days, this attachment is a must, assuming you want to digitize your collection. A slide adapter works by projecting the scanner's light through the adapter, off the internal mirror, and then through the slide—in short, you are using your scanner and the adapter as a slide projector so that the slide's image appears to the scanner as if it were reading a piece of paper.

Burning drive

Yes, we're pounding this point home again. Digital photos take up a lot of disk space. Your iPhoto Library is going to get really large and slow iPhoto down. Eventually, you're going to want to remove old photos from iPhoto, but you probably don't want to consign them to the bit-bucket (a digital wastebasket). After all, they're memories and you might want to look at them again some day — maybe to embarrass your kids when their teenage friends drop by.

Backing your digital photos up to CD or DVD is a compact and convenient archival method and allows you to free up the space they use. To accomplish this, you need a CD or DVD burner. Most Macs come with one these days, but if yours doesn't, you might consider getting an external burner. Apple made it even easier to back up to CD or DVD with iPhoto 2's Burn feature.

We recommend that you avoid USB burners — they're very slow and not that much less expensive than the much faster FireWire drives we see for $175 and up.

Tripods

Have you ever noticed that when professional photographers set up a studio shot or just about any other posed photo, their camera is on a tripod? The reason for doing this is to stabilize the camera so that nothing, including you clicking the shutter release, moves the camera or blurs the photo. The camera's shutter isn't open very long, but if the camera moves while it's open, a blurred (or worse) shot will result.

The standard rule for tripods is based on use with a 35mm camera. The rule states that you need to use a tripod any time the shutter speed is slower than the reciprocal of the lens focal length (in inches). Thus, if the lens focal length is 5 inches, you need a 1/5 second shutter speed. Most digital cameras have lenses equivalent to a 35mm film camera, so the rule applies.

This rule has a couple of addenda. One is that you should use a tripod whenever it is dark. The other is that you should use a tripod whenever you plan to have enlargements made. (Enlarging an image exaggerates any camera jitter effect.)

You'll find literally dozens of tripod brands and sizes available. Although you'll probably find your best prices on the Internet, buying a tripod without handling it is an iffy proposition. Knowing how much they weigh and how easy they are to set up and break down is critical. If the tripod is awkward to use or carry, you won't use it and then it's just money down the sewer.

A mini tripod is also a handy accessory. Dennis keeps one to use with indoor shots where he can set it on a counter or table.

When you look at tripods, consider how small they are when collapsed and how tall they are when extended. A tripod that extends to only 45 inches is probably going to be very uncomfortable for most adults to use (unless you have a flip-out LCD on your camera). Dennis is only 5'5" and finds any tripod shorter than 58 inches uncomfortable to use from a standing position. You should also consider the degrees of flexibility in the tripod's *pan head*, the little swivel stand to which you attach your camera. For example, if the pan head rotates on all three axes, you can get portrait orientation shots in addition to panning horizontally and vertically.

Lenses and filters

You've probably all encountered the terms *wide-angle lens* and *telephoto lens*. What these terms reference is the angle captured when you take a photo. For a typical 35mm camera, you have a standard focal length of 50mm, as shown in Figure 12-1. This approximates the 46-degree angle subtended by the human eye.

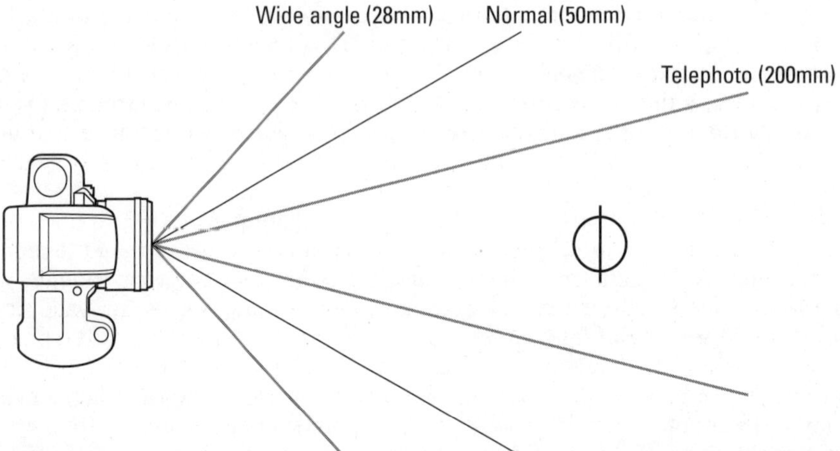

Figure 12-1: The human eye and a standard lens both capture a 46-degree field of view.

A wide-angle 35mm lens has a focal length between 24mm and 35mm, and a telephoto lens has a focal length between 80mm and 300mm. Think of this difference as zooming in (telephoto) and zooming out (wide-angle).

Focal lengths less than 20mm are called *super wide angle* and those greater than 300mm are called *super telephoto*.

If your camera supports attachable lenses and filters, you'll be able to take much better long-distance and close-up shots using telephoto and wide-angle lenses than using your camera's zoom feature — particularly if it is a digital zoom. Many digital cameras experience *barrel distortion* when shooting wide-angle shots using their zoom capabilities. A shot shows barrel distortion when the image center is spherized (rounded). For those of you who have used Photoshop or Photoshop Elements, the Spherize Filter produces the same effect.

You use filters to prevent certain wavelengths of light from entering your lens or to change the angle at which the light enters. For example, you can filter ultraviolet light with a UV filter and reduce haziness. Similarly, a neutral density filter in bright to very bright conditions, in effect, acts as sunglasses for your camera. A polarization filter changes the angle of light, reducing glare. Polarization filters are especially useful on sunny days, in the snow or at the beach.

What do you look for in a color printer

Here's another recommendation in the of-course category. If you never want a printed copy of your photos (or if you send them all off to Kodak for professional printing), then you won't need the color printer. However, we print a lot of our photos, even if just in contact sheets. We also use our photos in other documents, such as letters written in AppleWorks or Word, and Kodak doesn't print those. Nor do they print the greeting card formats iPhoto offers. (Personalized birthday cards are great.)

So what should you consider when looking for a printer? Obviously price is one consideration. The initial cost of a color inkjet can be very deceiving, though. As we mentioned in Chapter 9, the consumables are where the printer manufacturers make the money. Somehow, it just feels odd to spend $40 ($20 each for the black and color cartridges) every couple of weeks to refill a printer than only cost $79 to begin with, but if you're using the printer to print photos, it's not that bad a deal.

Consider that, at high quality on glossy photo paper, you get approximately 30 prints per cartridge at 8 x 10, with each cartridge costing about $20. With glossy photo paper costing between 50 cents and a dollar a sheet, an 8 x 10 ends up costing less than $2 (closer to $1.50, actually). This is less than half the $3.99 (plus tax and shipping) price that you pay to have Kodak do the job.

Another consideration is color fidelity and print quality. Although most of the better color inkjets (Epson, H-P, Lexmark, and Canon) print good photos with their standard four-color printers, the six-color printers produce better, crisper prints.

Some of these printers require replacing the entire cartridge when one color runs out; some of the newer printers have separate cartridges for each color. Adding up the costs of the individual color cartridges results in a higher price than the price of just one of the combined color cartridges. This is an unattractive alternative if your photos tend to deplete all colors somewhat evenly. However, if you tend to empty one inkwell faster than the others (maybe you use a lot of blue when printing ocean and sky), the separate cartridge approach can be quite attractive. You need to analyze your usage to determine which printer style suits you best.

Another consideration might be whether the printer supports wide format printing. If you plan to produce many large prints, a wide printer can come in handy. Dennis has a couple of 11 x 17 prints that he really likes from an Epson 1200.

Remember, there's no right printer for everyone. Pick the features you want and see what you can find with those features in your price range.

Software Acquisitions to Consider

iPhoto performs most of its functions really well, but there are a few gaps in its feature set. For example, it is the only one of the four major iApps that doesn't have a burn-to-disk feature. Although the 1.1.1 upgrade added Comments and user-assigned names for your photos, iPhoto still isn't a full-featured image database. Similarly, as we discussed in Chapter 10, iPhoto's image-editing tools are good but minimal. Additionally, iPhoto can really slow down when your Photo Library becomes large. You can address all of these shortcomings with various software products while still taking advantage of iPhoto's many best-of-breed features.

Toast 5 Titanium

Roxio's ever-valuable product, Toast 5 Titanium, is once again number one on our recommendation list. With the addition of the iPhoto 1.1.1 Toast Export plug-in, you have a quick and easy method of archiving photos and albums.

One program that comes with Toast is iView Media, a powerful image database application, which we'll be covering in our next recommendation.

A great feature of Toast is that you can use it to burn VideoCDs, discs that play in most set top DVD players, and provide VHS-quality video. You can drag any QuickTime movie, such as an exported slide show, onto Toast's VideoCD window, and it converts the movie to a VCD-compatible MPEG-1 file, all ready for you to burn and enjoy on your TV set. Using inexpensive CD-R media, you can share slide shows of your kids with their grandparents, of your vacation with friends and relatives, or your presentation with customers or coworkers.

Using VCD Builder, you can even add menus so that you can control the Video CD just like iDVD-created DVDs.

For more on the iPhoto 1.1.1 Toast Export plug-in, see Chapter 10. For more details on VCD Builder, see Chapter 17.

iView Media/iView MediaPro

iView Media is an organizational tool for images, movies, sounds, fonts, and other media files (including Web pages, AppleWorks documents, and many page layout documents). You import media into a *catalog*, iView's term for a multimedia database, as shown in Figure 12-2. iView only imports disk files, it doesn't recognize attached cameras or scanners unless you upgrade to the iView MediaPro product.

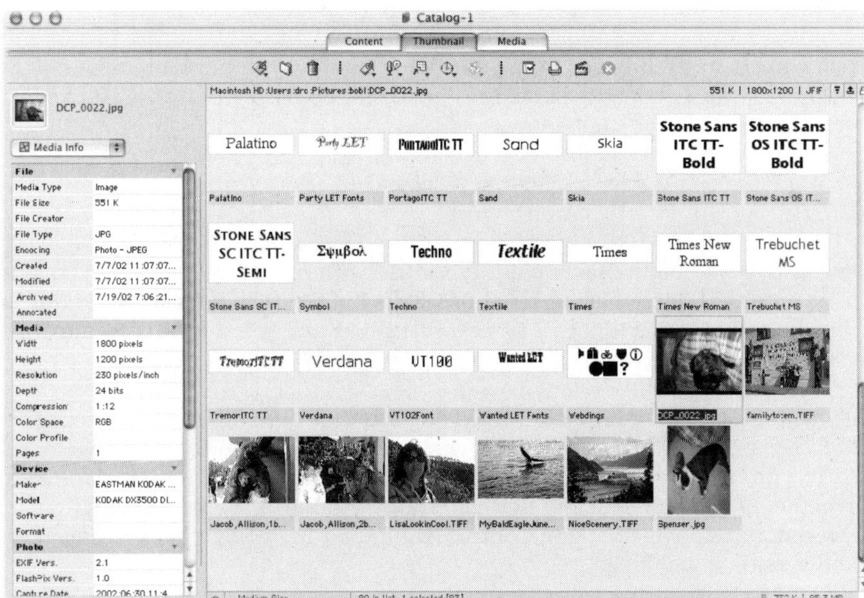

Figure 12-2: The iView catalog is like the iPhoto Library (on steroids).

iView MediaPro adds one nice option in its Import from Camera dialog: embedding a ColorSync profile into each image. ColorSync profiles make color-matching from screen to printer accurate.

With iView Media or MediaPro, you can archive your photos on CD, freeing up disk space, and when you want to access them, the program tells you which CD to insert. From here on, we're just going to write "the iView programs" when we mean either Media or Media Pro.

iPhoto's Comments feature is nice, but the iView programs support IPTC (International Press and Telecommunications Council) tags, a standard for annotating news data and graphic files, as well as recorded voice annotations, and 16 user-defined fields.

The AppleScripts available from www.apple.com/applescript/iphoto/ include a number of scripts for dealing with IPTC tags. So, even without direct support in iPhoto, you can still get there without another program.

iView's Slide Shows are more flexible than iPhoto's. You can set differing durations and transitions for individual slides, a feature unavailable in iPhoto.

When you create Web pages from your iView catalog, you have a template-driven exporter at your command, similar to those offered by the BetterHTMLExport plug-in from Drooling Cat.

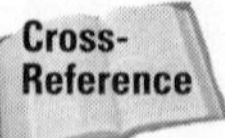

For more on plug-ins in iPhoto, see Chapter 10.

iView also has a built-in Backup utility for use with removable disks, such as the Zip, or onto CD-R media using Toast or OS X's built-in Disc Burner. While this isn't as nicely integrated as iPhoto 2's backups using Burn, it is a little more flexible, because you can add to your backup at a later time.

They're still not Photoshop, but the iView programs offer Sharpness; Hue Saturation & Lightness; Color Correction; and Invert (essentially creating a negative from a positive, or vice versa) tools to those available in iPhoto but don't include Red-Eye correction or the Enhance and Retouch tools. In addition to Revert to Original, the iView programs have a Version Control feature, letting you go back to any earlier saved version of an image.

If you're willing to forsake iPhoto's easy printing interface and deal with all the issues yourself, the iView programs offer template-driven printing, which let you define and print not just greeting cards, but CD jewel cases, Zip cases, and so forth.

The iView programs are very powerful, but lack much of iPhoto's ease of use. Also, you don't get the nice interface to Kodak prints or hardbound photo books present in iPhoto. Our primary photo use of iView is as an intermediate step between iPhoto and archiving the pictures. Another use is when we're trying to keep a project together (fonts, word processing documents, EPS or Illustrator files, and photos).

Adobe Photoshop 7/Photoshop Elements

Photoshop is the standard against which all other photo-editing programs are measured. With a complex, palette-filled interface (shown in Figure 12-3), Photoshop 7 is not considered an easy program for the new or occasional user. It is, most definitely, a tool targeted at the power user, and priced to match at $609 (list) or $149 for those upgrading from an earlier version.

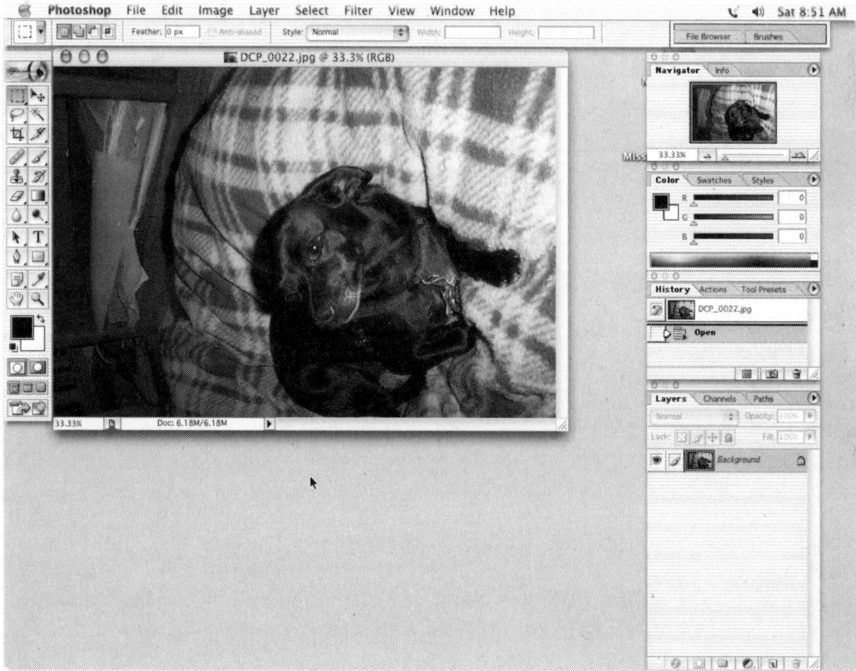

Figure 12-3: Photoshop offers palettes galore (and these are just the default set).

Photoshop Elements 2 (list price $99) retains much of Photoshop's palette-heavy interface and adds a few consumer-friendly options, such as the Quick Fix dialog that lets you remove red-eye as well as adjust lighting, contrast, color, and focus quickly.

Not only do the Photoshop products offer an incredibly rich editing environment, they also give you access to some really nice printing options. One of our favorites is the Picture Package, as shown in Figure 12-4. One 8.5 x 11 sheet of glossy photo paper filled with copies of your photo at the same or different sizes, just like the sheets you get when you order a photo package of your kid's school pictures. The number of templates available makes iPhoto's Print Sampler pale in comparison, especially because you can create your own templates.

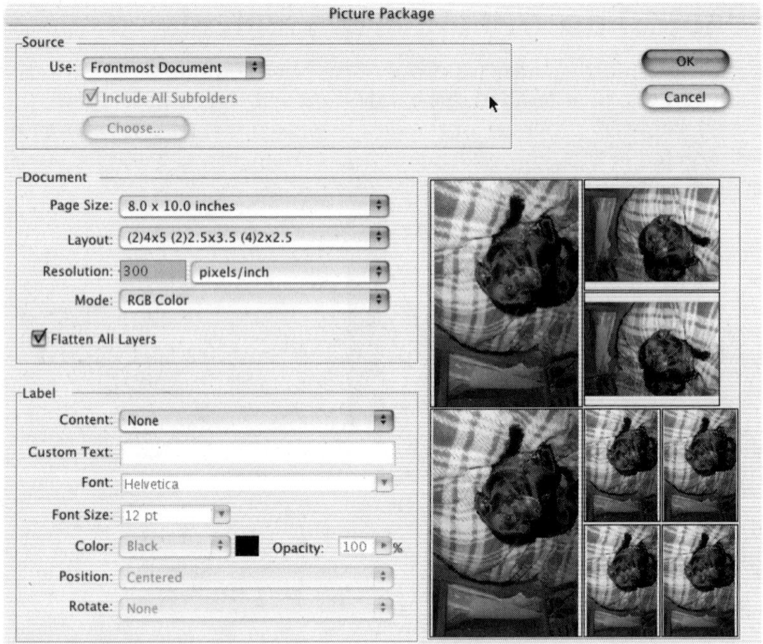

Figure 12-4: Get multiple prints in varying sizes on one sheet with Photoshop's Picture Package.

Photoshop is such a complex product, with so many features and capabilities, that books much larger than this one are devoted to it. Check out the *Photoshop 7 Bible* by Deke McClelland (John Wiley & Sons, Inc.) for tons of info. You can download a trial version of Photoshop from Adobe's Web site at `www.adobe.com/products/photoshop/main.html`.

GraphicConverter

Considered by many (we're among them) to be one of the best shareware programs ($35) around, GraphicConverter is bundled on many PowerMac systems just as AppleWorks is bundled on iMacs. As you might surmise from the name, GraphicConverter started out as an application to convert between the various graphic formats — there are literally hundreds of them. With the addition of painting and bitmap editing features as well as a very handy browser (shown in Figure 12-5), GraphicConverter can stand on its own as a powerful photo-editing tool.

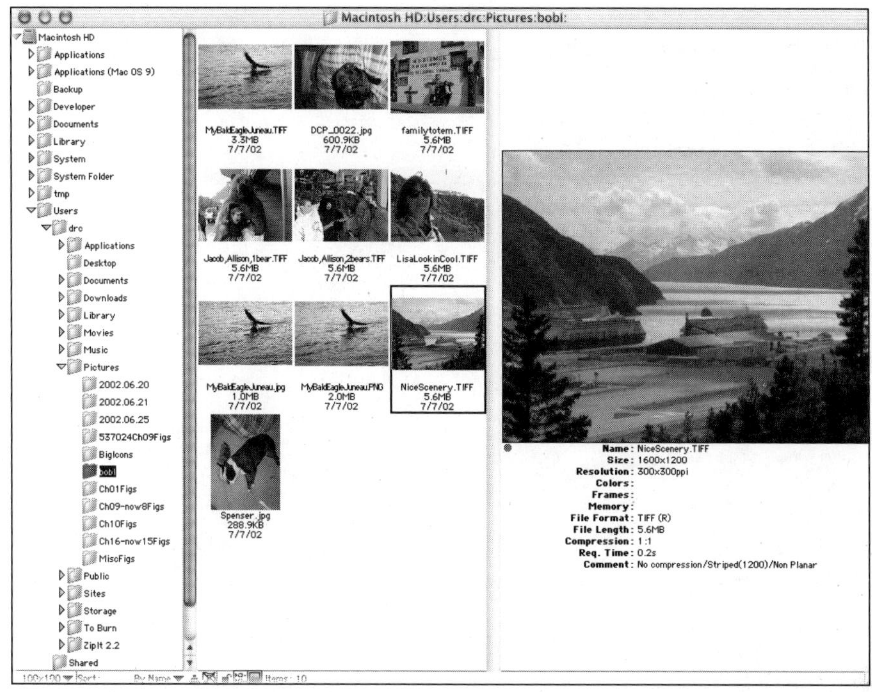

Figure 12-5: GraphicConverter's browser lets you move from image to image, wherever they are on your Mac.

Just double-click any thumbnail in the browser and an editing window opens for that picture, as shown in Figure 12-6.

Additionally, GraphicConverter has a rich AppleScript dictionary, allowing you to build programs to do multiple, complex operations on photos or groups of photos.

iPhoto Library Manager

Brian Webster (`http://homepage.mac.com/bwebster`) offers a wonderful freeware utility name iPhoto Library Manager. As the name implies, you can create multiple iPhoto Libraries and, using the iPhoto Library Manager, specify which you want to use the next time you open iPhoto. In addition to storing your photo libraries in places other than your Pictures folder, iPhoto Library Manager also sets up the permissions on your photo libraries so that other users can share them on your Mac.

Figure 12-6: GraphicConverter's editing environment is accessible from the browser.

iPhoto Librarian

A similar concept to the iPhoto Library Manager, Scott Schroeder's freeware offering from Scruffy Software (`http://homepage.mac.com/scrufmeister`), iPhoto Librarian lets you maintain multiple, separate Photo Libraries or even just one, if you want it somewhere other than your Pictures folder. Written in AppleScript, you double-click it, and it asks whether you want to use the Default Photo Library or a different one (Other). Select your Photo Library of choice and iPhoto Librarian launches iPhoto with your selected library.

SmartSound Movie Maestro

The biggest problem we have with the soundtrack feature on iPhoto slideshows is synchronizing the photo display so that the music doesn't seem to just cut off when we get to the last slide.

Although SmartSound's MovieMaestro ($49.95 from `www.smartsound.com`) doesn't completely resolve our second annoyance, it makes a good first step. After you create a soundtrack, you choose File ⇨ Save Sound and pick Soundtrack to iPhoto from the

Save dialog's pop-up list. The next time you open iPhoto, the soundtrack is in the pop-up list, ready for selection.

MovieMaestro's sole purpose is scoring movie clips. If you export your slideshow, you can use MovieMaestro to create precisely timed, customized soundtracks for your slideshow movie, as follows:

1. **In iPhoto, export your slideshow, making sure that the Add currently selected music to movie checkbox is cleared, as shown in Figure 12-7, then click Export.** The Save sheet appears.
2. **In the Save sheet, name your movie, and tell iPhoto where to save it.** Remember that your Movies folder is the default.

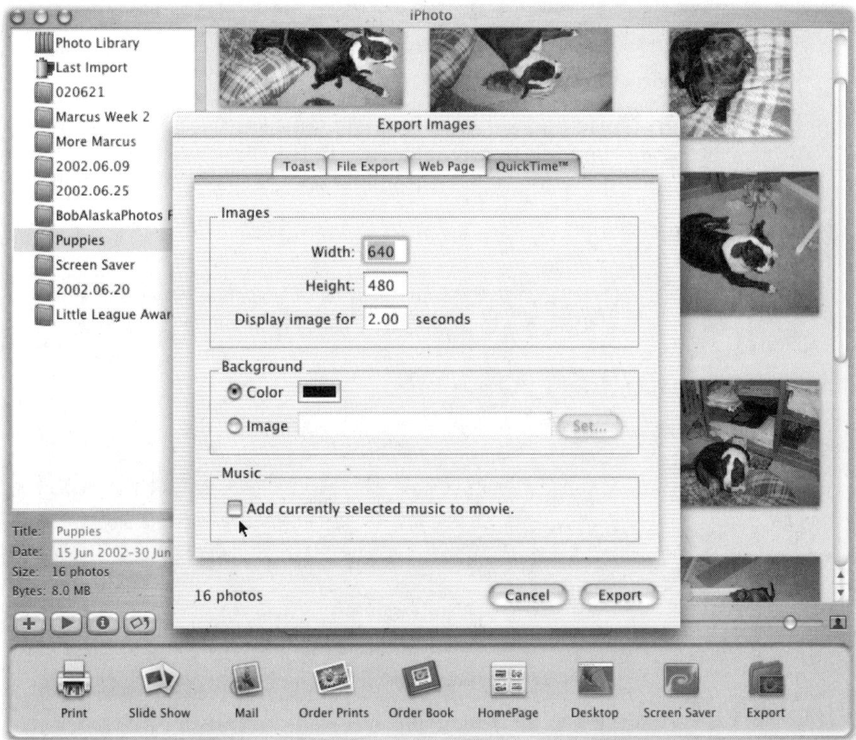

Figure 12-7: Start out with a silent slideshow.

3. **In MovieMaestro, select Create music for a movie.** Figure 12-8 shows this option.

Figure 12-8: Tell MovieMaestro that you're going to score an existing movie.

4. **Locate your movie and click Open.**
5. **Click Add Music and select the music you want your slideshow to use.** The music block is added to MovieMaestro's timeline, as shown in Figure 12-9, set to your slideshow's length. Optionally, you can select a different variation.

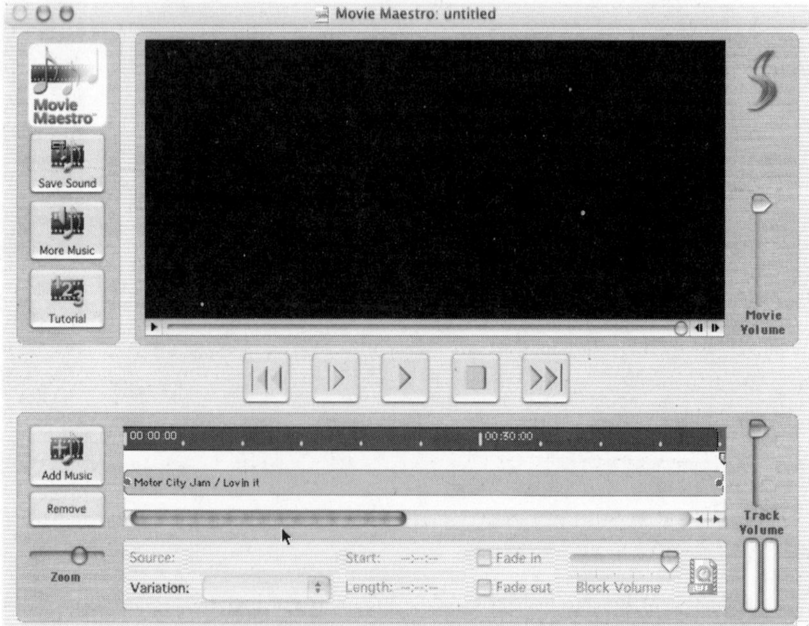

Figure 12-9: The music appears in MovieMaestro's timeline.

6. **Click Save Sound.** The Save pop-up menu appears.
7. **From the pop-up menu, choose Movie and Soundtrack, as shown in Figure 12-10, and click Save.** You're done. Your QuickTime movie now has a score, matching in length.

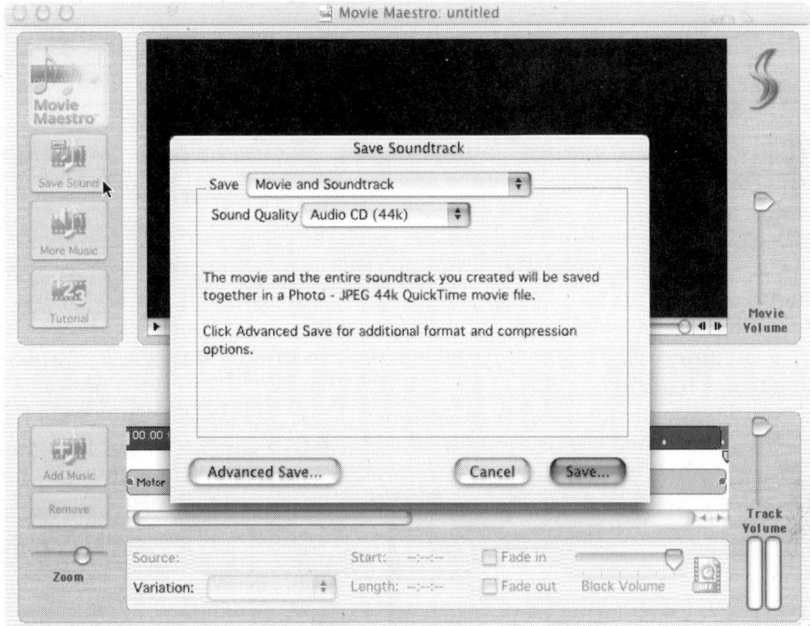

Figure 12-10: Save the movie and soundtrack together.

MovieMaestro is a neat product for scoring movies. If you outgrow MovieMaestro, its big brother, SonicFire Pro does even more, but requires more effort on your part.

Turn to Chapter 17 for additional information on MovieMaestro. You can find out some of the ways in which you can add high-quality soundtracks to your iMovies.

Educational Web sites

In addition to the Web sites we mention in previous chapters, here are more for your consideration.

Digital Photography Review (`www.dpreview.com`) is an excellent reference to all sorts of topics relating to digital photography. Between its Glossary, News, Learn, and Forum sections, you're almost certain to find answers or guidance when you have questions. Besides, learning about this stuff can be fun.

Although slanted toward Canon equipment, EF Lens 101 (`www.usa.canon.com/eflenses/lens101`) includes a wealth of information on lenses and a great, illustrated glossary of photo terminology.

Summary

In this chapter, you learned about purchases that can help you take better photos as well as how to bring old photos and slides into iPhoto, archive photos from iPhoto, free up space, and improve performance.

On the software side, you saw programs that significantly enhance your photo-editing options, printing options, and library management. Additionally, you encountered MovieMaestro, which helps with scoring your slideshows and the ever-useful Toast Titanium for backing up your Photo Library and burning slideshows to VideoCD.

Finally, you learned about a couple of Web sites to check when you have specific questions about photography, digital or otherwise, or if you just want to learn more about photography and lenses.

✦ ✦ ✦

P A R T

IV

iMovie

✦ ✦ ✦ ✦

In This Part

✦ ✦ ✦ ✦

CHAPTER 13

Introducing iMovie 3

✦ ✦ ✦ ✦

In This Chapter

Discovering digital video

Gathering the bare essentials

Exploring the iMovie window

Setting iMovie preferences

✦ ✦ ✦ ✦

Some applications just scream **Breakthrough**! MacPaint was the first one on the Mac, capturing hearts and piquing imaginations. Soon thereafter came the LaserWriter-PageMaker combination, and HyperCard.

Today, iMovie — at least in our humble opinion — is yet another breakthrough from Apple.

The first time Dennis sat down with iMovie and created something viewable and entertaining from a collage of typically disjointed home movies, he felt an excitement that he hadn't experienced with computers since the first time he sat down with a 128K Mac and MacPaint in 1984. Bob, who was still producing television commercials in Los Angeles in 1984, says he's been waiting almost 20 years for the ability to edit "near-broadcast quality" video on his Mac at a price he can afford.

Three years later there still isn't an application for Windows that can hold a candle to iMovie in either ease-of-use or bang for the buck. Each new version of iMovie just widens the gap between Mac and Windows; Microsoft's Movie Maker is, at best, a pale imitation; other Windows programs that do the things iMovie does cost a lot more and aren't as easy to use.

Discovering Digital Video

When we were growing up, our parents and grandparents were big on creating home movies (and compiling albums and boxes of still photos and slides). There wasn't a birthday party, trip to the zoo, or Little League game that didn't see one or more of them jostling for position with their movie camera, generally with portable lighting attached. Cameras using 8mm and 16mm film were state of the art for the home videophile, just as they had been for our grandfathers back when our parents were young. It wasn't until the late 1970s that home videotaping came into vogue, concurrent with the introduction and battle between Betamax (Beta) and VHS.

In spite of these advances, the technology was still analog. Tape replaced silver-based film, and VCRs replaced bulb-based projectors. iMovie uses even higher-quality digital video, often referred to as "DV."

Things went on like that, with little change beyond variations in tape size (VHS, VHS-C, and Hi8), for about a quarter century. Then, in the late 1990s, Apple (and a few others, including Sony) introduced a new technology called FireWire, (also known as IEEE 1394 and iLink), and several vendors (including Canon, Sony, and Panasonic) introduced new digital camcorders designed to use FireWire to transfer video from camcorder to computer. This put analog video gear on the endangered species list — in a few more years analog will seem as quaint as 8mm film or vinyl "high-fidelity" records seem to us today.

Professional filmmakers have been using custom-configured Macs and other computers to edit video for years, but until FireWire and digital camcorders came along, these systems required lots of additional (and very expensive) hardware and software add-ons. ($100,000+ configurations were not uncommon.)

All that has changed. Ever since Apple began to include FireWire and iMovie on all their computers and the price of digital camcorders dropped below $500 (though most are still priced higher, we've seen a couple on sale for around $300), the cost-of-entry for home users has become so affordable that almost anyone with the desire can now make a movie.

How affordable? Today you can get a basic iMac for around $800 and an inexpensive digital camcorder for under $500. So today you can get started with digital video for around $1300. To put that in perspective, Dennis's first VCR, which he bought in 1977, cost about the same as today's entry-level iMac. (And don't forget that the dollar was supposedly worth more then.)

Of course, most people will want more than the bare minimum system, but compared to prices just a few years ago, it will still be affordable. And don't forget: Your Mac can do more than just edit and play video, (unlike the projectors, splice blocks, razor blades, and film processing from days of yore).

Proliferating formats

When home VCRs first appeared, a battle ensued between two available formats, VHS and Beta. VHS was decidedly inferior to Beta in quality, but it had some things Beta did not — it was offered by a wide variety of vendors, it cost less, and it offered more storage per tape. Beta's quality advantage wasn't nearly enough to overcome these factors and VHS soon won the war.

Today we're experiencing a similar situation in digital video. There are multiple formats including DVD (Digital Video Disc or Digital Versatile Disk, depending on who you ask), VCD (Video Compact Disc), SVCD (Super Video Compact Disc), and variants of all three. Toss in upcoming MPEG-4-based formats and the field gets even more crowded.

DVD is the clear quality champion and you'll see blockbuster movies (and less well-known ones as well) for sale and rent on DVD at your neighborhood, well, Blockbuster Video. In the United States you'll be hard-pressed to find commercial VCDs and SVCDs for sale. But this isn't true in Asia and Europe, where VCDs and SVCDs are quite common, and in many cases, even more available than DVD. There are many reasons for this, but here are the two biggest:

- ✦ If you're a conspiracy theorist, you believe that the major movie studios have used their near-monopoly power to keep VCDs and SVCDs out of circulation in the United States.
- ✦ DVD media costs a lot more than CD media, even when you compare them per minute of video.

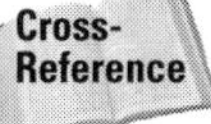

We'll talk about DVD in great detail in Part V. If you want to know more about VCD and SVCD, see Chapters 15 and 16.

Video compression

If you've looked at QuickTime in any detail, you've seen that it performs its magic of reducing the transfer rate of around 200MB/minute down to something you can watch enjoyably on a computer, and the resulting files take up a tiny fraction of the space for that same minute. It's all done with software called a *codec* (compressor-decompressor), with names like Sorenson, CinePak, Animation, MPEG, and a slew of others.

Video compression is achieved by eliminating redundant or (hopefully) unnecessary data from both the video frames and the audio track. In fact, if you merely encoded a digital video file's audio track as MP3 and create a JPEG image from each frame, the resulting file is considerably smaller than the original.

Video codecs are even more efficient than audio codecs, eliminating information that doesn't change from frame to frame and performing other tricks. Consider this: A VCD-compliant MPEG-1 encoded file is roughly 5 percent the size of the original DV stream! And even with all that compression and space saving, you still end up with VHS-quality video.

Gathering the Bare Essentials

Okay, we're really going to talk about the essentials for normal use, such as a digital camcorder or analog-to-digital FireWire converter; you'll need one or the other to move your video between your camcorder and your Mac.

You can use iMovie without such gear to create slideshows with transitions, music, and special effects, and if you don't have access to a camcorder or analog-to-digital converter (for importing analog video such as VHS or Beta), you can still have some fun with iMovie. But trust us, it gets boring real fast and you will barely scratch the surface of iMovie's capabilities.

What your Mac needs

Simply put, your Mac needs to meet certain minimum requirements to make productive use of iMovie. The following list describes what is necessary in Mac OS X.

- ✦ **iMovie 3:** This ships with every Macintosh currently manufactured by Apple, is included in the box with retail copies of MacOS X, and (at least currently) is available for free download from your iDisk's Software folder and from Apple's Web site.
- ✦ **A ton of free disk space:** This is critical — raw digital video consumes over 200MB of disk space per minute. Ten minutes of video take up better than 2GB of disk space. We feel that anything less than 10GB of free disk space will be uncomfortable. In fact, Dennis keeps a 30GB disk dedicated to iMovie projects and Bob has three 60GB FireWire hard drives he uses primarily for video.
- ✦ **FireWire:** Some older OS X-capable machines don't have it. If that describes your Mac, get a FireWire PCI card. If you have one of the early iBooks, one of the pre-FireWire iMacs, or the like and can't upgrade to FireWire, you won't be able to import or export your video footage.
- ✦ **Memory:** As with anything else, the more RAM you have in your Mac, the better. Although iMovie can run in a 128MB OS X machine, it may be slow, especially if other programs or processes are running. We suggest at least 384MB (more is better) of RAM to work efficiently with digital video.

What you need to connect to your Mac

We've already mentioned two possible input devices: digital camcorders and analog-to-digital converters. You'll need a FireWire cable to connect your input device to your Mac, but Apple was prepared for you and includes a 4-pin to 6-pin FireWire cable with each iMovie-capable Mac. This special cable, shown in Figure 13-1, has the normal (6-pin) FireWire connector to plug into your Mac and the smaller (4-pin) connector that almost every digital camcorder accepts.

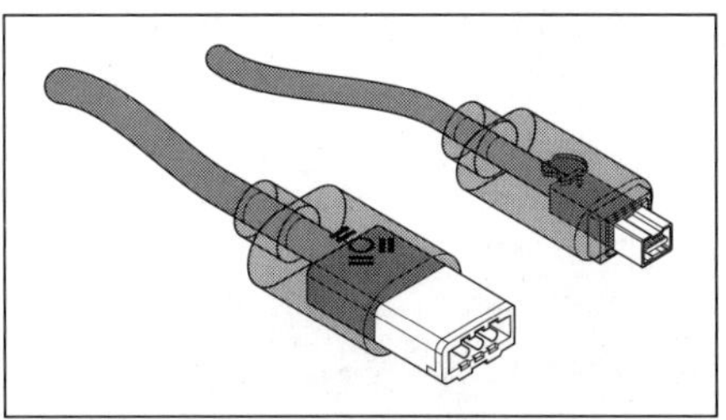

Figure 13-1: The Mac gets the normal FireWire connector (far left); the camera gets the smaller connector. The FireWire logo is shown on the right.

Note

Depending upon your camera model, the FireWire connector could be listed under a different name. On some models, it is called IEEE-1394, which is the name of the Institute of Electrical and Electronics Engineers standards document implemented in FireWire. On other models (Sony's, for example), it is called i.Link, which is Sony's trademarked name for their implementation. FireWire is Apple's trademark name, which they have licensed for free to the 1394 Trade Organization, along with the FireWire logo and symbol.

In case you are wondering what we mean by an analog-to-digital converter. Also known as *bridges* or *ADCs*, they are electronic devices that convert an analog stream of data to a digital stream and vice versa. Because iMovie can only deal with DV Streams as video input, whatever feeds it must provide a DV Stream, just as a digital camcorder would. The most popular of these bridges are the Dazzle Hollywood DV Bridge (`www.dazzle.com/products/hw_bridge.html`), the Canopus ADVC-100 (`www.canopus.com`). and the Formac Studio DV/TV (`www.formac.com`). If you can still find a Sony DVMC-DA2, it will also work, although Sony discontinued this product (which we think is a crying shame). The Formac Studio is more expensive than the Dazzle Hollywood or the Canopus, but it includes a 125-channel TV tuner, so you can actually use your Mac as a digital VCR and record TV shows to disk, although DV Stream format makes for some really large files at better than 200MB/minute. Figure 13-2 shows pictures of the Dazzle, Canopus, and Formac devices.

Nearly all digital camcorders include analog inputs, allowing them to act as pseudo analog-to-digital converters. Connect an analog source a camcorder or VCR to the analog inputs and transfer your analog footage to DV tape. You can then import the newly recorded DV footage to iMovie via FireWire.

Although it isn't 100 percent necessary, we strongly recommend that you upgrade your QuickTime version to QuickTime Pro as well. Having QuickTime Pro, or QT Pro, allows you to edit the QuickTime movies that you export from iMovie, even adding some special effects such as transparency. QT Pro also lets you perform far more format conversions than the basic QuickTime installation and lets you present your movies full-screen.

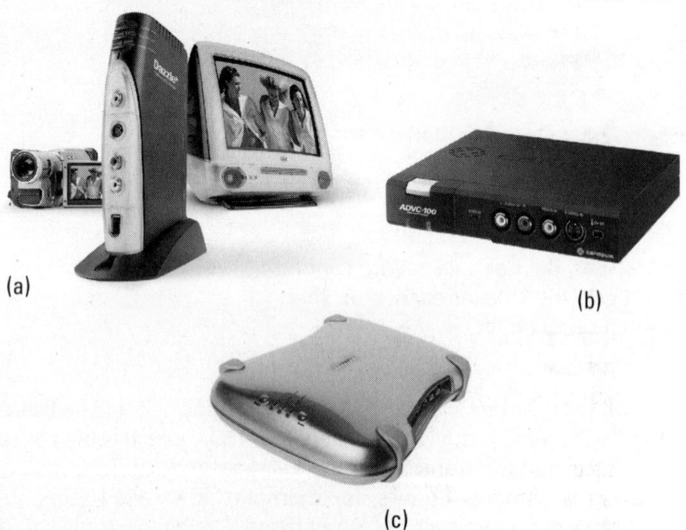

Figure 13-2: The Dazzle Hollywood DV Bridge (a); The Canopus ADVC-100 (b); The Formac Studio (c).
Photo courtesy of SCM Microsystems(a); Photo courtesy of Canopus (b)

Another strongly recommended add-on is a CD burner and a copy of Roxio's excellent Toast Titanium. Most current Macs include some sort of burner, but if yours doesn't, consider getting one as a way to save your finished and exported movies. One of the nicest benefits of Toast Titanium, in addition to being faster for burning your CDs (a lot less "preparation" than Mac OS's built-in CD burning), is that Roxio includes a VideoCD-compatible export option that lets you play your movies on many set top DVD players. Of course, if your Mac is equipped with a SuperDrive, you also have iDVD 3 and can burn DVDs. However, DVD-R media is a lot more expensive than CD-Rs at $3 for 90 minutes of DVD versus about 30 cents for 80 minutes of VCD.

You can find out about more details on the VideoCD-compatible export option in Chapter 15. See Part V for more about iDVD 3.

Jargon break

Although the following terms were discussed in Chapter 2, we want to make sure you understand them before we move on.

✦ **Clips:** Segments of a movie as they are stored on your disk.

✦ **Frames:** The smallest increment of duration used in iMovie. If you're dealing with NTSC (United States and Japan) video, there are 30 frames per second and with PAL video (just about everywhere else) there are 25 frames per second.

Actually, NTSC video has 29.97 frames per second, but we're going to round things off for the sake of simplicity.

✦ **Tracks:** A stream of video or audio. Although QuickTime supports tracks of other types, like text, iMovie only works with video and audio (you get one of the former and two of the latter).

Exploring the iMovie Window

We don't know if Steve Jobs was surprised by the vocal approval he heard when he announced that iMovie 3 would use a standard window rather than taking over your whole screen as previous versions did, but we weren't. The iMovie 3 window is shown in Figure 13-3.

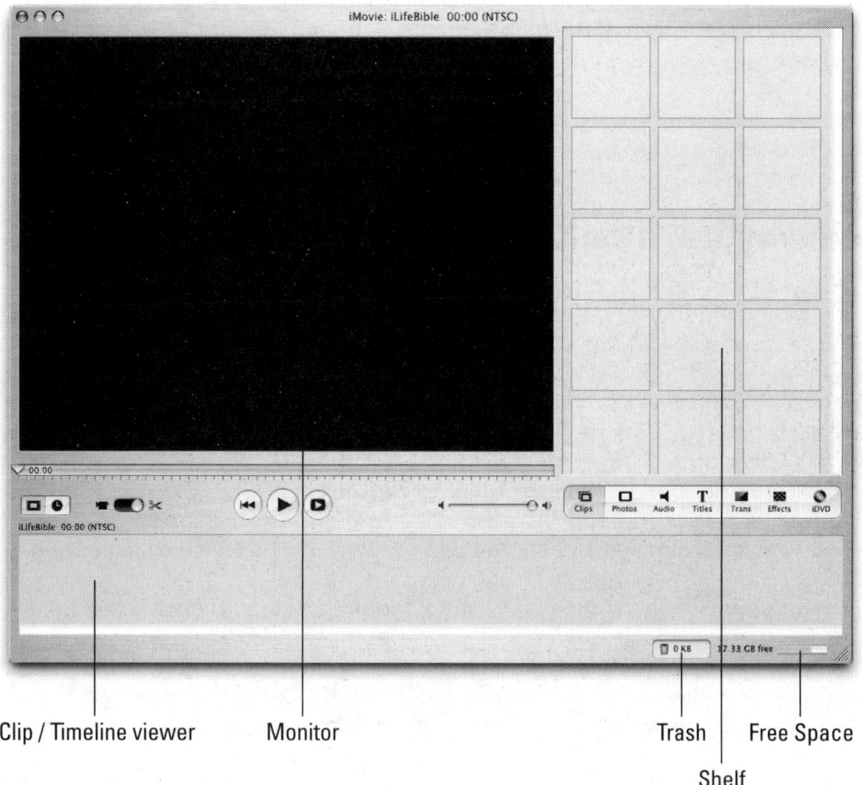

Figure 13-3: iMovie's window can be as big as your screen.

One nice feature of iMovie is that it remembers the last project (what iMovie calls a movie) you worked on. If that project is still available, iMovie opens it automatically when launched.

In addition to a lot of striped background, iMovie's window consists of four main areas:

✦ **Monitor:** It looks like a TV screen with some VCR controls beneath it and is where you view and edit your video footage. The camera/clip toggle switch controls what controls are visible on the monitor.

✦ **Shelf:** This is a clip storage location and the control center for adding iMovie transitions and special effects, accessing your iTunes and iPhoto Libraries, and passing your movie off to iDVD.

✦ **Clip viewer/Timeline viewer:** The area where you do your actual movie composition. The two indicated buttons control the viewer's appearance.

✦ **Status area:** This is where iMovie places its internal trash receptacle. The area displays the size of the files in the trash receptacle and how much free space remains on your iMovie project's disk.

In the next few pages, we'll begin to explore these areas; we'll explore them in excruciating detail in Chapters 14 and 15.

Viewing the monitor

The monitor is more than just where you view your clips or movies. It is also where you do much of the actual editing and deleting of clip segments. The monitor is also where you preview and import footage from your (connected) digital camcorder.

Figure 13-4 displays two views of the monitor, one in Camera mode, and the other in Clip Viewing mode. You won't see a lot of difference between them, except that the little toggle switch changes position and the Import button in Camera Mode changes to a scrubber bar in the Clip Viewing mode.

As you can see from Figure 13-4, the two modes have many items in common:

✦ **Screen:** Like the screen on your TV monitor, this is where clips or tapes play.

Note

When in Camera mode with nothing playing, the screen appears blue and indicates whether you have a camera connected. If a camera is connected, the screen shows where the tape is positioned in hours, minutes, seconds, and frames.

✦ **Play:** Click it to start playing a clip or tape. When in Clip Viewing mode, you click it again to stop play. In Camera mode, you can also click it to stop play, even though you have a separate Stop button (see later in this chapter).

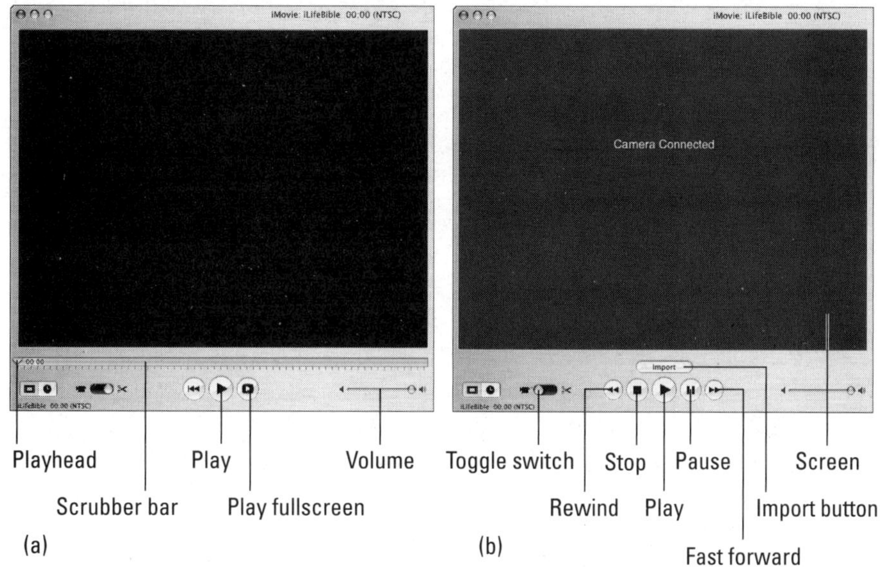

Figure 13-4: Monitor's Clip Viewing mode (a); Monitor's Camera mode (b).

- **Volume:** In Camera mode, you use this to control the level of sound input. When viewing clips, this control sets the sound output level.
- **Toggle Switch:** This two-position switch is where you tell iMovie that you want to work with the camera or with clips. Slide it to the little camera icon to make your FireWire-connected camera your input source. Move it to the film strip icon to tell iMovie you're going to work with clips.

Monitor items specific to Clip Viewing mode are as follows:

- **Home:** This button moves you to the beginning of the clip or sequence of selected clips.
- **Play Full Screen:** This little button, which is supposed to represent a "Play" arrowhead against a full screen backdrop, tells iMovie to fill your screen rather than just the monitor's miniscreen with your movie. Click anywhere onscreen while the clip is playing to return to the normal iMovie window.
- **Scrubber bar:** This aqua-colored bar with all the tick marks below it represents the length of your selected clip(s).

✦ **Crop markers:** You use these right triangles to select and delimit video segments within a clip for editing commands. Crop markers are initially adjacent and visible only when a clip is present.

✦ **Playhead:** This down-pointing arrowhead, with a time indicator to its right, moves along the scrubber bar to indicate your relative position in the clip(s) and the absolute position, timewise, within the clip(s).

Camera mode has a few other specialty items:

✦ **Rewind:** Just like on a VCR or a cassette player, this rewinds the tape or reverses direction of play in a tape.

✦ **Fast Forward:** Again, just like on a VCR, this button advances the tape at a faster rate.

✦ **Import:** Clicking this button tells iMovie to start retrieving data from your camera and storing it on your disk.

✦ **Pause:** Click this button to pause your camera. The current frame continues to display in the monitor screen.

✦ **Stop:** Click this button to halt the play or import process.

Seeing what's on the Shelf

The upper-right portion of the iMovie window is a veritable cornucopia of functions called the shelf, and what appears on the shelf depends upon which of the buttons along its bottom is selected. When iMovie first launches, you see the shelf as shown in Figure 13-5.

Each of the buttons invokes a different display and we're just going to introduce you to each of them here.

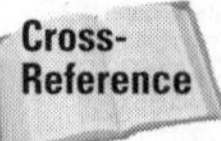

For full coverage of each button's functionality, see Chapters 14 and 15.

Clips

Most of the time, the shelf will probably look like Figure 13-5. Each of those little squares can hold one clip, has an editable name at its bottom, and displays the length of the clip in the upper left. The image in the middle represents the first frame of the clip. This incarnation of the shelf is called the *Clip pane*.

When you select a clip, its frame turns blue instead of white (it turned orange in previous versions of iMovie).

Figure 13-5: The shelf, in its clip pane persona (with one clip).

Unless you change the default preferences (see the "Managing your Import preferences" section later in this chapter), the clip pane is where imported camcorder footage always appears.

Photos

The next button, Photos, brings forth the iPhoto interface shown in Figure 13-6. In this persona, you have a portal to your iPhoto Library and all its albums. Additionally, you can apply the Ken Burns Effect to pan and zoom across your still images.

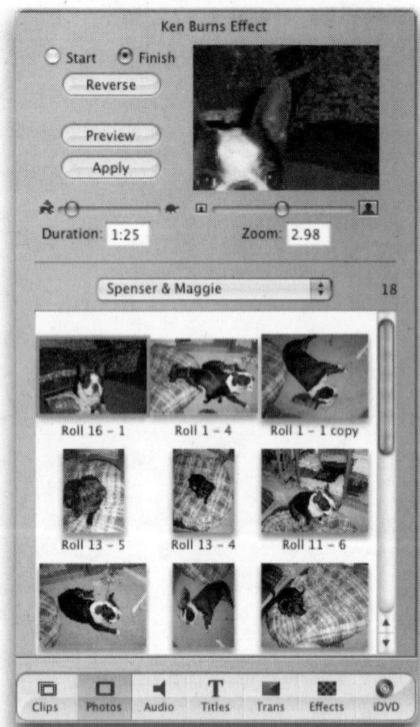

Figure 13-6: You can even access albums in your iPhoto Library here.

Audio

Narrations, background music, voice-overs, and the like can enhance many movies. iMovie provides the tools for all this in the shelf's Audio view, as shown in Figure 13-7. Audio view gives you access to Audio CDs, the Microphone, anything in your iMovie Sound Effects collection, and (ta-da) anything in your iTunes Library.

Titles

If you want to add credits or other text to your movie, this is the place. The shelf's Titles view, shown in Figure 13-8, gives you a wide range of titling and subtitling options.

Figure 13-7: iMovie gives you access to your iTunes Library and includes a small audio recording studio.

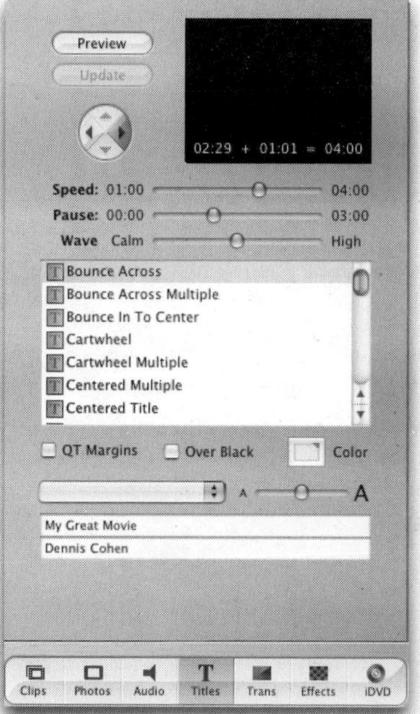

Figure 13-8: Add text titles and subtitles to your clips here.

Transitions

Clicking the Trans button alters the shelf's appearance, as shown in Figure 13-9. This is where you apply transition effects to clips, hopefully to the betterment of your movie.

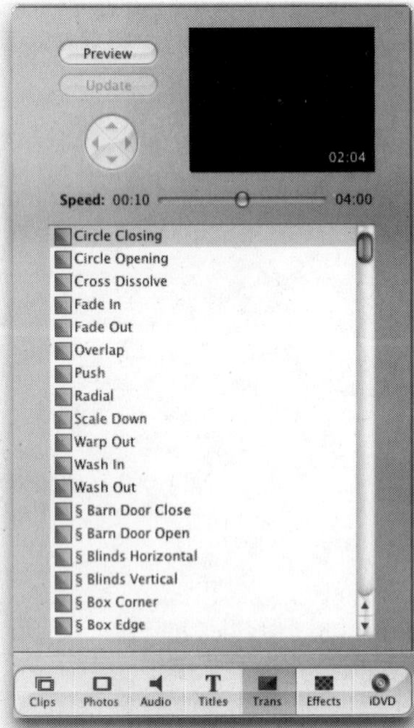

Figure 13-9: Select Transitions to apply special effects between your clips.

Effects

Special effects are what sell a lot of big-budget films, but the effects you employ from the shelf view (Figure 13-10) don't involve blowing up any trains, making people fly through the air, or morphing from one face to another. These effects adjust the coloring, lighting, and so forth in your clips.

iDVD

New in iMovie 3 are a direct interface to iDVD 3 and the brand-new chaptering feature. The iDVD pane, with one chapter marker, appears in Figure 13-11.

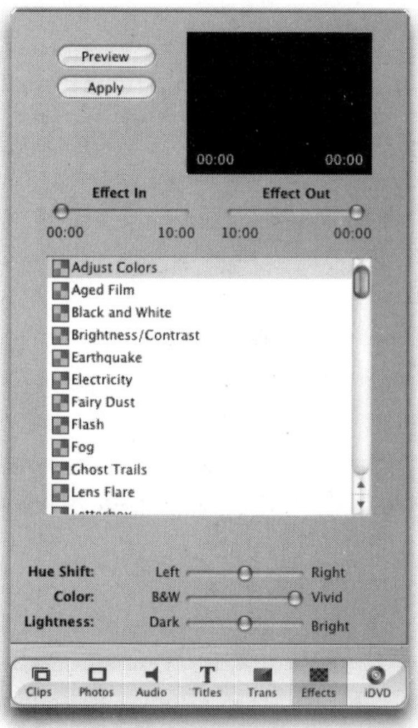

Figure 13-10: Apply visual effects here.

Figure 13-11: Create chapter markers in your movie so that iDVD can go to a specific scene.

The clip/timeline viewer

Stretching across the bottom of iMovie's window is a double-duty pane: the clip viewer/timeline viewer. The clip/timeline viewer (Figure 13-12, in its clip viewer persona) is where you assemble your movie and apply the effects, transitions, and titling introduced in the previous section.

The clip viewer

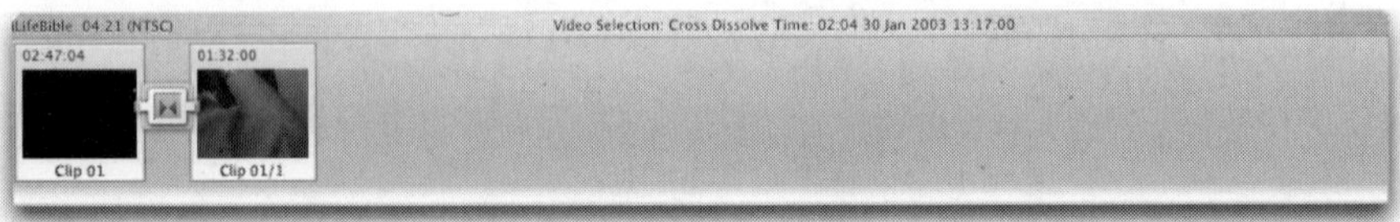

Figure 13-12: The clip viewer is where you assemble your movie and apply special effects.

You can recognize that the clip/timeline viewer is in clip-viewing mode when the film strip button shown here is highlighted. All the clips in your movie appear in sequence along the viewer, as do the effects applied. In Figure 13-12, there's a transition applied between the two clips. The name of your movie and its total length are displayed at the top left as well as whether your movie is NTSC or PAL format.

When you select a clip or transition, its name appears at the top center, along with other information, such as the date and time recorded and the clip's length. When you select multiple clips in the viewer, you only get to see that the selection comprises "<Multiple>" clips and what their total duration is.

The timeline viewer

Recognizable by its highlighted analog clock face, the timeline viewer (see Figure 13-13) is one of iMovie's most powerful tools. You can only add the majority of iMovie's best special visual effects, including fast- and slow-motion, in the timeline viewer.

Figure 13-13: Use the timeline to view the different tracks of your movie.

You use the timeline viewer to see what is happening at a specific point in your movie, to edit and manage the video track and two audio tracks, and to control the movie's speed and volume.

Unlike the clip viewer, where all clips take the same amount of space, every clip appears in a time-proportional bar in the timeline viewer's video track.

The Zoom slider, at the lower-left of the timeline viewer controls absolutely nothing in your movie, just the magnification used to view the timeline. It's called the timeline zoom, and you'll find it quite handy when you have really short clips or a really long movie. Setting it all the way to the left causes your entire timeline to fit in the viewer without activating the horizontal scroll bar.

In Chapter 15, you can find out how to use all of the timeline viewer's features, but your imagination is the only limitation on how you use these features. The timeline view is one of iMovie's most underrated features.

Status indicators

iMovie reserves a little bit of space at the bottom right of the window to keep you informed about how much data you've discarded but not yet erased (the iMovie Trash) and how much disk space you have left (the Free Space status bar). Figure 13-14 shows these status indicators.

Figure 13-14: The Free Space gauge (right) and the iMovie Trash (left) keep you informed about when you're running out of disk space and how much space you can free up.

The iMovie Trash

iMovie maintains its own Trash for discarded clips and clip segments as well as footage removed when applying transitions and effects. Similar to the Mac's Trash, the contents aren't really gone until you empty the Trash. Unlike the Mac's Trash, you can't open the iMovie Trash and directly retrieve the clip you want. You have to choose Edit ⇨ Undo (⌘-Z) as many times as necessary to get back to where you were when you deleted the clip.

Tip

iMovie allows 99 levels of Undo, which should be more than adequate in most cases. The downside is that you'll then have to manually redo each operation after the deletion that you want redone. The conclusion you can draw from this is that you shouldn't throw clips in the Trash until you're really sure that you don't need them any longer. Stick them in the Clips pane, maybe scrolled down to the bottom, if you just want to get them out of the way.

There is one sure way other than quitting from iMovie or changing projects to eliminate your ability to choose Edit ⇨ Undo. That guaranteed undo-killer is to Empty the iMovie Trash. Assuming that you have enough disk space (see the "What your Mac needs" section earlier in this chapter), we strongly recommend that you not empty iMovie's Trash until you're finished working on your project.

One really nice thing about iMovie's Trash is that you can see at a glance how much material is in it. iMovie displays how much it is holding just to the right of the Trash icon, as shown in Figure 13-14.

The Free Space status bar

The handy little thermometer to the left of the iMovie Trash tells you how much free space remains on the disk holding your iMovie project. It's even color-coded to give you a warning when space gets really tight.

✦ **Green:** You have more than 400MB of free space left. In other words, you can import about two minutes of video or more.

✦ **Yellow:** You have at least 200MB, but less than 400MB left. You should consider freeing up some disk space.

✦ **Red:** Okay, things are getting really tight. You're down to less than 200MB. You really need to start doing some housekeeping. Emptying the Trash might be a good start.

Apple claims that DV footage takes about 220MB per minute, other sources claim 200MB per minute or 210MB per minutes. In any event, that's a lot of space disappearing rather quickly when you're importing video from your camera, creating clips out of still photos, or otherwise adding clips to your project.

At 100MB, iMovie tosses an alert up on the screen beseeching you to start clearing some space. When you get down to 50MB or so, iMovie won't let you import any more footage until you free up some space.

Tip

We weren't kidding when we said that lots of free space is a must when you're working with iMovie and digital video. Although not everyone can afford to do so, investing in a large, fast secondary hard drive and dedicating it to iMovie projects is a very good idea. One problem with keeping your iMovie project on your startup disk is that this is also the disk that your Mac uses for virtual memory. If you have other programs running (that's what happens behind the scenes when you make use of iMovie's integration with the other iLife applications), it is possible that they will get swapped out to disk and the System will start taking disk space that iMovie is going to want. Of course, you could just not run other programs (like your e-mail program) while iMovie is running, but what's the fun in that?

Setting iMovie Preferences

iMovie 3 greatly simplified the iMovie Preferences dialog, going from a four-tabbed dialog to a single window with three sections: General, Import, and Advanced, as shown in Figure 13-15. Choose iMovie ➪ Preferences (⌘-,) to present the Preferences dialog.

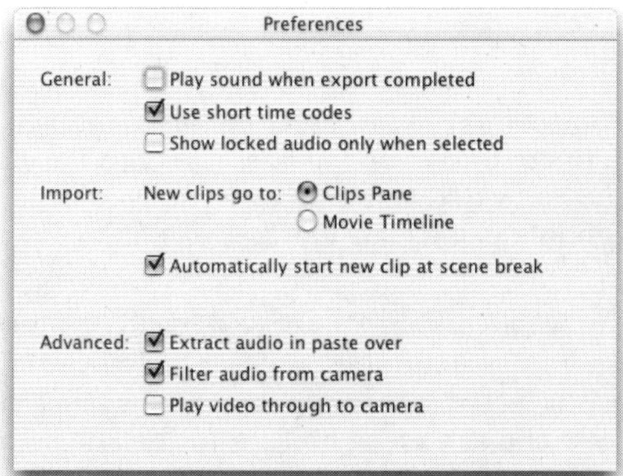

Figure 13-15: iMovie 3's Preferences dialog puts everything in front of you at once.

Checking out your General preferences

There are three checkboxes in the General section and they control how (and whether) specific information is made available, as follows:

✦ **Play sound when export completed:** When you check this box, you're telling iMovie that you want a notification sound when it completes an export (for example to QuickTime or to your camera) so that you can turn your attention back to iMovie.

✦ **Use short time codes:** This option is selected by default. Therefore, only as much of a time code (minimum being seconds and frames) as is necessary displays. Turning the option off adds the minutes field, even if it is not needed. It also causes the frames portion of the time code not to display in the status areas along the top of the clip/timeline viewer (they're still shown on the scrubber bars).

In previous versions of iMovie, this option deleted from the left any unnecessary numbers, but the frames were still displayed.

✦ **Show locked audio only when selected:** This option is also off by default. Enabling this option hides the fact that an audio clip is locked unless it is selected.

Managing your Import preferences

The Import section deals with clips you bring in from a digital camcorder and still clips you create by importing a graphic file.

✦ **New clips go to:** These radio buttons specify whether imported footage lands in the Clips pane or goes directly to the movie timeline. The Clips Pane is the default location. Unless you know that you want everything to be in the Timeline, in sequence, and without deleting any footage, we don't see a reason to change this preference.

✦ **Automatically start new clip at scene break:** This checkbox takes advantage of the fact that digital camcorders signal the start and end of a recording session (a scene). When this box is selected, a new clip is created when a start signal is detected. Starting a new clip at a scene break is the default setting.

Moving up to Advanced preferences

Although there are only three checkboxes, each of them enables some very cool features.

✦ **Extract audio in paste over:** With this feature, you can paste a length of video over an existing track, retaining the audio from the footage you're replacing. This comes in handy when you want to perform an intercut.

For more information on intercuts, see Chapter 16.

✦ **Filter audio from camera:** Tells iMovie to capture the audio when importing. One thing we know for sure, clearing this checkbox makes iMovie beep when we try to import from our cameras.

✦ **Play video through to camera:** You should select this option if you want iMovie to play your movie on both the Mac's screen and on your camera's screen. It is off by default.

Converting digital movies to analog

The Play video through to camera option gives you a really cool capability. You can use your digital camcorder as a *pass-through device* (a digital to analog converter) and record your movie directly on a VCR or play it on a TV set. Just follow these steps:

1. **Make sure that your camera is still connected via FireWire to your Mac and that you select Play video through to camera in the Advanced preferences.**
2. **Connect the AV-out port(s) on your camera to the red-white-and-yellow composite video connectors (they're often called RCA connectors) on your VCR or TV set (assuming that your TV set has RCA connectors for audio and video input).**

You're in even better shape if your camcorder and VCR or TV have S-Video connectors. In that case, don't connect the yellow (video channel) connector to the VCR/TV. Connect the S-Video cable instead. You'll get a better quality picture.

3. **Set the VCR or TV to the appropriate input setting.**
4. **Play your movie in iMovie and watch it on your TV or tape it on your VCR.**

Now, you know what your movie will look like when folks watch it on TV. You can create a videotape without what is called *generational signal loss*, which is why you lose quality with each copy of a copy when you use analog tape.

Summary

In this chapter, you learned a little about the evolution of home movies, from the film cameras and projectors of the mid-twentieth century, through the VCR era of the '80s and '90s, to today's digital era. You've also been introduced to the iMovie screen's many parts and faces, as well as iMovie's Preferences. The next few chapters delve more deeply into all these tools.

✦ ✦ ✦

CHAPTER 14

Getting Started with iMovie

✦ ✦ ✦ ✦

In This Chapter

Acquiring video from a digital camcorder

Working with clips

Importing images

Exporting your video

✦ ✦ ✦ ✦

We had a big decision to make about this section: Should we spend 50 to 100 pages telling you about composition, lighting, choosing a camcorder, and so forth? Or should we hit the high points of technique but focus on iMovie?

As you might guess, we're focusing on iMovie. Those peripheral issues, such as how to actually create footage you'd want to use in iMovie, can be found mostly in the Appendix. Some related topics, though, appear in this chapter as well as in Chapter 15 and Chapter 17. So, if you're the sort who normally skips sidebar material, you might want to rethink that position in these chapters.

Because we didn't want to detract from the fun stuff by adding a lot of non-iMovie details in this chapter, we're going to assume that you have a compatible digital camcorder, know how to use it, and how to light scenes, frame shots, and record usable sound in the field.

Acquiring Video from a Digital Camcorder

The first thing iMovie needs is video footage. If you don't have any pictures or video, you won't have anything to watch or anything with which to work. The intended (and most common) source of iMovie footage is from a digital camcorder.

Connecting your camcorder

In the last chapter, we showed you a picture of two FireWire connectors, a big one (six-pin) and a small one (four-pin). Most of you should have received a cable with these two connectors in the box when you purchased your Mac. Sometimes, you'll also get one with your camcorder, but if you didn't get a cable like this you're going to need to go out and buy one. Remember, it's called a 6-pin to 4-pin FireWire cable (it might be labeled IEEE-1394 or i.Link, instead of FireWire). Don't confuse it with a 6-pin to 4-pin USB cable or either of the two alternative (6-pin to 6-pin or 4-pin to 4-pin) FireWire cables. Just to make sure that you have its appearance firmly in mind, we're going to show you the connectors again in Figure 14-1.

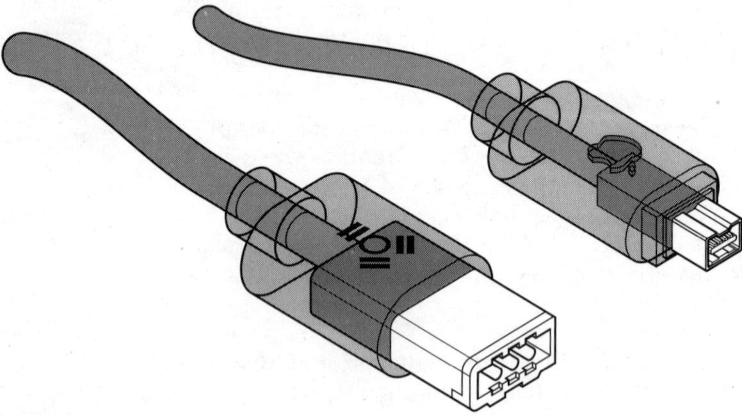

Figure 14-1: The FireWire connectors needed to hook your camcorder to your Mac.

You should insert the smaller square (4-pin) connector into your camcorder's FireWire port. This port may very likely be labeled IEEE-1394, i.Link, or DV in/out rather than FireWire. All these terms mean the same thing. You insert the larger wide (6-pin) end into one of your Mac's FireWire ports. The FireWire ports sport the FireWire logo shown in Figure 14-2.

Caution

Sometimes, if you connect the camera to another FireWire device rather than directly to your Mac, you can cause OS X to think that you've disconnected an external FireWire drive. We haven't heard of this happening when the connection is directly to the Mac. If you experience a dismounted drive when you connect your camcorder (or some other FireWire device, like an iPod), power the drive down and then restart it so that OS X receives a signal to mount it back on your Desktop. You should probably run Disk Utility's First Aid tool to make sure that your disk and its contents are okay.

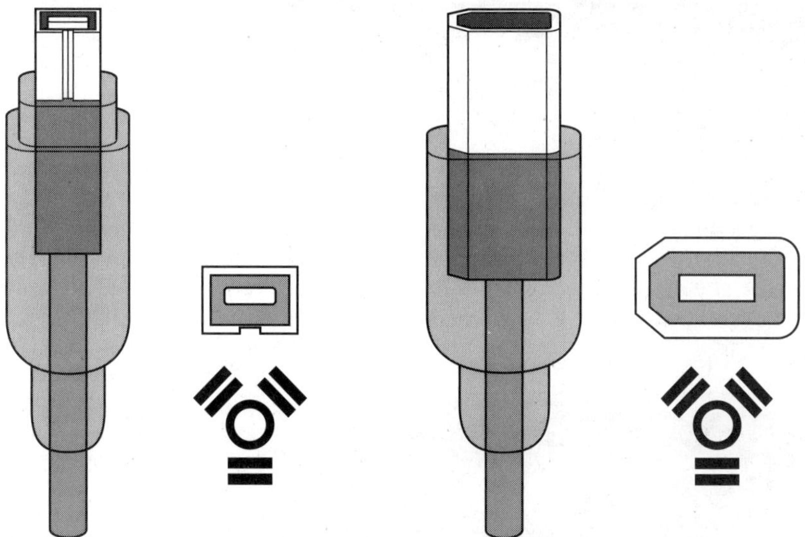

Figure 14-2: Insert the four-pin connector (left) into your camcorder and the six-pin connector (right) into the FireWire port on your Mac.

After you connect the cable at both ends, turn your camcorder on to its VCR (or VTR or Playback) setting rather than its Camera setting (we'll just call it the VTR mode from now on). You've probably already figured this out, but we'll tell you anyway, just in case: Don't run your camcorder on battery power while uploading to and downloading from iMovie. One reason is that running from battery drains the battery. For another, you'd really hate to have the camcorder shut down for lack of a charge in the middle of an upload or download.

Tip

Another real battery drain is using the camcorder's LCD display. That's really a shame, because the LCD is usually a lot easier to see and use than a viewfinder. If you're running low on battery power or think that you might be pushing your battery's limits later in your filming session, try to make do with the viewfinder.

Starting iMovie

The next step on the road to making your movie is to launch iMovie (kinda obvious, right?), which is probably in your Mac's Applications folder. Just click the Applications icon in a Finder window toolbar and look for iMovie. If you're going to use iMovie a lot, you might want to put iMovie's icon in your Dock as a (semi)permanent fixture, just like Apple did with iTunes and now (Mac OS X 10.2) does with iMovie, iPhoto, and iDVD. To do this, drag iMovie's icon to the spot in the Dock where you want the iMovie icon to be and let go. We keep ours between iTunes and iPhoto, as shown in Figure 14-3. From now on, all you have to do is click the iMovie icon in the Dock to launch iMovie.

Figure 14-3: If you use iMovie a lot, you should consider keeping it in the Dock.

However you choose to launch iMovie, the first time it starts up you'll see a screen similar to the one in Figure 14-4. Because you don't already have a project to open (this is your first time, right?), click the Create Project button, and iMovie presents you with the sheet shown in Figure 14-5. We're pleased to see that iMovie no longer offers that silly *<your name>*'s Movie that annoyed so many in previous versions.

Figure 14-4: Welcome to iMovie, choose your poison.

Save as:
Where: Movies
Cancel Save

Figure 14-5: iMovie's New Project sheet.

As much as we love iMovie (and we *really* do), it isn't without a few minor annoyances, and the New Project sheet you see in Figure 14-5 is one of them. Primarily, we don't like Save dialog that has the column browser hidden. Having the browser hidden, you can't see what names are already taken. Make it second nature to click the Reveal Browser button to the right of the Where pop-up menu.

Tip If you're fortunate enough to have a second internal hard disk with a lot of free space that you can use for iMovie, we recommend that you save your projects there. Keep that disk in your Favorites so that you can select it directly from the Where pop-up menu in the New Project sheet. A little later, we'll tell you why we specify an internal hard disk.

Okay, you now have a new project going as shown in Figure 14-6. Isn't that an empty, boring sight?

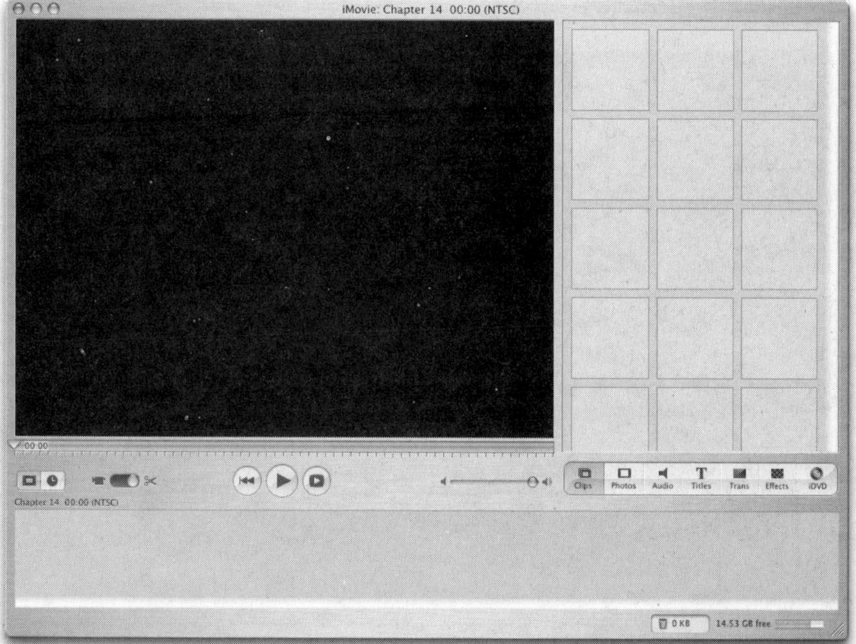

Figure 14-6: If this isn't starting with a blank canvas, we don't know what is.

If you haven't already done so, check out the "Exploring the iMovie Window" section in Chapter 13 to learn what all these screen areas are for.

iMovie will run in an 800 x 600 screen, but your monitor will be smaller. iMovie's window is designed to look best and be most functional at 1024 x 768 resolution.

Importing the video

If your camera is turned on and connected, the monitor should have a blue screen with the words Camera Connected centered horizontally and about 1/3 of the way down in white, possibly with a timer display in the upper right, as shown in Figure 14-7. If you don't see a blue screen, make sure that the toggle switch (to the left of the VCR controls) is in the camera position. If, instead of saying "Camera Connected" iMovie tells you "Camera Disconnected," you should check your cable connections to make sure that the connectors are fully inserted and check your camera to verify that it is turned on in its VTR setting. If you still don't see "Camera Connected," try turning the camera off and back on. Finally, if that fails, check at `www.apple.com/imovie` to verify that your camera is one that iMovie supports.

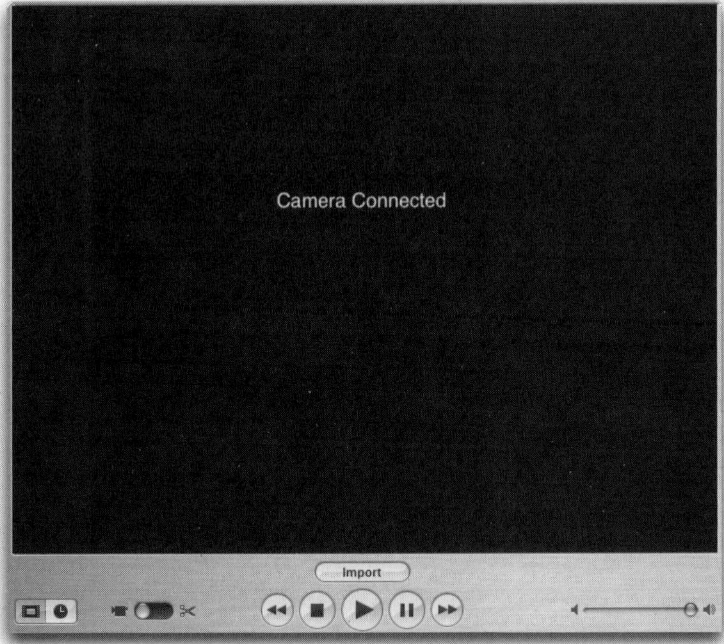

Figure 14-7: iMovie sees your camera and is ready for you to start importing.

You can also import video from disk files and, with a little work (okay, sometimes it's a lot of work) spent converting formats, from formats other than DV streams. We'll cover that in detail in Chapter 15.

Controlling your camera with iMovie

We really don't enjoy trying to manipulate the tiny membrane-style controls on our video camera with our fingernails when we want to rewind, fast forward, play, or stop the camera. We've even gotten to the point where we connect the camera in iMovie just to use its much easier controls to review our clips (and the bigger screen ain't bad, either).

We've watched and tried two different approaches to importing video. The first way is to just click the Import button and let iMovie import everything to disk, after which we go back and select the footage we want, discarding the rest.

By the way, if you don't have wasted footage, you probably didn't start shooting quickly enough or you stopped shooting too soon in at least some scenes. That's one reason professionals start shooting with that clapboard in view before the scene starts. They're making sure that they don't miss the beginning. They also shoot a couple of seconds after the director yells, "Cut," to make sure they don't lop off the ending.

The second method is a little more work upfront but doesn't fill our disk with nearly so much wasted footage. You should recall the Import Preference setting that tells iMovie to create new clips at scene breaks. With this on, iMovie starts a new clip each time the camcorder signals that a recording session started (in other words, each time the camera switched to Record or Pause was turned off).

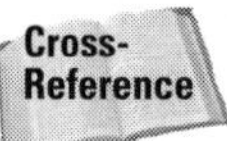

For more on the setting the Import Preference, see Chapter 13.

Scene changes aren't the only time iMovie automatically starts new clips. You'll also get a new clip after just short of 10 minutes of video, because iMovie won't allow a single clip to be larger than 2GB on disk.

Experience has taught us that what looks like more work isn't always. Professional filmmakers always shoot a lot more footage than they're going to need, just to make sure that they have everything they want. We suggest you follow their example. One of the corollaries to this approach is that you'll want to import manually rather than in bulk. This isn't actually as much work as it seems and it tends to use up a lot less disk space. Proceed as follows:

1. **Using the Play, Rewind, and Fast Forward buttons, position the tape to just before the footage you want.**
2. **Click Play.**
3. **When the tape starts running, click Import when you see the footage you want.** The Import button turns blue, a new clip appears on the shelf, and the clip's time code starts increasing.

Pressing the spacebar is the same as clicking Import.

4. **When the footage you want is complete, click Import (or press Space) again.** The Import button loses its blue coloring, and the footage stops importing. However, the tape continues to play until you click the Stop or Play buttons.

Repeat these steps (or just 3 and 4 if you leave the tape playing) until you've imported all the footage you want.

You might consider disabling the Importing preference that creates a new clip at scene breaks when manually importing if you know you have multiple scenes you want brought in as one item. In general we leave it enabled, but there are situations where we disable it for a session.

Knowing your timecodes

Although it is possible, an iMovie-compatible digital camcorder exists that doesn't keep a running *timecode*, we haven't seen one or heard of it. You've seen the little timer running in the upper-right corner (usually) while you're taping — that's the timecode. You also see it in iMovie when you're controlling the camera, as shown in Figure 14-8.

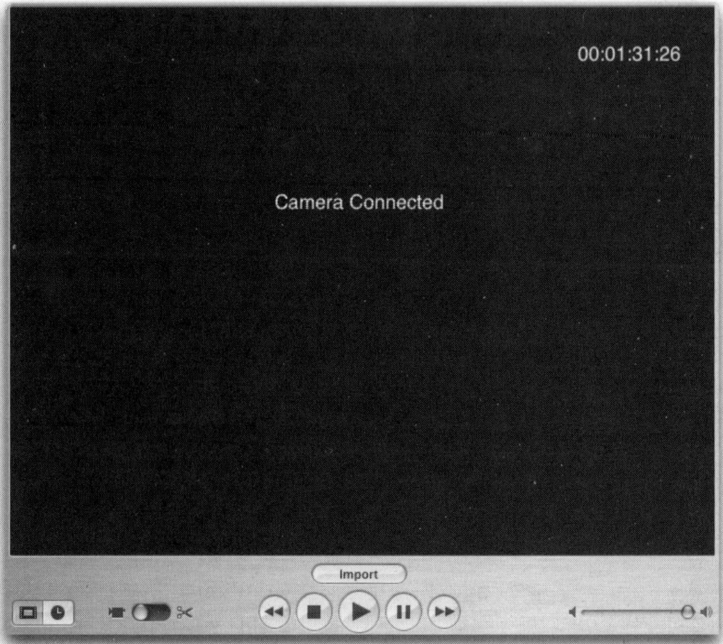

Figure 14-8: Finding your scene is a lot easier when you can tell time.

If you keep track of the timecodes for important scenes when you're recording, you'll find it much easier to locate the scenes you want when it's time to import your video. Just fast forward (or rewind) the tape to the noted timecode, and you're ready to start importing.

Make sure to take one precaution when you rely on timecodes. You should prepare the tape, which is called *blackstriping*. To blackstripe a tape, just record the length of it with the lens cap on. Doing this will write black to the entire tape, but your camera will record the timecodes for the entire tape. Now, no matter if you forward over a stretch of tape, the timecodes will still be continuous.

If you forget to blackstripe a tape, you can get around that in a few (awkward) ways. The first is to import everything from the tape (with New Clip at Scene Break enabled), blackstripe the tape, and then write everything back out. A second method would involve using two digital camcorders and copying from one to the other. You'll need a 4-pin to 4-pin FireWire cable for this, unless you're willing to lose quality by making an analog copy.

Working with Clips

Okay, you've imported your video and have a slew of clips sitting on the shelf. Now, the real fun (and work) begins: you get to start constructing your movie. Selecting clips on the shelf is about the most basic action you can perform on them, but it starts a chain of events in iMovie. First, iMovie switches into Edit mode (the toggle moves from DV to the filmstrip icon), and the beginning of the first selected clip appears in the monitor.

When you select a clip, its border turns blue. You can select multiple clips by holding down the Shift (or ⌘) key and clicking on the additional clips.

You need to select clips before you can edit them, add them to the Timeline viewer, or delete them (by dragging them to iMovie's Trash icon). Okay, we just told you how to delete a clip as well.

It is tempting, when the Trash icon tells you how many megabytes (or gigabytes) are sitting there, to empty the Trash (File ➪ Empty Trash or click the Trash icon). Be careful here! Not only does emptying iMovie's trash make the clips unrecoverable (unless you want to reimport them), but it wipes out iMovie's undo list, so you can no longer undo the last actions you performed, even if they had nothing to do with the clips you deleted. iMovie warns you, but we all know that confirmation dialogs are often OK'd without our actually reading them.

Renaming clips

We don't know about you, but names like Clip 3 don't tell us a whole lot about what the scene is. More than that, the thumbnail image you see (called the *poster frame*) in the clip often won't tell you enough about the clip for you to tell what the clip is about. For example, if you're filming your daughter's birthday party, how do you tell one clip from another when they all start out with a close-up of your little girl?

iMovie gives you a simple solution to this problem. You get to rename your clips. If you've used the AppleWorks 6 Presentations module, you already know how to do this, because the process is the same as renaming slides. For the rest of you, just follow the steps:

1. **Select a clip and click in the name area.** This makes it ready for editing as shown in Figure 14-9.

Figure 14-9: A clip that's ready to be given a useful name.

2. **Type a new name.** Keep the names short, though, because only about 12-14 characters are visible and longer names have some of the characters replaced with ellipses. (At least this is a step forward from only having ten characters show in previous versions.)

Well, that was pretty easy, wasn't it? Now, repeat the process for each of the clips you're going to use so that you can recognize them.

Editing clips

A movie that doesn't require some editing is rare. For example, you may want to remove unnecessary footage, such as a few extra frames at the start or end of a clip, or split a clip into two or more pieces so you can insert some other footage into the middle.

In Chapter 13, we discuss how the monitor's control buttons are a little different when you're in Edit mode. That's because they no longer have anything to do with your camera, they control how you view and work with your clips.

Another Way to Rename Clips

There's another way to rename clips. Choose File ➪ Show Info (⌘-I) or double-click the clip to display the Clip Info dialog shown here:

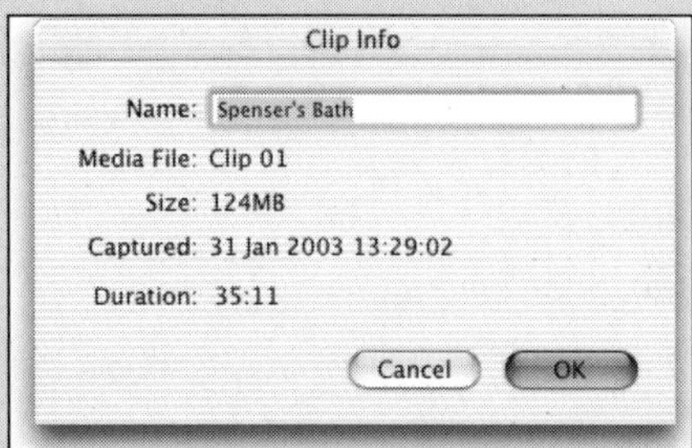

Just as in a Finder or iTunes Info window, select the part of the name you want to change and start typing.

The Clip Info window provides a bit more information, though, that can come in handy. After you've renamed a clip, the actual file on disk still has the original name. If you want to use the clip in another movie, you're going to need to know the name of the disk file, and this is where you can find it (it's on the *Media File* line). If you're curious as to how big the file is, when you imported it, or how long it is, you can see that information as well.

You can edit a clip on the shelf or in the Clip/Timeline viewer. iMovie 3 enables you to edit a sequence of clips selected in the Clips pane, something that wasn't allowed in previous versions.

The scrubber bar is your friend

That little blue bar located (Figure 14-10) between the monitor's screen and buttons is your most powerful tool when editing clips. With it, you position within a clip or select part of a clip.

Note

The tick marks below the scrubber bar don't actually tell you anything other than where you are within a clip or group of clips, relative to the total length. In other words, you have the same number of ticks (67) under a 3-second clip as you do under a 7-minute clip. Don't ask us where they came up with 67 as the number to use, either. (In iMovie 1, there were 123 ticks under the scrubber bar at 1024 x 768 resolution.)

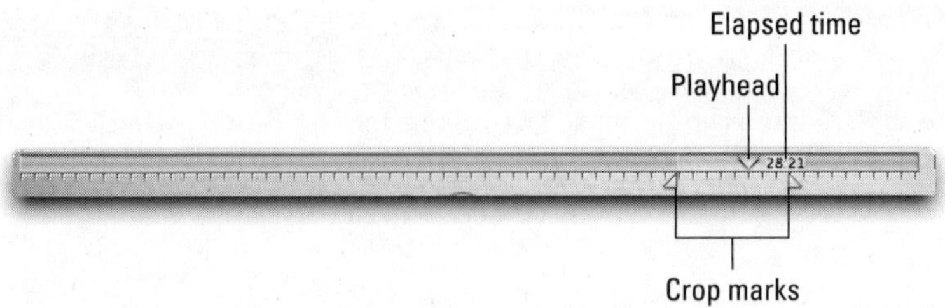

Figure 14-10: Use the scrubber bar to position your playhead.

iMovie gives you three ways to position the scrubber bar's playhead. You can

✦ **Click the scrubber bar:** Just click the point where you want to be. The playhead moves there, and the screen area displays that frame.

✦ **Drag the playhead:** This is called *scrubbing* and is where the scrubber bar gets its name. You'll actually see the frames flash by in the screen area.

✦ **Use the left and right arrow keys on your keyboard:** Each press moves you one frame backward (←) or one frame forward (→). Combining Shift with the arrow keys moves ten frames at a time in the corresponding direction and holding down the arrow keys keeps you moving continuously in the indicated direction.

Tip

You will likely find that the most effective method to position your clip is to scrub or click to approximately the position you want and then use the arrow keys to refine your position.

Use the crop markers to select portions of your clip for copying, cutting, or cropping (see the "Cropping clips" section later in this chapter). You can drag the crop markers to bound the desired clip segment. Even better, if the playhead and crop markers are positioned at one end of the segment you want, you can Shift-click the scrubber bar at the other end of your segment and iMovie selects the segment and moves the playhead to the point where you Shift-clicked.

Tip

You can use the left and right arrows (←, →) to position the crop markers just like the playhead. Click a crop marker and then use the arrow keys to move that marker one frame in the indicated direction (ten frames if you hold down the Shift key when pressing an arrow key).

Splitting clips

There are obvious uses for splitting clips, a couple of which are specific to working within iMovie. Among the obvious is when you want to interleave — that is, cut back and forth between — two scenes. Just split the clips and you can position the pieces in any order you please. The iMovie-specific reasons generally involve working with Transitions or other iMovie Effects and we'll get into that in the "Transitioning between clips," section later in this chapter.

Once again, iMovie makes your job easy, as follows:

1. **Position the playhead where you want the split to occur.**
2. **Choose Edit ➪ Split Video Clip at Playhead (⌘-T).**

We told you it was easy. You now have two clips with similar names. The first retains the name of the original clip, and the second is selected and has /1 appended to the name, as shown in Figure 14-11.

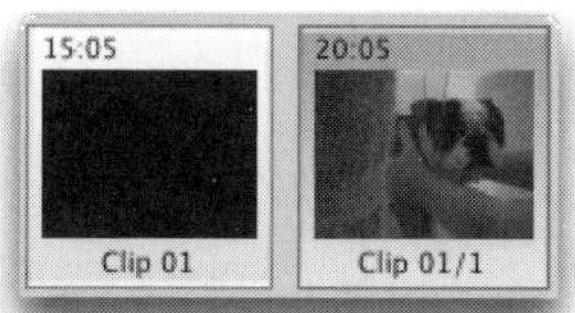

Figure 14-11: iMovie isn't exactly original when it names split clips.

Trimming or removing clip segments

You'll often want to trim a little from the start or end of a clip. Proceed as follows to trim from the end of a clip:

1. **Position both crop markers to the right end of the clip.**
2. **Position the playhead to the beginning of the extraneous footage.**
3. **Shift-click the playhead.** iMovie moves the left crop marker to the playhead, selecting everything from that point to the end of the clip.
4. **Choose Edit ➪ Clear or press the Delete key on your keyboard.** That footage is gone.

You should notice that the clip's length (in the shelf or clip viewer) indicates the new length, and the amount in the iMovie Trash has just increased.

To trim from the beginning of the clip, just reverse the process. With the crop markers at the left end of the scrubber bar, position the playhead at the end of the extraneous footage, Shift-click the playhead, and choose Edit ➪ Clear (or press Delete).

Although you could trim from both the beginning and end, you'll find cropping (described shortly) to be easier than performing two trims.

The obvious corollary to trimming a clip is that you can also remove a chunk from the middle. Just select the segment you want to remove and choose Edit ➪ Clear (or press Delete). The one major difference is that you'll now have two clips where you had one before. Notice that this is equivalent to splitting your clip and then trimming one or both.

Cropping clips

iMovie also gives you a convenient method to combine trimming from both ends at once, called *cropping*. Position the crop markers to bound the segment you want to keep and then choose Edit ➪ Crop (⌘-K). iMovie removes the footage from either end, leaving just your selection.

Cropping and clearing remove both the video and the associated audio. Sometimes you're going to want to retain the audio (maybe for narration over new video, like in a newscast). We'll show you how to do this in Chapter 15.

Of course, iMovie is a faithful Mac application, which means that you can also cut or copy then paste selected footage as well. When you copy (Edit ➪ Copy or ⌘-C) a segment and then paste it (Edit ➪ Paste or ⌘-V), a new clip appears on the shelf. What's cool about this is that you have now performed a crop without losing the original footage. Similarly, a cut (Edit ➪ Cut or ⌘-X) followed by a paste is the same as splitting and then splitting again.

Creating a still clip

We're sure that you've seen examples of still clips in movies and on television, even if you weren't aware that was what you were looking at. One common use for a still clip is when a scene transitions from what looks like a painting or daguerreotype into live action and full color. Another use is when you want to freeze a moment in your movie, such as a sign or a shocked expression.

Once again, iMovie makes creating a still clip simple:

1. **Position the playhead to the frame from which you want to create the still clip.**
2. **Choose Edit ➪ Create Still Frame (Shift-⌘-S), and you're done.**

iMovie names the first still clip Still 01 and numbers subsequent stills from there.

iMovie sets a still clip's duration as 5 seconds. This default used to be a preference setting, but is now cast in concrete; however, you can change duration once the clip exists in the Clip Info dialog, as shown in Figure 14-12.

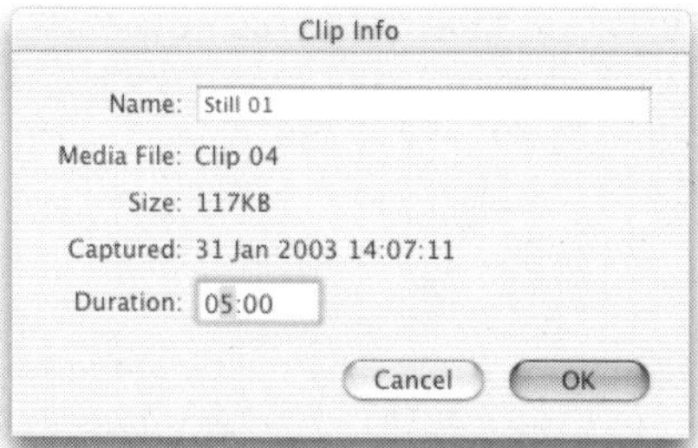

Figure 14-12: Change a still clip's duration in the Clip Info dialog.

Restoring a clip

Remember we told you that if you didn't empty iMovie's Trash, you could undo your way back to earlier states (up to 99 steps)? That method has some drawbacks, the greatest of which is that you end up undoing a whole lot of things that you might still want done to get a clip back to an earlier state. iMovie has a neat and easy solution to this quandary.

1. **Select the clip.** It doesn't matter whether it is in the shelf, in the clip viewer, or on the Timeline viewer.
2. **Choose Advanced ⇨ Restore Clip.** iMovie now alerts you, as shown in Figure 14-13, what it is going to do and how much data this will add to the beginning or end of the clip, and asks whether you want to proceed.

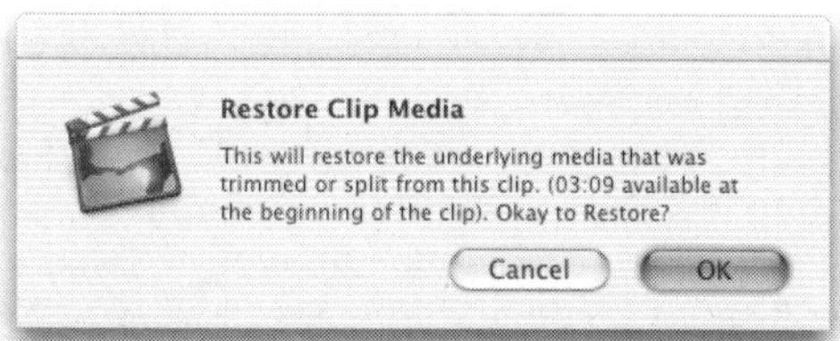

Figure 14-13: iMovie tells you how much material it will restore and asks whether to proceed.

3. **Click OK if you want to proceed.**

If you split the clip or removed material from the middle, you generate a second clip, which still exists and takes up disk space.

Reversing a clip

Here's an editing tool that falls into the category of special effects, and a pretty cool one at that when you use it appropriately. You can run a clip backwards as follows:

1. **Select the clip.** You can do this from the shelf, clip viewer, or Timeline viewer as appropriate.
2. **Choose Advanced ⇨ Reverse Clip Direction (⌘-R).** The clip reverses.

Now, when you play the clip in the monitor, everything in the clip runs backward, even the sound. If you don't want the sound to play backward, you must extract it first, as we describe in the "Extracting audio" section later in this chapter. If you look in the upper-right corner of a reversed clip icon's border, you will see a left-pointing triangle as shown in Figure 14-14.

Figure 14-14: Reversed clips sport a badge in their upper-right corner.

Working with the clip viewer

The Clips pane is a handy place to store clips, especially when you're working on them as described earlier in the "Editing clips" section. The Clip/Timeline viewer is where you assemble your movie, apply transitions and effects, and add titles and subtitles.

Moving your clips from the shelf to the clip viewer is, as usual, easy. Just select the clips in the shelf and drag them to the clip viewer. Being the obliging program that it is, when you select a clip (or group of clips) in the clip viewer, iMovie (again) presents you the opportunity to edit them in the monitor. But, far more than that, the Clip viewer tells you a lot about your selected clip. Figure 14-15 shows the clip viewer with all its informational displays. If you select multiple clips, the clip name is replaced by "<multiple>" and the recording date/time isn't displayed.

Now that you have your clips arranged in the clip viewer (hopefully, in the order you want them to play), it is time to start putting the polish on your movie: transitioning between clips, applying effect, and adding your titles, subtitles, and captions.

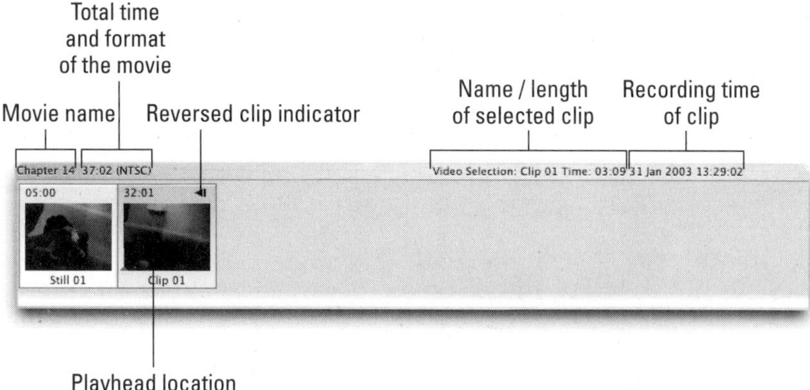

Figure 14-15: The Clip viewer tells you a lot about your selected clip(s).

If you have some clips with which to work, you might want to follow along through the next few topics and get a real feel for how transitions, effects, and titles work. We can eloquently describe them, but there is no way in a static medium (such as this book) that you can actually experience the visual effect they produce.

Transitioning between clips

Every situation in filmmaking is different. You can apply rules until you're blue in the face and get serviceable results, but creating a movie still involves art and feel. One place where you find this very evident is when you are moving from one scene to another. Do you apply a transition or not? If you choose to apply a transition, which one do you use? By the way, if you have no transition between scenes, you're said to have *cut* from one scene to the next.

Deciding to cut or transition

If you've got all your clips in the clip viewer, in the order you want them to occur, you're at a good starting point. One assumption that we're going to make is you already split your clips at scene breaks, if iMovie hadn't already done that for you.

iMovie provides a collection of common transitions: Circle Opening, Cross Dissolve, Fade In, Fade Out, Overlap, Push, Radial, Scale Down, Warp In, Warp Out, Wash In, and Wash Out as shown in Figure 14-16. Transitions exist between clips, becoming additional entities in the clip viewer and on the Timeline viewer. As you can see in the figure, each transition has a little icon to its left, but that icon no longer has any meaning — it's just used as a "handle" so that you can drag the transition into the Clip/Timeline viewer.

In previous versions of iMovie, the icon varied depending on whether the transition affected both clips, just the clip it followed, or just the clip it preceded.

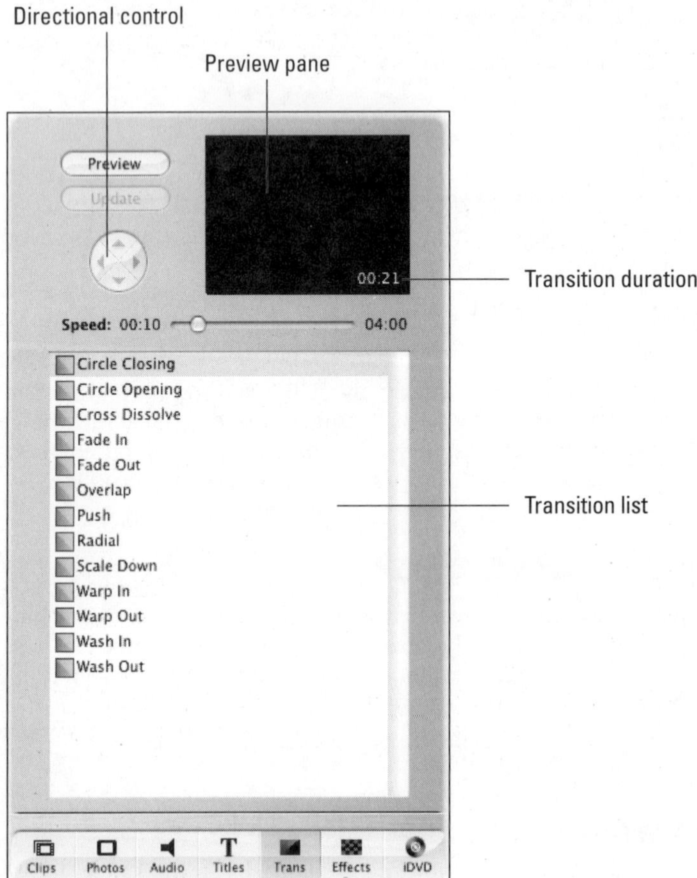

Figure 14-16: Select and control your transition in the shelf's Transitions panel.

You might be tempted to put transitions between every scene. Don't succumb, but don't consider yourself unusual, either. Transitions are like a shiny new toy, and the temptation to see how they look is almost unbearable. A transition's purpose is to segue your movie from one concept to the next, in other words, to indicate a change of focus. For example, you probably shouldn't put a transition between two clips during a battle scene or sporting event where all you did was change the camera angle. But, if you are moving from viewing the battle to what's occurring on the home front, you probably want a transition.

You use *transitions* to convey a change of focus or the passage of time. If you examine a movie closely, you'll find that cuts are used far more often than transitions and, with the addition of scoring or narration, the cuts are almost unnoticeable unless you're looking for them.

Checking out iMovie's transitions

As shown in Figure 14-16, iMovie comes with 13transitions, but you can add more from a commercial (or maybe shareware) package. Apple includes a link to third-party plug-in collections on the main iMovie page, `www.apple.com/imovie`. Here are the 13 supplied transitions and their descriptions:

✦ **Circle Closing:** This transition works on two clips, making the second clip appear as the first clip disappears in a shrinking circle. You might use this to indicate the end of a story line. It's particularly useful when going from the final scene to closing credits.

✦ **Circle Opening:** In this two-clip transition, the amount of the second clip that shows grows as the circle opens. We tend to reserve this transition to indicate the beginning of a scene or story line.

✦ **Cross Dissolve:** This transition works on two clips, making the first clip appear to gradually disappear, revealing the second clip running behind it. By setting the Speed, you can control how long the dissolve lasts. Cross Dissolves are especially effective for minor changes in time.

✦ **Fade In:** Use Fade In to cause a clip to gradually appear from a black background. Fade Ins are most useful when introducing the story or a significantly different scene, such as someone waking up the morning after another event.

✦ **Fade Out:** Fade Out causes your clip's end to fade to black and is effective at the end of your movie or to signal the end of a significant scene.

✦ **Overlap:** Working on two clips, an Overlap is similar to a Cross Dissolve. The primary difference is that the second clip now appears in front of the first clip. You primarily use overlaps to indicate a change of location.

✦ **Push:** Kind of a hokey transition, the second clip slides in and pushes the previous clip off screen. When you choose a Push, the Direction arrows become enabled, and you can choose whether things slide from left-to-right, right-to-left, bottom-to-top, or top-to-bottom. The only really good uses for this transition are in a slideshow presentation or when looking for a comedic touch.

✦ **Radial:** Another two-clip transition, the second clip replaces the first clips as a clockwise sweep is made. We don't particularly care for this one, but it does give the impression of a clock sweep, so you might find it useful to denote the passage of time.

✦ **Scale Down:** Another special-purpose, somewhat hokey transition, Scale Down causes the first clip to shrink down to a dot and disappear, revealing the second clip running behind it. Scale Down is also good for slideshows and might be useful if your film is science fiction.

✦ **Warp In:** Similar to Circle Closing, but using different shapes. This effect looks like the first clips is being sucked into the center of the second clip. We consider this a fairly hokey effect, but you might find a use for it.

✦ **Warp Out:** This transition resembles Circle Opening, albeit again with a different shape. Another special purpose visual effect.

✦ **Wash In:** Similar to a Fade In, but your clip appears from a white/gray background. This is a good transition in the same circumstances as a Fade In.

✦ **Wash Out:** This transition fades the clip it follows to white and is useful in the same cases that a Fade Out is useful.

The Circle, Warp, Wash, and Radial Effects were previously part of the freely downloadable plug-in pack available for iMovie 2.

Setting up and applying a transition

Unless you have selected clips in the clip viewer, iMovie assumes that you want to operate on the first clip or pair of clips in the Clip viewer, and those clips are the clips it'll use in the Preview pane for demonstration purposes. That's not a big deal if all you're interested in is seeing how the effects work, but if you want to see how the transition looks on the clips for which you intend it, select them in the Clip viewer (or Timeline viewer).

By clicking on a transition name in the Transition list, you tell iMovie to preview what it will look like in the Preview pane. Most of the time, previewing is a really good idea, because you're probably going to want to customize the transition a bit. There are two customizations possible: Speed and Direction, but Direction is only available to some transitions. For example, of the six transitions that come with iMovie, Direction is active only for Push.

✦ **Speed:** Also called duration. By moving the slider, you control how long the transition takes to complete. When you release the slider, iMovie displays the new preview. Just to be perfectly clear, the times on the slider are in seconds and frames. In general, iMovie neither allows a transition of less than 10 frames nor one longer than 4 seconds. The time you've selected displays in the lower-right corner of the Preview pane, which is a lot easier than estimating just how far you've moved the slider.

✦ **Direction:** This lets you specify the direction for movement-related transitions like Push.

When you're pretty sure that you have your project the way you want it, you should probably click the Preview button and check it one more time, this time in the monitor window so you don't have to squint so hard.

Note Be aware that the preview will not be as smooth as a finished transition. iMovie has to perform lots of computations to smooth things out and the preview is just an approximation.

Drag one-clip transitions on top of the clip they are to affect and drag two-clip transitions between the clips of interest. iMovie doesn't actually *render* (apply) the transition until you drag it into place in the Clip viewer (or Timeline viewer). While iMovie is performing the myriad calculations necessary to make the transition as seamless as possible, a small progress indicator (shown in Figure 14-17) appears below the transition's icon. The black bar gradually turns red as the rendering takes place.

Figure 14-17: The rendering progress indicator turns red as the rendering takes place.

With shorter or simpler transitions, the indicator often disappears before you even notice that it is there. As Macs get faster, the progress indicator's lifespan also grows shorter.

You can still edit or view other parts of your movie. However, you can't view the transition while rendering takes place. Be aware that rendering is a processor-intensive activity, so your Mac might be a little less responsive than usual while it concentrates on the rendering.

Now that you have your transition selected and rendered, you're obviously going to want to admire your handiwork. If it's a one-clip transition, you need only select it and the clip it affects in the Clip viewer (or Timeline viewer) and click the monitor's Play button. For two-clip transitions, select both clips (iMovie also selects the transition) and click the monitor's Play button. You could select just the transition in the timeline to play only the transition. If you do this, be aware that you won't see any context.

Tip

Transitions show up best if played back to your camera or an external monitor.

Note

If you select just the transition in the Clip/Timeline viewer, the Video Selection status at the top of the Clip/Timeline viewer reminds you which transition you employed.

Modifying and deleting transitions

If, after you've gone to all that effort creating and rendering a transition, you see that it isn't quite what you want, iMovie empowers you to modify it. Just select the transition in the clip viewer with the Transitions panel showing and you can modify any of the settings, even the selected transition. When you're done (or think you are), click the Update button and iMovie renders the new transition choice.

Deleting transitions is Mac-simple. If you added a transition last, you can choose Edit ➪ Undo (⌘-Z). Even if you've gone on and done other things, you can select the transition's icon and choose Edit ➪ Clear (or press Delete). The transition is gone, and iMovie returns any affected clips to their unmodified states (while storing the transition in the iMovie Trash).

Understanding Visual Effects

We noted (briefly) in Chapter 13 that what you find on the iMovie Effects panel (Figure 14-18) are not what we normally consider "special effects"—like a sunburst or a man morphing into a dog. What you can do here is affect the brightness, contrast, even color in your clips. When used in conjunction with transitions, you can emulate some of the classier visual effects of professional moviemakers.

iMovie comes with 19 built-in effects, but you can add more. Various third-party sources sell larger collections. We're big fans of the Gee Three Slick Transitions and Effects (`www.geethree.com`), which are inexpensive and give professional-looking results. Virtix (`www.virtix.com`), eZedia (`www.ezedia.com`), and CSB Digital (`www.csbdigital.com`) also have links on Apple's iMovie Web pages and offer some great packages, including free sampler packs.

Exploring the Effects panel

The Effects panel in Figure 14-18 is chock-full of possibilities. Some of the effects offer additional sliders below the list that you use to customize that particular effect. Others, such as Black & White, don't—what you see is what you get. As with transitions, every time you select an effect or change a setting, iMovie runs a preview of your effect in the (small) Preview pane at the upper-right of the panel.

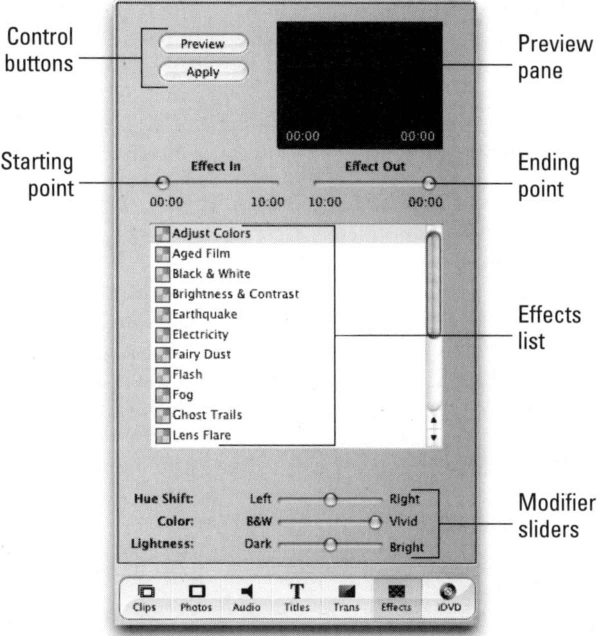

Figure 14-18: The Effects panel lets you choose, tweak, preview, and apply your effects.

Two sliders are present above the Effects list for all effects though: Effect In and Effect Out. Use Effect In to specify when the effect is to start relative to the beginning of the clip (0:00 says to start it at the beginning of the clip). Similarly, you use Effect Out to specify when the effect terminates relative to the end of the clip. That's a critical point: 0:00 means that it ends when the clip does, 1:15 indicates that it ends 1.5 seconds before the clip ends (30 frames to a second—it is 1.6 seconds if you're using PAL with its 25fps rate). So, if you know the timecode (from the time display next to the playhead) where you want the effect to end, you're going to have to do a little subtraction: length of clip minus the timecode.

Another behavioral oddity relating to effects is that if you specify that the effect is in effect (pun intended) for the clip's full length (Effect In = 0:00 and Effect Out = 0:00), then you sees a constant application of the effect, be it Sepia Tone, Soft Focus, or whatever. On the other hand, if either Effect In or Effect Out is not zero, you get a gradual increase (kind of like a fade in) effect to the effect (okay, we promise to stop abusing this pun opportunity).

You can apply multiple effects to the same clip, with the same or different in and out times. Although overuse of this capability can make your movie kind of tacky, judicious application, say sequential Color Shifts, can produce a stylish result.

Checking out iMovie's Effects

The 19 effects supplied with iMovie fall (pretty much) into three categories:

✦ **Brightness and Contrast Adjustments:** There's just one here, named (appropriately) Brightness/Contrast. This is very much like the Brightness and Contrast adjustments on your TV set. Increasing brightness makes everything closer to white whereas decreasing brightness makes everything darker, but at different rates. Dark pixels get darker faster than light pixels and light pixels get lighter faster than dark pixels. Increasing contrast makes dark pixels darker and light pixels lighter. Adjusting contrast can be helpful when you had too much light on your subject, washing out the image.

✦ **Color Adjustments:** Again, you just have one here with the original name, Adjust Colors. Three sliders, Hue Shift, Color, and Lightness appear beneath the list and provide this effect with great power to do good or evil.

- **Hue Shift** changes the colors in your image from red/yellow on the slider's left end toward blue/green at the right. If you have too much red/yellow/orange in the picture, moving the slider right a bit can help.
- **Color** adjusts individual pixels between pure (Vivid) and gray (B&W). Again, subtle changes are your best bet. A slight change toward black-and-white can give your movie an "aged" look, like some of the early color movies of the '30s and '40s.
- **Lightness** also creates a pixel shift. Unlike brightness, the shift rate is linear, everything lightening or darkening at the same rate.

✦ **Specialty Effects:** The remaining seventeen effects modify the clarity, fidelity, positioning, or presentation of your images.

- **Aged Film:** Gives the impression that the film is old, with a loss of clarity, fidelity, and resolution.
- **Black and White:** Consists of a simplified color adjustment all the way to black-and-white and has no additional controls.
- **Earthquake:** Gives a jitter effect to the clip.
- **Electricity:** Presents a blue electric flash striking into your clip. You can adjust the angle from which it enters.
- **Fairy Dust:** Looks like Tinker Bell's trail crossing your clip. You control the direction and length of the trail.

- **Flash:** Gives the impression of flash bulbs going off. You have control over how many times you have a flash, the duration of the flashes, and the brightness (intensity) of the flash.
- **Fog:** Makes it look like you're viewing your clip through a fog. You have control over how heavy the fog is (barely noticeable to a London pea-souper), whether there is a wind blowing the fog (and in which direction), as well as the color of the fog — from the worst L.A. smog (black) to a pristine cleanliness (white).
- **Ghost Trail:** Gives the appearance of, well, ghosts trailing across your clip. You control the length of the trail, how long the ghosts steps are, and how opaque the ghost effect is.
- **Lens Flare:** Presents a sweeping light reflection, as if someone were reflecting light off a mirror or through a lens across your clip. You control the sweep angle and how bright it is.
- **Letterbox:** Lets you create a letterbox effect, blacking out portions of the top and bottom. You control where the visible strip lies vertically, as well as how much gets blacked out.
- **Mirror:** The Advanced Mirror effect from iMovie 2's Plug-in Pack. You pick the horizontal and vertical axes through which the image gets reflected. This is easier to show than describe, so check out the image in Figure 14-19.

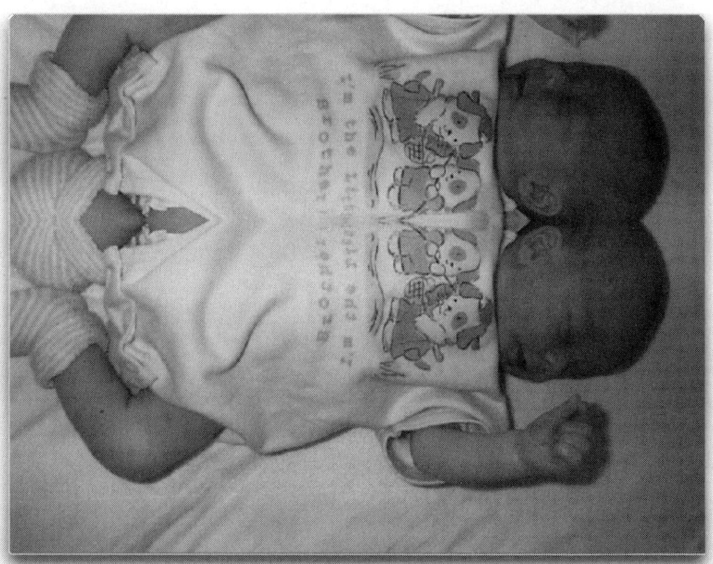

Figure 14-19: Mirror reflects through horizontal and/or vertical axes of your choice.

- **N-Square:** Reduces your image and tiles the reduced versions into an N×N array of miniatures. You control N with the Squares slider: Min is 2 x 2 and Max is 8 x 8.
- **Rain:** Gives the appearance of raindrops falling across your clip (but without the puddling or other accumulation). You control how heavy the rain appears to be and whether (and how much) wind is blowing.
- **Sepia Tone:** Gives your image the look of daguerreotypes from the Old West, with a brownish tinge to everything. Color experts call this shade of brown, sepia, hence the name, but we're guys and aren't supposed to know that much about color. Again, this effect has no additional controls.
- **Sharpen:** Adjusts each pixel (like Photoshop's Sharpen filter), making the image appear to have had a focus adjustment. You have one slider here, from Low (less sharpened focus) to High (very sharp focus). We tend to use this one frequently when we're going to export our movie to QuickTime (especially to VideoCD using Toast 5 Titanium's VideoCD export plug-in, which we'll discuss in Chapter 17).
- **Soft Focus:** The opposite of Sharpen. If you've used Photoshop's Blur filter, you've seen the effect. Adjust the slider to High if you want a really fuzzy picture, close to Low if you just want to soften some of the sharp edges that digital video sometimes produces.
- **Water Ripple:** The closest thing on the Effects panel to a classic special effect, this makes your picture look like you filmed it under water and that there is a current. No controls are available for this one.

Using Effect In and Effect Out

When applied to a full clip, most of the previous effects really don't appeal to us, or to experienced filmmakers of our acquaintance. Why, then, are they present in iMovie and why are we discussing them at such length? The answer is simple. When used as *transitional* effects these effects can be very, well, effective as the image changes gradually. The trick to making them transitional is to master the use of Effect In and Effect Out. Here are a few examples using Effect In to transition into a clip:

✦ Employing Sepia Tone and a still clip of the final frame, you can transition from a full-color motion picture to a daguerreotype-like still image. Set your Effect In time to late in the clip. Similarly, apply Sepia Tone to the entire still clip.

✦ Using Soft Focus, you can show what a delirious person's vision might be just before he or she passes out. Select the clip, select Soft Focus in the Effects panel, move the slider to High, and set Effect In time to the end of the clip. Of course, the clip needs to be 10 seconds or shorter, so prepare to split the clip if necessary.

✦ Selecting Brightness/Contrast and dragging both sliders all the way to the right, you can get the opposite of a fade-to-black—a total whiteout. Again, making sure that your clip is 10 seconds or less in length, set Effect In to the end of the clip and put on your polarized lenses.

Adjusting Effect Out lets you move from the effect to normal color and action. Here are a couple of examples that you might find useful:

✦ If you remember the TV series, *The Wild Wild West,* you'll remember scenes starting out as black-and-white stills, progressing to normal colors, and starting the action when full color was achieved. To emulate this effect, create a still clip of the opening frame and set it to Black & White. Then, in the real frame, set the Effect Out time to a few seconds after the start of the clip. (Yes, once again, you might need to split the clip so that the 10 second limit doesn't bite you.)

✦ You can achieve a gradual focus by setting Soft Focus to High and setting the Effect Out time to just a couple seconds into the clip. This effect is a cool way to emulate what someone who is just waking up might be seeing.

Finally, by tweaking both the Effect In and Effect Out on a clip, you can have the effect gradually take over at the beginning of a clip, be in place for a while, and then have the clip return to normal at the end. One possible use for this would be sliding into a hazy daydream perspective (Soft Focus) and then returning to full consciousness.

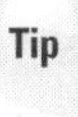

Tip

In the preceding discussion we frequently referenced the 10-second limitation on Effect In and Effect Out relative to a clip's beginning and end, respectively. This is one of the primary uses for splitting a clip. Because there is no perceptible difference between a clip that is one minute long or the same footage split into six ten-second clips when viewed, split the clip if it is at all advantageous. One use would be to have a visual effect, like Black and White or Water Ripple, be in complete sway for part of a clip (no gradual intro or exit). Just split out the segment you want, select it, pick your effect, and set the Effect In and Effect Out to 0:00.

When an effect has been rendered, the clip's frame bears a badge, seen here in the margin.

Adding text

The old saying goes, "A picture is worth a thousand words." We don't know how true that is, but when it comes to movie credits, everybody involved in a movie wants their name to appear on the screen, whether their picture is there or not.

Similarly, we expect to see a title appear, identifying the movie and, sometimes, the scene. The teletype intros on *JAG* and *X-Files* scenes as well as those in some action movies (*Clear and Present Danger*) really help set the scene.

In addition, we can't forget the subtitle. Subtitles don't have to be a language translation, either. You can use subtitles to identify characters in your movie when they first appear or use them to display the lyrics to a song as it plays. Is anyone else here old enough to remember "Sing Along with Mitch"?

You can't add a title to the portion of a clip containing a transition. If you *really* want a title inside the transition (it's usually an ugly idea, anyway), you have to add the title before applying the transition.

Exploring the Titles panel

As you can see in Figure 14-20, the Titles panel is the busiest we've seen yet. At the top is the ubiquitous preview area, with its miniature screen, the Preview button so that you can check your title out in the monitor before applying it, the Update button for when you want to tweak an existing title, and directional arrows for controlling the motion of animated title styles. In the center, you see a list of title (and subtitle) types. iMovie comes with thirty-four title and subtitle styles. GeeThree, for one, includes some additional title styles in their Volume 3 collection.

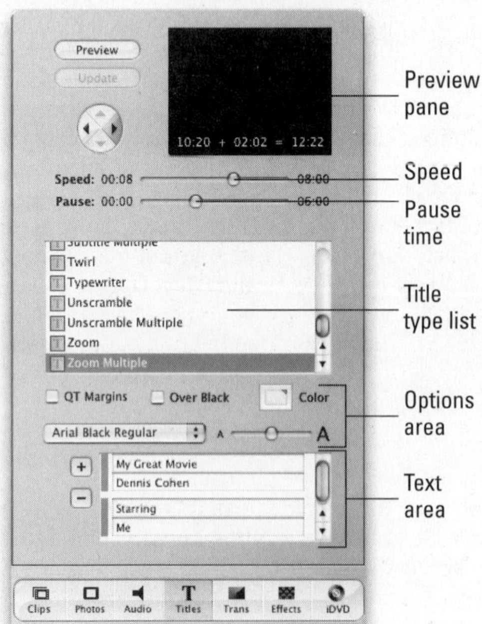

Figure 14-20: The Titles panel gives you lots of options.

Other than the two basic areas we just mentioned, the Titles panel contains three more areas of interest: the duration sliders (Speed and Pause), the options area (Color, Over Black, QT Margins, font, and size), and the text area.

The Duration sliders are used as follows:

✦ Set the Speed slider to how long the text should take to show up completely.

✦ Set the Pause slider to how long the text should remain on-screen once it has appeared. The Pause slider only enables when the title type involves some motion.

Tip

When the Preview pane reverts to black, you'll see the Speed and Pause times and their sum displayed in the bottom-right corner. By the way, if you find the slider names less than descriptive, don't feel like you're all alone. We feel the same way.

The Options area contains the following controls:

✦ **The Color button:** This is not a checkbox, but instead displays the currently selected text color. Click this square and you'll see the OS X (aka "Cocoa" color picker) (see Figure 14-21). Light text on a dark background and dark text on a light background look best. In fact, almost anything else approaches unreadable. Previous versions of iMovie only allowed selecting from a 32-color palette.

Note that like the Web, TVs aren't great at faithful color reproduction. In fact, there is an industry joke that NTSC actually stands for "Never Twice the Same Color."

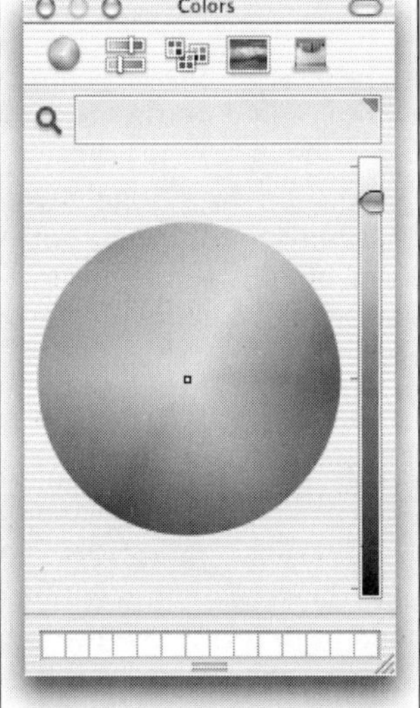

Figure 14-21: OS X's handy color picker lets you select your text color.

If you look closely, you'll see that iMovie adds a slight black drop-shadow to the text. This can make dark (particularly, black) text look a little strange.

✦ **Over Black:** This checkbox is really handy. By opting for Over Black, you create a new clip displaying your title text against a solid black background.

Note

Adding an Over Black title increases the length of your movie.

✦ **QT Margins:** This checkbox is a safety net of sorts. If you leave QT Margins off (the default), iMovie protects the text from appearing too close to the edge of the image. The 720 x 480 NTSC resolution in iMovie doesn't protect against the overscan common in TV sets. (There's more of the picture than is displayed within the TV screen's borders.) If you don't intend to display your video on a TV set, you can check QT Margins and iMovie lets your titles and subtitles sit a little closer to the screen's edges.

✦ **Font:** What can we say about the Font pop-up list that hasn't been said in hundreds of books? Use the pop-up to select a typeface for your text. (Please try to be tasteful.)

✦ **Size:** The Size slider (little A on one end, big A on the other) is pretty straightforward. Use it to decrease (slide left) or increase (slide right) the size of your title text.

The Text area is pretty straightforward as well. It either displays two lines of text, a scrolling list of two-line text groups, or a wrapping text input box, depending upon the Title type you select. (We'll discuss the supplied Title types next.)

Exploring iMovie's title types

With the 34 title types iMovie provides, most common titling and captioning needs are met. The following is a brief rundown of what you get in the box as it were:

✦ **Bounce Across:** Works with two lines of text. The directional arrow controls whether the text moves from left-to-right, right-to-left, top-to-bottom, or bottom-to-top. Set the Speed to determine how quickly the text moves, Pause to specify how long it sits centered, and Wave (a third slider) for how much the text undulates as it flows onto the screen.

✦ **Bounce Across Multiple:** This works just like Bounce across, but with multiple two-line blocks. Make sure that your clip is long enough to show all the blocks, based upon your Speed and Pause settings.

✦ **Bounce In To Center:** Works with two lines of text. The directional arrow controls the movement of the first line of text (the second line enters from the opposite edge of the screen). Set the Speed to determine how quickly the text moves and the Pause to set how long it stays onscreen once it has reached its final position.

✦ **Cartwheel:** This is similar to Bounce Across, except that the text seems to cartwheel (hence the name) in from the chosen side, pause, and then cartwheel off the other side.

✦ **Cartwheel Multiple:** The multi-block version of Cartwheel.

✦ **Centered Multiple:** Works with multiple two-line blocks. Each two-line group fades into view in the center of the screen as set by the Speed slider, sits there for as long as the Pause slider indicates, and then fades out to be replaced by the next two-line block until all your two-line blocks have been displayed.

✦ **Centered Title:** The same as Centered Multiple, but with just one two-line text group.

✦ **Converge:** Works with two lines and starts with the first (if the left directional arrow is selected) or last (if the right directional arrow is selected) characters in place. The remaining text slides into place.

✦ **Converge Multiple:** The multi-block version of Converge.

✦ **Converge to Center:** Similar to Converge, except that the middle of each line is in place and the remainder slides in from either side.

✦ **Converge to Center Multiple:** The multi-block version of Converge to Center.

✦ **Cross Through Center:** Starts with each line written from right-to-left and then the letters cross through the center until they are in place, reading from left-to-right.

✦ **Cross Through Center Multiple:** Okay, okay, you figured it out from the name).

✦ **Drifting:** Also works with just one two-line text group. The second line slides in the direction indicated by the directional arrow, the first line in the opposite direction until the two lines are centered onscreen and then the title fades out. There is no Pause option for this title effect.

✦ **Flying Letters:** Also works with just one two-line text group. The letters fly into position one at a time from the top-right corner if the directional arrow is down or from the bottom right if the arrow is up. The left and right arrows are disabled. After all the text is in place, the title will stay onscreen for the Pause time.

✦ **Flying Words:** Just like Flying Letters except that the text flies in a line at a time.

✦ **Gravity:** Starts with the text all jumbled at either the top or bottom and "falls" into place as though attracted by gravity (or a magnet).

✦ **Gravity Multiple:** The multi-block version of Gravity. We don't think very highly of the Gravity choices, but you might be doing a Warner Bros. cartoon parody and find a use for them.

✦ **Music Video:** One of our favorites, just because it lets you put large blocks of text onscreen at one time. There is no Pause time for this effect, but the Speed slider sets the duration. (No fade-in or fade-out is involved.) The text displays in the left half of the screen, pinned to the bottom and growing upward the more text you enter, as shown in Figure 14-22.

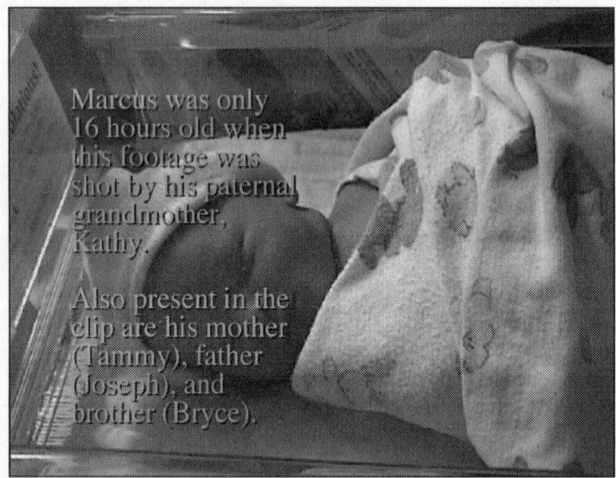

Figure 14-22: Music Video captions can span many lines of text.

✦ **Rolling Centered Credits:** Uses multiple two-line groups, with a twist. The first line of each group is right-justified at the screen's center (minus a little margin) and the second line is left-justified at the center (plus a little margin). This gives you side-by-side credits and is useful when you want to give the character name followed by the performer's name. You can have the credits roll up from the bottom or down from the top using the direction arrows. No Pause setting is available; you can only control how quickly the lines scroll.

✦ **Rolling Credits:** Similar to Rolling Centered Credits with the difference being that instead of aligning to the center of the screen, the first line is left-aligned, the second line is right-aligned, and they are connected by a row of periods.

✦ **Scroll with Pause:** A straightforward, means-what-it-says, effect. You get two lines of text that scroll in the direction you set, pause at center screen for the duration you specify, and then scroll out of view.

✦ **Scrolling Block:** One of our favorite effects. You can create large blocks of text (like with Music Video) and they scroll up or down the screen (centered horizontally). If we just had a perspective effect on this we could emulate the opening of a Star Wars movie.

✦ **Spread from Center** (and its multi-block version, **Spread from Center Multiple):** Start with the text as a line in the center of the screen. The text then slides out in both directions until it is in place.

✦ **Stripe Subtitle:** Changes the way some things work. For example, the color selection now describes the base color for the gradient stripe (dark on the left and fading out on the right) that spans the bottom third of your monitor (unless you choose a white, in which case the stripe will be black to dark gray) with the two lines of text displayed in white against this background, as shown in Figure 14-23.

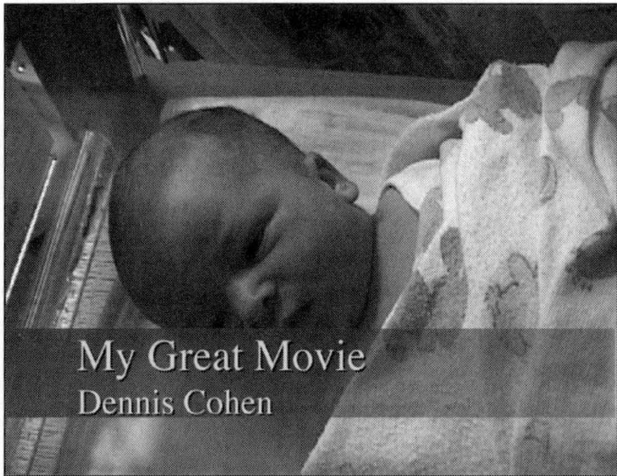

Figure 14-23: Striped Subtitles give you white text against a colored gradient stripe.

✦ **Twirl:** An unusual effect for which we haven't figured a good use. The text starts in place and then all the characters rotate clockwise (left-pointing arrow) or counter-clockwise (right-pointing arrow) around their baseline.

✦ **Typewriter:** The effect we're all familiar with from *JAG* and *X-Files* where letters and numbers appear one-at-a-time in the lower-left portion of the screen as if they're being typed on the screen (although you'll have to provide your own sound effects).

✦ **Unscramble** and **Unscramble Multiple:** This starts with the letters jumbled and they tumble into the correct (unjumbled) order. We've seen this effect used in a number of commercial motion pictures (usually comedies) and you might find these styles useful.

✦ **Zoom** and **Zoom Multiple:** This effect starts with small text in place, which grows to full size, based upon the Speed setting.

Assuming that you're displaying your title against a fairly static background or using Over Black, you can create some interesting variations. You might notice that Scrolling Block has no Pause option to display the text centered on your screen. To work around that, create a Scrolling Block title, extract a still frame with the text centered on your screen, split the original placing the extracted frame in the middle, and adjust its duration as desired. Using a similar technique, you can get around the 2-second limitation on Pauses. Like we said before, art (imagination) is a big part of making the most of iMovie.

Adding and removing titles

When you have the title the way you want it (that *is* what Preview is for), you're ready to add it to your movie. Drag the title type from the Title Type list to the left edge of the clip to which you want it applied. iMovie starts to render the title, displaying a progress bar as shown in Figure 14-24, right on the title clip.

If the title is shorter than the clip to which you're applying it, iMovie automatically splits the clip. If the title is longer than the clip, iMovie runs over into the next clip.

Figure 14-24: Title clips give frame-by-frame progress while rendering and sport a little T badge in the upper-right corner.

Title clips are marked with a T in the upper-right corner as you can see in Figure 14-24 and, if you create a new clip (as is often the case), it gets the name of the title.

Removing a title is really easy—just select it and choose Edit ➪ Clear or press Delete. iMovie even does your housekeeping for you, adding the content from the title clip back into the clip from which it came (assuming that it did its usual split). In short, deleting a title clip only deletes the rendering.

When you want to insert a subtitle, you're frequently going to find that you want it somewhere in the middle of the clip, not at the beginning where iMovie wants to put it. This reiterates our earlier advice: When in doubt, split a clip.

You can even combine title sequences, creating some interesting effects. For example, you can create a Flying Letters title for your male lead that flies in from the top (use just the first line of the two available) and another Flying Letters title for your female lead (use just the second line of the two available) that flies in from the bottom. The only thing you have to remember is that you can't set the second title up until you drag the first one down and start it rendering if you're using Over Black. If you're not using Over Black, you have to wait for the rendering to finish before you can add the next title.

Working with the Timeline viewer

There's a reason the Timeline view shares screen real-estate with the Clip view. Underneath the skin, they're the same thing. Virtually any action you can perform in the clip view can be performed in the Timeline view as well: transitions, effects, and titling are all doable in either view. The big difference is that the Timeline view has an awesome collection of editing tools available and gives you a more detailed view of how your movie is coming together. Where the clip view presents an outside view of your movie, the Timeline viewer is like Superman's x-ray vision and shows you the different tracks and lets you make adjustments at a much finer level.

Additionally, you can only apply some effects (those on the Audio panel) in the Timeline view because you need to access to the two audio tracks. There are a few other tasks you can perform only in the Timeline view and, while most of them have to do with audio, not all do so.

When we introduced the Timeline viewer in Chapter 13, we pointed out that iMovie does give you one cool special effect in the Timeline viewer: fast-mo and slo-mo. Just select your clip and move the slider. Clips that have had their speed altered appear in the clip viewer with a Fast Forward badge (double arrowhead) or Slow Down badge (vertical bar and arrowhead), as shown in Figure 14-25.

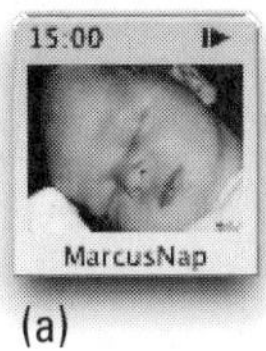

(a)

(b)

Figure 14-25: Speed-altered clips also sport badges: (a) indicates a slow-motion clip and (b) indicates a fast-motion clip.

Make a speed change the last thing you do to a clip. Any other effect, transition, or title applied to a speed-changed clip reverts the clip back to normal speed.

With the Edit Volume checkbox and the volume slider (or percentage textbox) at the bottom of the Timeline viewer, you can change a clip's volume. Maybe it was too soft or too loud when you recorded it, relative to the rest of your clips.

Using the Timeline viewer for transitions, effects, and titles

The only real differences between using the clip view and the Timeline view for these features are in appearance. For example, clip miniatures are smaller and harder to recognize in the Timeline viewer. The miniatures are also more spread out, so you'll probably need to change the Timeline viewer's zoom factor all the way left to get everything in view.

The behavioral differences are very minor. To apply a transition to the beginning of a clip, drag it to the left of the icon or, if you want to apply it to the end of a clip, drag to the right of the icon. Applying a title is roughly the same, but you get feedback where the title will go when a vertical line appears (let go if that's where you want the title). Similarly, for effects, just drag the effect to the clip's strip in the Timeline viewer.

Working with audio tracks

Now we're getting to the Timeline view's raison d'etre. Working with and manipulating your movie's individual tracks is how you distinguish your efforts from those of your grandfather with his 8mm Bell & Howell.

A simple but incredibly powerful iMovie feature involves separating the video and audio you've imported from your camcorder. Why, you ask, would I want to do this?

Suppose that you have background noise interfering with your kid's dance recital tape. You can separate the audio and replace it with a clean recording of the music, minus the jackhammer sounds from the construction going on outside or the gossipfest by the two parents in front of you whose kids have yet to do their performance.

Another handy use is best exemplified by a TV news show, where the reporter's voice describes what you're seeing on their news footage.

Extracting audio

Editing your existing audio begins with a single step. Select your clip in the Timeline viewer and choose Advanced ➪ Extract Audio (⌘-J). iMovie presents a progress dialog (shown in Figure 14-23), telling you that it is extracting audio and naming the clip from which the extraction is taking place. When the extraction is complete, you'll see a new audio clip (a purple strip) in the #1 audio track, as shown in Figure 14-26.

This audio clip will, at least until you start doing other things to it or the source video clip, be the same length as the video clip from whence it came and coincide with it in your movie's Timeline. Those cute little pushpin icons at the start of the separate video and audio clips are iMovie's way of telling you that the audio is pinned (iMovie calls it *locked*, but we guess OS X has overdone the padlock metaphor) to that point in the video. If you move the video, the audio will follow along.

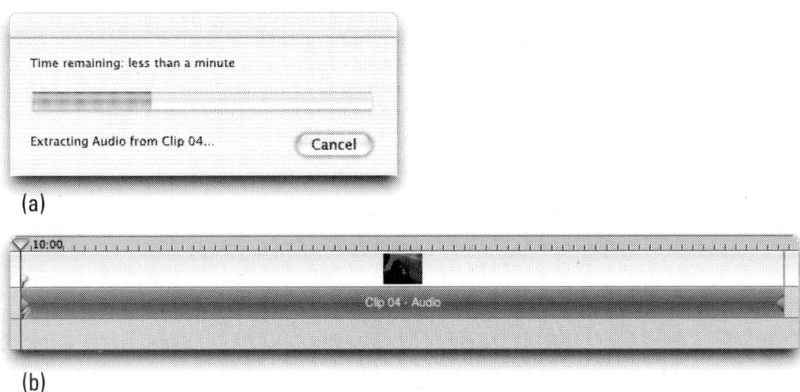

Figure 14-26: iMovie keeps you informed of the extraction progress (a); after extraction, you have separate, matched-up video and audio clips (b).

Removing, copying, cutting, and pasting audio

As with any other clip, one of the simplest things you can do with an audio clip is delete it. To delete the clip, select it (the pale purple gets darker), and choose Edit ➪ Clear (or press Delete). The only way to get a clip back is to use Edit ➪ Undo (⌘-Z).

Being the good Mac application that it is, iMovie also lets you select a clip and use the standard Mac editing commands: Cut, Copy, and Paste. If you cut (Edit ➪ Cut or ⌘-X), you remove the clip from the Timeline viewer but leave a copy in the Mac clipboard. Copying (Edit ➪ Copy or ⌘-C) leaves the clip in the Timeline viewer and places a copy in the clipboard. Paste (Edit ➪ Paste or ⌘-V) places a copy of what's on the clipboard in the Timeline viewer at the current playhead position (so be sure to move the playhead to where you want the audio to appear.

Tip

If you paste audio to a location where the video clip still has audio, you'll hear both audio tracks when you play the clip (or movie). This might (or might not) be what you want, but you should be aware of it. If you don't want the original video's audio track, extract and delete it before pasting the new audio clip.

Locking and unlocking audio clips

As we mentioned earlier in the "Extracting audio" section, iMovie locks the audio clip to the video clip from which it was extracted. You, too, can lock audio clips to video clips, actually to specific points within video clips. When you lock audio to a video clip, no matter what else happens in the movie, this audio clip starts to play at the marked point in that video clip.

Occasionally, you want to edit the video and have the audio associated with a new point on the Timeline viewer. (We cover this topic more in Chapter 15.) To achieve this, you need to unlock the audio from the video.

To unlock an audio clip:

1. **Select the locked audio clip.** The clip turns bright orange.
2. **Choose Advanced ➪ Unlock Audio Clip (⌘-L).** The pushpin disappears, revealing the triangular marker it was hiding the whole time.

After you accomplish your video editing, you're going to want to associate that audio clip with a new (video) point on the Timeline viewer and lock them together 'til death or your next editing brainstorm does them part.

To lock an audio clip:

1. **Select the audio clip.** Okay, there's a gotcha hidden here, especially if you have multiple audio clips in the track: You want to make sure that iMovie synchronizes the audio clip's start with the video position to which you're going to lock it down.
2. **Click in the playhead's tick bar above the end of the audio clip you're going to lock down before you click on the audio clip.** The playhead snaps to the start of the audio clip.
3. **Move the playhead to the position where you want the audio to start.** Use any or all of the standard playhead positioning gimmicks we've described.
4. **Choose Advanced ➪ Lock Audio Clip at Playhead (⌘-L) to lock the audio and video clips.** This makes the little pushpins appear.

Moving audio clips

iMovie only recognizes an audio clip's lock when a video edit affects the audio. This means that you can move even locked audio around in the Timeline viewer as you want; however, if the audio was locked, iMovie locks it to the point you place it. iMovie lets you select audio clips and move them by dragging or using the arrow keys.

Splitting and cropping audio clips

Further demonstrating that audio clips are really clips, you can split and crop them just as you can video clips. The only real difference is that the splitting and cropping occurs in the Timeline viewer rather than the monitor.

To split an audio clip:

1. **Select the audio clip in the Timeline viewer**
2. **Position the playhead where you want the split to occur by clicking along the playhead's tickline or dragging the playhead.** You can make fine adjustments to the playhead location with the arrow keys, just as you did when working with video clips in the monitor.
3. **Choose Edit ➪ Split Selected Audio Clip at Playhead (⌘-T).** If the clip is locked to the video, the left portion of the split clip will still be locked, but the right portion will be fancy-free, as shown in Figure 14-27.

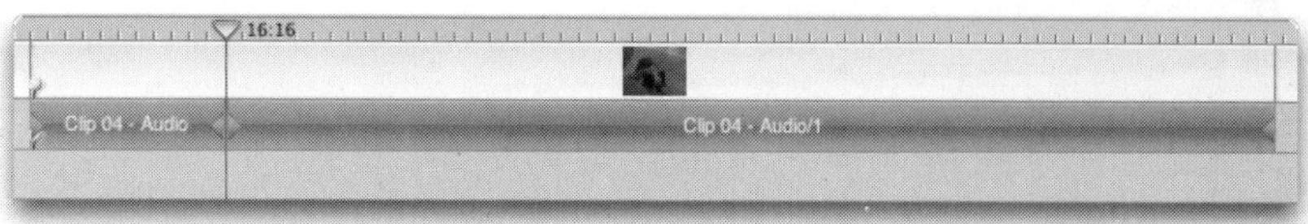

Figure 14-27: Only the beginning of a locked clip stays locked after splitting.

To crop an audio clip:

1. **Select the audio clip you want to crop.** There are inward pointing triangles at each end called crop markers. If the clip is locked, the pushpin might be hiding the beginning crop marker.
2. **Grab each crop marker in turn and move it toward the other one until you have the desired portion selected.** Portions outside the crop markers turn almost white, indicating deselection as shown in Figure 14-28. You can use the arrow keys for fine positioning of the crop markers.
3. **Choose Edit ➪ Crop (⌘-K).** This deletes the material outside the crop markers.

Figure 14-28: Move the crop markers to bracket the material you want to retain.

Strangely enough, even if you don't issue the Crop command, the material outside the crop markers is effectively deleted from your movie. Although it is still present, it won't play in your movie. So, if you aren't sure yet that you really want to delete it, don't issue the Crop command—you can check it out to see how it plays before you make up your mind. Then, if you decide to keep it, you can drag the crop markers back and restore it to your magnum opus.

Check out Chapter 15 for discussion of J-cuts, L-cuts, and intercutting—some of the really cool things you can do with audio editing.

Unleashing iMovie Audio effects

We're now going to hit the Audio panel, which we discovered in Chapter 13, but now you're going to learn how to use it. The Audio panel (shown in Figure 14-29) has two sections that we call, from top to bottom: Music & Sound Effects and Narration (or Voice overs).

Figure 14-29: The Audio panel lets you add sound effects, narrations, and background music.

That large scrolling list with the pop-up menu above it (which probably says "iTunes Library") is where you choose the source for imported Music & Sound Effects. At the top of the pop-up menu, you'll see all the albums in your iTunes Library. Beneath that are the iMovie Sound Effects section with two collections:

Skywalker Sound Effects — a really cool collection from the folks at Skywalker Ranch — and the more pedestrian Standard Sound Effects. Finally, if you have an audio CD inserted, the Audio CD item enable and the name of the album (if known) displays beneath it.

The Microphone line indicates audio input through the Mac's microphone, if you have one. You can record a narration in this manner, for example.

Adding sound effects and music

iMovie starts you off with 18 sound effects, with durations varying from a cat meowing for 18 frames to 6 seconds and 24 frames of footsteps. Pay special attention to those lengths, because one thing you can't do with the sound effects is edit them for length — the closest you can come is to fade it out or fade it in if it's too long.

Click a sound effect once to hear it through your Mac's speakers or, if you have headphones or external speakers attached, through them. You can use the volume slider in the monitor to adjust the playback volume.

As usual, adding a sound effect is Mac-simple. Just find the sound effect you want in the scrolling list and drag its name to the Timeline viewer, dropping it on either of the two audio tracks. An audio clip appears on the selected audio track, as shown in Figure 14-30.

Figure 14-30: Your sound effects appear in an audio track with the name of the effect and a sequential number.

Tip Although you can place a sound effect in either audio track, you're well-advised to keep them all in the same track for organizational purposes. We tend to reserve track one for soundtrack items and track two for background items like sound effects and background music. Obviously, you can do what you want, but as your movie grows, you'll benefit from a consistent approach. By the way, audio items on track 2 are colored brown, as opposed to the purple used for track 1.

Adding narration

Narrations, which iMovie refers to as *voice overs,* provide you with the tool to set the scene, documentary-style, or act as a master of ceremonies. That little Record button to the right of the Microphone volume indicators in Figure 14-29 looks simple, but conceals a great many headaches.

Dealing with the microphone

You might get lucky. Many Macs have a microphone built-in, but in some cases you're going to have to connect one, which raises a few issues of its own.

First, to find out if you have a built-in microphone, face your Mac with the Audio panel open and speak to it, (We promise not to tell the folks at Bellevue that you talk to your computer.) If your Mac has a functioning built-in microphone, you should see the little lights flicker in green and amber. This probably also means that you're running OS 10.2, because we haven't been able to get iMovie to recognize the internal microphone in OS X versions earlier than 10.2.

As a practical matter, many OS X Macs (especially those manufactured since January 2001) don't provide a built-in microphone or even the traditional line-in port through which you can connect a PlainTalk microphone (after about 18 months of computers with no line-in, Apple quietly reintroduced it in late 2002, but not on the iMacs and iBooks). This has undoubtedly saved a cubic centimeter or so inside your Mac, reduced the manufacturing costs by a couple of cents, and promoted the sale of such USB microphones as the iVoice (Macally Peripherals, `www.macally.com`), the Verse-704 (Labtec, `www.labtec.com`), or the iMic (Griffin Technologies, `www.griffintechnology.com`).

Note

Griffin Technology's iMic isn't really a microphone. It is a USB device into which you can plug almost any type of consumer microphone or speaker. So, if you have a microphone from some other piece of electronics, you can just plug it in and go to work. (Dennis *knew* that there was a reason to keep all those various recorders he owned over the years.)

Whether or not you have a built-in microphone, you're almost surely going to be better off with an external USB microphone. The sound quality of Apple's built-in microphones is really not adequate for a work of art you're going to produce in iMovie.

Sometimes, even a USB microphone won't give you the quality you want or you might not have one available (or want to spend the extra money on one). You do have another solution — your digital camcorder. You can record yourself speaking directly to it, import the clip, extract the audio, throw away the video, and be done with all the headaches. That, however, doesn't involve using Record Voice, so we'll get back on-topic now.

By default, iMovie stores your voice over recording on audio track 1, which is also where extracted audio gets placed. You can overlap audio clips on the track and both will play, but you'll have a difficult time discerning what ends where.

If you don't have a lot of experience speaking into a microphone, here are a few tips to help you achieve better results:

- ✦ Position yourself close to, but not directly in contact with, the microphone.
- ✦ Make sure that your throat is clear and that you're ready to start speaking.
- ✦ Test your microphone to make sure that it's working.
- ✦ Eliminate background noise by turning off printers, TVs, stereos, and so forth.
- ✦ Time a run-through of what you're going to say to make sure that you can fill the planned clip. Adjust your presentation or pace accordingly.
- ✦ Practice your presentation enough that you're familiar with it and that your speaking voice is natural when you are reading (or reciting) it.

Now that the prep work is done, you're ready to narrate. Here's what you do:

1. **Position the Timeline viewer's playhead where you want your clip to start.**
2. **Click the Record Voice button and begin speaking.** The Record Voice button changes to Stop.
3. **When you're done narrating, click Stop.**

Just as with imported video, iMovie limits an audio clip's length to just short of 10 minutes. But here, there's a difference. Instead of continuing the recording in a new clip, iMovie stops recording. Because you're aware of this, you should plan breaks in a narration exceeding this limit so that you can create multiple clips that flow smoothly from one to the next. (Paragraph breaks are a good place to stop a clip and start a new one.)

Adding background music

Successful movies (and videos) always, in our experience, have a great soundtrack. Whether it is a musical where a soundtrack is expected, science fiction (like *Star Wars*), or even a war story (like *Apocalypse Now*), there is background music setting the mood.

Getting your music from CD

Unless you're well-funded enough to hire musicians or musically gifted so that you can provide your own score, you're probably going to be looking for a music source. That generally equates into importing music from a CD or using MP3s from your readily available iTunes Library. There are some excellent scoring tools, such as SmartSound's MovieMaestro (`www.smartsound.com`), which we'll cover in Chapter 17, that provide access to professional-quality music without you risking a copyright violation lawsuit.

Copyright and You

Although iMovie (and iTunes) make it easy to use CD tracks for your own purposes, you should remember that repurposing the contents of a copyrighted commercial CD is likely to get you sued (and lawyers can be *very* expensive, even if you manage to win).

Fortunately, if your movie is going to be purely for the personal enjoyment of you and your family, the likelihood of any studio siccing their legal barracudas on you is pretty remote, even in the unlikely event that it ever comes to their attention. Although the music industry (and movies and TV) are pushing hard to eliminate its existence, the courts in the U.S. have long established a *fair use* clause slightly limiting the absolute power of copyright. Private, noncommercial usage of legally purchased recordings is generally considered as a fair use (as opposed to the legal principle called "fair use").

Note the "noncommercial" and "private" qualifiers. Using copyrighted material in a corporate video does not fall under any definition of fair use. In such a scenario, you must obtain permission or acquire a license from the copyright holder to use their work. Unfortunately, artists rarely own the copyrights to their work, and dealing with the legal departments of Sony, Disney, or other media giants is not a pleasant, speedy, or inexpensive endeavor.

One prospect is to acquire royalty-free recordings. Now, royalty-free doesn't mean totally free—it just means that once you purchase them, they're yours to use. Collections of royalty-free music are available from many sources: Sonic Desktop (`www.smartsound.com`), Media Tracks (`www.media-tracks.com`), and Fresh Music (`www.freshmusic.com`) are just a few, and more pop up all the time. Do a search for *royalty-free music* on Google and find dozens of sources.

Because we're not lawyers, you should not assume that what's in this sidebar constitutes legal advice. These are generally accepted guidelines at this time, but very little in copyright law is cut-and dried, and new precedents are set and new laws written all the time. If you have any doubt, consult an attorney.

Whether or not you have copyright issues and regardless of their status, actually adding CD tracks for use in your movie is, as usual, quite simple. As you can see in Figure 14-31, the Audio CD interface offers a familiar look and familiar controls. You can select tracks in the scrolling list. Clicking the Place at Playhead button starts the process of extracting the music from the CD and placing it in audio track 2.

Importing audio files

CD audio isn't the only way to get your music into iMovie. Up until iMovie 2.1.1, any audio file you imported had to be an AIFF file, then iMovie also started importing MP3s directly. Now, with the integration of your iTunes Library into iMovie 3, you can use any audio track available in iTunes.

Slightly more expensive, but an expense we strongly encourage, is to upgrade your QuickTime to QuickTime Pro. This is $30 well spent if you're going to do much with iMovie or iTunes. With it, you can translate a myriad of audio formats into AIFF or MP3.

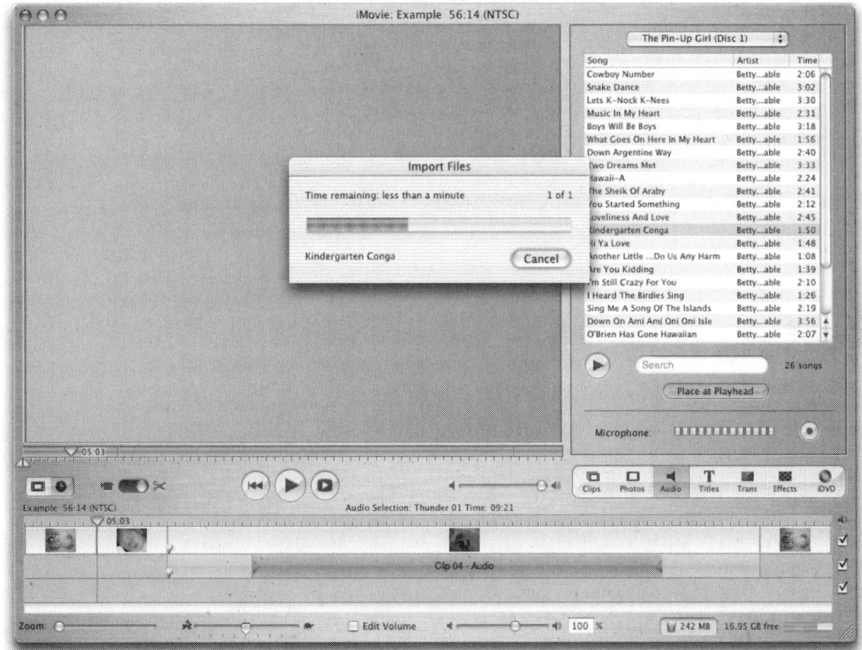

Figure 14-31: Select the track you want to add to your movie from the scrolling list and iMovie imports it for you.

Tip

We'll discuss this more in Chapter 17, but if you own Toast 5 Titanium, you also have access to a wonderful little utility called CD Spin Doctor which enables you to bring in audio from such analog sources as cassette tapes and vinyl LPs, assuming that you have either a line-in jack on your Mac or something like the Griffin iMic to which you can connect your legacy hardware. (That's a polite term for "old-fashioned stuff.")

After you manage to get the audio file into iTunes, you're just a couple short steps away from having it in your soundtrack. With the Audio panel showing in the Shelf, do the following:

1. **Position the Timeline viewer's playhead where you want the imported audio to begin.**
2. **Select the file you want to import and click the Place at Playhead button.** iMovie starts to import the file and displays a progress dialog while it does so.

We told you it was just a couple short steps. You can actually reduce this to one step by eliminating playhead positioning. Just select the track in your iTunes Library and drag it to the Timeline viewer, as shown in Figure 14-32. iMovie displays a small song badge accompanied by the song name and a yellow, vertical bar indicating where the clip will go.

Figure 14-32: You can just drag songs from your iTunes Library right into the Timeline.

Importing Images

Depending upon how old you are (or how technologically advanced your school was), you might remember traditional slideshows, where the teacher placed a collection of slides in a circular tray atop a slide projector and let it project the pictures on the same roll-down movie screen where you watched 8mm and 16mm educational (read "boring") films. If your grandparents were anything like ours, they also had a slide projector and just looked for an excuse to embarrass you by showing candid shots of you to friends and family.

Apple seems obsessed with slideshows. You can make them in AppleWorks using the Presentation module. You can make them in QuickTime Player Pro. iPhoto makes slideshows as well and exports them as QuickTime movies. iDVD also makes slideshows. But, you can make even better slideshows using iMovie than with any of these other applications. (Okay, QuickTime Player Pro matches up pretty close in capabilities, but it is way more difficult to use.) With iMovie, you control the picture and you control the sound. Each image can have its own duration. You can vary the soundtrack and apply the transitions, captions, and effects you want. In short, you can do anything with the images in your slideshow that you can do with any other movie. In fact, with the available Ken Burns Effect, you can do even more by adding pan and zoom effects to your slides.

As we'll describe in "Getting an image into iMovie the easy way", later in this chapter, creating a basic slideshow in iMovie isn't as easy as it used to be because you can no longer bring your slides in directly as still frames, but you gain some flexibility with the Ken Burns Effect. Whether that flexibility is worth the additional effort is a function of how often you need or want the Ken Burns Effect in your slideshow.

Here are some other uses for still images in iMovie:

✦ **Create a Ken Burns Effect:** The very cool Ken Burns Effect, topping the panel shown in Figure 14-33, lets you pan and zoom across a still image, giving the impression of live action.

✦ **Create your own, customized title screens:** Maybe you want Over Blue instead of Over Black. You can create slides, shorten their duration, and then, using Transitions, create some very cool titles.

- **Importing the slides from a presentation:** You can do this to avoid having to shoot a slide presentation with your camcorder when filming the boss's presentation to the Board of Directors.
- **Create your own video storybooks:** This is great for entertaining the kids.

One thing Apple made incredibly easy in iMovie 3 is importing your photos from iPhoto. The secret to this is the new Photo pane on the shelf, as shown in Figure 14-33. The top of the pane, as you can see, is labeled the "Ken Burns Effect" after the man who used the pan and zoom across stills to such great effect in his Civil War documentary works. The bottom of the pane is your window into your iPhoto Library, including all your albums. Unlike the iTunes interface on the Audio panel, it doesn't include iPhoto's search capabilities so you can't search for a keyword or comment when trying to locate a picture.

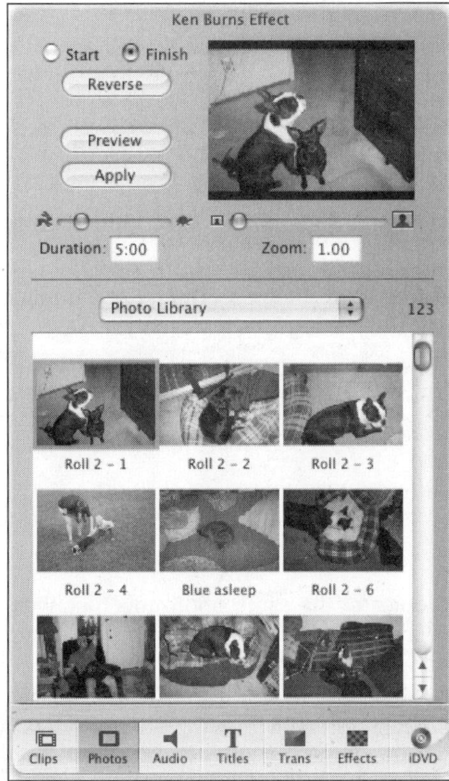

Figure 14-33: Your entire iPhoto Library is at your fingertips, with the Ken Burns Effect integral to the import process.

Using the Ken Burns Effect

We've mentioned the Ken Burns Effect enough. It's now time to give you the low-down on how to use it, but using it is really pretty easy. Using it well, on the other hand, takes an artistic eye or a lot of experience — in the wrong hands, you can easily make your audience suffer vertigo (of course, that might be the effect you're trying to achieve).

Proceed as follows to pan & zoom a still photo with the Ken Burns Effect:

1. **Select your photo from your iPhoto Library.**
2. **In the Duration textbox, or using associated slider, set a length for your clip.** The minimum value that iMovie accepted is 0:03 (three frames), and the maximum allowable duration is 60:00 (one minute).
3. **Click the Start radio button.**
4. **Adjust the Zoom using either the textbox or the slider.** The allowable range is from 1.0 (no zoom) to 5.0 (5× zoom).
5. **Slide the picture in the Pan & Zoom preview box (the pointer turns into a hand when you enter the box) until you have your desired beginning image in place.**
6. **Click the Finish radio button and repeat Steps 4 and 5 for your ending image.**
7. **Click Preview to make sure you have your desired effect.** Repeat any of the preceding steps necessary to tweak the settings if they aren't right.
8. **After you have things the way you want them, click Apply.** iMovie copies your photo to the Clip/Timeline viewer and starts to render it. Meanwhile, it is selected and displays in the monitor.

The Reverse button does pretty much what you would expect it to do — it swaps the Start and Finish settings. You can then click Apply, and iMovie re-renders the clip.

Tip One neat trick is to chain multiple copies of the same photo together, with the Finish settings for one becoming the Start settings for the next. This lets you navigate multiple parts of a picture, smoothly.

You can do some really neat tricks with the Ken Burns Effect — let your imagination run free. You might be surprised how much life you can get out of a still image.

Getting an image into iMovie the easy way

Every photo you import from your iPhoto Library has the Ken Burns Effect (we'll call it the KBE) applied as iMovie renders the photo into a clip. That photo will have the same duration as set for the KBE, will be zoomed at the start of the clip the same amount as the KBE Start zoom, will have the KBE Finish zoom applied at the end, and will have corresponding KBE Start and Finish positioning.

You can import from the iPhoto Library as discussed in "Getting an image into iMovie the hard way" a little later in this chapter.

Don't get us wrong, because we think the Ken Burns Effect is great, and we use it a lot; however, we really wish there were an "off" switch so that we could, when we wanted, just import the photo as an old-fashioned still frame (the way it worked in iMovie and iMovie 2). Of course, you can still achieve the same result in a couple of ways. You can:

- ✦ Set the KBE duration to what you want and the start and end zooms to 1.0, with the photo centered in the frame. This won't be exactly the same as was available in iMovie 2, because the photo is now a rendered clip of fixed duration rather than a still frame. However, your audience will never know the difference.
- ✦ Set either the start or end zoom to 1.0 with a centered photo and then, after the clip's been rendered, position the playhead and choose Edit ➪ Create Still Frame (Shift-⌘-S). Following which, you should trash the rendered clip.

If you employ the second method, set the duration in the KBE to 0:03 (three frames), which is the minimum length allowed. The result is a short rendering time, a plus for a clip you aren't going to keep around, anyway. Also, you can now select the still frame and, using File ➪ Get Info (⌘-I), set the duration to what you want.

In either case, it seems like an awful lot of work to go through to achieve a simple goal, especially because you then need to reestablish your normal KBE settings. Additionally, because iMovie renders the photos into video clips, the import takes a lot longer than bringing in a still frame did previously.

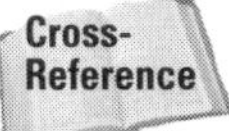

In Chapter 17, we show you a little trick to make the default behavior be "KBE off."

If, like Dennis, you have a camera that doesn't use a 4:3 aspect ratio, the KBE zoom settings can come in handy. Dennis sets the zoom to 1.16 for his 1800 x 1200 pictures, centered in the frame, and the KBE automatically trims them to 1600 x 1200, while eliminating the letterbox effect.

To add a photo to your movie, just drag the thumbnail image from the Photos panel into the Clip/Timeline viewer.

Getting an image into iMovie the hard way

You can use the ever-handy File ➪ Import File (Shift-⌘-I) command as the portal through which your images pass. iMovie can import many different graphics formats: Macintosh PICT, Compuserve GIF, JPEG, Adobe Illustrator, TIFF, and BMP are directly usable. (That last one is Windows bitmap format, for those of you who've never had to deal with the dark side of computing.) Also importable, but not available for the Ken Burns Effect are Adobe Photoshop and PDF.

Actually, some Photoshop (PSD) files can receive the pan & zoom, just not the multi-layered ones. Similarly, the rare multilayered TIFF file shows only the top layer, just as PDF shows only the first page.

Realistically, you will probably encounter still images you want in other formats: PNG (Portable Network Graphics), WMF (Windows Metafile), or QTIF (QuickTime Image File) to name just a few. Upgrading to QuickTime Pro lets you convert anything QuickTime can read, but that still leaves a whole bunch of formats you can't handle. One superb shareware program for converting files between formats (and not a bad little image editor, either) is Lemke Software's GraphicConverter (`www.lemkesoft.de`).

Even assuming that you can get the image in the right format, you still have one hurdle to leap: size and resolution. Images imported into iMovie should be 72dpi (dots per inch), sometimes referred to as 72ppi (pixels per inch), resolution. They should also be 640 x 480 pixels in size.

"But," you exclaim, "I read in Chapter 2 that NTSC TV resolution is 720 x 480 pixels! What's with this 640 x 480 stuff?" The answer to that question is that TV screens are not like your computer screen; pixels on a TV aren't squares, they're rectangles that are narrower than they are tall. iMovie makes the compensation automatically when dealing with video so that you don't see a distorted image on your computer and those 720 horizontal TV dots fit in 640 computer dots. Thus, if you feed iMovie a 640 x 480 still image, it makes the conversion to 720 horizontal TV dots when it generates your clip.

If your image is larger than 640 x 480, iMovie scales it down in size so that it fits within the 640 x 480 space. So long as the width to height ratio is 4:3 (yeah, a little bit of your elementary school math is going to come in handy), you'll have a picture that looks like your image. If the ratio isn't 4:3, you're going to have some black bars either on the sides or on the top and bottom. For example, if your picture was 1800 x 1200 (like those produced by Dennis's Kodak digital camera), you'll get a picture that looks like the one in Figure 14-34. You'll get the same matting, except that it might be on all four sides, if you import an image that is less than 640 x 480 in size. iMovie won't scale up because that produces blotchiness (technical term for "it don't look good").

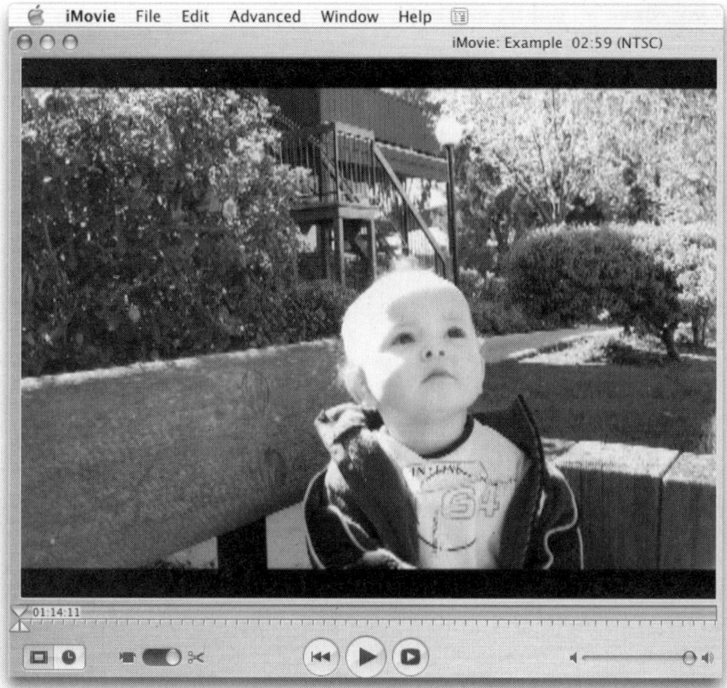

Figure 14-34: iMovie pads your image to fit in a 640 x 480 rectangle, after scaling it down if necessary.

One of the options in iPhoto's export dialog is to scale the image to be no larger than 640 x 480. If you use that option, iPhoto does the scaling for you and saves iMovie from doing so. This is especially handy if you're exporting multiple images from iPhoto for use with iMovie.

Tip

We're going to assume that you've read or are going to read the iPhoto chapters or that you're familiar with at least one graphics program for creating and editing your images. There is one more caveat about your images that is pretty specific to iMovie (or at least, to digital video). Just as there is a *Web-safe color palette* to use when creating Web pages if you want them to show up correctly in all browsers, there is a NTSC color-safe palette in some applications (Adobe's Photoshop is one). If you don't have such an application, just stick to colors where the red, green, and blue components are all 200 or lower out of the possible 255. Playing through to a TV (see Chapter 13) is a good way to see what your colors look like. If they shimmer or seem to bleed, you've probably exceeded the threshold. You might also run into problems with small checked patterns or narrow striped patterns. Some cynics say that NTSC stands for "Never The Same Color."

Assuming that you have a conforming image that you want to include in your movie, importing it is really easy:

1. **Choose File ⇨ Import File (⌘-I).** This presents the Import File dialog as shown in Figure 14-31.
2. **Locate and select your file, applying one of the Show filters seen in Figure 14-31, if you wish.**
3. **Click the Import button.**

You now have a new still clip on the shelf. Everything that you learned earlier about working with still clips is in play.

Exporting Your Video

After you've sweated and slaved over your video, making it just so, you probably want to share it with the world (or at least your family and friends). You can export it back to your camcorder and, using the analog connections from it, either play it on the TV or record copies of your masterpiece on a VCR. Exporting back to your camcorder also lets you archive your movie on a tape, letting you delete the project from your hard disk and free up the gigabytes of hard disk space your movie consumes (so that you can start on your next magnum opus). If e-mail or a Web page is the distribution medium you choose, you can export it to QuickTime and let people view it on their computers. Apple makes a version of QuickTime that runs on Windows computers, too. Finally, you can pass it on to iDVD and burn DVDs to pass out to friends, family, customers, or whoever your intended audience might be.

As you'll see in Chapter 17, when we talk about Toast Titanium, there's also the world of VideoCDs, but that involves a QuickTime export as well and doesn't qualify as a fourth topic here.

Exporting back to a camera

The process of exporting back to your camera is really straightforward, but there are a few things to do first and a few decisions to make.

Probably the first thing to do is run through your movie one more time, making sure that everything is just the way you want it. Even if you make this check, you'll probably have some gaffes in the movie, even the Hollywood blockbusters do, with their legions of editors and professionals poring over the footage. That doesn't mean that you shouldn't try your best to eliminate the really silly errors.

Note: If you have Video Play Through to Camera turned on and a TV monitor hooked up to your camera, you can verify both audio and video with a single check pass. Another advantage of previewing on a TV set is that you'll get a chance to catch any problems arising from using QT Margins for your titles and subtitles as well as any color problems.

We generally use a fresh tape to hold our finished product, keeping the raw footage tape in case we ever want to grab something from it that we didn't include in this movie. (Yes, that foresight has paid off more than once.)

Note: The one lesson it did take us a while to learn was, Label the <expletive-deleted> tapes! Inserting, checking, and ejecting tapes gets really annoying really quickly when you're trying to find the footage you know you have *somewhere*.

At any rate, you have the movie just the way you want it, the camera is hooked up and powered on with a tape inserted and positioned to where you want to start recording — you're ready to start exporting.

When iMovie exports to your camera, it converts all your tracks back into a single DV Stream file sent via FireWire to your camcorder. The multitasking in OS X means that you can still use your Mac to do things, but unless you have a really fast Mac, response might be a bit sluggish.

Here's how to export to your camera:

1. **Choose File ➪ Export (Shift-⌘-E).** This presents the iMovie: Export dialog shown in Figure 14-35.

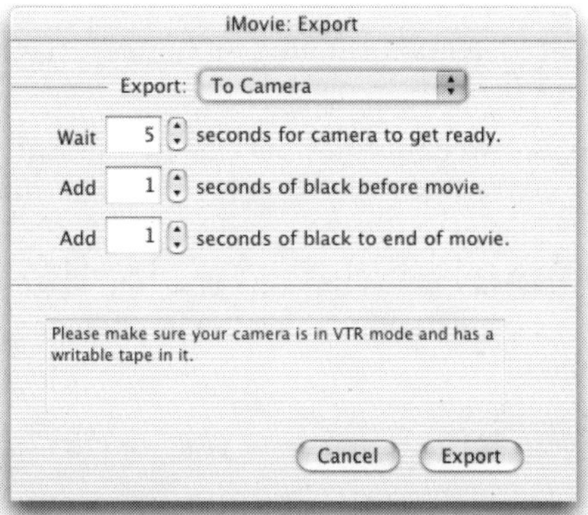

Figure 14-35: The Export Movie dialog defaults to Camera as your destination.

2. **Check the message box in the middle of the dialog.** iMovie tells you whether it is ready to start exporting (Figure 14-35) and reminds you to have a tape in your camera and your camera in VTR mode.
3. **Assuming that you're now ready to export (double-check your connections), make sure that the three text boxes reflect the settings you want:**
   - **Wait *nn* seconds for camera to get ready:** This tells iMovie how long to wait after you click Export and send the Record command to your camcorder before data should start flowing. The reason for this is that, as we're sure you've seen by now, the tape might take a few seconds to get up to speed and start recording.
   - **Add *nn* seconds of black before movie:** We always use this option. By placing the black on the tape, future exports to VHS (or Beta, if you're one of the very few stalwarts) will have a little bit of slack time to get past the tape leader and get the videotape up to speed.
   - **Add *nn* seconds of black to the end of the movie:** This is particularly useful if you're not using a new tape and are recording over something else. At least, you'll have a bit of black to signal the transition from your work to the old material and at best, you'll avoid messed-up timecodes on the tape resulting from overlapping recordings.
4. **Click the Export button.** After the movie starts exporting, you sees it playing on the Monitor's screen while an Exporting to Camera progress dialog displays its sideways thermometer.

If anything interrupts the export, your export is pretty much guaranteed to be useless. Here are some things to do or not do which should improve the likelihood of a successful export:

✦ Plug your camera into an outlet instead of running off battery. Having the camera shut down for a lack of juice is easily avoided.

✦ Don't do anything else on the FireWire bus. Connecting and disconnecting FireWire devices will virtually guarantee a signal going through that will terminate your export.

✦ Don't touch the cables or connectors between your Mac and your camera. (Don't let the kids, cats, or dogs near them, either.) A simple jiggle could interrupt the connection for a moment.

For information on transferring your DV footage to your VCR, turn to Chapter 15.

Exporting to QuickTime

One of Apple's greatest and least understood accomplishments is their QuickTime technology. Most people think of it as just the QuickTime Player, but that Player is just a single window into many QuickTime capabilities.

To use some geek terms, QuickTime defines some APIs (application programming interfaces), codecs (compressors-decompressors), and a flexible and extensible document format (QuickTime Movie format). We get into what QuickTime is and how it works in Chapter 17 when we talk about QuickTime Pro and why you should upgrade to it.

If you know a lot about how to use QuickTime, you can tweak the QuickTime export settings to be just what you want. However, 99 percent of the time, iMovie's canned settings are going to be all you need.

As with exporting to camera, you need to make some preparations in terms of previewing your movie before exporting to QuickTime. In fact, they're mostly the same ones. A couple things, though, should be remembered:

✦ **Titles and captions should be in a fairly large and distinct font.** It is unlikely that you're going to export to QuickTime at 640 x 480 resolution, so the text is going to shrink, possibly a lot. Eighth-inch (roughly 9 point) text at 640 x 480 is only going to be three sixty-fourths of an inch tall if you export at 240 x 180 (the Web Movie, Small setting) and even smaller if you export it at the small e-mail setting. Similarly, titles and captions are more distinct Over Black than against motion when you reduce the image's size.

✦ **Make sure that you have enough free disk space to save the QuickTime movie.** The Free Space indicator tells you how much space is available on the disk containing your project. You'll need to go outside iMovie to find out the free space on other volumes.

  Figuring out how much space you need is where guesswork and experience are going to come into play. As a rough rule of thumb, the e-mail option takes about 1MB per minute, small Web movies take about 4MB per minute, the CD-ROM setting chews up about 10MB per minute. A full-quality movie is essentially the same size as your DV Stream — about 200+MB per minute.

Take a look at the canned Export to QuickTime settings shown in the Formats pop-up menu displayed in Figure 14-36.

✦ **E-mail:** Down to 10fps and only 6.25 percent the resolution of your original, the video is going to be hard to see and pretty ragged. Additionally, the audio is now mono at 22Khz, so you've got fair degradation there as well. The sole virtue of this format is that you can get a little over three minutes of video into a message that fits in most 5MB mailboxes.

Note

Although a .Mac mailbox, for example, can hold 15MB of messages, that doesn't mean you can make the movie close to 15MB. Attachments like pictures, files, or video to e-mail messages have to be encoded for transmission and encoding adds between 30 and 40 percent to the size of the file. Additionally, the mac.com mail server does not accept any individual message (including attachments) larger than 3MB.

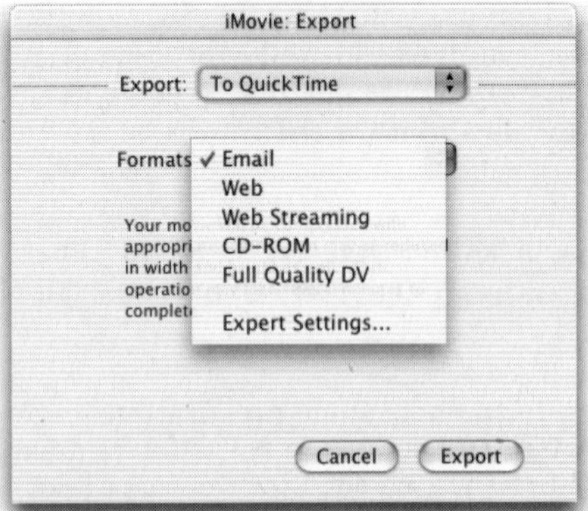

Figure 14-36: iMovie provides five common QuickTime export configurations (and an Expert option where you do all the work).

✦ **Web:** Running at 12 frames per second versus your video's 30fps, you should get motion reminiscent of some (non-realistic) cartoon animation with images at about 14 percent the resolution you started with. While the sound is still stereo, the sample rate has been cut in half to 22Khz (approximately that of FM radio).

✦ **Web Streaming :** With the exception of streaming hints (which we'll discuss in Chapter 15) being added, this is the same set of options that you see previously in Web.

✦ **CD-ROM:** At last, full CD-quality stereo sound. At 320 x 240 resolution, we're also getting back into the realm of watchable video where we can discern some detail. At 15fps, the motion should be fairly smooth, assuming you weren't filming a martial arts matchup.

✦ **Full Quality DV:** You now have the same quality picture and sound as your original, because to all intents it is your original. This is only really useful if you're going to work on the movie with another DV application like iDVD, Final Cut Pro, or DVD Studio Pro.

Our Bible editors love step-by-step instructions, so we'll now walk through the steps to QuickTime export:

1. **Choose File ⇨ Export (Shift-⌘-E).** This displays the iMovie: Export dialog.

2. **Choose To QuickTime from the Export pop-up menu and watch the options change.** To see the change in options, compare Figure 14-35 and Figure 14-36.

3. **Choose the type of movie from the Formats pop-up menu.**

4. **Click the Export button.** An export progress dialog appears. Plan to wait a long time for this to complete. Times between five and twenty minutes per minute of video are not uncommon, even on relatively fast Macs, when QuickTime is performing significant compression.

Exporting for iDVD

We'll be covering exporting for iDVD more in Part V, but the basics are the same as when exporting to QuickTime. Make sure everything is the way you want it in your movie, just as you did for the camera and QuickTime.

Make sure that you have enough disk space. An iDVD export chews up over 200MB per minute of video, so be sure that you have as much space free as your project folder uses.

Now, for the final step-by-step in this chapter:

1. **Choose File ⇨ Export (Shift-⌘-E).** This opens the iMovie: Export dialog.
2. **Choose To iDVD from the Export pop-up menu, if your version of iMovie includes it.** Alternatively, you can choose Full QualityDV as described previously in the "Exporting to QuickTime" section.
3. **Because iMovie 3 prepares projects for iDVD automatically every time you save (File ⇨ Save or ⌘-S), click the Export button.** An export progress dialog appears.

   Because iMovie isn't doing any compression, you might expect this to be a pretty quick process, but it isn't necessarily. Even doing a Finder copy of that much data takes a while (remember, over 200MB per minute of video).

Whew! Now we're ready to go on to more advanced things you can do with iMovie. We'll see you in Chapter 15, where we're going to lead off with creating chapter markers for use with iDVD (the final button on the shelf).

Summary

In this chapter, you learned to connect your camcorder, import video from it, and export video back to it. You also saw how to work with the Clip/Timeline viewer's two persona, and the shelf in all its faces: adding titles, subtitles, transitions, effects, photos, and audio. You learned to do basic clip editing in the monitor and to add and work with still clips. We also covered exporting to camera, QuickTime, and iDVD.

✦ ✦ ✦

Getting Advanced with iMovie

✦ ✦ ✦ ✦

In This Chapter

Adding chapters for iDVD use

The cutting room floor

Working with non-DV video

Plugging into iMovie

Becoming expert with QuickTime Export

Postproduction tricks with QuickTime Pro

Putting your movie on the Web

✦ ✦ ✦ ✦

Using what you've learned in Chapters 13 and 14, you can already make better home movies than your parents or grandparents ever dreamed of making. But, we've barely touched the surface. Using iMovie, you can easily produce movies that could be mistaken for professional work, and we aren't talking about cheesy B-movies, either.

Now that you know how to use iMovie's tools, we're going to discuss how to achieve your artistic production goals. In other words, what to do and when to do it.

In addition, you'll learn how to add chapter markers for use by iDVD, use non-DV video clips, extend iMovie's capabilities with plug-ins, become an expert at QuickTime exports, use QuickTime Pro to add some cool special effects to your movie after you get done with it in iMovie, and make your movie available on the Internet.

If you didn't need your hands free to work the mouse, we'd tell you to sit down, buckle in, and hang on.

Adding Chapters for iDVD Use

Dennis loves using iMovie to edit and prepare his footage, whether the target is DVD, Video CD, or Super Video CD. He also likes iDVD but has tended to use Video CDs more than DVDs for his longer efforts for one reason: You can place scene selection menus in movies, just like you find on commercial DVDs. To do this, you need *chapter markers*, which are cues that run along the length of the footage, usually at the beginning of a song or a video scene, that tell the CD or DVD where to begin playing. You generally place chapter markers into a VCD before authoring and burning the disc. In the past, iDVD didn't support chapter markers. That's all changed now, with iMovie 3 and iDVD 3. In fact, the lack of chapter markers was one of the major reasons Bob uses Final Cut Pro and DVD Studio Pro for most of his efforts.

Clicking the iDVD button below the shelf presents the panel seen in Figure 15-1. This very simple panel packs a lot of punch. Just move the playhead in the monitor or Timeline view to the place you want the chapter marker to occur. Next, click Add Chapter. In response, iMovie:

✦ Numbers your chapters.

✦ Inserts a thumbnail of the frame where the chapter marker goes.

✦ Offers a default name for the chapter title. The chapter title defaults to the name of the clip, but you can edit the name, and probably should.

✦ Displays the timecode in your movie where the chapter marker occurs.

Figure 15-1: The iDVD Panel is where you create and maintain your movie's Chapter Marker list.

iMovie also keeps the markers in timecode order, so if you go back and add another marker, earlier in your movie, iMovie inserts it in chronological order, as shown in Figure 15-2.

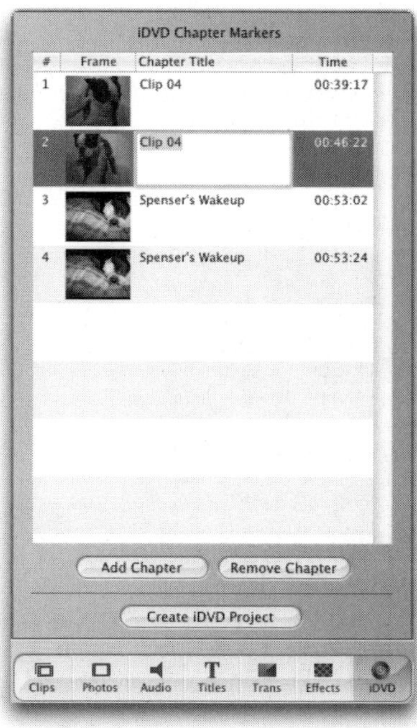

Figure 15-2: When you add a marker earlier in a film, it appears in timecode order, ready for you to rename it.

iMovie even communicates with iDVD and tells it to create a new project for your movie. Although we cover iDVD in Part V of this book, in Figure 15-3, we show you a default iDVD project's scene selection menu, which iMovie creates when you click the Create iDVD Project button.

There is a limit of 36 chapter markers per movie. This is a restriction imposed by iDVD's limit of six buttons per menu. Because of this limitation, the main menu can only have six buttons pointing to scene selection menus and each of those can only contain six buttons. Even with the "New Math," 6 x 6 is still 36.

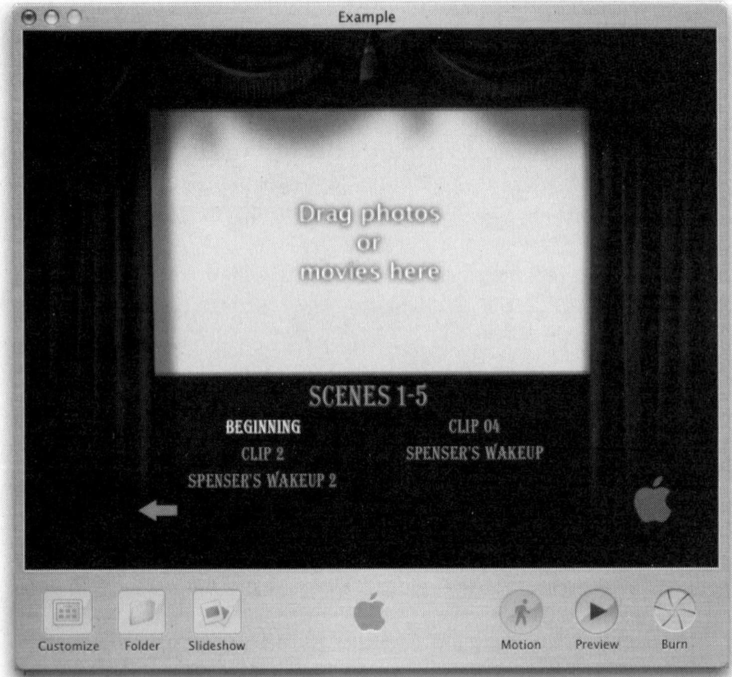

Figure 15-3: iDVD creates a new project with a scene selection menu at iMovie's request.

The Cutting Room Floor

The best footage in the world won't do you any good unless you can put it together and present it for people to enjoy. And the secret to making an average movie good or a good movie great is the editing.

The art of the intercut

First, you need to get familiar with the terminology. A *cut* is the break from one clip to the next, without transition. More than that, though, you need to know about special cutting techniques where you cut from one clip's video to another while retaining the first clip's audio. This is usually called *intercutting*, a technique most often used with documentaries, presentations, and news broadcasts. We don't know about you, but most people (including us) get really bored if the camera stays trained on a speaker as he or she drones on about the new frammis their company is announcing. However, if the presentation continues, but the picture changes to one showing the frammis in operation, we get a little more interested. Steve Jobs and the folks at Apple have this down to a fine art. Just watch Steve when he announces Apple's latest and greatest products. The video footage cuts back and forth between him and the products, but his soundtrack is in play the whole time. Of course, they're doing this live, using multiple cameras and switching between them on signal. But you can do this too, with intercutting.

Tip

You can also use this technique to create your own lip-synching effect or, more likely, to reshoot some video that didn't turn out too well, and mate it with good audio.

Cutaways and reaction shots

The cuts used for a Steve Jobs–type presentation or when the video changes from the performer to the audience are called *cutaways*. The latter (when people are involved) are also called *reaction shots*.

Note

To get a real reaction shot requires two or more cameras. Otherwise, you're not catching the actual reaction, you're staging a response and (other than in fiction) that is considered ethically dubious, which is a polite term for fraudulent.

Cut-ins

Another really handy intercut is called a *cut-in*, or *insert*. In reality, all this means is that you cut to a close-up. For example, you are filming Tiger Woods teeing off on the 72nd hole of the U.S. Open and then cut-in to a close-up of the driver impacting the golf ball.

One of the intercut's beauties is that you don't have to use two video clips. In many cases, such as a presentation or a lecture, you can cut to a still image. When your boss is talking about the departmental budget, you can cut to a chart. When we prepare a presentation about a software program, we can cut to a clip of the screen doing what we're discussing.

Tip

There are two convenient ways to get a movie of your screen. One is to hook your computer's video out to play to a TV. (Just stick a VCR in between to record the action.) Many Macs (like the iBooks) come with the circuitry to make this easy. The second method is a software solution: Snapz Pro X from Ambrosia Software (`www.AmbrosiaSW.com`) takes QuickTime movies of your screen that you can then import into iMovie. If you have one of Apple's desktop G4 models or a PowerBook G4, you might have received a licensed copy with your computer.

Transitioning Between Intercuts

A really common use of intercuts with still images is inserting customized title and credit clips in your movie's opening sequence. This is one situation where you might consider transitioning between the still and live action.

One technique we particularly like is used in a lot of TV shows. You have an opening scene and there is a short freeze of an actor and their name (maybe even the character name) and then the action continues. Using the following steps, you can create this effect:

1. With your opening sequence displayed in the Timeline viewer, click Advanced ➪ Extract Audio or ⌘-J. This extracts the audio

2. Advance the playhead to where you want your first "freeze" and choose Edit ➪ Create Still Frame (Shift-⌘-S). Write down the timestamp.

3. Select the still clip in the shelf and set its duration in the Clip Info dialog (File ➪ Show Info), as shown in the following figure.

With the still clip selected, set its "play time" in the Clip Info dialog.

4. With the clip still selected in the shelf, choose Edit ➪ Copy (⌘-C). If you don't want to retain the clip on the shelf for later use, you may use Edit ➪ Cut (⌘-X) instead.

5. Advance the playhead back to the time you wrote down in Step 2 and choose Advanced ⇨ Paste Over at Playhead (Shift-⌘-V).

6. Repeat Steps 2 through 5 for as many items as you wish.

There's one thing of which you should be careful: Don't let your last title freeze extend past the end of the clip. Doing so will cost you part of your next clip's video or, if this is the only clip in the Timeline viewer, can result in video sans audio.

Now it's a simple matter to go back to your various title clips and, using what you learned in Chapter 14, add the text and apply the title style. One side effect of this approach is that the still clip and the resumed action are often similar enough that the image appears jumpy. This is a time to smooth your intercut with a transition. A short fade-in transition (maybe 10 to 12 frames) at the start of each resumed action clip should do the job.

You might also want to use Photoshop or AppleWorks to create customized title slides employing styles not available in iMovie. The Presentations module in AppleWorks 6 is great for this, because 640 x 480 is the default slide size. Save your stills in an importable format and then import them, one at a time, into iMovie. Once they're on the shelf, follow Steps 3 through 5 for each of the clips, except that now you have to pick their insertion points.

Cross-cutting

Another cut technique that you'll see a lot in battle scenes and sporting events is *cross-cutting*, where the perspective changes from one camera angle to another on the same action. It's also used in the opening credits of some movies.

There are a couple of obvious techniques resulting in a cross-cut effect. The simplest is to just split the clip into multiple clips and remove one or two of them. The downside of this method is that you won't be synchronized with the audio (or the audio will also have gaping holes). This style works best when you aren't going to use the original clip's audio and plan to replace it with a soundtrack of your choice. The following steps explain this technique:

1. **Place the original clip in the Timeline viewer and click Advanced ⇨ Extract Audio or ⌘-J.** Doing this extracts the audio of the clip.

2. **Select the video clip and choose Edit ⇨ Copy (⌘-C).** A copy is placed on the Clipboard.

3. **Select a clip in the shelf and choose Edit ⇨ Paste (⌘-V).** A copy is placed on the shelf.

Note The reason you have to select something on the shelf is so that iMovie will know where to paste it. Otherwise, it ends up back in the Timeline viewer because that's where you were working.

4. **Select the shelf copy of your clip.** The shelf copy appears in the monitor screen.
5. **Locate the desired split location and choose Edit ➪ Split Video Clip at Playhead (⌘-T).** You now have two clips, one ending at the split point and the other starting at the split point.
6. **Repeat Steps 4 and 5 until you have all the pieces you want.** Name the clips you're going to use so that you can recognize them easily for the following steps.
7. **Select the first clip you're going to use and choose Edit ➪ Cut (⌘-X) or Edit ➪ Copy (⌘-C).** If you cut, the clip disappears from the Timeline.
8. **Position the playhead on the Timeline viewer and choose Advanced ➪ Paste Over at Playhead (Shift-⌘-V).** The copied (or cut) clip reappears in the Timeline, starting where you had the playhead positioned.
9. **Repeat Steps 7 and 8 with the playhead positioning at the end of the previously pasted clip.**
10. **Either trim the existing audio to match the new sequence length or replace it with a soundtrack of the proper length.**

You can shorten this process quite a bit if you know that you aren't going to use the clip's audio, as follows:

1. **With the Timeline view showing, select the clip that you're going to use and turn its Volume off.** Select Edit Volume and drag the Volume slider at the bottom of the Timeline view.
2. **Switch to the clip view and do your splitting.** Drag the pieces you don't want to use to the iMovie Trash.
3. **Switch back to the Timeline view and add your soundtrack.** See Chapter 14 or the previous steps to add your soundtrack.

Note

While writing this chapter originally, Dennis took a little break to watch *Windtalkers* (he's a history buff with a strong interest in WW II) and, maybe because it was fresh in his mind, he noticed the movie credits were in a sequence of landscape jump cuts against a subtle audio background, each cut introduced with a short fade in. If you watch movies and are aware of these techniques, you'll start to notice them, too, without even trying.

The coolest cuts of all

Similar in many respects to an intercut, are the *J-cut* and the *L*-cut. With the J-cut, the audio track begins before the video, reminiscent of the letter *J* shape. With the L-cut, the audio continues after the video ends, looking like the letter *L*.

Applying J-cuts

The J-cut is a common effect in movies and on TV. You're watching a scene and hear a phone ring just before the scene transitions to the person going to answer it. Now that you've seen how to perform intercuts, performing a J-cut is a breeze:

1. **Place the two clips you're going to work on in the Timeline viewer.** Make sure that the zoom factor lets you see both clips without scrolling.
2. **If your first clip has audio, choose Advanced ➪ Extract Audio Extract.** This extracts the audio from the first clip.
3. **Extract the audio from the second clip.**
4. **Decide whether you need the audio from the clip.** If you don't need any audio from this clip, choose Edit ➪ Clear (Delete) and skip to Step 12. If you do need the early audio from the clip, select the second audio clip and unlock it (Advanced ➪ Unlock Audio Clip or ⌘-L) from its video clip. Your Timeline viewer should now resemble Figure 15-4.

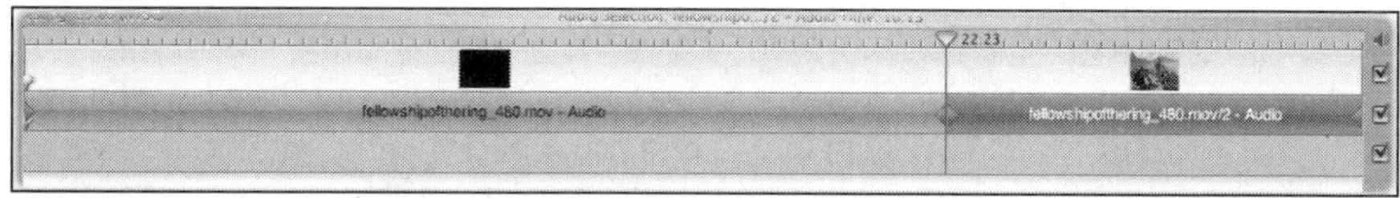

Figure 15-4: Unlock the audio track before proceeding.

5. **Create a temporary third clip.** If you don't have one handy, choose Edit ➪ Create Still Frame (Shift-⌘-S). Place your third clip in the Timeline viewer after the second clip.
6. **Position the playhead at the end of the second clip.** See Figure 15-5 for an example.

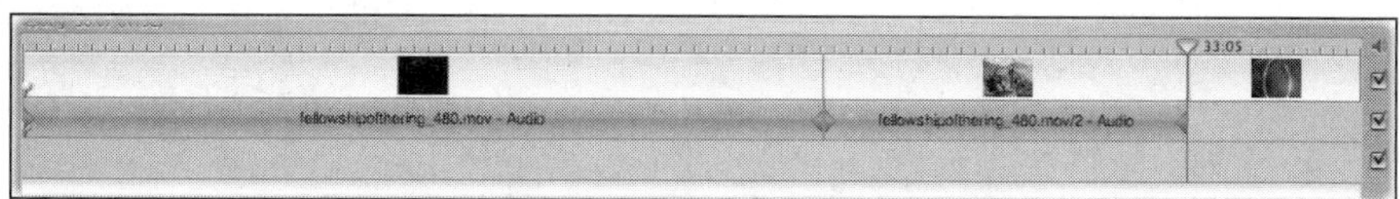

Figure 15-5: Move the playhead to the end of the second clip.

7. **With the second audio clip selected, move the playhead exactly one frame forward.** Pressing → one time works best.
8. **Choose Advanced ➪ Lock Audio Clip at Playhead.** The audio clip's end will now be locked to the temporary clip, as shown in Figure 15-6.

Figure 15-6: Attach the audio clip to the video clip that follows.

9. **Using the monitor's crop marks, select the second video clip and remove the requisite amount of video for your desired overlap.** Notice that the two audio clips now overlap beneath the first video clip, as shown in Figure 15-7.

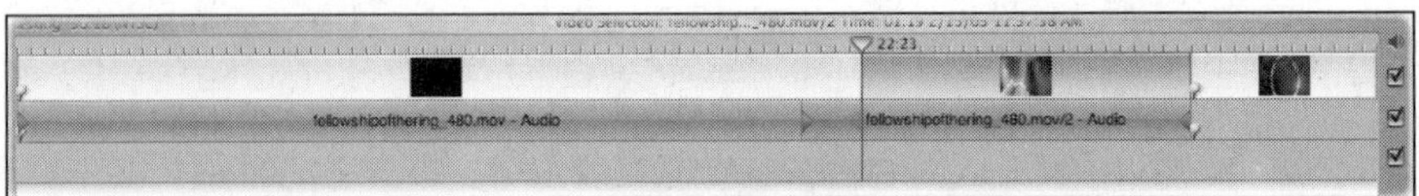

Figure 15-7: You've made the audio clips overlap.

10. **Select the second audio clip and press ← one time.** The audio clip unlocks from the third video clip, moves back one frame, and locks its ending to the second video clip's ending. If the third clip was a placeholder, you can get rid of it now.
11. **Temporarily drag the second audio clip to down to the second audio track so you can see the first audio clip's crop marker (see Figure 15-8).** Select the first audio clip and drag its right crop marker left to the beginning of the second clip's audio. Then drag the second audio clip back up. Remember that audio cropping of this type doesn't remove the audio; it merely tells iMovie not to play it.

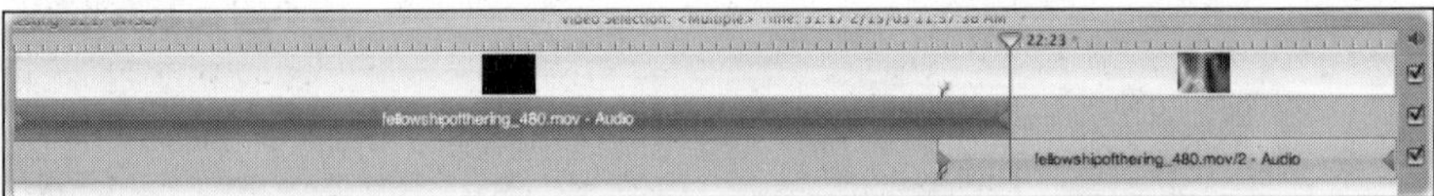

Figure 15-8: Use the second audio track to temporarily hold the second clip's audio.

Note Only perform Steps 12 and 13 if you jumped here from Step 4.

12. **Select the second video clip and, using the monitor's crop markers and Edit ➪ Clear (Delete).** Now remove the amount of video by which you want the audio to overlap.

13. **Move the second audio clip so that its end is once again synchronized with the end of the video clip.** Obviously, it is helpful to know just how much you eliminated in Step 12. With that knowledge and a little time arithmetic, you can position the audio clip precisely where you want it.

If you ask, "But why don't I just lock the ends of the second video and audio clip before I eliminate the early frames?" the answer is iMovie doesn't move the audio clip over. We're not sure if it's a bug or feature, but the obvious doesn't work here.

Applying L-cuts

More common and a lot easier than a J-cut is the L-cut. You see it in narrations and presentations all the time where the speaker keeps talking, but the picture changes to show what he's talking about. The place we see this most is on TV, when some sporting event or (un)important news bulletin has cut into one of the programs and then we're told, "Now rejoining our regularly scheduled programming..." with the program's picture on-screen just before the audio comes back. To perform an L-cut:

1. **Place the two clips you're going to work on in the Timeline viewer.** Make sure that the zoom factor lets you see both clips without scrolling.
2. **Extract the audio from both clips.** You do this by choosing Advanced ➪ Extract Audio Extract.
3. **Verify that each audio clip is locked to the beginning of its respective video, as shown in Figure 15-9.**

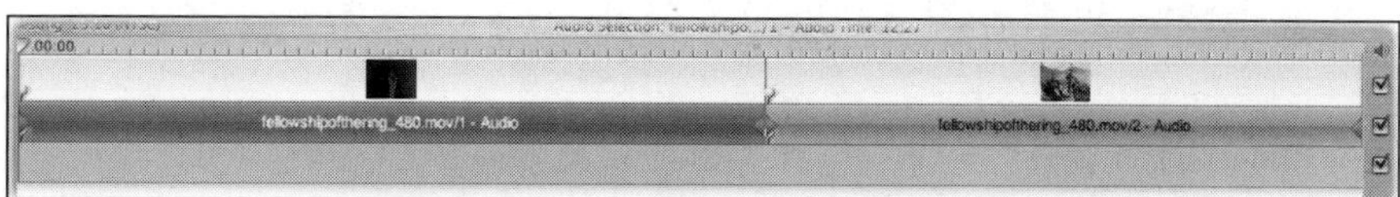

Figure 15-9: Start with the audio and video clips separated, but locked.

4. **Select the first video clip and, using the monitor's crop markers and Edit ➪ Clear (Delete), remove the desired amount of video from the end.** If you don't mind some audio overlap, you're finished; however, usually you'll want to clear out the overlapping audio from the second clip.
5. **Drag the first audio clip down to the second audio track.** See Figure 15-10 for an example of this.
6. **Select the second audio clip, making it the only selected item.**
7. **Position the playhead at the end of the overlapped portion.** See Figure 15-11 for an example.

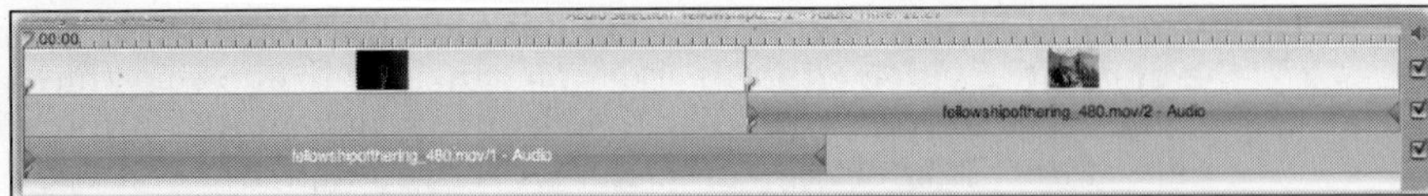

Figure 15-10: Drag the first audio clip temporarily to the second track.

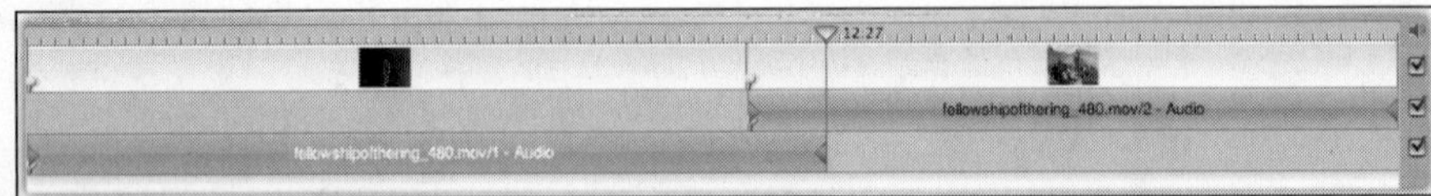

Figure 15-11: The playhead should be at the very end of the overlapped audio.

8. **Choose Edit ➪ Split Selected Audio Clip at Playhead (⌘-T).**
9. **Select only the portion that overlaps the first clip and remove it by choosing Edit ➪ Clear (Delete).**
10. **Select the second audio clip's remains and choose Advanced ➪ Lock Audio Clip at Playhead (⌘-L), and, to be tidy, drag the first audio clip back up to the first audio track.** You're done!

If you find the audio cut from the first to the second clip a bit abrupt, you can always use iMovie 3's audio volume editing abilities to fade an audio clip in or out.

A little bit softer now: Using Fade In and Out

iMovie 3 provides far more audio editing punch than its predecessors. You still need to use the Timeline view to get at the audio features, but after you're there, look out! Where there once was a simple Fade In and Fade Out control, you now have the ability to adjust the volume of *any* portion of any (and every) clip.

The keys to this particular audio hot rod can be found in the rather unassuming Edit Volume checkbox. Click it and suddenly you'll see horizontal lines (called "volume level bars") inside each clip, as shown in Figure 15-12.

Figure 15-12: The volume level bars appear inside your clips when you click Edit Volume.

If you select at least one clip, the volume slider to the right of the Edit Volume checkbox comes alive. Slide it back and forth and watch the volume bars of the selected clips bob up and down. This makes putting a music track under a narration that you've recorded using iMovie's Record feature (described in the previous chapter, "Getting Started with iMovie") easy. And then you can lower the music's volume so that it doesn't drown out the melody of your award-winning voice-over.

But it gets better. Much better. As we said, you can adjust the volume of any portion of any clip. As an example, we'll show you how to fade the clip's audio in and out — yes, this feature *seems* a little harder to use than the previous iMovie versions' much more limited Fade In and Fade Out control, but you can actually master it very quickly and it is also a lot more fun to use.

1. **In the Timeline view, click the Edit Volume checkbox.**
2. **Select the clip to which you want to add the audio fades.**
3. **Click the clip's volume level bar where you want the fade in to end.** A round marker appears where you clicked and a small square control handle appears to its left, as shown in Figure 15-13.

Figure 15-13: The volume level markers appear when you click on a clip's volume level bar.

4. **Drag the square control handle to the left (toward the beginning of the clip) and down.** The volume level bar redraws itself to show the shape of the fade-in, as shown in Figure 15-14. You can drag the round marker farther to the right if you want the fade in to take more time.

Figure 15-14: You can adjust the volume level markers to create an audio fade-in.

5. **To make the audio fade out, click on the volume level bar at the end of the clip.** Again, a round marker appears with a small square control handle to its left.
6. **Drag the round marker down.** The volume level bar again shows the shape of the fade. If you want the fade to take more time, drag the small square control handle farther left.

You aren't limited to adjusting the audio volume at the beginning or ending of a clip, though. You can add volume level markers anywhere in a clip that you want, and you can add a lot of them. It's like a Ken Burns effect for sound!

Working with Non-DV Video

iMovie is made to work with DV Streams, pure and simple. If you're going to feed it video, that video must be DV. So, what's this hoohah about working with non-DV video?

Sometimes you don't get a choice about your source material's format. You might get a QuickTime clip from a client that they want included in the movie. One example might be a PowerPoint presentation that was saved as a QuickTime movie. At other times you might find some video on the Web and (after getting all the requisite permissions, of course) wish to include it in your movie.

Fortunately, iMovie 3 can convert many video file formats into DV Streams "automagically" by way of the File menu's Import command. It does this by silently using the QuickTime software already installed on your Mac. Almost any video file that QuickTime can export can be imported into iMovie.

In those increasingly rare cases where iMovie's QuickTime-enabled import doesn't work, you must convert the file into a DV Stream in some other way A number of commercial products such as Media Cleaner (Discreet Systems, `www.discreet.com`) can perform this task, though they're pretty pricey. Nevertheless, if you need to repurpose some MPEG files (either MPEG-1 or MPEG-2) or some of the other formats not included in QuickTime Pro's arsenal, Media Cleaner is a product that we recommend.

If the Cleaner price seems a bit steep to you, there are freeware (open-source) applications that do very nearly as well, but with a much less friendly interface. One we particularly like is ffmpegX (`homepage.mac.com/major4`).

What (and Why) Are All These Formats?

If you've ever been given a word-processing or spreadsheet document that your software doesn't understand, you've probably cursed either the person who gave it to you, your software for not recognizing the format, the software developers for creating multiple formats that are not compatible, or some combination of the above. Although each of these formats was developed for a reason, they are only trouble for you now. Think of formats as languages. If you're monolingual, you need a translator or interpreter to understand what was said in languages other than your own. Although iMovie on its own is monolingual when it comes to video, it uses QuickTime's multilingual capabilities to translate video into its own language; similarly, it uses iTunes' multilingual capabilities for audio.

Apple developed QuickTime to deal with time-based data (video and audio, primarily). To facilitate dealing with time-based data, QuickTime also defines a container format, recognized by the .mov file extension. One of the things the MOV format does is tell which compressor was used to create the data and which decompressor you need to extract it. On Windows, AVI files fall into the same general category—they hold data and information about the compressors-decompressors. In either case, unless you have the needed decompressor, the data won't do you much good.

Basically, all movies are a sequence of images (like flip-cards) with attached sound. The devil, as they say, is in the details. To make these movies consume less space on your disk and less time to transmit across a network, you use compression to compact repetitive data and eliminate superfluous data. Various compressors and compression algorithms have been developed, are being developed, and will be developed in the future to optimize the compression to meet specific goals.

For example, you need to compress data you're going to stream over the Internet not just for the number of bytes, but also for how fast you can decompress it at the receiving end so that you can play data as you receive it. This compression often creates an emphasis on space savings. On the other hand, data stored on disk might strike a different balance, trading some of that space savings for more decompression speed—after all, the data is all present, and we can read from a disk a lot faster than we can receive data across the Internet.

Most of the time, you have a video track and an audio track in the container and you need decompressors for both. The Motion Picture Experts Group (MPEG) adds yet another complication to our lives with their MPEG-1 and MPEG-2 formats: *multiplexed* (also known as *muxed*) tracks. Therefore, the video and sound are interwoven into a single track. That's why, if you try to use QuickTime Pro to convert a MPEG file to a DV Stream, you'll lose the audio. The conversion process doesn't separate the two types of data and only passes on the one it deems more important.

Microsoft and RealNetworks also complicate matters with proprietary formats (ASF, WMV, and the like from Microsoft and the various RM types from Real). If their player is out there (particularly, Microsoft's) on almost every computer sold, the broadcasters have an incentive to pay for the tools that can deliver content to those players.

Converting compatible formats

QuickTime Pro, at least according to Apple, recognizes and plays QuickTime movies, MPEG files, and AVI files. We qualified that statement for several reasons:

✦ QuickTime files, those with filenames ending in .mov, .qt, or .moov usually, are QuickTime container files. You may, sometimes, encounter QuickTime files that your perfectly up-to-date QuickTime Pro won't open and you'll be told that you might have difficulty with a track because the required compressor couldn't be found, as shown in Figure 15-15.

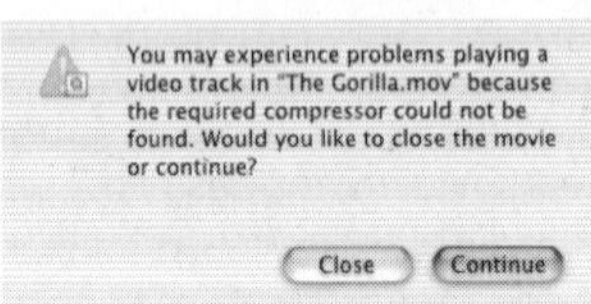

Figure 15-15: QuickTime sometimes can't find the compressor for a QuickTime file.

The simple reason behind this is that whoever created this QuickTime file did so by using a compressor that isn't part of the standard distribution. One common source of this error is when you encounter QuickTime movies created with the freeware tool DivX Doctor II, which uses a freeware compressor called 3ivx Decoder for OS X (which will probably have a version number in the middle of its name).

✦ MPEG files are those whose names end in .mpg and cover a wide range of possibilities. QuickTime recognizes and plays most MPEG-1 files. Although we haven't encountered an uncorrupted MPEG-1 file that causes QuickTime to hiccup, we have seen reports in newsgroups and on mailing lists, so we can't discount the possibility that such exist. The real problem arises from the fact that MPEG-2 files, used for SVCD (Super VideoCD) and DVD discs also employ the .mpg extension. QuickTime 5.x doesn't understand MPEG-2. QuickTime 6 does, but it requires that you purchase a $20 add-on decoder. Also, new in QuickTime 6, is support for MPEG-4 files. MPEG-4 is mostly used for streaming video as it generates small files that retain impressive quality.

✦ AVI is the Windows equivalent of QuickTime (it stands for Audio-Video Interleaved) format. Apple claims that QuickTime understands AVI files and if there is a gross overstatement anywhere in the marketing materials for QuickTime, that's it! AVI is a catch-all file extension used for files encoded with the various Indeo compressors from Intel (some of which have never been ported to the Macintosh), various DivX formats comprising another half-dozen or so compressors, and some other minor variations. QuickTime Pro only recognizes a few of the Indeo compressors. The others display a message similar to Figure 15-15 unless you find suitable compressors from other sources.

Now that we've looked at all the things that can go wrong, we'll tell you that most of the time things just work.

Knowing what to import

You can import any video file that QuickTime Player can play into iMovie. That doesn't mean that you'll necessarily like the results. *GIGO* (Garbage In, Garbage Out) is more clearly demonstrated in a few situations other than video. Files saved for distribution on CD, over the Web, or in e-mail typically exhibit some compromises in terms of resolution, frame rate, and compression. If the movie isn't smooth and clear when played at 640 x 480 resolution in QuickTime Player, it won't be any better when you import it into iMovie. (Use Movie ⇨ Double Size or ⌘-2 to get a 320 x 240 up to 640 x 480.) Similarly, you save most QuickTime movies at a frame rate significantly lower than 30fps, resulting in jumpiness when you export to NTSC's 30fps DV frame rate. Finally, if the compression ratio you use is more than 4:1, you're going to see blurry images when you import it.

As a case in point, Microsoft added a Save as QuickTime feature in PowerPoint 2001 and improved it in PowerPoint for OS X. This feature should have resulted in a lot more iMovie QuickTime imports. Saving a presentation as a QuickTime file means that you can tape the boss (or be taped, yourself) delivering a presentation and import the actual presentation. With a little judicious intercutting as described earlier in this chapter ("The art of the intercut"), and you can create a great business video, one that just a few years ago would have required professionals and cost a small fortune to produce.

At least, that's the theory. In practice, you need to have quality input files before you can import them. The main problem with PowerPoint's QuickTime settings is that they overcompress. Using PowerPoint's Business Plan template as an example, we saved it as a 640 x 480 QuickTime movie. In Figure 15-16, you can see what it looks like in QuickTime and how blurry (it's called pixilation) the text appears after you import it into iMovie. Apple's new Keynote product seems to be better behaved in this area.

"Aha!" you cry, noticing that the DV Stream is wider (720 x 480) than the QuickTime movie, "Things got distorted in the translation." Well, that's not the case, we're forced to say. As you can see in Figure 15-17, we also saved the presentation at 720 x 480 resolution and then exported that, with similar sorry results.

The lesson here is that you should still import the presentation as 640 x 480 still images and do your magic completely within iMovie. You'll lose PowerPoint's special effects, but you can't have everything (yet).

(a)

(b)

Figure 15-16: A 640 x 480 QuickTime movie created by PowerPoint (a); the same movie after conversion to iMovie's native DV Stream format (b).

(a)

(b)

Figure 15-17: A 720 x 480 QuickTime movie created by PowerPoint (a); the same movie after conversion to iMovie's native DV Stream format (b).

If you own and use Apple's new Keynote presentation software, you're a lot better placed to import its presentations that have been saved to QuickTime.

What then, does work well when you import into iMovie? You can bring PCI and USB video capture cards and devices into iMovie with good results, so long as they work at 640 x 480, 30fps, and use a lower than 4:1 compression ratio. You can also make some slideshows in QuickTime Pro employing masks and other special effects that aren't available in iMovie. We'll show you one of them later in this chapter under "Postproduction Tricks with QuickTime Pro." Because QuickTime Pro lets you set all the parameters necessary, getting DV-friendly files is pretty easy.

Plugging into iMovie

Way back in 1986, when Apple and Bill Atkinson were preparing WildCard's birth as HyperCard, it was obvious that Mac users (particularly "power users") wanted to extend the capabilities of their software. HyperCard introduced XCMDs (external commands) to satisfy that lust and, as a result, created a cottage industry. Adobe and other developers saw this and put a plug-in architecture together for their products — there are, literally, hundreds of plug-ins for PhotoShop. Much of the really cool stuff you do with your Web browser (watch movies on the Web, read PDF files, play music, view Flash animations, and so forth) results because your browser supports plug-ins. No fool, Apple realized that the Effects, Transitions, Titles, and such provided with iMovie were not going to quench your directorial thirst. Thus, iMovie also has a plug-in architecture.

Previous versions of iMovie only came with a few standard effects, transitions, and title styles, although Apple did provide additional ones in optional plug-in packs that the company made available for download. iMovie 3, however, comes with those formerly optional plug-ins built in. But if that cornucopia of editing goodies doesn't sate your creative hunger, a number of third-party developers offer still more iMovie plug-ins, and Apple provides links to several of them on its iMovie Web page. Some of the latter even provide free sampler packages that you can download and try out.

While we're writing this, there are collections from four companies: GeeThree, Virtix, CSB Digital, and eZedia. All four have some really cool transitions and effects, but (at least for the moment), one of our favorites is eZeMatte from eZedia. Being able to overlay a still on top of our clips opens all sorts of possibilities: framing, fancy titles and credits, or applying a logo just touch the surface. Another favorite is GeeThree's picture-in-picture from "Slick Transitions & Effects — Volume 4." GeeThree's Slick Motion used to be one of Bob's favorites, but the Ken Burns Effect in iMovie 3 pretty much supplanted Slick Motion.

Installing plug-ins

How and where you install iMovie plug-ins depends on whether the plug-ins come with an installer application. If there is an installer package, run it and you're done. If there isn't an installer, the process still isn't very difficult:

1. **Locate the Library folder in your Home directory.**
2. **Find and open the iMovie folder.** If it doesn't exist, create it.
3. **Drag the plug-ins to the Plug-ins folder.** If the Plug-ins folder doesn't exist, create it.

Now, wasn't that easy? When you launch iMovie, you see the new effects, transitions, titles, and sounds appear in the appropriate shelf panels. Figure 15-18 shows a typical iMovie Plug-ins folder; note that you can further subdivide the Plug-ins folder into appropriate folders: iMovie looks through them all to find what it needs.

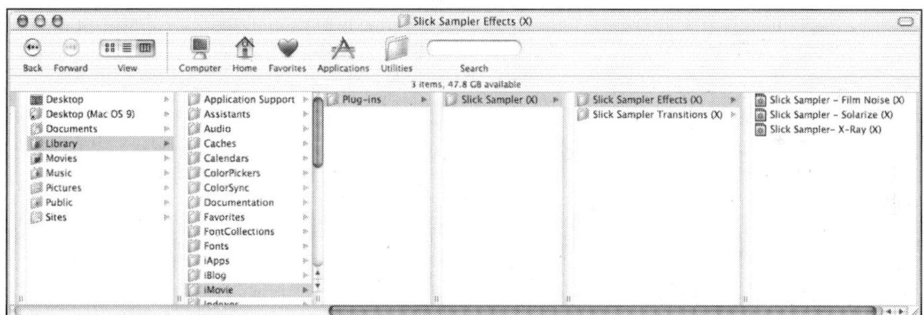

Figure 15-18: The iMovie Plug-ins folder in your Home's Library is where you place additional iMovie effects, transitions, and title styles.

Adding other stuff to iMovie

Apple also provides a number of sound effects for use with iMovie. Just click the Audio Effects button on the iMovie Web page and you can pick and choose the one(s) you want. On the same Web page, you can find links to several companies that offer commercial sound effects and music, which you can purchase for your iMovie use. Additionally, Apple makes Freeplay Music's (`www.freeplaymusic.com`) collection of 2100 royalty-free songs available on your iDisk.

Tip

If you haven't sprung for a .Mac account yet, you really should consider it. Go to Apple's site `www.mac.com` and create yours. In addition to the mac.com e-mail address, the iDisk is a phenomenal resource, even if you never use it for storage or as a Web site. Apple makes a lot of software, both their own and third-party, available in the Software folder on every iDisk.

Becoming Expert with QuickTime Export

As we saw in Chapter 14, iMovie comes with canned settings for what Apple considers the most common QuickTime Export configurations: small e-mail attachments, small Web pages, medium-sized CD movies, and huge DV-quality movies to watch from your hard disk.

Expert Settings is another option. Unlike previous versions of iMovie, iMovie 3's Expert Settings feature presents the same QuickTime export interface that's available in other QuickTime applications on your Macintosh, such as QuickTime Player Pro. You need to understand what you're trading off and what you're trying to accomplish, because you'll be making all the decisions here.

To get to the standard QuickTime export settings follow these steps:

1. **Choose File ➪ Export (Shift-⌘-E).**
2. **From the Export pop-up menu, choose To QuickTime.**
3. **From the Formats pop-up menu choose Expert Settings.**
4. **Click the Export button.**

You'll see QuickTime's standard Save exported file as dialog (Figure 15-19).

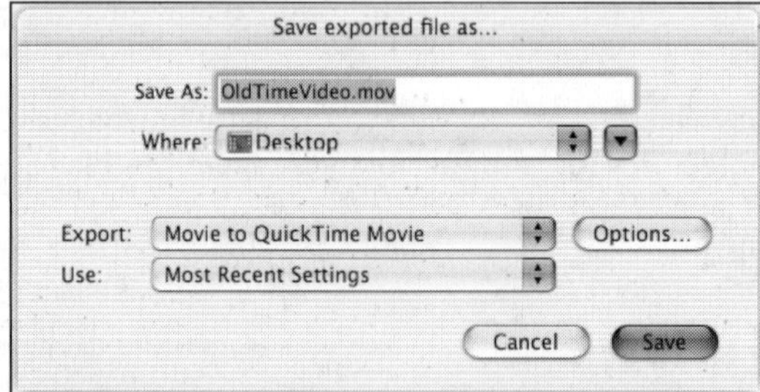

Figure 15-19: The Save exported file as dialog provides access to all of QuickTime's compression and conversion features in a deceptively compact space.

From this dialog, you can save your iMovie as a QuickTime movie — or you can use its Export pop-up menu to save the file in any one of the other formats that QuickTime can produce. As you can see from Figure 15-20, there are a number of them. For example, you can save movies in the new MPEG-4 format that plays on a variety of digital devices (imagine your iMovie playing on a digital telephone screen), or you can save the video as a sequence of still pictures (with a couple of reams of paper and a pile of ink cartridges you can make the ultimate flipbook animation), or you can save just the audio portion of the movie (producing a soundtrack album of your cinematic masterpiece is just a few clicks away). But this section is about QuickTime movies, so that's the focus here.

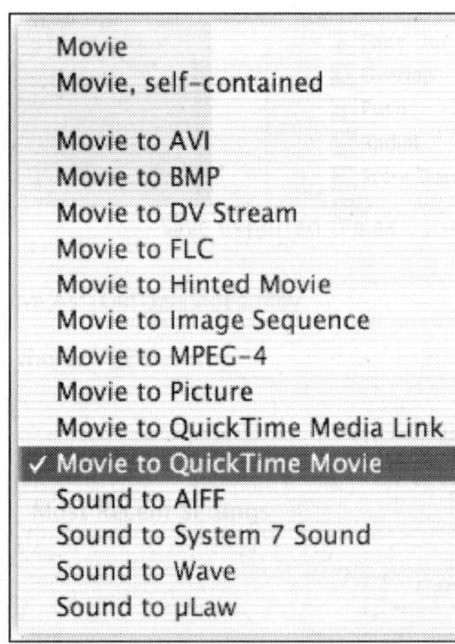

Figure 15-20: QuickTime can save your iMovie as a QuickTime movie – or as a whole lot of other things.

You'll also notice that the dialog also provides a Use pop-up menu that lets you pick from several preconfigured output settings — although if you wanted to use presets, you wouldn't have used Expert Settings in the first place, would you? However, the Most Recent Settings choice on the Use pop-up is handy if you plan to export several movies using the same specialized settings.

It's the Option button that gets you to the compression settings. Click this and you'll see QuickTime's Movie Settings dialog (Figure 15-21).

The Movie Settings dialog is divided into three areas: Video, where you decide what to do with the video; Sound, where you specify compression, sampling, and channels for your sound; and Prepare for Internet Streaming for setting your movie up for access from a Web page. You can tell QuickTime not to bother exporting the audio or the video, or not to worry about making the file ready for the Internet, just by unchecking the appropriate checkbox.

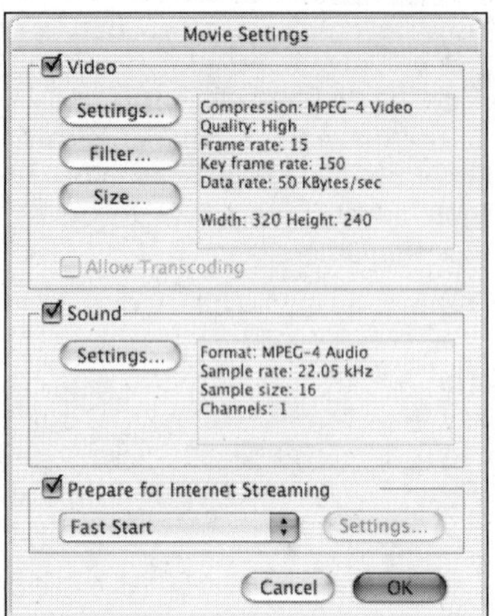

Figure 15-21: The Movie Settings dialog puts you in complete control of your movie's export.

Determining image video settings

The Video settings area has three powerful buttons: Settings, Filter, and Size. You'll probably want to ignore the Filter button; it provides access to QuickTime's own video effects and filters, but most likely you'll have already used iMovie's effects and transitions before you even get here. However, you almost certainly *will* want to use the Size and Settings buttons.

The Size button brings up a small dialog that lets you specify the width and height in pixels of the exported movie. Unfortunately, as a consequence of providing iMovie 3 users complete access to the standard QuickTime export settings, a useful feature of earlier iMovie versions has been lost — a special button in the Size dialog that let you constrain the output dimensions to a 4:3 ratio. Instead, you'll have to do the math yourself (good thing the Mac has a built-in Calculator program!).

The ratio of width to height is called the *aspect ratio*. Standard TV has a 4:3 aspect ratio, and you need to use that ratio in most cases. But you don't have to. Freedom is a wonderful thing.

Clicking the Settings button presents the Compression Settings dialog shown in Figure 15-22. The topmost Compressor pop-up presents a long list of compressors you might use, similar to the one in Figure 15-22. (We have a couple of choices in the figure in addition to those offered by a basic QuickTime Pro installation and a couple of new choices are missing; because QuickTime has a plug-in component architecture of its own, this menu is always subject to change.) We're not going to cover all of them, just the ones appropriate to video — some of them, like BMP and

JPEG, are compressors that apply to still images rather than video. Here are the major video compressors:

✦ **Animation:** A lossy compression format. The more you compress your video, the more the quality suffers. At its High and Best quality settings, you don't achieve much compression. As its name implies, it is probably best suited to cartoon-like images and image sequences.

✦ **Cinepak:** One of the oldest compressors available. If you use it, it's certain that any user with QuickTime installed, even really old versions, can view your work. The downside to Cinepak is that it doesn't achieve a lot of compression and what it does achieve is lossy. You should have at least one, preferably two or three, key frames per second, at least 12 (preferably 15) frames per second, and a data rate of at least 150KB per second. A 320 x 240 video, at 150KB/sec, 15fps, and a key frame every 7 frames consumes about 12MB per minute.

✦ **DV-NTSC/DV-PAL:** Generates files about the same size and quality as they are in iMovie. Reducing the frame size to 320 x 240 and the frame rate to 15fps only reduces your space consumption by about 50 percent to about 100MB/min. These formats are best suited as an intermediate format to feed to third-party video postprocessing tools. We discuss some of those in Chapter 17.

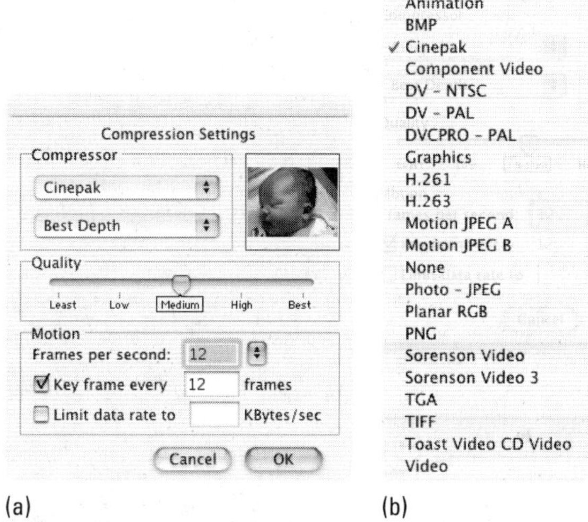

(a) (b)

Figure 15-22: The (video) Compression Settings dialog (a); Lots of choices in the Compressor pop-up menu (b).

✦ **H.261:** Developed over ten years ago (1990) by the ITU (International Telecomm Union). It's optimized for streaming data, particularly those with data rates that are a multiple of 64Kbits/sec. It is particularly well-suited for ISDN connections.

✦ **H.263:** One of your better trade-off choices. You can get about the same or slightly better quality in half the space that Cinepak uses. You don't require as many key frames for good results.

✦ **Motion JPEG A/Motion JPEG B:** Extensions to video of JPEG image compression. Using Motion JPEG, each frame is a JPEG-compressed image. The difference between the A and B variants is that Motion JPEG-B doesn't support markers to denote start-of-image. This format is common in many PCI- and USB-based capture cards.

✦ **MPEG-4 Video:** A cross-platform scalable compression standard developed by the Motion Picture Experts Group. MPEG-4 Video is new to QuickTime 6. In fact, the MPEG-4 file format is actually based upon Apple's QuickTime format. MPEG-4 provides one of the better, more compact compression schemes around. However, because it is an industry standard that has yet to be approved by a committee, it will always be a step or two behind the latest and greatest video compressors. The quality is good. This compressor is going to be an increasingly important one to consider as time goes by, especially for Internet streaming. However, unless your audience has QuickTime 6 installed, forget about this one for now.

✦ **Sorenson:** Since its inclusion with QuickTime 4, Sorenson has been the quality champion, at least until Sorenson 3 showed up with QuickTime 5.0.2. Sorenson, — more accurately, Sorenson 2 — comes with a performance price tag. Compressing can take a long time. Playback requires QuickTime 4.0 or later and, if you want decent performance, a G3 or better processor. While this isn't a problem for you, using Mac OS X, not all of your audience is guaranteed to be so well prepared.

✦ **Sorenson 3:** Significantly improves on Sorenson 2's performance, delivering equivalent quality in about half the time. The software bar has been raised, though, requiring QuickTime 5.0.2 or later to view Sorenson 3-compressed movies. Both Sorenson and Sorenson 3 offer another advantage. They play back well when scaled up to double their size. This means that a 320 x 240 movie still looks good at 640 x 480.

✦ **Video:** Another of the older compressors. This compressor is a good choice when compatibility with older versions of QuickTime and older, slower Macs is a consideration. Video's main failing is that it doesn't achieve significant compression. At 12fps and 320 x 240 resolution, 25MB/minute is not uncommon.

Actually establishing your video compression options is pretty easy. Just follow these steps:

1. **Choose the compressor from the upper Compressor pop-up menu.** See the previous sequence for more details.
2. **Choose the number of colors from the lower Compressor pop-up menu.** Number of colors is sometimes expressed as the Bit Depth.
3. **Use the Quality slider to set the desired quality.** The higher the quality you set, the larger the resultant file.
4. **Specify the speed of play in the Frames per second text field (or select from the adjacent pop-up menu).** A rate between 12 and 24fps is usually a good choice for CD-based movies. 24fps is the frame rate associated with film and generally results in a very high-quality playback, if the computer is fast enough to support that speed. If there is a lot of action (a hockey game, for example), you might want to use higher frame rates as well.

Note

iMovie uses the American television standard frame rate of 30fps (more accurately, the standard is really 29.97fps, but you can think of it as 30). Using a lower frame rate means that iMovie will drop frames. This is not bad because your goal is to reduce the size of your output file and dropping frames is a sure way to do that. However, keep in mind that frame rates that divide evenly into 30 (such as 7.5, 10, or 15) spread the frame loss out more evenly, resulting in a less jumpy looking picture.

5. **Set the key frame rate in the Key frame every *nn* frames text box. Make sure that you select the checkbox.** Most video compression is achieved by computing differences from a reference image (called the key frame). The more variation there is, the less advantage this technique achieves. You can actually get to the point where the differences record comprises more data than a complete image. We tend to use at least one key frame per second (generally two or three if the image isn't relatively static).
6. **If available (for example, Animation disables it), you can select the Limit data rate checkbox and specify an upper limit for how fast you want to move data.** Here, the "x" in CD drives designated 2x, 8x, and so on comes into play. Many older drives are 1x (by definition) and, if compatibility with those drives is an issue, you should keep the data rate under 150KB/sec (probably far under).

Specifying audio compression

If QuickTime's default audio settings are not to your liking, click the Audio section's Settings button to display the Sound Settings dialog shown in Figure 15-23. As you can see, this dialog doesn't have quite as many variations for you to consider.

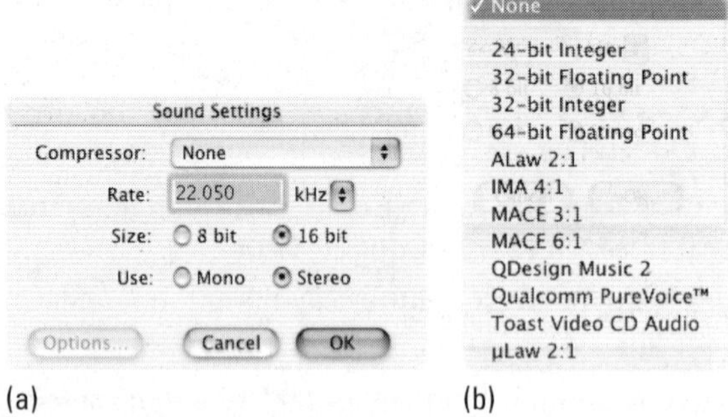

Figure 15-23: The Sound Settings dialog (a); choose one from the Compressor pop-up menu (b).

You can save space by lowering the quality of your audio (but video compression has a much higher impact on size). How you plan to distribute your movie has a major impact on the audio settings you choose.

1. **Choose an audio compressor from the Compressor pop-up menu.** The choices follow:
    - **24-bit Integer/32-bit Floating Point/32-bit Integer/64-bit Floating Point:** Primarily intended for use with processor-specific hardware and software storage. They aren't generally useful for video editing.
    - **ALaw 2:1:** Similar to >Law 2:1 (see last in list), but is based on European digital telephone standards.
    - **IMA 4:1:** Highly recommended for CD-based movies. It compresses rapidly at about a 4:1 ratio and works well with both the Mac's AIFF format and the WAV format common on Windows.
    - **MACE 3:1/MACE 6:1:** The Macintosh Audio Compression and Expansion codecs that have been part of the Macintosh Sound Manager seemingly forever (a long time, anyway). Included with QuickTime 3.0 or later, they are general-purpose, cross-platform choices and work well when older hardware might be in play, but they are seldom used these days.
    - **MPEG-4 Audio:** This is not shown in Figure 15-23. This option brings the high-quality AAC audio compressor to QuickTime. It provides excellent music compression that many users consider to be better than MP3, and it can do it at a much lower data rate. QuickTime's MPEG-4 audio support is still in its early stages, and this compressor will only be getting better as time goes on. But, until more people download QuickTime 6 and its successors, this option may not be the best choice for a movie that you want to distribute to a widely diverse audience.

- **QDesign Music 2:** As the name implies, this option is optimized to compress music. This compressor enables the Sound Settings Options button, which you can click to set a target data rate between 8Kbps and 48Kbps. The compressor works well for streaming music because it can deliver near-CD-quality sound over a 28.8Kbps modem connection (though not with video included).
- **Qualcomm PureVoice(tm)**, in contrast to QDesign Music 2, is optimized for the spoken voice. Supporting only mono settings, it can greatly compress spoken audio. It's based on the same CDMA (Code Division Multiple Access) technology used in cellular telephones. When you choose this compressor, you have access to the Options button, which will let you specify 9:1 or 19:1 compression and whether to optimize for streaming.
- **>Law 2:1:** Purely 16-bit audio, with the low (2:1) compression rate used in the United States and Japan for digital telephony. It is generally a poor choice for video due to its low compression but does have the advantage of being fast and not very lossy.

2. **Choose your sample rate.** You can do this either from the pop-up button or by typing it into the Rate textbox.
3. **If applicable, specify whether to use 8-bit or 16-bit sound on the Size line.**
4. **Specify Mono or Stereo sound as appropriate (if the choice is available).**
5. **Click OK and return to the Expert QuickTime Settings dialog.** The dialog now reflects the choices you've made.
6. **Assuming that you're done, click OK to dismiss the dialog.**

We discuss the "Prepare for internet" option later in this chapter, under "Putting Your Movie on the Web."

Postproduction Tricks with QuickTime Pro

Now that you have a movie exported to QuickTime, you might think that you're done. You could be right as the movie is now ready to be viewed by users with a compatible QuickTime version installed on their computers.

If, however, you've ponied up the big bucks to upgrade your QuickTime Player to the Pro version (trust us, it is $30 well worth spending). You'll be able to get at some additional QuickTime specific editing features that iMovie doesn't provide. The control center for these QuickTime features is the Properties dialog (Movie ⇨ Get Movie Properties, or ⌘-J), shown in Figure 15-24.

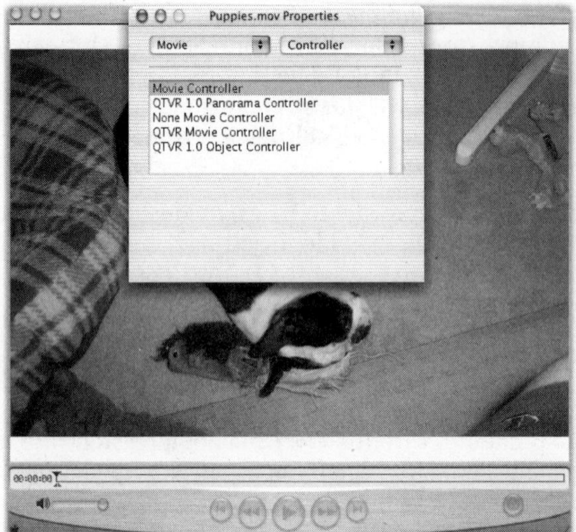

Figure 15-24: QuickTime Player Pro's Properties dialog.

The key to the Properties dialog is the pair of pop-up menus at the top. Although they appear to be peers, the pop-up on the right changes depending upon what you select from the left-hand pop-up. By default, you open to the Movie selection in the left pop-up menu. At this point, your choices in the right pop-up are

✦ **Annotations:** Where you can add textual information such as a copyright notice, a date stamp, or a myriad of other possibilities. If you want to annotate your movie, click the Add button, shown in Figure 15-25, to display the Add Annotation dialog. Select the category in the scrolling list at the top and enter your text in the textbox at the bottom of the dialog. When ready, click Add.

  When annotations are selected in the Properties list, you can choose to Edit or Delete them as well.

✦ **Auto Play:** You are presented with one checkbox, labeled Auto Play Enabled. If you select this checkbox and open the movie, the movie starts playing automatically (at least on Macs where that feature is available and enabled).

✦ **Colors:** Only useful if you plan to play your movie on computers that don't support thousands or millions of colors (for example, 256, or 8-bit, video). You can attach a color palette to your movie by clicking the Set button and navigating to the color palette file. In today's computing world, this selection is an anachronism.

✦ **Controller:** Shown in Figure 15-24. This is where you specify which type of QuickTime Player window the user should see when opening your movie. For movies created with iMovie, the only two of interest are Movie Controller (the default) and None (which just eliminates the scrubber bar and the VCR-like controls from the window).

Figure 15-25: Click the Add button to include annotations, such as copyright information.

✦ **Files:** Tells which files are used for the movie. On a movie resulting from an iMovie export to QuickTime, these are just the files you double-clicked to launch QuickTime.

✦ **General:** Just informs you how many tracks are in your movie, their speed, and their size.

✦ **Preview:** Lets you specify the portion of your movie to display in an Open dialog's Preview pane or the Mac OS X Finder's column view.

✦ **Size:** Refers to dimensions, such as 640 x 480 or 320x 240. You will be informed of both the default (Normal) size and the current size, in case you've chosen to resize the Player window.

✦ **Time:** Tells you where the playhead is (Current Time), how long the movie is (Duration), the timestamp of a current selection's beginning (Selection Start), and how long the selection is (Selection Duration).

Although much of this is very interesting (and useful) information, it really doesn't get you any closer to using QuickTime Pro's special effects. They work on individual movie tracks, not on the movie as a whole. Select a video track (as shown in Figure 15-26) and the right-hand pop-up menu changes a bit. Two of these, Graphics Mode and Size, allow for some interesting effects.

Figure 15-26: With Video Track selected in the left-hand pop-up menu, you have many options available in the right-hand pop-up menu.

Masking out part of the screen

Somewhat of a contradiction, you use transparency to black out part of your video image. Actually, block out is more accurate than black out, because you specify the single color to ignore in an image.

Note

There is no fudge factor or tolerance on the color chosen. You must specify the color exactly. An RGB color specification of 0, 0, 128 is not going to affect any other shade of blue, no matter how close they appear to the male eye. (We've given up on underestimating the female ability to distinguish between two colors that most men would find identical.)

What we're going to describe here is a fairly simple example: putting a speech balloon, like the ones in comic books, on a section of our video. Starting with the image in Figure 15-27, we're going to add a balloon of text saying, "But I don't wanna get up!" above and to the right (partially hiding the fan base).

1. **Using your graphics program of choice, create the thought balloon and make everything other than the text and the balloon's outline the color that you want to have disappear.** To make this process easy, black is our transparency color, and we'll put the text and balloon in any other color or combination, as shown in Figure 15-27b (okay, we'll choose white). You should make the image file 640 x 480 (or whatever size your video track is) at a 72dpi resolution.

   We used GraphicConverter, but you can accomplish this equally well with AppleWorks, Photoshop, Corel, or many other programs.

2. **Save the file as a PICT image.**
3. **Open your movie in QuickTime Player and find out how long it is.**
4. **Choose File ⇨ Import, locate the PICT file you created in the Open dialog box (or sheet) and click the Open button.**
5. **Choose File ⇨ Save (⌘-S), name the movie you've just created, and click Save.**
6. **Select the entire movie (Edit ⇨ Select All or ⌘-A) and choose Edit ⇨ Copy (⌘-C).**
7. **Switch to the QuickTime Player window with your real movie.**
8. **Place the playhead where you want the overlay to take effect.**

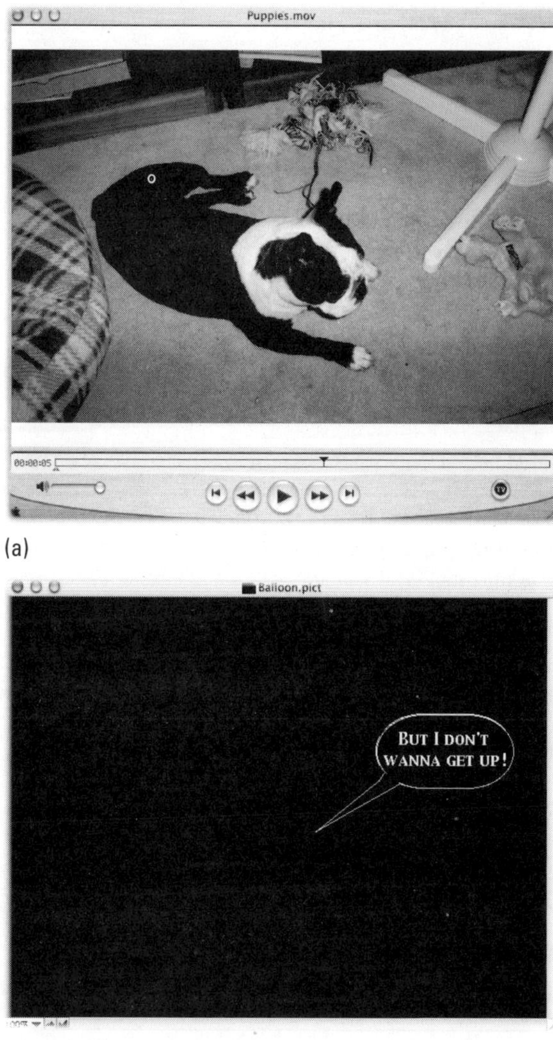

Figure 15-27: Our movie (a); our mask, as created in GraphicConverter (b).

9. **Holding down the Shift key, drag the playhead to the end of the sequence you want overlaid.** Your window should resemble that in Figure 15-28. (The very light gray in the scrubber bar might not show up well in the figure, so look for the crop markers.)

Figure 15-28: Use the crop markers to select the frame sequence you want masked.

10. **While pressing the Option and Shift keys, choose Edit ➪ Add Scaled (or, for the suitably dexterous, just press Option-Shift-⌘-V).** Add Scaled only appears in the Edit menu if you press both Option and Shift. With just the Option key down, Add appears in the menu, but this addition adds just one second.

Now, because the mask is hiding your movie, it's time to make it (at least partially) transparent:

11. **Choose Movie ➪ Get Movie Properties (⌘-J).**
12. **In the left pop-up, choose Video Track 2 (the track you just added).**
13. **In the right pop-up, choose Graphics Mode and select transparent from the list.**
14. **Click the Color button and, using your color picker of choice (we chose RGB), specify the color you want to make transparent.** In our case, it was black (0, 0, 0).
15. **Click OK and see the result, as shown in Figure 15-29.**

We're sure that you can come up with many variations on this theme if you unleash your imaginations. Remember, any colors other than your mask color remain.

Tip

If you want a black-and-white mask to apply to the whole track, there is a shortcut. Choose your video track in the left pop-up, choose Mask from the right pop-up, click the Set button, and select the image you want to use for a mask.

Figure 15-29: But Spenser doesn't wanna get up!

Making better subtitles with Text Tracks

Subtitles and captions can really augment a movie. iMovie gives you some pretty nice styles for the subtitles, but they aren't exactly flexible about mixing fonts, text styles, and sizes within a single subtitle (to put it mildly). QuickTime's Text Tracks are a lot more freewheeling in this regard, but you're stuck with the text appearing on a black bar at the bottom of your screen, reminiscent of closed caption TV.

To use Text Tracks, follow these steps:

1. **Create your text, using all the formatting you deem appropriate in a text editor.** TextEdit is a pretty good choice for OS X, as is SimpleText in OS 9.
2. **Select the text and choose Edit ⇨ Copy.** This places your text on the system clipboard.
3. **Switch to your QuickTime movie and position the playhead where you want the text to first appear.**
4. **While pressing Shift, drag the playhead to the point where you want the text to disappear.** Adjust the crop markers as necessary if you missed your spots by a bit.
5. **While pressing Shift and Option, choose Edit ⇨ Add Scaled (Option-Shift-⌘-V).**

Now, wasn't that easy? When you play your movie back, the text appears as shown in Figure 15-30.

Figure 15-30: Closed captioning, with style.

You can even do some resizing and skewing of the text track, just go to the Properties menu to tweak it by following these steps:

1. **Choose Movie ➪ Get Movie Properties (⌘-J).**
2. **Choose the text track from the left pop-up menu and then choose Size from the right-hand pop-up.**
3. **Click the Adjust button and some red handles appear around the caption.** These handles are a little strange but, if you drag the corner handles, you can resize the caption horizontally or vertically. If you drag the circled X handles, you skew or rotate the caption.

If you have multiple lines of text (kind of like the flashing billboard signs you see on the highway) where you want one line to show up and, when it disappears, have the next line appear, and so forth. That, too, is made to order for QuickTime text tracks. In this case, you start by making your story a QuickTime movie, as follows.

1. **Create your text file and save it.** Each paragraph is considered a text frame and given a two-second duration.
2. **In QuickTime Player, choose File ➪ Import and select your text file in the Open dialog box.**

3. Select the entire movie (Edit ➪ Select All or ⌘-A) and choose Edit ➪ Copy (⌘-C).

4. Switch back to your original QuickTime movie.

5. While pressing Option, choose Edit ➪ Add (Option-⌘-V).

You have just added a multiframe text track to your movie.

Putting Your Movie on the Web

There is a human compulsion to chronicle our lives for future generations. Prehistoric man did it with drawings on cave walls, the early Egyptians used hieroglyphics in and on their tombs, Renaissance man kept diaries and journals, and people of the mid- to late-twentieth century took photographs and made home movies. One commonality among those methods is that only a small number of copies exist (sometimes only one) and distribution is extremely limited. Now, with digital movies and photographs, in conjunction with e-mail and personal Web sites, distribution is almost unlimited. In the past few years, we've received digital photo and movie substitutes via e-mail and Web links for the ubiquitous Christmas letters, birth and wedding announcements (not necessarily in that order), and vacation summaries that used to arrive in the mailbox.

We're going to ignore e-mail here, assuming that you know enough about your individual e-mail client to attach a file for transmission. Besides, there are just too many possible e-mail clients for us to try to cover them all.

Ah, but the Web is a different story. Just as you saw how to create Web pages using iPhoto in Chapter 10, you're now going to see how to create Web pages to let people watch your movies.

You have two restraints on unfettered Web movie hosting: space and bandwidth. Unless you have your own Web-hosting server, with lots of hard disk space, your ISP is going to constrain you to somewhere between 2MB and 20MB. Usually. AOL is at the low end, with 2MB per member name. Apple's .Mac far exceeds the upper end with 100MB. Most ISPs offer between 5MB and 10MB. You can, however, opt to pay your ISP a greater monthly fee for expanded service, including more Web hosting space. Likewise, unless you know that the folks visiting your page have broadband access, for example, DSL and cable-modem, large, high-quality movies are going to take a long time to download for viewing. Even with broadband, there are limits. Dennis has a rather fast (150KB/sec) cable modem connection, for example, and he still sometimes runs into bottlenecks with some larger (say 640 x 480) movies. So, a variation of computing's golden rule, using the same acronym, is in order: KISS (keep it small, sonny/sister).

You have three ways to make your movie accessible through a Web page:

- ✦ **You can make it downloadable via a hyperlink.** People download it and view it with QuickTime Player on their Mac.
- ✦ **You can make it downloadable via an embedding command.** Here, it looks like part of your Web page and people view it using their browser's QuickTime plug-in.
- ✦ **You can make it stream.** This means that your visitor views your movie in real time, while it is being transmitted.

For convenience sake, choose Web Movie, Small or Streaming Web Movie, Small as your Export format.

When exporting a movie for the Web, you should avoid using spaces or special characters—those other than letters, numbers, hyphens, and underscores—in the filename. In fact, because many Web servers are hosted on Unix systems (which are case-sensitive in nature), you may want to use only lower-case characters in the filename. Also, be sure to include the .mov filename extension so that Windows computers recognize that the file is a QuickTime movie. If you want to include spaces, your HTML is going to have a whole bunch of "%20" entries in the middle of the name to make sure that Web browsers and servers can find your file.

Creating the HTML for a downloadable movie

You're going to need to know something about coding HTML to follow along here, but it isn't that difficult. If you just want to make the movie downloadable from your Web page, your task is a piece of cake. All you have to do is add a hyperlink similar to this one:

```
<a href="my_movie.mov">Click here to download my movie.</a>
```

For quite awhile, it was considered common to use all uppercase characters for tags and attributes. With the computing world migrating from HTML to XML, we're doing a 180. Tags and attributes must be lowercase, now. In our code snippets, we're going to follow modern convention. In the expository text, we use upper-case references on occasion, where we want to make sure the reference stands out from the surrounding text. (Sometimes the simple font change just isn't enough.)

Of course, as a courteous Web page designer, you would probably include a little more information such as the size and, maybe, an icon (like a filmstrip picture) to make the fact that it is a movie absolutely clear. The following code does that job, assuming you had an image file named filmstrip.gif present in the directory with your Web page:

```
<a href="my_movie.mov"><img src="filmstrip.gif" alt="filmstrip
icon" width="18" height="16"></a>
<a href="my_movie.mov">Click here to download my movie
(2.1MB)</a>
```

Figure 15-31 shows what a simple Web page with this code in it might look like when seen in Microsoft Internet Explorer 5.1.4.

Figure 15-31: Click either the text link or the QuickTime filmstrip icon to download the movie.

Embedding a movie in your Web page

If you know that visitors to your page have the QuickTime plug-in installed for their Web browser, you can use the EMBED tag. The EMBED tag has lots of options, covered in exquisite detail on Apple's Web site. Check out www.apple.com/quicktime/authoring/embed.html if you want to know everything about this tag. For our purposes, we're going to use a subset covering common usage.

For example, we're going to demonstrate using the SRC attribute for a still image with the HREF attribute accessing the real movie, just like the big guys (Apple's Web pages) do. You use the EMBED tag's CONTROLLER attribute to specify the presence (="TRUE") or absence (="FALSE") of the QuickTime control strip along the movie's bottom.

If you want the QuickTime controller to be present, increase the height by 16 pixels so that everything fits.

Figure 15-32 shows a simple variation of our example page with the movie embedded on the page (including a controller) and no click-on-me still image.

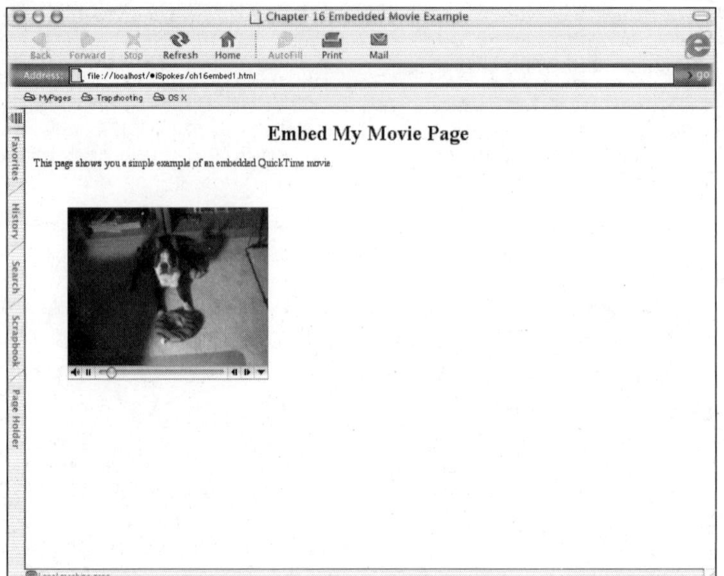

Figure 15-32: Embedding the movie on your Web page is a straightforward exercise.

The HTML for this page follows:

```
<!DOCTYPE HTML PUBLIC "-//W3C//DTD HTML 4.01 Transitional//EN"
        "http://www.w3.org/TR/1999/REC-
html401-19991224/loose.dtd">
<html lang="en">
<head>
   <meta http-equiv="content-type" content="text/html;
charset=iso-8859-1">
   <title>Chapter 16 Embedded Movie Example</title>
   <meta name="generator" content="BBEdit 6.5.2">
</head>
<body>
<h1 align="center">Embed My Movie Page</h1>
<p>
This page shows you a simple example of an embedded QuickTime
movie.
</p>
<embed controller="true" width="320" height="256"
src="spenserwontplay.mov">
</body>
</html>
```

As you can see, Dennis uses BBEdit as his HTML editor of choice. However, you can use anything that saves your HTML as plain text. Be sure, if you use TextEdit that you save as text rather than RTF. The code isn't fancy, but it gets the job done. You'll notice that this movie starts playing while it is loading. If you don't want it to start playing until your page's visitor clicks the Play button, add the `autoplay="false"` attribute to your `embed` tag.

Not so very long ago, Microsoft changed the way that its Explorer browser on Windows used plug-ins. It just so happened that this change broke the QuickTime plug-in. As a result, Apple had to provide a new ActiveX component to fix the problem, but it meant that the `EMBED` tag had to be wrapped in an `OBJECT` tag with certain special attributes to make sure that the ActiveX component would be downloaded if it was needed. The whole sordid tale is spelled out in great detail on a page at Apple's QuickTime Tools & Tips site (`www.apple.com/quicktime/tools_tips/tutorials/activex.html`). By now, most Windows Internet Explorer users have the necessary QuickTime ActiveX plug-in, but if you want to make sure that they do, you can adapt the example code that Apple provides.

Figure 15-33 shows an almost identical page, but with a one-frame "poster" movie, awaiting your visitor's click to load the real movie. You want to turn off the controller here so that your visitor doesn't click it to make the poster frame play. You also need to include a `TARGET` attribute, so that the browser knows to load the `HREF` into the same space as the `SRC` when clicked.

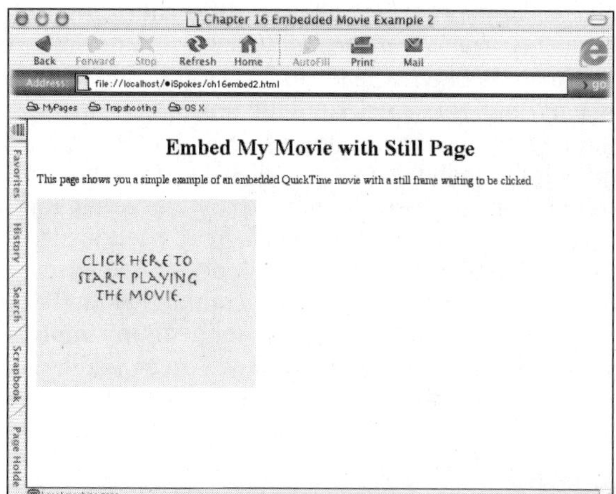

Figure 15-33: Click on the still to load your movie and start it playing.

The HTML source for this page follows:

```
<!DOCTYPE HTML PUBLIC "-//W3C//DTD HTML 4.01 Transitional//EN"
        "http://www.w3.org/TR/1999/REC-
html401-19991224/loose.dtd">
<html lang="en">
<head>
   <meta http-equiv="content-type" content="text/html;
charset=iso-8859-1">
   <title>Chapter 16 Embedded Movie Example 2</title>
   <meta name="generator" content="BBEdit 6.5.2">
</head>
<body>
<h1 align="center">Embed My Movie with Still Page</h1>
<p>
This page shows you a simple example of an embedded QuickTime
movie with a still frame waiting to be clicked.
</p>
<embed controller="false" autoplay="false" width="240"
height="180" src="ch16embed2.mov" target="myself"
href="spenserwontplay.mov">
</body>
</html>
```

Streaming your movie

Streaming is one of those abstract concepts that can mean different things to different people; a handy property for those who want to sell you something. One sort of streaming, the kind that QuickTime has been able to do for a long, long time, is not streaming at all but really downloading: the QuickTime file downloads, in its entirety, to your computer, and begins playing as soon as enough of it arrives for your QuickTime software to play it through without pausing. The fact that the file starts playing before completely being received is what led the marketing folk at Apple to call this technique "streaming." The virtue of this form of pseudo-streaming, more properly called "progressive download," is two-fold: it doesn't require a special streaming server (any Web server can do), and it isn't completely limited to the speed of the network connection — a user with a slow connection simply waits longer (sometimes, a lot longer) before the file starts to play. The embedded QuickTime files we described in the preceding section are examples of progressive download.

True streaming, on the other hand, requires a special server that can transmit the file in real time. In fact, streaming uses a special protocol called RTSP, which stands for "real time streaming protocol." QuickTime can perform true streaming as well as progressive download pseudo-streaming. True streaming behaves like a hose: if more water comes out than can fill your bucket, you lose the excess and it is gone. Similarly, a user watching a true QuickTime stream with a connection that isn't fast enough to handle the stream loses frames, sound quality, and possibly the whole connection — the bucket overflows. Therefore, you should prepare a streaming file so that its data rate is no larger than the connection speed of its intended audience. For modem users, that rate is very low and is only seldom practical for video.

Given those limitations, why would anyone want to stream a file? For several reasons. First, with a streaming file, the entire file never completely downloads to the user's machine: the data comes in, plays, and disappears. Not completely downloading the movie to the user's machine is very appealing for those who don't want to make it easy for users to copy their intellectual property. Second, because users don't have to wait for the file to download, they can move the controller around from one end of the movie to the other and the streaming server starts sending the part of the file represented by the controller's current position: you don't have to wait through a long download to see the end of a movie — just drag the controller to the end and the streaming server sends it to you. Streaming is particularly useful for large files, or for live broadcasts.

To stream a QuickTime movie, you need to prepare the movie for streaming and you need a QuickTime streaming server on which to place the movie. We'll assume that you have access to the latter.

To make sure that a file is ready for streaming, follow these suggestions:

✦ **Make sure that the data rate of the compressed movie is suitable for the connection speed that your audience is going to have.** Realistically, this should fall into the 50KB/sec range for DSL or cable modem users; if dial-up modem users are going to view the file, the data rate can't be higher than 5KB/sec, which isn't very much. You'll want to have a small frame, a low frame rate, and material that looks okay in that size and at that speed (forget about action films; "talking heads" are more suitable for this medium).

✦ **Hint your file for streaming.** Doing this places additional information into the movie file that the streaming server uses to make the stream more efficient. The hints make the file bigger, but the hinting information itself isn't streamed. iMovie hints your movie for you when you use its QuickTime export feature to create a streaming Web movie. If you export your movie using the QuickTime expert settings, you can hint it yourself. The Prepare for Internet Streaming section of the Movie Settings dialog (Figure 15-21) has a pop-up menu with a Hinted Streaming option. Choose this option when you export your file, and your movie becomes hinted.

Viewing a streaming file is not very hard with QuickTime Player. Just choose File ➪ Open URL in New Player (⌘-U) and enter the movie's URL in the dialog. Note, though, that streaming movies do not use the http protocol that you are probably accustomed to, but they do use the rtsp protocol, so your URL will look something like this: `rtsp://www.somestreamingserver.com/somedirectory/streamingfile.mov`.

When you begin playing a streaming movie, QuickTime Player shows you how the connection is progressing (Figure 15-34).

Figure 15-34: QuickTime Player keeps you informed when preparing to play a streaming video.

Embedding a streaming movie takes a little more work, because the `embed` tag isn't really set up to use an rtsp URL in its `src` attribute. Instead, you need to create a *reference movie*, which is a QuickTime movie that points to the real movie. You place that movie on your Web server and link to it in your `embed` statement's `src` attribute; the browser's QuickTime plug-in follows the reference movie's internal pointer to find the streaming movie.

Creating a reference movie is simple. Open the streaming movie in QuickTime Player Pro, stop playing, drag the controller back to the beginning, and save the movie on your computer. You end up with a small (about 1KB) reference movie file.

Putting your iMovies on your iDisk

If you've signed up for a .Mac account, the .Mac focus points squarely at your iDisk. One of the folders Apple places on every iDisk is the Movies folder, another is Public, and a third is Sites. Any one of these folders is a suitable repository for iMovies you want to share — it just depends upon *how* you want to share them.

We're not going to provide screen shots of the .Mac Web pages for two reasons. First, they change appearance frequently as .Mac evolves. Second, the permissions forms to use the screen shots take a lot of time away from preparing the book. (Besides, dealing with lawyers isn't good for our blood pressure.)

The simplest method is to place your movie in the Public folder. Then, users who know your .Mac username (not your password) can access your movie by mounting your iDisk Public folder on their desktops. They can either play it from there, although that can result in stuttering playback if the connection isn't fast enough to download the movie before it finishes playing, or (more likely) they can copy it down to their disk to enjoy over and over.

Creating a FileSharing Web page

If your friends or family are .Mac-deprived, they can still see what's in your Public Folder if you create a FileSharing Web page, a quick and easy task.

1. **On the main iDisk page, click the link for Sharing Your Public Folder** (which used to be called Publish Personal Folder). Doing so takes you to the HomePage page with the FileSharing tab already selected.
2. **Pick a theme.** At present there are two themes, identical except for color: graphite and magenta.
3. **In the page that appears, click the Edit button and customize the text in those areas where text boxes appear.**
4. **Click the Publish button.** Anyone with a Web browser can access the contents of your Public folder at `http://homepage.mac.com/yourname/FileSharing.html`. Figure 15-35 shows Spenser's (Dennis's Boston Terrier) file sharing page.

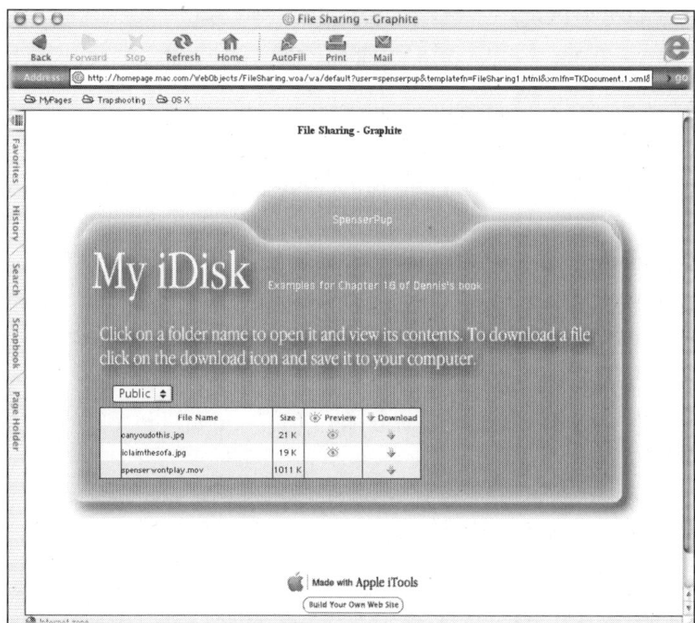

Figure 15-35: .Mac makes it easy to get files from a member's Public folder.

Using the .Mac HomePage Web page

If you want to make your movie available via the .Mac HomePage Web page mechanism, copy the movie to your Movies folder (the one on your iDisk, not the one in your Home directory). .Mac makes it easy to create a Web page to present your movie without you having to learn any HTML. Follow these steps:

1. **Fire up your Web browser, log in to .Mac, and click the HomePage button or icon, to present the HomePage page.** (Even though it sounds like it, we're not stuttering.)
2. **Click the iMovies button under the Create a Page heading.** This displays the various Themes (templates). At the time we're writing this, Apple offers seven themes.
3. **Click a theme.** This presents the page customization screen.
4. **Click Change Text and enter a title and short description for your movie page.**
5. **Click the QuickTime area's Choose button.** If you don't see the movie(s) you've uploaded to your Movies folder in the list, click the Update button. If you need to add the movies to your Movies folder and you don't have your iDisk open, click the Open My iDisk button.
6. **Select your movie from the list and click the Preview button.** Your Web browser shows you the page in its current state and starts to download your movie. This preview should give you a good idea what visitors with connections similar to yours will experience.
7. **If you like what you've created, click the Apply button.** This returns you to the Themes page.
8. **If you want to see how the whole page will look, click Preview.**
9. **When you're satisfied with your creation, click Publish.** .Mac congratulates you on your fine work and tells you the URL for the page you just created.

The pages (HTML files) for sites you create are stored in your iDisk's Sites folder. You can open those files in a text editor if you want to modify them, or if you're new to HTML, to learn from them.

Summary

In this chapter, you learned some advanced audio- and video-editing techniques. You also saw how to work with and convert non-DV video and how to enhance iMovie with plug-ins. We also presented you with a crash course in using QuickTime Export's Expert settings and how to do postproduction editing of your movie with QuickTime Pro. Finally, you learned how to publish your movies on the Web, both as progressive downloads and as streaming media.

✦ ✦ ✦

CHAPTER 16

More iMovie Tips, Tricks, and Techniques

✦ ✦ ✦ ✦

In This Chapter

Sharing clips between projects

Making menu-driven VideoCDs

Plan your shoot and shoot your plan

Taping tips for better footage

✦ ✦ ✦ ✦

This chapter provides you with tips about shooting the most optimal footage before you get to the editing stage, reusing clips from one movie in another, and — with the help of a couple of add-on software products — how to create a "poor-man's DVD" — a menu-driven VideoCD that you can play in many set top DVD players and can navigate using the player's remote control.

We've covered iMovie's editing capabilities to a fare-thee-well in Chapters 13–15, and in Chapter 17, we'll show you all sorts of things you can acquire, either free or by using a little plastic (or cash), to make your movie-making more productive.

Sharing Clips between Projects

TV and movie studios keep large libraries of what they call *stock footage*. These are clips and scenes that they reuse in multiple productions, such as crowd scenes, car crashes, and explosions. You can create your own stock footage libraries with iMovie if you know a little bit about how iMovie stores its clips.

Adding clips to your iMovie project

iMovie offers you three ways to add stock footage to your iMovie project. You can choose File ⇨ Import, the original (and slow) method to import DV Stream files into iMovie. You can drag the clips' Finder icons to the Clips pane. Finally, you can copy or move the clip into project's Media folder.

If you choose the third method, you see an alert similar to the one shown in Figure 16-1 the next time iMovie opens your project. However, the number and names of clips vary depending upon how many you moved into the Media folder. Click the Move File To Clip Pane button, and your footage appears on the shelf, as shown in Figure 16-2. A really nice feature of this method is that iMovie picks up the names you've given the clips.

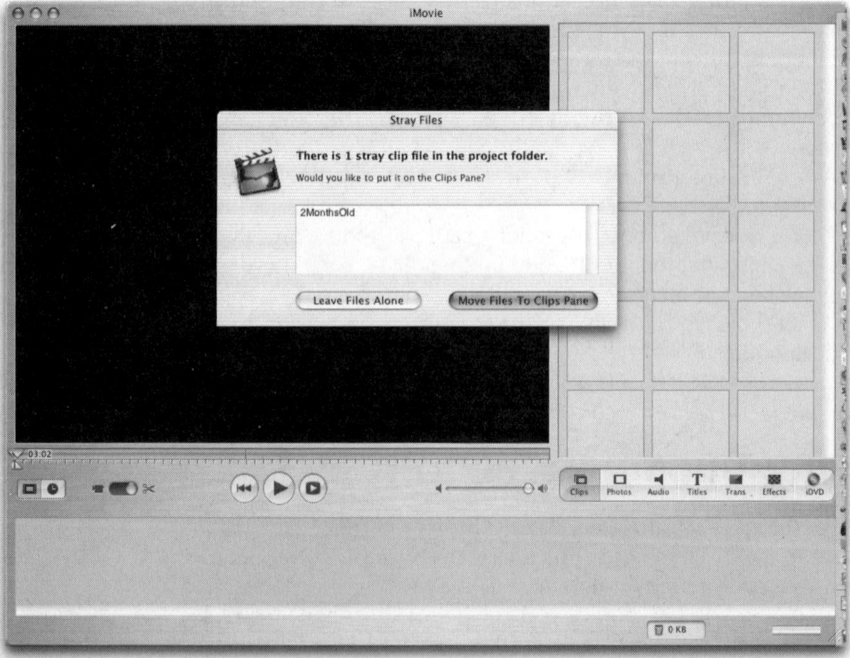

Figure 16-1: iMovie offers to add clips you move into the Media folder to your Clips pane.

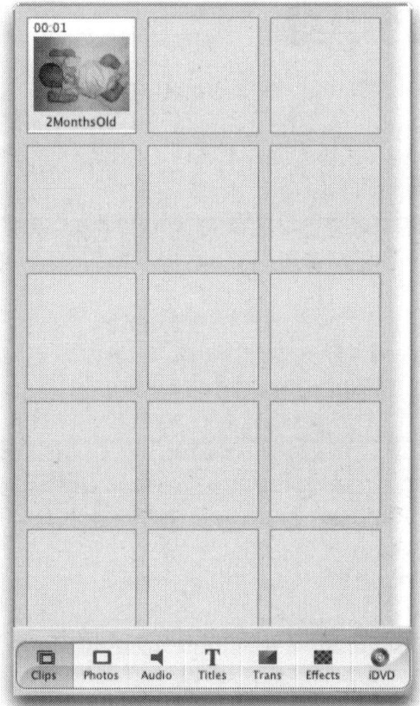

Figure 16-2: iMovie even displays them with the names you gave them.

Renaming clip files

Unfortunately, iMovie doesn't rename the clip files in the Media folder when you rename them on the shelf or in the clip viewer, so you'll have to know which clips you want to rename in the Finder. You probably don't want your collection of stock material to all be named Clip 01, Clip 02, and so on. You have three ways of changing the name of a clip:

✦ **Using QuickTime Player.** One way is to open each clip in QuickTime Player to determine which one it is and then name it accordingly.

✦ **Using the Finder's Column view.** An even faster way is to switch to Column view in the Finder and check out the live previews appearing when you select a file. This option doesn't work if you have multiple files selected.

✦ **Using the File menu.** You can choose File ⇨ Get Info on the clips in iMovie 3 and then, in the Finder, rename the displayed filename.

Rename the clip's file in the Finder. Doing a Save or Save As in QuickTime Player won't retain it as a clip file that iMovie "adopts." iMovie has to re-render it when you import the file.

Making Menu-Driven VideoCDs

VideoCDs are an inexpensive and handy format in which to distribute your iMovie work. You can write up to 80 minutes of VHS-quality video on a standard 700MB CD-R or CD-RW blank. Best of all, you can write VideoCDs on any CD burner with the help of added software that can write VideoCD format or, generically, Multitrack CD-ROM XA format (of which VideoCD is a special case). We strongly recommend Toast Titanium (`www.roxio.com`) and will assume its presence in the following discussion.

Like the DVD-R media used by iDVD, CD-R-based VideoCDs work in *most* DVD players, though not always the same machines. For example, one of Dennis's DVD players will play VideoCDs (and SVCDs) written to CD-R media, but won't play the DVDs written to DVD-R media by iDVD or DVD Studio Pro. On the other hand, his neighbor's DVD player plays the DVD-Rs, but doesn't recognize the CD-R or CD-RW media on which he writes VideoCDs. Check out `www.vcdhelp.com` for a breakdown of which players support which formats and disk types.

You can just put multiple movies on the VideoCD and, when you stick them in your DVD player, they'll play one after another. This method is effective, but it isn't particularly interesting. iDVD can create menu-driven DVDs, but they aren't really comparable to the menu structures on commercial DVDs—you're limited to six menu buttons per screen and only the basic navigational tools iDVD provides. With the help of a wonderful freeware utility, VCD Builder by Johan Lindström (`homepage.mac.com/johan`), you can create VideoCDs that support chapters, and you have control over the menu layout and navigation. And, if you're a programmer-type, Lindström even makes the source code available on his Web page.

You can find out more on menu-driven DVDs in Part V. For more on VCD Builder, turn to Chapter 17.

VCD Builder is donation-ware. Johan doesn't charge for it, and there are no annoying reminders, limitations, or registration dialog, but he is set up to accept donations through PayPal if you consider it worthwhile. We did.

Planning for chapters

DVD players play one movie after another from a VideoCD. This stream is continuous, with no pause between movies. By taking advantage of this behavior and the fact that we can override the default behavior with a VCD menu structure, we're well on the way to creating VideoCDs that behave like commercial DVDs.

First, you break your movie into scenes in iMovie and export each of those scenes as a self-contained VideoCD-compatible MPEG file using Toast's VideoCD Export plug-in as described in the "Have a little Toast with your iMovie" section in Chapter 17. After you have your entire movie exported as separate mini-movies, you're ready to start constructing your VideoCD.

Note

In Chapter 17, we show you a way to create SVCD-compatible files from your movie, thanks to our new Mac friends from the Unix world. VCD Builder also creates SVCD disc images, all set to be burned by Toast for use on many set top DVD players (once again, check at `www.vcdhelp.com` for your player's compatibility with VCD, SVCD, CD-R, CD-RW, and DVD-R).

Building a menu-driven VideoCD

VCD Builder lets you designate a movie or picture as a menu, something that you can have playing until you interrupt it with a command via the remote control or until you have it automatically advance to the "next" movie. For our purposes, we're going to assume that you use a picture for the menu. We tend to use Photoshop or Photoshop Elements to create our menu pictures (640 x 480 frame size at 72 dpi resolution), but you can use any program that creates QuickTime-readable image files of the appropriate size.

For those of you wondering why we use the 640 x 480 resolution rather than 720 x 480 for DV Stream video, it is because the video stream pixels aren't square like those on a computer monitor; iMovie, QuickTime, and VCD Builder interpolate them into the 640 horizontal, square pixels that are displayed. If you supply a 640 x 480 digital photo, it will be converted to the rectangular pixels required for DV when rendered.

Understanding sequences

You create *sequences* in VCD Builder, specifying a picture, a movie, or group of pictures and movies that exist as a unit and play in order. You can then connect the sequences to move from one to another (called the *target sequence*), as follows:

- ✦ **Play:** Jump to the target sequence when the remote control's Play button is pressed.
- ✦ **Stop:** Jump to the target sequence when the remote control's Stop button is pressed. On some DVD players, the Menu button rather than the Stop button invokes this command.
- ✦ **Previous:** Jump to the target sequence when the remote control's Previous button is pressed.
- ✦ **Next:** Jump to the target sequence when the remote control's Next button is pressed.
- ✦ **1...9:** Jump to the target sequence when the remote control's corresponding numeric button is pressed.

✦ ***n-m*:** The first digit represents the target sequence and the second digit represents the chapter number.

✦ **Timeout:** Jump to the target sequence when the source sequence finishes playing. If there is no Timeout connection, the Next connection takes control, and if the Next connection isn't present, the Stop action takes over.

Building sequences

Figure 16-3 shows a simple VideoCD with a menu and three additional sequences, the third of which is being connected back to the menu using a Timeout connection. Creating the connection is simple:

1. **Hold down the Control key and click and drag from the source sequence to the target sequence.** When you release the mouse button, the circular menu, shown in Figure 16-3, appears.
2. **Move the mouse to the icon for the desired connection type (its name appears in the center) and click it.** The menu disappears and the connection shows in its place.

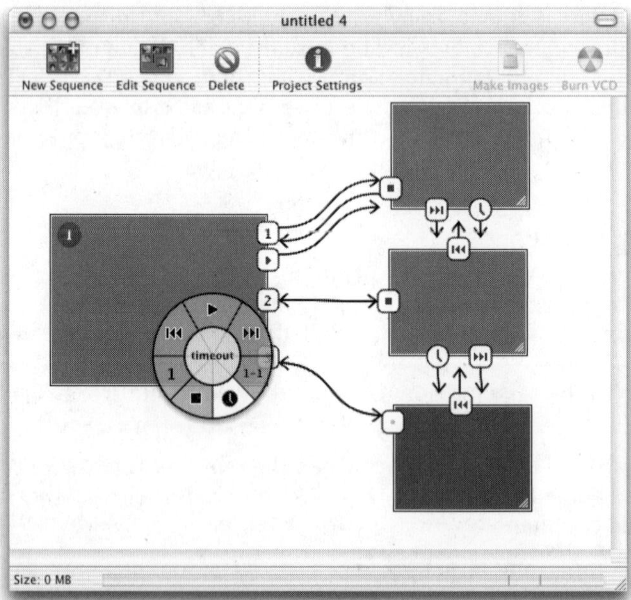

Figure 16-3: Connecting your sequences is a simple control-click and drag.

3. **Now that you have your structure, you can start filling the sequences with content.** In the simplest case, the one we're describing here, drag your menu picture to the box with the number one badge on it and drag each scene, in order, to the corresponding sequence boxes. For more involved sequences, such as a menu that cycles through four images or one that automatically advances to the next item after a specified length of time follow Steps 4, 5, and 6.
4. **Double-click a sequence box.** The window displays, as shown in Figure 16-4.

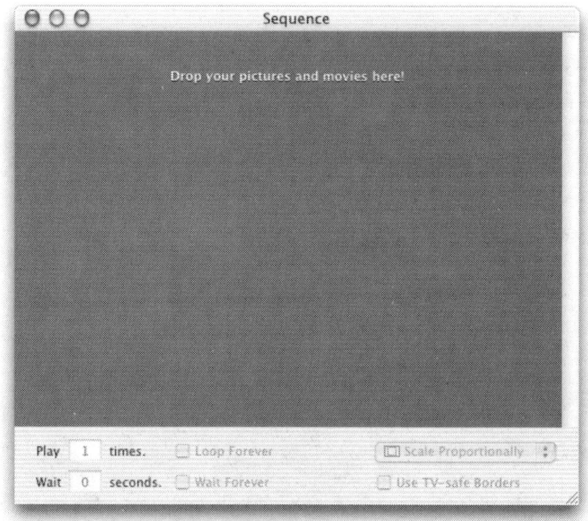

Figure 16-4: This window is where you build the sequences that give the boxes their name.

5. **Drag your pictures and/or movies into this window to populate the sequence.** If you don't like the order, you can drag the thumbnails around, as shown in Figure 16-5, to reorder them.
6. **Using the pop-up menu, you can choose whether your images are scaled or cropped to fit in the display area.** You can also check the Use TV-safe Borders box for any image that you think might have important information falling outside the viewable area on a TV set.

If you don't want to break your scenes out into separate movies, you don't really have to do so. VCD Builder 1.1 added internal chaptering support, as shown in Figure 16-6.

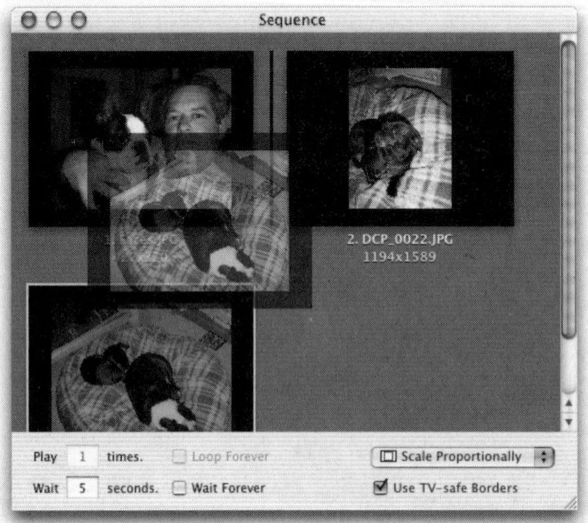

Figure 16-5: Drag your images and clips around to get them in the order you want.

Figure 16-6: You can place chapter markers in your movies within VCD Builder.

Double-click a movie sequence and click the timeline point where you want a chapter marker. You can drag it if you didn't get it right where you wanted it. Of course, you'll have to know the timecodes for your scene breaks, but keeping such a record (in fact, a project notebook) is a good idea, anyway.

Burning a VideoCD

After you have all your sequences populated, save and name your project file. By doing this, the VideoCD you create will have the name you want rather than "Untitled." Now, click the Burn VCD button in the window's toolbar (refer to Figure 16-3). VCD Builder starts converting your still images to VideoCD-compatible form (your movies must already be in VideoCD-compatible MPEG-1 format) and creating the various tracks for your VideoCD. After those image files are created, VCD Builder launches Toast Titanium with the format set to Multitrack CD-ROM XA, and the image files load into Toast. Click Toast's Burn button when you're ready. Sit back and wait for your masterpiece to emerge.

VCD Builder creates the image files regardless of whether you click the Make Images or Burn VCD toolbar button. If you don't want to launch Toast, click Make Images instead. This is handy if you're using some burner software other than Toast or if your CD burner drive is busy doing something else. (Dennis sometimes watches a DVD while he has VCD Builder creating his VideoCD images.)

With a little imagination, you can see that one menu can point to another menu, which gives you the flexibility to create really complex projects, just like commercial DVDs.

Plan Your Shoot and Shoot Your Plan

If you follow the Boy Scout motto, "Be Prepared," you're well on your way to shooting better video. Before you shoot, make sure that you have extra tape, a well-charged battery, a spare battery, a microphone or two (always beneficial) as well as lenses or filters for the expected (or unexpected) lighting conditions. Additionally, have a tripod handy or some other tool to provide a steady base for your camera.

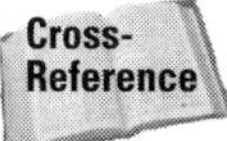

See Chapter 17 for some lens and filter suggestions.

If you can recharge your camera's battery when you detach it from the camera, take a spare battery or two and the charger. There is nothing more aggravating than to run out of juice while taping. If you see your battery power running down quickly, close the LCD and use the viewfinder. Using the viewfinder might be a little harder on you, but it will extend your battery life significantly.

As an example, assume that you're planning to shoot footage of your kid's school play or recital. Arrive early and stake out a good camera location or two — ones where you won't have audience members' heads popping into the frame. Arrange to place a microphone or to tap into the auditorium's sound system so that you can pick up the sound.

If you're actually creating a movie rather than taping a staged or extemporaneous event, storyboard the project. Determine what shots you will need for the different scenes and set up camera locations and lighting to make them work. If you need an external microphone, find a place to position it so that it will pick up the sound without intruding on the scene. Finally, whenever possible, shoot multiple takes of scenes, possibly from different angles, or, if you're fortunate enough to have two video cameras available, tape from two positions. In either situation, you'll have a fallback position if something doesn't come out the way you had hoped and, in the latter case, you can cut from one camera angle to the other for a better cinematic effect when you edit your footage in iMovie.

With more and more people running around with camcorders, you may be able to borrow someone else's tape to mix with your own when you're both recording the same event. This worked out really well when Dennis and two friends were taping a Little League playoff game – they pooled their tapes and were able to cut to different angles and distances on plays without missing any of the action.

Most people have seen those scenes from movies about making movies where the assistant holds up a clapboard with the act, scene, and take information on it while the director calls out "Roll'em!" Having that clapboard on film accomplishes two goals: Labeling the footage and making sure that the camera is rolling before the action starts. You can cut out the introductory footage later — editing is really easy in iMovie, as you've seen — but if you miss the start of the scene, you can't get it back. Get the camera running early and let it run past the end of the scene. Having the extra footage on either end means that you always have the footage you need.

Taping Tips for Better Footage

The three best tips we can give you to improve the quality of your footage are to use a tripod, optimize your lighting, and get the best sound capture you can. Regardless of how good iMovie might be for movie editing, it can't make a silk purse out of a sow's ear (the acronym for this is GIGO — garbage in, garbage out).

Bouncing is bad

Nothing is more amateurish than footage in which the picture jiggles up and down or weaves when you pan the action. A tripod is your best friend when you want a solid base from which to shoot. And, with a good panhead on it, you can smoothly follow the action.

If your budget can handle it and you need to move with the action, invest in a Steadicam (`www.steadicam.com`), about $900, or some other gyro-stabilized attachment so that you can simultaneously walk and shoot footage that won't make your audience seasick when they watch it.

If you don't have a tripod or some other (expensive) stabilizing device, try to improvise using a wall, table, bench, automobile hood, or some other solid, stationary object. When moving the camera to follow the action, rotate as slowly and smoothly as possible.

Excessive bouncing can make your audience nauseous, and so can frequent or rapid zooming. You can avoid unnecessary zooming by framing your shot with the zoom before you start shooting whenever possible. If you must use the zoom while taping, zoom as slowly as possible.

When given a choice between optical and digital zooming, there really isn't a choice. Ignore the fact that digital zoom even exists. As discussed in Chapter 12, digital zoom is just a magnification and interpolation by your camera—you lose resolution, and the end result is usually fuzzy and blurry. Turn it off if your camera allows you to do so.

Getting good lighting

Never forget that your camera, an electronic device, doesn't see light the same way your human eye sees it. Just because your eye dilates enough to make you think that there's enough light for a night (or indoor) scene, doesn't mean that your camera will agree.

First, whenever possible get extra lighting on a scene. Use reflectors or fill lights to eliminate shadows.

Learn which adjustments your camera allows. Many camcorders have settings for low-light conditions, low-contrast settings, and what is called *white balance*, which is filtering out color casts.

The human eye filters out color casts associated with individual lighting sources. Sunlight usually has a blue cast, incandescent lights tend toward yellow, and fluorescent lights gravitate toward green. While our eyes filter these before we notice them, the camera's optical sensors don't, and you're likely to get some strange tints in your footage if you don't white balance your camera when taping under different lighting conditions.

Most good digital camcorders provide a menu of preprogrammed settings for common lighting conditions. They might be called Programmed Auto-Exposure (AE) Settings (Sony), Presets (Canon), or something similar. For example, Dennis's Sony provides the following AE settings:

✦ **Spotlight:** Prevents objects, such as people's faces, from washing out to white when shot under a strong light.

✦ **Soft portrait:** Brings out the subject while softening the background.

✦ **Sports lesson:** Minimizes jitter on fast-moving objects, such as a baseball pitch or a tennis serve.

✦ **Beach & ski:** Prevents faces from appearing dark when under bright light or before a reflective background, such as a ski slope or a sunny summer beach.

✦ **Sunset & moon:** Maintains atmosphere when recording bright objects, for example, fireworks, against a dark background.

✦ **Landscape:** Lets you focus on distant objects, even if nearby objects are present, such as the glass in a window through which you might be taping.

✦ **Low lux:** Brightens subjects in low light conditions.

You should read your camcorder's manual, no matter how poor the English, and learn what capabilities your camera offers. Every make and model has some variation in the features available. Check the manual out, learn what your camera offers, and try out the various settings to become familiar with them.

Tip

Your camera might also have some special effects, such as Sepia or Solarize. Avoid them! You can do a much better job with iMovie's Effects panel, especially if you acquire some of the add-on effects you'll see covered in Chapter 17.

Huh? What'd they say? (getting clean audio)

Your digital camcorder comes with a built-in (probably stereo) microphone, and you might think that takes care of obtaining your audio. For simple jobs, it very well might — assuming that you are relatively close to the verbal action, that there isn't a lot of ambient noise, such as cars, trains, and peripheral conversations, and that your subjects speak loudly and clearly enough for the microphone picks them up.

Note

Camera-integrated microphones occasionally pick up some camera sounds that you might not even hear. For example, if you're using a zoom lens, the motor makes a whirring sound and is next to the microphone input.

You can only do so much to fix bad sound without spending tens of thousands of dollars on high-tech audio-editing gear like you see in various police and spy shows (*CSI: Crime Scene Investigation* and *The Agency* come to mind), where they isolate the perfect pieces of an audio mish-mash. Even with that equipment, working with good audio in the first place is still easier.

The question before us is, "How do we get great audio?" The answer, at least the first step, is to get the microphone as close to our sound source as possible without generating feedback.

Tip

Most camcorders have a headphone jack and its purpose is to let you hear the sound the way the camera hears it. When taping, have your headphones on and plugged in to this jack. Now, you'll be able to hear what the camera is capturing and you can make adjustments before you get to postproduction with damaged audio.

Second, if possible, don't rely on your camera's built-in microphone. Even an inexpensive clip-on mic does a better job in many cases. Microphones fall into various categories:

- **Cardioid:** These microphones have a heart-shaped (hence the name) pickup pattern. Although directed forward, they pick up ambient sounds from the sides and rear. Camcorders with built-in cardioid mics are more susceptible to camera sounds, such as the tape transport mechanism and zoom lens operation.
- **Directional:** Microphones, such as the shotgun mic, that have a very focused field.
- **Super-cardioid:** The type of microphone present on most camcorders. Super-cardioid is a compromise between the cardioid and directional mics, and they eliminate the sound from behind the mic.
- **Omnidirectional:** Microphones that pick up sounds from all directions equally well. Many clip-on and lavaliere mics fall into this category.

Bob created Figure 16-7 to illustrate these four types of microphones.

Remember that the patterns in Figure 16-7 are cross sections and that the pattern is equally true whether you think of it as a vertical slice, horizontal slice, or anything in between.

If you know your subjects are going to be (relatively) stationary, you might consider a boom mic, even if it is a roll-your-own boom made by dangling a super-cardioid mic from a hook, just out of the picture.

Lots of microphones come with foam covers. The covers aren't just to protect the mic from getting dinged, they're really wind-guards used to filter out the sound of wind and some speech side effects, like the popping sound of *p* and *b* or the sibilance of *ss*.

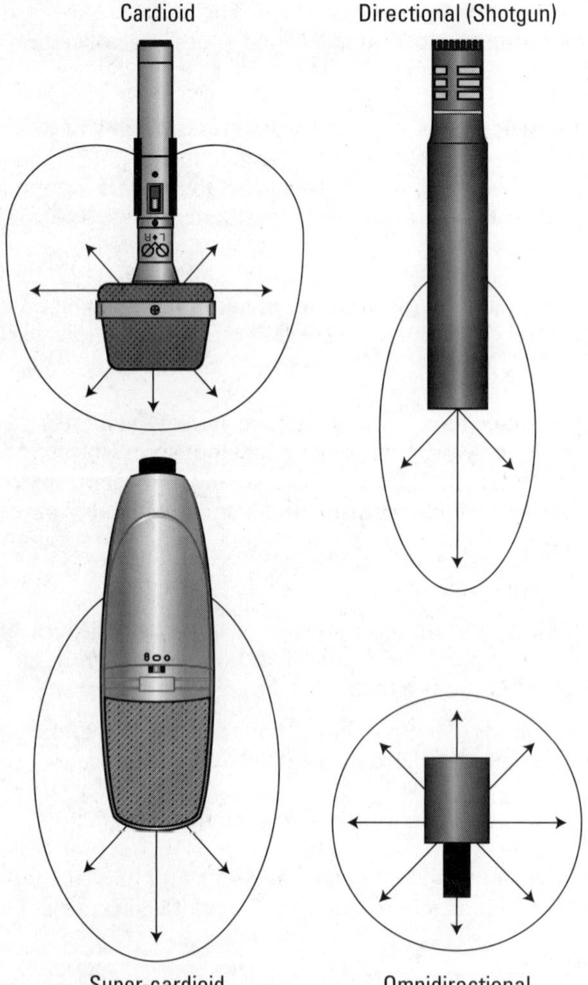

Figure 16-7: Two-dimensional cross sections of microphone pickup patterns.

Changing Undocumented iMovie Preferences

First, we're going to say that this material is not for the faint-of-heart nor for those of you who don't feel comfortable getting your hands dirty going around what Apple intended to be user-accessible. In pre-OS X days, this meant using a tool like ResEdit, which always included admonitions about working only on a copy because you could really break things. Today (or at least in this context), it means editing your iMovie 3 Preferences file.

The Preferences dialog displayed when you choose iMovie ➪ Preferences (⌘-,) doesn't even touch the surface of all the settings in your actual iMovie preferences file (`~/Library/Preferences/com.apple.iMovie3.plist`).

Just so you can't say that we didn't warn you, here's the standard admonition: Work on a *copy* of your preferences file. If you've installed the Apple Developer Tools CD that came with your copy of OS X, double-clicking the plist file should launch Property List Editor. If, however, you haven't installed the tools, you can edit the plist file with a plain text editor (even TextEdit, if you're careful to set it to plain text rather than rich text), it just won't be as clear. Figure 16-8 shows what you'll see after the Property List Editor window opens and you click the disclosure triangle next to Root. We're only going to discuss a few of the settings available. A few dozen other settings are in this plist file, most of which we wouldn't want to touch, so we aren't going to even talk about them.

✦ **AppleSavePanelExpanded:** As you might have guessed from an earlier comment, one of the first things we change is the AppleSavePanelExpanded setting from NO to YES. This displays the column browser when the Save sheet appears, so you no longer have to click the disclosure button next to the Where pop-up menu to navigate to your destination folder.

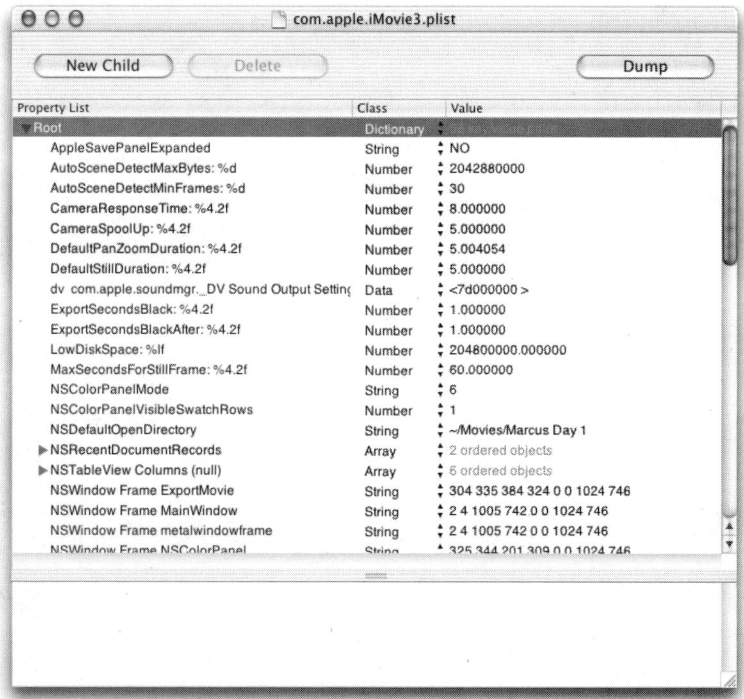

Figure 16-8: Property List Editor shows you a lot more preference settings than were accessible in the Preferences dialog.

✦ **Option autoApplyPanZoomToImportedStills: %d:** In Chapter 14, we decried the lack of an "off" switch for the Ken Burns Effect. An off switch is present in the Property List Editor. Look for the line "Option autoApplyPanZoom ToImportedStills: %d". This Boolean (logical) value is set to YES. If you change that to NO, then photos that you drag in from iPhoto, from the Finder or via the File ➪ Import (Shift-⌘-I) command are simply still frames with the duration set in the Ken Burns Effect area. This import is *very* fast because no rendering takes place. If you want the Ken Burns Effect on a particular still, just select the still frame and click the Apply button in the Photos panel's Ken Burns Effect area.

✦ **The LowDiskSpace:** This setting tells you at what point iMovie is going to start complaining that you're running out of space to import and render. The default, as you can see, is 204,800,000 (a little under 200MB). You probably shouldn't lower this figure, but you might want to get warned a little earlier. On Dennis's PowerBook, for example, this is set to 409,600,000 so that he gets the notification about two minutes before he's out of space rather than one minute.

✦ **MaxSecondsForStillFrame:** One other item of possible interest is MaxSecondsForStillFrame, which defaults to 60. If, for some reason, a one-minute maxima on your stills is not to your liking, you can change this value. 30 seconds, to match the Ken Burns Effect slider's behavior, might be more convenient.

Summary

In this chapter, you discovered how to share clips between projects. You also learned how to use VCD Builder together with Toast Titanium to create professional-quality, menu-driven VideoCDs, including chapter markers. We also gave you some tips and techniques for creating better footage to use in iMovie. Finally, we showed you how to modify some of your iMovie settings for which Apple didn't provide a Preferences dialog option.

✦ ✦ ✦

CHAPTER 17

Enhancing Your iMovie Experience

✦ ✦ ✦ ✦

In This Chapter

Hardware enhancements

Software enhancements

✦ ✦ ✦ ✦

Adding certain accessories, both hardware and software, that enhance your iMovie usage are no-brainers: A digital camcorder with a FireWire connector falls into that category.

What else can you do, though, to enrich your iMovie-making? In this chapter, we list items that we think should be at the top of anyone's list and a few items that we just think are cool.

Hardware Enhancements

There was a time when hardware was expensive, especially hardware for video editing. You're lucky. You already have the two big-ticket items: FireWire-equipped Mac and your digital camcorder.

That doesn't mean you can't find good ways to use your credit cards (and maybe earn some frequent-flyer miles or cash rebates along the way) in your quest for great iMovies.

Adding RAM

We both believe that most Macs ship with just enough memory to let you use them. iMovie can run on a 256MB iMac with OS X, but it operates noticeably better on that same Mac with 384MB, better yet with 512MB, and even better with 640MB or 768MB — well, you get the idea.

You probably won't see much difference when importing video, but more memory speeds even that process up a bit. You'll see the biggest performance gains when you render clips, transitions, and special effects or export your video using one of the QuickTime codecs. Processor-intensive operations such as these thrive on large amounts of RAM.

Boosting mass storage

iMovie gobbles disk space. We know we've told you this before, but it's something we feel cannot be overemphasized.

It's almost comical to remember the first iMovie-equipped iMac DVs with their 6GB or 10GB drives. Unless you stripped all the preinstalled software except iMovie and what it needed to run, you only had room for between 15 and 45 minutes of video before your disk was full. Today's 20GB, 40GB, and 60GB internal drives are a big improvement, and they practically guarantee room for at least one or two iMovie projects. But it still won't take long to fill a hard disk if you don't monitor and manage its contents carefully.

Furthermore, if you're going to use iDVD to burn a DVD-R disc, you're going to need even more free disk space for the special files that iDVD generates. All of a sudden, a one-hour video requires (at least temporarily) at least 25GB of disk space. So a 20GB drive won't come close to having enough space for the job, and a 40GB drive may be too small if you already have a lot of stuff on it.

See Chapter 18 for more on using iDVD to burn your own DVD.

Another problem with using your main drive for digital video work is *disk fragmentation*. As files are written, rewritten, removed, and replaced, you get to the point that pieces of your files are scattered all over the disk, resulting in much slower read and write operations as the Mac has to bounce the disk's read head around from place to place on the disk. We offer our configurations next as ones that address the disk fragmentation problem with the minimum of pain on our part.

You can purchase software, such as Norton Utilities or Alsoft's PlusOptimizer, to defragment your drives. In fact, these are good programs to have even if you aren't dealing with huge digital video files. However, defragmenting takes a lot of time, especially when you have to reboot to run the optimization software.

Dennis has these three drives in his old G4/400 (which has 896MB of RAM):

- ✦ An 8.5GB SCSI drive that holds OS X, his applications, and other basics
- ✦ A 20GB ATA drive used for accumulated data (like the files for this book)
- ✦ A 30GB ATA drive dedicated (almost exclusively) to iMovie work

Now that Dennis has a new flat-panel iMac G4/800 with a 60GB drive, the G4/400 isn't getting as much use for digital video. (It doesn't have a SuperDrive and it's a lot slower than his new iMac.) Still, that configuration worked great for over a year-and-a-half. Even with the 60GB drive (and 768MB of RAM), the iMac also has a 30GB FireWire drive connected — it makes a great place to export the movies for iDVD. When Dennis is done creating and burning a DVD, he can erase the files, leaving an unfragmented drive from which to work the next time.

Bob, on the other hand, thinks it's a waste of time and energy to defragment. He has an external 60GB FireWire dedicated to video. When a project ends, he burns or backs up what he needs, then erases the hard disk. That defragments it quite nicely for the next project, thank you very much.

Burning drives

Distributing your movies on CD or DVD is a cost-efficient way to send out high-quality copies to family and friends. It's also a great way to distribute business and promotional materials you create in iMovie to coworkers and clients. Unlike videotapes, you can duplicate digital video CDs without *generational loss* (the signal degradation that occurs when copying analog data). This means that you can keep making copies as the need arises and not worry about deteriorating quality. You can also write CDs faster than you can write videotape. CDs and DVDs are also an excellent archival medium, taking up very little space while holding large amounts of data. Because they are random-access media, it's also much quicker to retrieve something from a CD or DVD than it is from a (sequential access) taped backup.

Apple currently includes CD-R/RW burners in most Mac models, but if you don't have one in yours, we strongly encourage you to get one. The SuperDrive is both a CD-R/RW burner and a DVD-R burner and this is a great combination. Purchased in quantity, CD-R media, even including jewel cases and labels, can be had for under $1 per unit.

Getting out of the shadows

Dark indoor shots or heavy shadowing in outdoor clips can ruin a scene. This is where lighting kits, fill lights, and reflectors come in handy.

For those troublesome indoor scenes, consider a portable lighting kit, especially one where the key light fits on your camera's *accessory shoe*, that little slotted mount on the top of most digital camcorders. Some very nice kits, ranging up in price from a few hundred dollars, are available from Lowel (`www.lowel.com`), Cool-Lux (`www.cool-lux.com`), and NRG Research (`www.nrgresearch.com`).

Almost any photography store stocks fill reflectors. Two popular manufacturers are Photoflex (`www.photoflex.com`) and Bogen Photo Corporation (`www.bogenphoto.com`).

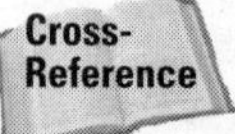

For more information on reflectors, see Chapter 12.

Keeping a steady hand

Even more than with still photography, keeping the camera steady while taping is critical. Most digital camcorders have some built-in stabilization control, minimizing motion caused by trembling hands, but using a tripod beats the built-in adjustments all to heck.

If you need to move around while taping, a tripod won't help. This is where a stabilizer should enter your picture. Ranging from about $250 for entry-level models to thousands of dollars for professional units like those shoulder-mounted mounts you see TV news cameramen using in popular films, stabilizers use gyroscopes and gimbals to eliminate undesirable motion.

Manufacturers of popular models include SteadyTracker (`www.steadytracker.com`), GlideCam (`www.glidecam.com`), and Kenyon Labs (`www.ken-lab.com`).

Filtering and focusing

Unlike better film and digital still cameras, most digital camcorders don't have interchangeable lenses. Many camcorder manufacturers offer a partial solution with attachable lens *adapters* and *filters*.

Adapters let you attach different lens types, such as wide-angle or telephoto lenses, to your camcorder.

Filters help you deal with varied lighting conditions and come in multiple flavors. Here are some of the more useful:

- ✦ **UV (Ultraviolet) filters:** Reduce haze by decreasing the UV rays that gets through to the camera's CCD.
- ✦ **ND (Neutral Density) filters:** Best described as "sunglasses for your camera," these filters improve contrast and detail in bright to very bright sunlight.
- ✦ **Polarization filters:** Change the angle at which light enters the lens, and thus reduce reflected glare. These filters allow you to tape through windows or a watery surface.
- ✦ **Diffusion filters:** Soften a scene. Romantic scenes and reminiscences are often shot through a diffusion filter, providing that slightly hazy effect.
- ✦ **Center Spot filters:** A special kind of diffusion filter. They diffuse the periphery while leaving the scene's center in sharp focus.

Check with your camcorder's manufacturer to see what, if any, adapters, lenses, and filters are available from them. Another good source to check is Tiffen (`www.tiffen.com`), probably the largest manufacturer and supplier of filters in the business.

Software Enhancements

The wonderful world of software provides numerous opportunities to do more with your iMovies. Best of all, many of the programs are free or quite inexpensive (although a few can put a serious dent in your plastic).

Going Pro with QuickTime

QuickTime Pro is a $30 (okay, $29.95 + tax) upgrade to the QuickTime that came with your Mac or that you downloaded for free. You don't get a disk, manual, or anything you can touch physically for that money; what you do get is a multicharacter unlock code, tied to your name, which unlocks extra features in QuickTime. For the record, the features that put the Pro in QuickTimePro are worth paying for:

- ✦ Exporting to multiple formats
- ✦ A cornucopia of editing tools
- ✦ The ability to present your movie full-screen

If you're serious about making cool iMovies, QuickTime Pro's $30 price tag is money extremely well spent. Figure 17-1 shows Bob entering his QuickTime Pro registration information, just to show how easy it is. (We smudged out his serial number, so you'll have to obtain your own.)

For more on the extra features that QuickTime offers, see Chapters 14 and 15.

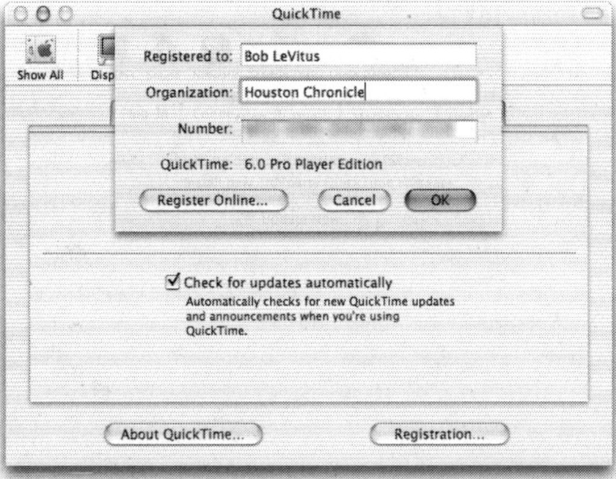

Figure 17-1: A QuickTime Pro upgrade requires just your name, company, and serial number.

The new MPEG-4 compressor, available through the Expert settings, produces high-quality streaming video relatively quickly. The downside of this compressor is that all your viewers need to have QuickTime 6 or another MPEG-4 decompressor, and there just aren't that many of them available yet.

Figure 17-2 shows a menu's eye glimpse of the extra commands available after you upgrade to QuickTime Pro.

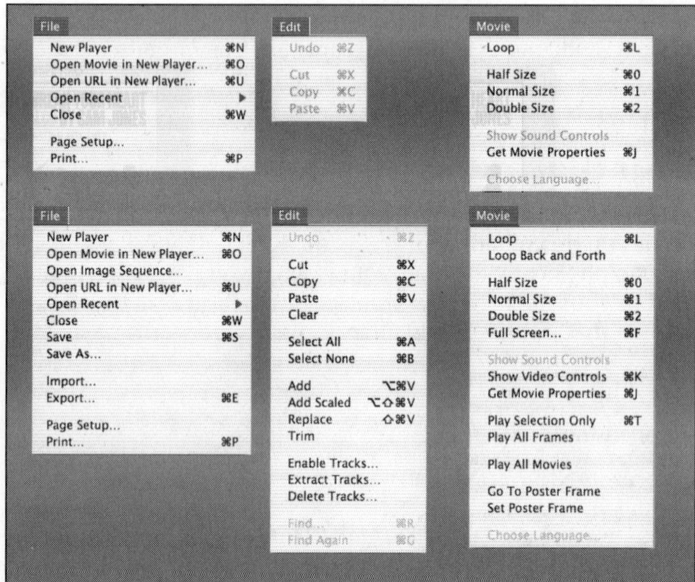

Figure 17-2: Comparing the File, Edit, and Movie menus from regular (free) QuickTime (top row) and QuickTime Pro (bottom row).

Have a little Toast with your iMovie

As we've said repeatedly in this book, Roxio's Toast 5 Titanium is "must have" software if you burn more than an occasional CD. For use with iMovie, Toast 5 Titanium includes a VideoCD QuickTime codec, which adds another choice, as shown in Figure 17-3, to the Save dialog's Export pop-up menu when you choose Expert Settings. (Dennis's Export pop-up probably includes more choices than yours, because he collects codecs.)

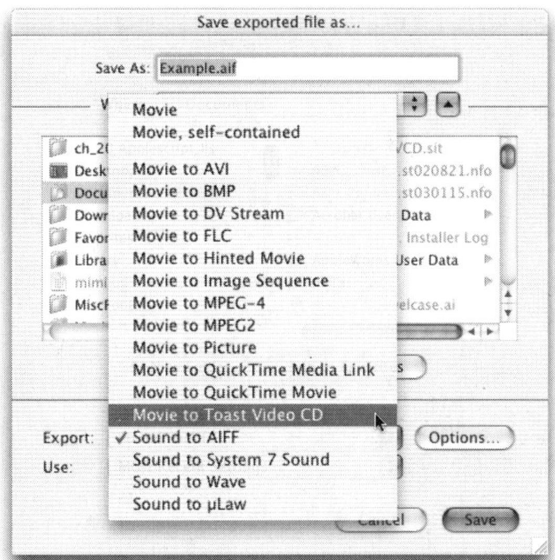

Figure 17-3: Choose Expert Settings from the QuickTime pop-up menu and, in the Save exported file as dialog, your Export pop-up menu sports a Movie to Toast Video CD choice.

Also in the package are useful utilities, such as a Roxio-specific version of the Discus disk-labeling software, the Audion MP3 player application, CD Spin Doctor for extracting songs from cassette tapes and LPs, and iView Media for managing collections of digital media. Although iView Media doesn't do everything that iPhoto does, iView Media is a more powerful and flexible photo database that also manages movies, sounds, and fonts.

If your iMovie usage is anything like Dennis's, you'll accumulate various clips that you'll want to use in more than one movie. Because keeping track of which clip does what is not exactly one of iMovie's strengths, you can use iView to store thumbnails of your clips and retrieve the one you want when you want it.

Because Toast can write so many different CD formats, some of the tools we'll tell you about a little later in this chapter in the "Free software" section create files for Toast to let you write Super VideoCDs (SVCDs), a very high-quality format playable on many set top DVD players.

Check it out at `www.roxio.com`. You can find this software in most stores for $69 when a promotion is running.

Although it isn't, technically, an iMovie adjunct, we would feel remiss if we didn't include a plug for El Gato Software's EyeTV unit in this book, and this seems like as good a place as any. The EyeTV is a TV tuner and MPEG-1 encoder in one $199 unit that connects to your Mac via USB. If your goal is to convert old analog tapes

(VHS or Beta, for example) to Video CD, this is the easiest and fastest method we can think of. Just play the tape on your VCR and let EyeTV record it, in either VCD format on your hard disk. After it's on your disk, just tell EyeTV's software to hand it off to Toast for burning as a Video CD.

Adding effects, transitions, and scoring

There's something about visual effects, transitions, and soundtracks that appeals to people. Just as early Mac users went overboard with fonts, something new at the time to the general computer user, new iMovie users strive to try out all the effects and transitions they can get their hands on. We tried them all, eventually settling on the ones that work for our purposes, but that hasn't stopped us from looking for new effects and transitions.

Effects and transitions

If the ones that come with iMovie 3 don't satisfy your cravings, check out these cool offerings:

✦ **eZedia (`www.ezedia.com`):** Their first effect is called eZeMatte ($29) and it is one of Dennis's favorites. You can use eZeMatte to overlay any image over an iMovie clip. If you want to make it seem like you're looking through a window, overlay a window frame. Add customized logos, if you wish, just like the networks do. The second eZedia plug-in is a variation on eZeMatte called eZeScreen ($39). The difference is that instead of overlaying a graphic, you can overlay a QuickTime movie. If the fixed logo capability of eZeMatte isn't enough for you, something like the animated Cartoon Network logo might be more to your taste. Better yet, you can do picture-in-picture by overlaying a small QuickTime movie in the corner. These aren't special effects in the car-exploding category, but they're getting a lot closer to special effects than the standard iMovie visual effects.

✦ **GeeThree (`www.geethree.com`):** We both really like Slick Transitions and Effects for iMovie (Volumes 1 through 4). In fact, Bob likes them so much that the folks at GeeThree quote him on their Web page: "An essential, no iMovie user should be without it!" They're $29.95 each for Volumes 1 and 2 and $49.95 each for Volumes 3 and 4, with discount pricing for multiple volume combinations. Each pack contains over 50 transitions and effects. Although you don't get to supply your own frames and overlays as you do with eZeMatte, some of the effects in Slick Collection 2 are frames. Volumes 3 and 4 were released just before this book went to press.

✦ **CSB Digital (`www.csbdigital.com`):** With two iPlugins Special Effects Packs, you'll surely find something useful or at least interesting. For example, spy Camera could be useful if you want a "night-vision goggles" image. CSB Digital is a British company and quotes their prices in Pounds Sterling. Doing a rate conversion, the packs are about $15.30 each or $26 for the pair.

✦ **Virtix (www.virtix.com):** Showcasing their Bravo collection of iMovie effects ($24.99) and Echo collection of iMovie transitions ($24.99), Virtix also offers a Zoom effects package and a Pan & Scan effects package at $19.99 each. Having discovered Virtix's offerings after the GeeThree packages, we were a little jaded and didn't get as excited by them as you might. The Bravo and Echo collections are quite well-done, with a bundle price of $39.99.

Each of these companies also offers a sampler pack of free effects, hoping that you'll like what you see so much that you'll purchase the whole package. It is quite likely that many of you will make their hope a reality.

Scoring

For those more inclined to background music than visual effects, SmartSound (www.smartsound.com) offers Movie Maestro ($49.95) to help you create perfectly synchronized, custom movie soundtracks for your movies. In the following simple three-step process, you can create a soundtrack:

1. **Export a reference file.** Web Movie, Small is what SmartSound recommends.
2. **Open and score it in Movie Maestro, which does almost all the work for you.**
3. **Click Movie Maestro's Save Sound button and choose SoundTrack to iMovie from the Save Soundtrack dialog's Save pop-up menu.**

Voila! You now have the score, properly positioned on Track 2 in the Timeline view, all set for you to export your movie in any available format. Dennis has been having a lot of fun with Movie Maestro. SmartSound includes a little over two dozen audio tracks for use with Movie Maestro and offers additional CD collections at $29.95 each. (Six CD collections were available when we wrote this, but more are surely on their way.)

Software that puts a dent in your plastic

When you want to go in and tweak individual frames or sequences, add animated effects, or add special effects like transparency to your finished film, Adobe Systems (www.adobe.com) offers Adobe After Effects for about $650. Wiley already has a book larger than this one, just to cover all the things this high-end program can do— check out the *After Effects 5 Bible* by J. J. Marshall and Zed Saeed for the complete scoop. (It even includes a DVD-ROM rather than a CD.)

Final Cut Pro and Final Cut Express offer some of the same tweaks as After Effects along with a suite of video- and audio-editing tools. Both are great if you want to step beyond the simple effects possible with iMovie.

Free software

Because OS X's underpinnings are Unix, we have access to the work of a large software development community. An even greater benefit is that much of this software is free. Unfortunately, most Unix software is written for the command-line interface and doesn't provide the user experience Mac users expect. Many considerate developers are putting nice front-ends on these tools, though, and our software horn of plenty is starting to brim over with the fruit of those labors.

Of particular interest to iMovie users are encoders, particularly ones that generate formats unavailable from QuickTime Pro. MediaPipe (`http://mediapipe.sourceforge.net`) is a framework to handle media under OS X, and it comes with a few encoders:

- ✦ **MPEG-2:** The encoding method used for DVDs. MPEG-2 is also used for SVCDs, which, in addition to playing in many set top DVD players, are burned on standard CD-R media, making them much less expensive. SVCDs don't require a SuperDrive, just a CD burner and Toast.
- ✦ **MP3:** A format with which we should all be familiar by now. It stands for MPEG-1 layer 3 audio and has become ubiquitous. Many newer CD and DVD players include firmware to play MP3-formatted CDs.
- ✦ **MP2:** MPEG-1 Layer II, the standard for VCD and SVCD audio streams.

Note

Due to licensing restrictions imposed by the Motion Picture Experts Group on MPEG-2 encoders, the MPEG-2 encoder is distributed in source code form and not as an executable binary. Those licensing restrictions (and accompanying fees) are the reason the MPEG-2 decoder for QuickTime is a separate $20 option. You need to have the Apple Developer Tools installed to compile the encoder. If you purchased Mac OS X, the Developer Tools are one of the CDs in the box. If OS X came installed on your Mac and you haven't already done so, you'll need to download the tools from `www.apple.com/developer`. Create a free Apple Developer Connection account to download the tools.

You can create VCDs containing multiple MPEG-1 files using Toast 5 Titanium's VideoCD setting. Similarly, you can create multiple SVCD image files from MPEG-2 files using GNU VCDToolsX and burn those with Toast's Multitrack CD-ROM XA setting. These tools, as the name implies, are ports of GNU (Gnu's Not Unix) programs. Jesper Nilson, the fellow who's brought them to OS X, updates them regularly, and you can find the most recent version and documentation at `www.sbpr.a.se/systemjammers/vcdtoolsx`. The documentation and documentation links are thorough, but it is quickly obvious that English is not the author's native tongue, so some sentence construction is a bit awkward. As with anything GNU-based, the source code is also available for the intrepid among you who want to tweak things.

If you want to encode for DivX, MPEG-1, or MPEG-2, or transcode between formats, check out ffmpeg (`http://homepage.mac.com/major4/`). With a number of Presets (preconfigured settings for standard delivery formats), ffmpeg is great for converting video and audio files from one format to another.

Another handy tool is VCD Builder by Johan Linström (`homepage.mac.com/johan`). Using VCD Builder, you can create menu-driven VCDs and SVCDs by building *sequences* (boxes) and connecting them with lines showing the control flow. You can even use still pictures for some of the sequences — VCD Builder converts those stills to an appropriate format for you; however, you'll need to have compatible MPEG-1 and MPEG-2 files for your movies as VCD Builder won't convert those for you. When you have the disk structure you want, you can generate image files to be burned later or you can click VCD Builder's Burn VCD (or SVCD, if your files are MPEG-2) button to have it create the images and pass the data to Toast. Then, all you'll have to do is click Toast's Record button and tell it at what speed to burn.

Summary

In this chapter, you learned about some of the hardware you can purchase to help you make better movies and some other hardware to improve iMovie's performance. You also learned about software, for purchasing or just to download, to help you create even better iMovies and make even better use of the iMovies after you've exported them.

✦ ✦ ✦

iDVD

P A R T

V

✦ ✦ ✦ ✦

In This Part

✦ ✦ ✦ ✦

Introducing iDVD

In This Chapter

Understanding DVDs

Exploring the iDVD window

Setting iDVD preferences

iDVD is a remarkable program that enables you to make your own menu-driven DVDs, with up to 90 minutes of video content, just like the big studios — almost. We say "almost" because iDVD maxes out at 90 minutes of video per DVD-R. Also, you have little or no control over compression levels and are limited to six buttons per screen.

Of course, such things are trivial with iDVD's $999 big brother, DVD Studio Pro, which lets you do anything and everything you see on studio release DVDs. Still, you can make amazing DVDs with nothing more than a Mac, a copy of iDVD, and some still or moving digital images.

DVD History and Background

Just a few years ago, if you went into your neighborhood Blockbuster or Wherehouse, the unit of currency in video entertainment, from wall-to-wall, was the videotape. Today it's the ubiquitous DVD, also known as the *Digital Video Disc* or *Digital Versatile Disc*, depending on whom you ask. DVDs hold the same place in the video world that CDs hold in the audio world. They're the high-quality, state-of-the-art delivery medium for your video entertainment. They're everywhere, and most frequent renters (and buyers) will only *settle* for videotape if they can't get their hands on the movie's DVD version for the following reasons:

- **Random Access:** Which means you can jump to any scene you want nearly instantly.
- **No Rewinding:** With DVDs you don't get yelled at or penalized for being unkind because there's no need to rewind.

✦ **Interactivity:** The best reason of all, most DVDs are somewhat interactive: You use the DVD player's remote control to navigate and activate (point and click) buttons on the screen.

✦ **Quality:** The image quality on a DVD can be much higher than is available on a videotape.

DVD's predecessor in the consumer digital video market is the LaserDiscs, which are the size of LPs and much heavier. In fact, comparing LaserDiscs to DVDs is like comparing LPs to CDs. DVDs hold more and can display a higher-quality picture, just as CDs hold more than an LP and produce better audio. Besides, DVDs and CDs have the same physical dimensions, just like LaserDiscs and LPs.

In January 2001, Apple introduced the first affordable personal computer on which you could burn a DVD that could be viewed on most major DVD players — the $3,499 PowerMac G4/733. This was a major price breakthrough and not just in the Macintosh world. Before the G4/733 with SuperDrive, the cheapest DVD burner alone cost two or three times that much and software for making DVDs was expensive and rare. At the time we're writing this, you can get an eMac with SuperDrive and iLife for $1499 or a 1GHz iMac (similarly equipped) with a 17" flat-screen display for only $1799.

The SuperDrive was actually Pioneer's new (at the time) A103, and for the first few months, the only way to get one was inside one of these G4/733s — Apple bought every A103 drive Pioneer could build. After production caught up with demand, the retail price of an A103 fell to around $1,000. Soon other companies were competing in the DVD-R market, driving the street price of a SuperDrive, a second-generation Pioneer A-105 at this writing, even lower to under $400.

Note

The original A103 was a 1x burner, with 60 minutes of video taking 60 minutes, plus overhead, to burn. The A104 is a 2x burner and the A105 is a 4x burner. To achieve those burn rates, your DVD-R media also has to be rated for that speed. Apple released an update for various models, in particular flat-panel iMacs with SuperDrives, to enable compatibility with 4x media (but the 4x media burns at 1x speed on the older SuperDrives).

As of this writing, external DVD-R drives *do not work with iDVD*. If you want to burn DVDs with video and play them on a set top DVD player, you need to buy a Mac with a built-in SuperDrive. iDVD does not recognize third-party external FireWire SuperDrives; you'll need the $999 DVD Studio Pro or some other solution to burn DVDs.

Blank DVD-R media started out costing $10 per disc or more, but as DVD-R became more popular, the price quickly fell to today's more reasonable $2 to $3 a disc (in 3-packs and 5-packs) — Apple-labeled 5-packs are $15.

The SuperDrive alone wasn't enough to popularize the DVD burning technology. It would have been far less useful had Apple not included a neat little piece of software called iDVD.

Understanding DVDs

Most people think that DVDs are simply just another media with higher-quality video and audio than videotape. Better quality *is* a part of the draw, but DVDs are much more than that.

DVDs also specify a disc layout that allows for alternative audio tracks. For example, one DVD can contain a movie with English, French, Spanish, German, Japanese, and other soundtracks. You can also have subtitles available in multiple languages.

We already mentioned interactivity, and that's key. DVDs are the first consumer media choice with the interactivity that used to be tied exclusively to computers or a Web connection like WebTV.

And all that is just for video DVDs. You can also use DVDs like a giant CD-ROM to hold data—4.7GB of data on a single DVD-R is the equivalent of about seven CDs (a little more than seven 650MB CDs, a little less than seven 700MB CDs). They're even called DVD-ROMs. In iDVD 2.1, Apple added the feature of being able to create *hybrid* DVDs, which are DVDs that have a DVD-ROM section where you can place data files. This feature is still present in iDVD 3.

When we write "DVD," we are referring to the video DVD format that you watch on a DVD player. When we want to talk about a data DVD that you access via your Mac (or a suitably equipped PC), we'll call it a "data DVD" or "DVD-ROM." (Boy, isn't that original?)

DVDs aren't just about movies. You can also include slideshows on the DVD. Apple even has AppleScripts available for download at `www.apple.com/applescript/idvd` that take photos from iPhoto and create a slideshow on the DVD for you. You can even add your own background music to iDVD menu screens and slideshows.

Assuming that you have your content—the movies you want to burn to a DVD—you still need software that does three things:

- ✦ Creates the menu buttons and other interactive features for the DVD
- ✦ Encodes your video to meet the specifications required for DVD players
- ✦ Burns the DVD on your DVD burner in the case of iDVD, that's a built-in SuperDrive

iDVD provides all these features, and more, through a simple, straightforward user interface.

Authoring a DVD

The process of creating a DVD is called *authoring*. You aren't creating or editing the content that will be watched; it's assumed that you already did that in another program, such as iMovie 3. When you use iDVD, you're building a framework for your content.

Here are some of the authoring tasks you'll get to know quite well in Chapters 19 and 20:

- ✦ Importing content
- ✦ Creating on-screen menu buttons
- ✦ Choosing background images
- ✦ Selecting music or audio for menus
- ✦ Choosing a frame or sequence to represent each button
- ✦ Choosing a shape and label for each button

Those are just a few of the things we mean when we talk about authoring in iDVD.

DVD-R burning application

After you have your authoring completed and the material encoded (well, iDVD has encoded it for you — there's nothing you need to do), the remaining step is to burn it to a DVD-R.

iDVD only works if there is an internal SuperDrive present. As long as you've got one, you're ready to start. Just insert a blank DVD-R disc, click iDVD's Burn button, click it again when it changes to the radioactive icon, and then sit back and wait for the burn to complete.

Unfortunately, unlike burning a CD-R or CD-RW, burning a DVD can't (yet) be accelerated so that you can burn 64 minutes in 8 minutes using 8x speed. Burning a DVD happens at 1 x, 2 x, or 4 x speed, so burning 60 minutes of DVD video will take at least 15 minutes, depending on the SuperDrive model in your Mac and the rated speed of the DVD-R media, plus a little bit of time to write the menus and the other support files that the DVD specification requires, plus close out the burn. And that time estimate assumes that the encoding is complete before you tell iDVD to burn the disc.

Most of What You Need to Know About MPEG

This part gets a little acronym-crazy and more than a little geeky. It's all background material you don't really need to know before you roll up your sleeves. We put it here in this sidebar in case you're interested.

Uncompressed digital video gobbles up hard disk storage at better than 200MB per minute. Without compression, you could fit roughly only 23 minutes of video on a DVD, and that wouldn't leave room for interactive menus or anything else.

The Motion Picture Experts Group (MPEG) has developed and standardized a number of compression formats for video and audio. The best known of these are

- **MPEG-1:** Used on VideoCDs.
- **MPEG-1 Layer 3 audio:** More commonly known as MP3, and used for audio content.
- **MPEG-4:** The new standard for streaming media.
- **MPEG-2:** The format used for DVDs and Super VideoCDs.

You can't use just any MPEG-2 file for a DVD. The frame rate and frame size have to be right, and both the audio and video bit-rates must fall within specified ranges.

If you want all the gruesome details concerning what is required for a DVD's MPEG-2 and just about anything else related to MPEG-2, we recommend these three Web sites:

- **VCDHelp.com (**`www.vcdhelp.com`**):** This site's a little or a lot biased towards Windows solutions, but the specification and link information is comprehensive and it has a great database of DVD players, citing features and compatibility with different formats and media.
- **MPEG Home Page (**`mpeg.telecomitalialab.com`**):** The home of MPEG.
- **Berkeley Multimedia Research Center (**`http://bmrc.berkeley.edu/frame/research/mpeg/mpeg2faq.html`**):** A great frequently asked questions (FAQ) collection at UC Berkeley.

iDVD will adjust all the parameters to make the movie you give it match the DVD specifications and then it will encode it. No fuss, no mess, and no fiddling with settings.

Best of all, iDVD will do the encoding in the background while you continue working, either in iDVD or in another application. Frequently, by the time we're done creating our menu structure and annotating things, the encoding is done.

Exploring the iDVD Window

Each of the applications in this book has a slightly different feel. iTunes has a window where buttons appear, change, and disappear based upon what's selected in the source list. iMovie has one window, but controls change based upon whether you're in camera or clip-editing mode, which shelf panel you have exposed, and whether you're working with the clip view or Timeline view. iPhoto has one window (or two, if you set your preference for a separate editing window) and an always-present tools panel whose contents change based upon your mode. iDVD has a static, nonresizable window, but has a drawer that slides out the left side when you click the Customize button, similar to the drawer in OS X's Mail program.

The main window

When you first launch iDVD, you see the window shown in Figure 18-1. This simple window, with its project pane and six buttons, is really approachable. However, those six buttons conceal a lot of functionality.

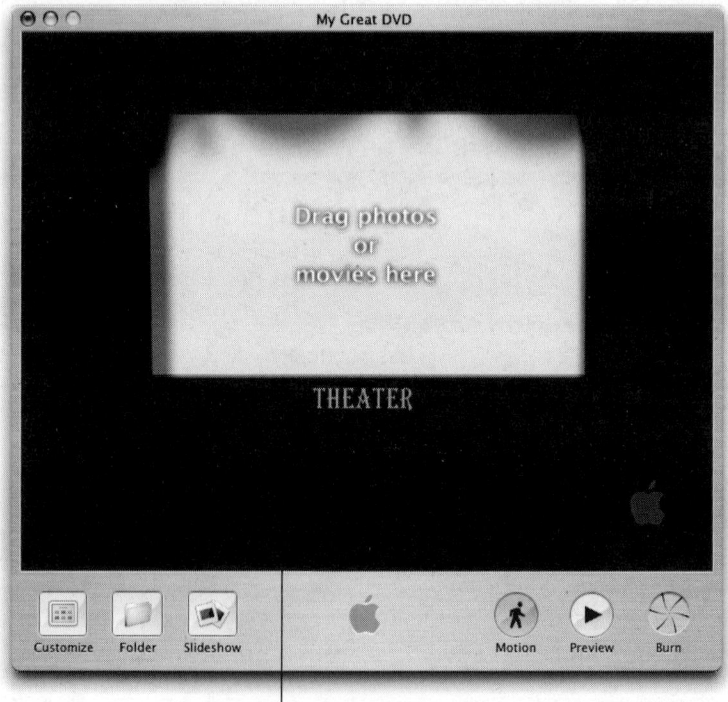

Figure 18-1: iDVD's window, ready for you to start creating your project.

The parts of the window are as follows:

✦ **Project pane:** This is where you build your DVD project. It displays the menus or screens that will be on your finished DVD.

✦ **Customize:** This button slides out the Customize drawer if it's closed or shuts it if it's open.

✦ **Folder:** Creates a new folder button. iDVD allows up to six buttons on a single menu. Clicking on a folder button moves you to a new menu, which can also have up to six buttons on it.

✦ **Slideshow:** As we mentioned earlier in this chapter, you can create slideshows as part of your DVD.

✦ **Motion:** Turns Motion menus on and off. One of the coolest features added in iDVD 2.0 was motion menus. Not only can you animate your menus, but you can also make your menu buttons play segments from the movies they represent. iDVD adds a number of new themes with Motion menus.

✦ **Preview:** Click this button and iDVD displays a floating window resembling a DVD remote control, as shown in Figure 18-2. Using this control, you can preview your project just as if it were burned and playing in OS X's DVD Player application.

For introductory information on the Customize and Slideshow buttons, see "The Customize drawer" and "The Slideshow pane" sections in this chapter. For more about processing details on the Customize, Slideshow, and Motion buttons, see Chapter 19.

Figure 18-2: Preview your DVD before burning with this remote control window.

✦ **Burn:** If you remember the Burn CD button in iTunes, this button will be very familiar. It looks the same and it works the same. Click it once, and the shutter opens, displaying a pulsing orange and black button reminiscent of the radiation warning symbol. Click it again, and the burn will commence.

The Customize drawer

Clicking that little Customize button in iDVD's lower-left corner opens the Customize drawer shown in Figure 18-3. The Customize drawer has six buttons: Themes, Settings, Audio, Photos, Movies, and Status. Collectively, iDVD refers to the Audio, Photos, and Movies buttons as the *iMedia buttons*.

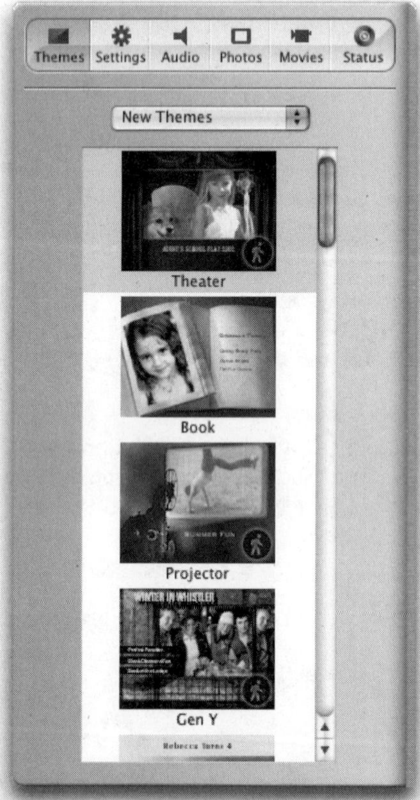

Figure 18-3: The Customize drawer, with the Themes button selected.

Choosing a theme

What is a *theme?* In iDVD, themes are templates that define the look and feel of your project. Near the top of the Themes pane is a pop-up menu where you can filter the themes displayed in the scrolling list. iDVD comes with 24 new themes, as well as the 14 themes available from iDVD 2. Choose from the pop-up menu to show all the themes, just the new themes, just the old themes, the default theme, or your defined Favorite themes in the scrolling list. These themes fall into four categories:

✦ **Motion:** Surprisingly, these are themes with motion menus.

✦ **Picture-only:** Themes that provide a static background for your menus. The buttons can still have motion.

✦ **Picture with audio:** A picture theme with an associated soundtrack. Claim Check is an example of a Picture with audio theme.

✦ **Drop Zone:** Contain one or more *Drop Zones*, or areas of the background in which you can place movies, slideshows, or graphics. Drop Zone themes come with text buttons, but you can change these to motion or still image buttons in the Customize drawer's Settings panel. Postcard is an example of a Drop Zone theme.

Customizing a theme

You can change Apple's categories by adding or deleting audio, or changing from image to video or vice versa, in the Settings pane as shown in Figure 18-4.

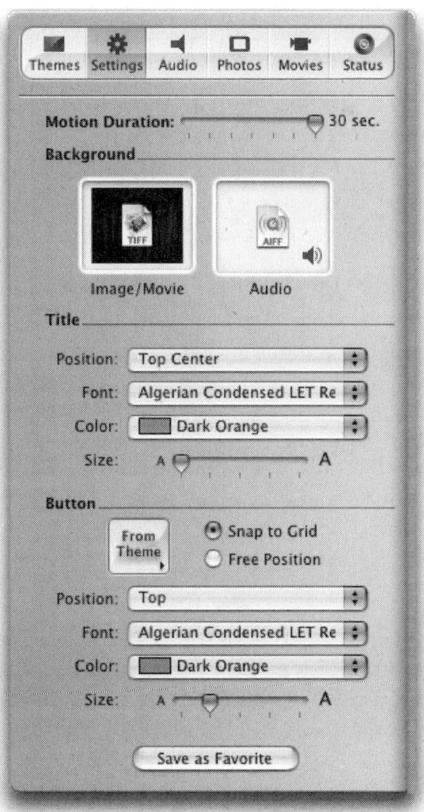

Figure 18-4: Modify a theme to your heart's content in the Settings pane.

The Settings pane is divided into four parts, the main area and three sections:

✦ **Background:** This section contains two *wells:* Image/Movie and Audio. Simply drag a media file and drop it onto the appropriate well.

- **Image/Movie:** Drag the graphic or video you want to appear behind your menu buttons and drop it on the Image/Movie well.
- **Audio:** Drag the sound file (AIFF, MP3, or WAV) you want as background music when your menu buttons are on screen and drop it onto the Audio well.

✦ **Title:** This section contains pop-up menus to specify the menu title's position, font, and text color, plus a font size slider.

✦ **Button:** The section has a variety of controls:

- **Pop-up button:** Located in the upper-left corner, this lets you select a shape for your buttons.
- **Snap to Grid** and **Free Position:** These radio buttons specify whether iDVD positions your buttons in a nice neat grid, or whether you get to position them where you want them.
- **Position, Font, Color pop-ups** and **Size slider:** These features do for button labels what the corresponding controls do for titles in the Title section.

The main tab has two controls on it:

✦ **Motion Duration:** Drag this slider to set a playtime for the menu background's video and accompanying audio from 0 to 30 seconds.

✦ **Save in Favorites:** This is a handy button. When you have customized a theme that you might want to reuse, you can save it as a Favorite and can recall it at a later time. These themes appear in the Themes pane's scrolling list when you choose Favorites from the pop-up menu.

We'll be covering these features in glorious detail in Chapter 19 and Chapter 20.

Checking project status

In iDVD 2.0, the Project Status pane displayed the Project size and Encoder Status. iDVD 2.1 added a pop-up menu with Encoder Status and DVD-ROM Contents, as shown in Figure 18-5. iDVD 3's Status panel is unchanged from the 2.1 version.

Figure 18-5: iDVD lets you add data files to your DVD-ROMs.

- **Project size:** Displays, both graphically and textually, how much space you've used on the DVD image. The text display shows both time and gigabytes consumed out of the total available time/space.
- **DVD-ROM Contents:** Enables you to utilize extra space on your DVD for data storage. For example, you can place the JPEG files used in a slideshow on the disc as data so that friends with a computer (and a DVD drive) can copy the images to their hard disk.
- **Encoder Status:** Displays encoding progress for each of the movies on your DVD.

Adding media to your DVDs

iLife's application integration comes to full flower in iDVD 3. The iMedia buttons provide access to your iTunes Library (Audio), your iPhoto Library (Photos), and your iMovies (Movies).

Checking out the Audio panel

The Audio panel, shown in Figure 18-6, is a straightforward conduit to your iTunes Library as well as all your playlists. Using the small knob between the album list area and the song list area, you can modify how much space each takes up relative to the other (the total is fixed). Below the song list, you have a Play button so that you can preview the songs before adding them to your iDVD project and a Search box, similar to the one in iTunes, so that you can search your Library for a particular tune.

Figure 18-6: The Audio panel provides access to your iTunes Library.

Looking at the Photos panel

Just as the Audio pane is a doorway into your iTunes Library, the Photos panel provides access to your iPhoto Photo Library, as shown in Figure 18-7. The topmost scrolling list is your iPhoto Album List. Below that, you'll find a scrolling list of image thumbnails for the item selected in the Album List. At the bottom is a Search box, so that you can search comments, keywords, and titles for particular character sequences (often words).

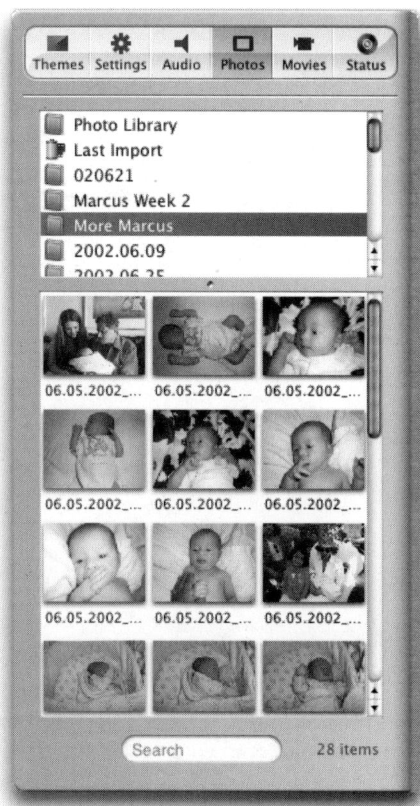

Figure 18-7: Browse or search your iPhoto Library in the Photos panel.

Viewing the Movies panel

The Movies pane, shown in Figure 18-8, is a previewing interface to the movies you might want to add to your iDVD project. Initially, the Movies pane includes only your Movies folder in its list of folders to search. You can augment this list in your iDVD Preferences' Movies panel, as described in "Setting iDVD Preferences" later in this chapter.

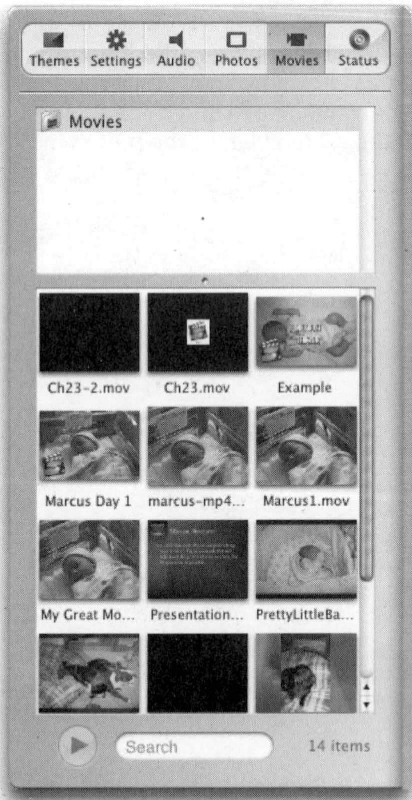

Figure 18-8: iDVD displays all your importable movies from a list of folders.

iDVD does *not* drill down, or even acknowledge, subfolders of folders in your list. If you have folders of movies within your Movies folder, for example, you cannot preview them until and unless you add the subfolders to your folder search list.

To preview a movie, select it in the thumbnail list and click the Play button or double-click the thumbnail. To find a movie, you need to know at least part of its name. Type that text into the Search textbox and press Return — iDVD commences searching. The thumbnail list displays only those movies that match your search string.

The Slideshow pane

Clicking the Slideshow button creates a Slideshow button in the Project pane. Double-clicking the slideshow's button replaces the Project pane with the Slideshow pane, as shown in Figure 18-9. Click the Return button to go dismiss the Slideshow pane.

Each slideshow is limited to a maximum of 99 images.

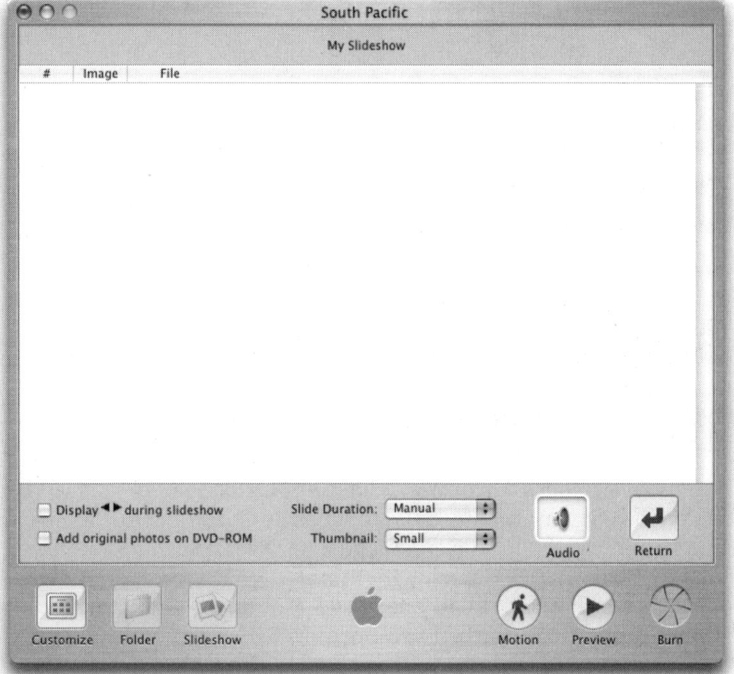

Figure 18-9: This is where you build your iDVD slideshows.

Setting iDVD Preferences

iDVD has few preferences for you to set, but some of them are quite important. Choose iDVD ➪ Preferences (⌘-,) to display the dialog shown in Figure 18-10.

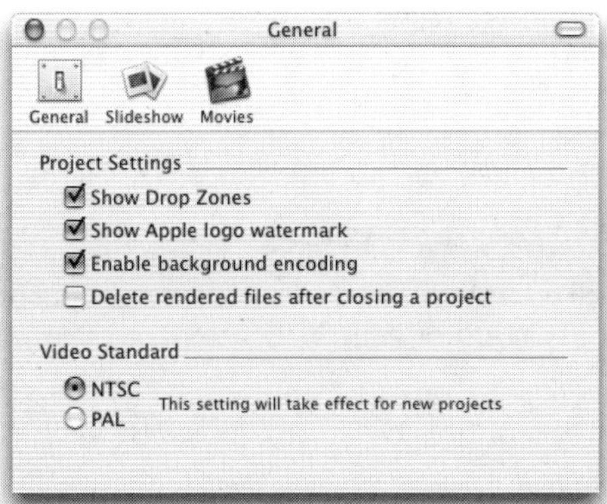

Figure 18-10: iDVD's General Preferences dialog.

The iDVD Preferences dialog is divided into three panes, with a toolbar button to display each pane.

The first pane is the General pane, which deals with how iDVD operates behind the scenes. This pane comes with two sections:

✦ **Project Settings section:** Contains four checkbox items:

- **Show Drop Zones:** When this box is checked, iDVD displays the message, "Drag photos or movies here" within the Drop Zone's borders.
- **Show Apple logo watermark:** Selecting this checkbox displays the pale white Apple logo as a watermark in the lower-right corner of the screen. Leave it there if you want folks to know that your DVD was made on a Mac or uncheck the box if you don't feel like advertising. Bob usually leaves it on, but he also ends most of his movies with a huge credit proclaiming, "Made with Mac OS X!"
- **Enable background encoding:** Selecting this checkbox tells iDVD to start encoding your menus and media as soon as possible and to encode while you're working. This can make iDVD's response to input a bit sluggish on slower Macs or Macs with minimal RAM; however, it means that you won't have to wait nearly so long (or at all) to start burning your DVD when you do click the Burn button.
- **Delete rendered files after closing a project:** Selecting this option tells iDVD to eliminate the encoded files it created when you close the project. Selecting this option can also free up a great deal of disk space, because the MPEG-2 files are generally about 25 to 50 percent the size of the DV files from which they were encoded (between 50MB and 100MB per minute of video). The downside of selecting this checkbox is that the next time you open the project, iDVD has to encode the files again.

iDVD encoded files are hidden (invisible), so you can't easily find and delete them in the Finder.

✦ **Video Standard section:** Has two radio buttons that determine whether new projects will be created as NTSC (American/Japanese television standard) or PAL (most of the rest of the world's TV standard).

The Slideshow pane in the Preference dialog has two options (shown in Figure 18-11).

✦ **Always add original slideshow photos to DVD-ROM:** Selecting this option tells iDVD to automatically include a copy of all the slides in any slideshows you create in the DVD-ROM (data) portion of your DVD.

✦ **Always scale slides to TV-Safe area:** Selecting this option tells iDVD to make sure that your slides fit in the portion of the screen which will be visible on a properly adjusted TV set.

As we discussed in Chapter 14, the video frame is wider than will fit on a TV screen, and parts of the image will be cropped when you show your movie on TV. The TV Safe area is that portion that will be within your TV screen's borders.

The Movies pane has two sections, shown in Figure 18-12:

✦ **When importing movies section:** Has three radio buttons:

- **Automatically create chapter marker submenu:** Tells iDVD to (obviously) create a submenu for the chapter markers whenever a movie containing chapter markers is imported.
- **Never create chapter marker submenu:** Tells iDVD to ignore any chapter markers in imported movies.
- **Ask each time:** iDVD's cue to query you about creating a chapter marker submenu whenever a movie with chapter markers is imported.

✦ **Look for my movies in these folders section:** This is where you manage the folder list seen in Customize's Movies panel (refer to Figure 18-8).

- **Add:** Click Add to select folders in a standard Open dialog (we think it should be a Choose dialog, but the only difference is the name at the top and the label on the button).
- **Remove:** To remove a folder from the list of searchable directories, select it in the list box and click Remove.

iDVD reminds you that your Movies folder is always searched. Also, remember that the search doesn't search subfolders, so if you have subfolders of your Movies folder that you want searched, add them here.

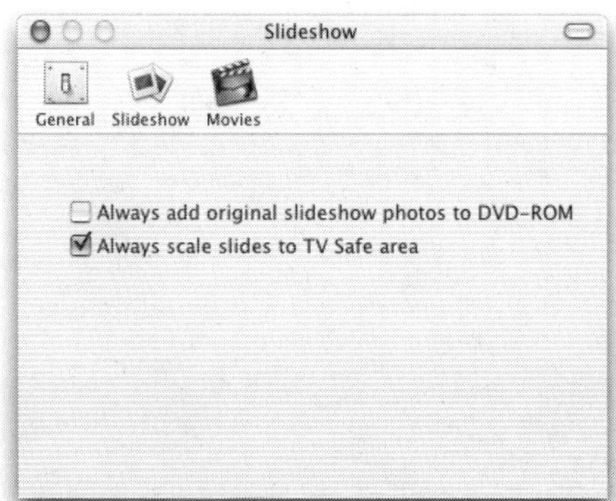

Figure 18-11: iDVD's Slideshow Preferences dialog.

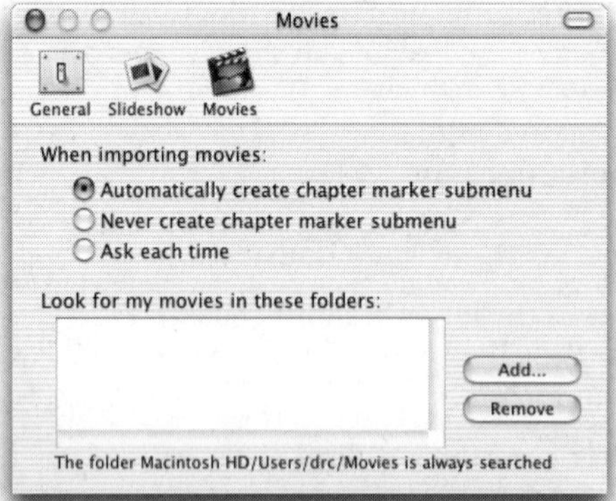

Figure 18-12: iDVD's Movies Preferences panel.

Summary

In this chapter, you learned what a DVD is and what is involved in creating one. You were introduced to the high points of the iDVD window, the Customize drawer, and the Slideshow pane. Finally, you saw what iDVD Preference settings are available and what they do.

✦ ✦ ✦

CHAPTER 19

Getting Started with iDVD

In This Chapter

Creating DVD menus

Creating a slideshow

Previewing your DVD

Burning a DVD

Whether you have a bunch of family movies you want to share, product demonstration films to distribute, or a set of presentations to deliver, DVDs are a superb medium. iDVD can help you package your content in an attractive, easy-to-use form.

You could just make QuickTime movies, stick them on CD or DVD, and send them out for use on a computer. You know, open in the Finder (or Windows Explorer), find the file the user wants, and play it — *if* they have the correct player(s) and codec(s) installed. You could, but it would be wrong. Not only do you have to worry about whether your audience is computer-savvy enough to deal with what you send them, but a Finder/Windows Explorer interface also isn't very attractive packaging.

One of our favorite introductions to DVD sites is Apple's own Seminars Online (`www.seminars.apple.com/seminarsonline`). One of their free seminars is *DVD Authoring Made Simple,* and the advice they give on the DVD creation process is great, breaking the authoring process up into five steps:

1. Plan what you want to present and how you want to present it.
2. Create your content. This includes not just the raw video, but also your menu backgrounds, audio, and other graphics.
3. Encode your video and audio content.
4. Author your DVD. This means creating an easily navigable, interactive layout and structure.
5. Record the DVD (burn to disc).

iDVD does Step 3 for you while you're working on Step 4. We give you a few tips on planning in Chapter 21. For creating content, refer to the 15 iTunes, iPhoto, and iMovie chapters that have led you to this point in the book.

Creating DVD Menus

One huge DVD advantage over videotape is that DVDs are *random-access* and tape is *sequential-access*. You can instantaneously jump from one point to another on the disc, unlike videotape, which requires you to wait while fast-forwarding and rewinding tape. Taking advantage of DVD's quick access, you create menus containing buttons that take your audience from one item to another with a click or two on the remote control, just like clicking the links on a Web page to navigate a Web site. In fact, authoring a DVD is very much like designing a Web site.

Just as a Web page will have a background color or graphic, a DVD menu screen will have a background image or movie, possibly with a soundtrack. A menu's content consists of text and buttons that are very much like links on a Web page.

Before you get started with anything else, choose File ➪ Save Project As (Shift-⌘-S) or File ➪ New Project so that you'll have your own project and won't be monkeying around with the Tutorial project. Either you or someone else in your home or office may actually want to use the tutorial in the future.

What's your theme?

To help get you started, iDVD 3 includes 38 templates (24 new ones and 14 retained from iDVD 2), called *themes*, for your interactive menu structure. Maybe we're unusual in this respect (we don't think so, though, after talking to other people), but we seldom like any of the designs supplied in templates accompanying software products; however, iDVD actually does quite well in this respect. Of the 38 templates, there are at least a dozen we might actually use, at least as a starting point. (We'd probably change the font or music, for example.) The presupplied themes are shown in Figure 19-1.

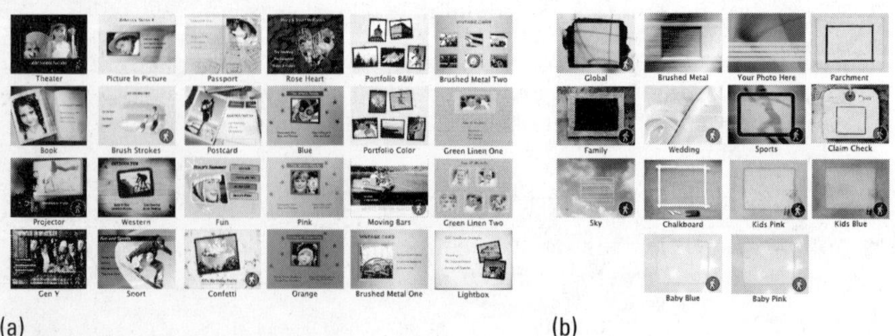

Figure 19-1: iDVD's 24 new themes (a) and 14 old themes (b).

There are more than a dozen other themes present in the iDVD application (the themes that came with iDVD 1.0), but they aren't immediately available to you. We'll tell you about them in Chapter 21.

Just so you know, that little "running man" icon in the lower-right corner of some theme icons isn't part of the theme; it indicates that the theme either has a motion menu, an audio track, or both. From iDVD's perspective, there are four kinds of themes:

✦ **Drop Zone themes:** Include an area where you can drop movies or still images to customize a portion of the background. By default, they have text buttons only, but you can change that in the Customize drawer's Settings panel.

✦ **Motion themes:** Short videos, up to 30 seconds in length, that loop in the background. They might have associated audio or they might be silent.

✦ **Picture only themes:** Sport a static background picture with no motion or sound.

✦ **Picture with audio themes:** Picture themes with a sound track that loops in the background.

Note

Introduced in iDVD 2, menu screens with video rather than still images as the background are called *motion menus*. Drop Zone themes were introduced in iDVD 3 and allow you to, among other things, create hybrid motion/still menus—partly static and partly motion.

You select your theme from the Customize drawer's Themes panel, and you open the Customize drawer by clicking the Customize button or choosing Project ➪ Show Customize Panel (Shift-⌘-B). When the Customize drawer is open, this menu item toggles to Hide Customize Panel.

Caution

Unlike some other drawer-savvy applications, such as OS X's Mail program, the Theme drawer *always* opens out of the iDVD window's left side, even if it would be completely off-screen. If you're going to use the Theme drawer, be sure to leave room on the left for it to appear. Fortunately, every OS X machine that supports iDVD also supports at least 1024 x 768 resolution and iDVD 3 requires that resolution as a minimum, so there will be room.

Menus are composed of backgrounds, text, drop zones, and buttons. The background can be a still picture or a video clip, and it can have an audio track associated. The text is just a title for your menu; you can't place text annotations on the menu.

Tip

If you want text on a menu, such as instructions or descriptive prose, like those sported by professionally produced DVDs, you'll either need to make it part of your background image or clip, or create it as a still image and place it in a drop zone. This isn't quite as dynamic as the moving menu text on *X-Men* or the like, but it's as close as you're going to come with iDVD 3. You can come a bit closer by creating a short, animated video sequence of your text in iMovie and placing that in a drop zone. (You need DVD Studio Pro or some other high-end – read expensive and complicated – DVD-authoring tool to create menus containing text frames that do everything you might wish.)

Drop zones are areas of the background into which you can place still images or video. You might think of them as a window through which you can see some or all of what's on the other side of the background. When you drop an image or movie into a drop zone, iDVD displays as much of your image as the drop zone's frame allows. As you move the pointer over the drop zone, it turns into a hand, so that you can reposition the contents by grabbing (clicking) and dragging.

Buttons can be still pictures, video clips, text, folders (links to subsidiary menu screens), or navigation aids. Buttons also have (optional) associated text, called *labels*. Even if they include a sound track, the sound doesn't play in the menu—just think of the cacophony that would result from six movie sound clips playing at once!

Note

IDID creates and maintains Navigation buttons. Although you have no control over buttons, you can change their appearance by choosing another theme, or by changing settings in the Customize drawer's Settings panel.

Don't worry if you don't like the themes iDVD offers. You can modify the themes to your heart's content. You can even change them to the point that you create your own, and we show you how in "Customizing your theme," a little later in this chapter.

Adding movie content

There's little simpler than adding a movie to your DVD. You can drag its icon into iDVD's Project pane or choose File ➪ Import ➪ Video and then navigate a file selection sheet to locate and select your movie. But the best way, in our opinion, is to use the Customize drawer's Movies panel to select your movie. Of course, if you haven't added your movie's folder to your search paths, you're back to importing or dragging.

Tip

We think that dragging and dropping is by far easier than using the Open sheet, and faster too. But if your monitor is space-constrained or you really like using the Open sheet, by all means use the Import Video method.

After you've added a movie to the Project pane, iDVD creates a button in the Project pane. Depending upon the theme, the button could be just text, an outlined object displaying one frame of your movie, or an outlined object that plays up to 30 seconds of your movie in miniature, as shown in Figure 19-2.

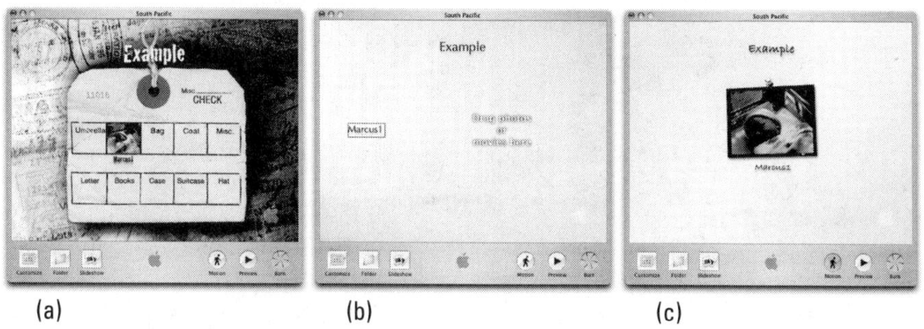

Figure 19-2: A still image button (left), a text button (middle), and a movie button (right).

Because the figures in a book such as this just capture an instant in time, you'll have to take our word for it that the still image button and the movie button are different.

If you're anything like us, a lot of your DVDs are going to contain numerous short movies. After all, at $3 a pop you don't want to waste 90 percent of the disc by including only one 6-minute movie.

iDVD allows a maximum of only six buttons per menu. To work around this constraint, you create folders which, when clicked, take you to a subordinate menu screen that can, again, have up to six buttons, and so on. As with almost each of its actions, iDVD provides two ways to add a folder:

✦ Click the Folder button in the iDVD window.

✦ Choose Project ➪ Add Folder (Shift-⌘-N).

As we stated in the beginning of this chapter, the first step in creating a DVD is to plan. Planning your DVD's menu structure by deciding which buttons go on which menu and how you want your menus organized is important. It's really annoying to have to remove a button that you've set up the way you want to make room for a folder button, only to find that you have a new home for the removed button and that you have to recreate the button.

Using either method, the result is the same. iDVD adds a button with the standard OS X folder icon on it (My Folder in Figure 19-3).

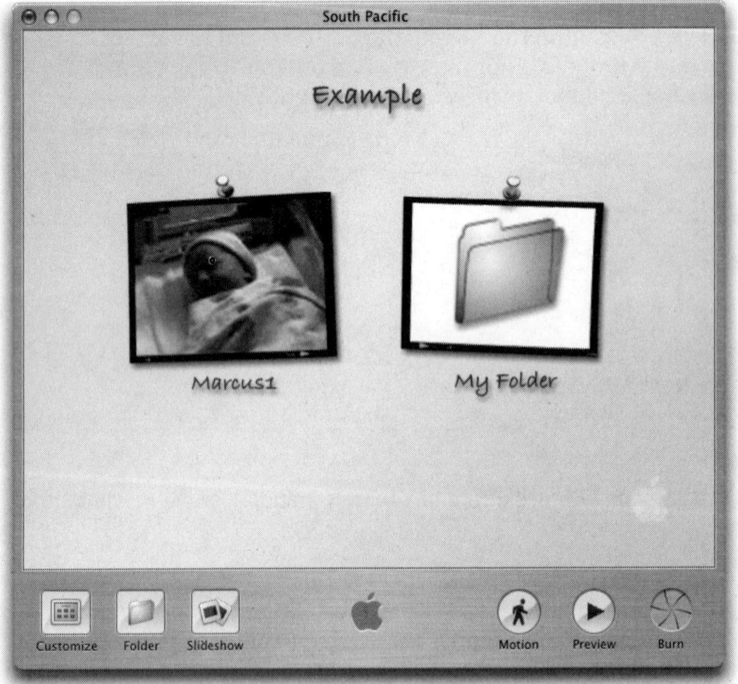

Figure 19-3: Folders let you create a hierarchical structure and work around iDVD's six-buttons-per-menu limitation.

Neither of us is fond of the default folder icon's appearance even when used in the Finder. We think it looks really tacky on a beautiful DVD menu, so here's how you can put your own graphic in its place: Just drag a graphic file's icon from the Finder or from the Customize drawer's Photos panel into the button and you have a custom folder button.

Make sure your aspect ration is correct (4:3). If it is not, iDVD will zoom the image to fill the frame and crop anything that falls outside.

A movie button is automatically given the movie's name, minus any file extension such as .mov. You might want to leave those names in place, but you're surely going to want to change the menu's title from "Click to edit text" and any folders' names from My Folder. To change any of these names, just click them and edit the text in standard Mac fashion.

Customizing your theme

If all you could do is use the themes the way Apple supplied them, iDVD would be really boring and our job would almost be done, but you can customize themes so much that Apple wouldn't even recognize them and save them under new names for future use. You can even save these modified or new themes so that other people using your Mac can use them.

You're probably a little ahead of us and have already figured out that you use the Customize drawer's Settings panel to perform this magic. Before you jump to the Settings panel, pick an existing theme as your starting point—one that has at least a vague resemblance to what you have in mind, even if it's only a motion menu or a font you want to use. Anything you can use from a theme means a little less to change.

Drop zone themes get customized a little differently. If you replace the background with a still by dragging a photo from the Photos panel, the drop zone is immutable, as shown in Figure 19-4. However, if you drag a photo or movie from the Finder into the Image/Movie well, the drop zone disappears (actually, it gets covered over).

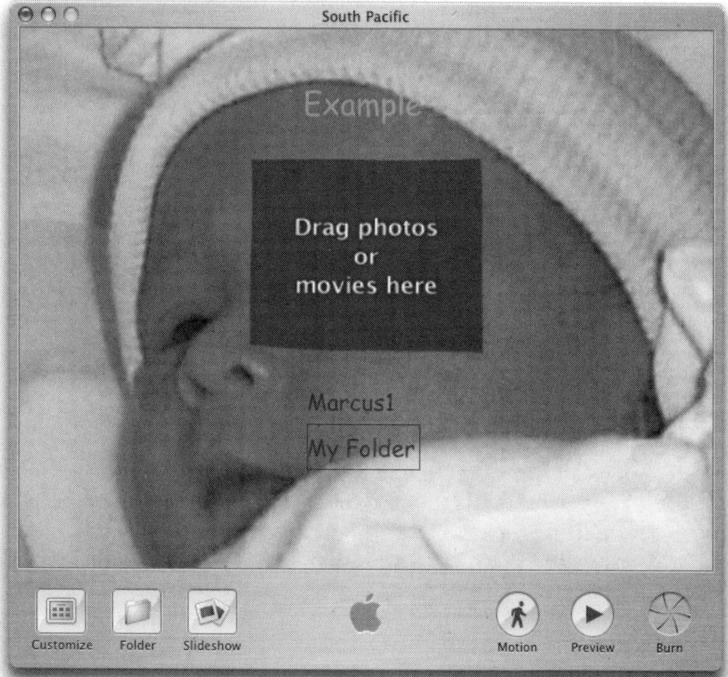

Figure 19-4: The size, shape, and position of the drop zones remain intact when you replace the background from the Photos panel.

Changing the background

Although several iDVD themes have attractive backgrounds, they probably aren't quite right for your DVD. For example, none of them fit a sports theme like your kids' soccer season highlights or an event theme like a graduation ceremony. iDVD makes it easy for you to replace the background. You can do so in one of four ways:

✦ **Via the Photos panel or Finder:** Drag a picture from the Photos panel or the Finder onto the Project pane's background.

✦ **Via the Image/Movie well:** Drag a picture or clip to the Image/Movie well. See Figure 19-5 for an example.

✦ **By choosing File ➪ Import ➪ Background Video:** A file selection sheet appears over the Project pane.

✦ **From the file selection sheet:** Navigate the file selection sheet to locate and select your new background movie or image. The image appears as your background.

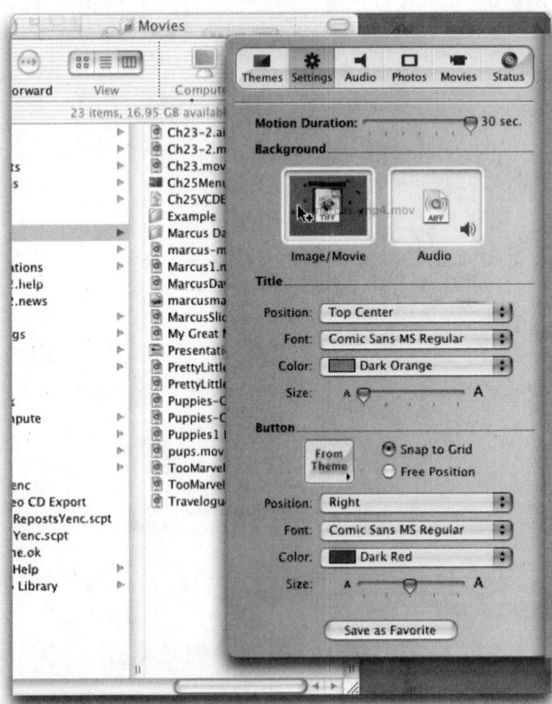

Figure 19-5: Change your theme's background by dragging a movie or image file to the well.

There is a minor difference, as mentioned earlier in this chapter, between the first method and the last two: Using the first method, drop zones are retained and using the last two they are concealed.

After you perform one of these four options, the old image is replaced and, if the movie has a soundtrack, the audio will be used, as shown in Figure 19-6. You can see the word Movie on the filmstrip icon in the Audio well to indicate that the movie's audio track is being employed. If you don't want the audio portion to play while your background is in use, just drag the icon out of the Audio well, let go, and watch it disappear in a puff of smoke.

If you want just the audio track, you can drag the movie to the Image/Movie well and, after its two tracks are in place, drag the thumbnail out of the Image/Movie well. The movie's sound will still be present in the Audio well until and unless you remove or replace it.

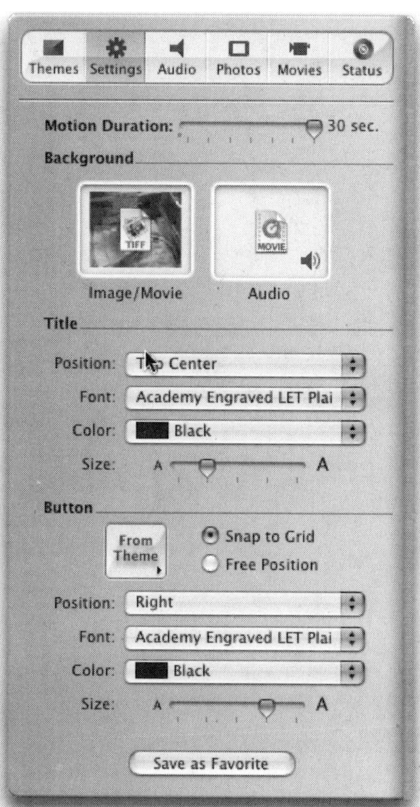

Figure 19-6: iDVD replaces the background with the clip you chose and uses the clip's soundtrack, if present for the audio.

Tip

Use QuickTime Player or some other program with a timeline to determine just how much of the clip should play. You are allowed up to 30 seconds, in 1-second increments. Use QuickTime Pro or iMovie to create a small clip that looks good when looping, because abrupt scene changes can be jarring in the background.

Understanding the TV safe area

Most TVs don't display the full width and height of the picture received. Depending upon the TV set and the signal, the portion of "lost" picture will vary. Just as iMovie uses QT Margins (see Chapter 14) to help you stay within the portion you can count on seeing displayed, iDVD defines a TV safe area for your assistance. To have iDVD place a thin red border around the TV safe area for you, as shown in Figure 19-7, choose Advanced ➪ Show TV Safe Area (⌘-T). To hide it, choose Advanced ➪ Hide TV Safe Area (⌘-T). Of course, if your DVDs are all meant to be watched using your Mac's (or a less fortunate Windows-using friend's) DVD Player software, you don't have to worry about the TV Safe area.

Figure 19-7: Stay within the borders to make sure that the content shows up on screen.

Adjusting menu titles

A menu screen has only one line of text, called the *title*. That's not one paragraph or even one sentence—it is one line! Nevertheless, iDVD gives you a lot of control over how that line appears. Using the controls in Figure 19-8, you can control the following title elements:

- ✦ **Font:** You change the font you want for your title using the Font pop-up menu.
- ✦ **Font size:** You adjust its size using the Size slider in the Font pop-up menu. You really only have five choices for size, which are the tick marks on the slider.

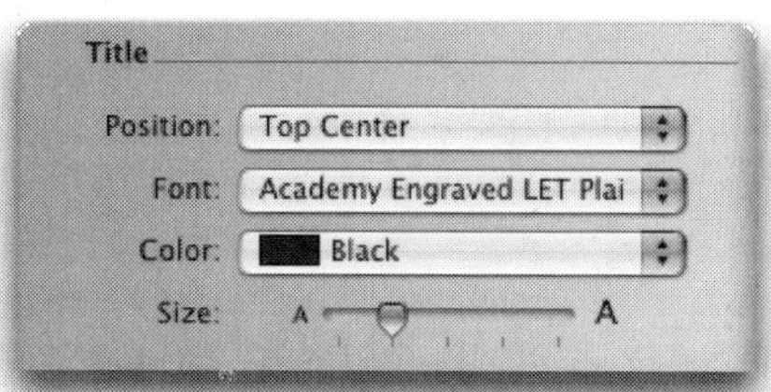

Figure 19-8: Position and manage your title's appearance with these controls.

- ✦ **Font color:** You choose the font color from the Color pop-up, as shown in Figure 19-9. You have 18 color choices: Black, White, and two shades each (light and dark) of eight more colors.
- ✦ **Location on the menu:** The Titles section's Position pop-up menu helps you change this element.

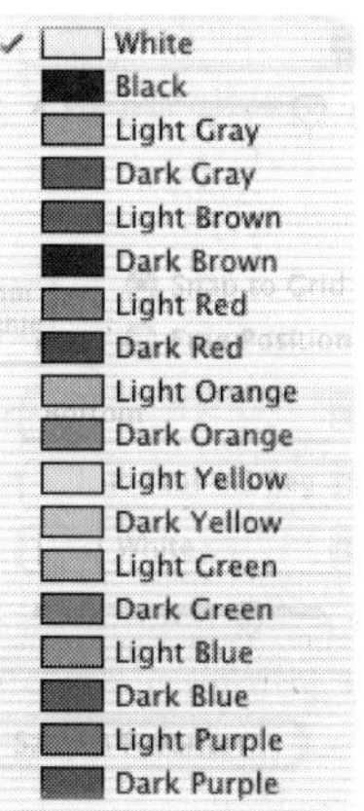

Figure 19-9: You have a limited but useful selection of title text colors.

The Title section's Position pop-up menu gives you five choices to change the location of your title on the menu, as shown in Figure 19-10:

✦ **No Title:** If you don't want a title line on your menu, choose this.

✦ **Top Left:** Left-justifies the title about one line below the top of the TV safe area.

✦ **Top Center:** Centers the title horizontally about one line below the top of the TV safe area.

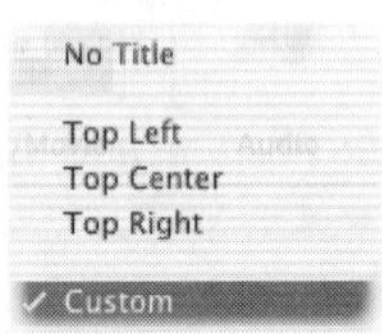

Figure 19-10: The Title section's Position pop-up menu.

✦ **Top Right:** Right-justifies the title about one line below the top of the TV safe area.

Justification and centering apply only to the area available, excluding any drop zones that are present. Thus, if a drop zone consumes much of the left half of your screen, centering will center it within the right half.

✦ **Custom:** Lets you drag the title wherever you want on the menu, even outside the TV safe area.

Configuring your buttons

A menu's buttons are links to content and any other menus. iDVD enforces a consistent appearance between buttons on a single menu but lets you define that appearance with the controls shown in Figure 19-11.

At first glance, the Button section's controls look just like the Title section's, with a couple of additions. For Font, Color, and Size, that's an accurate impression. The Position pop-up menu's contents, though, have changed, as shown in Figure 19-12.

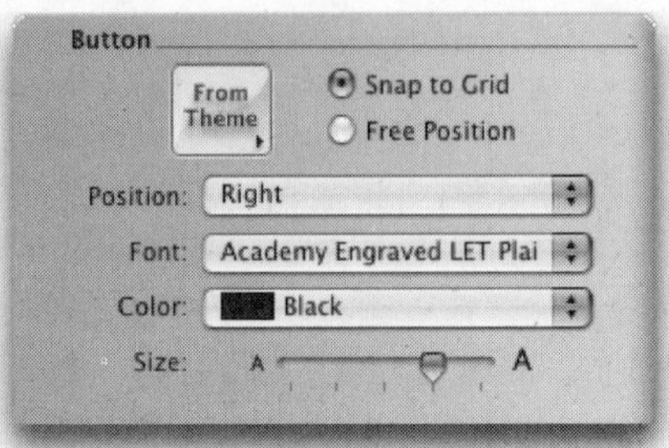

Figure 19-11: You get the same text controls for buttons as you do for menu titles, as well as a couple of extras.

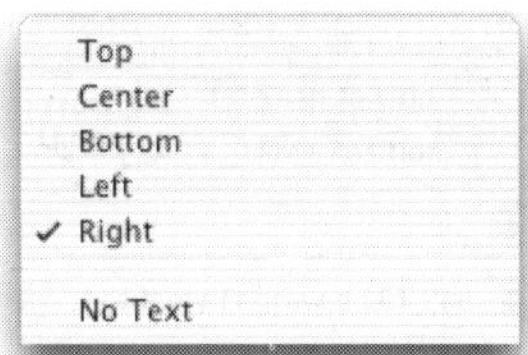

Figure 19-12: The Button section's Position pop-up menu.

Your button position choices reflect the relationship between the button and its caption, as follows:

✦ **Top, Bottom, Left, and Right:** Indicate that the caption will be centered adjacent to that button edge.

✦ **Center:** Tells iDVD to center the caption across the middle of the button. With the elimination of the Text Only button option from iDVD 2, Center is your means to place a caption in the middle of a button rectangle having no image, imitating the buttons in a Drop Zone theme.

✦ **No Text:** Means that the button will not have a caption.

No, we don't know why the Text Only option for buttons was removed from the product. Of course, because there are still themes with text only buttons, you can use one of them as your starting point when you want text only buttons.

The two radio buttons control placement of the buttons within the menu, as follows:

✦ **Snap to Grid:** Tells iDVD to place the buttons within the TV safe Area aligned according to the grid the underlying theme defines.

✦ **Free Position:** Lets you arrange the buttons wherever your artistic sense dictates within the menu, even outside the TV safe area.

The unlabeled pop-up button in the Button section's upper-left specifies the frame used for the button, as shown in Figure 19-13.

Figure 19-13: Choose a frame style for your menu's buttons from this pop-up menu.

Caution If you choose From Theme in this pop-up menu, any changes you made to the buttons' position, font, color, size, or placement changes back to those defined by the theme, so you might think of this choice as a revert option. Also, because it behaves this way, you may want to choose your button shape before you do any further customizing.

When you add one of your movies to a menu, iDVD creates a button, and that button displays your movie clip unless your theme uses a Text Only button style. iDVD provides one more button customization (or two, depending on how you look at it). Click the button, and a small controller appears, as shown in Figure 19-14. Clear the Movie checkbox and your button no longer plays. Move the slider to the frame you want for your still image (if Movie is cleared) or the frame where you want the button to start playing. You can also drag a still image or a short clip into the button's frame to replace the default display without affecting the movie that plays when the button is selected on your DVD or in Preview mode.

Figure 19-14: Control what your buttons display.

Saving your favorite themes

When you have set up your theme the way you want it, you should consider saving it for use in other iDVD projects. That's where the Save as Favorite button comes into play. Click Save as Favorite, and iDVD drops a sheet, as shown in Figure 19-15. On this sheet, you can name your theme and, optionally, make it available to other iDVD users.

Figure 19-15: Save your theme for later use.

If you don't select the "Shared for all users" checkbox, iDVD grinds away, saving a copy of the Theme in the Library/iDVD/Favorites folder in your home directory. Select this option and iDVD saves the theme in the Library/iDVD/Favorites folder at the root level of your hard disk so that any account on your Mac can access it.

The Replace existing checkbox tells iDVD whether to replace any older Favorite with the same name when you save this item. If you don't check this box, you see the alert shown in Figure 19-16. If you check this box, iDVD blithely replace the existing version.

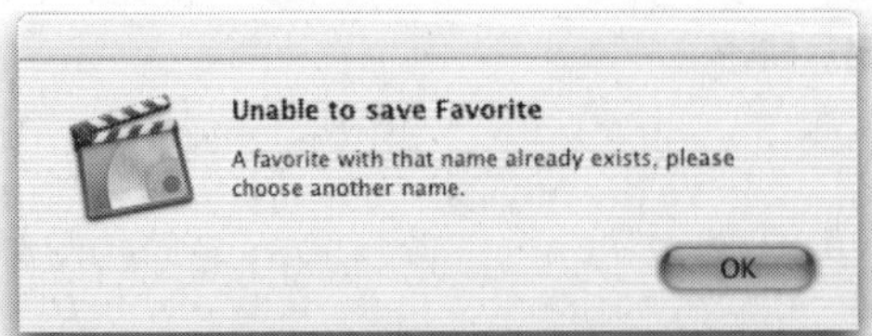

Figure 19-16: iDVD won't save the favorite over an existing favorite of the same name if the Replace existing box is unchecked.

Now, if you select the Customize drawer's Themes panel and choose Favorites from the pop-up menu, you find your theme with a small "favorites" badge, seen here next to this paragraph, in its lower-left corner.

Note You can't remove a favorite from within iDVD. To eliminate favorites you no longer want, delete them in the Finder. Remember: Personal favorites are in your home directory's Library/iDVD/Favorites folder and shared favorites are in the hard disk's Library/iDVD/Favorites folder.

Just in case you have your artistic breakthrough partway through the project, iDVD gives you a way to apply your new theme to all your project's menu screens after the fact and in one fell swoop. Simply choose Advanced ➪ Apply Theme to Project. Right below that helpful menu choice is Apply Theme to Folders, which (as the name implies) converts all your folder menu screens to the new theme while leaving the main menu as is. Of course, if you're the do-it-yourself type, you can go from menu to menu, applying the theme by selecting it in the Theme panel.

Creating a Slideshow

Slideshows are great tools to display snapshots or presentations in a visually appealing manner and the inclusion of a soundtrack can actually make a slideshow into entertainment. But, whether the folks at Apple are convinced that slideshows are integral to everyone's digital life or they simply have a slideshow fetish is not clear. QuickTime Player Pro, AppleWorks 6, iMovie, iPhoto, and now iDVD and Keynote all prominently promote slideshow creation. If you want to create slideshows, you now have a wealth of tools at your disposal.

Dennis still makes most of his slideshows in iMovie for the flexibility it provides, or in iPhoto, just because it is so easy; Bob likes to use Final Cut Pro for his slideshows, but he knows it's overkill. That said, iDVD makes slideshow creation really simple if you don't need the kinds of slide-to-slide customization and precision timing offered by iMovie or Final Cut Pro. To create a slideshow, follow these steps:

1. **Click the Slideshow button or choose Project ➪ Add Slideshow (⌘-L).** Either route creates a button named My Slideshow, as shown in Figure 19-17.
2. **Click the My Slideshow button once.** A frame, a slider, and a name-editing box appear. Use the editing box to rename your slideshow's button and the slider to set how long (up to 30 seconds) a miniature of your slideshow plays in the button. The frame just indicates that this is the currently selected button.
3. **Double-click the slideshow's button to replace the Project pane with the Slideshow Editor, shown in Figure 19-18.** Again, you have two ways to add photos or other image files to your slideshow.
4. **Drag the photos from the Finder (or another drag-enabled application, like iPhoto) or choose File ➪ Import ➪ Image.** As usual, we prefer dragging but feel free to use the menu if you prefer.

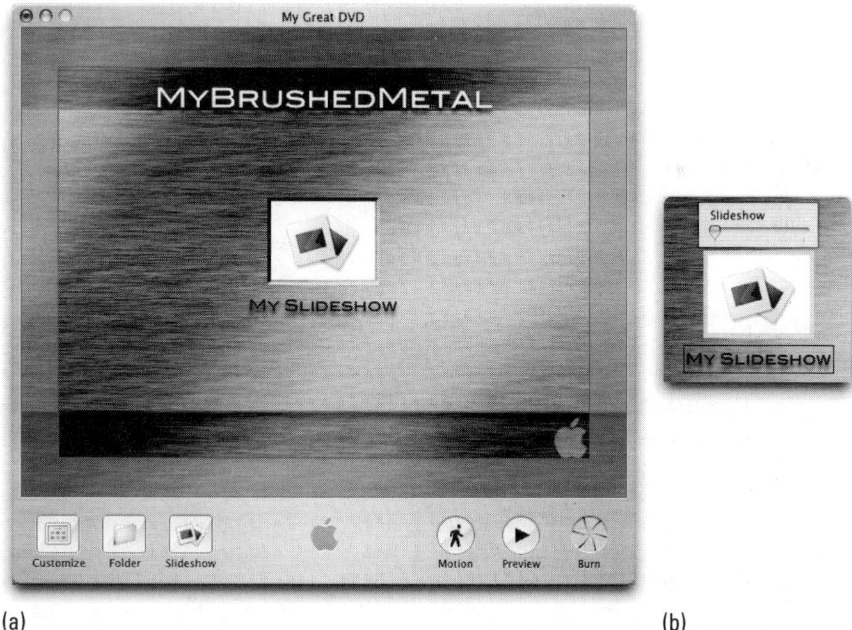

Figure 19-17: A slideshow button on your menu (a) and what a single click displays (b).

Figure 19-18: The Slideshow Editor.

Should you choose to use the File ➪ Import ➪ Image command, don't let the singular name Image fool you. You can select multiple items in the Open dialog, as shown in Figure 19-19. To select multiple contiguous items, click the first item in the range and then Shift-click the last item. To select noncontiguous items, ⌘-click them. When you have your photos selected, click the Open button or press Return or Enter.

Note

AppleScript support was added in iDVD 2.1. To show off its scriptability, one of the free scripts Apple made available (`www.apple.com/applescript/idvd`) is the iPhoto to iDVD Slideshow script. Just drag items from iPhoto to the script's icon and, using the script's preferences, iDVD adds the photos as an iDVD slideshow with a number of the options preset. With the Photos panel available in iDVD 3, this script is of interest only for historic and educational reasons. You can modify it to work with other applications.

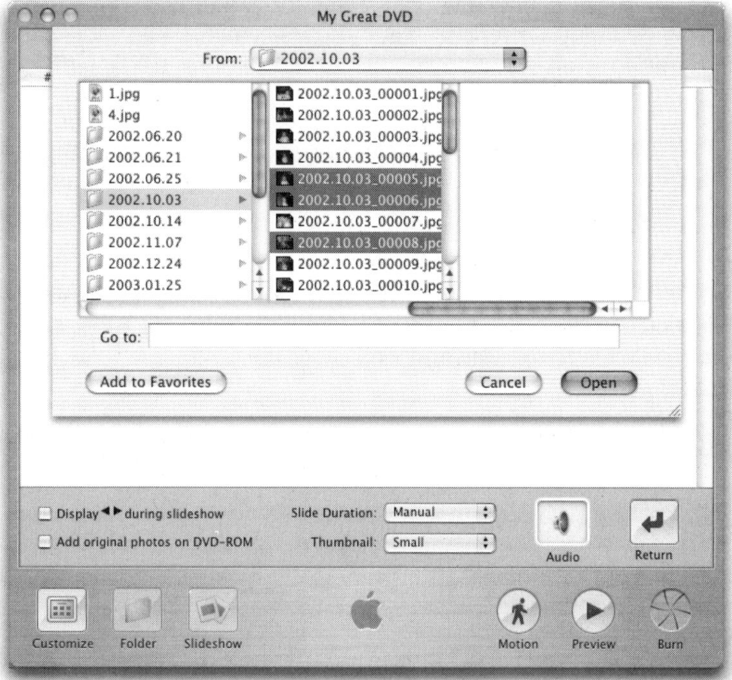

Figure 19-19: You can select multiple items when importing images.

5. **Select desired options from the bottom of the Slideshow Editor.** The Slideshow Editor has six controls that you can adjust:

   • **Display ◀ ▶ during slideshow:** This option places arrowheads on the screen for previous and next slide. These arrowheads are not clickable, just a reminder to your viewer to use the previous and next buttons on their remote control to move from slide to slide.

   • **Add original photos to DVD-ROM:** Selecting this option tells iDVD to include copies of each image in the data portion (DVD-ROM) of your DVD when you burn the disc. Doing this allows people to whom you give copies to insert it in their computers (assuming they have a DVD reading drive) and copy the originals to their hard disks.

- **Slide Duration:** This pop-up menu enables you to choose how long each slide should play. If there is an audio track, you have an extra choice: Fit To Audio. This is a handy choice because it tells iDVD to divide the length of the audio track by the number of slides so that the last slide finishes at the same time as your song. When you choose Manual from this pop-up, viewers must advance from slide to slide manually, using their DVD player's remote control; this is iDVD's default behavior.
- **Thumbnail:** Choose whether to show Small or Large thumbnails in the Slideshow Editor using the Thumbnail pop-up menu.
- **Audio:** Drop an AIFF, WAV, or MP3 file in this well to use it as your slideshow's audio track. In fact, you can drag pretty much any QuickTime-compatible file to the well and iDVD uses the first audio track it finds in the file.

After you have images in your slideshow, dragging a song to the Audio well switches the Slide Duration menu choice from Manual to Fit To Audio.

- **Return:** Click this button when you want to exit the Slideshow Editor.

iDVD has certain behaviors and limitations that affect how imported images appear in slideshows. Keep the following things in mind when importing images:

✦ **iDVD scales the image to fit the screen:** Images that don't have a 4:3 aspect ratio are going to display a letterbox effect. You should consider matting portrait images against an attractive background to avoid large black stripes on the sides, for example. Similarly, images smaller than 640 x 480 exhibit jaggies and other artifacts as they're enlarged. The upside is that larger images, such as 1280 x 960 or 2048 x 1536, scale down beautifully, so you don't need to scale larger images before importing them and, if you tell iDVD to save them to DVD-ROM, the full-resolution image will be stored.

✦ **You can reorder the images in your slideshow at any time before burning:** Just drag them in the Slideshow Editor, as shown in Figure 19-20.

✦ **If you choose Fit To Audio, manually advancing the slide (or moving back) moves the audio playhead:** This happens because each slide is linked to a specific portion of the audio track. iDVD is trying to synchronize the video and audio to end together.

✦ **You're limited to 99 slides in a slideshow:** If you have more than that, you're going to have to break them up into multiple slideshows or cull the list down to 99 (or fewer).

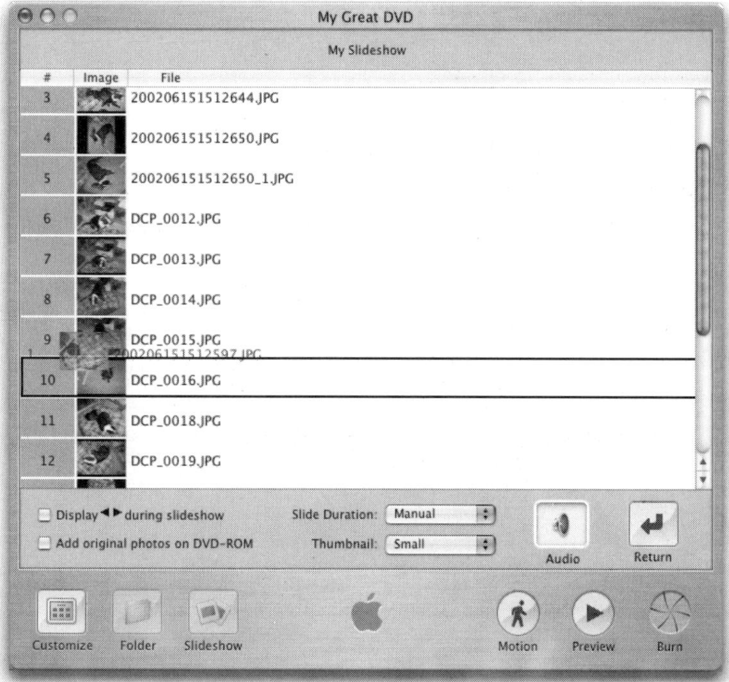

Figure 19-20: Reorder your slides by dragging them in the Slideshow Editor's list.

- **Changing your Preferences setting to Add Slideshows to DVD-ROM does not affect existing slideshows:** However, it automatically selects the Add to DVD-ROM checkbox for new slideshows.
- **For proper viewing on a TV screen, you should choose iDVD ⇨ Preferences and ensure that the "Always scale slides to TV safe area" checkbox is selected:** This results in a letterbox effect when you Preview your slideshow. See "Previewing Your DVD" later in this chapter.

Video is great, but some subjects display better in a slideshow. For example, infants don't really move enough to make video truly entertaining, but a slideshow with a musical background works great when showing off the newborn. Similarly, a slideshow is a wonderful way to commemorate a prom night. Of course, there are also the more pedestrian business slideshow uses, like presentations and catalogs. Maybe Apple isn't obsessed, just observant.

Previewing Your DVD

One frequent complaint about iDVD 1.0 was that you had to burn your DVD to see what it would look like, and at $10 a burn (the price hadn't dropped to $5 or $3 yet), creating DVDs could quickly get expensive. iDVD 2.0 responded to this criticism with the Preview button, shown in the margin to the left of this paragraph, and iDVD 3 retains it (if it ain't broke, don't fix it). When you click the Preview button, it turns blue, and a remote control appears, as shown in Figure 19-21.

Figure 19-21: Preview your DVD before burning using the on-screen remote control.

iDVD's on-screen remote control has three groups of buttons and a slider:

✦ **Four arrow buttons:** You use the four buttons surrounding the Enter button to navigate to and select buttons on your menu. Your keyboard arrow keys and the Return and Enter keys are synonymous with these remote control buttons.

✦ **Previous Slide, Pause/Play, Stop, and Next Slide:** You can find these buttons in a row just above the navigation buttons. The Pause button toggles to Play when clicked.

✦ **menu**, **title**, and **exit:** Clicking menu takes you to the menu for the currently playing movie; otherwise it does nothing. Clicking title takes you to your main DVD menu (if you have multiple menus). Clicking exit terminates Preview mode.

Clicking either menu or title while watching a movie or slideshow and then clicking menu again returns you to your movie or slideshow at the point you interrupted play.

Tip

You can also exit Preview mode by clicking the Preview button.

✦ **Volume slider:** At the bottom of the remote control is a volume slider, which controls the volume of your preview.

If you're like us, you find the motion menus distracting while you're creating your DVD structure (besides the fact that they slow things down), so you probably turn them off while authoring. Remember to turn them back on by either clicking the Motion button or choosing Advanced ➪ Motion (⌘-J) before entering Preview mode. If you don't, you won't see the DVD the way you intend. Instead, it plays without motion menus, motion buttons, or menu audio.

Burning Your DVD

You've created your DVD, previewed, edited, and previewed it again until you're certain that everything is just the way you want it, and now the moment of truth has arrived. It's finally time to burn your DVD.

The interface to burning a DVD should be really familiar to you — it's the same interface you see for burning CDs in iTunes.

Before you burn your DVD, on the Customize drawer's Status panel, check to see how much progress iDVD has made toward encoding your content, as shown in Figure 19-22. You can also see how much of your DVD this opus uses. When you see a lot of the disc going to waste, you might decide to include some items in the DVD-ROM portion and let the disc do double-duty — movie *and* storage.

For more on burning CDs in iTunes, refer to Chapter 4. For more on DVD-ROM capabilities, turn to Chapter 20.

When you click the camera-shutter-like Burn button (shown left), it opens in an iris effect to reveal a pulsing button, reminiscent of a radioactive materials label. Click the pulsing button and you'll see one of the two alerts shown in Figure 19-23.

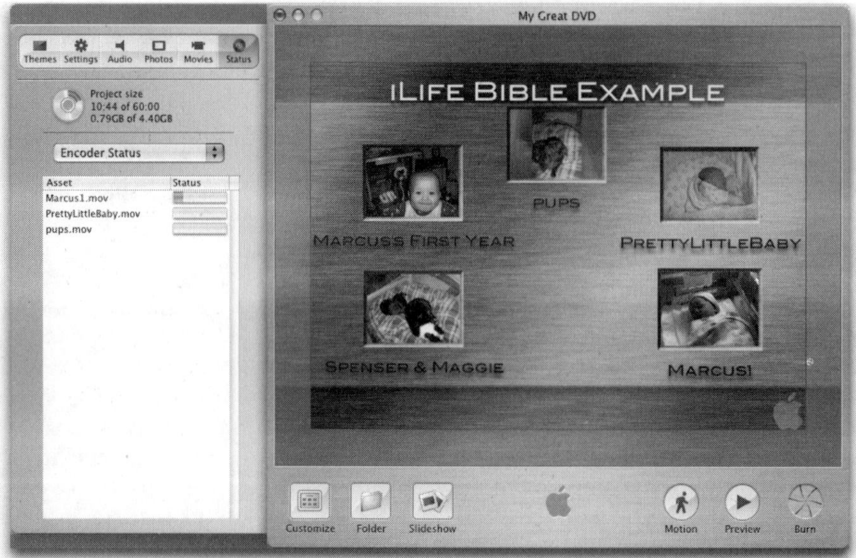

Figure 19-22: Check to see how much of your disc is being used and how much progress has been made encoding your content.

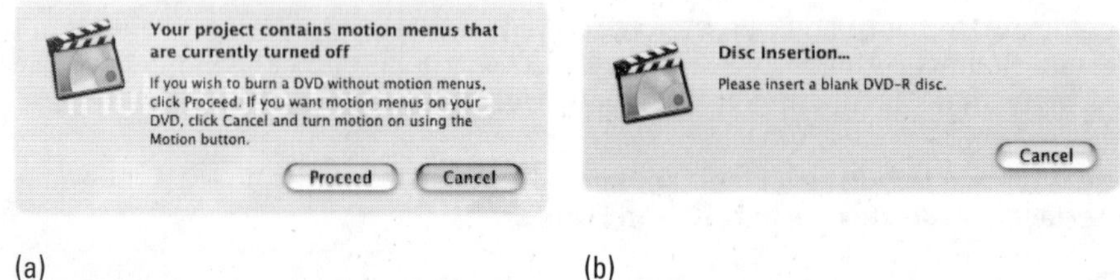

(a) (b)

Figure 19-23: If you have Motion turned off, iDVD gives you a gentle reminder when you click Burn (a); otherwise, you'll be prompted to insert a DVD-R (b).

Assuming that you have Motion turned on and that you inserted a blank disc, iDVD starts the burning process either immediately or as soon as it's done encoding your DVD's content. We wish that we could tell you the process is fast, but it depends on how much content is being burned, how fast your Mac is, which model of SuperDrive you have in your Mac, and the speed rating of your DVD-R media. The original SuperDrive used the Pioneer A103 mechanism and it burned at 1x. In other words, burning 30 minutes of video took 30 minutes plus some overhead time. The A104 SuperDrives can burn at 2x speed, so that same 30-minute disc only takes 15 minutes plus the overhead when using DVD-Rs rated at 2x or better. At the time we're writing this (February 2003), the A105 is state-of-the-art and, if you use 4x-rated media, you'll get that same 30-minute burn done in 7.5 minutes (plus overhead).

Here's our standard recommendation: Add more memory if your encoding takes a long time. You can, as Apple says, run iDVD on a 256MB Mac, but we found that upgrading from 256MB to 768MB in Dennis's flat-panel iMac cut the encoding time by almost 50 percent. Encoding to MPEG-2 is a time-consuming, processor-intensive, memory-gobbling operation and anything you can do to give the encoder more memory or a faster processor will help.

Summary

In this chapter, you've learned the basics of authoring, previewing, and burning your DVD. You've seen how to select and customize themes, add video content, create a hierarchical menu structure, create slideshows, operate iDVD's remote control when previewing, and burn your DVD.

✦ ✦ ✦

CHAPTER 20

Getting Advanced with iDVD

✦ ✦ ✦ ✦

In This Chapter

Storing data on your DVD

Monitoring your DVD's status

Using iDVD Companion

AppleScripting iDVD

✦ ✦ ✦ ✦

iDVD 3.0 is a marketer's dream and a Bible author's nightmare. It's simple, elegant, useful, and easy-to-use. And you get great results even if you barely know what you're doing.

Although this makes iDVD easy to sell to users (and, we suspect, reduces Apple's support costs), it makes it tough for us authors. How do we cover the advanced functionality when the program offers exactly zero advanced features?

In fact, for a time we thought this was going to be the shortest chapter either of us had ever written. Rescuing us from this dilemma, Apple released iDVD 2.1 in July 2002 and finally gave us some advanced features to cover, including DVD-ROM data storage on your DVD, using AppleScript to automate iDVD and communicate with other programs, and a handy utility program, iDVD Companion (written in AppleScript Studio and with source code available), to help you construct and rearrange your iDVD menus. Then, in January of 2003, with iDVD 3.0.1, Apple gave us chapter markers, and integrated iDVD more closely with the other iLife applications by adding media browsers.

Storing Data on Your DVD

Just as you can create multitrack CDs where part of the disc is an audio CD and part is a data CD, you can create multitrack DVDs. iDVD 2.1 added this capability to iDVD's feature set. But you aren't limited to just the slideshow images. You can add any files you want to the DVD-ROM portion, so long as there is available space.

Refer to Chapter 19 to find out how to have iDVD automatically add a slideshow's images to your disc's DVD-ROM portion.

To add data to your DVD, follow these steps:

1. **In the Customize drawer, click the Status button.** The Status panel appears.
2. **Click the pop-up menu just below the disc usage image and choose DVD-ROM Contents.** Don't ask us to explain why a data collection and management function is in the Customize drawer. The best answer we can come up with is a guess: There wasn't anyplace better to put it. Actually, that guess applies to the Status tab in general, which we finish covering a little later in this chapter.

   iDVD creates a Slideshows folder in the DVD-ROM portion as the resting place for the images added when you have iDVD automatically add a slideshow's image files, either in the Slideshow pane or in your iDVD preferences.
3. **In the Finder, locate the files you want included and drag them onto the Customize drawer's Status panel.** See Figure 20-1. These files can be anything: MPEG-1 versions of your movies, Microsoft Office documents, AppleWorks documents, MP3 files, and so on.

Figure 20-1: You manage your disc's DVD-ROM portion in the Customize drawer's Status panel.

You need to have the original files available when you choose to burn the DVD so that iDVD can verify that they haven't changed since they were encoded. This means that files on removable media or network servers must be present when you burn a DVD referencing them.

In an unusual move for iDVD, no menu item or button is available for adding other items to the DVD-ROM portion. All you have available is the method we usually find the easiest, drag and drop. See Figure 20-2.

Depending upon how long it takes, a progress sheet might appear briefly over the Project pane.

Although you can't tell in the black-and-white image, iDVD even color-codes the relative amount of disc space used in the little disc icon (upper-left of the Status panel). The DVD content is green and the DVD-ROM content is blue.

4. **If you change your mind about including some file(s) on the DVD-ROM, just select the ones you don't want and press the Delete key.** The files are removed from the Status panel.

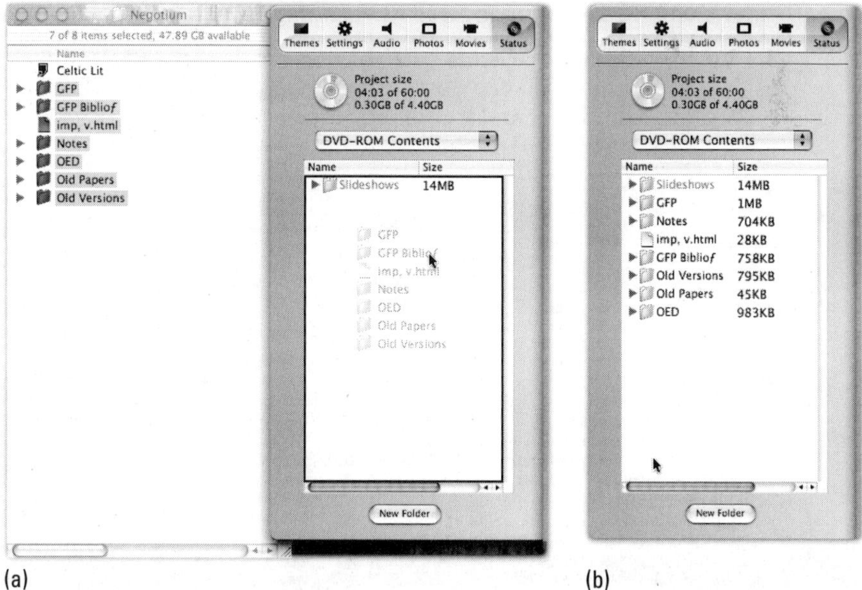

Figure 20-2: Drag your files into the DVD-ROM Contents area (a); iDVD adds them to your project (b).

You can even use the New Folder button (at the bottom of the Status panel) to create folders in the DVD-ROM and reorganize the files by dragging files into or out of folders, just like a Finder list view.

Monitoring Your DVD's Status

When it comes to monitoring what's on your DVD, iDVD suffers from a multiple-personality disorder with part of the information in the Customize drawer and part of it in the Project Info dialog. If you're just putting one or two movies on the DVD, monitoring what's present probably isn't too critical, but with larger projects that include multiple movies and slideshows, you will want to use iDVD's monitoring capabilities to verify that your DVD's content matches your project checklist. To monitor the status of your DVD:

1. **Choose DVD-ROM Contents from the Customize drawer's Status panel pop-up menu.** See the previous section for further instructions. Doing this allows you to find out what's on the DVD-ROM portion.
2. **Switch the pop-up menu back to Encoder Status.** This allows you to see how far along the background MPEG-2 encoding has gotten.
3. **Choose Project ⇨ Project Info (⌘-I).** This displays the Project Info dialog shown in Figure 20-3. You do this when you want to know what files are being used in your project and where they reside on your Mac.

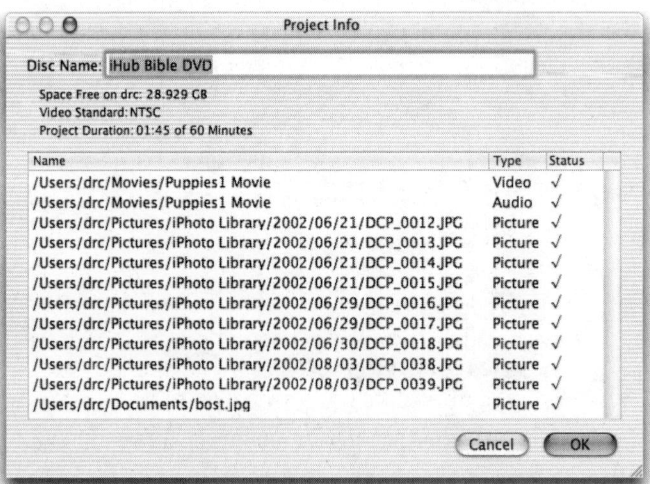

Figure 20-3: The Project Info dialog displays a list of all your project's files.

We find it strange that Status is in the Customize drawer rather than part of the Project Info dialog. Apple's gotten really good at creating tabbed dialogs, keeping related information and functionality together and their reasons for not doing so here escape us.

iLife Integration

With iDVD 3, Apple dramatically enhanced the integration of iDVD with the other iLife applications, iPhoto, iTunes, and iMovie. iDVD uses media browsers to let you directly import images from iPhoto, movies from iMovie, and songs from iTunes, in addition to importing them from the Finder.

iDVD lets you browse your media files by clicking the Customize button, then clicking on the Audio, Photos, or Movies buttons at the top of the Customize drawer. The media browsers make it simple to locate a particular file, then drag and drop it where you want to use it. All three of the media browsers have a search field at the bottom of the drawer. Type part of the name of a file, and any files that don't match disappear from the list.

- **Audio:** Clicking Audio allows you to browse your iTunes library, selecting a playlist or the entire library from the top, with the artists, names, and times of each song displayed in three columns below. Click on a column heading to sort by that heading. Click the Play button in the bottom of the drawer to preview a song.

  You can add music to a slideshow by double-clicking the button of the slideshow you want to enhance, then clicking the Customize button to open the Customize drawer. Next, click Audio and drag a song from the iTunes browser to the Audio well at the bottom of the Slideshow editor.

- **Photos:** Clicking this button displays the iPhoto media browser. This browser lets you browse your entire iPhoto collection. Images from the currently selected album are displayed as thumbnails.

  You can customize a menu button by dragging an image from the iPhoto browser to the button. In addition, you can replace the background image of a menu by dragging an image from the iPhoto browser to the iDVD window.

- **Movies:** Clicking this button lets you browse the movies in your Movies folder, or any other folders you've added to your iDVD Preferences. Remember, iDVD doesn't see movies contained in subfolders; if you want to be able to browse those, you'll have to add them individually to the Preferences.

For more on setting iDVD preferences, refer to Chapter 18.

Create a Slideshow Using the iDVD Media Browsers

The easiest way to turn an iPhoto album into a slideshow with background music is to use the iPhoto and iTunes browsers. To do so:

1. **Click Customize.** Doing this opens the Customize drawer.
2. **Click the Photos button.** Doing this selects an album to convert to a slideshow.
3. **Drag an album from the album list to the iDVD window.** You'll see a Slideshow button appear with the name of the album you selected.
4. **Double-click the new slideshow's button.** The Slideshow editing window displays, which allows you to add music to your slideshow.
5. **Click the Audio button in the Customize drawer.** Your iTunes Library and playlists display.
6. **Select a song and drag it to the Audio well in the lower third of the Slideshow edit window.** The duration of the slides is automatically set to fit the length of the audio file. However, you can change the order in which they appear by clicking and dragging the thumbnails in the Slideshow editor.

Using iDVD Companion

Although the iDVD themes do a good job arranging buttons against the provided backgrounds, most people will probably not use the themes out of the box. They will opt for their own backgrounds and will arrange the buttons to the best effect. This involves using the Free Position setting in the Customize drawer's Settings panel.

Unfortunately, free position means just that — drag the button into place and let go. There are no rulers, no grid, and none of the other alignment aids we've come to expect in a design layout environment. You do everything by eyeballing the result and hoping that what you've done is close enough.

The remedy is a wonderful little accessory program called iDVD Companion. iDVD Companion was first introduced as part of iDVD 2.1's AppleScript support and is a free download from `www.apple.com/applescript/idvd/companion.html`. A collection of AppleScripts, packaged together by AppleScript Studio into a normal OS X application (Cocoa, if that matters to you), iDVD Companion gives you several nice enhancements:

✦ **Controls:** A variety of alignment and placement controls for your buttons

✦ **Back buttons:** Access to the Back button on subordinate menus

✦ **AppleScripts:** Import songs from iTunes to use as background music, photos from iPhoto to use as backgrounds or button images, and albums from iPhoto to create a slideshow

Figure 20-4 shows iDVD Companion running with iDVD in the background.

Figure 20-4: iDVD Companion provides a palette to adjust iDVD menu buttons and titles.

Employing the iDVD Companion palette

iDVD Companion's tabbed palette (Figure 20-5) enables you to move selected buttons, optionally including the menu title, up, down, left, or right in 1-, 6-, 36-, or 72-pixel increments using the Nudge tab.

You can choose Edit⇨Select Back Button (⌘-B) to reposition the Back button, something not allowed in the iDVD application's interface.

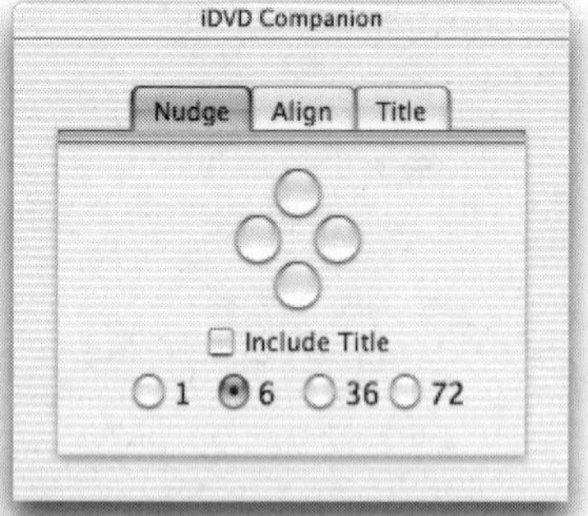

Figure 20-5: Nudge selected items by set increments.

The Align tab (see Figure 20-6) enables you to align the edges of two or more selected buttons. If you have only one button selected, nothing happens except that you hear whatever alert sound you set in your OS X sound preferences.

Figure 20-6: Align the left, right, top, or bottom edges of multiple selected buttons.

Use the Title tab to specify an absolute position for your menu's title (Figure 20-7). When you first display the Title tab, iDVD Companion fills in the current title position. The position is measured in pixels from the top-left corner of the Project pane.

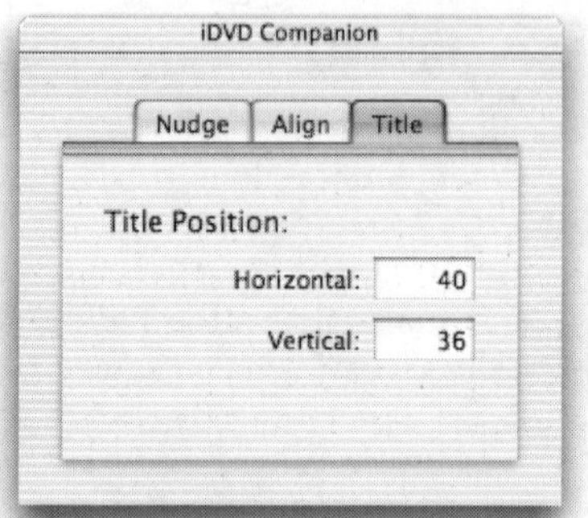

Figure 20-7: Precisely position the menu title using the Title tab.

Using the iDVD Companion menu bar

In addition to providing a palette full of positioning tools, iDVD Companion adds even more features in its menus.

File menu

The File menu has only one choice: Generate Projects. This choice sprouts a submenu, which (as of the initial release) has only two templates. The first generates a template of slideshows, as shown in Figure 20-8. The second option, Single Movie (iMac) when used with iDVD 3, results in an error message because the referenced theme graphics aren't present.

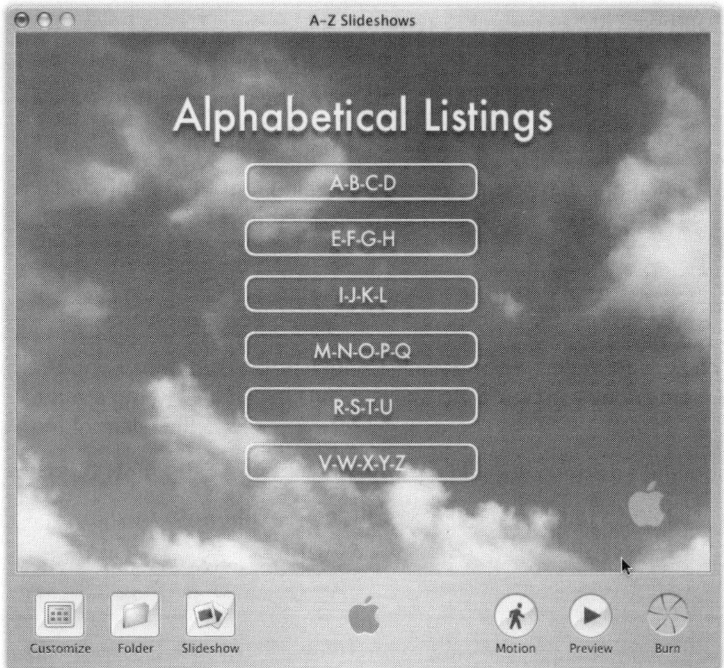

Figure 20-8: Create an alphabetic arrangement of your slideshows.

Edit menu

The iDVD Companion's Edit menu doesn't sport any of the traditional Undo, Cut, Copy, or Paste commands; those are left to iDVD's Edit menu. What you get are the handy Select Back Button (⌘-B) command, unavailable in iDVD. Additionally, you find a few time- and click-saving commands, including Delete Every Button, Select All Buttons (⌘-A), and Deselect All Buttons (⌘-D). Keep in mind that if you select Delete Every Button, there's no Undo available.

Go menu

The Go menu relieves you of having to navigate your project's menu structure to find a specific menu or slideshow. Choosing Go ➪ Go To Menu (⌘-G) displays a list of all your project's menus, assuming that you have named them as described in the "Menu menu" discussion later in this section. Just select the one you want, and Companion tells iDVD to display that menu. Similarly, choosing Go ➪ Go To Slideshow (Option-⌘-G) displays a list of your slideshows so that you can select the one you want to appear in the Project pane, as shown in Figure 20-9.

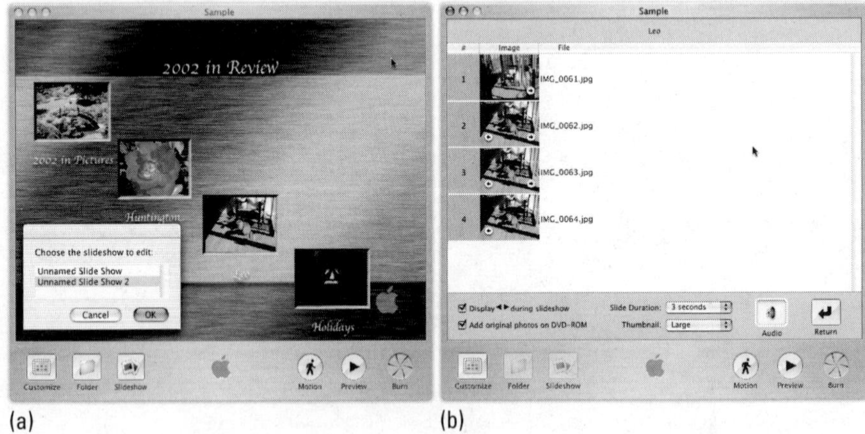

Figure 20-9: Choose your slideshow (a); iDVD Companion directs iDVD to position it in the Project pane (b).

As you can see in Figure 20-10, Unnamed slideshow isn't a very helpful designation. Use the Button ➪ Name Selected Button command described a little later in this section so that you can tell your slideshows apart.

Theme menu

The Theme menu's first two choices, Choose Theme (⌘-T) and Toggle Motion (Option-⌘-M) aren't very interesting because their equivalents are readily available in iDVD's interface. However, the Layouts submenu provides you with four scripts to arrange the current menu's buttons, assuming that there are four buttons:

- ✦ **4 Corners:** Places your buttons at the four corners of the TV safe area.
- ✦ **4 Center Diamond:** Places your buttons in a diamond (rhombus) arrangement, with one on the top row, two in the middle row, and one on the bottom row.
- ✦ **4 Across Top:** Places your buttons along the top row within the TV safe area.
- ✦ **4 Across Bottom:** Analogous to 4 Across Top, except that the buttons are now at the bottom of the TV safe area.

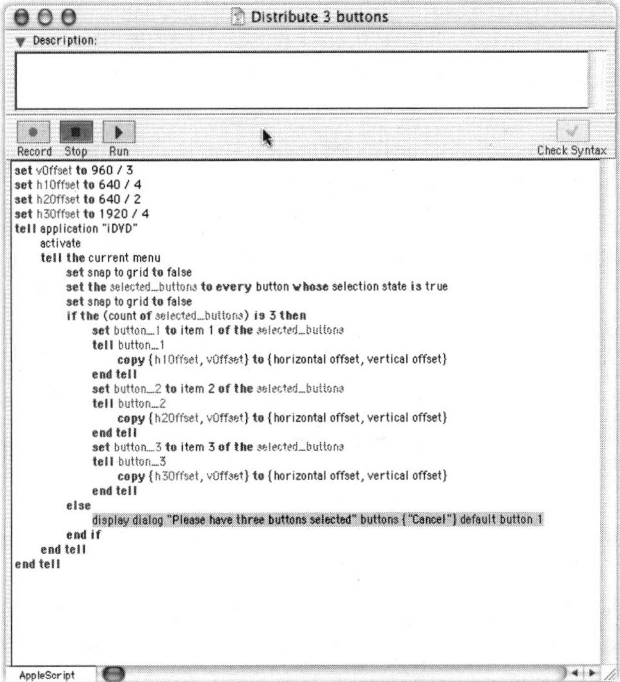

Figure 20-10: Our little AppleScript distributes three buttons evenly.

You'll get an AppleScript error message that the variable `button_list` is not defined. This is not a fatal error, and your existing buttons will be positioned according to the chosen layout.

Menu menu

The Menu menu offers eight choices:

✦ **Name Current Menu (⌘-N):** You name your menus to make them accessible via the Go menu's Go To Menu command.

✦ **Snap To Grid • On (⌘-–):** Equivalent to clicking the Snap to Grid radio button in the Theme drawer's Customize tab.

✦ **Snap To Grid • Off (⌘-=):** Equivalent to clicking the Free Position radio button in the Theme drawer's Customize tab.

✦ **Import Audio From iTunes (Option-⌘-I):** This option brings iTunes to the front, while displaying a floating window, and enables you to select a track from your iTunes Library. Click Transfer in the floating window and iDVD comes to the front with that audio track playing as your current menu's background audio.

- **Import Image From iPhoto (Option-Shift-⌘-I):** Enables you to select an image from your iPhoto Library to use as the current menu's background.
- **Import Album From iPhoto:** Enables you to select an iPhoto album to use as a slideshow in iDVD.
- **Delete Background Image (Option-⌘-D):** Removes any background image, reverting to the theme's original background.
- **Delete Background Audio (Option-Shift-⌘-D):** Removes any background audio file you've added to the current menu.

You might get an AppleScript error message telling you that the album contains no images if you use the Import Album From iPhoto menu and the script will fail. Don't worry, your images are fine.

Button menu

The Button menu offers three choices:

- **Name Selected Button (Option-⌘-N):** This does as the name implies. As noted previously, this is really handy when you have a lot of slideshows.
- **Set Button Position (Option-⌘-P):** Enables you to precisely position a button on the menu. The position is relative to the menu's upper-left corner and a menu is 640 x 480 pixels.
- **Swap Button Positions (Option-⌘-S):** Requires that you have two buttons selected. If so, it will swap their positions within the menu.

AppleScripting iDVD

We're not going to attempt to teach you AppleScript here. If you want to learn AppleScript, we direct you to `www.apple.com/applescript`, where you'll find an abundance of tutorial references as well as online and downloadable documentation. This discussion assumes that you have at least a passing acquaintance with AppleScript, what a script is, and how Script Editor works.

iDVD 2.1 introduced the first scriptable version of iDVD. iDVD Companion, described earlier in this chapter, provides a wealth of example scripts, most of which are available as separate downloads from `www.apple.com/applescript/idvd`, where you'll also find several additional sample scripts.

If you get error messages when attempting to open iDVD's AppleScript Dictionary in Script Editor, check `www.apple.com/applescript/idvd` for the Scripting Terminology updater. Early releases of the iDVD 2.1 updater did not include this critical resource. The problem was fixed in iDVD 3.

We don't know about you, but we find modifying existing scripts the easiest way to start scripting a new application. We encourage you to peruse the sample scripts to find snippets that do something similar to what you want and tweak to your heart's content. Before you know it, you'll be creating useful and original scripts.

One of our biggest quibbles with iDVD is the lack of fine control over button placement and alignment. iDVD Companion provides some useful tools to ease our pain, but it is sometimes a bit cumbersome. What we're going to do is write a little script that distributes three buttons horizontally, spaced about the horizontal center, and one-third of the way up from the bottom.

This boils down to aligning the center of each button with specific grid points. Vertically, the center should be two-thirds of the way down from the top of the screen. Because a screen is 480 pixels tall, the button centers should be 320 pixels from the top. Similarly, we are placing buttons one-fourth, one-half, and three-fourths of the way across the 640-pixels wide screen. Doing that arithmetic, we find that the centers of the buttons should be 160, 320, and 480 pixels, respectively, from the screen's left edge.

As you can see in Figure 20-10, we perform these computations at the top of the script. After that, we make sure that iDVD won't override our computations with its preset grid coordinates. Next, it's just error-checking to make sure that exactly three buttons are selected and telling the buttons where to position their origins (centers).

Note

In iDVD 2.1, the offsets were based on the button's lower-left corner. The iDVD 3.0 dictionary has the origin being the button center, which makes the computation much simpler; however, you need to modify existing scripts that position based on these offsets.

If the user has selected more or fewer than three buttons, the alert dialog shown in Figure 20-11 appears.

Figure 20-12 shows before and after images of what happens when the script runs with three buttons selected.

As you peruse the example scripts and let your imagination soar, you'll come up with ideas to make your iDVD use even easier. Give it a shot. Programming AppleScript isn't as hard as you might think. Just remember that computers, even Macs, are just incredibly literal and obedient idiots. If you forget to tell them to do something, they don't do it; they do *exactly* what you tell them, without understanding nuance or assuming anything.

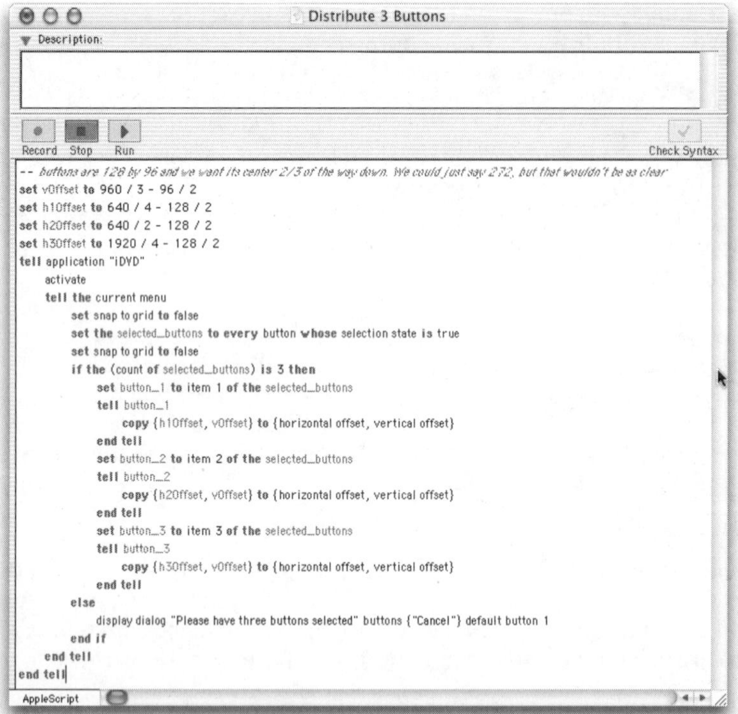

Figure 20-11: We have to let them know that they must select exactly three buttons.

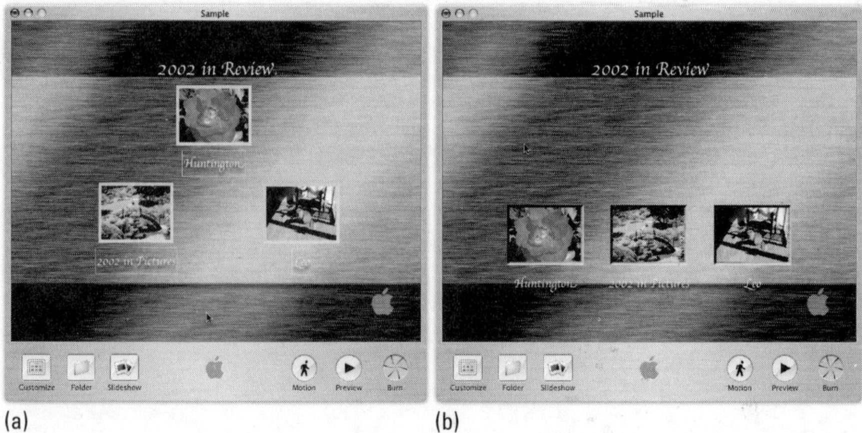

Figure 20-12: Our menu with three buttons selected (a); our menu after iDVD has positioned the buttons (b).

Summary

In this chapter, you learned how to use the DVD-ROM portion of your DVD and how to monitor your DVD's status as iDVD does its work. You learned to use the media browsers. You saw how to take advantage of the AppleScript capabilities Apple includes and how to use the very handy little utility, iDVD Companion, built with AppleScript Studio, to access some iDVD capabilities not present in its menus.

✦ ✦ ✦

CHAPTER 21

iDVD Tips, Tricks, and Techniques

✦ ✦ ✦ ✦

In This Chapter

Inside projects

Inside themes

Planning your iDVD project

Inside encoding and compression

✦ ✦ ✦ ✦

We have to tell you up front: This is going to be a relatively short chapter and you may even find it a bit geeky. iDVD is a great entry-level program for authoring, encoding, and burning your DVDs, but it's pretty much "what you see is what you get" and Chapters 19 and 20 pretty much exhausted iDVD's repertoire. Even the Advanced menu isn't very advanced.

There are currently no tools to create themes from scratch. All you can do is customize the ones included with iDVD. And you can't control the encoding process other than to force a lower bit rate by putting more than 60 minutes of content on your DVD.

What we do in this chapter is tell you how DVD projects and themes are constructed. Next, we give you a few tips on planning your projects. Finally, we finish up by covering a couple of esoteric points about MPEG-2 encoding and Photo-JPEG.

Inside Projects

When you create an iDVD project you get a document icon just as you do when you create an AppleWorks document or a FileMaker Pro database, right? Well, almost right. Unlike most documents, an iDVD project is really a folder that the OS X Finder treats like a single file, just as it does with most applications.

You can see this by Control-clicking the project file, as shown in Figure 21-1, and noticing the contextual menu's Show Package Contents item.

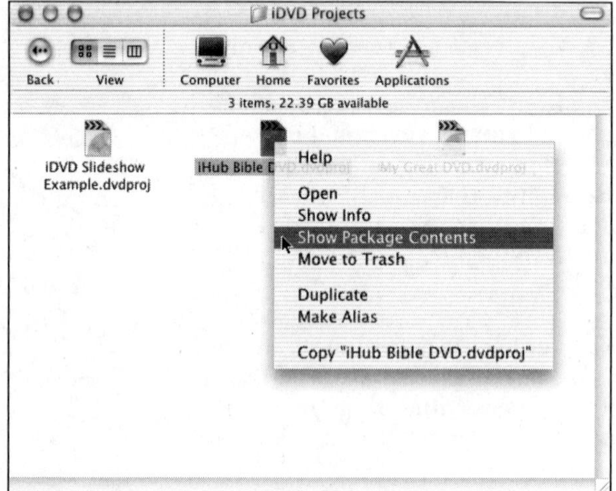

Figure 21-1: iDVD projects are really special folders, called *packages*.

Choosing Show Package Contents opens a new Finder window in icon view. We've switched to list view and ⌘-Option-clicked the Contents folder's disclosure triangle to display all the Completed Tutorial project's levels in Figure 21-2. The project's main menu screen is shown in Figure 21-3.

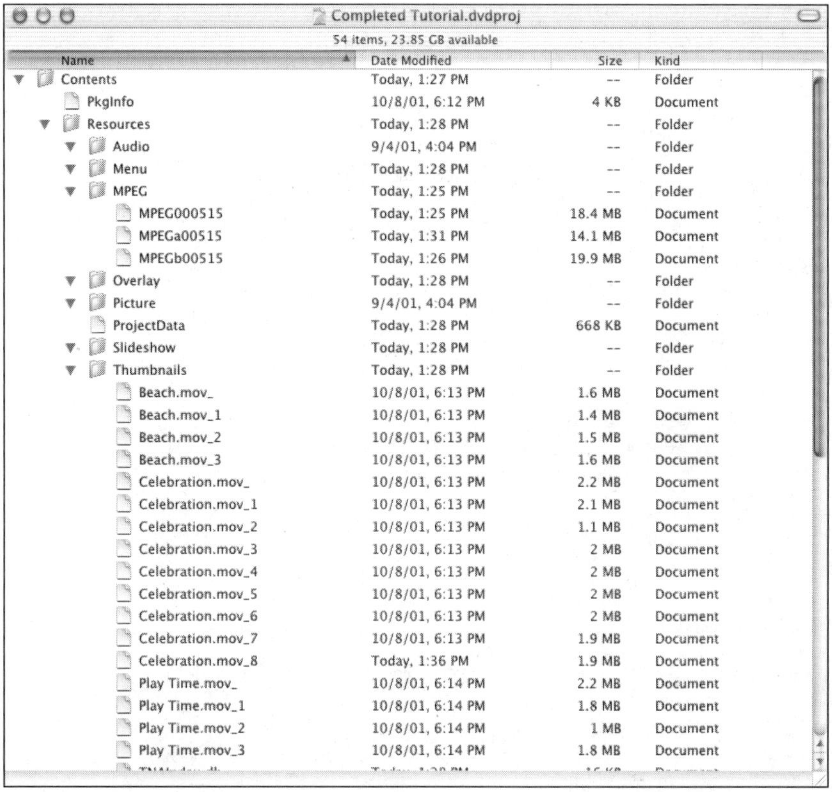

Completed Tutorial.dvdproj

54 items, 23.85 GB available

Name	Date Modified	Size	Kind
Contents	Today, 1:27 PM	--	Folder
PkgInfo	10/8/01, 6:12 PM	4 KB	Document
Resources	Today, 1:28 PM	--	Folder
Audio	9/4/01, 4:04 PM	--	Folder
Menu	Today, 1:28 PM	--	Folder
MPEG	Today, 1:25 PM	--	Folder
MPEG000515	Today, 1:25 PM	18.4 MB	Document
MPEGa00515	Today, 1:31 PM	14.1 MB	Document
MPEGb00515	Today, 1:26 PM	19.9 MB	Document
Overlay	Today, 1:28 PM	--	Folder
Picture	9/4/01, 4:04 PM	--	Folder
ProjectData	Today, 1:28 PM	668 KB	Document
Slideshow	Today, 1:28 PM	--	Folder
Thumbnails	Today, 1:28 PM	--	Folder
Beach.mov_	10/8/01, 6:13 PM	1.6 MB	Document
Beach.mov_1	10/8/01, 6:13 PM	1.4 MB	Document
Beach.mov_2	10/8/01, 6:13 PM	1.5 MB	Document
Beach.mov_3	10/8/01, 6:13 PM	1.6 MB	Document
Celebration.mov_	10/8/01, 6:13 PM	2.2 MB	Document
Celebration.mov_1	10/8/01, 6:13 PM	2.1 MB	Document
Celebration.mov_2	10/8/01, 6:13 PM	1.1 MB	Document
Celebration.mov_3	10/8/01, 6:13 PM	2 MB	Document
Celebration.mov_4	10/8/01, 6:13 PM	2 MB	Document
Celebration.mov_5	10/8/01, 6:13 PM	2 MB	Document
Celebration.mov_6	10/8/01, 6:13 PM	2 MB	Document
Celebration.mov_7	10/8/01, 6:13 PM	1.9 MB	Document
Celebration.mov_8	Today, 1:36 PM	1.9 MB	Document
Play Time.mov_	10/8/01, 6:14 PM	2.2 MB	Document
Play Time.mov_1	10/8/01, 6:14 PM	1.8 MB	Document
Play Time.mov_2	10/8/01, 6:14 PM	1 MB	Document
Play Time.mov_3	10/8/01, 6:14 PM	1.8 MB	Document

Figure 21-2: Even a small project is made up of lots of files and folders.

Notice that the Thumbnails and MPEG folders hold most of your data. Encoded movie files go, as the name suggests, in the MPEG folder. The Thumbnails folder is the repository for all your buttons and the scaled-down, soundless clips that play in them.

However, the really important file is the one called ProjectData. It doesn't include a filename extension nor does it sport a traditional file type (like "TEXT"), but it is an XML file and it describes the entire project's structure, as illustrated in Figure 21-4.

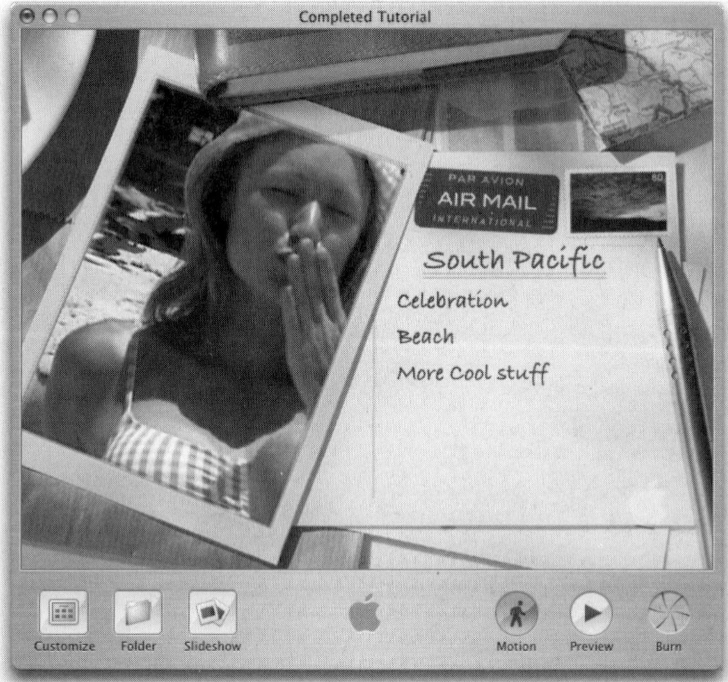

Figure 21-3: The Completed Tutorial project's main menu.

Caution

If this book were in color, we'd put this warning in big red letters: Don't modify the ProjectData file or anything else you find in the project's package. From your perspective, this is read-only data and the best you can hope for is to not break things if you fiddle with it. The only time we recommend even looking in the ProjectData file is when iDVD can't find some of your content. You might be able to get a clue what you misplaced that iDVD needs.

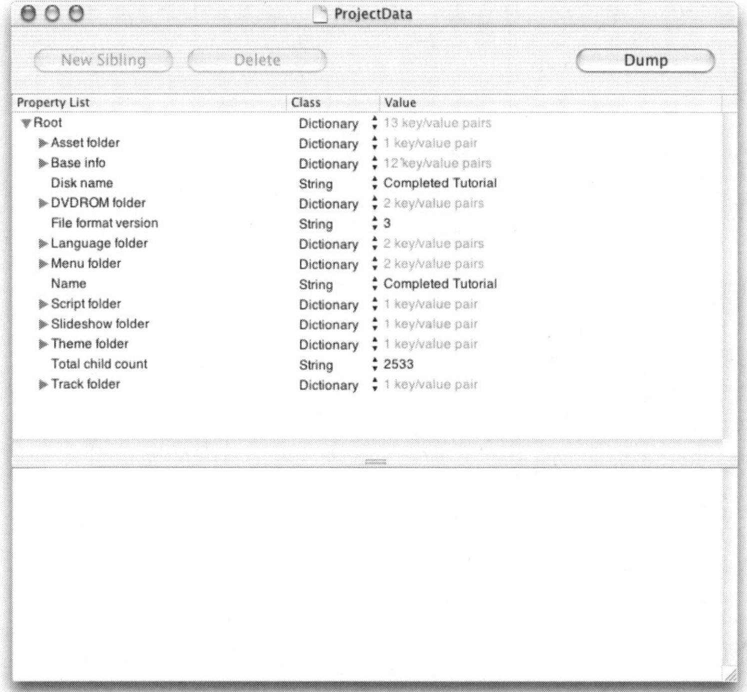

Figure 21-4: ProjectData's top two levels are displayed in Property List Editor.

Inside Themes

Themes, like projects and the iDVD application, are packages. In fact, if you look inside the iDVD application package's Resources folder, you'll see the 48 themes stored in iDVD's Themes panel (when All is chosen), and you'll find another 18 themes that don't appear, as shown in Figure 21-5. The inaccessible themes are numbered 901 through 919, with no 904. These themes were created for the iDVD 1.0 application.

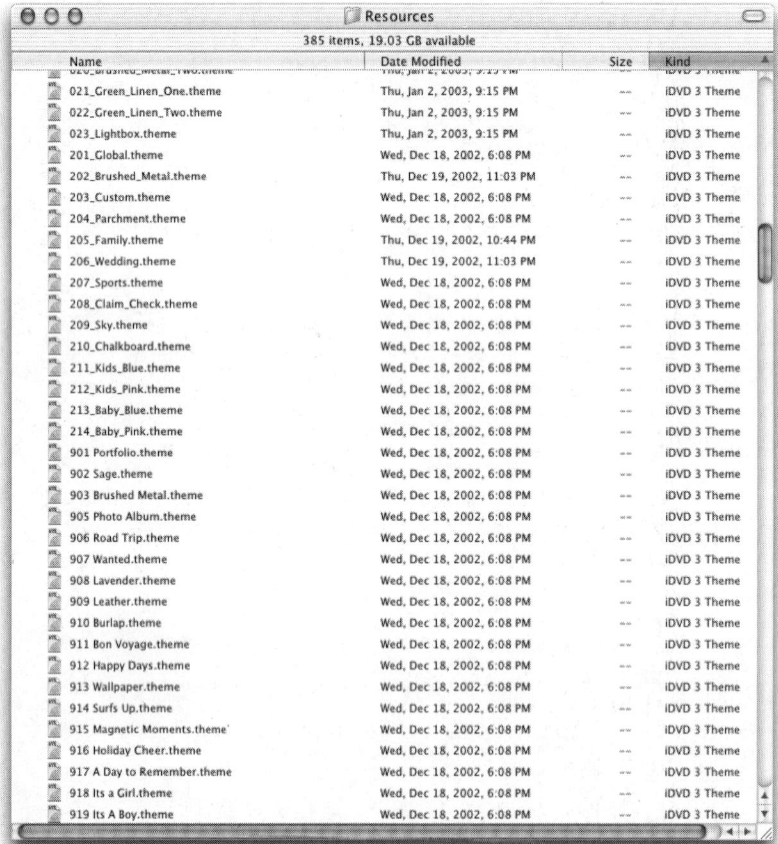

Figure 21-5: iDVD stores its themes in the application package.

Borrowing a background

It's really a shame that some of these themes aren't available in the Themes drawer. For example, the Happy Days theme is great for commemorating a birthday party, and Surfs Up has a beautiful background. We have to assume Apple had some reason for leaving them out, because they consume a little over a megabyte each of disk space, in the application package. At the moment, the only use (other than a hack we'll tell you about in a bit) we have is borrowing some of the backgrounds to use in our own customizations, as follows:

1. **With iDVD not running, Control-click the iDVD icon and choose Show Package Contents.** The content of the package appears.
2. **Navigate down through the Contents folder to the Resources folder.** You see the themes available to you, as well as a number of other files and folders.

3. **Control-click the theme whose background you want to borrow and choose Show Package Contents.** The content of the package appears.
4. **Navigate down through the Contents folder into the theme's Resources folder.** You'll see a number of TIFF files (extension .tif), as well as many other files.
5. **Select the Background.tif file and, holding down the Option key, drag it to the Desktop or some other conveniently accessible location.** This creates a copy of the Background.tif file.
6. **Close all of the theme's folders and all of the iDVD package folders you've opened.**
7. **Launch iDVD and open the Customize drawer if it isn't already open.** The Customize drawer appears out of the iDVD window's side.
8. **Click the Settings button to display the Settings panel.**
9. **Drag the Background.tif file into the Image/Movie well, as shown in Figure 21-6.** The background in iDVD's window is now the image in Background.tif.

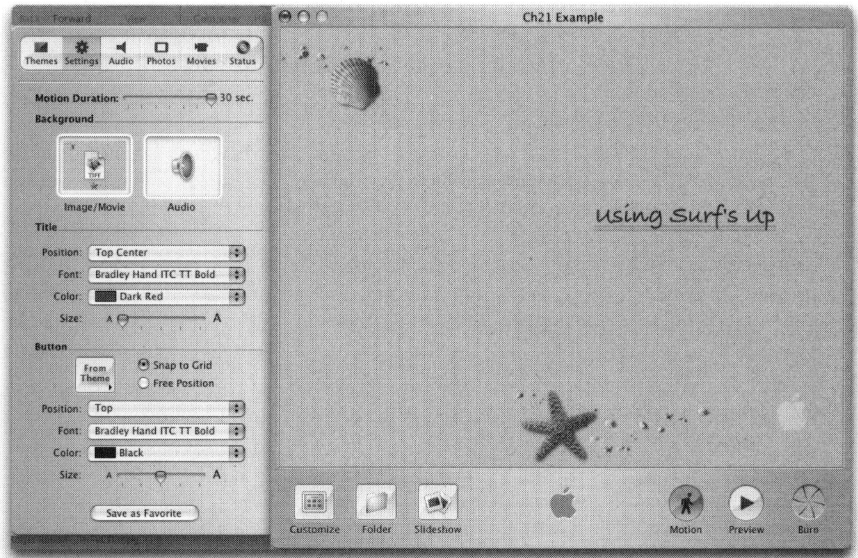

Figure 21-6: You now have the background from Surfs Up, perfectly proportioned and sized, in your menu.

Creating custom themes seems like a solid niche product for an enterprising developer with XML skills. We hope to see a small cottage industry developing before long. At the time we're writing this, only one such entrepreneur has stepped forward—more about this in Chapter 22.

Resurrecting an iDVD 1 theme

You can, with just a little effort and care, make one or more of the iDVD 1 themes available. Proceed as follows:

1. **Press the Option key and drag the themes you want to your home directory.** Doing this makes a copy of the theme for you to work on.
2. **Control-click on the theme copy and choose Show Package Contents.** The Contents of the package appears.
3. **Navigate down into the Resources folder within the Contents folder.** You'll see a number of files and folders. The folders bearing a language name and the extension .lproj are the ones with which we're going to be concerned.
4. **Open the language folder for your version of iDVD and find the Description.plist file.** In this example, we open the English.lproj folder.
5. **Open Description.plist with Property List Editor (if you have the OS X Developer tools installed) or a plain text editor like BBEdit.** Almost at the end of the file, you'll find an entry that says the version is 1.

You can edit the `Description.plist` file with TextEdit, but you have to be extra careful to make sure that you save it as plain text. TextEdit likes to convert things to RTF and that would make the file unusable by iDVD.

6. **Change the 1 to a 2 and save the file.** See Figure 21-7 for an example. This tells iDVD that the theme is suitable for use, just as those iDVD 2 themes displayed in the Old Themes list.
7. **Close the theme's window(s) and move it to your home directory's Library/iDVD/Favorites folder.** You may have to create the folder, if one does not exist.

8. **Change the filename extension from** `.theme` **to** `.favorite`**.** This tells iDVD to list it in the Favorites list. Now if you launch iDVD and open the Customize drawer's Themes panel, you'll find Road Trip, or whichever themes you edited, available after the built-in themes as shown in Figure 21-8 when All is chosen in the pop-up menu. If you choose Favorites from the panel's pop-up menu, only those themes in the Favorites folders are shown.

```
            <array>
                <string>{x=160;y=270;width=128;height=96}</string>
                <string>Roadtrip</string>
            </array>
            <array>
                <string>{x=350;y=270;width=128;height=96}</string>
                <string>Roadtrip</string>
            </array>
        </array>
        <array>
            <array>
                <string>{x=65;y=116;width=128;height=96}</string>
                <string>Roadtrip</string>
            </array>
            <array>
                <string>{x=255;y=116;width=128;height=96}</string>
                <string>Roadtrip</string>
            </array>
            <array>
                <string>{x=445;y=116;width=128;height=96}</string>
                <string>Roadtrip</string>
            </array>
            <array>
                <string>{x=65;y=270;width=128;height=96}</string>
                <string>Roadtrip</string>
            </array>
            <array>
                <string>{x=255;y=270;width=128;height=96}</string>
                <string>Roadtrip</string>
            </array>
            <array>
                <string>{x=445;y=270;width=128;height=96}</string>
                <string>Roadtrip</string>
            </array>
        </array>
    </array>
    <key>buttonSize</key>
    <integer>2</integer>
    <key>labelPosition</key>
    <integer>4</integer>
    <key>selectColor</key>
    <integer>0</integer>
    <key>title</key>
    <string>Road Trip</string>
    <key>titleColor</key>
    <integer>3</integer>
    <key>titleFont_Localizable</key>
    <string>Machine ITC TT</string>
    <key>titlePosition</key>
    <integer>3</integer>
    <key>titleSize</key>
    <integer>3</integer>
    <key>title_Localizable</key>
    <string>Road Trip</string>
    <key>version</key>
    <integer>2</integer>
</dict>
</plist>
```

Figure 21-7: Using BBEdit to change the Road Trip theme's version to 2.

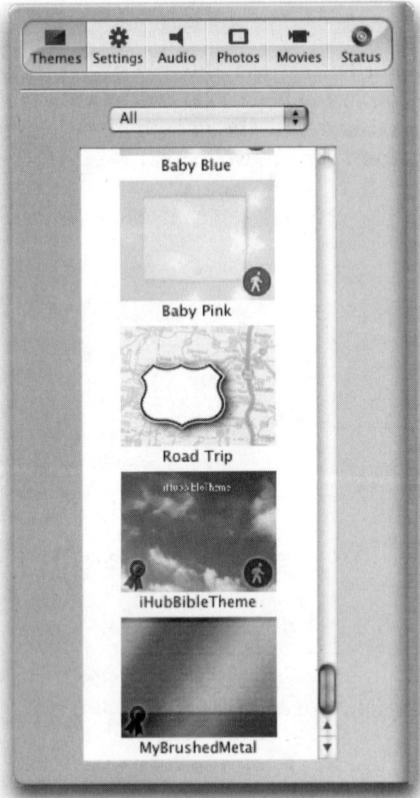

Figure 21-8: The resurrected theme is now available to you.

Planning Your iDVD Project

We can appreciate how easy and tempting it is to just throw a few buttons onto a menu screen, click Burn, insert the blank DVD-R, and sit back awaiting the finished DVD. In fact, we've even done it ourselves when we needed something (anything) quickly.

But, if you want your DVDs to be something special, you'll have to put a little work into planning your DVD. Assuming that you already have your content, you need to plan your presentation. Just as high-priced restaurants receive critical acclaim for average food, mediocre service, and minuscule portions when the meal is properly presented, you can receive kudos for everyday footage and slideshows if you package and present them properly.

Choosing software

Bob likes to use an outliner to organize the whole project. Because he does his writing in Microsoft Word, he tends to use Word's outliner; you, on the other hand, might also consider OmniOutliner, a really Aqua-beautiful OS X-only outliner from the Omni Group (www.omnigroup.com) or even the outliner included in AppleWorks. Meanwhile, Dennis is rapidly switching from pads of quadrille paper filled with barely recognizable sketches to OmniGraffle (also from the Omni Group) to diagram what he wants on his DVDs.

This section illustrates Dennis's use of iDVD. It is more geared to combining iMovie footage and photos he already has on hand into DVDs for friends and family.

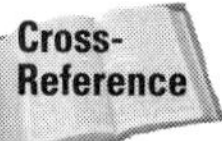

We'll get more into Bob's approach in Chapter 24, because he starts with planning the movie creation process as well as the DVD authoring.

Planning your project

You can plan your project using the following steps, which assumes you already have your content:

1. **Gather your content.** The first step you need to do is collect your content into one place. You could navigate your hard disk to find all the pieces as you build your DVD, but you'll be making your job harder than it needs to be. Additionally, if your content is all in one folder and you keep your iDVD project file in that folder, backing up your work becomes easy. (You do back up, don't you?)

2. **Find music to complement or enhance your menus and slideshows.** For example, Rocky Balboa running up the steps wasn't a great scene until it was driven by the music. If you have a .Mac account, Apple and FreePlay Music make 1.3GB of music available in varying clip lengths, providing a wealth of choices at the right price—free (or, almost free, as .Mac does have a price). Alternatively, you can search the Web for other free or inexpensive music sources or use a commercial product like Sonic Desktop's Movie Maestro or SonicFire Pro (www.smartsound.com) to create a soundtrack.

3. **Organize your menus and buttons so that your audience can easily find what they're looking for.** Keeping movies with movies and slideshows with slideshows is a good start, but you can do more. Figure out the sequence in which the content is best viewed and arrange the buttons to match. Your audience can still select randomly, but at least you'll be giving them a starting point if they don't know ahead of time which movie they want to view.

Inside Encoding and Compression

Although encoding and compression are two separate concepts, most people use them interchangeably, and incorrectly. *Encoding* converts the form of the data on which it acts and may result in a data set that is larger or smaller (or even the same size) than the original. For example, when you convert the analog signal from a VCR to digital form using a digital camcorder as a pass-through device, you are digitally encoding the signal. When you attach a file, for example a picture, to an e-mail message, your mail software encodes the attached file into a form compatible with Internet mail protocols. *Compression,* however, makes things smaller and falls into two categories:

✦ **Lossless compression** means that the original data can be completely reconstructed from the compressed copy. Compression and archival software like StuffIt and Zip use lossless compression.

✦ **Lossy compression** means that unnecessary data is discarded as part of the compression process. (Well, you hope the data is unnecessary.) MP3, JPEG, and MPEG are examples of lossy compression schemes. The more data (quality) you're willing to discard, the smaller the resulting file, possibly to the point where the data loss is easily visible, as shown in Figure 21-9.

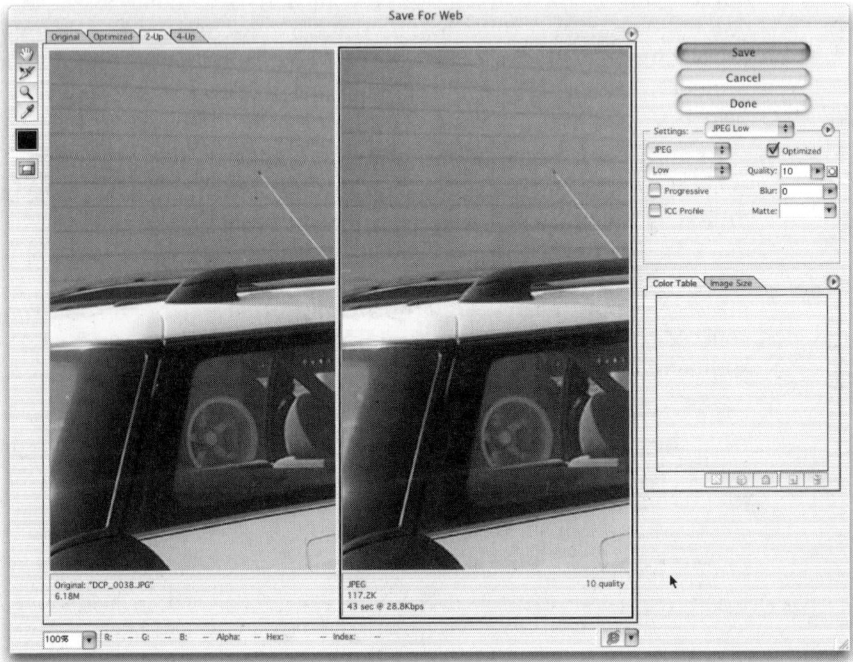

Figure 21-9: You can see the artifacts and blurring around the auto antenna when heavy JPEG compression is used in this Photoshop 7 before and after screen shot.

The Motion Pictures Experts Group (MPEG) is an industry coalition responsible for defining such standards as MP3 (MPEG-1 Layer 3 audio), MPEG-1 (used on VideoCDs), MPEG-4 (used for streaming media), and MPEG-2 (used for DVDs and Super VideoCDs).

We're not going to delve into all the mathematics and mind-numbing specifications describing MPEG-2. If you want that level of detail, check out `http://mpeg.telecomitaliab.com` or `http://bmrc.berkeley/frame/research/mpeg/mpeg2faq.html`.

Just because a file is compressed and encoded as an MPEG-2 file doesn't mean that you can burn it to a DVD. The frame size has to be right for either NTSC or PAL, as does the frame rate (frames per second, or fps). More than that, though, the data bit rate has to fall within a specified range. Table 21-1 gives a requirements and features breakdown for both NTSC and PAL DVDs.

Table 21-1
DVD Specifications

	NTSC	***PAL***
Bit Rate	Up to 9.8 Mbit/sec MPEG-2. May be CBR or VBR.	Up to 9.8 Mbit/sec MPEG-2. May be CBR or VBR.
Frame Size	720×480	720×576
Frame Rate	29.97 fps	25 fps
Audio	Up to 8 audio tracks containing Dolby Digital, DTS, PCM (uncompressed audio), MPEG-1 Layer2; but one track must either have DD or PCM Audio (48 kHz).	Up to 8 audio tracks containing Dolby Digital, DTS, PCM (uncompressed audio), MPEG-1 Layer2; but one track must either have DD or PCM Audio (48 kHz).

Both AIFF and WAV are examples of PCM (Pulse Coded Modulation) audio.

iDVD 3 uses constant bit-rate encoding at one of two preset speeds. The higher speed fits 60 minutes of video on a DVD-R, and the lower is set to record 90 minutes per disc.

Even after attending to all these technical details, we're still not ready to burn a DVD. The DVD disc format requires that certain files need to be in specific places and that a naming convention is enforced. Fortunately for all of us, iDVD takes care of that bookkeeping as well, meaning that we don't have to do anything specific except to click the Burn button telling iDVD to finish up.

Basic MPEG Compression

We're going to get more than a little nerdy in this discussion. Unless you're prepared to follow along, bail out now.

Movies are filmed at 24 fps and, as an analog medium, which means that there are 24 distinct images recorded every second. When you view television (we'll assume NTSC for this discussion, only the numbers change for PAL), you see almost 30 fps. That 30 fps is misleading, though, because 60 frames are actually transmitted each second, with alternating frames containing the even and odd scan lines, which your TV then *interlaces*, or reassembles in order, back into an image.

Encoders, in our case MPEG-2 encoders, perform a mathematical analysis of each frame, determining how to encode the data for optimum results. Much of the analysis is similar to that in JPEG compression, where the encoding software decides which data can be eliminated without visually degrading the image quality.

But, no frame is an island. The encoder also compares each frame with the frames around it, analyzing the differences and deciding in which of three ways to encode the frame:

✦ **Intraframes:** Contain the frame's complete image data, which, obviously, means that compression is minimal. Think of it as a reference frame.

✦ **Predicted frames:** Contain just enough data to tell the DVD player's decoder how to reconstruct the image based upon the most recently displayed intraframe or predicted frame.

✦ **Bidirectional frames:** Tell the decoder to use the surrounding intraframes and predicted frames to interpolate (approximate or average out) the frame contents.

The more variation from frame to frame, the more intraframes required and, as a result, less compression achieved. All of this analysis, which requires more than one pass through the data, takes time. That's why encoding is so slow. There is an upside to this time expenditure, though. Almost no analysis needs to be done at decoding time, and your DVD player can easily reconstruct the images and display them without having the picture stutter.

If you want to delve even deeper into this process, we recommend `www.howstuffworks.com/video-format.htm`. Actually, we recommend the How Stuff Works site in general. It's a great reference and answers most of our questions about how things work (probably how it got its name).

Summary

In this chapter, you learned about how iDVD projects are constructed and that both projects and themes are implemented as packages. You also saw how to obtain access to the iDVD 1 themes that still reside within the iDVD 3 application package. Then, we gave you some tips on planning your iDVD project. Finally, you saw, briefly, how compression works and how DVDs come to be.

✦ ✦ ✦

CHAPTER 22

Enhancing Your iDVD Experience

✦ ✦ ✦ ✦

In This Chapter

Hardware enhancements

Software enhancements

✦ ✦ ✦ ✦

If any of the iLife applications in this book could be considered "high-end," it would be iDVD, which seems odd because iDVD is pretty much a one-trick pony. In fact, if Apple hadn't added the capability to write data DVDs in version 2.1, we would have called it just that.

Because iDVD has so few basic functions, and the fact that iDVD is only available on Macs with *internal* SuperDrives, you'll understand why there are fewer hardware and software add-ons for iDVD than other iApps.

Most of what you need to get the most out of iDVD with the least effort is covered in Part IV and, to a lesser extent, Part II and Part III. We touch on a few items here that aren't covered elsewhere (and a couple that were, but bear repeating) and then get on to Part VI.

Hardware Enhancements

iDVD works only with internal SuperDrives, the Pioneer A103, A104, and A105 model DVD-R/CD-RW burners. For a very short time there was a third-party enhancement from Other World Computing that enabled iDVD to work with external drives, but Apple's lawyers had that software withdrawn from the market. That is not, however, the same thing as saying that iDVD requires that your SuperDrive be one that came with your computer from Apple.

Pioneer A105 (SuperDrive)

If your Mac didn't come with a SuperDrive, you're not necessarily out in the cold, forced to pay $1,000 for DVD Studio Pro if you want to create and burn DVDs. You can replace your

Mac's original internal CD or DVD drive with a Pioneer A104 or A105, if you're comfortable working with hardware or know someone who is and who can do so without voiding your Apple warranty.

Bob did just that to one of his Macs, a G4/500 that came out before the SuperDrive became available and was equipped instead with a DVD-RAM drive. He removed that drive (and sold it on eBay) and installed a Pioneer A104 in its place. iDVD couldn't tell the SuperDrive (er, A104) didn't ship with the computer and worked flawlessly.

Note

It still does. He sold it to a friend who uses it daily in his recording studio. The friend reports that the Pioneer drive is still going strong.

You can find internal A104 and A105 drives for approximately $300-$400 at the time we're writing this, sometimes with rebates that get the price down even further. For an additional $70 or so, you can get a FireWire enclosure into which you might place your original drive and continue to use it as an external — a particularly attractive option if you ever desired to have two optical discs mounted simultaneously. Both of us have external drives in addition to our built-in drives — we frequently find the need (or have the desire) to access one CD (or a DVD) while another is burning in the background.

DVD players

If you're using iDVD, then you're burning DVDs to play in what Apple refers to as "most standalone DVD players." We're not going to argue with the use of "most" in this context, because it is almost certainly accurate; however, it is a bit misleading if you think it means "almost all" rather than "a majority of."

Note

Dennis's experience with DVD-R compatibility has been mixed. His Konka plays VCDs, SVCDs, CD-R, and CD-RW, but doesn't recognize DVD-R discs. His neighbor's GE doesn't recognize any of the above, just commercially pressed DVDs and VCDs. But his Philips and the neighbor's Apex play just about everything. Price and brand name also don't tell the story. There are some expensive Sony models, for example, that don't recognize various media and others (both expensive and not) that do. Bob's Samsung set top DVD player will play everything he burns on a DVD-R disc, but not a VCD. His neighbor's older Panasonic DVD player doesn't play most DVD-Rs but does play VCDs just fine. And his father's DVD player (who knows what kind *that* was) wouldn't play anything Bob burned — neither DVD-R nor VCD.

Before purchasing a DVD player, check out `www.vcdhelp.com`. Although the site is mostly geared to VideoCD variants and Windows users of digital video software, it has the most extensive compatibility database concerning standalone DVD players we've seen or heard of. You can check out whether they support DVD-R, DVD-RW, CD-R, CD-RW, VideoCD, SVCD, and a raft of other features. Additionally, the user commentary that gives tips on street price for the models as well as any other quirks that have been encountered is very valuable. It's not as formal as *Consumer Reports,* but we love the depth of detail and the honesty of some reviews. We really love useful information that also entertains.

Media

While no longer the price leader, Apple-labeled DVD-R blanks were the first (relatively) inexpensive media available for DVD recording. Some other brands, including TDK and GQ (Fry's "house" brand) are now selling for less. We've actually seen them advertised for under $1.50 each, in quantity purchases (spindles of 25 or 50). Our experience with Apple DVD-R discs has been uniformly excellent, but we've experienced a few "coasters" when using other brands.

Note

Want details? Dennis had two out of ten TDKs fail, and Bob had half of the generic pink DVD-R disks someone gave him fail. And don't even ask about DVD-RW (rewritable) discs. Bob's tried most of the brands and had more failures than successes. Not to mention how DVD-RW discs burn slowly and erase even more slowly. He gave all of his away and sticks to DVD-R for now.

At this point, we would advise you to stick with Apple-labeled discs for anything important. If you wish to experiment with less costly brands, try small quantities first to see how they work for you before purchasing a spindle or other large lot.

Tip

It's even more critical with DVDs than with CDs to protect the shiny surface from scratching, fingerprints, and the like. Keep them in their protective sleeves or cases when you're not playing them and, for goodness sake, purchase sleeves or cases to use when you buy spindles. A ruined DVD is not just five times the cost of a ruined CD, but it's also a loss of almost seven times as much data.

Software Enhancements

Because iTunes, iMovie, and iPhoto are already covered in this book (they come with OS X, and iDVD requires OS X), we're not going to include them in our recommended software acquisitions, but they're tools you'll find very useful when creating your DVD's content. Some of the items we'll mention have been recommended or discussed elsewhere in the book, but we hope that we'll be providing a new context here.

QuickTime Pro

Two of iDVD's best features are motion menus and drop zones. Using QuickTime Pro, you can create nice movie files for use as a motion menu or for playing in a drop zone. As we've belabored, iDVD puts rather restrictive controls on what text elements may appear in a menu and restricts those to one line each; however, with QuickTime Pro, you can create multiline or animated text for a more professional-looking menu.

For more QuickTime Pro post production tricks, see Chapter 15. There, you will find a basic sampler of things you can do with QuickTime Pro and a movie file, the exact kind of file that you drag into iDVD for use as a motion menu.

Photoshop or Photoshop Elements

If you want a still menu rather than a motion menu, you can obviously use iPhoto when you want to select an already-existing graphic. To customize one of these photos in any way, however, such as by adding text or creating a composite of multiple photos, you need a good graphics-editing tool. Adobe Photoshop and Adobe Photoshop Elements are considered by most to be about the best of breed; if they're not the best, they're definitely the industry standard.

Photoshop has a few more bells and whistles and, if you need those features for other tasks, by all means spend the $600+ that Photoshop costs. Although we both own Photoshop 7 and think very highly of it, Photoshop Elements (at $99) does everything we need for iDVD and photo retouching with iPhoto, as well as a lot more.

In fact, the combination of Photoshop Elements and QuickTime Pro is a decent little menu-creation toolbox.

iDVD Companion

We cover iDVD Companion in Chapter 20, but we really feel that it bears repeating here. iDVD Companion will unlock, through the wonders of AppleScript, features that iDVD just doesn't make available in its standard interface. This is a free download from Apple at `www.apple.com/applescript/idvd`.

Actually, iDVD Companion just touches the surface of what you can do with iDVD when you bring AppleScript into the arena. If you don't already know how to write AppleScripts, work through Apple's online and downloadable tutorials at `www.apple.com/applescript` and check out the example AppleScripts available alongside iDVD Companion.

iDVD ThemePaks

As we noted in the last chapter, one intrepid soul (Todd Siechen) thus far has published iDVD add-on themes. At the time we're writing this, he has 16 themes divided into two packages available and has announced two more packages to be available soon. These new packs should be for sale by the time this book is available. Check out `www.idvdthemepak.com/` to see what Todd offers. You can also download a free theme, Street, to try out (see Figure 22-1). The packages are available in NTSC or PAL for $29 per pack (8 themes) or for $54 for two packs. The Road Trip theme in ThemePAK 2, for example, is a really attractive interface to a motor vacation DVD.

When you run the installer for a ThemePAK theme, the theme is placed in your iDVD Favorites folder. But, it shows up under a new item in the Themes panel, Theme Pak, as shown in Figure 22-1.

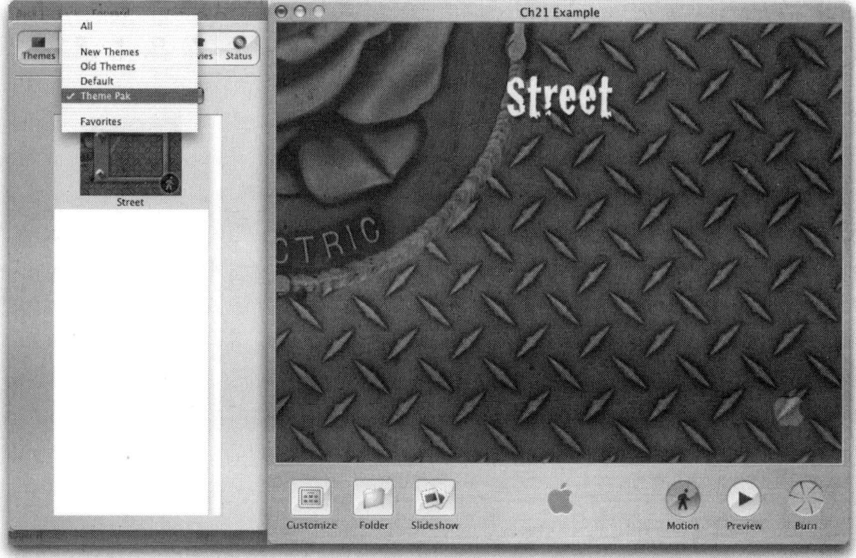

Figure 22-1: Themes from iDVDThemePAK get their own menu entry in the Themes panel pop-up menu.

Check these themes out. We think that you'll find some you like.

Note A last-minute addition, just before we went to press, introduces another third-party theme provider. Check out `www.idvdthemes.com` for their offerings. Similarly, iDVDThemePAK.com has added two more packages of themes to their offerings.

Summary

In this chapter, we reminded you how iDVD Companion and AppleScript can increase your control and options within iDVD. We also showed you what to look for and where to look when purchasing a DVD player or blank media. You learned that QuickTime Pro and Photoshop (or Photoshop Elements) can help you make better still or motion menus for your DVDs. Finally, we pointed you to sources for additional iDVD themes.

✦ ✦ ✦

P A R T

VI

Putting It All Together

✦ ✦ ✦ ✦

In This Part

✦ ✦ ✦ ✦

Using the Four "i"s Together

In This Chapter

Although each of our four featured applications are useful all by themselves, there's a reason Apple refers to this constellation (and a couple of other applications) as "spokes on your digital hub."

All by themselves, spokes are just sticks (or rods), useful for a variety of purposes. Attached and working together they let you do even more. For example, you can use songs from iTunes or images from iPhoto in your iMovie and iDVD productions. You can even, with a little help from QuickTime Pro, take your iMovie's soundtrack and create a soundtrack CD in iTunes, just like the studios do with their movies.

In this chapter, we also explore other ways to leverage the capabilities of one iApplication to enhance another.

What's the Score?

When the movie is released, picture studios releases a CD containing the movie's musical score. Although your productions are not on the same scale or scope as those of Universal, MGM, or Warner Bros., you can emulate them in this respect. Just as one example, assume that one or more of your family is part of a play or recital, and you want to make a movie of the event.

Because you're making a movie, it seems likely that you'll distribute it on DVD, VideoCD, and/or videotape to reach the widest audience. However, you might also consider distributing just the audio portion, all packaged up as a commemorative CD, or just an album to carry around on your iPod.

Note

In the case of a musical recital or a live performance, we're going to assume that you positioned your microphones or audio pickup, as we advised in Chapter 16, and have a clean audio feed. The old adage of "garbage in, garbage out" is especially true in audiovisual work. Barring extraordinarily expensive equipment, a lot of time, and the assistance of an audio specialist, there isn't too much you can do to make a bad audio track sound decent and, if you missed recording the audio, you're probably out of luck.

Tip

If you know you're going to get only one take, try to have a backup recording going. Maybe you have a friend or family member who also has a digital camcorder or even a tape recorder. Sometimes redundancy is a virtue.

What we're going to show you isn't really snazzy or state-of-the-art, but it works. Follow the steps and have QuickTime Pro handy — you'll have a sound track that you can turn into a CD with multiple tracks:

1. **In iMovie, with your movie in the Clip/Timeline Viewer, choose File ⇨ Export Movie (⌘-E).** The Export Movie dialog appears.
2. **Select To QuickTime in the Export Movie dialog's Export pop-up menu.** A Save-style dialog appears.
3. **Select Expert from the Formats pop-up menu.** The Expert QuickTime Settings dialog appears.
4. **In the Save exported file as dialog, select Sound to AIFF from the Export pop-up menu.** See Figure 23-1. Click the Options button and the Sound Settings dialog makes an appearance.

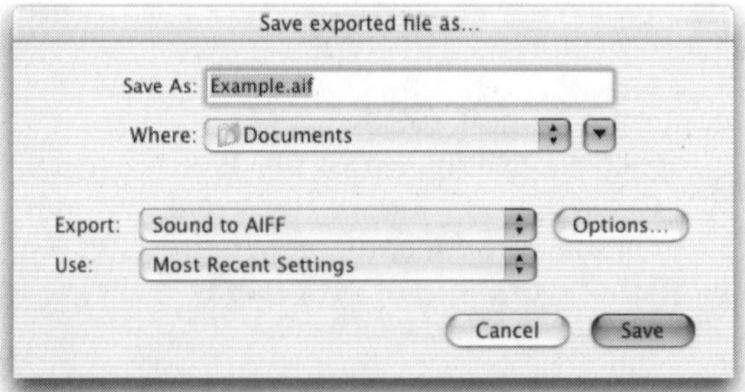

Figure 23-1: Make sure that the audio settings are appropriate for your high-quality soundtrack.

5. **Either by typing or choosing from the pop-up menu, set the Rate to 44.100 kHz.** See Figure 23-2. Make sure that you select 16 bit and Stereo for the Size and Use.

6. **Click OK.** This dismisses the Sound Settings dialog.
7. **In the Save exported file as dialog, name your movie and select a location.** If your desired location isn't available in the Where pop-up menu, click the disclosure button we point out in Figure 23-3 to display the usual Save dialog's file browser.

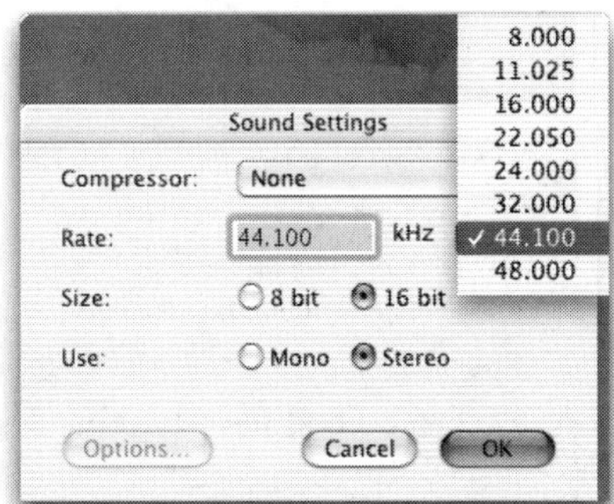

Figure 23-2: Set the audio to 44.1 kHz, 16 bit, Stereo for CD-quality sound.

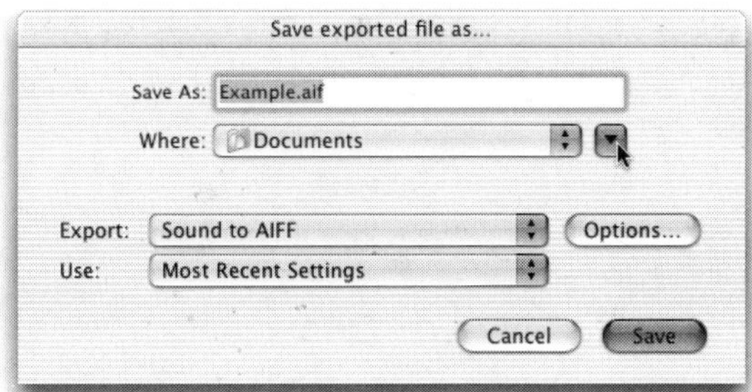

Figure 23-3: Click the indicated button to display the Finder-like column view.

We *really* wish that there were a preference setting so that all Save dialogs can be forced to open with the column view displayed. We frequently want to save files someplace other than the directories in the pop-up list. At least, with the tip in Chapter 16, you can make that behavior the default for iMovie's own Save sheet.

8. **Wait for QuickTime to export your movie.** When it's done, quit from iMovie and open the movie you just saved in QuickTime Player.

9. **Using the techniques described in the "Postproduction Tricks with QuickTime Pro" section in Chapter 15, select the section of your movie with the audio you want to use for your first track.**
10. **Choose Edit ➪ Copy (⌘-C).**
11. **Choose File ➪ New Player (⌘-N).** A new, untitled, QuickTime player window appears on your screen.
12. **Choose Edit ➪ Paste (⌘-V).** Your new movie's audio track is now the same as the selection made in Step 10.
13. **Choose File ➪ Export (⌘-E).** The Save exported file as dialog appears.
14. **Choose Sound to AIFF from the Export pop-up menu, and name the file you're creating. Click Save to store the file on disk.** See Figure 23-4. To make things easier later on, you should save this file and subsequent files to a folder created for this project.

If you prepend numbers in the track names, you won't have to reorder the tracks in Step 17.

15. **Repeat Steps 9 through 14.** Do this for as many songs or audio selections you want to create.
16. **Quit from QuickTime Pro and start iTunes.** The iTunes window appears.
17. **Drag the folder containing your songs to the iTunes Source pane.** This creates a new playlist, as shown in Figure 23-5.

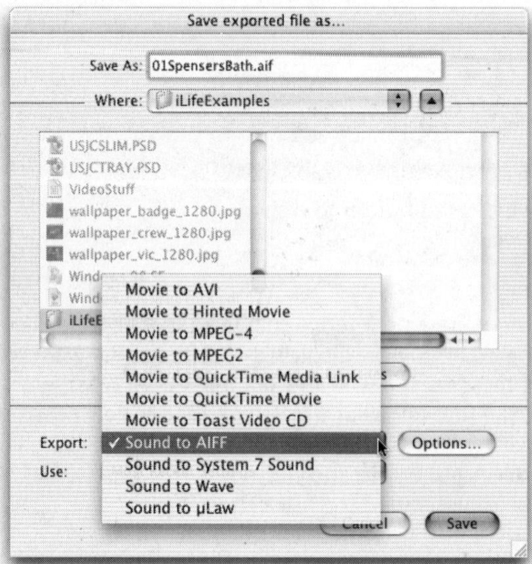

Figure 23-4: Save the movie's audio track as an AIFF file by choosing Sound to AIFF from the Export pop-up menu.

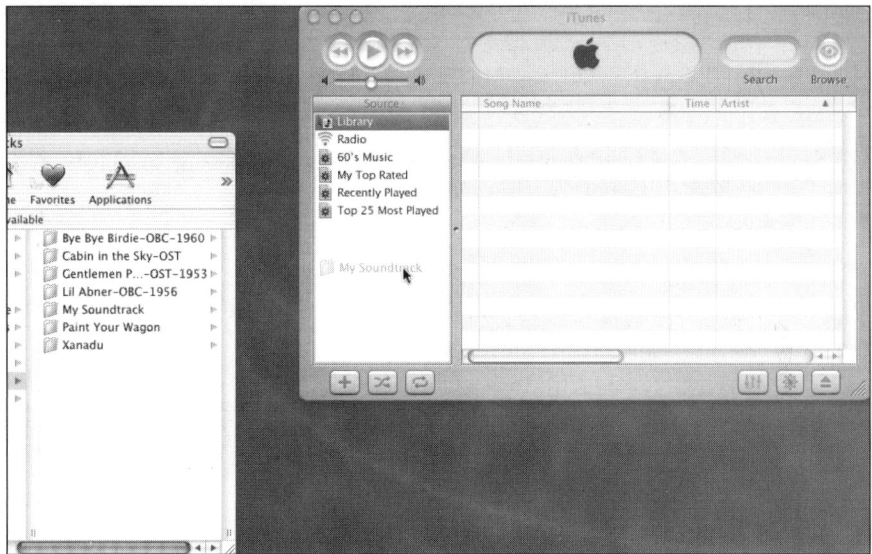

Figure 23-5: Create a playlist containing the AIFF files you've created.

18. **Select your new playlist in the Source pane.** Proceed as described in the "Making Your Own CDs" section in Chapter 4.

Congratulations! You've just created your soundtrack album — look out, AOL/Time-Warner!

Slip, Slideshowing Away

Slideshows are everywhere — screensavers, travelogues, business presentations, family reminiscences, you name it. And, if Apple has its way, slideshows will be even more common. In AppleWorks 6, Apple eliminated the communications module, replacing it with a Presentations feature. Microsoft includes PowerPoint as a major part of their Office for the Mac product. QuickTime 6 creates slideshows from folders of images. iPhoto creates slideshows from your photo collection. iMovie creates slideshows out of still images you import. iDVD also has a very nice slideshow feature. Apple even has the fabulous Keynote presentation package, a standalone, state-of-the-art presentation creation tool. In fact, you have so many slideshow tools available that you could be whirling around trying to figure which application to choose.

Here, we give you the definitive answer as to which slideshow tool to use. That answer is, "it depends," because many factors weigh into the determination. There are three critical questions to ask: What is the subject? Where is it going to be viewed? How much flexibility do you need to build into your slideshow?

If your slides are mostly text and business-related graphics, such as charts and the like, your best bet is a presentation tool: Keynote, PowerPoint, or the AppleWorks Presentation modules are great choices. We won't get into them here, as they are not germane to this book. Check out *Macworld Microsoft Office 2001 Bible* by Bob LeVitus and Dennis R. Cohen or *Macworld AppleWorks 6 Bible* by Steve Schwartz and Dennis R. Cohen (both published by Wiley Publishing, Inc.) for coverage of PowerPoint and AppleWorks presentations, respectively. We are not yet aware of a book on Keynote.

We categorize slideshows as basic or complex depending upon whether they are viewing-oriented or message-oriented.

Creating basic slideshows

We categorize slideshows as basic if they are *viewing-oriented*. Screensavers and kiosk-oriented travelogues are basic slideshows. This is because each image displays for the same amount of time, everything is automated to go from one slide to the next and, possibly, loop back to the beginning after displaying the final slide.

Using iPhoto to create one theme slideshows

Using iPhoto is probably your best choice if a single, simple slideshow is sufficient for your needs. A simple, themed slideshow with a title such as "Our Day in Mazatlan" with a musical accompaniment is made to order for iPhoto. Just organize the pictures you want in an album, as described in Chapter 9, and pick your music. You can watch these shows in iPhoto or you can export them. They also make great screensavers, if you've updated to Mac OS X 10.2 (Jaguar).

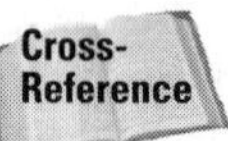

For more on creating a slideshow, see Chapter 9. For more on sharing a slideshow, see Chapter 10.

Using iDVD to create slideshow sets

The preceding example, "Our Day in Mazatlan," could also be part of a set of vacation slideshows: Mazatlan, Acapulco, On Ship, and so on. Using the Photos panel in iDVD's Customize drawer, you can set each album up as an iDVD slideshow and then burn them to a DVD.

If you don't have iDVD and a DVD burner, though, you're not left out in the cold, so long as you have Toast Titanium and a CD burner. Using the wonderful freeware utility, VCD Builder, you can create inexpensive menued VideoCDs that compares favorably with the iDVD productions. Just proceed as follows:

1. **Create your slideshow in iPhoto.** See Chapter 9 for the details.
2. **Export the slideshow using the Toast-supplied QuickTime component to create a VideoCD-compatible MPEG-1 file.** See Chapter 10 for the details.
3. **Repeat Steps 1 and 2.** Do this until you've created all the slideshows you want.

4. **Create your menu screen in AppleWorks, GraphicConverter, Photoshop Elements, or any other handy graphics editor.** We tend to like captioned miniatures of each show's title slide, but your mileage may vary.
5. **Launch VCD Builder and create your sequences**. Alternatively, you can use one of the templates. Chapter 16 covers using VCD Builder.

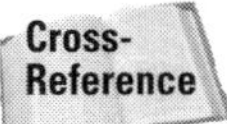

To learn how to make menu-driven VCDs, see Chapter 16.

Dennis used this method to create a collected slideshows VideoCD featuring his friends' first baby, Marcus. (You've seen pictures of Marcus several times in this book.) He also created a nice label and CD jewel case cover, and Marcus's family really loved the result. In other words, VideoCDs and DVDs of this sort make great gifts.

Creating complex slideshows using iMovie

Product presentations, where individual slides might have different on-screen durations, and other information-purveying slideshows fall into the *complex category.* Complex slideshows are more message-oriented presentations.

When you want variable intervals for on-screen images, multiple soundtracks, or varied transitions and effects (such as captioning), be prepared to do a little more work and use iMovie.

The additional work arises mostly because each image has to be separately imported. We can only hope that the next version of iMovie has useful AppleScript support. (We were disappointed that AppleScript support didn't arrive with iMovie 3.)

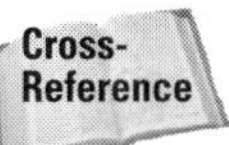

Chapter 14 covers getting your pictures into iMovie and setting durations for each slide.

Employing iMovie's voice recording capability and taking advantage of the two audio tracks, you can easily have a background music track while narrating your presentation, travelogue, or photo essay. Add iMovie's transitions, titling, and other special effects (including those available via plug-ins) and you have a presentation tool for digital images that fills a gaping hole between Keynote and the iPhoto slideshow.

On those occasions where you want complete control while giving the presentation, go with iDVD and set the slideshow to be manually advanced. You now have all the flexibility of the rotary slide projector and remote control. This method is great for classroom or lecture hall presentations, where the slideshow's purpose is to illustrate your presentation but the timing is variable and backtracking might be desired. Just remember, if you're going to be backtracking, you probably don't want a background music track.

If you want that extra special effect in your slideshow, you might want to check out Slick Motion from GeeThree (www.geethree.com). It's part of their Slick Transitions and Effects Volume IV.

Feeding iDVD

Although iDVD can leverage all three of our other applications, it's a one-way street. iTunes is a provider, iPhoto and iMovie are both providers and consumers, but iDVD consumes, period. But, when all is said and done, iMovie is iDVD's favorite source.

iTunes can provide music for your iDVD menus and slideshows. iPhoto can provide photos for slideshows and images for still menus.

When you say "DVD" to most people, they think "Movie." For this reason, it's obvious that iMovie is iDVD's supplier of choice. DVD Studio Pro offers a lot though, like extensive control over the encoding process, allowing longer movies on a DVD. What isn't so obvious is that iMovie's also a great place to create the up-to-30-second clips you'll want for your motion menus.

You don't even have to have video footage to create these motion menus. You can use iMovie-created, or iPhoto-created and exported, slideshows for the menus (Slick Motion can be useful here as well).

Summary

In this chapter, you learned at least one way to create a soundtrack recording from your movies. You also discovered how to decide which of your army of slideshow tools to employ for different tasks. Finally, you saw some ways to provide fodder to iDVD, such as using iMovie to create short (up to 30 second) movies to use as buttons and motion menus.

✦ ✦ ✦

Chapter 24

Making Movies and DVDs Like the Pros

✦ ✦ ✦ ✦

In This Chapter

Storyboarding the movie

Shooting extra footage

Setting the stage in iMovie

Choosing transitions

Planning the DVD

✦ ✦ ✦ ✦

Granting the fact that the vast majority of iMovie and iDVD use is casual, we still see serious use made of these basic, but highly functional, applications. Aspiring performers create music videos, students develop documentaries and original dramas as film projects, and businesspeople assemble presentations for clients or stockholders. Visiting Apple's iMovie Web pages at `www.apple.com/imovie` links you to all sorts of more-than-merely-casual projects.

The one commonality among all these projects is that they were planned and executed, using all (or almost all) the production techniques employed by professional moviemakers.

You don't need to perform all the steps we're going to talk about on every project, but you do need to know what those steps are so that you make an informed decision when you skip one.

Storyboarding the Movie

Before you remove your camcorder's lens cap, plan your project. We know that planning can be really boring and that you might begrudge the time you would rather spend doing the fun stuff.

There are two kinds of lazy: *smart lazy* and *just plain lazy.* We like to be smart lazy, and that means spending a little time upfront so that we don't have to spend a whole lot more time down the road trying to do the things we forgot, redoing things we messed up due to inadequate preparation or understanding, and trying to fit all the parts together.

Collecting your notes

Bob is a habitual note-taker. He has little notepads filled with ideas, many of which come when he isn't in front of the computer. Dennis tends more toward self-stick notes as a recording device for his ideas. We both transcribe our notes onto our Macs, though, when we return to our digital comfort zone.

We strongly recommend that you do something similar. It doesn't have to be fancy, but if you have the notes in front of you, you have a reminder of the things you still have to accomplish and there's less likelihood that something will fall through the cracks.

In journalism, they teach that the five *W*s are the backbone of any news story: who, what, when, where, and why. Creating a movie isn't that different. Your project's *what, why,* and *who* are generally referred to as your goals and objectives. (What's your subject? Why are you doing this? Who is your target audience?) If you keep these points in mind, you'll be able to tailor your movie for maximum benefit. We cover the *when* and *where* next.

Outlining or charting your project

Bob keeps folders for each project and a project checklist is in each of those folders, used for tracking all his ideas as well as keeping a status list. Dennis doesn't keep a checklist or status list; he keeps a chart full of boxes and arrows.

Bob started using ThinkTank 512 back in the Mac's early days and became addicted to outlining. His books, presentations, videos, you name it, all have outlines stored somewhere on his Mac (or on an archive disk). Figure 24-1 shows part of one of Bob's video project outlines.

Note You can see the short film that resulted from this outline at `http://homepage.mac.com/boblevitus/iMovieTheater1.html` if you're interested.

Because our publishers insist on Microsoft Word documents, we both spend a goodly portion of our digital lives in Microsoft Word. And, because Bob spends so much time in Word, he tends to use Word's outline mode to maintain his lists. Now, Word's outliner, like most of Word, is very powerful but not really too intuitive. If you choose outlining, but either don't use Word or don't feel comfortable using it, you might consider the AppleWorks outliner or OmniOutliner, a beautiful product of the Omni Group designed specifically for OS X. (It's $21.12, but there's a free demo available at `www.omnigroup.com/applications/omnioutliner`.) Bob agrees, and though he's proficient at outlining in Word, often uses this simple but powerful application instead.

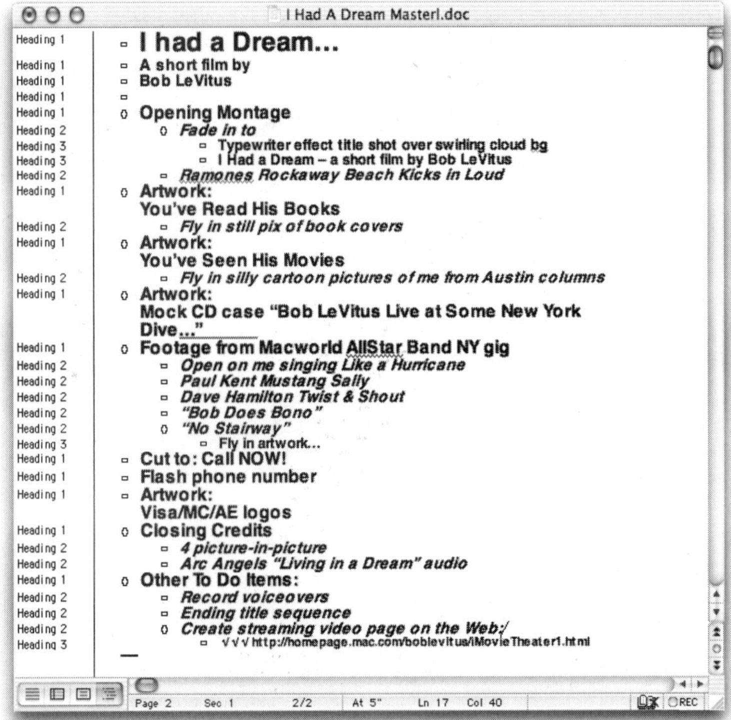

Figure 24-1: Bob plans and tracks projects using a Microsoft Word outline.

Dennis comes from the old programmer's school and started his career when flowcharting a software project was de rigueur. He still charts his projects, but has changed tools a number of times. Currently, his tool of choice is OmniGraffle, also from the fine folks at Omni Group. Figure 24-2 shows part of a project chart in OmniGraffle.

Professionals might use a *PMS*, or *Project Management System* to track the costs, activities, and schedule for their project and, if you're so inclined, you can do the same. Neither of us has gone that far because we're satisfied with the tools we have, but Intellisys Project Desktop (shareware, $59, from Intellisys, Inc. `www.webintellisys.com`) has gotten good reviews and looks quite capable at first glance.

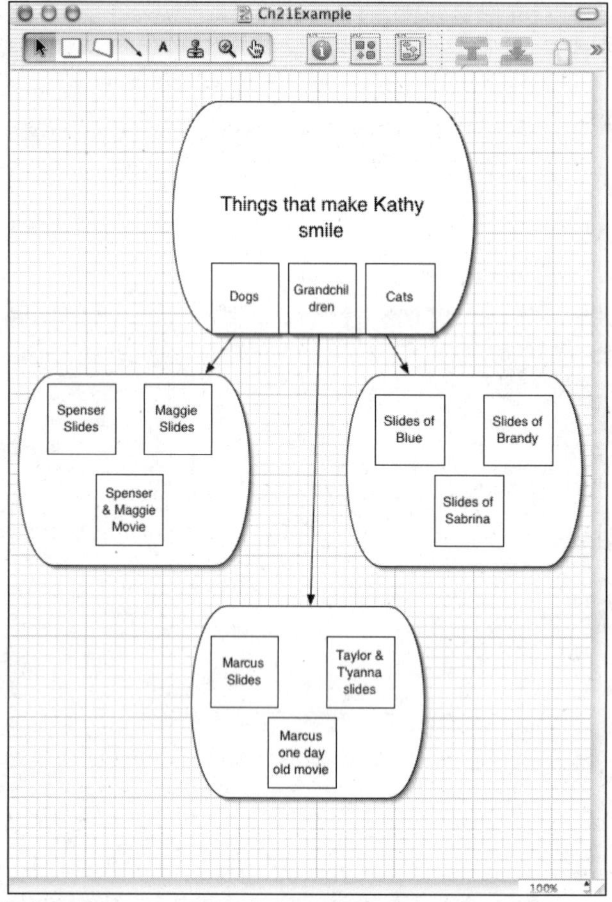

Figure 24-2: If you like a visual overview, consider OmniGraffle.

Dennis developed and maintained PMS software during part of his software development career. He warns that if you choose to use such a tool, the reports you get are only as accurate as the data you supply. Unless you are really fastidious in planning the project and entering all the data accurately, you can draw some really erroneous conclusions from the output. Until you become comfortable with their use and have tracked the history of a few completed projects to make sure you've got the hang of organizing your data, don't rely too heavily on the schedule projections or the cost estimations.

It's really of no consequence what method or tool you use to keep track of your project, but it is very important that you track it somehow. If not, we can guarantee that it won't be as good as it might be and it will almost surely take longer to complete.

Does your movie need a script and, if so, do you and your cast have it? Have you established a *shot list* (list of locations and scenes to remind you what you're shooting, where, and when)?

The shot list should also have your camera positions and angles charted out. Getting the right angle on a scene and taking maximum advantage of lighting helps a lot.

Scripts

This is unusual in the world of computers, but these scripts don't involve writing code. If your movie has planned dialogue, you need a script. Even narration should have a written script — extemporaneous narrative does not flow as well.

Besides, scripts aren't just about the spoken word. Scripts also provide direction to the performers and the camera person/people. You can make this as formal as you wish, using professional script-writing software, such as Final Draft AV (`www.finaldraft.com`). Alternatively, you could just scribble out the dialogue and directions on a sheet of paper or an envelope (hey, it worked for Lincoln with the Gettysburg Address). Or, you can do something in between, maybe using Word or the word processor in AppleWorks.

Shot lists

Sometimes, though, you won't have any dialogue or scripted action. In those rare cases, you should consider a script subset — the shot list. Figure out the scenes you're going to require and the best angles from which to shoot and write them down.

If you do this, you won't miss any shots you need. You might shoot additional footage and even use that in addition to or in place of something you planned, but at least you'll get what you know you want.

For example, if you know you're going to be shooting footage of a horse race, decide whether you want footage of the horses' heads, full body shots, and/or shots focused on pounding hooves.

Storyboards

In a full-fledged, professional production, there will be a series of artist conception drawings, sometimes referred to as mockups, laying out precisely the look being sought. In a very casual movie, the storyboard might just be written descriptions of the various elements.

Because the desired end-result is a DVD, you'll actually need two storyboards: one for the movie and one for the DVD's menus. Figure 24-3 shows the mockup Dennis created for a gift DVD and the DVD menu implementing it.

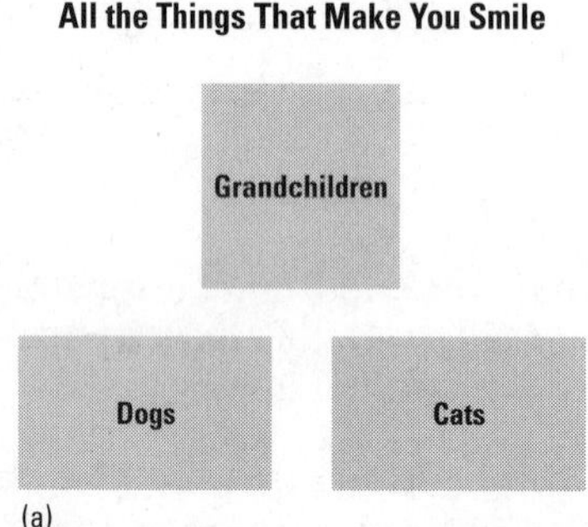

(a)

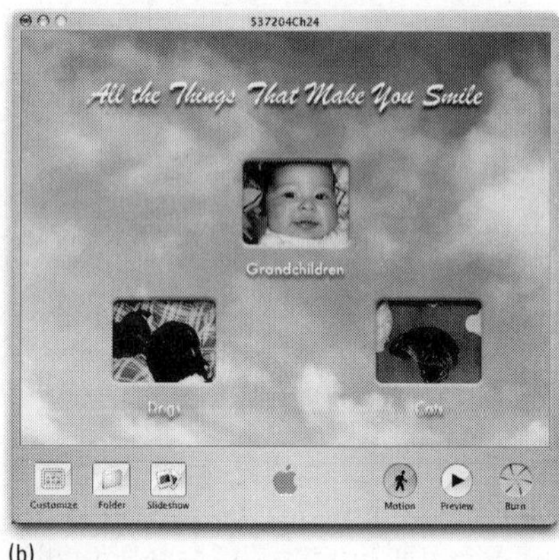

(b)

Figure 24-3: The concept (a); the implementation (b).

Budgets

Sometimes you're going to need to purchase or lease equipment, license music, hire actors or writers, purchase tapes and media, or rent a location. Even the simplest and cheapest DVD production requires at least a tape (even a recycled one) and blank media. Consult your script and project plan (chart or outline), then list the things you're going to require.

If you stop to really think about it, you're going to be spending something on the project and, the larger the project, the more money you're apt to spend and the more different things you'll find to spend it on.

Plan for these expenses. If your budget can't handle what you come up with, at least you'll know it before you blow the dough on a project you can't afford to finish and you can revise your plan accordingly.

Schedules

The old adage says, "Time is money." We don't know if that's literally true, but there are a lot of similarities when it comes to creating and delivering a video project.

After you've figured out what shots you need to take, when you need to take them, and so forth, chart this all out. If there's a deadline on this project, you might find that you don't have time to do everything you want to do. In that case, you should refine your goals, revise your script and shot list, and redo the schedule.

Do you have enough tape? Have you got all the cables, microphones, batteries, and lights you'll need for the shots you plan to take? How about a tripod or gyro-stabilizer? Keeping abreast of what you'll need to shoot your footage is also an important part of your planning process.

We both tend to keep kits containing these sorts of things ready, just so we'll have them when they're needed. It's really frustrating to go on location and have to stop shooting because our battery went dead and we didn't have a spare. Also, when we're shooting stationary indoor scenes and there are convenient electrical outlets, we keep the camera plugged in. Why run down the battery and have to recharge or replace it later?

Shooting Extra Footage

Whenever possible, shoot more than you think you need. Not only will starting a little early and stopping a little late guarantee that you don't miss the beginning or ending of your scene, it might also provide you with some useful framing shots. And don't forget, when you use transitions like the dissolve, you need extra frames on the beginnings and ends of shots to accommodate them.

Similarly, when shooting background and transitional scenes, shoot them from different angles and, maybe, with different filters or lenses. You can often stumble across a good alternative effect for your movie.

Finally, whenever you have the opportunity to film extra footage of interesting scenes as *file shots*—scenes that you can use generically in future projects—do so. Random people walking down the street, cars in traffic, cable car riders in San Francisco, subway riders in New York—all of these can be used over and over again to set a context.

Setting the Stage in iMovie

Now that you've got something resembling a plan of attack and you've shot some footage, you're ready to start editing, right? Well, maybe.

Assuming that you've dotted all the i's and have your tape ready to feed into iMovie, there's still at least one step to do. Clear all the disk space you're going to need for your project before you get started. Although it probably isn't practical for everyone, we recommend having a dedicated hard disk that you can erase or reformat before you start a project. As noted elsewhere, that's what we both do.

Plan for iDVD's limitations

Remembering some of iDVD's limitations while creating your movie can pay large dividends. To that end, the greatest limitation is that iDVD burns movies at only one of two constant rates. You either get 60 minutes or 90 minutes of video per DVD. Go one second over the 60 minutes and everything gets encoded at the 90 minutes speed. If you're filming high-action scenes (a youth hockey game, for example), you can lose some quality if you don't edit down to fit 60 minutes. Another, less obvious limitation, is that you can only have 36 chapters in a movie. While that should be enough in most cases, you need to keep it in mind when marking all the places in your movie you think the viewer might wish to jump to.

You can use iMovie to extract the relevant audio, video, and still images from your movie. Additionally, you can use tools like Movie Maestro (see Chapter 17 to score the menu's video). You should remember that motion menus only play the first 30 seconds of video and audio (repeating it ad nauseam), so you should plan accordingly and avoid jarring breaks in either the video or audio portions. Similarly, you can create motion buttons (but without audio) that cycle through a scene of up to 30 seconds.

Another somewhat obvious use for extracted still images is the making of CD jewel case covers, inserts, and even posters.

Choosing Transitions

Less is more. iMovie provides a buffet table of transition choices and, with the addition of various available third-party collections, you can turn the selection into a menu of unmanageable dimension. Most of these transitions look cool when viewed in isolation, but they rarely do anything to enhance your movie and often detract from the continuity.

We covered transitions and the philosophy behind them pretty thoroughly in the "Working with Clips" section of Chapter 14; you should review that material before selecting and applying transitions.

Professional cinematographers use transitions sparingly and, when they do choose a transition, they tend to be very subtle — usually a fade or dissolve. We try to emulate the masters and use the more noticeable transitions only in special circumstances — slideshow presentations are good venues for radial and push transitions, for example.

Tip

Radial is also a good transition when you're going for a sci-fi effect, like Clark Kent staring at a wall and then the scene shifting to what's on the other side of the wall.

Because adding transitions alters your movie's length, you should apply your transitions before scoring your movie. You don't want the audio to be mangled in the transition.

Planning the DVD

The storyboard layout we discussed earlier in this chapter (and embodied in Figure 24-3) is only one part, even if it's the biggest part, of planning your DVD. Creating useful storyboards will tell you how many menus you will need and how they're organized. What it won't tell you is what movies and still images you'll be using for your menus, nor what background music your menus will play. The following list gives you suggestions on some items to consider when planning your DVD:

✦ **Format:** iDVD isn't too fussy concerning which QuickTime-compatible format your video is in, but you'll get much better results with a video frame rate of 29.97 and using uncompressed 48-kHz audio for NTSC discs. PAL movies should have a 25-fps frame rate. iMovie makes this easy for you with the To iDVD choice in its iMovie: Export dialog's Export pop-up menu, shown in Figure 24-4.

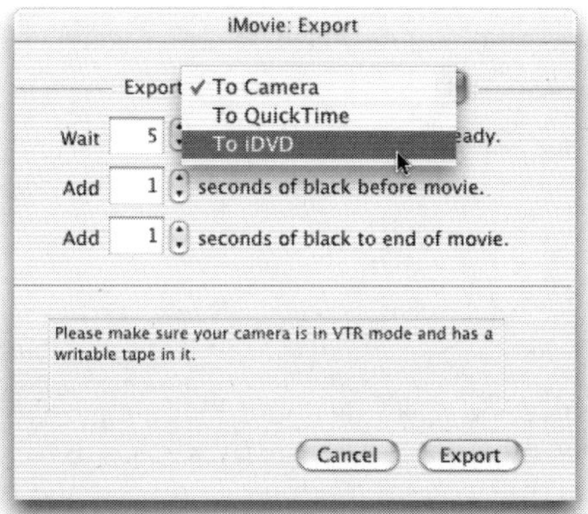

Figure 24-4: iMovie makes preparing a movie for iDVD a simple menu choice.

✦ **Resolution:** When creating menus from still images, or when creating slideshows, remember that resolution is critical to good results. Images should be 640 x 480 to fill the screen. Once again, iMovie can make this easy for you if you extract your still images from the movie — they'll always be the right dimensions. If, however, you use a different source for your stills, you should use a graphics-editing program to make sure that the pictures are 640 x 480 and 72 ppi. Of course, iPhoto will do this for you easily. Just select the image in iPhoto, click Share, click Export, select the File Export tab in the Export Photos dialog, and then select the Scale images no larger than radio button, as shown in Figure 24-5.

✦ **Folder Structure:** We also recommend that you have a single folder serving as the repository for all your DVD's parts: stills, audio, and video for use in your menus, folders for any slideshows, and a folder for any material you intend to include on your DVD-ROM portion. Having all this material co-located reduces the likelihood that you'll misplace or, accidentally of course, delete something you're going to need.

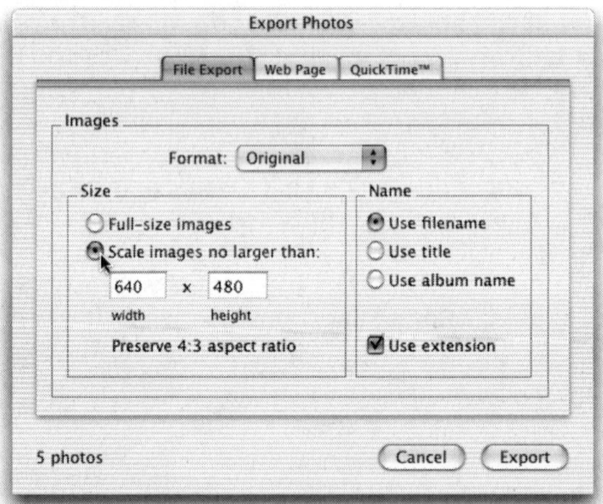

Figure 24-5: You can use iPhoto to scale your images to 640 x 480.

Summary

In this chapter, you learned the things you need to know about planning and organizing a DVD project. You're the only one who can decide which steps you're going to omit, but at least you'll know what it is that you aren't doing and what the repercussions might be.

✦ ✦ ✦

CHAPTER 25

Taking Slideshows Beyond iPhoto

✦ ✦ ✦ ✦

In This Chapter

Adding a little control over iPhoto slideshows

Taking slideshows to VideoCD

✦ ✦ ✦ ✦

Slideshows are such a pervasive topic throughout this book that our publishers felt that they deserved a chapter of their own, tying the threads together and showing you some of the other ways to create, use, and share your slideshows. We happen to agree.

The digital slideshows you can create with iPhoto, iMovie, iDVD, and QuickTime Player Pro (as well as numerous applications dedicated solely to creating slideshows and presentations) have come a long way from the overhead projectors, slide viewers, slide trays, and rotary attachments of our youth. Organizing digital photos takes far less time, and we don't have to worry about losing or scratching the originals. Nor do we have the slightest concern about the risk of dropping them and getting them out of order. Additionally, we can now add precisely timed musical backgrounds or narrations to complement the slides. Finally, we have all sorts of visual special effects at hand, a mixed blessing that can either enhance a presentation or make our audience question our aesthetic judgment.

Getting More Control over iPhoto Slideshows

We think that iPhoto provides the easiest venue we've ever seen for creating attractive slideshows. Just stick the photos in an album, rearrange them in the order you want, add background music if you like, and click the Slideshow button to view your work. Until computers can read your mind, what could be simpler?

However, there are three limitations to an iPhoto slideshow that become apparent as soon as you start wanting to use them for anything other than a kiosk-style presentation.

The first and most glaring limitation is that every slide appears on-screen for the same predetermined duration; and, second, a user's manual control over the slideshow's presentation is limited to clicking the mouse to terminate it.

Using manual controls

Fortunately, a few undocumented keystrokes provide you a modicum of manual slideshow control:

- **spacebar:** Pause/resume the slideshow.
- **↑:** Make the slideshow faster by decreasing slide duration in 1-second increments (to a 1 second minimum).
- **↓:** Make the slideshow slower by increasing slide duration in 1-second increments (to a 30 second maximum).
- **←:** Pause the slideshow and go to previous slide.
- **→:** Pause the slideshow and go to next slide.

After you pause (spacebar) use ← and → to move back and forth from slide to slide, just like you would with a hot-bulb slide projector and remote control clicker. If you look closely, you can see the dimmed pause, forward, and back buttons in the lower-right portion of Figure 25-1.

Any soundtrack you have playing continues uninterrupted while the slideshow is paused.

Assigning a soundtrack to a slideshow

The third limitation is that you can assign only one soundtrack to a slideshow. If, for example, your slideshow were composed of Mediterranean vacation slides, you might want Spanish music for the photos taken in Barcelona, Italian for Rome and Venice, and Greek for Athens. iPhoto prevents you from doing this, but you can get around this limitation by using an audio-editing program to put together the music you want. QuickTime Player Pro lets you edit AIFF and MP3 files, creating composites. You'll just need to compute how long each segment will be and in what order you want them to appear. For example, if you have 15 slides from Barcelona, 20 from Rome, 18 from Venice, and 18 from Athens, and each is going to be on-screen for three seconds, you'll require 45 seconds of Spanish music, 1 minute 54 seconds of Italian, and 54 seconds of Greek.

Figure 25-1: They're not really obvious, but control buttons appear when you have a paused slideshow.

To create this composite soundtrack, proceed as follows:

1. **Open your three song files in QuickTime Player Pro.**
2. **Select segments of the appropriate length in each song's window.** Figure 25-2 shows QuickTime Player Pro with the three song windows open and durations selected.
3. **Choose File ➪ New Player (⌘-N).** This creates a new song window as shown in Figure 25-3.

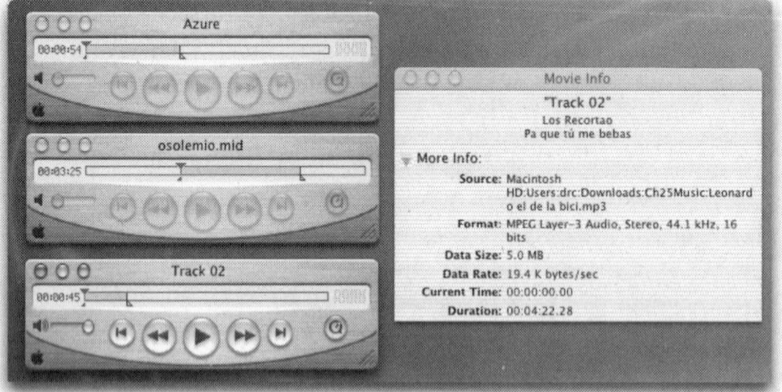

Figure 25-2: Select a portion of each song of the appropriate length.

Figure 25-3: Create a new player window to hold your composition.

4. **Choose Edit ➪ Copy (⌘-C).** Doing this copies the file to the Clipboard.
5. **Select your new window and choose Edit ➪ Paste (⌘-V).** The playhead advances to the end of the selection just pasted, as shown in Figure 25-4.

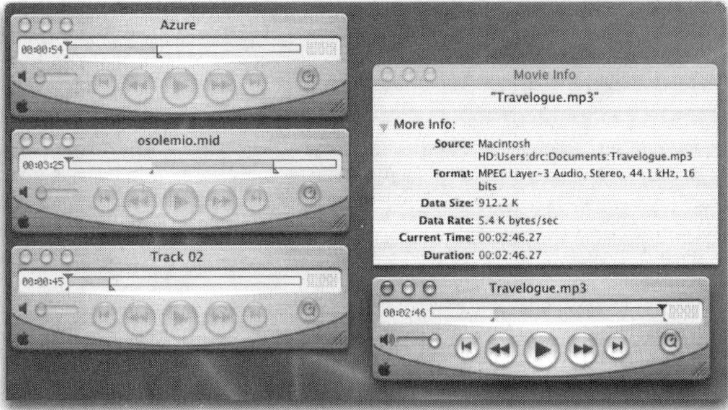

Figure 25-4: The playhead moves to the end, ready to accept your next paste.

6. **Repeat Steps 4 and 5.** You need to repeat Steps 4 and 5 for each song window in turn.
7. **Choose File ⇨ Save.** This saves your new song window. Also, give your new song a name.
8. **Open iTunes and add the new song to your iTunes Library.** See Chapter 4 if you've forgotten how to add a song to the iTunes Library.

Alternatively, if you've purchased Movie Maestro or a similar product, you can create your own musical soundtracks from the clips they provide and add those to your iTunes Library.

See Chapter 17, for more on creating musical soundtracks and adding them to your iTunes Library.

Playing your soundtrack

When you have the soundtrack you desire, just choose it in iPhoto's Slideshow dialog, as follows:

1. **With your slideshow album selected, click iPhoto's Organize button.** This switches iPhoto into Organize Mode, so that the Organize tools (including Slideshow) appear.
2. **Click Slideshow.** The Slideshow Settings dialog appears.
3. **Select the song from your iTunes Library.** See Figure 25-5.

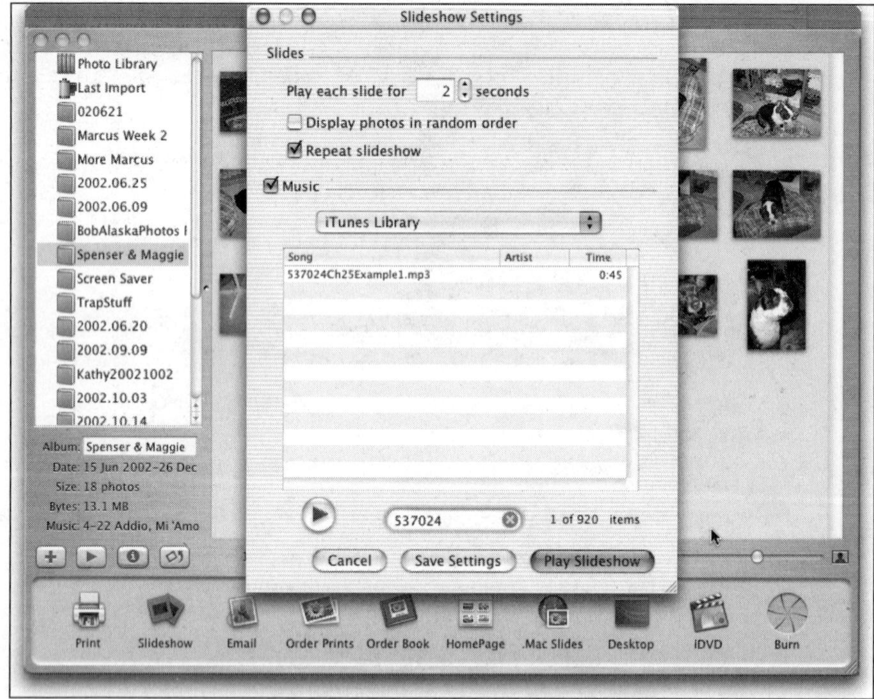

Figure 25-5: Find the song in your iTunes Library and select it.

4. **Click Save Settings in the Slideshow Settings dialog.** You do this if you want the song associated with this slideshow in the future. Alternatively, you can click Play Slideshow if you just want to check it out.

The slideshow starts playing with your soundtrack, and that music will be associated with this slideshow until you change it.

Taking Slideshows to VideoCD

Not having a SuperDrive and, thus, access to the iDVD application doesn't mean that you can't create slideshow CD collections for your friends and family to view on TV using their DVD player. Besides a CD burner, all you need is Roxio's Toast Titanium, which includes a handy little QuickTime component that turns QuickTime movies into VideoCD-compatible MPEG-1 files, and the freeware application VCD Builder.

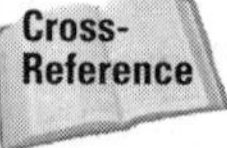

For more on MPEG-1 files, see Chapters 16. For more on the VCD Builder, see Chapter 17.

Follow the directions in Chapter 10 to export your slideshows to QuickTime. VideoCDs expect image resolutions of 320 x 240, so you should export at a resolution that is an even multiple of 320 x 240. We tend to prefer 640 x 480 as that's a good size to preview on the Mac's screen.

VideoCDs actually expect 352 x 240 images, but that resolution applies to rectangular pixels instead of square. QuickTime does the conversion for you.

Converting QuickTime to VideoCD

After you have exported your slideshows, the first step is to convert the QuickTime movie to VideoCD. This process is very simple and straightforward:

1. **Launch Toast Titanium.** The Toast Titanium window appears.
2. **Choose Video CD from Toast's Other button pop-up menu.** See Figure 25-6.

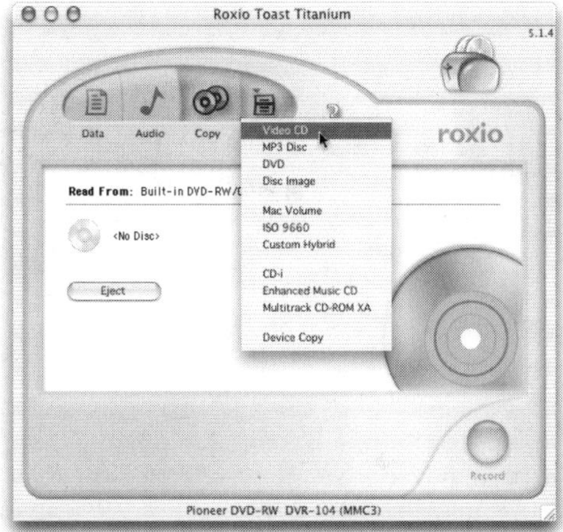

Figure 25-6: The Other button hides a pop-up menu where you can choose Video CD as the destination format.

3. **Drag your movie into Toast's window.** The window is the white area, as shown in Figure 25-7. The Toast Video CD Options dialog appears.
4. **Use the settings in Figure 25-8 in the Toast Video CD Options dialog.** You only use these setting if you are in the United States or Japan. If you're in a PAL country, choose PAL (25 fps) from the Format pop-up menu.

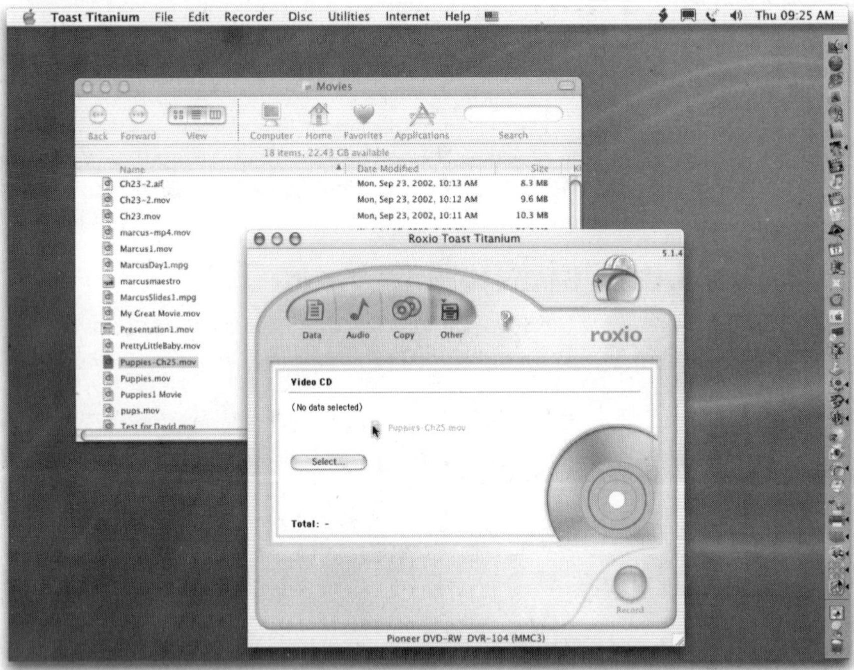

Figure 25-7: Drag the movie to be converted.

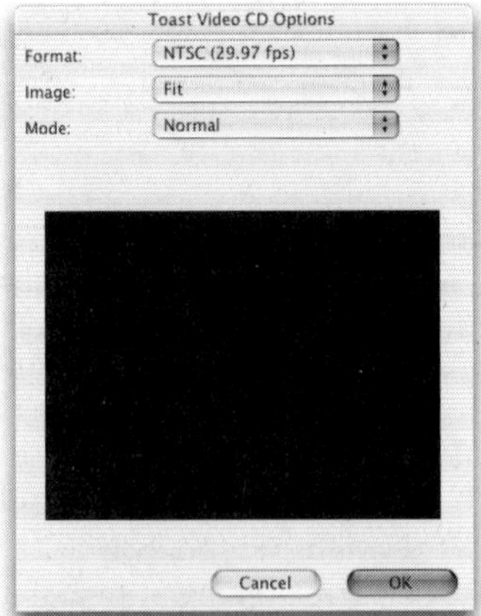

Figure 25-8: Use these settings for a good-looking VideoCD.

5. **Click OK.** A Save Video CD Stream As dialog now appears.
6. **Select a location for your VideoCD file.** The file will have a .mpg filename extension. If you don't like the name suggested by Toast, rename it.
7. **Click Save.** Toast displays a progress bar, as shown in Figure 25-9 as it creates your VideoCD file. When the encoding is complete, the progress bar disappears.

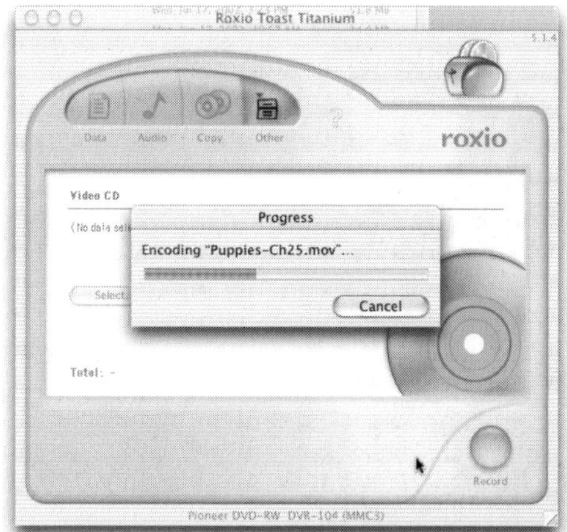

Figure 25-9: Toast encodes your movie into a VideoCD-compatible MPEG-1 file.

8. **Repeat Steps 3 through 6.** You repeat these steps for as many slideshows as you wish to encode.

You could, at this point, just burn the VideoCD and when you put it in a DVD player, the slideshows will play, one after the other, with no user intervention, as if they were one long movie. But, we want to make a VideoCD that behaves more like a DVD (navigated via menus), so you need to exit Toast and do a little more work.

You could also use QuickTime Player Pro's Export command and choose Movie to Toast Video CD from the "Save exported file as" dialog's Export pop-up menu for each slideshow, but we think dragging into the Toast window is easier.

Creating menus

First, select a representative image from each slideshow's collection of photos to use in your menu and decide whether you want your menu to be a rotating sequence of pictures or a collage. We tend toward the collage view, because it is the way almost all DVDs offer their scene selections. Therefore, you're going to need to use a graphics program (Photoshop or Photoshop Elements, GraphicConverter, or AppleWorks are all reasonable choices) to create your (preferably, 640 x 480) menu picture. VCD Builder can scale other sizes to fit, but most graphics programs have optimized scaling routines that might be preferable. Because the editing and saving methods differ from program to program, we'll leave you to use whatever method makes you most comfortable and just illustrate, in Figure 25-10, what a sample menu might look like. (We used Photoshop Elements.)

Figure 25-10: Create a menu screen that will help your viewers find the slideshow they want.

Building the VideoCD

Now that you have your menu screen and the various MPEG slideshow movies, you're ready to create your VideoCDs as follows (using the three slideshow example matching the menu in Figure 25-10):

1. **Launch VCD Builder.**
2. **Click New Sequence.** A rectangle with a 1 in the upper-left corner appears, as shown in Figure 25-11.
3. **Drag your menu's icon to the rectangle.** Notice that, by default, VCD Builder will place it within the TV Safe area.

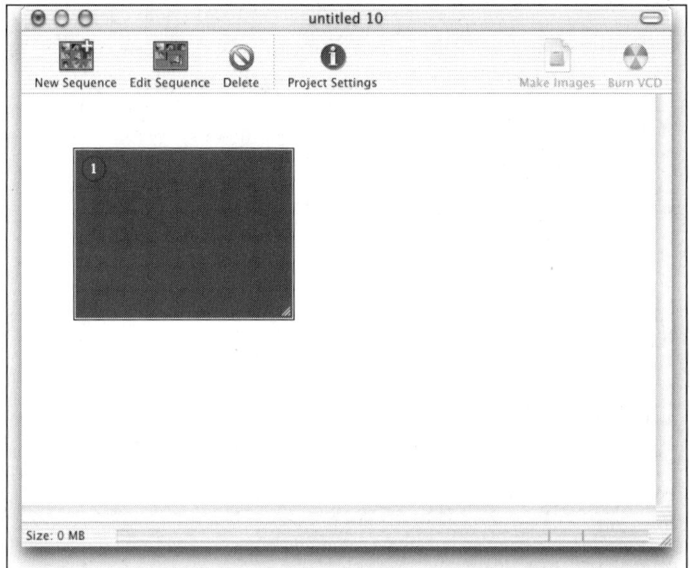

Figure 25-11: Create the first sequence to hold your menu.

Note

If you want to turn off the TV Safe area, double-click the sequence rectangle, select your image in the window that appears, and deselect the Use TV-safe Borders checkbox.

4. **Click New Sequence and drag the rectangle to a nonoverlapping position.** A new sequence box appears in the VCD Builder window.
5. **Drag your first MPEG file's icon to that rectangle.** The first frame of your MPEG file will display in the rectangle.
6. **Holding down the Control key, click in the menu rectangle and drag into the new rectangle and let go.** A circular selection menu appears, as shown in Figure 25-12.
7. **Click the numeric section to make your choice.**

Note

The bottom of the window keeps you informed as to how large your VideoCD is at each step.

8. **Holding down the Control key, click in the slideshow's rectangle and drag into the menu's rectangle, and let go.** This creates a connection between the two sequences and the circular selection menu again appears.

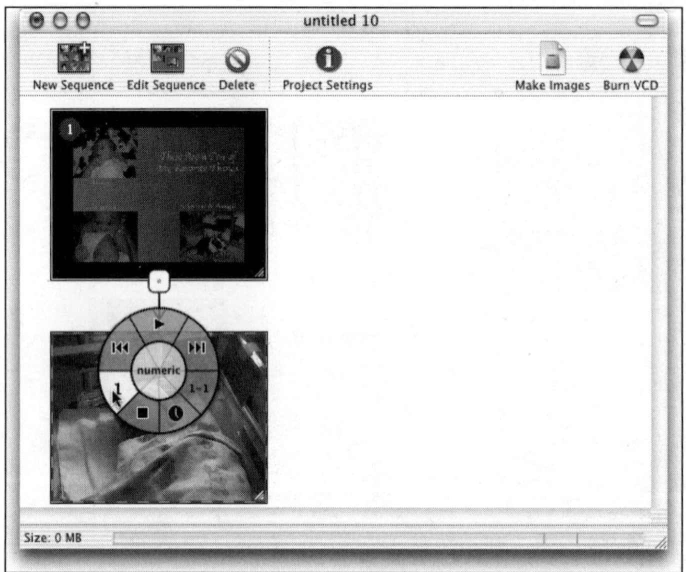

Figure 25-12: Choose the numeric button for your DVD player's remote control that corresponds to the selected slideshow.

9. **From the circular menu, select the Timeout section.** The Timeout section looks like a clock dial. The Timeout action is taken when the sequence finishes playing.

10. **Repeat Steps 4 through 8.** You do this for each of your slideshows. You should now have a window resembling the window shown in Figure 25-13.

    Optionally, you can create Next and Previous connections between the slideshow rectangles, if desired, to respond to clicking the DVD player's remote control's next and previous buttons.

The movie rectangles show the first frame of your movie. This will often be pure black. You can double-click it to get its name and size if you forget which is which.

11. **Choose Project ➪ Save (⌘-S) or Save As (⌘-Shift-S).** You do this to give your project and the VideoCD a name.

12. **Click Save.** Doing this stores the vcd project file on disk.

13. **Click Burn VCD to burn the VCD files in Toast.** VCD Builder presents a Save sheet where you must specify a name and location for the temporary image files. After you have done so, click Save.

14. **Sit back and wait for VCD Builder to finish creating the images.**

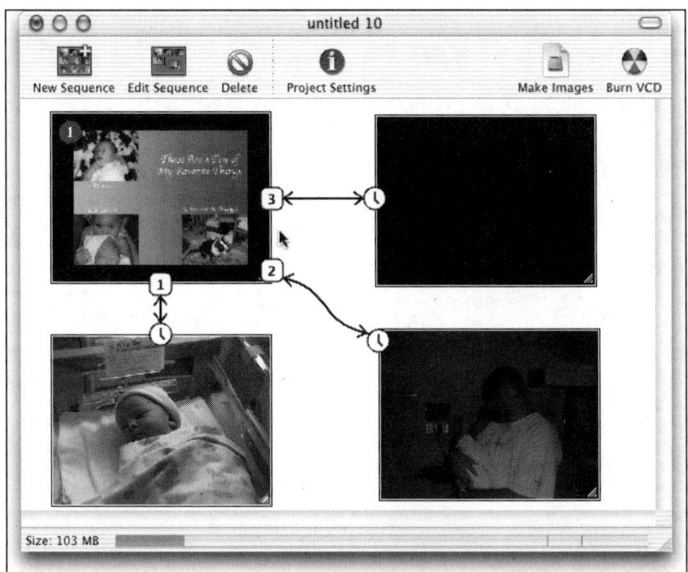

Figure 25-13: Each of your slideshows is now connected to the menu and will return to the menu when completed.

15. **When VCD Builder launches Toast, it sets Toast to Multitrack CD-ROM XA format, and load the image files.** The Toast window comes to the front.

    Click the Burn button. Remember to feed your CD burner a blank disc when prompted.

16. **Click Burn Disc in the dialog that appears.** Doing this tells Toast to proceed. Now, all you have to do is wait for your VideoCD to be burned.

The "temporary" files aren't really temporary. They remain on your hard disk until you throw them away, which is handy if you later decide to burn more copies; just be aware that these large files can consume disk space pretty quickly.

You now have a VideoCD that behaves almost identically to a DVD created in iDVD. Some differences include that you have more control over the sequence and flow of control on the VideoCD, but that you don't have the manual slideshow operation via the remote control you get from an iDVD-created slideshow.

Just as with an iDVD creation, you can mix and match slideshows and movies on the same VideoCD. Because VideoCD takes up significantly less space than DVD, the 80 minutes that you can put on a VideoCD comes very close to the 90 minutes available to iDVD, at a fraction of the cost.

Creating an SVCD

If you want to come closer to DVD quality on your CDs than VideoCD allows, which is essentially VHS quality, consider creating SVCDs. Although a little more effort is involved, and the tools are a bit nerdy, the process is actually pretty easy.

First, we recommend that you install the current version of ffmpeg from `www.versiontracker.com` or `homepage.mac.com/major4/`. ffmpegX is updated frequently, and 0.0.6f was current while we were writing this (early February, 2003). Due to licensing restrictions, various components must be downloaded separately, however, major4 has made that process as painless as possible by providing an installer (shown in the following figure), which tells you what to download from which location. When you point the installer at the downloaded tools, the installer calls Terminal, which asks for your Administrator password so that it can complete the install.

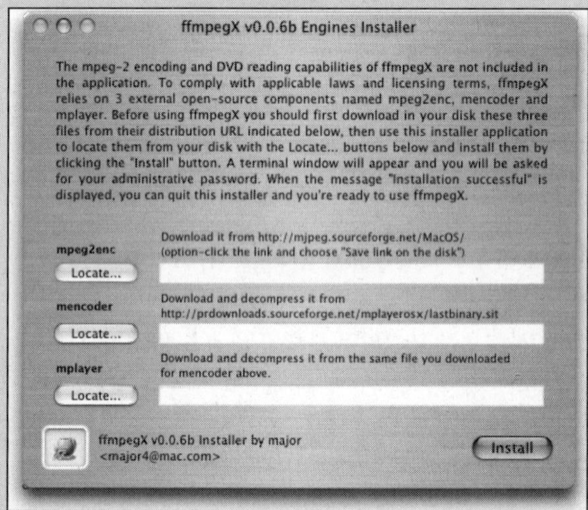

After you have the engines installed, just copy the ffmpeg application to your Applications directory. This can be either the main one or one in your Home directory.

Because the display area for NTSC SVCDs is 480 x 360, you can see that larger images are preferable, keeping in mind the scaling that will take place in your slideshow. When you save your slideshow to QuickTime, you choose 640 x 480 or, or if your images are large enough, 960 x 720.

Launch ffmpeg and click the Open button, selecting your source movie. Then, click the Save As button and name the file you wish to create. ffmpeg will supply the filename extension. Click the Quick Presets button, as shown in the following figure and choose SVCD (NTSC). If you're in PAL territory, select SVCD (PAL). ffmpeg sets all the geeky parameters and options for you in all four tabs. Finally, click the Encode button. ffmpeg launches Terminal and passes the various tools the information needed to create your SVCD.

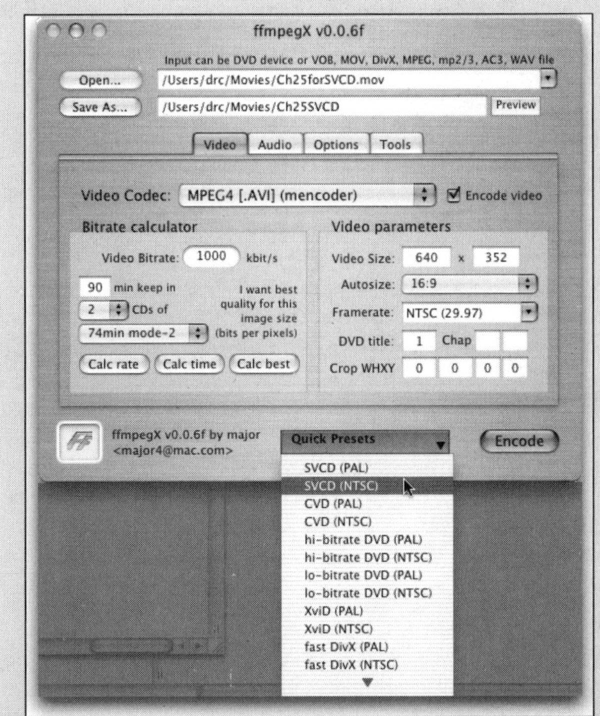

If your filenames or the paths to them include various special characters, such as parentheses or single- or double-quote marks, the tools in Terminal will be unable to proceed.

After grinding away for a while, you'll find a number of similarly named files in your designated destination directory. The one with the name you gave and an extension of `.mpg` is your desired result. The others are irrelevant to this process and can be discarded. You can create SVCDs in VCD Builder by using these MPEG-2 files. You cannot, however, mix MPEG-1 and MPEG-2 files and get a usable disc.

Summary

In this chapter, you learned a few undocumented iPhoto slideshow keystrokes. You also saw a way to create customized audio tracks for your slideshow. Finally, you saw how to create a menu-driven VideoCD or Super VideoCD slideshow disc that looks very similar to (and operates similarly to) an iDVD-created DVD.

✦ ✦ ✦

When You Outgrow the "iStuff"

✦ ✦ ✦ ✦

In This Chapter

When iTunes isn't enough

Moving beyond iPhoto

Moving beyond iMovie

Authoring beyond iDVD

✦ ✦ ✦ ✦

Apple designed and positioned the iLife applications really well. They provide a 100 percent solution for 90 percent of all users and a 90 percent solution for the other 10 percent.

But what happens when you or a particular project falls in those 10 percent areas? That's what we cover in this chapter.

In our opinion, not one of the applications to which you might need to migrate approaches any of the iLife components in design elegance or ease-of-use, but that's one price you'll have to pay for increased power and flexibility. The other is measured in dollars, or whatever your national currency might be. Make no mistake about it; some of the steps up can result in some very real sticker shock.

When iTunes Isn't Enough

We're going to be really blunt here: iTunes is the application you're least likely to outgrow. Now in its third major version release, it's lost none of its ease of use and has added numerous power-user features. At least in our opinions, no other application we've seen or heard of matches iTunes' feature set.

That's not to say that you won't (possibly) find a need to augment iTunes. There are some gaps in its feature set. For example, it has no tools to import music from LPs or cassette tape, just CDs. Similarly, it has no tools for actually editing your audio files.

However, as a ripping, mixing, playing application, it is without peer. Throw in its integration with MP3 players (in particular the iPod), and you have the king of the MP3-playing hill.

What happens though, on those occasions that your MP3 or even your original source material contains hisses, pops, or clicks? At that point, you need an audio-editing tool. There are a number of such tools available, but we're going to focus on two: one shareware (Sound Studio) and one commercial (Roxio's Jam).

Sound Studio

Written by Lucius Kwok and distributed by his small company, Felt Tip Software (www.felttip.com), Sound Studio is a small, but feature-packed audio recording and editing utility. You can download it from Version Tracker and other fine shareware outlets and try it out for up to two weeks to determine whether it is worth the $49 price to you.

Figure 26-1 shows you what Sound Studio looks like with a song loaded. We aren't going to even attempt to tell you how to use Sound Studio. It comes with a 30+-page PDF user's manual as well as other useful documentation on the Sound Studio Web pages, including how-to descriptions for many common tasks.

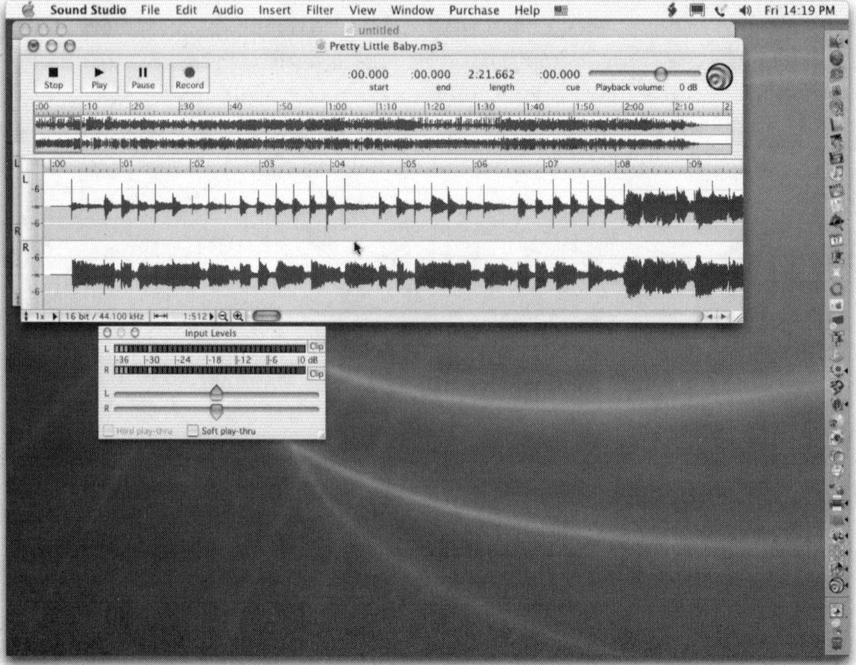

Figure 26-1: Felt Tip Software's Sound Studio is an affordable, yet powerful audio-editing utility.

Roxio's Jam

No longer available as a standalone product, Jam is part of Roxio's Toast with Jam product ($189). Also included is BIAS Peak LE VST, a collection of highly optimized waveform editing tools. Using Peak, you can enhance your audio with various special effects, such as concert reverb (the pulsing echo you experience when listening to a live concert) and noise reduction.

Roxio offers licensed Toast owners an upgrade path to Toast with Jam for $100. (They call it $99.95.)

We all know that we can use iTunes or Toast to burn audio CD-Rs that play in most CD players, but those CDs don't necessarily conform to all the Red Book standards for a CD-DA master disc — one that a CD duplicator can use to mass-produce "real" CDs. This is where Jam steps up to the plate. It has all the tools required to construct discs from which you can create master discs. Figure 26-2 shows Jam with a playlist ready to master.

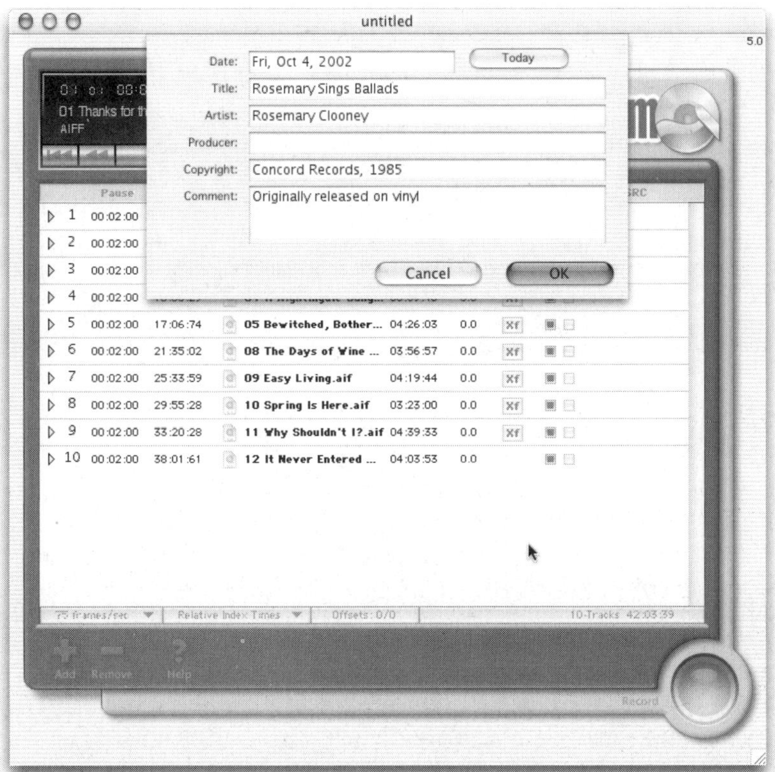

Figure 26-2: Create Red Book-compliant CD-DA master discs with Jam.

Moving Beyond iPhoto

Don't get us wrong, we both love iPhoto and use it regularly. However, iPhoto's still young and has some serious limitations for heavy users. iPhoto gets really slow with large photo libraries and has a limited chest of editing tools. Although its lack of archiving facilities is an issue, the Burn button introduced in iPhoto 2 made that complaint irrelevant. Other shortcomings are iPhoto's inability to handle multiple libraries and its very basic editing tools.

Handling multiple libraries

Various freeware and shareware authors have provided *kludges* (technospeak for nonwarranted workarounds) to handle multiple libraries. In our opinion, the power-user solution to this problem is iView Media or iView Media Pro. If you're having problems with iPhoto's performance as your Library grows, take a look at iView Media or iView Media Pro. (Remember, iView Media is bundled with Toast Titanium.) It could solve all your distributed storage problems.

For more on kludges as well as iView Media or iView Media Pro, see Chapter 12.

If that's the only way you're outgrowing iPhoto, we would encourage you to use one of the iView Media applications as an adjunct to iPhoto. iPhoto's sharing and organizational tools are just too nice to forego.

On the other hand, if you need to consolidate your photos with other supporting files, such as Word documents, audio files, movie projects, or presentations, then you'll probably have to make iView Media Pro your command center and use iPhoto as the occasional adjunct. For example, if you want a coffee table book, iView Media Pro does not have this feature.

Getting around iPhoto's editing tools

iPhoto's other glaring weakness is its editing tools. Although they're useful for basic photo manipulation, they're not what you want for fine control or more sophisticated touchup jobs. Apple recognized this limitation, so iPhoto lets you specify another application to employ as your photo editor. To do so, perform the following steps:

1. **Choose iPhoto ⇨ Preferences (⌘-,).** The Preferences dialog appears.
2. **Click the Other radio button under Double-clicking photos opens them in.** This selects the button and enables the text box and Select button.
3. **Click the Select button and nominate your photo-editing application of choice in the Choose dialog that appears.**

Obviously, the top dog in the photo-editing pack is Adobe's Photoshop 7. If you're a professional graphics person, you probably have and use Photoshop on a daily basis. For the rest of us, though, Photoshop Elements 2 provides just about any Photoshop feature you might want, often in a more accessible form, and at one-sixth the cost. Although Dennis owns both Photoshop and Photoshop Elements, he does almost all his photo retouching in Elements. Photoshop only gets brought into play when he's dealing with scans of photos that were in bad shape — times when even tools like iPhoto 2's Retouch brush to repair imperfections are just not enough.

If you have a G4 "Pro" unit produced in 2002 or later, it is quite likely that Apple provided you a licensed copy of the wonderful shareware graphics tool, GraphicConverter. While GraphicConverter isn't Photoshop, it has a number of very nice features. One of Dennis's favorites is that you can tell exactly where you are in the photo, which is very handy when trying to make a selection of a specific size. Figure 26-3 gives an example of this feature, and shows a 1024 x 768 selection cropped out of an 1800 x 1200 photo.

Figure 26-3: Know where you are and your selection sizes at all times by choosing Picture ➪ Show Position.

Thorsten Lemke, GraphicConverter's author frequently updates the program, adding new features and additional supported formats in addition to fixing the rare bug that gets reported. Check at `www.lemkesoft.de` to determine the current version. You'll probably want to upgrade.

Assuming that you were not blessed with a copy on your Mac, we would encourage you to consider purchasing a copy. Not only is it one of the best shareware applications available, the support Thorsten provides his customers is top-notch. For $35, it is one of the best software deals out there.

Moving Beyond iMovie

Video is where moving to a more feature-rich program can get really expensive. The two major contenders in this arena are Adobe Premiere ($599) and Apple's Final Cut Pro ($999). We're both big fans of Adobe's products, but just don't see getting Premiere without also purchasing After Effects for the special effects and compositing functions. Even with the reduced bundle price of $999 when you buy them together, you're still paying as much as you would for Final Cut Pro, probably the finest personal computer video-editing software available on any platform.

Dennis hasn't outgrown iMovie yet, especially because he's augmented it with the wonderful plug-ins available from GeeThree, Virtix, and eZedia. He's combined this with the plethora of tools appearing out of the Unix-verse for post-processing his video. However, Bob uses Final Cut Pro a lot. Figure 26-4 shows a screen shot of the Final Cut Pro/Final Cut Express editing table metaphor.

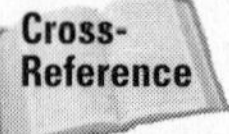

For more on GeeThree, Virtix, and eZedia, see Chapter 17.

Recently, Apple introduced Final Cut Express ($299) as a "cut-down" version of Final Cut Pro, designed to straddle the gap between iMovie and Final Cut Pro. We haven't had enough time to fully assess Final Cut Express, but it could easily be a solution for you, if iMovie 3 doesn't provide enough control.

Some of the features Final Cut Pro brings to the table include chapter markers and support for multiple formats including OfflineRT, a way of storing over 40 minutes of video in 1GB of hard disk for offline editing while still being able to reconnect it to the original DV source.

Figure 26-4: Final Cut Pro and Final Cut Express simulate a professional film editor's worktable.

Authoring Beyond iDVD

If your DVD-authoring goals include making movie DVDs like the big shots in Hollywood, you'll outgrow iDVD fairly quickly. Once again, outgrowing a video product can quickly get expensive. DVD Studio Pro, at $999, is the professional-quality authoring solution. There's a hidden catch to this, making it even more expensive. You'll almost certainly have to upgrade to Final Cut Express or Final Cut Pro as well, so your movies will have the multiple tracks, marker (chapter) points, and so forth not provided by iMovie. Note that iMovie's chapter markers interface only with iDVD 3. Figure 26-5 shows a typical DVD Studio Pro project in progress.

DVD Studio Pro includes a few bonus items as well. You get a QuickTime Pro license, in case you didn't already upgrade. Final Cut Pro also includes a QuickTime Pro license. Here are a few other programs and a music library that you might find useful:

✦ **A.Pack:** A wonderful audio-encoding utility, enabling you to encode many different formats into Dolby Digital, ready for use on your DVD.

✦ **Subtitle Editor:** A sweet tool for creating multiple subtitle tracks for your movies, depending upon which language the viewer selects.

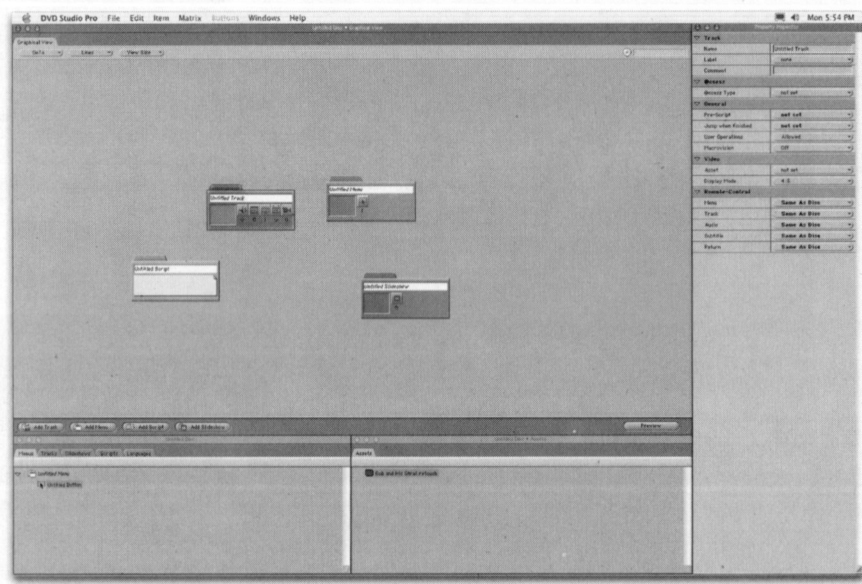

Figure 26-5: Professional DVD authoring features are at hand when using DVD Studio Pro.

- ✦ **Peak DV:** A full version of the audio-editing application included with Roxio Jam (described earlier in this chapter), provides every software feature you might need to edit your projects' audio.
- ✦ **CorelDRAW Graphics Suite 11:** Lets you build layered menus or even use it to touch up your photos and slides.
- ✦ **FreePlay Music Library:** This is a free library and also available to paid-up .Mac account holders via their iDisks. It is a huge collection of license-free music.

Although not nearly so popular nor, in our opinion, quite as powerful as Adobe Photoshop 7, Corel's CorelDRAW Graphics Suite 11 provides a huge feature set and is the closest thing to a competitor Photoshop has.

Summary

In this chapter, you saw some of the software available to handle the growing pains when one or more of the iApps just doesn't provide the power you crave. You've also seen that the next step up can be very expensive.

✦ ✦ ✦

System Requirements

A program's hardware and OS requirements lists are nebulous blends of facts. In some cases, they list the minimum configuration on which you can even hope to launch the program. Other times, they'll merely describe the minimum configurations on which the publisher has tested or certified the software as usable — the reality might be lower, but if it is, you're on your own with respect to support because the publisher won't acknowledge your configuration. And, once in a while, there will be parenthetical "recommendations" for more memory or a newer OS release than the minimum. As a rule of thumb, we treat these recommendations as the *real* minimum requirement for use where we won't be drumming our fingers on the table and muttering.

What we're going to do in this appendix is list Apple's requirements for these four wonderful applications and add our own editorial comments as to what we consider reality.

What Do I Need for iTunes?

Apple's listed requirements for iTunes 3.0.1 (current at the time we're writing this) are

- Mac OS X version 10.1.4 or later
- Mac with built-in USB ports
- 400MHz G3 or better
- 256MB RAM
- Supported CD-RW drive if you wish to create your own CDs

These requirements come pretty close to reflecting our view, too, with one exception. We don't think that 256MB of RAM is enough to avoid frustration, especially if you want to have anything but the Finder and iTunes running. In fact, the slower your processor (and for OS X, 400MHz G3s are pretty darned slow), the more RAM we recommend. On a 400MHz G3 PowerBook, like Dennis's, 256MB wasn't enough to keep him from muttering imprecations — upgrading to 640MB made iTunes and everything else very pleasant, but 384MB seemed okay. Also, most everything runs a little better in Mac OS X 10.2 (Jaguar) than in earlier OS releases, so we also recommend stepping up to Jaguar, though it isn't as critical if you have enough RAM.

Although Apple says you need a "built-in USB port," many users have reported success using iTunes with a third-party USB card in their earlier-model Macs. So while Apple may not support it officially, you may very well be able to run iTunes on a Mac that doesn't offer a built-in USB port.

What Do I Need for iPhoto?

iPhoto 2.0 is the current version as we're typing this material and Apple's requirements list is short:

- Mac OS X version 10.1.5 or later (10.2.2 or later recommended)
- Macintosh with built-in USB ports
- Compatible camera, printer, or other device
- 400MHz G3 or better recommended
- 1024 x 768 minimum screen resolution recommended
- 256MB RAM

Technically speaking, you don't need a camera, a printer, a SmartCard reader, and so on to make use of iPhoto. iPhoto works with almost any graphics you provide it — at least those in standard, QuickTime-compatible formats — so you could get them off the Web, via e-mail, or off of CD. With the on-demand printing and the book features, you don't need a printer, either. Having said that, the suggested items are good accessories to have for iPhoto.

Again, iPhoto works with OS X, 10.1.5, but you'll be happier with 10.2.2 or later. Similarly, the more RAM you can feed it the better on any system, especially those with slower processors. Dennis found 640MB on the 400MHz G3 Powerbook to be tolerable, so long as the Library didn't grow too large. 256MB on an 800MHz flat-panel iMac G4 was agonizingly slow with just about 100 photos in the Library. Upgrading to 768MB alleviated that frustration — even with 1,500 photos in the Library, in over 30 albums, response is quite zippy.

Again, while Apple says you need a "built-in USB port," many users have reported success using iPhoto with a third-party USB card in their earlier-model Macs. So while Apple may not support it officially, you may very well be able to run iPhoto on a Mac that doesn't offer a built-in USB port.

What Do I Need for iMovie?

While we're writing this material, iMovie 3.0.2 is the current version. Apple's listed requirements for iMovie are

- 300MHz G3 or better with built-in FireWire port(s)
- CD or DVD drive
- Mac OS X 10.1.5 or later with 256MB of RAM or more (Mac OS X 10.2.2 or later recommended)
- 1024 x 768 minimum screen resolution
- QuickTime 6.1 or later
- 2GB or more of available disk space

iMovie is a program where we think that Apple's giving you a list of the bare minimums. 200MB of disk doesn't come close to being a realistic number. That's only enough room for about one minute of video and it would leave your Mac groaning and moaning with the disk full very shortly. We think that you should have as much (fast) hard disk space available as possible, but a realistic minimum would be 200MB *more* than the space needed for the video itself (at 200MB/minute). Thus, for a 10-minute movie, you should try to have at least 2.2GB of available disk space, and that doesn't include the space you'll need if you choose to export the finished product to QuickTime or VideoCD. We also think that doubling the recommended memory gives a more realistic starting point if you want decent performance. Again, we've both gotten our best iMovie experiences in OS X, version 10.2.2.

What Do I Need for iDVD?

iDVD is currently at Version 3.0, with the following requirements list:

- Mac OS X, version 10.1.5 or later (10.2.2 or later recommended)
- Any Power Macintosh G4, G4 iMac, or eMac containing a built-in Apple SuperDrive
- 1024 x 768 minimum screen resolution

- ✦ 2GB free hard disk space
- ✦ 256MB RAM (384 MB recommended)

We consider the OS requirement accurate, but have experienced noticeable performance improvements under Jaguar (10.2 or later). The hardware requirement is accurate, although (as we've noted elsewhere) replacing a built-in CD or DVD drive with a Pioneer A104 or A105 unit seems to work. The recommendation for 384MB RAM, in our opinions, is barely a workable minimum, and the listed minimum of 256MB will have you tearing your hair out. As always, the more RAM the better. This is especially true if you want to run iDVD Companion, or any other software, simultaneously.

✦ ✦ ✦

Late-Breaking News: iTunes 4

✦ ✦ ✦ ✦

While this book was going to press, Apple announced and released iTunes 4. Because we felt this material was important and should be included in the book, but did not want to delay getting you all the information, we're covering the iTunes 4 changes and additions in this appendix.

Fortunately, everything we showed you how to do with iTunes 3 still works with iTunes 4. Apple added features and capabilities without changing existing behavior, which (for once) makes our job a little easier.

What Do I Need for iTunes 4?

Apple's listed requirements for iTunes 4 (as of May 2003) show very little change from those for iTunes 3:

- Mac OS X Version 10.1.5 or later (10.2.4 recommended)

Note In fact, some features, as we'll describe in the body of this appendix, require 10.2.4 (but iTunes 4, itself, does not).

- Mac with built-in USB ports
- 400MHz G3 or better
- 256MB RAM
- Supported CD-RW drive if you want to create your own CDs

These requirements come pretty close to reflecting our view, too, just as they did with iTunes 3 (see Appendix A) with one exception. We still don't think that 256MB of RAM is enough to avoid frustration, especially if you want to have anything but the Finder and iTunes running. In fact, the slower your processor (and for OS X, 400MHz G3s are pretty darned slow), the more we recommend as much RAM as you and your wallet feel comfortable providing.

What's New in iTunes 4?

The first change you may notice when you launch iTunes 4 the first time is small and cosmetic, but the iTunes 4 Dock icon's "note" is now green.

The major new features in iTunes 4 are:

- You can purchase and download individual songs or albums from Apple's online Music Store directly to your music library (so far, this requires a credit card with a United States address).
- You can use Rendezvous to share your music between computers on your network. This Rendezvous sharing requires Mac OS X 10.2.4 or later. You can even stream them from any other iTunes 4-using computer whose IP address you can access.
- MPEG-4 Advanced Audio Coding (AAC) is now available. Encoding AAC requires QuickTime 6.2 or later. Although AAC becomes the default encoding format, you can still import using MP3, AIFF, or WAV by setting your Preferences.
- If you're running OS X 10.2.4 or later and have an internal SuperDrive, you can back up your music to DVD-R or DVD-RW disks. These DVDs work in your computer, but not in commercial DVD players. You can also back up to data CD-R and CD-RW discs from within iTunes 4.

Apple says that some third-party DVD burners might also work, but they don't provide any information on which ones those might be.

- View song and album artwork for your purchases from the Music Store, or add artwork of your own to songs in your library.

The main iTunes window has a few minor but immediately obvious differences. There is now a Music Store entry in the Source list and an added button, Show or hide song artwork, below the Source list. These two items are shown in Figure B-1. Additionally, you'll see that the font used in the Source and Song lists now obey your anti-aliasing preferences (also visible in Figure B-1).

Shopping at the Music Store

Clicking the Music Store Source list entry initiates an Internet connection to Apple's Online Music Store. After setting up your account (necessary only the first time you connect), you'll see a window similar to that in Figure B-2. (You'll undoubtedly have different playlists than Dennis, and the featured songs and albums change regularly.) The Music Store display area is really just a specialized Web browser, and you navigate the Music Store as you would any other Web site.

Figure B-1: The Source list now sports a Music Store item, and there is a new button below the Source list.

You can purchase individual songs for 99¢ each or download entire albums for varying prices (most are about $9.99), as shown in Figure B-3. The per-song pricing should be a blessing to the hordes who complain about having to purchase a whole CD for $12 or $18 when they only want one or two songs from that CD. With 1-Click purchasing turned on (the default), when you opt to purchase an album or song you see the alert shown in Figure B-4. As usual, iTunes offers you a "stop bugging me" checkbox, but we don't recommend using this unless you're willing to risk accidental clicks charging your credit card and starting a download. The music from the Apple Store is AAC-encoded (MPEG-4 Advanced Audio Encoding). AAC encoding gives MP3-equivalent quality at a lower bit-rate and thus smaller size. Although we obviously haven't sampled everything (we don't have that kind of budget), the songs we've downloaded have all been 128-bit encodings, and they sound at least as true as 192-bit or higher MP3 encodings. When the download starts, the iTunes Status display shows which song is downloading and the progress, as shown in Figure B-5.

You can sample the first 30 seconds of each individual song over your Internet connection by double-clicking the song in the Music Store's browser list.

It's probably a little underhanded, but for some albums (in particular Classical and Jazz, with their long tracks), purchasing the individual songs is cheaper than purchasing the entire album.

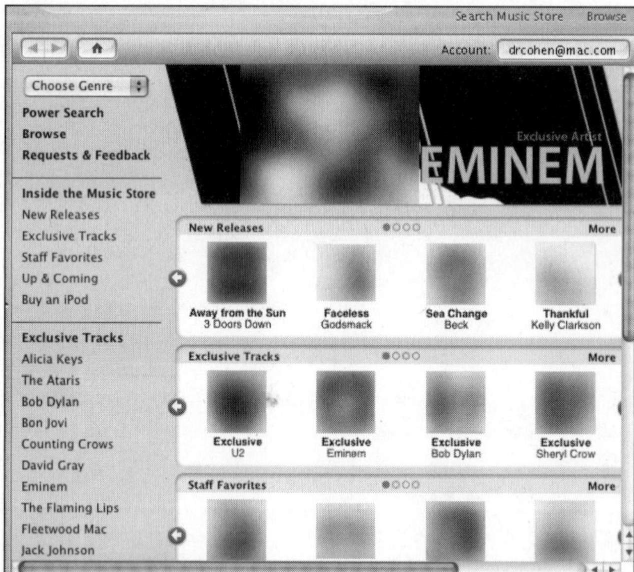

Figure B-2: iTunes now has a Web browser built in for use with the Music Store.

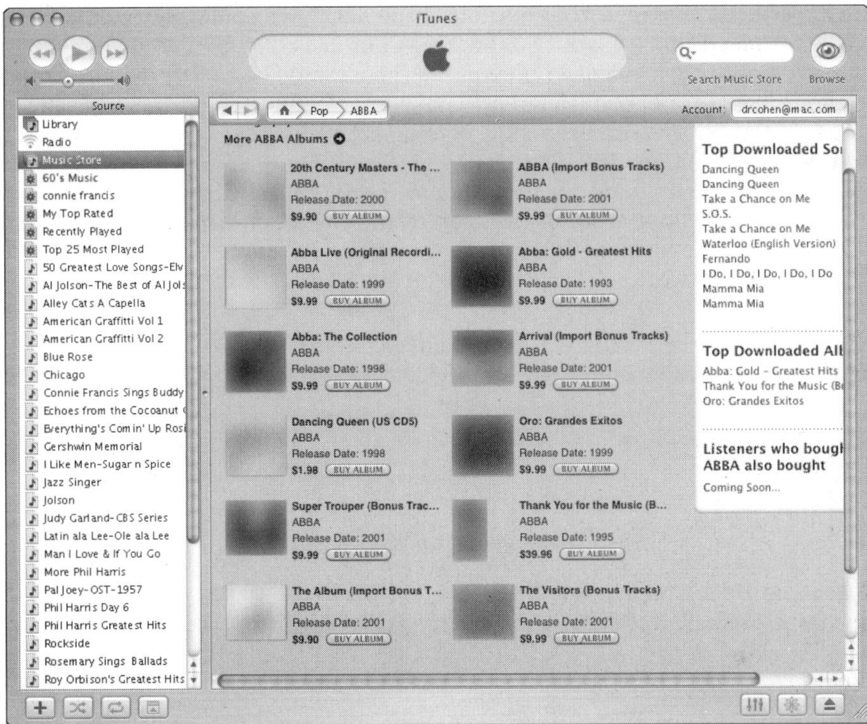

Figure B-3: You can purchase entire albums, too.

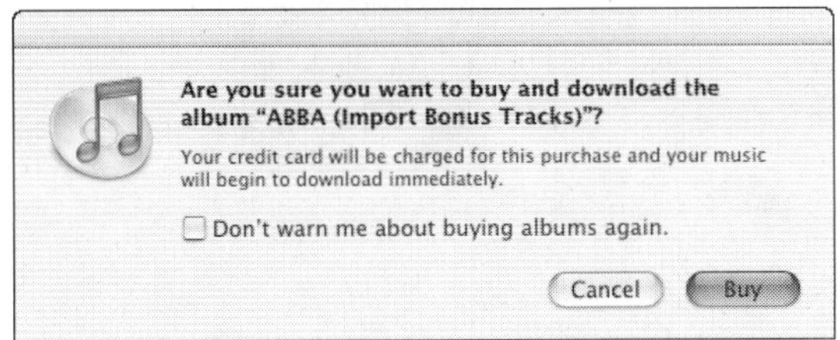

Figure B-4: iTunes gives you a chance to back out from a misclick.

Figure B-5: The Status display lets you know your download progress.

After you've downloaded your first purchase, you have a new playlist directly below the Music Store in your Source list — Purchased Music (see Figure B-6). Click the Purchased Music playlist and you see the alert in Figure B-6. We activated the stop bugging me checkbox here fairly quickly. Selecting one of the songs and choosing File ➪ Get Info (⌘-I) presents the iTunes 4 revamped Info dialog, as shown in Figure B-7. The Summary tab replaces the iTunes 3 Info tab and now displays the CD cover that accompanies your purchase. The iTunes 3 Tags tab has been renamed as the Info tab in iTunes 4, and Options remains unchanged. The Artwork tab (Figure B-7) lets you add customized artwork, including your own digital photos or scans. The Artwork tab's slider controls the size of the artwork display.

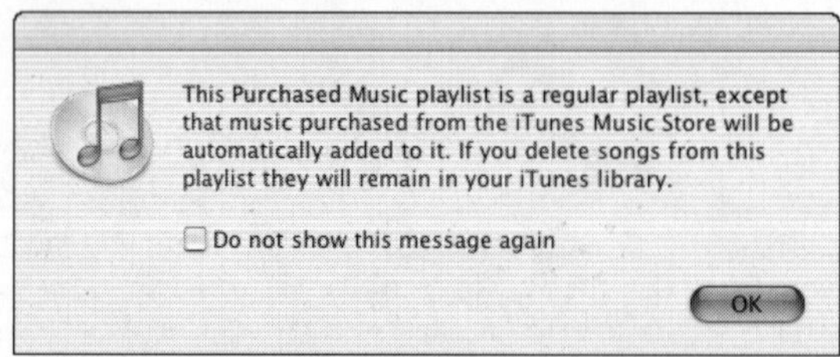

Figure B-6: iTunes 4 reminds you what the Purchased Music playlist is, every time you select it.

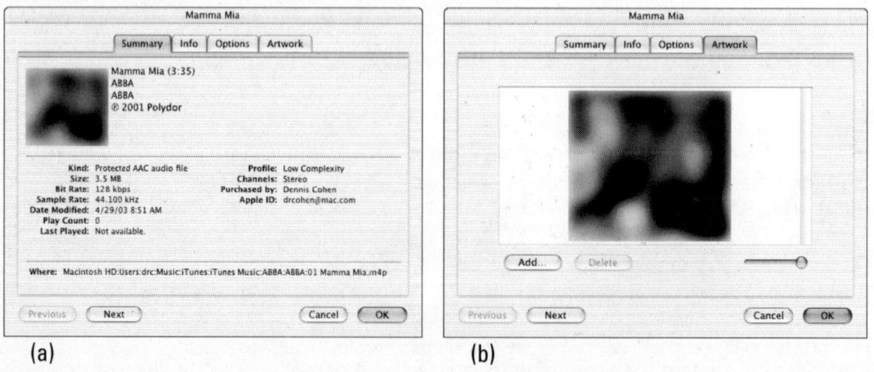

Figure B-7: The Info dialog's Summary tab (a) and Artwork tab (b).

Each of the songs you purchase has DRM (Digital Rights Management) information within it. iTunes uses this information to prevent certain copyright abuses. You can use individual songs in as many personal mix collections as you want and burn those, but you can only burn an individual playlist containing one or more purchased tracks ten times. You can download songs to as many iPods as you like, but can only authorize three Macs to play purchased songs at one time. You can, however, remove a Mac's authorization by choosing Advanced ➪ Deauthorize Computer, freeing up a slot to use with a different computer. All of these authorizations are managed via connections to the Music Store, so you have to have a connection to authorize or deauthorize computers.

iTunes Preferences Changes

Choose iTunes ➪ Preferences (⌘-,) to open the iTunes 4 Preferences dialog. The General and Effects panes are unchanged, but if you have QuickTime 6.2 Pro or later installed, there is a new AAC Encoder item in the Importing pane's Import Using pop-up menu (Figure B-8). The Burning pane also grew a new option: burning a Data CD or DVD (also Figure B-8). Additionally, the Advanced pane lets you set the buffer size for streaming music. *Streaming music* is music that you share with other iTunes 4 users over a network. The major additions, though, are the Sharing and Store panes (Figure B-9).

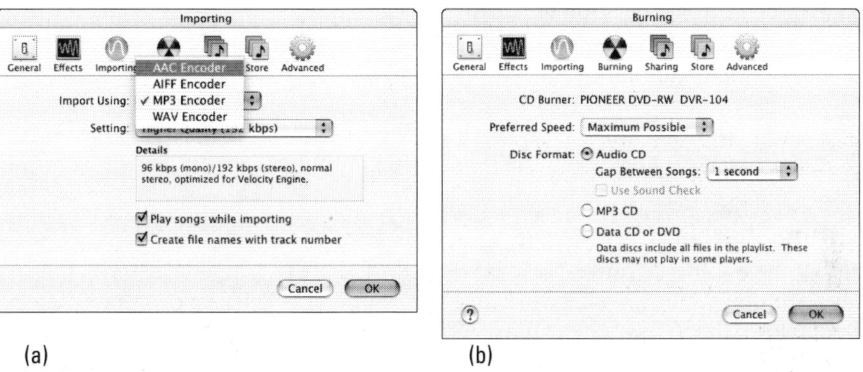

Figure B-8: Your Importing preferences have a new encoding choice (a), and your Burning preferences now let you specify a data CD or DVD format (b).

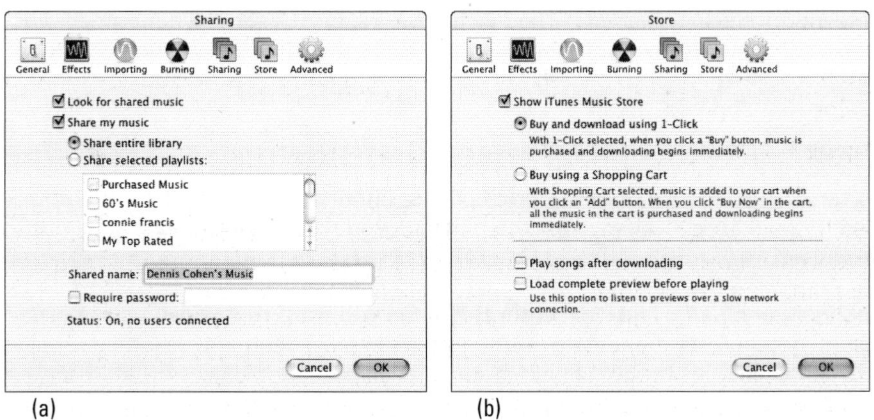

Figure B-9: New in iTunes 4 are Sharing (a) and Store (b) preference panes.

Setting Store preferences

The Store preferences pane is straightforward. If you uncheck the Show iTunes Music Store checkbox, the Music Store no longer appears in your Source list. If you decide that you want to use the store, you need to choose iTunes ⇨ Preferences, select the Store pane, and select the checkbox. The two radio buttons give you a choice of 1-Click purchasing (the default) or Shopping Cart purchasing. With 1-Click, each purchase is a separate credit card charge, which would really lengthen a credit card statement if you do much shopping at the Music Store, but the Music Store consolidates purchases made in a 24-hour period into one charge. The downloading starts immediately, and you can continue shopping while it downloads. Using the Shopping Cart lets you change your mind when you see how many songs and albums you've accumulated, but using it means that nothing starts downloading until you check out by clicking the cart's Buy Now button.

If you're on a dialup connection, you'll probably want to select the Load complete preview before playing checkbox. Doing this causes iTunes to download the full 30-second clip before playing it, but eliminates all delays while you're waiting for your connection to catch up.

Play songs after downloading is obvious. When you select it, each song you purchase starts to play when the download completes.

Setting Sharing preferences

One of the coolest features (at least in our opinion) is iTunes 4's Sharing. If you have multiple Macs on a network and are running OS X 10.2.4 or later on each of them with iTunes 4, you can share your iTunes libraries or playlists with other users. In fact, you can even share with users over the Internet, if you know their IP addresses.

The Look for shared music checkbox determines whether your copy of iTunes will check the network for shared iTunes libraries and playlists and then list them in your Source list. Just click the disclosure triangle to see the contents. If you know the IP address of another user who is sharing their music, you can choose Advanced ⇨ Connect to Shared Music (⌘-K) and enter their IP address in the dialog that appears.

Selecting Share my music tells iTunes that either your entire library (Share entire library radio button) or specified playlists (Share selected playlists radio button combined with checkboxes for the playlists you want shared) should be published to the network.

In the Shared name text box, enter the name you want to have appear in other users' Source lists to indicate your shared library. Selecting the Require password checkbox enables the text field where you can enter a password that other users will need to know to access your library. Figure B-10 shows the dialog that appears when iTunes attempts to access a password-protected library.

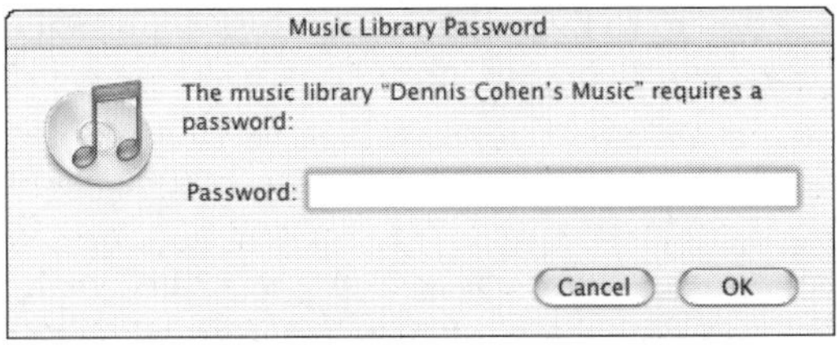

Figure B-10: You can restrict sharing to only those users who know the password you set.

Sharing music

When you check the Share my music box option in Sharing preferences, the computer sharing the songs must have iTunes 4 running in Mac OS X 10.2.4 or later.

Note

If you use OS X's built-in firewall and iTunes 4, you may find that, although iTunes can find other sharing computers, you can't actually view playlists and play music. This is because the firewall defaults to blocking port 3689, which iTunes uses for both local (Rendezvous) and remote (IP) music sharing.

Remedying this problem is easy. Launch System Preferences (clicking its Dock icon is the easiest way), click the Sharing icon, and then click the Firewall tab. Click New and then choose Other from the Port Name popup menu. Type in 3689 for the port number and give it a name, such as "iTunes Sharing" in the dialog that appears. Close the dialog and you should be sharing as originally intended.

When you share a playlist or library, you need to authorize any content purchased from the Music Store to play on that computer, as shown in Figure B-11. You may have as many as three computers simultaneously authorized to play specific tracks. If you want to authorize a fourth computer, you need to choose Advanced ➪ Deauthorize Computer on one of the existing three. You can even deauthorize the one on which the content actually resides, a useful way to make one (probably older) Mac a song-server — you just can't play the song on that Mac until you reauthorize the computer.

Figure B-11: You can only play rights-managed songs on Macs you authorize.

For non-protected songs, you can serve up to five other computers simultaneously. You cannot share Audible.com spoken word content, nor can you share QuickTime soundtracks.

Backing up your music

From iTunes introduction, one of its biggest selling points was that you could burn audio CDs. iTunes 3 added burning MP3 CDs, which lets you store about 10 times as many songs on a single CD-R and still play it in many standalone CD and DVD players (those that play MP3s as well as CD-DA). But, until now, there has never really been a built-in backup function.

As mentioned earlier, burning data CDs and DVDs has been added to iTunes 4 in the Burning preferences. So as not to break the existing interface, you can still only burn from a playlist, which means that if you want to back up your entire library to a DVD-R, you need to create a playlist that contains your entire library. Give the playlist the name you want the backup CD to have, because that's the name iTunes will use when burning the disc. Then, with your Burning preferences set to burn Data CDs and DVDs, you can burn the playlist to disc. Borrowing a page from iPhoto 2's Burn command, discs that you burn in this manner mount as iTunes playlists when you insert them in your Mac, as shown in Figure B-12. In fact, if iTunes isn't running, inserting the disc will start iTunes. Unfortunately, you still can't nest playlists, so the burned disk has no organizational structure to it—just a lot of songs in a flat directory. Even worse, it doesn't reflect any play order that you might have created until you click the sequence number (farthest left) column header.

Figure B-12: CDs and DVDs burnt as data discs mount as playlists in the iTunes 4 Source list.

Here's hoping that hierarchical backups become available in the next version.

Adding and viewing artwork

Apple added a nice aesthetic touch in iTunes 4. You can now associate artwork with your individual songs. Songs purchased from the Apple Music Store come with the album cover scan linked to each song. You can add one or more images to any song in your Library via the Info dialog's Artwork tab, as follows:

1. **Select the first song to which you want to attach artwork.** Yes, you have to add the artwork one song at a time using this method.
2. **Choose File ➪ Get Info**. Alternatively, you can press ⌘-I. The Info dialog appears.
3. **Click the Artwork tab.**
4. **Drag the art file's icon from the Finder into the large list box**. You can also click Add and navigate in the Choose a File dialog that appears to select your artwork.
5. **Repeat Step 4 as many times as you want to add as many pictures to that song as desired**. Figure B-13 shows a song with two images associated.

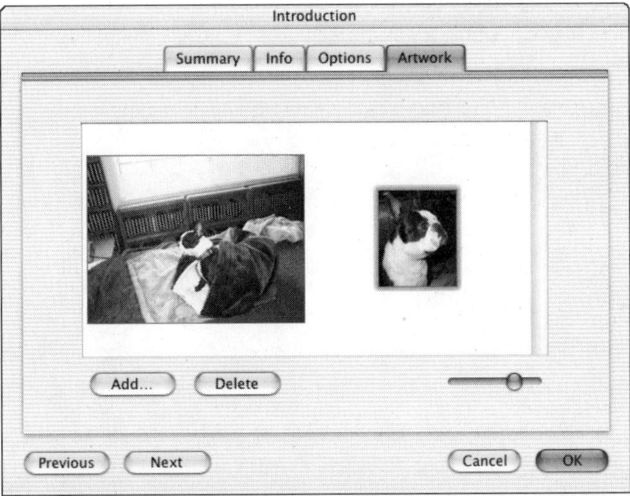

Figure B-13: This Introduction track has two pictures associated with it.

6. **(Optional) Click the Previous or Next buttons to move to another song and repeat Step 4 for those to which you want to add images.**
7. **Click OK when done.**

Now, when you're in the main iTunes window, select a song and click the Show or hide song artwork. button to reveal the artwork pane. If, as in Figure B-14, the song has artwork attached, the first image displays in the artwork pane. If the song has more pictures attached, the next (right-pointing) arrow will be enabled and you can press that to cycle through the images. When you move to the second image, the previous (left-pointing) arrow will be enabled, so that you can move backward through the artwork. That's all there is to it, almost. You don't actually have to go through the Get Info process—you can drag artwork directly into the artwork pane. In fact, that's how you can add the same piece of art to multiple songs, simultaneously.

Click a piece of artwork in the Hide and show artwork. pane to open it, full-size, in its own window.

Figure B-14: Use the Artwork pane to add or view artwork.

✦ ✦ ✦

Index

B

Continued

Continued

Continued

Continued

J

K

L

N

O

P

Continued

W

X

Z